Pearl Harbor to Guadalcanal

HISTORY OF U. S. MARINE CORPS

OPERATIONS IN WORLD WAR II

VOLUME I

by

LIEUTENANT COLONEL FRANK O. HOUGH, USMCR

MAJOR VERLE E. LUDWIG, USMC

HENRY I. SHAW, JR.

Historical Branch, G–3 Division, Headquarters, U. S. Marine Corps

Foreword

With the recent completion of our historical monograph project, the Marine Corps historical program entered a new phase. This book is the first of a projected five-volume series covering completely, and we hope definitively, the history of Marine operations in World War II.

The fifteen historical monographs published over a period of eight years have served to spotlight the high points in this broad field. The basic research which underlay their preparation will be utilized again in this project. But a monograph by its very nature aims at a limited objective, and in its concentration on a single battle or campaign necessarily ignores many related subjects. All too often it has been difficult to avoid conveying the impression that the specific operation under discussion was taking place in a vacuum. Thus, while much valuable history has been written, the story as a whole remains untold.

This lack the present project aims to rectify. The story of individual battles or campaigns, now isolated between the covers of separate publications, will be largely rewritten and woven together in an attempt to show events in proper relation to each other and in correct perspective to the war as a whole. In addition, new material, especially from Japanese sources, which has become available since the writing of the monographs, will be integrated into the story. Only when the broad picture is available can the significance of the Marine Corps' contribution to the final victory in the Pacific be fairly evaluated.

Now a word about Volume I which sketches briefly the development of the Marine Corps' amphibious mission from its inception and then carries the story of World War II through Guadalcanal. As logistical officer of the 1st Marine Division, I was privileged to take part in this, our first effort to strike back at the Japanese. Looking rearward from the vantage point of later years when our materiel superiority was overwhelming, it is difficult to visualize those lean first months in the Pacific when there was never enough of anything, and Allied strategy of giving top priority to Europe meant that there would not be for some time to come. Thus our initial offensive quickly and richly earned the nickname "Operation Shoestring." But the shoestring held during those early critical days when its holding appeared highly questionable; and when it did, the ultimate outcome of the war in the Pacific ceased to remain in doubt.

R. McC. PATE
GENERAL, U. S. MARINE CORPS
COMMANDANT OF THE MARINE CORPS

Preface

This book covers Marine Corps participation through the first precarious year of World War II, when disaster piled on disaster and there seemed no way to check Japanese aggression. Advanced bases and garrisons were isolated and destroyed: Guam, Wake, and the Philippines. The sneak attack on Pearl Harbor, "the day that will live in infamy," seriously crippled the U. S. Pacific Fleet; yet that cripple rose to turn the tide of the entire war at Midway. Shortly thereafter the U. S. Marines launched on Guadalcanal an offensive which was destined to end only on the home islands of the Empire.

The country in general, and the Marine Corps in particular, entered World War II in a better state of preparedness than had been the case in any other previous conflict. But that is a comparative term and does not merit mention in the same sentence with the degree of Japanese preparedness. What the Marine Corps did bring into the war, however, was the priceless ingredient developed during the years of peace: the amphibious doctrines and techniques that made possible the trans-Pacific advance—and, for that matter, the invasion of North Africa and the European continent.

By publishing this operational history in a durable form, it is hoped to make the Marine Corps record permanently available for the study of military personnel, the edification of the general public, and the contemplation of serious scholars of military history.

This initial volume was planned and outlined by Lieutenant Colonel Harry W. Edwards, former Head of the Historical Branch, G-3 Division, Headquarters, U. S. Marine Corps. Much of the original writing was done by Lieutenant Colonel Frank O. Hough, formerly Head of the Writing Section, Historical Branch. Three historical monographs, Lieutenant Colonel Robert D. Heinl, Jr.'s *The Defense of Wake* and *Marines at Midway*, and Major John L. Zimmerman's *The Guadalcanal Campaign*, were adapted to the needs of this book by Major Verle E. Ludwig, who also contributed considerable original writing of his own. Mr. Kenneth W. Condit wrote the chapter on landing craft development and shared, with Colonel Charles W. Harrison and Major Hubard D. Kuokka, the authorship of the chapter treating the evolution of amphibious doctrine. The buildup of Pacific outpost garrisons, the opening moves of the war, and the record of Marines in the defense of the Philippines were written by Mr. Henry I. Shaw, Jr. The final editing was done by Colonel Harrison, present Head of the Historical Branch.

A number of the leading participants in the actions described have commented on preliminary drafts of pertinent portions of this manuscript. Their valuable assistance is gratefully acknowledged. Special thanks are due to those people who read and commented on the entire volume: Lieutenant General Edward A. Craig, U. S. Marine Corps, Retired; Dr. John Miller, Office of the Chief of Military History, Department of the Army; Captain Frederick K. Loomis, U. S. Navy, Naval History Division, Office of the Chief of Naval Operations, Department of the Navy; and Colonel Heinl, who initiated the original program of monographs dealing with Marine actions in World War II.

Mrs. Edna Clem Kelley and her successor in the Administrative and Production Section of the Historical Branch, Miss Kay P. Sue, ably handled the exacting duties involved in processing the volume from first drafts through final printed form. The many preliminary typescripts and the painstaking task of typing the final manuscript for the printer were done by Mrs. Miriam R. Smallwood and Mrs. Billie J. Tucker.

Most of the maps were prepared by the Reproduction Section, Marine Corps Schools, Quantico, Virginia. However, we are indebted to the Office of the Chief of Military History, Department of the Army, for permission to use Maps Nos. 3, 14, 15, 20, 21, and 23–27, which were originally drafted by its Cartographic Branch. Official Defense Department photographs have been used throughout the text.

E. W. SNEDEKER
MAJOR GENERAL, U. S. MARINE CORPS
ASSISTANT CHIEF OF STAFF, G-3

Contents

PART I INTRODUCTION TO THE MARINE CORPS

CHAPTER   PAGE

1. Origins of a Mission 3
2. Evolution of Modern Amphibious Warfare, 1920–1941 8
3. Development of Landing Craft 23
4. Marine Occupation of Iceland 35
5. The Marine Corps on the Eve of War 47

PART II WAR COMES

1. Prewar Situation in the Pacific 59
2. Japan Strikes 70
3. The Southern Lifeline 84

PART III THE DEFENSE OF WAKE

1. Wake in the Shadow of War 95
2. The Enemy Strikes 106
3. Wake Under Siege 121
4. The Fall of Wake 132
5. Conclusions 150

PART IV MARINES IN THE PHILIPPINES

1. China and Luzon 155
2. Bataan Prelude 172
3. The Siege and Capture of Corregidor 184

PART V DECISION AT MIDWAY

1. Setting the Stage: Early Naval Operations 205
2. Japanese Plans: Toward Midway and the North Pacific . . . 214
3. Midway Girds for Battle 216
4. Midway Versus the Japanese, 4–5 June 1942 221
5. Battle of the Carrier Planes, 4 June 1942 226

PART VI THE TURNING POINT: GUADALCANAL

CHAPTER	PAGE
1. Background and Preparations	235
2. Guadalcanal, 7–9 August 1942	254
3. Tulagi and Gavutu-Tanambogo	263
4. The Battle of the Tenaru	274
5. The Battle of the Ridge	294
6. Action Along the Matanikau	310
7. Japanese Counteroffensive	322
8. Critical November	341
9. Final Period, 9 December 1942–9 February 1943	359

APPENDICES

A. Bibliographical Notes	375
B. Chronology	382
C. Marine Task Organization and Command Lists	387
D. Marine Casualties	395
E. First Marine Division Operation Order—Guadalcanal	396
F. Military Map Symbols	399
G. Guide to Abbreviations	400
H. Unit Commendations	404
Index	413

ILLUSTRATIONS

Continental Marines	6
Marines of Huntington's Battalion	6
Marines in France in World War I	12
Bandit-Hunting Patrol in Nicaragua	12
Experimental Amphibian Tractor	25
Early Version of Landing Craft	25
Air Evacuation of Wounded in Nicaragua	49
Army Light Tank Landing at New River, N. C.	49
Pearl Harbor Attack	72
Japanese Landing on Guam	72
Japanese Patrol Craft Lost at Wake	135
Japanese Naval Troops Who Took Wake	135
Japanese on Bataan	174
Aerial View of Corregidor Island	186
Effect of Japanese Bombardment of Corregidor	186
An Army B-25, One of Doolittle's Raiders	208
Japanese Carrier *Shoho*	208

ILLUSTRATIONS—Continued

	PAGE
Camouflaged Lookout Tower at Sand Island	222
Japanese Cruiser *Mikuma*	222
Crude Sketch Map of Guadalcanal	246
Equipment for the 1st Marine Division	251
Marine Raiders and the Crew of the Submarine *Argonaut*	251
The Original Henderson Field	255
Unloading Supplies at Guadalcanal	255
Tulagi Island	272
Tanambogo and Gavutu Islands	272
Marine Commanders on Guadalcanal	278
LVT Bridge Built by Marine Engineers	282
Solomons Natives Guide a Patrol	282
90mm Antiaircraft Guns of the 3d Defense Battalion	296
105mm Howitzer of the 11th Marines	296
Raiders' Ridge	309
Marines of the 2d Raider Battalion	309
The Pagoda at Henderson Field	312
Cactus Air Force Planes	312
Five Blasted Japanese Tanks	331
Marine Light Tanks	331
Japanese Torpedo Plane	338
Naval Gunfire Support	338
37mm Guns of the Americal Division	361
1st Division Marines Leave Guadalcanal	361

MAPS

1. Scene of Battle	Map Section
2. Japanese Capture of Guam, 10 December 1941	77
3. South Pacific	91
4. Defense Installations on Wake, 8–23 December 1941	97
5. Landing on Wake Island, 23 December 1941	Map Section
6. Situation on Wilkes Island, 0300–Dawn, 23 December 1941	145
7. Japanese Landing on Bataan	Map Section
8. Corregidor with Inset Showing Manila Bay	Map Section
9. Marshalls, Gilberts, and Eastern Carolines	206
10. Midway Islands, June 1942	Map Section
11. Solomon Islands with Inset Showing Santa Cruz Islands	244
12. Makin Raid, 17–18 August 1942	284
13. Guadalcanal and Florida Islands	Map Section
14. Initial Dispositions, 7 August 1942	Map Section
15. Landings in Tulagi Area, 7 August 1942	Map Section
16. The Perimeter, 12 August 1942	287

MAPS—Continued

	PAGE
17. Battle of the Tenaru, 21 August 1942	289
18. The Perimeter, 12–14 September 1942	300
19. Edson's Ridge—First Phase, 12–13 September 1942	304
20. Edson's Ridge—Final Phase, 13 September 1942	307
21. Matanikau Action, 24–27 September 1942	314
22. Matanikau Offensive, 7–9 October 1942	318
23. October Attacks on the Perimeter	Map Section
24. Push Toward Kokumbona, 1–4 November 1942	344
25. Koli Point, 4–9 November 1942	Map Section
26. Battle Area, December 1942–January 1943	Map Section
27. XIV Corps Plan—First January Offensive	Map Section
28. Capture of Kokumbona and Advance to the Poha River, 23–25 January 1943	Map Section
29. Final Phase, 26 January–9 February 1943	370

PART ONE

Introduction to the Marine Corps

CHAPTER 1

Origins of a Mission

In a sense, Marines may be said to have existed in ancient times when the Phoenicians, and subsequently the Greeks and Romans, placed men aboard their ships for the specific purpose of fighting, in contrast to the crews who navigated them and the rowers who propelled them. However, Marines in the modern sense date to Seventeenth Century England where, in 1664, a regiment of ground troops was raised specifically for duty with the fleet as well as ashore. This unit bore the somewhat ponderous title: "Duke of York and Albany's Maritime Regiment of Foot." Over a period of many decades of expansion and evolution, during much of which nobody knew for certain whether it belonged to the Army or the Navy, this basic unit developed into the corps known today as the Royal Marines.

By the time of the American Revolution, the status of the British Marines had jelled firmly. Thus, when the American Colonies revolted and began setting up their own armed services, they modeled these much along the lines of the similar components of the mother country, these being the forms with which they were most familiar and which suited them best temperamentally. This was true of the Continental Marines and to an even greater degree of the Marine Corps, reactivated under the Constitution in 1798.

In the days of wooden, sail-propelled ships the functions of the Marines became well defined. At sea they kept order and were responsible for internal security. In combat they became the ship's small-arms fighters: sniping from the fighting tops, and on deck spearheading boarding parties in close action or repelling enemy boarders. Ashore they guarded naval installations, both at home and abroad, and upon occasion fought on land beside Army components. Amphibious-wise, they were available as trained landing parties, either to seize positions on hostile shores, or to protect the lives and property of nationals in foreign countries. Both the British and U. S. Marines have seen much such service.

At the time of this writing the Marine Corps is 181 years old, according to its own reckoning, though its service has not been continuous. Marines celebrate their Corps' birthday on 10 November, this being the date in the year 1775 when the Continental Congress authorized the raising of two battalions of Marines for the Continental service. The scanty records extant show nothing to indicate that those battalions were actually raised, but many Marines were recruited for service on board the ships of the infant Navy where they performed creditably in all the major sea actions of the Revolutionary War, staged two important amphibious landings in the Bahamas, and ashore participated in the Trenton-Princeton campaign under General Washington.

The Continental Marines, like the Navy and all but a minuscule detachment of the Army, passed out of existence following the close of the Revolutionary War. How-

3

ever, foreign pressures brought the Navy back into existence in 1798 under the recently adopted Constitution, and on 11 July of that year the Marine Corps was reactivated as a separate service within the naval establishment.

Since that date Marines have fought in every official war the United States has had—and scores of obscure affairs that lacked official blessing but in which, to quote the eminent Marine writer, John W. Thomason, Jr., ". . . a man can be killed as dead as ever a chap was in the Argonne."[1] They have served as strictly naval troops, both ashore and afloat, and participated in extended land operations under Army command, notably in the Creek-Seminole Indian Wars of the 1830's, the Mexican War, both World Wars, and in Korea.

All over the world, Britian's Royal Marines were seeing much the same type of service. For a century or more the courses of the two corps ran parallel, and they were as functionally alike as it is possible for any two military organizations to be. Individual members of these services had so many interests in common that, as one British writer put it, they had a tendency to "chum up"[2] when ships of the two nations put in to the same ports. Even the present U. S. Marine emblem (adopted in 1868) derives from that of the Royal Marines; though at a glance they appear entirely different, the basic motifs of both are the fouled anchor and globe: the Eastern Hemisphere for the British, the Western for the U. S. Much in common existed at top level, as well, and over the years the two organizations developed a very close and most cordial relationship that exists to this day, despite the strange evolutionary divergence that set in between them.[3]

The transition of navies from sail to steam began evolutionary developments which profoundly altered the nature of all shipboard duties, and temporarily threatened both corps with extinction. From this the Royal Marines emerged burdened with a miscellany of often incongruous duties never envisioned in the old days, and considerably emasculated by lack of a single mission of overriding importance. That the effect on the U. S. Marines was precisely the reverse resulted from the fundamental difference in the problems facing the two nations which required U. S. Marines to carve out a special mission for themselves, though they traveled a long, uneven road in bringing this to full fruition.

The basic problem that confronted the early steam navies was that of obtaining fuel. Sail-propelled men-of-war, on which all naval experience and tradition up to that time was based, could operate at sea almost indefinitely, putting in only to replenish provisions and water, readily available at nearly any port of call anywhere in the world. But sufficient coal to support large-scale steamship operations could be obtained only from well stocked bases, and a fleet's operating radius thus became limited by the location of such bases. If an enemy lay beyond that radius, the fleet might as well be chained to a post so far as getting at

---

[1] Capt J. W. Thomason, Jr., *Fix Bayonets!* (New York: Charles Scribner's Sons, 1955 ed.), xiv.

[2] LtCol M. Rose, RMA, *A Short History of the Royal Marines* (Deal, England: Depot Royal Marines, 1911), 22.

[3] LtCol R. D. Heinl, Jr., "What Happened to the Royal Marines?," *USNI Proceedings*, February 1949, 169.

him was concerned, unless the source of supply could be projected farther in his direction.

To the British Empire, on which "the sun never sets," this posed no serious problem; it had, or could build, all the bases it needed without leaving its own territory. But the United States, with few outlying possessions, had genuine cause for concern. In order to give the fleet significant operating range in the Pacific, the Navy in 1878 set up a coaling station in Samoa, and in 1887 the government concluded a treaty with Hawaii permitting the establishment of another at Pearl Harbor.

But the United States had no deep-seated interest in the Far East during this era, and no serious apprehension of an attack from that direction. The Navy's principal concern lay in the possibility of being obliged to enforce the Monroe Doctrine in the Caribbean or South Atlantic. As early as 1880, far-sighted naval officers began turning their thoughts toward this mission. The cost of maintaining permanent bases in those areas would have been prohibitive, so the problem boiled down to devising a plan for seizing advanced bases when and where strategy dictated their need and developing these as quickly as possible to withstand attack. The scattered, under-strength U. S. Army of that era could not supply sufficient trained ground troops on the short notice necessary to make such operations effective, so the Navy faced the problem of developing ground troops of its own for service with the fleet.[4]

It would seem, particularly with benefit of today's hindsight, that the Marine Corps would be the logical choice for the development of this mission. However, this was not so apparent at the time. Marines had never participated in this type of operation on anything resembling the scale envisioned, and they comprised a very small unit as compared to the bluejackets. One school of thought contended that the advanced base function should be performed entirely by Navy personnel under command of naval officers, in the interests of unity and other considerations.[5] The controversy, strictly on the theoretical level, waxed warm and sometimes acrimonious, giving rise at length to one of those perennial efforts to eliminate the Marines altogether.[6]

However, the advent of the Spanish-American War found the Navy wholly unprepared to cope with the advanced base problem. It was the Marine Corps that promptly organized an expeditionary battalion, including its own artillery component, for the seizure of Guantanamo Bay, Cuba, in order to enable the U. S. Fleet to operate indefinitely in the Caribbean waters. At Key West this unit underwent training in minor tactics, basic weapons, and musketry, and then landed in the target area on 10 June 1898, ten days before the first Army troops arrived off the coast of Cuba. There the Marines quickly secured a beachhead and successfully defended it against a numerically superior enemy.

---

[4] E. B. Potter (ed), *The United States and World Sea Power* (New York: Prentice-Hall, 1955), 577–578, hereinafter cited as *U. S. & Sea Power*.

[5] For detailed discussion of this controversy, see W. H. Russell, "The Genesis of FMF Doctrine: 1879–1899," *MC Gazette*, April–July 1951.

[6] LtCol R. D. Heinl, Jr., "The Cat with More than Nine Lives," *USNI Proceedings*, June 1954.

CONTINENTAL MARINES *present a stirring sight as they charge in this symbolic painting of Revolutionary fighting by H. Charles McBarron, Jr. (USMC 304045)*

MARINES OF HUNTINGTON'S BATTALION, *first troops ashore in Cuba in 1898, captured Guantanamo Bay, used thereafter as an American naval base. (USMC 4982)*

So expeditiously and efficiently was this operation conducted that its contribution to the speedy and decisive culmination of the war would be difficult to evaluate. This also greatly strengthened the Marine Corps' claim to the Navy's amphibious mission, a claim that gained still further strength by Admiral Dewey's subsequent statement that if a similar Marine component had served with his fleet at Manila Bay, the whole painful and protracted Philippine Insurrection might have been avoided.

The Spanish-American War signaled emergence of the United States as a world power. Possession of the Philippines caused the Navy to reappraise the whole Far East situation. The USS *Charleston*, convoying Army troops to Manila, paused en route to seize the Spanish island of Guam to serve as an advanced coaling station,[7] and annexation of Hawaii followed shortly.[8] Additional advanced bases were established in the Philippines themselves as soon as the situation permitted.

This increasing consciousness of the Navy's widespread commitments and responsibilities brought about the evolutionary developments which culminated in the early 1940's in the amphibious assault doctrines and techniques "which finally made possible what Major General J. F. C. Fuller has called 'the most far-reaching tactical innovation of [World War II].'"[9]

---

[7] Seizure of Guam required no landing force. The Spanish governor had not learned about the declaration of war and mistook the token naval bombardment for a courtesy salute and hurried out to the *Charleston* to apologize for his inability to return it for lack of ammunition. He promptly surrendered the island upon being apprised of the facts.

[8] Prior to the Spanish War, the question of the annexation of Hawaii had been under negotiation off and on for many years between that government and the United States. In a treaty signed in 1875, Hawaii had been declared "an American sphere of influence."

[9] Quoted in *U. S. & Sea Power*, 587.

Evolution of Modern Amphibious Warfare, 1920–1941

EARLY DEVELOPMENTS

The success of the Guantanamo Bay operation and the very real possibility that the United States' new position in world affairs might lead to repetitions of essentially the same situation led high-level naval strategists to become interested in establishing a similar force on a permanent basis: a force capable of seizing and defending advanced bases which the fleet could utilize in the prosecution of naval war in distant waters—waters conceivably much more distant than the Caribbean. This in turn led to the setting up of a class in the fundamentals of advanced base work at Newport, Rhode Island in 1901. During the winter of 1902–1903 a Marine battalion engaged in advanced base defense exercises on the island of Culebra in the Caribbean in conjunction with the annual maneuvers of the fleet. Expeditionary services in Cuba and Panama prevented an immediate follow-up to this early base defense instruction, but in 1910 a permanent advanced base school was organized at New London, Connecticut. A year later it was moved to Philadelphia.[1]

By 1913 sufficient progress had been made in advanced base instruction to permit the formation of a permanent advanced base force. Made up of two regiments, one of coast artillery, mines, searchlights, engineers, communicators, and other specialists for fixed defense, and the other of infantry and field artillery for mobile defense, the advanced base force totalled about 1,750 officers and men. In January of 1914 it was reinforced by a small Marine Corps aviation detachment and joined the fleet for maneuvers at Culebra.[2] But the analogy between advanced base training and the amphibious assault techniques that emerged in World War II is easily overdrawn. Prior to World War I the primary interest was in defense of a base against enemy attack. There was no serious contemplation of large-scale landings against heavily defended areas.

This all but exclusive concern for the defense of bases was clearly borne out by the writing of Major Earl H. Ellis. Ellis, one of the most brilliant young Marine staff officers, was among the farsighted military thinkers who saw the prospect of war between the United States and Japan prior to World War I. Around 1913, he directed attention to the

---

[1] J. A. Isely and P. A. Crowl, *The U. S. Marines and Amphibious War* (Princeton: Princeton University Press, 1951), 21–22, hereinafter cited as *Marines and Amphibious War*.

[2] *Annual Report of the Major General Commandant of the Marine Corps, 1914* (Washington: GPO, 1914). Hereinafter all annual reports from the Office of the Commandant will be cited as *CMC AnRept* (year).

problems of a future Pacific conflict. To bring military force to bear against Japan, Ellis pointed out, the United States would have to project its fleet across the Pacific. To support these operations so far from home would require a system of outlying bases. Hawaii, Guam, and the Philippines, which were the most important of these, we already possessed. Their defense would be of utmost importance and would constitute the primary mission of the Marine advanced base force. Ellis discussed in considerable detail the troops which would be required and the tactics they should employ.

In addition to the bases already in the possession of the United States, Ellis foresaw the need of acquiring others held by Japan. To the Marine Corps would fall the job of assaulting the enemy-held territory. Although he did not discuss the problems involved nor take up the tactics to be employed, Ellis foreshadowed the amphibious assault which was to be the primary mission of the Marine Corps in World War II.[3]

The infant Advance Base Force was diverted to other missions almost as soon as it was created. Hardly were the Culebra maneuvers of 1914 completed when the Marines were sent to Mexico for the seizure of Vera Cruz. The next year they went ashore in Haiti, and in 1916 unsettled conditions in Santo Domingo required the landing of Marines in that country. Expeditionary service in these two Caribbean republics was to constitute a heavy and continuing drain on Marine Corps resources which might otherwise have been devoted to advanced base activities.

The expansion of the Marine Corps to about 73,000 officers and men during World War I served as a temporary stimulant to the Advance Base Force. In spite of the demands for manpower resulting from the sending of an expeditionary force to France, the Advance Base Force was maintained at full strength throughout the war. By the Armistice it numbered 6,297 officers and men.[4]

UPS AND DOWNS OF THE NINETEEN TWENTIES

Marines returning from overseas late in 1919 picked up where they left off three years before. At Quantico the Advance Base Force, redesignated the Expeditionary Force in 1921, stood ready to occupy and defend an advanced base or to restore law and order in a Caribbean republic. In that year it included infantry, field artillery, signal, engineer, and chemical troops, and aircraft. A similar expeditionary force was planned for San Diego, but perennial personnel shortages prevented the stationing of more than one infantry regiment and one aircraft squadron there during the 1920's.[5]

Nothing seemed changed, but delegates of the Great Powers, meeting at Versailles to write the peace treaty ending World War I, had already taken an action which was to have far-reaching consequences for

---

[3] Earl H. Ellis, "Naval Bases" (MS. n. d.). The date and origin of this MS and to whom it was addressed are obscure, but it appears that the work is either a lecture or a series of lectures with the following divisions: "1. Naval Bases; Their Location, Resources and Security; 2. The Denial of Bases; 3. The Security of Advanced Bases and Advanced Base Operations; 4. The Advanced Base Force."

[4] LtCol C. H. Metcalf, *A History of the United States Marine Corps* (New York: Putnam's. 1939), 456–460, 472.

[5] *CMC AnRepts*, 1921–29.

a future generation of Marines. In the general distribution of spoils, the former German island possessions in the central Pacific had been mandated to the Japanese. At one stroke the strategic balance in the Pacific was shifted radically in favor of Japan. That country now possessed a deep zone of island outposts. Fortified and supported by the Japanese fleet, they would constitute a serious obstacle to the advance of the United States Fleet across the Pacific.

Earl Ellis was one of the first to recognize the significance of this strategic shift. In 1921 he modified his earlier ideas and submitted them in the form of Operations Plan 712, "Advanced Base Operations in Micronesia." In this plan Ellis stressed the necessity for seizing by assault the bases needed to project the Fleet across the Pacific. He envisioned the seizure of specific islands in the Marshall, Caroline, and Palau groups, some of which were actually taken by Marines in World War II. He went so far as to designate the size and type of units that would be necessary, the kind of landing craft they should use, the best time of day to effect the landing, and other details needed to insure the success of the plan. Twenty years later Marine Corps action was to bear the imprint of this thinking:

> To effect [an amphibious landing] in the face of enemy resistance requires careful training and preparation, to say the least; and this along Marine lines. It is not enough that the troops be skilled infantry men or artillery men of high morale; they must be skilled water men and jungle men who know it can be done—Marines with Marine training.[6]

The Commandant, Major General John A. Lejeune, and other high ranking Marines shared Ellis' views. "The seizure and occupation or destruction of enemy bases is another important function of the expeditionary force," he stated in a lecture before the Naval War College in 1923. "On both flanks of a fleet crossing the Pacific are numerous islands suitable for submarine and air bases. All should be mopped up as progress is made. . . . The maintenance, equipping and training of its expeditionary force so that it will be in instant readiness to support the Fleet in the event of war," he concluded, "I deem to be the most important Marine Corps duty in time of peace."[7]

The 1920s, however, were not the most favorable years for training in amphibious operations. Appropriations for the armed services were slim, and the Navy, whose cooperation and support was necessary to carry out landing exercises, was more intent on preparing for fleet surface actions of the traditional type. Still, a limited amount of amphibious training was carried out in the first half of the decade.

During the winter of 1922, a reinforced regiment of Marines participated in fleet maneuvers with the Atlantic Fleet. Their problems included the attack and defense of Guantanamo Bay, Cuba, and the island of Culebra. In March of the following year, a detachment of Marines took part in a landing exercise at Panama, and a battalion of Marines and sailors practiced a landing on Cape Cod that summer.

Panama and Culebra both witnessed landing exercises early in 1924, with a Marine regiment participating. This set of exercises was the high point of train-

---

[6] OPlan 712, AdvBOps in Micronesia, 1921.

[7] MajGen J. A. Lejeune, "The United States Marine Corps," *MC Gazette*, December 1923, 252–253.

ing reached in the twenties. It marked the advent of serious experimentation with adequate landing craft for troops and equipment. However, it was most notable for the great number of mistakes made in the course of the exercises, such as inadequate attacking forces, insufficient and unsuitable boats, lack of order among the landing party, superficial naval bombardment, and poor judgment in the stowage of supplies and equipment aboard the single transport used.[8]

The last landing exercise of the era was a joint Army-Navy affair held during the spring of 1925 in Hawaiian waters. It was actually an amphibious command post exercise, undertaken at the insistence of General Lejeune to prove to skeptical Army officers that the Marine Corps could plan and execute an amphibious operation of greater than brigade size. A force of 42,000 Marines was simulated, although only 1,500 actually participated. It ran more smoothly than had the previous exercise, but still was handicapped by a lack of adequate landing craft.[9]

Even this meager amphibious training came to an end after 1925. New commitments in Nicaragua, in China, and in the United States guarding the mails served to disperse the expeditionary forces. By 1928 the Commandant announced in his annual report that barely enough personnel were on hand at Quantico and San Diego to keep those bases in operation.[10]

Whatever the shortcomings of the work in amphibious doctrine and technique during the 1920's, the Marine Corps scored a major triumph when its special interest in the field became part of the official military policy of the United States. *Joint Action of the Army and Navy*, a directive issued by the Joint Board of the Army and Navy in 1927, stated that the Marine Corps would provide and maintain forces "for land operations in support of the fleet for the initial seizure and defense of advanced bases and for such limited auxiliary land operations as are essential to the prosecution of the naval campaign."

Further, in outlining the tasks to be performed by the Army and Navy in "Landing Attacks Against Shore Objectives," this document firmly established the landing force role of the Marine Corps: "Marines organized as landing forces perform the same functions as above stated for the Army, and because of the constant association with naval units will be given special training in the conduct of landing operations."[11]

ACTIVATION OF THE FLEET MARINE FORCE

The recognition of a mission did not create the doctrine nor the trained forces to carry it out, and, in 1927, neither was at hand. In January 1933 the last Marine had departed from Nicaragua, and withdrawal from Haiti was contemplated. Troops were now becoming available for training in landing operations, but before any real progress could be made, one preliminary step was essential. A substantial permanent force of Marines with its

---

[8] *Marines and Amphibious War*, 30–32.

[9] BriGen Dion Williams, "Blue Marine Corps Expeditionary Force," *MC Gazette*, September 1925, 76–88; LtGen M. B. Twining ltr to ACofS, G–3, HQMC, 25Jan57; BPlan JA&Nav Exercise, 1925, Problem No 3, Blue MarCor ExpedFor, 8Jan25.

[10] *CMC AnRept*, 1928.

[11] The Joint Board, *Joint Action of the Army and Navy* (Washington: GPO, 1927), 3, 12.

MARINES IN FRANCE IN WORLD WAR I, *part of the 4th Marine Brigade of the 2d Infantry Division, prepare to move up to the front line trenches.* (USMC 4967)

BANDIT-HUNTING PATROL *in Nicaragua in 1929 typifies Marine activities between the World Wars when the Corps served as a Caribbean riot squad.* (USMC 515283)

own commander and staff would have to be organized for the purpose, otherwise training would be constantly interrupted by the dispersal of the troops to other commitments.

No one recognized this more clearly than the Assistant Commandant, Brigadier General John H. Russell. He assembled a staff at Quantico to plan the organization of a force which could be rapidly assembled for service with the Fleet. In August of 1933 he proposed to the Commandant that the old "Expeditionary Force" be replaced by a new body, to be called either "Fleet Marine Force," or "Fleet Base Defense Force." The new force, while an integral part of the United States Fleet, would be under the operational control of the Fleet Commander when embarked on vessels of the Fleet or engaged in fleet exercises afloat or ashore. When not so embarked or engaged it would remain under the Major General Commandant.

Russell's recommendations were promptly approved by the Commandant and by the Chief of Naval Operations. The designation "Fleet Marine Force" (FMF) was preferred by the senior naval staffs, and the Commandant was requested to submit proposed instructions for establishing "appropriate command and administrative relations between the commander in Chief and the Commander of the Fleet Marine Force."[12] The decision became official with the issuance of Navy Department General Order 241, dated 8 December 1933.

This directive could well be called the Magna Carta of the Fleet Marine Force. It stated:

1. The force of marines maintained by the major general commandant in a state of readiness for operations with the fleet is hereby designated as fleet marine force (F. M. F.), and as such shall constitute a part of the organization of the United States Fleet and be included in the operating force plan for each fiscal year.

2. The fleet marine force shall consist of such units as may be designated by the major general commandant and shall be maintained at such strength as is warranted by the general personnel situation of the Marine Corps.

3. The fleet marine force shall be available to the commander in chief for operations with the fleet or for exercises either afloat or ashore in connection with fleet problems. The commander in chief shall make timely recommendations to the Chief of Naval Operations regarding such service in order that the necessary arrangements may be made.

4. The commander in chief shall exercise command of the fleet marine force when embarked on board vessels of the fleet or when engaged in fleet exercises, either afloat or ashore. When otherwise engaged, command shall be directed by the major general commandant.

5. The major general commandant shall detail the commanding general of the fleet marine force and maintain an appropriate staff for him.

6. The commanding general, fleet marine force, shall report by letter to the commander in chief, United States Fleet, for duty in connection with the employment of the fleet marine force. At least once each year, and at such times as may be considered desirable by the commander in chief, the commanding general, fleet marine force, with appropriate members of his staff, shall be ordered to report to the commander in chief for conference.[13]

However significant the creation of the FMF may have been in terms of the future, its initial form was modest enough. The Commandant was obliged to report in August 1934 that the responsibility for maintaining ship's detachments and garrisons abroad, and performing essential

---

[12] CNO ltr to CMC, 12Sep33; *Marines and Amphibious War*, 33–34.

[13] Navy Dept GO 241, 8Dec33.

guard duty at naval shore stations, prevented the Marine Corps from assigning the component units necessary to fulfill the mission of the FMF. At this time the total number of officers and men in the FMF was about 3,000.[14]

"THE BOOK" COMES OUT

With the creation of the FMF the Marine Corps had finally acquired the tactical structure necessary to carry out the primary war mission assigned to it by the Joint Board in 1927. The next order of business was to train the FMF for the execution of its mission.

But the training could not be very effective without a textbook embodying the theory and practice of landing operations. No such manual existed in 1933. There was a general doctrine by the Joint Board issued in 1933, and, though it offered many sound definitions and suggested general solutions to problems, it lacked necessary detail.

In November 1933, all classes at the Marine Corps Schools were suspended, and, under the guidance of Colonel Ellis B. Miller, Assistant Commandant of the Schools, both the faculty and students set to work to write a manual setting forth in detail the doctrines and techniques to be followed in both training and actual operations. Under the title, *Tentative Manual for Landing Operations*, it was issued in January 1934.

On 1 August 1934, the title was changed to *Manual for Naval Overseas Operations* and some changes were effected in the text. A few months later this publication, now retitled *Tentative Landing Operations Manual*, was approved by the Chief of Naval Operations for "temporary use . . . as a guide for forces of the Navy and the Marine Corps conducting a landing against opposition."[15] In mimeographed form it was given relatively limited distribution within the Navy, but wide distribution within the Marine Corps. Comments were invited.

The doctrine laid down in this remarkable document was destined to become the foundation of all amphibious thinking in the United States armed forces. The Navy accepted it as official doctrine in 1938 under the title of *Fleet Training Publication 167*, and in 1941 the War Department put the Navy text between Army covers and issued it as *Field Manual 31–5*.

Remarkable as it was, the Marine amphibious doctrine was largely theory when it was first promulgated at Quantico in 1934. To put the theory into practice, major landing exercises were resumed. They were held each winter from 1935 through 1941 on the islands of Culebra and Vieques in conjunction with fleet exercises in the Caribbean, or on San Clemente off the California coast. A final exercise of the prewar period on a much larger scale than any previously attempted was held at the newly acquired Marine Corps base at New River, North Carolina, in the summer of 1941. These fleet landing exercises provided the practical experience by which details of landing operations were hammered out.

In light of its importance, here might be as good a place as any to consider briefly the more basic aspects of this doctrine as conceived in the original manual and mod-

---

[14] *CMC AnRept*, 1934.

[15] NavDept, *Tentative Landing Operations Manual*, 1935, hereinafter cited as *Tentative Landing Operations Manual*.

ified by experience in fleet exercises up to the outbreak of the war. Amphibious operations and ordinary ground warfare share many of the same tactical principles. The basic difference between them lies in the fact that the amphibious assault is launched from the sea, and is supported by naval elements. While water-borne the landing force is completely powerless and is dependent upon the naval elements for all its support: gunfire, aviation, transportation, and communication. In this initial stage only the naval elements have the capability of reacting to enemy action. As the landing force, however, is projected onto the beach, its effectiveness, starting from zero at the water's edge, increases rapidly until its strength is fully established ashore.

COMMAND RELATIONSHIPS

This basic difference between land and amphibious operations created a problem in command relationships which has plagued amphibious operations from earliest times. During the initial stage when only naval elements have the capability of reacting to enemy action it has been generally and logically agreed that the over-all command must be vested in the commander of the naval attack force. It has, however, not been so generally agreed in the past that once the landing force is established ashore and capable of exerting its combat power with primary reliance on its own weapons and tactics that the landing force commander should be freed to conduct the operations ashore as he sees fit.

The authors of the *Tentative Landing Operations Manual*, writing in 1934, evidently did not foresee that this particular aspect of command relations presented a problem that required resolution.[16] They simply defined the "attack force" as all the forces necessary to conduct a landing operation and added that the attack force commander was to be the senior naval officer of the fleet units making up the attack force. His command was to consist of the landing force and several naval components, organized as task groups for the support of the landing. These included, among others, the fire support, transport, air, screening, antisubmarine, and reconnaissance groups. The commanders of the landing force and of the several naval task groups operated on the same level under the over-all command of the attack force commander throughout the operation.

This initial command concept was destined to undergo a number of modifications and interpretations which will be discussed in this history as they occur. The first important change did not come about until toward the close of the Guadalcanal campaign.[17]

NAVAL GUNFIRE SUPPORT

There is nothing new in the concept of using the fire of ships' guns to cover an amphibious landing of troops during its most vulnerable phase: before, during, and after the ship-to-shore movement. Our

---

[16] Unless otherwise noted the material in the remainder of this chapter is derived from *Tentative Landing Operations Manual; FTP-167, Landing Operations Doctrine, U. S. Navy* (Washington: Office of the CNO, 1938) and changes 1 & 2 thereto; 1st MarBrig ltr to CMC, 5Jun39 and encl (a) thereto; 1st MarBrig Flex 6 Rept, "Notes from Critique for Makee Learn Problem at Culebra, 14–15Feb40;" 2d MarBrig Minor Landing Exercises Rept, San Clemente Island, Calif, 17Apr–6May39.

[17] See Part VI of this history.

own history contains many examples of this technique, notably: two landings of U. S. troops in Canada during the War of 1812 (York and Niagara Peninsula, summer 1813); General Scott's landing at Vera Cruz in 1847 during the Mexican War; several amphibious operations during the Civil War, *e. g.*, Fort Fisher in 1865; and Guantanamo Bay during the Spanish-American War in 1898.

However, the evolution of modern weapons posed difficult problems of a technical nature, and the much belabored Gallipoli operation seemed to indicate that these were insoluble. High-powered naval guns, with their flat trajectory and specialized armor-piercing ammunition, proved no true substitute for land-based field artillery, and much study and practice would be required to develop techniques which would make them even an acceptable substitute.

Nevertheless, a rudimentary doctrine concerning naval gunfire support evolved during the years between 1935 and 1941. But it evolved slowly and none too clearly. Experimentation indicated that bombardment ammunition, with its surface burst, was better suited to fire missions against most land targets, while armor-piercing shells could be employed to good effect against concrete emplacements and masonry walls. The types of ships and guns best adapted to perform specific fire missions—close support, deep support, counterbattery, interdiction, etc.—were determined. And some progress was made in fire observation technique.

Three types of observers were provided for: aerial, shipboard and, once the first waves had landed, shore fire control parties. For the greater part of this period the latter were made up of personnel of the firing ships, inexperienced in such work, untrained, and wholly unfamiliar with the tactical maneuvers of the troops they were supporting. Not until 1941 were trained Marine artillery officers with Marine radio crews substituted, the naval officers then serving in a liaison capacity.

Other considerations of a naval nature served as further limiting factors on the NGF support concept. The necessity for the support ships to have a large proportion of armor-piercing projectiles readily available with which to fight a surface action on short notice restricted the accessibility of and limited the amount of bombardment shells carried. In turn, the probability of enemy air and submarine action once the target area became known caused much apprehension in naval minds and dictated the earliest possible departure of the firing ships from the objective. An example of this apprehension at work came to the fore early in the Guadalcanal campaign.[18]

Furthermore, tradition dies hard in any service. The traditional belief that warships exist for the sole purpose of fighting other warships dates far back in history, with one of its leading exponents the great Lord Nelson with his oft-quoted dictum: "A ship's a fool to fight a fort." This supposed vulnerability of surface vessels to shore-based artillery remained very much alive in the minds of naval planners. So they dictated that support ships should deliver their fires at maximum range while traveling at high speed and maneuvering radically—not exactly conducive to pin-point marksmanship.[19]

In sum, these considerations, the starting concept of naval gunfire support with which we

---

[18] See Part VI, Chap 2, of this history.
[19] *Marines and Amphibious War*, 38.

entered World War II, added up to this: a bombardment of very short duration, delivered by ships firing relatively limited ammunition allowances of types often not well suited to the purpose, from long ranges while maneuvering at high speeds. Obviously, the best that could be expected would be area neutralization of enemy defenses during troop debarkation and the ship-to-shore movement, followed by a limited amount of support on a call basis, with this, too, to be withdrawn as soon as field artillery could be landed.[20]

Area neutralization—that was the basic concept, with deliberate destruction fire ruled out. A blood bath would be required to expunge this from "The Book."

AIR SUPPORT

As the Marine Corps developed the various techniques contributing to a smooth landing operation, it had to give more and more consideration to the fast growth of military aviation as a powerful arm.

Even the original *Tentative Landing Operations Manual* considered the vulnerable concentrations of troops in transports, landing boats, and on the beach and called for a three-to-one numerical superiority over the enemy in the air. Later, in *FTP-167*, the ratio was increased to four-to-one, primarily to wipe the enemy air threat out of the skies and secondarily to shatter the enemy's beachhead defense and to cut off his reinforcements.

Considerable emphasis was placed, however, on direct assistance to the troops themselves. This included such supporting services as guiding the landing boats to the beach, laying smoke screens, and providing reconnaissance and spotting for naval gunfire and artillery. Most importantly, it included rendering direct fire support to the landing force until the artillery was ashore and ready to fire.

For this air war, employment of Marine squadrons on carriers was considered ideal but, due to a limited number of carriers, was not always a practical possibility. Planners even considered moving Marine planes ashore in crates and assembling them, after the ground troops had seized an airfield.

Hence, the *Tentative Landing Operations Manual* called for the Navy to carry most of the initial air battle. Marine pilots, however, might be employed with Navy air units. Actually, in order to exercise Marine air, most of the early training landings had to be scheduled within round trip flying distance of friendly airfields. Although by 1940 Marine carrier training operations were becoming routine, the heavy reliance upon Navy carrier air over Marine landings lasted throughout the war.

As noted before, close coordination of air with ground received great emphasis in the Marine Corps. Even in Santo Domingo and Haiti and later in Nicaragua, Marine pilots reconnoitered, strafed, and bombed insurgent positions, dropped supplies to patrols, and evacuated wounded. The *Tentative Landing Operations Manual* incorporated this teamwork into its new amphibious doctrine, and the landing exercises of the late 30's developed aviation fire power as an important close ground support weapon. By 1939, Colonel Roy S. Geiger advocated and other Marine Corps leaders conceded that one of the greatest potentials of Marine aviation lay in this "close air support."

The challenge became that of applying the fire power of Marine air, when needed,

---

[20] SM-67, *Naval Gunfire in Amphibious Operations* (Quantico: MCEC, MCS, 1955), 2.

to destroy a specific enemy front line position without endangering nearby friendly troops.

Refinement of this skilled technique as we know it today was slow because of many factors. There was so much for pilots to learn about rapidly developing military aviation that close air support had to take its place in the busy training syllabus after such basic drill as aerial tactics, air to air gunnery, strafing, bombing, navigation, carrier landings, and communications, and constant study of the latest in engineering, aerodynamics, and flight safety.

Also, whenever newer, faster, and higher flying airplanes trickled into the Marine Corps in the lean thirties, they were found to be less adaptable for close coordination with ground troops than the slower, open cockpit planes which supported the patrol actions of Nicaragua.

In Nicaragua the aviator in his open cockpit could idle his throttle so as to locate an enemy machine gun by its sound, but in the maneuvers of 1940 pilots flashing by in their enclosed cockpits found it difficult to see what was going on below or even to differentiate between friendly and "enemy" hills.[21] In Nicaragua, the Marine flier was most often an ex-infantryman, but 10 years later many of the new Navy-trained Marine aviators were fresh from college and knew little about ground tactics. The lack of a real enemy to look for, identify, and to shoot at hindered attempts at precision, especially since air-ground radio was not yet as reliable as the old slow but sure system where pilots read code messages from cloth panels laid on the ground or swooped down with weighted lines to snatch messages suspended between two poles.

The main key to development of close air support lay in reliable communications to permit quick liaison and complete understanding between the pilot and the front line commander. Part of the solution lay in more exercises in air-ground coordination with emphasis on standardized and simplied air-ground communications and maps. By 1939 an aviator as an air liaison officer was assigned to the 1st Marine Brigade Staff. While both artillery and naval gunfire, however, employed forward observers at front line positions, air support control was still being channeled slowly through regimental and brigade command posts.[22] In the same year one squadron sent up an air liaison officer in the rear seat of a scouting or bombing plane to keep abreast of the ground situation and to direct fighter or dive bomber pilots onto targets by means of radio.[23] This was better but not best.

Meanwhile, war flamed up in Europe. Navy and Marine planners took note as the Germans drove around the Maginot line with their special air-ground "armored packets" in which aviation teamed up with the fast, mobile ground elements to break up resistance.[24] By this time the Marines were working on the idea of plac-

---

[21] From Culebra came the report, "1st MAG as a whole performed in a creditable manner, although at one stage they were impartial in their attacks." 1st MarBrig Flex 6 Rept, "Notes from Critique for Makee Learn Problem at Culebra, 14–15Feb40."

[22] LtGen Julian C. Smith interview by HistBr, G–3, HQMC, 25Jul56.

[23] Col R. D. Moser interview by HistBr, G–3, HQMC, 31Aug56.

[24] WD G–2 Memo for C/S, 23Sep41, I. B. 130, Air-GrdOps, Tab C; CinCLant Flex 6 Rept, 13Jun40, 14–15.

ing radio-equipped "observers" on the front lines to control air support for the troops. But the Leathernecks were already in the war before the first standardized Navy-Marine Corps instructions on their employment appeared.[25] Also at that time, on Guadalcanal certain infantry officers were given additional duty as regimental "air forward observers." They were coached on the spot by aviators of the 1st Marine Aircraft Wing.[26]

THE SHIP-TO-SHORE MOVEMENT

The ship-to-shore movement was visualized by the *Tentative Landing Operations Manual* in a manner which resembled closely a conventional attack in land warfare: artillery preparation, approach march, deployment, and assault by the infantry. It stressed that this movement was no simple ferrying operation but a vital and integral part of the attack itself and demanded a high order of tactical knowledge and skill.

The two major problems in the ship-to-shore movement are the speedy debarkation of the assaulting troops and their equipment into the landing boats and the control and guiding of these craft to their assigned beaches. To facilitate the first, the *Tentative Landing Operations Manual* directed that each transport on which combat units were embarked should carry as a minimum sufficient boats to land a reinforced infantry battalion.[27] Thus each transport and its accompanying troops would be tactically self-sufficient for the assault landing, and the loss of one ship would not be a crippling blow. To expedite their debarkation the Marines generally went over the side via cargo nets rigged at several stations on the ship.

To solve the second major problem in the ship-to-shore movement, that of controlling and guiding the landing craft to their proper beaches, the *Tentative Landing Operations Manual* provided for: (1) marking the line of departure with buoys or picket boats; (2) a designated control vessel to lead each boat group from the rendezvous area to the line of departure, towing the boats in fog, smoke, or darkness, if necessary; (3) wave and alternate wave guide boats; (4) each boat to carry a signboard with its assigned letter and number indicating its proper position in the formation; and (5) for a guide plane to lead the boat waves in.

The system for the control of the ship-to-shore movement was still substantially the same as prescribed in the *Tentative Landing Operations Manual* when the Marines made their first amphibious landing of World War II at Guadalcanal on 7 August 1942.

COMBAT UNIT LOADING

"Combat unit loading" of transports is the key to amphibious logistics as developed by the Marine Corps. This is a practical process designed to make supplies and equipment immediately available to the assault troops in the order needed, disregarding to a large extent the waste of cargo space which results. In contrast is commercial loading which is equally

---

[25] USN, CSP-1536, 5Sep42.

[26] 1st MarDiv, Final Report on Guadalcanal Operation, 1Jul43, Phase V, Annex D, OPlan 2-42, 5. The directive on appointing air forward observers was dated 2Oct42.

[27] This general concept that troops and their landing craft should be transported together to the objective area remained valid through-

out the war, although at times it was necessary to deviate from it.

practical in utilizing every cubic foot of cargo space available but prevents access to much of the cargo until the ship is unloaded.

Highest priority items for combat unit loading vary somewhat with the nature and problems of a particular operation. Relative priorities must be worked out with minute care. The responsibility for handling this was given to a Marine officer designated transport quartermaster (TQM) aboard each amphibious assault ship. He had to know not only the weight and dimensions of each item of Marine gear carried but had to familiarize himself with the characteristics of the particular ship to which he was assigned: exact location and dimensions of all holds and storage spaces in terms of both cubic feet and deck space. This familiarity required at times accurate remeasurement of holds and loading spaces as modifications, not shown in the ship's plans, had often been made in the ship's internal structure. Initially, the *Tentative Landing Operations Manual* directed that the TQM should be an officer of the unit embarked, but such were the variations in ships that it subsequently proved more feasible to assign a Marine officer, thoroughly familiar with Marine gear, permanently to a particular ship with which he would become equally familiar through experience.

Practical experience with combat loading between 1935 and 1941 generally confirmed the soundness of the doctrines set forth in the *Tentative Landing Operations Manual*. Application of these doctrines in the fleet landing exercises was limited, however, by several factors, chiefly the lack of suitable transports. In addition, an uncertainty at times as to ports of embarkation and dates of availability of ships sometimes entangled planning procedures. As a result, there was no ideal approximation of wartime combat loading.

SHORE PARTY

One of the most serious problems encountered in early landing exercises was congestion on the beaches as men and supplies piled ashore. To keep such a situation reasonably in hand requires a high degree of control; control difficult to achieve under such circumstances, even when the enemy remains only simulated. Assault troops must push inland with all speed not only to expand the beachhead, but also to make room for following units and equipment to land and to provide space in which personnel assigned strictly beach functions can operate.

To solve this problem the *Tentative Landing Operations Manual* provided for a beach party, commanded by a naval officer called a beachmaster, and a shore party, a special task organization, commanded by an officer of the landing force. The beach party was assigned primarily naval functions, *e. g.*, reconnaissance and marking of beaches, marking of hazards to navigation, control of boats, evacuation of casualties, and, in addition, the unloading of material of the landing force from the boats. The shore party was assigned such functions as control of stragglers and prisoners, selecting and marking of routes inland, movement of supplies and equipment off the beaches, and assignment of storage and bivouac areas in the vicinity of the beach. The composition and strength of the shore party were not set forth except for a statement that it would contain detachments from some or all of the following landing force units: medical, supply, working details, engineers, military police, communications, and chemical. The beach party and the shore party were independent of each other, but the *Tentative Landing Operations Manual* enjoined that the fullest cooperation be observed between the beachmaster and the shore party commander, and the personnel of their respective parties.

It was not indicated from what source "working details" for the shore party would come, but in practice, since there was no other source, the policy of assigning units in reserve the responsibility for furnishing the labor details quickly developed. This in effect, however, temporarily deprived the commander of his reserve.

No realistic test of the shore and beach party doctrine took place during the early fleet landing exercises. Although some material was landed on the beach, it generally consisted of rations and small quantities of ammunition and gasoline. Not until 1941 were adequate supplies available and the maneuvers on a large enough scale to provide a test of logistic procedures. The results were not encouraging. "In January of 1941 . . . the shore party for a brigade size landing . . . consisted of one elderly major and two small piles of ammunition boxes," wrote a Marine officer who "suffered" through those years. "The ship-to-shore movement of fuel was a nightmare. We had no force level transportation, [no] engineers and no supporting maintenance capability worthy of the name. In short, the combination of the parsimonious years and our own apathy had left us next to helpless where logistics were concerned."[29]

Major General H. M. Smith, the landing force commander at the New River exercise in the summer of 1941, reported that "considerable delay in the debarkation of troops and supplies was caused by lack of personnel in the Shore and Beach Parties . . . . Roughly, the supplies except for subsistence it was possible to land . . . were insufficient to sustain the forces engaged for more than three days."[30]

General Smith, who had a deep respect for logistics, was determined to correct these deficiencies. "It is evident," he reported to Rear Admiral Ernest J. King, Commander in Chief, Atlantic Fleet, "that special service troops (labor) must be provided for these duties in order to prevent reduction of the fighting strength of battalion combat teams . . . . The present doctrine results in divided authority between shore party commanders." He recommended that "the beach and shore party commanders be consolidated into one unit, a Shore Party, under control of the landing force."[31]

Solution to the problem of divided authority came from a joint board of Army, Navy, Marine Corps, and Coast Guard officers appointed by Admiral King. Its recommendations closely followed those of General Smith and were accepted *in toto* and published on 1 August 1942 as *Change 2 to FTP 167*. The principal changes were: (1) joining together of the beach and shore parties under the title Shore Party, as a component of the landing force; (2) designating the beach party commander as the assistant to the shore party commander and his advisor on

---

[29] BriGen V. H. Krulak ltr to ACofS, G–3, HQMC, 5Mar57.

[30] CG LantPhibFor PrelimRept to CinCLant on New River Exercise 4–12Aug41, 27Aug41.
[31] *Ibid*.

naval matters; and (3) transferring the responsibility for unloading boats at the beach from the naval element to the landing force element of the shore party.[32]

Marine Corps Headquarters solved the labor force problem by adding a pioneer (shore party) battalion of 34 officers and 669 enlisted men to the marine division.[33] This change occurred on 10 January 1942, too late for the personnel concerned to gain practical experience in large-scale exercises in the techniques of handling vast quantities of supplies or to test the adequacy of the strength and organization provided. At Guadalcanal this lack came close to having serious consequences.[34]

General Smith was not content merely to submit his shore party recommendations to Admiral King. At his direction, the logistics staff of the Amphibious Force Atlantic Fleet prepared a detailed Standing Operating Procedure (SOP) covering all phases of logistics. Issued as Force General Order No. 7-42, SOP for Supply and Evacuation, it served as the basic guide to combat loading and shore party operations during the Guadalcanal operation.[35]

By 7 December 1941 the Marine Corps had made long strides towards amphibious preparedness. It had a doctrine which had been tested in maneuvers and found to be basically sound. Many of the errors in implementation had been recognized and corrected; still others were awaiting remedial action when war broke out. But the simulated conditions of the maneuver ground were now to be abandoned. The Marines and their doctrine were now to submit to the ultimate test of war.

---

[32] *Ibid.*
[33] Marine Corps T/O D-94, 10Jan42.
[34] See Part VI of this history.
[35] Krulak, *op. cit.*; Twining, *op. cit.*

CHAPTER 3

Development of Landing Craft

INTRODUCTION

The amphibious warfare doctrine laboriously developed by Marines between the two World Wars could never have been successfully executed without special equipment to transport the assaulting troops and their supplies from ship to shore and to land them on an enemy-defended beach.

No one was more aware of the need for such equipment than the Marines. Shortly after the end of World War I they induced the Navy to undertake design studies on two landing craft, one for personnel and one for materiel. Troop Barge A, as the first of these types was called, was tried out at Culebra in the winter of 1923–24. A shallow draft, twin-engined, 50-foot craft with a rated speed of about 12 knots and a carrying capacity of 110 fully equipped Marines, it had good beaching qualities and could retract from the beach with aid of a stern anchor. Three years later the second type, a 45-foot artillery lighter, was built and tested. Equipped with two parallel hinged ramps in the stern, it could be beached successfully stern-to and 155mm guns and other pieces of heavy Marine equipment unloaded. It lacked a power plant, however, and had to be towed by another craft.[1]

Another item of equipment tried out in 1924 was the Christie "amphibian tank." Afloat, this unusual machine was driven by twin-screw propellers at a rated speed of seven knots. On short, as a tractor, it could make 15 mph; or, where good roads were available, the demountable tracks could be removed, and on wheels it could do 35 mph. It functioned well enough on land and in the sheltered waters of rivers. But in the open sea, under conditions that must be realistically anticipated for an assault landing, it proved so unseaworthy that the Marine Corps directed its attention to other types.

The construction of these types of amphibious equipment constituted a beginning, however humble, towards the solution of the problem of transporting troops and equipment from ship to shore. But a shortage of funds made it impossible to follow up these developments until 1935, when appropriations became more plentiful as a result of the naval expansion program begun in the first Roosevelt administration.

LANDING BOATS

With the publication of the *Tentative Landing Operations Manual* in 1934 and the resumption of landing exercises the following year, work on the landing craft

---

[1] LtGen K. E. Rockey ltr to ACofS, G–3, 21Jun57; 2dLt W. B. Trundle rept on experiments with Beetle Boat to CG, MarCorExpedFor, 3Mar24; Senior Member, BoatCom ltr to Pres, MCEB, 21Jul36, both in War Plans Sec HQMC files, folder "Landing Boats and Barges, 1924–1939," hereinafter cited as *War Plans Files, 1924–39*.

was resumed. Three types of boats for landing operations were contemplated by Marine planners of the mid-thirties. These included fast, small, surf boats to lift the leading waves; standard Navy boats and life boats of merchant vessels for the bulk of troops; and barges and lighters for heavy material.[2]

Steps to solve the first problem, provision of special troop landing boats, were initiated in 1935. The Marine and Navy officers who tackled the problem that year had to start pretty much from scratch, for Troop Barge A, a promising early development, fell victim to the size and weight restrictions imposed by naval ships in those days. Navy thinking and planning for the development of amphibious equipment was restricted by the types of ships then serving the fleet. Troop transports were practically nonexistent, so it was planned as an emergency measure to lift Marine landing forces in battleships and cruisers. A length of 30 feet, the size of davits on these ships, and a weight of five tons which was the maximum capacity of the davits, were therefore imposed as basic requirements for all new landing craft.

In an effort to explore the suitability of existing commercial craft for landing operations, the Navy, at the request of the Marine Corps, agreed to test as wide a variety of small craft from the yards of private builders as the limited funds available would permit. Bids were advertised, and nine replies were received, four of which met with the approval of the Marine Corps Equipment Board and were accepted.[3]

Tests of these approved types were conducted at Cape May, New Jersey, in the summer of 1936. But the experiments fell short of the original intention, "to test as wide a variety of forms as was practicable," because Andrew Higgins, a New Orleans boat builder with a promising design, declined to submit a bid. In 1926 Higgins had designed a special shallow draft craft called the *Eureka* for the use of trappers and oil drillers along the lower Mississippi and Gulf coast. It had a tunnel stern to protect the propeller and a special type of bow, called by Higgins a "spoonbill," which enabled it to run well up on low banks and beaches and retract easily. In 1934 the inventor had visited Quantico to interest Marines in his boat, and the Navy was now particularly anxious to test it with other comparable types of small craft.[4]

The four boats which showed up at Cape May for the test were of two general types. The sea skiff, a boat employed by Atlantic coast fishermen, was represented by the Bay Head, Red Bank, and Freeport boats. This type appeared in theory to offer a solution to the landing craft problem, as it was normally launched and landed through the heavy surf of the Atlantic beaches in fishery work. The other boat, a sea sled built by the Greenport Basin and Construction Company, was a high speed craft not normally employed in surf nor landed on beaches. The test board, comprising representatives of the Navy general line, Bureau of Construction and Repair, Bureau of Engineering, the Coast Guard, and the Marine Corps, reported that none of the boats were wholly satisfactory. They eliminated the sea sled en-

---

[2] CMC to Chief BuC&R, 24Nov36, 2d endorsement to ComInCh ltr to CNO, 14Oct36. *War Plans Files, 1924-39.*

[3] *Ibid.*

[4] Asst Chief BuC&R ltr to Higgins Industries, 21Oct36, S82-3 (15) BuShips files.

DEVELOPMENT OF LANDING CRAFT

EXPERIMENTAL AMPHIBIAN TRACTOR *developed for the Marine Corps in 1924 began the long line of test vehicles that culminated in the LVT.* (USMC 13562)

AN EARLY VERSION OF THE LANDING CRAFT *used in World War II which resulted from joint Navy-Marine Corps experiments in the 1920's and 30's.* (USMC 515227)

tirely and recommended that the three remaining craft be modified and sent to the Fleet for further tests.[5]

These tests took place at Culebra during Flex 4 in the winter of 1938. Though superior in speed and beaching ability to standard Navy boats, the modified fishing craft still had serious drawbacks. Owing to their exposed rudders and propellers

---
[5] CMC to Chief BuC&R, 24Nov36, 2d endorsement to Cominch ltr to CNO, 14Oct36, *War Plans Files, 1924–39*.

they tended to dig in when retracting. They were so high forward that Marines debarking had to drop 10 feet from the bow to the beach. They were, moreover, all unsuitable for lowering and hoisting.[6]

In the light of the drawbacks revealed by tests, the Bureau of Construction and Repair undertook the construction of a boat embodying all the best features of the fishing craft.[7] This was the beginning of a long and unsuccessful effort by the Bureau to develop a satisfactory landing craft. The "Bureau Boat" in various forms showed up regularly at Fleet Landing Exercises from 1939 through 1941, but efforts to get the "bugs" out of its design were abandoned in 1940.

Experiments with standard Navy ships' boats proceeded simultaneously with the development of special types. From the first they proved unsatisfactory. After five of them foundered in a four-foot surf at San Clemente during Flex 3, efforts to adapt standard Navy boats for beach landings were abandoned. The fact was that, having been designed for other purposes, none of them were suitable for beaching operations. As the Commanding Officer of the 5th Marines concluded: "Navy standard boats are totally unsuited for landing troops of the leading waves, even under moderate surf conditions. They are in no sense tactical vehicles, lacking in speed and maneuverability and are extremely difficult to handle in surf.

---

[6] CG 1st MarBrig Flex 4 Rept, 12Mar38; BriGen V. H. Krulak ltr to Head HistBr, G-3, HQMC, 1Feb57, w/attached comments.

[7] CMC to Chief BuC&R, 24Nov36, 2d endorsement to Cominch ltr to CNO, 14Oct36, *War Plans Files, 1924-39*.

They do not permit the rapid debarkation of troops at the water's edge."[8]

By 1938 a beginning had been made towards the solution of the landing craft problem. As a result of the early experiments the Marines had proved to their own satisfaction what they had suspected all along—that none of the standard Navy boats could be adapted satisfactorily for the landing through surf of troops or heavy equipment. Nor were the experimental models based on commercial craft, though superior to Navy boats, a satisfactory means for landing of assault waves on a defended beach. These results, though negative in character, at least cleared the way for concentrating development on specially designed landing craft.

The fruitful line of development came into view with the re-entrance of Andrew Higgins into the picture. In October 1936, about a year after declining to bid on the experimental landing boat contract, Higgins had written the Navy offering his *Eureka* as a troop landing craft. As funds for the purchase of experimental boats had been exhausted, the Navy was unable to purchase the Higgins craft at that time.[9]

A year later Commander Ralph S. McDowell, who was responsible for landing craft development in the Bureau of Construction and Repair, learned of the *Eureka* boat. He wrote Higgins inviting him to visit the Navy Department and discuss this boat if he ever came to Washington. Higgins and his naval architect

---

[8] CO 5th Mar Flex 3 Rept, 26Feb37.

[9] Asst Chief BuC&R ltr to Higgins Industries, 21Oct36, S82-3 (15) BuShips files.

caught the first train for Washington. They spent about a week in McDowell's office working out a conversion of the standard *Eureka* into a landing craft. As funds for the purchase of experimental boats had been exhausted, the Navy Department at first refused to purchase the Higgins craft. But after the inventor offered to build a boat for less than cost, the Department relented, found the necessary funds, and gave Higgins a contract for one boat. Higgins delivered it to Norfolk in 30 days.[10]

The *Eureka* was tested in surf at Hampton Roads in the spring of 1938[11] and made its first maneuver appearance at Flex 5 in 1939 where it competed against several Bureau boats and the by now venerable fishing craft. Marines were enthusiastic about its performance. "The Higgins boat gave the best performance under all conditions. It has more speed, more maneuverability, handles easier, and lands troops higher on the beach," reported the commanding officer of the 1st Battalion, 5th Marines. "It also has greater power in backing off the beach; not once was the boat observed having difficulty in retracting."[12]

Lieutenant Commander R. B. Daggett, the representative of the Bureau of Construction and Repair at Flex 5, did not share the Marines' enthusiasm for the Higgin's *Eureka*. "The Higgins . . . boat is too heavy. . . . The speed is too slow. . . . All the Higgins boats have 250 horsepower with accompanying excessive gasoline consumption for the speed obtained,"[13] he reported to his bureau.

Daggett's preference was for a modified Bureau boat built by the Welin Company. The other Bureau types and the fishing boats he found unsatisfactory, and as the Marine Corps and the Bureau were in agreement, on this point at least, these craft were discarded.

Neither the Marine Corps nor the Bureau of Construction and Repair was to have the last word at Flex 5. The Commander Atlantic Squadron, as represented by his Landing Boat Development Board, recommended further tests for the Bureau and *Eureka* craft. Accordingly at Flex 6 the following year the drama was reenacted. Again the Marines declared the *Eureka* to be "the best so far designed." The Atlantic Squadron, shifting slightly from dead center, decided that the Higgins "was the best all-around boat for the purpose intended . . . [but] the Bureau was almost as good."[14]

By 1940 money for naval purposes was beginning to be more plentiful, and the Navy was now willing to purchase landing

---

[10] Capt Ralph S. McDowell, USN, interview by HistBr, G-3, HQMC, 19Jun57; Asst Chief BuC&R ltr to Higgins Industries, 21Oct36, S82-3 (15) BuShips files.

[11] LCdr G. H. Bahm ltr to CNO, 7Jun38, S82-3 (15) BuShips files.

[12] CO 1/5 Flex 5 Rept No 14 to CG 1st MarBrig, 15Mar39.

[13] LCdr R. B. Daggett memo to Chief BuC&R, 13Feb39, encl to Chief BuC&R ltr to CNO, 16Feb39, *War Plans Files, 1924–39*.

[14] Comments & Recommendations of Umpires and Observers, Flex 6, January-March 1940; Experimental Landing Boat Group Officer ltr to ComLantRon, 10Mar40, *War Plans Files, 1940–41*.

craft in quantity. But in view of the fact that the Fleet was unable to make a clear-cut recommendation for either the Bureau or Higgins types, the Navy let contracts for the first 64 landing craft on a fifty-fifty basis.[15]

The question was finally settled in September 1940. The Navy was now converting large merchant ships for use as troop transports. These ships were equipped with davits capable of handling 36-foot boats, and as the *Eureka* of 36-foot length had twice the capacity of the 30-footer then in service and could make the same speed without an increase in horsepower, the Navy decided to adopt the larger as standard.[16]

After five years of work the Marines finally had the landing craft they wanted. The one feature that kept the Higgins boat from fulfilling the ideal that they had built up in their minds was the difficulty of emptying it on the beach: all troops, equipment, and supplies had to be unloaded over the fairly high sides. During a visit to Quantico in April 1941, Higgins was shown a picture of a Japanese landing craft with a ramp in the bow by Major Ernest E. Linsert. Higgins became enthusiastic about the idea and returned to New Orleans determined to examine the possibility of installing a ramp in the bow of his 36-foot *Eureka*. Linsert, who was serving as Secretary, Marine Corps Equipment Board, recommended to the President of the Board, Brigadier General Emile P. Moses, that the Marine Corps procure a ramp-bow 36-foot *Eureka*. Upon receiving the approval of Marine Corps Headquarters, Moses and Linsert went to New Orleans to assist Higgins, who had agreed to make a prototype, converting a standard 36-foot *Eureka* into a ramp-bow boat at his own expense.

On 21 May, informal tests were conducted on Lake Pontchartrain. The new craft proved to be seaworthy. She beached and retracted with ease, and while on the beach the ramp was lowered and personnel and a light truck were debarked and reembarked. On the recommendation of the Navy Department Continuing Board for the Development of Landing Boats,[17] a special board of Marine Corps and Bureau of Ships officers was appointed to conduct official acceptance tests. With General Moses as senior member the board carried out the tests during the first week in June. The ramp-bow craft passed with flying colors.[18]

Thus was born the precursor of the LCVP (landing craft vehicle, personnel), the craft which, in the opinion of General H. M. Smith, " . . . did more to win the war in the Pacific than any other single piece of equipment."[19]

---

[15] DeptContBd for Dev of Landing Boats Rept to CNO, 18May40, and BuShips ltr to Cdt 5th Naval Dist, 8Jul40, both C-S82-3(15) BuShips files.

[16] CNO ltr to Chief BuShips, 23Sep40, 2455–130–60 HQMC files.

[17] This board had been created by SecNav on 12Jan37 to coordinate landing craft development. It was composed of representatives of the CNO, BuC&R, BuEng. and MarCorps.

[18] LtCol E. E. Linsert interview by HistBr, HQMC, 3Jun57, hereinafter cited as *Linsert interview*; BriGen E. P. Moses msg to CMC, w/ endorsements, 21May41, 2455–130–60 HQMC files; MajGen E. P. Moses ltr to ACofS, G-3, HQMC, 11Apr57; CNO ltr to CMC et al, 2Jun41, 2455–130–60 HQMC files.

[19] Gen H. M. Smith, *Coral and Brass* (New York: Charles Scribner's Sons, 1949), 72.

LIGHTERS AND BARGES

The design of a successful tank lighter proved a longer and more difficult process than did the development of the personnel landing craft. The old 45-foot artillery lighter, developed in 1927, was considered to have a limited usefulness for landing heavy equipment in the later stages of an operation, but the Marine Corps hoped to obtain a lighter, self-propelled craft particularly suited to landing tanks during the early stages.[20]

As a stop-gap measure, Marines at Quantico came up with a device to adapt the standard Navy 50-foot motor launch for landing light vehicles and artillery. "Boat Rig A," this contraption was called. It consisted of a platform fitted within the hull of the boat, together with a portable ramp by means of which the vehicle could go ashore over the bow when the craft beached. The ramp was carried into the beach broken down, where it was assembled and hitched up for debarkation. This completed, it would be disengaged and left on the beach to accommodate the next boat coming in. The ramp could be assembled and made ready for use by eight men in about 10 minutes. On subsequent trips, it took about four minutes to connect the ramp to the boat. Under ideal conditions vehicles up to five tons in weight could be landed from a 50-foot motor launch using Boat Rig A. In calm water Boat Rig A worked fairly well, but when it was tried out at Culebra in 1935, it proved so top heavy that it nearly capsized in a moderate swell. The experiment was accordingly written off.[21]

With the failure of Boat Rig A, the Marine Corps turned its attention to developing a self-propelled lighter designed specifically for landing tanks and heavy equipment through the surf. In December 1935 the Commandant requested the Bureau of Construction and Repair to design such a craft. It was to be capable of landing the 9,500-pound Marmon-Herrington tank which the Marine Corps was then considering. Negotiations dragged on for more than a year, until in April both the Marine Corps and the Bureau had agreed upon a design. A 38-foot craft, it made its first appearance at a fleet landing exercise in 1938.[22] The Marines reported it to be "a distinct improvement over previous experimental designs. It is self-propelled, has sufficient speed, and is sound and practicable in construction. It is equally adaptable for landing artillery and is an efficient cargo carrier."[23]

A 40-footer, built at the Norfolk Navy Yard in the autumn of 1938, showed up at Culebra the following winter for Flex 5. It was used successfully in transporting ashore tanks and trucks of the types then standard in the Marine Corps. Under the conditions encountered at Culebra in 1939, both the 38- and 40-foot lighters were judged to be ". . . good sea boats, handle well, have sufficient power and speed, and are capable of retracting themselves from the beach by use of their stern anchors. . . . Both types . . . proved suitable for landing tanks and motor vehicles. The new

---

[20] CMC to Chief BuC&R, 24Nov36, 2d endorsement to Cominch ltr to CNO, 14Oct36, *War Plans Files, 1924–39.*

[21] *Marines and Amphibious War,* 47; *Tentative Landing Operations Manual,* 78–80.

[22] CMC ltr to Chief BuC&R, 19Dec35, S82-3(16) BuShips files; Senior Member, BoatCom ltr to Pres, MCEB, 21Jul36; CNO ltr to Chief BuC&R, 8Jul36; CMC ltr to Chief BuC&R, 17Apr37; Chief BuC&R ltr to Cdr R. H. English, 7Apr37, all in *War Plans Files, 1934–39.*

[23] CG 1st MarBrig Flex 4 Rept, 12Mar38.

lighter proved superior to the old in respect to ease and safety of loading in a seaway as well as cargo-carrying capacity."[24]

All tank lighter experiments conducted up to the end of Flex 5 had been built around the Marmon-Herrington tank. This vehicle, adopted by the Marine Corps in 1935, had been designed to fit within the weight limitations imposed by the Navy for amphibious equipment. Lightness was just about the only virtue possessed by this tank. By 1939 the Marine Corps had given up on it and was testing the Army light tank for its suitability in amphibious operations. As the Army tank weighed about 15 tons, it could not be carried in any of the tank lighters then in existence. The Navy accordingly produced a new model 45-feet in length, capable of carrying one Army and two Marmon-Herrington tanks.[25]

One of the new 45-footers was completed in time for a trial at Culebra during the winter of 1940 in Flex 6. The tests lacked somewhat in realism, however, because none of the Army-type tanks were available. The new lighter performed adequately as a carrier of the Marmon-Herrington tank, for other vehicles, and miscellaneous heavy equipment. At the end of Flex 6, General Smith recommended to the Commandant that ". . . 20 of the 45-foot lighters be constructed, at the earliest practicable date, for use by the Atlantic Squadron in landing operations."[26]

In the fall of 1940 the Navy contracted for the construction of 96 45-foot tank lighters. After the contract had been awarded, doubt arose as to the seaworthiness of the basic design. During a landing exercise in the Caribbean, one of the 45-footers capsized and sank when the Army-type tank it was carrying shifted to one side in a moderate sea.[27]

In the spring of 1941 the Marine Corps found itself in urgent need of all the lighters it could lay its hands on for use in a proposed amphibious landing in the Azores.[28] None of the 96 lighters ordered by the Navy had been delivered, and not more than eight or ten were expected in time for the operation. Therefore, on 27 May 1941 the Navy Department Continuing Board for the Development of Landing Boats recommended that Higgins be given an opportunity to convert one of his 45-foot *Eureka* boats into a tank lighter by installing a ramp in the bow. If this craft met service tests he would be awarded a contract for 50 tank lighters. The Secretary of the Navy gave his approval on 29 May, and Higgins received this order by telephone the next day.[29]

Higgins rushed through the conversion, completing it in time for testing and acceptance during the first week in June by the same board of Marine Corps and Bu-

---

[24] CO 1/5 Flex 5 Rept No 14 to CG 1st MarBrig, 15Mar39.

[25] BuC&R ltr to Cdt Norfolk Navy Yard, 6Jul39, *War Plans Files, 1940–41*.

[26] CG 1st MarBrig ltr to CMC, 29Apr40, *War Plans Files 1940–41*.

[27] ComLantRon ltr to CNO, 13Dec40, 2455–130–60 HQMC files; Senate Report No. 10, Part 16, Additional Report of the Special Committee Investigating the National Defense Program, 78th Congress, 2d Session, hereinafter cited as *Senate 10*.

[28] See Part I, Chap 5 of this history.

[29] CNO ltr to CMC *et al*, 2Jun41, 2455–130–60 HQMC files; *Senate 10*, 139; Capt R. B. Daggett, USN, interview by HistBr, G–3, HQMC, 20May57, hereinafter cited as *Daggett Interview*.

reau of Ships officers who had come to New Orleans to test the 36-foot ramp-bow *Eureka*. At the New River exercises that summer the Higgins tank lighters proved to be of excellent basic design. "They were found to be fast, subject to ready control and retraction, relatively light, and equipped with a reliable power plant," reported General Smith.[30] They also proved to be too hastily constructed. The ramps were so weak that several collapsed, and the sill was too high for efficient handling of vehicles. Higgins, who was present, was confident that he could correct the deficiences.[31]

Before the reports of the New River exercises had been received by the Navy Department, a contract had been let for 131 additional tank lighters. These were of a 47-foot Bureau design, a prototype of which had never been built. As a result of the good showing of the Higgins tank lighter at New River, this contract was later reduced to ten. Higgins was the low bidder, and built one craft to Bureau specifications, although he was convinced that the design was unseaworthy. His fears proved to be well founded when the tests were carried out. By this time, however, the tank lighter program had again changed direction.[32]

On 4 October 1941, the Auxiliary Vessels Board of the Navy had reported that there was no lighter capable of landing the newly developed Army 30-ton medium tank. The Secretary of the Navy directed the Bureau of Ships to remedy this deficiency. Accordingly, in December existing tank lighter contracts were changed to provide 50-footers in lieu of the 45-foot Higgins and 47-foot Bureau types still to be built. Both Higgins and the Bureau produced designs of 50-foot craft. Before any deliveries could be made, President Roosevelt, at a White House Conference on 4 April 1942, directed the procurement of 600 additional 50-foot tank lighters by 1 September for the North African operation. The Bureau of Ships, to meet this commitment, ordered 1,100 of its own design.[33]

Since this order was earmarked for service in a projected Army operation, the Army showed keen interest in a test of the two types held near Norfolk on 25 April 1942. Each carried a 30-ton tank, elaborately lashed down in the Bureau lighter, merely blocked in place in the Higgins. Wind velocity ran 18 to 23 miles per hour, with wave heights estimated between 1½ and 2 feet. Both lighters showed a speed of 10 miles an hour over a measured 1½-mile course. What happened after that is described by the Army observer who made the trip in the Higgins type:

As we neared the [antisubmarine] net it became apparent that the Navy Bureau-type tank lighter was in trouble. She appeared to have a tendency to dive when headed into the seas and was taking considerable water aboard. She stopped several times and members of the crew could be seen manning hand pumps and attempting to better secure the tank in the lighter. Once when under way and making a wide turn, it appeared that the lighter was going to overturn. Some of the crew was seen straddling the higher bulwark and the coxswain had left the pilot house and was steering the vessel from the rail.

While this was going on, our [Higgins] lighter was standing by, as was a picket boat and two

---

[30] CG PhibLant ltr to CinCLant, 9Sep41, FMFLant files.

[31] CNO ltr to CMC *et al*, 2Jun41, 2455-130-60 HQMC files; *Daggett Interview; Linsert Interview;* CinCLant ltr to CNO, 7Oct41, FMFLant files.

[32] *Senate 10,* 139–140.

[33] *Ibid.,* 157.

Higgins 36-foot boats. None of these vessels was experiencing any difficulty. The Higgins tank lighter was maneuvering around in sharp turns into the sea, through the wave troughs.

We then [after Bureau lighter turned back] opened the engines up to 1,900 r. p. m. and proceeded past Little Creek to Fort Storey. The lighter took no water except a little spray. Performance was excellent in all respects. The lighter was beached in the surf and the tank ran off onto the beach despite poor handling by the coxswain who finally allowed the lighter to broach to. In spite of this the vessel had such power and retraction qualities [as] to get back into deep water.

As far as comparison of characteristics of the types of tank lighters are concerned, it may be stated that in the May 25 tests there was no comparison. . . .[34]

As a result of these tests, the Bureau hastily notified all yards to shift to the Higgins type. Thus the Higgins 50-footer became the standard tank lighter of the Navy, the prototype of the LCM (landing craft, mechanized) as the Marines knew it in World War II, and as they know it today in enlarged form.

AMPHIBIOUS VEHICLES

Another vehicle which was to play a vital role in the amphibious operations of World War II was the amphibian tractor (amtrack, LVT). It was built in 1935 by Donald Roebling, a wealthy young inventor living in Clearwater, Florida. The "Alligator," as Roebling called his creation, was a track-laying vehicle which derived its propulsion afloat from flanges fixed to the tracks, essentially the principle of early paddle-wheel steamships. Originally intended as a vehicle of mercy, for rescue work in the Everglades, the "Alligator" was destined for fame as an instrument of war.

The Marine Corps first took notice of the "Alligator" in 1937, when Rear Admiral Edward C. Kalbfus, Commander, Battleships, Battle Force, U. S. Fleet, showed Major General Louis McCarthy Little, then commanding the Fleet Marine Force, a picture of the strange vehicle appearing in *Life* magazine. General Little was quick to grasp its potentialities and sent the picture and accompanying article to the Commandant. He, in turn, passed it along to the Equipment Board at Quantico.[35]

The Marine Corps had not forgotten the old Christie amphibian, of such bright promise and disappointing performance. Here appeared to be a possible answer. The Board dispatched its secretary, then Major John Kaluf, to Florida to see the vehicle perform and to consult with Mr. Roebling. Kaluf was favorably impressed, and on this basis the Equipment Board reported to the Commandant that ". . . subject boat has possibilities for use in landing troops and supplies at points not accessible to other types of small boats." In May 1938 the Commandant cited this opinion in recommending to the Navy that ". . . steps be taken to procure a pilot model of this type of amphibious boat for further tests under service conditions and during Fleet Landing Exercise No. 5."[36]

Both the Navy Board and the Bureau of Construction and Repair endorsed the recommendation unfavorably on the grounds of economy. The boat develop-

---

[34] *Ibid.*, 163.

[35] *Linsert Interview;* LtCol V. J. Croizat, "The Marines' Amphibian," *MC Gazette,* June 1953, 42–43 (Croizat takes his information from Linsert).

[36] CMC ltr to Senior Member, NavDept ContBd for Dev of Landing Boats, 18May38, *War Plans Files, 1924–39.*

ment program was at last well under way, and it seemed unwise to divert any of the limited appropriations to a purely experimental project. CNO concurred in the recommendation of the Board.[37]

Marine interest in the amphibian tractor persisted, however, and in October 1939, General Moses visited Roebling at his shop in Clearwater, Florida. He inspected the latest model tractor, and persuaded Roebling to design a model including desired military characteristics.[38]

In January 1940, Roebling had completed the new design. An appropriation was secured from the Bureau of Ships, and work started on the first military model of an amphibian tractor. In November the completed machine was delivered at Quantico where it was demonstrated for the Commandant and a large party of high ranking officers of the Army and Navy.[39] It measured up in every respect save one. Its aluminum construction was not considered rugged enough for hard military use. Still the tractor was so impressive in every other respect that the Navy contracted with Roebling for 200 of the machines constructed of steel. As Roebling did not have the facilities for mass manufacture, he subcontracted the actual construction to the Food Machinery Corporation which had a plant in nearby Dunedin. The first vehicle, now designated LVT(1) (Landing Vehicle Tracked), came off the assembly line in July 1941.[40]

Quantity procurement of LVT(1) did not halt further development of amphibian tractors. By October 1941, the prototype of LVT(2) had put in an appearance, but volume production of the new model was delayed by the entry of the United States into the war. To achieve maximum output, the design of LVT(1) was "frozen" shortly after Pearl Harbor and the vehicle put into mass production.[41]

This early LVT(1) was unarmed, though capable of mounting machine guns. The Marines, now that they had made a start, wanted something more: an armored, turreted model capable of mounting at least a 37mm gun and serving as the equivalent of a seagoing tank in landing operations. At Clearwater in January 1940, Roebling sketched a turreted version of the LVT, the plans for which Major Linsert, Secretary of the Equipment Board, later completed.[42]

Nothing more was done about the armored LVT until June 1941, when the Commandant recommended that such a vehicle be developed, using the existing LVT as a basis. The new vehicle should be " . . . capable of sustained point-blank combat against shore-based weapons . . . . It should be able to approach a defended beach from the sea, land, over-run enemy weapons, destroy them, and continue operations ashore to support our ground troops."[43] Armor protection against .50 caliber machine-gun fire and an armament

---

[37] *Ibid.*, and endorsements thereto.

[38] Pres MCEB ltr to CMC, 29Aug40, 2455-130-20 HQMC files; *Linsert Interview;* Croizat, *op. cit.*

[39] *Linsert Interview;* Croizat, *op. cit.*

[40] Chief BuShips ltr to Cdt 5th Naval Dist., 6Dec40, 2455-130-60 HQMC files; SecNav ContBd for the Dev of Landing Vehicle, Tracked, "History of Landing Vehicle Tracked," 1Dec45, hereinafter cited as *LVT Hist.; Daggett Interview.*

[41] *LVT Hist.*

[42] Croizat, *op. cit.*

[43] CMC ltr to CNO, 27Jun41, and CNO 1st endorsement thereto to Chief BuShips, 15Jul41, 2455-130-20 HQMC files.

including a 37mm antitank gun and three .30 caliber machine guns would be required to accomplish this mission. The Chief of Naval Operations approved the project and directed the Bureau of Ships to perfect a design.

Bureau engineers began development in cooperation with Roebling and the engineers of the Food Machinery Corporation. But theirs was not to be the first armored LVT completed. Working independently and at its own expense, the Borg-Warner Corporation produced model "A," the first turreted amphibian tractor. Design work on the Roebling-Food Machinery model, LVT(A)(1) was not completed until December 1941, and the prototype did not emerge from the Food Machinery plant until June 1942. It was an LVT(2) hull mounting a 37mm gun in a standard light tank turret. It was quickly put in production, and the first vehicle rolled off the assembly line in August 1943.[44]

The craft described here were, of course, only a few of the wide variety of boats and beaching ships that performed yeoman service in all theaters during World War II. These ranged in size from the big lumbering LST (Landing Ship, Tanks, or "Large, Slow Target"), originated by the British, to the Army-developed DUKW, an amphibious truck propeller-driven afloat. But Marines played no notable part in the development of any of these, and none had appeared during the period covered by this volume. They will be described in subsequent volumes as they came to play their part in the tactical picture of Marine operations.

---

[44] *LVT Hist;* Croizat, *op. cit.*

CHAPTER 4

Marine Occupation of Iceland[1]

"It has been said," wrote Winston Churchill, "'Whoever possesses Iceland holds a pistol firmly pointed at England, America, and Canada.'"[2] At the time of which he wrote, the "pointed pistol" threatened most immediately the British lifeline: the northern convoy route between Great Britain and the Western Hemisphere, upon which the island kingdom was dependent for most of the materials to sustain its war effort as well as much that was needed for its very subsistence. Iceland perched on the flank of these shipping lanes, which were under heavy attack by German submarines. Hostile air and naval bases on the island would almost certainly render the northern route unusable, and put pressure, perhaps intolerable pressure, on the longer and more vulnerable southern route.

At the outbreak of the war Iceland enjoyed the status of autonomous parliamentary monarchy, sharing the same king with Denmark. When the Nazis overran the latter nation in April 1940, the Icelandic Parliament voted to take over the executive power of the Danish King and to assume control of foreign affairs. The strategic island became, for all practical purposes, a completely independent republic[3]—and a wholly defenseless one without even the pretense of an army or navy. This state of affairs gave rise to considerable concern in London and Washington, more genuine concern than it caused initially among the insular-minded Icelanders.

To the British the threat appeared very desperate indeed. Early in May they determined to occupy Iceland, and the need for speed and secrecy fused decision and action.[4] There was no time to stand on

---

[1] Unless otherwise noted the material in this chapter is derived from the 1st MarBrig(Prov) Rept of Activities 16Jun41–25Mar42, 26Mar42; 6th Mar(Reinf) Repts of Activities 25May–30Nov41, 13Dec41; 5th DefBn Repts of Activities 7Jun41–28Feb42, 27Feb42; Correspondence files dealing with Marine occupation of Iceland; J. L. Zimmerman, Notes and MSS on Marine occupation of Iceland (located at NRMC, Job 14051, Box 9, Folders 129–130), hereinafter cited as *Zimmerman MSS*; Gen O. P. Smith, Diary and Narrative covering the occupation of Iceland, hereinafter cited as *Smith Narrative*; S. Conn and B. Fairchild, "The Framework of Hemisphere Defense," MS of a forthcoming volume in the series *United States Army in World War II* (located at OCMH), hereinafter cited as *Hemisphere Defense*; B. Fairchild, MS chapters titled "Planning the Iceland Operation: The Army's First Task Force," "Establishing the Iceland Base Command," and "Bermuda and the North Atlantic Bases," part of a forthcoming volume of the same series; W. L. Langer and S. E. Gleason, *The Undeclared War* (New York: Harper & Brothers, 1953), hereinafter cited as *Undeclared War*.

[2] W. S. Churchill, *The Grand Alliance* (Boston: Houghton Mifflin Company, 1950), 138.

[3] On 16May42 the Parliament announced that Iceland would not renew its union with Denmark and in 1944 the island became in name as well as fact a republic.

[4] J. R. M. Butler, *Grand Strategy: Volume II—History of the Second World War* (London: HMSO, 1957), 262.

ceremony; despite Churchill's bland assertion that the British occupation of Iceland was effected "with the concurrence of its people,"[5] they had, in fact, not been consulted beforehand. "As the attitude likely to be adopted by the Icelandic Government toward such an 'invasion' was in some doubt they were not informed of the proposed expedition."[6] Indeed the first inkling the natives had that anything out of the ordinary was afoot came when early-rising fishermen discovered a British destroyer nosing up to a jetty in the harbor of the island capital, Reykjavik. At 0620 on 10 May, a reinforced battalion of Royal Marines landed and occupied the town, moving so swiftly that it was able to seize the German Consulate before the hapless Consul could destroy his papers.

According to plan, the Royal Marines were to take the situation in hand in order to pave the way for larger occupation forces. They were relieved in ten days by a Canadian Army brigade which was first reinforced and later replaced by British units. By the time Iceland began to loom large in U. S. defense plans, the big, bleak, sparsely-populated island was occupied by nearly 25,000 British troops. Hvalfjordur, a deep inlet of the sea 30 miles north of Reykjavik, became the site of a vital naval fueling and repair base, while the principal airfields, also near the capital, were home bases for squadrons of patrol bombers that hunted the German submarines.[7]

As reverse followed reverse, however, the British increasingly felt the need for the return of their troops from Iceland to the home islands, seriously threatened with invasion and under heavy air attack. The prospect of British withdrawal caused some alarm among the Icelanders and led to diplomatic soundings of the American position.

On 18 December 1940 the Icelandic Minister of Foreign Affairs, V. Stefansson, arranged a private meeting with the U. S. Consul General, Bertel E. Kuniholm. After firm assurances that his proposal was strictly unofficial, the Minister suggested to Kuniholm that the United States might consider the possibility of declaring Iceland part of the area covered by the Monroe Doctrine, in effect joining the island to the Western Hemisphere.[8] Kuniholm duly reported the tentative proposition to Washington and nearly a month later he received a cautious reply from the Secretary of State which advised him that no action was likely to be forthcoming in the near future but that he should neither encourage nor discourage further approaches along this line.[9]

In unheralded American-British staff conversations which took place in Washington in the first months of 1941, plans were laid for Allied action in case the U. S. should be drawn into the war beside Britain. Under these plans the defense of Iceland was to become the re-

---

[5] Churchill, *loc. cit.*

[6] Maj D. B. Drysdale, RM, ltr to LtCol J. L. Zimmerman, 7Sep54, in *Zimmerman MSS*, Folder 130.

[7] Butler, *op. cit.*, 262, 287, 402, 469.

[8] Although the location of the eastern boundary of the Western Hemisphere is a subject of debate among geographers, most maps of this period show Iceland as clearly within the Eastern Hemisphere. Secretary Hull, however, remembered associates bringing him maps (at the time Hitler seized Denmark) which showed Greenland wholly and Iceland partly within the Western Hemisphere. *The Memoirs of Cordell Hull*, 2 vols (New York: The Macmillan Company, 1948), I, 73.

[9] *Ibid.*, I, 754.

sponsibility of the United States; Army troops were to relieve the British as soon as practicable after the outbreak of war, but certainly no sooner than 1 September 1941, as the Army did not feel it would be ready to take on such a commitment until then.[10] But as the spring of 1941 wore on, American measures in aid of Britain, such as Lend-Lease and the progressive extension of the Neutrality Patrol into the mid-Atlantic, brought the U. S. closer and closer to conflict with Germany. Open and increasing support of the British seemed to suit the public mood; a survey of public opinion taken by the Gallup Poll in early May showed that an overwhelming majority (75%) of the American people favored helping Britain even if such a course was sure to lead the nation into war with Germany.[11] The stage was thus set for what one exhaustive study of this period has called an "overt act of participation in the European conflict."[12]

By late spring Britain felt her back against the wall. Churchill asked President Roosevelt to send American troops to Iceland to replace the British garrison. The President agreed provided an invitation to the American occupation force was forthcoming from the Icelandic Government. Churchill undertook to produce this invitation, but the process proved more one of extraction than of production. Icelandic reluctance to "invite" a foreign force to occupy the island very nearly upset a timetable already in operation.

On 4 June, the President ordered the Army to prepare a plan for the immediate relief of British troops in Iceland. The question of where the troops were going to come from arose immediately. Although the Army had reached a strength of nearly a million and a half men, the great bulk of its soldiers were raw recruits gathered in by Selective Service and recently called up National Guardsmen. Under existing legislation these men could not be sent beyond the Western Hemisphere unless they volunteered for such service. Equipment in nearly every category was in short supply, even for training purposes. The Army needed its comparatively small force of regulars to form cadres for new units. To withdraw these cadres for an expeditionary force would throw the whole immense training program out of gear.

A review of the Army's immediate capabilities convinced the President that the Marine Corps would have to furnish the initial occupation force for Iceland. Since all Marines, both regular and reserve, were volunteers, there were no geographical restrictions on their use. On 5 June, Roosevelt directed the Chief of Naval Operations (CNO), Admiral Harold R. Stark, to have a Marine brigade ready to sail in 15 days' time. The organization of this brigade was facilitated by the fact that a reinforced infantry regiment slated for expeditionary duty was at that moment en route from the west coast to the east.

At this time the Marine Corps was heavily committed to a program of organizing, equipping, and training two divisions, one on each coast. Since the infan-

---

[10] M. E. Matloff and E. M. Snell, *Strategic Planning for Coalition Warfare—United States Army in World War II* (Washington: OCMH, 1953), 46, hereinafter cited as *Strategic Planning*.

[11] E. Roosevelt and J. P. Lash (eds.), *F. D. R.: His Personal Letters 1928–1945*, 2 vols (New York: Duell, Sloan and Pearce, 1950), II, 1158.

[12] Langer and Gleason, *op. cit.*, 575.

try regiments of both divisions were still forming, they were considerably understrength, and it had been necessary to reinforce the east coast's 1st Marine Division when it was tabbed for a major role in a proposed landing operation. On 24 May, the Commandant drew on the 2d Marine Division at Camp Elliott, California, for the necessary regiment, and Colonel Leo D. Hermle's 6th Marines (Reinforced) was selected "for temporary shore duty beyond the seas."[13] The regiment was brought up to full strength by substantial drafts from the 2d and 8th Marines,[14] and on 28 May it joined its assigned reinforcing artillery, tank, and service elements. Six days after he received his orders, Colonel Hermle had his command combat loaded; the ships, three large transports and four destroyer transports, sailed from San Diego on 31 May.

When it had embarked, this regiment had orders to report to the Commanding General, I Corps (Provisional), FMF, Atlantic Fleet. At that time, its most probable mission appeared to be either the seizure of Martinique or the occupation of the Azores, both discussed in the following chapter. Momentous events, however, were developing in Europe, and these served to change the whole pattern of the war, as well as the mission of the regiment. Both British and American intelligence indicated that Hitler was getting ready to attack Russia, and soon. Such an event would automatically cancel any immediate threat to Gibraltar and render the Azores venture pointless. President Roosevelt, in fact, ordered a suspension of planning for the Azores operation on 7 June, while preparations for the movement to Iceland proceeded apace.

While the 6th Marines' convoy was still in the Pacific heading for the Panama Canal, the wheels were set in motion to complete the organization of the projected brigade. One other major unit, the 5th Defense Battalion at Parris Island, was designated for duty in Iceland; its commanding officer, Colonel Lloyd L. Leech, flew to Washington on 7 June for a two-day round of briefing and reports. The battalion's antiaircraft guns and gunners were what was wanted, so when the order assigning the 5th Defense to I Corps (Provisional) was published on 10 June the 5-inch Artillery Group was shown as being detached. In addition to the 6th Marines (Reinforced) and the 5th Defense Battalion (less 5-inch Artillery Group), the budding brigade received a company of engineers, a chemical platoon, and a platoon of scout cars from the 1st Marine Division at New River. The port for the hurried assembly of ships, materiel, and men was Charleston, S. C.

The men of the 5th Defense Battalion had some inkling of their probable area of employment; Colonel Leech's warning order phoned from Washington on the 8th had directed that special attention be paid to provision of warm clothing. On board the 6th Marines' transports, however, speculation was rife that the regiment was heading for the Caribbean, perhaps for Guantanamo Bay, but more popular was the rumored destination of Martinique. When the convoy turned north after clearing the canal, passed the western end of Cuba, and headed for Charleston most of the "scuttlebutt" still held out for a tropical objective. Need-

---

[13] 6th Mar (Reinf) Repts, op. cit., 1.

[14] "The rule was that [these] men must have been in the service for one year and must have clear records. The other regiments 'played ball' in this respect and we received good men." Smith Narrative, 17.

less to say, the issue of winter clothing after the regiment arrived at Charleston on 15 June came as a real "shocker." The severely limited time to assemble and load out the Iceland force made this cold weather gear "the darndest collection of winter clothing ever assembled;"[15] there were bits and pieces of everything.

On the day following the arrival of the 6th Marines in Charleston the 1st Marine Brigade (Provisional) was formally organized; its commander was Brigadier General John Marston. The troop list included:

Brigade Headquarters Platoon
Brigade Band
6th Marines
5th Defense Battalion (less 5-inch Artillery Group)
2d Battalion, 10th Marines
Company A, 2d Tank Battalion (less 3d Platoon)
Company A, 2d Medical Battalion
Company C, 1st Engineer Battalion
1st Platoon, Company A, 2d Service Battalion
3d Platoon, 1st Scout Company
Chemical Platoon

On 18 June, General Marston arrived in Charleston from Quantico, bringing with him a small headquarters detachment and his instructions from the CNO for the operation of his brigade in Iceland. These orders, dated 16 June, gave him a simple and direct mission:

> In Cooperation with the British Garrison, Defend Iceland Against Hostile Attack.[16]

The question of over-all command in Iceland had, of course, risen early in the top-level negotiations. The British wished the brigade to be placed directly under their control since they had the major force on the island, but Admiral Stark thought that it would be going too far for U. S. troops, ostensibly neutral, to be placed under the command of an officer of a belligerent power. Marston's orders, therefore, read that he would coordinate his actions "with the defense operations of the British by the method of mutual cooperation,"[17] while reporting directly to the CNO.

The brigade spent a week in Charleston, most of it devoted to loading supplies that arrived from camps and depots all over the eastern half of the U. S. The Army might not be sending any troops in this first contingent, but a good portion of the weapons and equipment that went out with the Marines was taken from Army units.[18] On 22 June, the last cargo that could be handled within the time limits set was loaded and at 0800 the four transports and two cargo vessels carrying 4,095 officers and men set sail for Argentia, Newfoundland.

At sea a formidable escort force including battleships, a couple of cruisers, and ten destroyers joined up.[19] Five days out of Charleston, the convoy arrived at Argentia and hove to awaiting further orders. These orders were not forthcoming until 1 July, when the Icelandic reluctance to actually "invite" American occupation was finally compromised in a much-qualified statement by the island's Prime Minister to President Roosevelt that the presence of U. S. troops was "in accordance with the interest of Iceland."[20] This left-handed invitation was the go-ahead

---

[15] MajGen H. R. Paige ltr to ACofS, G-3, HQMC, February 1957.

[16] CNO Serial 069312 to CG, 1st MarBrig (Prov), 16Jun41.

[17] Ibid.

[18] G-4 draft memo for TAG, "Transfers of Equipment to the U. S. Marine Corps," 5Jun41.

[19] U. S. Atlantic Flt OPlan F-41, 20Jun41, 1-2.

[20] Msg sent by Prime Minister Herman Jonasson of Iceland to President Roosevelt, 1Jul41.

signal and the brigade was headed east by dawn on 2 July. The Marines were going with the blessing of Churchill who had written the President earlier that:

> I am much encouraged by . . . your marines taking over that cold place and I hope that once the first installment has arrived you will give full publicity to it. It would give us hope to face the long haul that lies ahead.[21]

The President made the desired announcement on 7 July as the convoy anchored in Reykjavik harbor, pointing out that the Americans were there "to supplement, and eventually to replace, the British forces," and that an adequate defense of the strategic island was necessary to ward off a potential threat to the Western Hemisphere.[22] A third, but unannounced, purpose of this American occupation was the acquisition of a naval and air base in Iceland to facilitate the prosecution of our antisubmarine war in the North Atlantic.[23]

While the threat of German attack was always present, the likelihood of it happening steadily lessened as the year wore on.[24] On the day that the 1st Brigade left Charleston, Germany attacked Russia. Hitler repeatedly in the months that followed indicated that he wanted to avoid provoking the U. S. into war while he concentrated on the offensive in Russia. His submarine commanders were given orders to spare American shipping as much as possible, even though it had been publicly announced that U. S. Navy vessels were affording protection to British and Canadian ships that joined American convoys headed for Iceland. Still Hitler decreed that there would be no accounting for the submarine commander who sank an American vessel by mistake. Up until the actual U. S. entry into the war this partial immunity of American vessels from attack held good.[25]

The fact that Hitler had decided to go easy on U. S. ships in the North Atlantic was naturally not known to American naval commanders. There was considerable pressure to get the brigade and its equipment unloaded in the shortest possible time and the convoy headed back for the States. This unloading proved an onerous task. There was little local labor. Marines had to furnish all working parties and the men toiled around the clock, helped not a little by the fact that at this time of year it was light 24 hours a day.

Only two ships could be docked at Reykjavik at a time and the places beside

---

[21] Quoted in Hull Memoirs, op. cit., II, 947.

[22] S. I. Rosenman (ed), *The Public Papers and Addresses of Franklin D. Roosevelt*, 13 vols (New York: Harper and Brothers, 1950), X, 255–256.

[23] S. E. Morison, *The Battle of the Atlantic—September 1939–May 1943—History of the United States Naval Operations in World War II* (Boston: Little, Brown and Company, 1947), 78, hereinafter cited as *Battle of the Atlantic*.

[24] An estimate of the situation prepared by a special board convened by the brigade shortly after its arrival in Iceland attributed to the Germans the following capabilities: To land in force from air or sea; to conduct bombing attacks; and to conduct raids by surface vessel and submarines. The board concluded, however, that as long as the British Home Fleet operated in superior numbers in the water surrounding Northern Scotland, the Orkney, Shetland, and Faroe Islands it would be impossible for the Germans to support a force of any size in Iceland. 1stMarBrig(Prov) Estimate of the Situation (Defense of Iceland), 5Aug41.

[25] "Fuehrer Conferences on Naval Affairs, 1939–1945," *Brassey's Naval Annual 1948* (New York: The Macmillan Company, 1948), 220ff. See the transcripts for the conferences of 21Jun41, 9Jul41, 25Jul41, 17Sep41, and 13Nov41 for the continuity of German policy regarding American shipping.

the wharves were reserved for the cargo vessels which carried heavy equipment of the 5th Defense Battalion. The rest of the convoy rode at anchor in the harbor, while men and supplies were lightered ashore to a gently sloping pebble beach near the city. Early on 12 July the job was finished, the convoy sailed, and the Marines had their first real chance to look around them.

They drew small reassurance from what they saw. The Icelandic landscape was something less than prepossessing, at least to men raised where soil produces vegetation and a tree is a tree. No trees above dwarf height grow on Iceland's rugged, mountainous terrain, and vegetation is limited to a little sheep pasturage on the comparatively flat stretches. It has been described as the most volcanic region in the world. Craters, many of them occasionally active, pock its surface, and lava flows lace across it.

The most unpleasant thing about Iceland's weather is its very uncertainty; the mountains usually insure that the same kind of weather rarely exists simultaneously all over the island. Although the temperature range is moderate, the humidity is consistently high, and precipitation frequent but erratic. About the only constant is the assurance of steady winds, which may change abruptly to gale force.[26]

The island is slightly smaller in area than Kentucky, but barely supported a population of about 120,000 at the time of the occupation. Along its 2,300 miles of jagged coastline were a number of small fishing villages; and except for the area around Reykjavik where there was a roadnet, all communication was by sea. The prim little capital boasted about 38,000 inhabitants, two movie houses, and one first class hotel; as a liberty town for nearly 30,000 British and American troops it boasted nothing. The only living things the island had in abundance were sheep and ponies,[27] and the Marines never developed a taste for mutton and were forbidden to ride the runt-sized steeds. Altogether, it was probably good for morale that the Marines did not know at this time that they were destined to see Iceland—and nothing but Iceland—for eight dreary months to come.

Even before the first brigade unit set foot on shore, the Marines learned what the term "mutual cooperation" meant to the British. They could not have been more cordial, generous, and helpful. As the brigade was woefully short of motor transport, the British put more than 50 trucks at its disposal, together with drivers familiar with the region and the traffic problems peculiar to Iceland—and left them in the hands of the Marines for several weeks. They also furnished rations and turned over several of their permanent camps to the new arrivals, moving into tent camps to make room.[28]

The enthusiastic reception by the British included a highly prized offer by their

---

[26] In a hurricane on 15Jan42, wind velocities of over 125 mph were recorded. It did an enormous amount of damage. Ships were driven on the rocks and huts and other buildings which were not firmly anchored were blown away. Paige, *op. cit.*

[27] Most of the information on Iceland's climate and terrain was taken from Col L. P. Hunt, "Report of two-day reconnaissance of Iceland, June 12–13, 1941," 18Jun41.

[28] "Our reception by the British has been splendid. They have placed at our disposal all of their equipment and have rationed us for ten (10) days to cover the period of disembarkation." BriGen J. Marston ltr to MGC, 11Jul41.

commander, Major General H. O. Curtis, to provide the Marines with the distinctive polar bear shoulder insignia of the British force. General Marston accepted for the brigade and noted later that:

> The mutual cooperation directive worked, to the entire satisfaction of the British Commander and the Brigade. The British complied with our requests and we complied with theirs. It was as simple as that. A British commander less sympathetic than General Curtis might have upset the applecart but under that talented officer no incident of conflict occurred.[29]

In their new camps the Marines made their first acquaintance with the Nissen hut, an introduction that was to ripen into familiarity that rarely reached the friendship stage. In the months to come the men of the brigade were to build and maintain roads and construct defenses; they were to become very practiced at the art of the stevedore; but most of all they were to become efficient builders of the ubiquitous Nissen hut. The hut itself "was an elongated igloo covered with corrugated iron roofing and lined with beaver board"[30] designed to accommodate about 14 men. It was possible to erect several huts in combination to accommodate larger numbers of men or for use as offices, mess halls, recreation rooms, and classrooms.

For the first week ashore the Marines were fully occupied getting their camps established and then they were fitted into the British scheme of defense. Initially, the brigade's primary mission was to serve as a mobile reserve although its lack of transportation meant that most of its mobility would be dependent on foot power.[31] The various units, which were spread out over a good part of the countryside around Reykjavik, were also responsible for local defense of their bivouac areas, a responsibility that grew to include long segments of coastline when the British units defending these possible landing points were later relieved.

The machine guns and 3-inch guns of the 5th Defense Battalion were integrated into the British antiaircraft defenses around the airfield and harbor and remained a part of this system for the rest of the Marines' stay. As a result, the 5th Defense spent most of its time performing the duties for which it was constituted; its state of training was good and it improved as a result of a steady round of gun watches and drills and frequent though unproductive enemy aircraft alerts. In contrast, the men of the 6th Marines and its reinforcing units had reason to think that they were on one gigantic and never-ending working party, and the regiment labelled itself a "labor regiment" in its August report to General Marston.

A welcome break from the steady grind of labor details occurred on 16 August when Prime Minister Churchill visited Iceland en route to England following his famous Atlantic conference with President Roosevelt. He was accompanied by an imposing array of high British rank: Admiral of the Fleet Sir Dudley Pound, First Sea Lord; General John Dill, Chief of the Imperial General Staff; and Air Chief Marshal Sir Wilfred Freeman, Vice Chief of Air Staff. After paying their respects to local officials, they at-

---

[29] MajGen J. Marston ltr to ACofS, G-3, HQMC, 31Jan57.

[30] *Smith Narrative*, 34.

[31] Iceland Force memo IF/168/1/G to CG, 1st MarBrig, 16Jul41; 1st MarBrig OpOrd No 3-41, 16Jul41.

tended a large joint British-American military review held in their honor. Of this event Churchill wrote later: "There was a long march past in threes, during which the tune 'United States Marines' bit so deeply into my memory that I could not get it out of my head." [32]

The reason for the continuous round of camp construction was two-fold. First, somebody had to build the camps to accommodate the expected influx of Army troops; neither the British nor the Icelanders were in a position to do so. The process of simple elimination gave the Marines the job. Second, it soon became apparent that the Marines themselves were going to stay for a while and a good part of their time had to be spent preparing their own facilities for the onset of winter.

A common, indeed, official, belief that the Marines were going to be relieved in September by Army troops held strongly for about a month after the brigade arrived in Iceland. There were numerous evidences that this was the intention of the top planners when the concept of the Marine Corps furnishing the initial occupation troops was first broached. By mid-August, however, it became evident that the Army would not be able to provide enough men to relieve the brigade and that the lack of readily available troops would make the role of those who did arrive one of reinforcement rather than relief. The British, who were supposed to return to their home islands, had to stay on to bolster the defenses. The crux of the Army's dilemma was the fact that not all of its men were available for assignment; "the passage of legislation in August 1941 permitting the retention in service of the selectees, Reserve officers, and the National Guardsmen still left the problem of restriction on territorial service—a problem which was to remain with the Army until Pearl Harbor brought a declaration of war." [33]

There was really not too much trouble taking care of the first Army contingent to arrive, a small force of about 1,000 men built around a pursuit squadron and an engineer battalion. Their convoy made port on 6 August and the units, which came under Marston's command, moved into a camp set up for them by the Marines. However, preparations for the arrival of a second Army echelon of brigade strength due in mid-September meant that every Marine available had to turn to on camp construction. It was the difficulties attendant upon the raising of this second force that led to the decision to hold the Marines in Iceland.[34]

The commander of the Army troops of the September echelon was senior to General Marston; according to the original occupation plan, the principle of unity of command was to hold in Iceland, and under it the senior officer present, regardless of service of origin, would have assumed operational control over all American troops. Acording to this concept, Army Major General Charles H. Bonesteel would simply have superseded General Marston and all hands would have carried on as before. But in the interim between June and September, the Army Chief of Staff, General George C. Mar-

---

[32] Churchill, *op. cit.*, 449.

[33] *Stategic Planning*, 51.

[34] AG memo to ACofS, War Plans Div, 6Sep41. In order to field the force that finally reached Iceland in September, the Army had to draw on posts and stations all over the U. S. AG WrnO to Army commanders concerned, 14Aug41 (located at TAGO).

shall, had decided that unity of command did not go far enough, at least as far as Iceland was concerned. He determined that if General Bonesteel was to have full responsibility for the American occupation, then he should also have full administrative as well as operational control over all the troops in Iceland.

Such a transfer of the Marines from Navy control could be effected by executive order, as had been done by President Wilson in the case of the Marines serving in France in World War I. Unfortunately, from the Marines' point of view, this transfer involved a great deal more than a simple change of command. It brought them under the Army's administrative and disciplinary system which differed considerably from that of the Navy and with which they were unfamiliar.

The Commandant, who had seen the system at work in World War I, protested vigorously. On 4 September he wrote Admiral Stark:

> The proposed change will not only necessitate a complete revision of this plan [unity of command] but would introduce many administrative difficulties, with no corresponding advantages in so far as command relations are concerned. A complete change of the administrative system would again be required when the First Marine Brigade is detached from the Army.[35]

And again on 5 September:

> In view of the existing situation in Iceland and the probable nature of other operations to be conducted by the Navy elsewhere, the proposed plan has many undesirable ramifications. If carried to its logical conclusion, it will mean, at best, frequently shifting Marine units from the Navy to the Army and back again, with much administrative grief. It will probably change our concept of command relations in joint operations.[36]

---

[35] MGC memo for Adm Stark, 4Sept41.
[36] MGC memo for Adm Stark, 5Sep41.

But it was a losing fight. Marshall stated that he had no intention of establishing a precedent and remained adamant. The Commandant did not learn of the proposed change until it was practically an accomplished fact, and the support he received from the CNO was lukewarm. The actual transfer of command took place on 24 September and General Holcomb was directed to report to the Secretary of War on all matters pertaining to the brigade.[37]

The resultant administrative difficulties did not prove to be as bad as Holcomb and many others had feared. The changeover was more of an annoyance than it was a definite hindrance; after all, as one battalion commander commented later, "while administration difficulties may be bothersome they can be handled."[38] In the course of trying to master Army procedures, General Marston wrote the Asistant Commandant:

> They have a tremendous amount of paper work which the Marine Corps seems able to avoid. The barrage of force orders coming out of staff sections is appalling. Of course we are getting along all right but it will be months before we are oriented in the new direction ... If the future develops another situation similar to that of this Brigade in Iceland, I hope that you will be able to have the transfer deferred with at least two months notice so that the officers concerned can get themselves oriented in preparation for the jump.[39]

One of General Bonesteel's first acts as the Commanding General of the new Iceland Base Command was to send a letter of appreciation to the 1st Marine Brigade (Provisional) which extended his "sin-

---

[37] Presidential directive to SecWar and SecNav, 22Sep41.
[38] MajGen W. A. Worton ltr to CMC, 1Feb57.
[39] BriGen J. Marston ltr to BriGen A. A. Vandegrift, 10Oct41.

cere thanks for the splendid assistance [given] in the preparation of the various campsites and in numerous other ways prior to and during our arrival in Iceland. The amount of hard and extended labor involved is fully recognized and deeply appreciated."[40]

The onrush of winter made it necessary for all troops to devote a good part of their time to camp maintenance and weatherizing. And as supplies continued to come in for the depots being built up near Reykjavik, working parties had to be provided to empty ships as well as to construct the storehouses needed to protect the equipment. Days rapidly shortened until there were only four hours of a sort of hazy daylight to accomplish necessary functions.

With the continued requirements for camp construction and preparations for an arctic winter, the brigade was not able to conduct a satisfactory training program.

Every possible opportunity was seized by unit commanders, however, to improve the state of readiness of their men. Many of the specialists, of course, like the communicators, engineers, and service personnel received considerable on-the-job training. While large-scale exercises were not possible, small units operated together as the press of construction allowed. In particular, a considerable amount of range firing of crew-served weapons was accomplished. When the 3d Battalion of the 6th Marines was moved to a camp too far away from Reykjavik to make it feasible to use its men for working parties, the commanders of 1/6 and 2/6 agreed to alternate in furnishing working parties "in order to get in a minimum amount of training."[41] The 3d Battalion, encamped in a pass that lay right in the path of winter winds howling out of the mountains near Hvalfjordur, was forced to "button-up" for the winter almost as soon as it shifted in September.

The lack of adequate unit training has been emphasized by some critics of the Marines' employment in Iceland. Training did not stop; it was hampered and curtailed by the weather and the requirements of working details, but it did go on despite all the very real obstacles. The men, trained and indoctrinated as amphibious assault troops, however, were perturbed when they heard the news of Pearl Harbor while huddled around the stoves in their Nissen huts. Were they to be left forgotten in the wrong ocean?

Once the war broke out in earnest the Navy, too, did not view with favor the employment of a Marine Brigade on a defensive mission in Iceland. The Marines were needed in the Pacific and pressure was put on the Army to get them relieved. Plans were laid to send a convoy with 8,000 men from New York on 15 January to provide the brigade's relief and return transportation. But, like so many previous false starts, this was not to be. Several of the ships in this convoy were diverted elsewhere and the resulting troop lift was only enough to relieve one battalion. General Marston picked 3/6, which cheerfully turned over its wind-blown billets to the Army troops and embarked on 28 January. The battalion left Iceland on the 31st and reached New York on 11 February.

A start had been made and the brigade began negotiations to turn over its camps,

---

[40] CG, IBC ltr to CG, 1st MarBrig(Prov), 27Sep41, quoted in *Zimmerman MSS*, Folder 129.

[41] Gen O. P. Smith ltr to ACofS, G-3, 7Feb57.

defense mission, and heavy equipment to the Army. The convoy carrying the final relief put into Reykjavik on 3 March, and the Marines began loading out the following day. At 1010 on 8 March, General Marston closed his CP on shore and opened it on board the USS *McCawley*; at noon that date the brigade returned to the jurisdiction of the Navy. It is interesting to note that this is the only instance in World War II where a Marine unit was "detached for service with the Army by order of the President." In the many joint operations that followed, all services adhered to the principle of unity of command. General Bonesteel recognized the Marines' dislike for the "detached service" concept but in a final letter to General Marston commended the brigade whose "every officer and enlisted man gave his whole hearted support and cooperation to our efforts to a much greater extent than mere compliance with instructions implied."[42]

The brigade landed at New York on 25 March and was immediately disbanded. The 5th Defense Battalion was ordered to Parris Island, the 6th Marines to the Second Division at Camp Elliott, and the supporting units to their parent organizations wherever those might be.

Thus passed into history an uncomfortable and at times frustrating mission, the military value of which was not clearly apparent at the time. The Marine Corps' expansion program in late 1941 and early 1942 was admittedly hampered by the absence of such a sizeable body of well-trained regulars and reserves. The brigade had relieved no appreciable number of British troops, which had been the original purpose of the American occupation. There is no concrete evidence that the Germans ever seriously considered attacking Iceland, although it is conceivable, even if somewhat unlikely, that the knowledge of the presence of the brigade might have deterred such an attack. The military value of the Iceland occupation stemmed from rigorous service in the field. In the many scattered and detached posts, heavy responsibilities fell on the shoulders of the young company grade officers and NCOs. Adversity developed and strengthened leadership. Once the brigade reached Iceland there was a minimum rotation of officers and men. This stability of personnel gave the commanders an opportunity, seldom afforded in peacetime, to develop teamwork and unit *esprit de corps*. Upon return to the United States, almost all ranks received a promotion and all units of the brigade were drawn on heavily to provide leaders for newly activated units. The 6th Marines furnished large drafts to the raider and parachute battalions, as well as to units of the 2d Division.

The military know-how, discipline, and qualities of leadership developed in Iceland were invaluable in providing cadres of experienced Marines around which to form these new units. As a result, the 6th Regiment, which sailed from San Diego for New Zealand in late October 1942, contained only a very small percentage of "Iceland Marines." The military wealth had been shared.

---

[42] CG, IBC ltr to CG, 1st MarBrig(Prov), 1Mar42, quoted in *Zimmerman MSS*, Folder 130.

CHAPTER 5

The Marine Corps on the Eve of War [1]

THE INEVITABLE CONFLICT: DEFENSIVE EXPANSION

While war came to Europe in September 1939, the United States did not formally enter the struggle against the Axis Powers for another 27 months. The formal declarations of war did not, however, project the nation directly from a state of isolation and indifference into active belligerency. Although the United States declared its neutrality—our aim being to avoid conflict while guarding against totalitarian penetration of the Western Hemisphere—we were gradually drawn deeper and deeper into short-of-war operations in support of Great Britain and her allies.

Initially, the Administration moved with caution. In the years following the "war to end all wars," disappointment in the League of Nation's failure and the world-wide depression of the 1930's had served to increase our isolationist tendencies. Aware of the national sentiment,[2] President Roosevelt initiated a program for gradually increasing the armed services, strengthening our bases, and developing a foundation for the expansion of our national resources and industry. On 8 September 1939, seven days after Hitler's armies crossed into Poland, the President officially declared a limited national emergency. As the rising tide of Nazi aggression swept over Europe in 1940 and 1941, Americans awakened more and more to the peril and supported increasingly the national policy of strengthening our armed forces.

As of 30 June 1939, two months before Hitler's armies launched their *Blitzkrieg*, Marine Corps strength stood at 19,432 officers and enlisted,[3] of whom 4,840 (including aviation components) were assigned to the Fleet Marine Force. FMF ground forces were organized in two units optimistically designated "brigades," each in actuality an understrength infantry regiment [4] reinforced by skeletonized supporting elements: 1st Brigade based on the east coast (Quantico), 2d Brigade on the west coast (San Diego). Each brigade had the support of a Marine aircraft group of corresponding numerical designation, and FMF aviation further boasted a scouting squadron (VMS-3) based in the Virgin Islands.

However, conversion of international tension into armed conflict in Europe resulted in a marked quickening of United

---

[1] Unless otherwise noted the material in this chapter is derived from *CMC AnRepts*, 1939–1941.

[2] The Roper Poll in September 1939 showed that extreme interventionist sentiment was limited to 2.5% of the total population; 37% preferred to have nothing to do with the warring nations. R. E. Sherwood, *Roosevelt and Hopkins, An Intimate History* (New York: Harper and Brother, 1948), 128.

[3] Table DGB-2200-DJF prepared by PersAcct Sect, RecordsBr, PersDept, HQMC, 26Nov54.

[4] 5th and 6th MarRegts of WWI fame, based on the east and west coasts respectively.

States defense efforts. And from that point on the Commandant's Annual Reports reflect a steady succession of upward revisions in personnel planning until by 30 November 1941 total strength stood at 65,881, the number, give or take a few, with which the Marine Corps would enter the war against the Axis Powers a week later at Pearl Harbor.

But of greater significance than the increase in over-all strength was the growing proportion of that strength represented by the Fleet Marine Force. Fiscal 1940 saw the numbers of the Corps' striking arm more than doubled: from 4,525 to 9,749; and this figure in turn had more than tripled by 30 November 1941, reaching 29,532. One factor largely responsible for this impressive increase was mobilization in November 1940 of the entire Organized Marine Corps Reserve, both ground and air, thus making available a large number [5] of officers and men, at least partially trained, for incorporation into the FMF with a minimum of delay.

This increased strength made possible organization of a unit larger than the Marine Corps had ever operated before: the triangular division, consisting of three infantry regiments, an artillery regiment, supported by engineer, reconnaissance, and signal units plus medical and other service troops. Thus on 1 February 1941 the brigades stationed on the east coast and west coast were officially activated as the 1st Marine Division and 2d Marine Division respectively. To effect the necessary expansion, cadres were drawn from existing units around which to build and train new units of the same type. This proved a slow and laborious process, and months passed before either division could be built up to authorized strength.

Growth of Marine Aviation kept pace with that of the ground forces, and again that pace looked faster on paper than it was in actuality. Simultaneously with the conversion of the two brigades into divisions, the east coast and west coast FMF aircraft groups, based at Quantico and San Diego respectively, were activated as the 1st and 2d Marine Aircraft Wings (MAW). But, as with the divisions, bringing them up to authorized strength proved no overnight process.

Initially, each could boast only a single aircraft group of mixed composition, designated MAG–11 and MAG–21 respectively. On the eve of Pearl Harbor, FMF air personnel numbered 2,716 officers and enlisted out of a total aviation strength of 5,911.[6] These were divided among the two wings and the detached squadron in the Virgin Islands. The 1st MAW had remained based at Quantico. But the coming of war found the 2d MAW scattered far and wide, with a squadron at Wake Island, a detachment at Midway Island, and the balance of the wing at Ewa, on Oahu, T. H.[7]

Though the two divisions and two wings comprised the Marine Corps' principal striking arm, considerations of im-

---

[5] Total of 5,241 officers and enlisted.

[6] The two groups were identical in composition but slightly unequal in strength. Each contained 2 fighter, 2 scout-bomber, 1 observation, and 1 utility squadrons. MAG–11 had 100 operational aircraft to 90 for MAG–21. The Virgin Islands detachment operated 8 utility-scouting planes, bringing the total of FMF aircraft of all types to 198. Altogether, Marine Aviation included 13 squadrons and 204 operational planes of all types.

[7] "Administrative History of U. S. Marine Corps in World War II" (MS in HistBr Archives), 158, hereinafter cited as *AdminHist*.

AIR EVACUATION OF WOUNDED *from Ocotal, Nicaragua was pioneered by Marine aviators who presaged the mass evacuation techniques of World War II.* (USMC 5173)

ARMY LIGHT TANK *is unloaded from its landing craft during joint Army-Marine amphibious exercises at New River, N. C. in August 1941.* (SC 125129)

mediate urgency diverted many FMF personnel into other activities. The United States had no intention of defending America on its own soil as long as the situation permitted any other choice. The Navy already possessed several outlying bases and hoped to obtain more, for security of which it relied on the Marines. Hence there evolved a type of organization specially adapted to this duty: the Marine defense battalion, which was primarily an artillery outfit whose main armament consisted of antiaircraft and coast defense guns.[8] The first four of these, with consecutive numerical designations, were activated during fiscal 1940. By the time of Pearl Harbor the number had reached seven with two more in process of formation.[9]

Concurrent with increased numbers came increased responsibilities. The Navy, too, was expanding at an unprecedented rate, diverting more Marines from the FMF to perform the Corps' traditional functions: security of naval installations ashore and service afloat. By 30 November 1941, ships' detachments had grown to 68, manned by a total of 3,793 Marines.[10]

Ashore the Navy's stepped-up training programs, particularly in naval aviation, created more and more bases, security of which imposed a serious additional drain on Marine man power. In fiscal 1940 the Corps was called upon to provide guard detachments at four new naval air stations in the Continental United States and three in U. S. overseas territories.[11] The following fiscal year added another four air stations, a naval ammunition depot, a naval supply depot,[12] and 18 other new installations ranging in character and location from David Taylor Basin, Carderock, Maryland, to Naval Magazine, Indian Island, Washington. Furthermore, garrison detachments were detailed to twelve stations overseas, as will be discussed subsequently.

Simultaneously with filling the Navy's demands, the Marine Corps assumed additional security problems of its own as existing bases expanded and new ones were established. (See below.) Thus, the period under discussion saw the activation of seven new guard companies of a non-FMF character: at Quantico, San Diego, Dunedin (Florida), and Bremerton (Washington).

GROWTH OF MARINE TRAINING AND OPERATIONAL BASES

Inevitably the problems of housing, training, and equipping rapidly expanding manpower imposed increasing pressure on the Corps' existing facilities, pegged as these were to peacetime needs and the economy of depression years.

Following World War I, activities strictly Marine Corps in nature had been concentrated generally at the recruit training depots at Parris Island and San Diego,[13] and at the operational bases at Quantico and San Diego, where the East

---

[8] The genesis of the defense battalion was attributable to two factors: (a) the acceptance of the advanced base concept and its logical tactical requirements; and (b) during the pre-World War II period, while the nation was apathetic towards rearmament and/or military expansion, an increase in Marine strength, under the guise of a defense force, was politically more acceptable.

[9] CNO ltr to CMC, 9Dec41, Encl (a).

[10] Compilation from muster rolls closed 30Nov41 (located at Unit Diary Sect, HQMC).

[11] NAS Key West and Jacksonville, Fla.; Tongue Point, Oreg.; Alameda, Calif.; Sitka and Kodiak, Alaska; and San Juan, Puerto Rico.

[12] NAS Cape May, N. J.; Miami, Fla.; Corpus Christi, Tex.; and Quonset Point, R. I.; NAD Burns City, Ind.; NSD, Oakland, Calif.

[13] Generally, all recruits from east of the Mississippi were trained at Parris Island, all from west at San Diego.

Coast and West Coast components of the Fleet Marine Force were stationed. FMF aviation was based nearby at MCAS, Quantico, and NAS, San Diego.

Marines first laid eyes on Parris Island early in the Civil War when they participated in the naval expedition which seized adjoining Port Royal. This served as an important naval base throughout the war, but the Navy did not begin construction of installations on the island proper until 1883. The first record of a separate Marine detachment setting up there permanently occurs in June 1893. The post did not begin functioning, however, in its present capacity until November 1915 when the East Coast Marine recruit depots were transferred there from Norfolk and Philadelphia.

Retained as a permanent base after World War I, Parris Island continued its role as the point of initial contact with military life for all newly enlisted Marines from the East. Partly for this reason, its facilities were maintained at a fairly high level during the lean years of the 1920's and 1930's. Nevertheless, the flood of recruits soon overflowed existing facilities and forced a rapid expansion. Thus in 1940–41, even as the full training program continued and was intensified, new barracks, a new post exchange, and a new rifle range were added to those already operating at full capacity.

The Recruit Depot, San Diego, which had operated as such since August 1923, experienced similar problems and arrived at similar solutions. As events proved, both of these bases managed to keep abreast of the expansion program throughout the war and thus accomplish their basic missions.

Much of San Diego's success in its primary mission was owed to the activation of nearby Camp Elliott in mid-1940 to furnish advanced training and serve as a base for West Coast elements of the FMF. Until then San Diego had housed both of those activities, and with the speeding-up expansion program they were beginning to get in each other's way. The first FMF units began the transfer early in 1941 and greatly eased the pressure; though, as will be seen, Camp Elliott itself was eventually pressured out of existence.

Quantico, acquired by the Marine Corps immediately following U. S. entry into World War I, found its difficulties less readily resolved. During the interim between wars, this post assumed a position of paramount importance in the development of Marine amphibious doctrine and techniques, and in the training of Marine officers and technicians. The passage of years saw additional educational units move in until the Virginia base became the center of higher learning for the Marine Corps.

Advent of the national emergency soon made it apparent that no practicable physical expansion would enable Quantico to continue these activities, all rapidly growing and intensifying in scope, and at the same time serve as home base for east coast FMF units, especially when operational forces were to reach division size. Parris Island, hard pressed to keep abreast of its own problems, could do little to relieve the presure. Clearly the situation called for construction of an entirely new and extensive base for FMF operations on the eastern seaboard. This required Congressional approval, which was obtained on 15 February 1941.

The site selected lay in the New River-Neuse River area of the North Carolina coast. The surveying and purchasing of land began immediately. By the end of April this preliminary work had been completed, and construction of Tent Camp #1, Marine Barracks, New River commenced. The isolated location of the area made development an enormous task. Transportation to the site was almost nonexistent, electric power lines were either lacking or greatly overloaded and able to provide but a fraction of the current needed. And the necessary labor could be obtained only by offering special inducements to workers. Both the Marine Corps and civilian contractors approached these problems to such good effect that by the summer of 1941 the far-from-completed camp had reached a stage of development that made it available for use.

The fledgling 1st Marine Division, still understrength,[14] moved in shortly after its return from maneuvers in the Caribbean. There it participated in a series of amphibious exercises, one with the Army's 1st Infantry Division, the first of four Army divisions to receive such training jointly with Marine units or under the direction of Marine officers.

Men of the Marine division pitched in to improve camp conditions while continuing their intensive training for combat.

---

[14] While the table of organization listed three, the 1st MarDiv had only two infantry regiments at this time.

Civilian contractors pushed construction of permanent buildings so effectively that soon various specialized training and schooling facilities and other units began transferring to the new base from both Quantico and Parris Island. The 1st Marine Division, however, had long since departed beyond the seas by the time Marine Barracks, New River, reached the stage of development where the powers that be saw fit to dignify it, late in 1942, with the name Camp Lejeune.

Like the division, the 1st Marine Aircraft Wing began outgrowing its Quantico facilities long before it achieved full strength. Even while development progressed at New River, the Marine Corps obtained authorization for a new air base nearby. Cunningham Field, Cherry Point, North Carolina, was designated a Marine Corps Air Station for development purposes on 1 December 1941, and work began on what would become by commissioning day, 20 May 1942, a vast new base capable of handling the greater part of a completely built-up Marine aircraft wing.[15]

On the west coast, Camp Elliott, less hampered than Quantico by a multiplicity of activities, proved capable initially of handling the vastly increased load of advanced training, though the camp was expanded and developed to many times its original size in the process. Its 29,000 acres housed the 2d Marine Division from its activation until its departure for the Pacific. It also became the home of the Marine Corps' first tank training center and the infantry training center for numerous replacement drafts.

---

[15] *AdminHist*, 159.

OVERSEAS COMMITMENTS: ATLANTIC[16]

During the years between wars, the pervasive spirit of pacifism which led to repeated attempts by this country to cooperate in reduction of naval armaments and in international treaties militated against adequate defense preparations, as did budgetary restrictions. Such peace as these measures achieved proved uneasy at best, but the fact that the U. S. lived up to its agreements, whereas some other nations did not, contributed toward making our defense program a shadow of what it might have been. This was particularly serious in the Pacific, as will be seen. But in 1939–41, with war flaming through Europe, the more immediate danger lay in the Atlantic where Hitler's submarines appeared nearly invincible.

In the fall of 1939 the United States armed forces were barely adequate for the defense of the Western Hemisphere. As long as the national sentiment did not sanction total rearmament and military expansion, the administration was forced to rely on existent means and a partial mobilization of both manpower and material. Unfortunately, the lull in military operations in Europe during the winter of 1939–1940 seemed to justify public apathy and made the problem of rearmament more difficult for the President and his military planners.

Britain's historical dominance of the Atlantic sea lanes had given us a false sense of security there, and permitted the United States to commit a major part of the Navy to guard against Japanese aggression in the Pacific. However, the German offensive in the spring of 1940 served to jolt Americans from their complacency. German troops overran Denmark, Norway, the Low Countries, and France. President Roosevelt recognized the danger in this and caused a shift in our military policy to provide greater security in the Atlantic.

During the summer and fall of 1940, Congress stepped up the procurement of aircraft, mobilized the reserves, passed selective service legislation, and launched the two-ocean navy building program. But completion of these measures would take time, and we had no assurance that the Axis partners would sit idly by and enjoy the fruits of their initial aggression. To implement the rearmament program, President Roosevelt adopted the policy of aiding Britain and Russia (after June 1941) while continuing diplomatic relations with Germany and Japan. With industry expanding and the armed forces increasing in size and equipment, the Administration did everything short of war to bolster Britain's tottering position.

In the fall of 1940 Britain and the United States completed negotiations which culminated in one of the most extraordinary military deals in history. Britain, holding numerous Caribbean possessions, desperately needed additional convoy vessels to protect her vital Atlantic supply line against submarine depredations; the U. S., possessor of numerous overage destroyers, wished to strengthen defense of eastern approaches to the mainland and the Panama Canal. As a result of this situation, on 2 September 1940 the U. S. agreed to swap 50 of these destroy-

---

[16] Unless otherwise noted the material in this and the following sections is derived from *Hemisphere Defense; Undeclared War; Strategic Planning; Battle of the Atlantic*.

ers [17] in return for 99-year leases on certain base sites in various strategically placed British possessions: the Bahamas, Jamaica, Antigua, Saint Lucia, Trinidad, and British Guiana.

Since plans called for development of these sites into naval activities of varying nature, the first Americans to move in were Marines of the several security guard detachments. The same held true in the case of two additional bases not included in the destroyer deal: at Argentia (Newfoundland) and in Bermuda. Thus, while in the throes of expanding the FMF, the Marine Corps found itself saddled with still more garrison duty beyond the continental limits of the United States.

DEFENSE OF THE WESTERN HEMISPHERE: MARTINIQUE

The fall of France and the Netherlands alarmed the United States to the danger that New World possessions of these countries [18] might fall into Germany's hands should Hitler force the conquered nations to cede them, or to provide servicing there for German U-Boats operating in the Atlantic.

Martinique, the administrative and economic center of France's colonies in the Caribbean, became the focal point of American interest and concern. For should the three French warships there, including the aircraft carrier *Bearn* (loaded with 106 American-manufactured fighter planes destined for pre-Vichy France), be taken over by the enemy, the security of British and American shipping in the Atlantic would be seriously threatened. Furthermore, the French High Commissioner for the Antilles, Rear Admiral Georges Robert had declared his allegiance to the Vichy government and was emphatic in his refusal to accept American and British offers of "protection."

One solution, and one which was immediately discarded, called for an American break with Vichy and the occupation of the islands by American forces. It was not expected, however, that Admiral Robert would yield without a fight—and we were not ready to scrap our neutral policy and draw accusations of Yankee imperialism from friendly Western Hemisphere nations. Dire necessity, however, required some plan of operation. On 8 July 1940, the Joint Planning Committee completed a plan for an expeditionary force, to be readied for embarkation from New York on or about 15 July. The 1st Marine Brigade [19] was earmarked for the initial landing force, to be followed by a task force based on the Army's 1st Infantry Division.

While the expeditionary force was readied, officials of the Departments of State and Navy worked out a compromise to relieve the tense situation. The Ameri-

---

[17] These were 1,200-ton, flush-deck four-stackers, vintage of World War I, many of which had been laid up since that struggle and had to be recommissioned. By the time the trade was completed (10Apr41), the U. S. had become more deeply involved and threw in an additional 10 escort vessels of the "Lake" class Coast Guard cutter.

[18] Dutch Guiana, Aruba, and Curacao; French Guiana on the South American continent; Saint Pierre and Miquelon off Newfoundland; Martinique, Guadeloupe, and several smaller islands in the West Indies.

[19] The 1st MarBrig then based at Guantanamo Bay, Cuba, was composed of 5th Mar, 1st Bn, 10th Mar (artillery), 1st EngBn, 1st MedBn, three provisional (casual) companies, BrigHqCo, and one company each of service troops, chemical troops, tanks, and motor transport.

can representative in negotiations that followed, Rear Admiral John W. Greenslade, arrived at an agreement with Admiral Robert to maintain the *status quo;* and the "hot" Martinique problem was temporarily resolved without the United States being forced into military action.

However, heightened tensions during the late summer of 1940 again indicated the possibility of French connivance with Germany. Accordingly, late in October 1940 the President " . . . asked the Navy to draft a plan for an emergency operation. . . ."[20] This plan called for an assault on Martinique, by a naval force including a landing party of some 2,800 Marines of the 1st Marine Brigade, to be supported by two reinforced Army regiments. Later plans increased the size of the force; revised estimates were based on the possibility of more than token resistance from the seven to eight thousand French soldiers and sailors on the island.

Fortunately, the operation against Martinique died stillborn. Admiral Greenslade reached a new "gentlemen's agreement" with Admiral Robert, although there were frequent instances later when President Roosevelt still thought it might be necessary to occupy the island. The Marine Corps remained prepared for possible action until Admiral Robert surrendered his command to American Vice Admiral John S. Hoover in June 1943.

THE AZORES

As early as spring 1940, President Roosevelt was deeply concerned over the possibility of a German invasion of the Portuguese Azores. These islands lie athwart the vital shipping lanes between the United States and the Mediterranean, and Europe and South America. While the Army considered them of little value in Western Hemisphere defense considerations, their danger was measurable by their value to Germany. From air bases and naval facilities in the islands, German aircraft and submarines could sortie after the bulk of British shipping.

Our deep concern for the safety and integrity of the islands led to a series of discussions with both the British, Portugal's ally, and the Lisbon government. By October 1940, United States Army and Navy planning officers had drafted a plan for a surprise seizure of the Azores. However, the plan to land one reinforced division was built on sand: the Army did not have the necessary troops to commit, nor did the Navy have adequate ships to transport and support the landing force. And, politically, it was contrary to American policy at this time to become a *de facto* participant in the European war.

By May 1941 intelligence estimates from Europe again indicated the possibility of a German movement into the Iberian peninsula and German occupation of the Azores and adjacent islands. On the 22d of that month, President Roosevelt directed the Army and Navy to draft a new plan for an expedition to occupy the Azores. This plan (GRAY), approved by the Joint Board on 29 May, provided for a landing force of 28,000 combat troops, half Marine and half Army; the Navy was responsible for transporting and supporting the force. Major General H. M. Smith, USMC, would command the landing force, under Rear Admiral Ernest J. King, the expeditionary commander.

However, while these preparations were being made, other factors developed and

---

[20] Quoted in *Hemisphere Defense,* Chap IV, 6.

altered the original mission of the mixed force. Portugal was opposed to an American occupation of the Azores, and United States planners became preoccupied with the threat of German efforts to occupy South America, particularly Brazil. The succeeding weeks witnessed a change in both the urgency for the Azores operation and in the mission of the Marine complement of the Azores force.

During the early part of June, intelligence sources in Europe produced creditable evidence that Germany did not plan to invade Spain and Portugal but intended rather to attack in the opposite direction. Russia would be Hitler's next objective. The forecast of the German plans put an end to American fears for the safety of the Azores, and permitted the United States to divert the Marines to Iceland.

DISTRIBUTION SUMMARY

How thin the Marine Corps had to spread its manpower in order to fulfill its many commitments is indicated by the table that follows showing the distribution effective 30 November 1941, on the eve of Pearl Harbor. The fact that the figures quoted do not add up to total Corps strength is accounted for by omission of minor categories involving individuals or small groups of men.

Continental U. S. (non-FMF)

Major Marine Corps Bases [21]	14,707
Posts & Stations (43)	10,089
Headquarters & Staff	780
Recruiting (4 districts)	847
Total	26,423

Overseas (non-FMF)

Posts & Stations (24)	3,367
Tactical Units [22]	5,498
Shipboard Detachments (68)	3,793
Total	12,658

Fleet Marine Force, Continental U. S.

1st MarDiv	8,918
2d MarDiv (less dets)	7,540
2d DefBn	865
1st MAW	1,301
2d MAW (less dets)	682
Miscellaneous	633
Total	19,939

Fleet Marine Force, Overseas

5 DefBns (Pacific)	4,399
2d MAW (elements) (Pacific)	733
2d MarDiv (elements) (Pacific)	489
Total	5,621
Total above categories	64,641
Total strength Marine Corps	65,881

[21] Quantico, Parris Island, San Diego, Camp Elliott, New River.

[22] 4th Mar (Philippines), 801; 1st SepBn (Philippines), 725; 1st MarBrig(Prov) (Iceland), 3,972.

PART TWO

War Comes

CHAPTER 1

Prewar Situation in the Pacific

SUMMARY OF NEGOTIATIONS [1]

In the late years of the 19th Century and the early decades of the 20th, Japan set out to gain more territory. Consistently following a policy of encroachment in Asia and the Pacific, and retreating only when confronted with the threat of superior force, the Japanese Empire steadily grew in size and strength. Warning signals of an impending clash between Japan and the Western nations with extensive interests in the Orient became increasingly evident. In the 1930's when these nations were gripped by economic depression and their military expenditures were cut to the bone, Japan struck brazenly.

In 1931 Japanese troops invaded Manchuria and no concerted international military effort was made to halt the seizure. An ineffectual censure by the League of Nations, far from discouraging Japan, emboldened her to further action. Angrily, the Japanese delegates stalked out at Geneva and gave formal notice of intention to withdraw from the League. The country thickened its curtain of secrecy which shrouded the League-mandated islands awarded Japan as its share of the spoil of German possessions lost in World War I. In 1934 the Japanese served notice that they would no longer abide by the limitations of the Washington Naval Disarmament Treaty of 1922. Finally, in 1937, Japan attacked China and horrified the world with the excesses committed by her soldiers in the infamous Rape of Nanking. But still there was no effective military action to curb this rampant aggression.

In this period Japan was not without supporters. Germany and Italy, bent on similar programs of territorial aggrandizement in Europe and Africa, made common cause with the Japanese. These "Axis" powers signed a mutual assistance pact in 1937, ostensibly aimed at the Communist Cominform, but in essence as a show of strength to forestall interference with their plans of conquest. In August 1940, after the outbreak of war in Europe and the fall of France, Germany forced the Vichy Government to consent to Japanese occupation of northern Indo-China. The three predatory nations combined again in less than a month, this time in the Tripartite Treaty of 27 September which promised concerted action by the Axis in case of war with the United States.

The United States, traditionally a friend of China and a supporter of an "Open Door" policy in Asia, strongly opposed Japanese moves to establish hegemony over the strife-torn Chinese Republic.

---

[1] Unless otherwise noted the material in this section is derived from Senate Doc No. 244, 79th Congress, 2d Session, *Report of the Joint Committee on the Investigation of the Pearl Harbor Attack* (Washington: GPO, 1946), hereinafter cited as *Pearl Harbor Rept* and the Committee's record of 39 volumes of hearings and exhibits, hereinafter cited as *Hearings Record*; G. N. Steiger, *A History of the Far East* (Boston: Ginn and Co., 1944).

While the political sentiment of the majority of Americans in the late 1930's would condone no direct military intervention, the government and the nation were openly sympathetic to the Chinese cause. Both moral and legal embargoes against munitions shipments to Japan were put into effect and increasing amounts of material aid given to China. American pilots, including members of the armed forces, were permitted to volunteer to fly for the Chinese Air Force against the Japanese.[2]

By early 1941 Japan was hurt in pride, purse, and potency as a result of American political and economic measures taken to halt its expansion. In March a new Ambassador, Admiral Nomura, was sent to Washington to negotiate a settlement of Japanese-American differences. He was confronted with a statement of four principles which represented the basic American position in negotiations. These were:

(1) Respect for the territorial integrity and the sovereignty of each and all nations;
(2) Support of the principle of noninterference in the internal affairs of other countries;
(3) Support of the principle of equality, including equality of commercial opportunity;
(4) Nondisturbance of the *status quo* in the Pacific except as the *status quo* may be altered by peaceful means.[3]

In retrospect, it seems obvious that there was little likelihood of Japan accepting any of these principles as a basis for negotiations. At the time, however, considerable and protracted effort was made to resolve differences. Postwar evidence indicates that the Japanese Premier, Prince Konoye, as well as Ambassador Nomura were sincere in their efforts to achieve a peaceful solution of the threatening situation in the Pacific. It was not Konoye, however, who called the turn in Imperial policy, but the Japanese Army. And the Army adamantly refused to consider any concession that might cause it to lose face.

After Germany attacked Russia in June 1941, the longtime threat of Soviet intervention in Japan's plans for expansion was virtually eliminated. The Japanese Army moved swiftly to grab more territory and to add to its strength. Southern Indo-China was occupied and conscripts and reservists were called up. In the face of this fresh evidence of Japanese intransigence, President Roosevelt froze all Japanese assets in the United States, effectively severing the last commercial contact between the two nations.

In October the Army forced the Konoye Cabinet to resign and replaced it with a government entirely sympathetic to its position.[4] The new premier, General Tojo, sent a special representative, Saburu Kurusu, to Washington to assist Nomura and revitalize negotiations. The Japanese diplomats were in an untenable position. They were instructed, in effect, to get the United States to accept Japanese territorial seizures on Japanese terms. Their mission was hopeless, but behind its facade of seeming interest in true negotiations, Tojo's government speeded up its preparations for war. As far as the Japanese leaders were concerned, war with the United States was a now or never proposition, since American-inspired economic sanctions would soon rob them of the necessary raw materials, particularly

---

[2] *United States Relations with China* (Washington: Dept of State, 1949), 24.

[3] *Hearings Record*, Part 2, 1103–1104.

[4] M. Kato, *The Lost War* (New York: A. A. Knopf, 1946), 48.

oil, which they had to have to supply their military machine.

The only event that might have halted Japanese war preparations would have been a complete abnegation by the United States of its principles of negotiation. On 22 November Ambassador Kurusu received the third and last of a series of communiques from Japan setting deadlines for successful negotiations. He was informed that after 29 November things were "automatically going to happen."[5]

As far as the Japanese were concerned negotiations were at an end and the time for direct action had come. The two Japanese envoys were carefully instructed, however, not to give the impression that talks had been broken off. The stage had been set for "the day that will live in infamy."

After an extremely thorough investigation of the negotiations during this period prior to the outbreak of the war, a Joint Congressional Committee summed up the duplicity of Japanese negotiations in this succinct statement:

> In considering the negotiations in their entirety the conclusion is inescapable that Japan had no concessions to make and that her program of aggression was immutable.[6]

JAPANESE WAR PLAN [7]

Both the United States and Japan had developed plans for war in the Pacific long before December 1941. Each nation considered the other to be its most probable enemy. There was, however, a fundamental moral difference between the respective war plans. The Americans planned for defense and retaliation in case of attack; the Japanese intended to strike the first blow. (See Map 1, Map Section)

Japan's prime objective was economic self-sufficiency, and the prize she sought was control of the rich natural resources of Southeast Asia and the islands of the East Indies, her "Southern Resources Area." The Japanese were well aware that invasion in this area would bring them into conflict with a coalition of powers. The lands they aspired to conquer were the possessions or protectorates of Great Britain, Australia, New Zealand, the Netherlands, and the United States. By means of surprise attacks, launched simultaneously on a half dozen different fronts, the Japanese expected to catch the Allies off-balance and ill-prepared.

The obvious threat of war with Japan had not been ignored by any of these Allied nations, but the tremendous advantage of choice of time and place of attack rested with the aggressor. Japan intended to strike during a period when most of the resources in men and material of the British Commonwealth were being devoted to the defeat of the European Axis partners. The Netherlands, which existed only as a government-in-exile, could contribute quite a few ships but only a small number of men to a common defense force. And the United States, most certainly Japan's strongest enemy, was heavily committed to support the Allies in Europe and the Near East. Moreover, that nation was only partially mobilized for war.

The initial Japanese war concept did not envisage the occupation of any terri-

---

[5] *Hearings Record*, Part 12, Exhibit No. 1, 165.

[6] *Pearl Harbor Rept*, 49.

[7] Unless otherwise noted the material in this section is derived from *Pearl Harbor Rept; Hearings Record*, Part 13, Exhibits 8–8D, Japanese Records; USSBS (Pac), NavAnalysisDiv, *Campaigns of the Pacific War* (Washington: GPO, 1946), hereinafter cited as *Campaigns of the Pacific War*.

tory east of Tarawa in the Gilberts. All operations beyond the limits of the Southern Resources Area were designed to establish and protect a defensive perimeter. The cordon of strategic bases and island outposts was to stretch from the Kuriles through Wake Atoll to the Marshalls and Gilberts and thence west to the Bismarck Archipelago. The islands of Timor, Java, and Sumatra in the East Indies were to be seized and Japanese troops were to occupy the Malayan Peninsula and Burma.

The major force which might prevent or delay the accomplishment of the Japanese plan was the United States Pacific Fleet based at Pearl Harbor. Recognizing the threat posed by the American naval strength, the Commander in Chief of the Japanese Combined Fleet, Admiral Isoroku Yamamoto, directed that a study be made of the feasibility of a surprise aerial attack on Pearl, timed to coincide with the outbreak of war. In February 1941 the first staff considerations of the projected raid were begun, but the actual details of the operation were not worked out until September when it seemed increasingly obvious to the Japanese high command that war was inevitable and that they needed this bold stroke to insure the success of initial attacks.

On 3 November the Chief of the Naval General Staff, Admiral Osami Nagano, approved the draft plan, and on the 5th commanders of fleets and task forces were given their assignments. Orders were issued to selected task force units to begin moving singly and in small groups to Hitokappu Bay in the Kuriles on or about 15 November. Ten days later a striking force, its core six large fleet carriers transporting the pick of the Japanese Navy's planes and pilots, sortied from the secluded anchorage bound for the Hawaiian Islands. The approach route lay well north of the search areas patrolled by American planes based at Midway and Wake and out of normal shipping lanes.

The tentative day of attack, X-day, had been set for a Sunday, 7 December (Pearl Harbor time). Japanese intelligence indicated that most of the Pacific Fleet would be in port on a weekend. Tallies of the ships present at the Pearl Harbor Naval Base received from the Japanese consulate at Honolulu were transmitted to the attack force as late as 5 December. Vice Admiral Chuichi Nagumo, the striking force commander, received orders from Yamamoto on 2 December confirming the chosen date. There was still time to turn back; if the approaching ships had been discovered prior to 6 December they had orders to return. No one saw them, however, and the carriers arrived at their launching point right on schedule.

At midnight of 6–7 December, the Japanese Combined Fleet Operation Order No. 1 informed its readers that a state of war existed with the United States, Great Britain, and the Netherlands.

AMERICAN WAR PLAN [8]

A nation's war plans are never static. The constantly changing world political scene demands continual reevaluation and amendment. In the 1930's, American war

---

[8] Unless otherwise noted the material in this section is derived from *Pearl Harbor Rept;* Navy Basic War Plan—Rainbow No. 5 (WPL–46), 26May41 and Appendix I, Joint Army-Navy Basic War Plan Rainbow No. 5, quoted in full in *Hearings Record*, Part 33, Exhibit No. 4; MarCorps Plan C–2, Rainbow No. 5, 5Jun41, Plans & Policies Div Files; M. S. Watson, *Chief of Staff: Prewar Plans and Preparations—United States Army in World War II* (Washington: HistDiv, DA, 1950); S. E. Morison,

PREWAR SITUATION IN THE PACIFIC

plans were concerned primarily with courses of action to be taken in the event of a conflict in one theatre and against one nation or a contiguous group of nations. In these so-called "color plans," each probable enemy was assigned a separate color designation; Japan became Orange. With the advent of the Axis coalition, American military men began thinking in terms of a true world war. As these new plans evolved they were given the name Rainbow to signify their concept of a multi-national war.

The United States was deeply involved in the war in Europe soon after its outbreak, if not as an active belligerent, then as the arsenal of the democracies. By the spring of 1941 American naval vessels were convoying shipments of war materiel at least part of the way to Europe and they were actively guarding against German submarines a Neutrality Zone that extended far out into the Atlantic. The intent of these measures and others similar to them was clearly to support Britain in its war against Germany, Italy, and their satellites. There was little question where the sympathies of the majority of Americans lay in this struggle and none at all regarding the position of their government.

On 29 January 1941, ranking British and American staff officers met in Washington to discuss joint measures to be taken if the United States should be forced to a war with the Axis Powers. It was regarded as almost certain that the outbreak of hostilities with any one of the Axis partners would bring immediate declarations of war from the others. By insuring action on two widely separated fronts, the Axis could expect at the very least a decreased Allied capability to concentrate their forces. The American-British conversations ended on 27 March with an agreement (ABC-1) which was to have a profound effect on the course of World War II. Its basic strategical decision, which never was discarded, stated that:

> Since Germany is the predominant member of the Axis Powers, the Atlantic and European area is considered to be the decisive theatre. The principal United States military effort will be exerted in that theatre, and operations of United States forces in other theatres will be conducted in such a manner as to facilitate that effort .... If Japan does enter the war, the Military Strategy in the Far East will be defensive.[a]

The defensive implied in the war against Japan was not to be a holding action, however, but rather a strategic defensive that contemplated a series of tactical offensives with the Pacific Fleet as the striking force. A new American war plan, Rainbow 5, was promulgated soon after the end of the American-British talks. Almost the whole of the Pacific was made an American strategic responsibility and the Army's primary mission under the plan was cooperation with and support of the fleet.

A listing of the contemplated offensive actions of Rainbow 5, which included the capture of the Caroline and Marshall Islands, would be interesting but academic. The success of the Japanese raid on Pearl Harbor forced a drastic revision of strategy which effectively postponed amphib-

---

The Rising Sun in the Pacific 1931–April 1942—History of United States Naval Operations in World War II (Boston: Little, Brown and Company, 1948), hereinafter cited as *Rising Sun in the Pacific*.

[a] Para 13 of ABC-1 quoted in *Hearings Record*, Part 33, 958.

ious assaults in the Central Pacific. Certain defensive measures which were mentioned in the plan, however, were implemented prior to the outbreak of war and in most of them Marine forces figured prominently.

Some of the Marine defense battalions, tailored to meet the needs of garrisons for isolated island outposts, were already in the Pacific by the time Rainbow 5 was published. The plan called for the development of bases, primarily air bases, at Midway, Johnston, Palmyra, Samoa, and Wake. All of these islands, which were under control of the Navy, were to have Marine garrisons. Guam, in the center of the Japanese-held Marianas, which had long had a small Marine barracks detachment, was decisively written off in the war plan; its early capture by the Japanese was conceded. The rest of the islands were placed in a category which called for defense forces sufficient to repel major attacks.

The purpose of establishing bases on these islands was twofold. Samoa was to help protect the routes of communication to the Southwest Pacific; Johnston, Palmyra, Wake, and Midway were to serve as outguards for the Pacific Fleet's home port at Pearl. (See Map 1, Map Section)

MARINE GARRISONS [10]

The Navy did not start cold with its advance base development scheme for the four island outposts of the Hawaiian Group. A blueprint for base expansion in the Pacific had been laid out in the report of the Navy's Hepburn Board, a Congressionally authorized fact-finding group which, in the spring of 1938, made a strategic study of the need for additional United States naval bases. The potential utility of Midway, Wake, Johnston, and Palmyra was recognized,[11] and surveys were conducted and plans made for the construction of base facilities, airfields, and seadromes during 1939 and 1940. The responsibility for developing garrison plans and locating coastal and antiaircraft gun positions was given to Colonel Harry K. Pickett, 14th Naval District Marine Officer and Commanding Officer, Marine Barracks, Pearl Harbor Navy Yard. The fact that Colonel Pickett personally surveyed most of the base sites insured active and knowledgeable cooperation at Pearl Harbor with requests from the islands for men and materiel to implement the garrison plans.

Although they were popularly referred to in the singular sense, a custom that will be continued in this narrative, each of the outposts was actually a coral atoll encompassing varying numbers of bleak, low-

---

[10] Unless otherwise noted the material in this section is derived from CNO Serial 070412, 23Jun41, "Policy regarding employment of Marine Defense Battalions in the Pacific Area" (located at NRMC); CNO Serial 091812, 25Sep41, "Employment of Marine Defense Battalions"; CO, 1st DefBn ltr to OIC, HistDiv, HQMC, 29Dec43; CO, 3d DefBn ltr to OIC, HistDiv, HQMC, 4Feb44; MD, 1st DefBn, PalmyraIs. Annual Rept of Activities, 1Jul43; Hist of the 7th DefBn, 21Dec42; 1st SamoanBn, MCR, Annual Rept of Activities, 1Jul42; LtCol R. D. Heinl, *The Defense of Wake* (Washington: HistSec, PubInfoDiv, HQMC, 1947), hereinafter cited as *Defense of Wake*; LtCol R. D. Heinl, *Marines at Midway* (Washington: HistSec, PubInfoDiv, HQMC, 1948), hereinafter cited as *Marines at Midway*.

[11] House Doc No. 65, 76th Congress, 1st Session, "Report on the Need of Additional Naval Bases to Defend the Coast of the United States, its Territories and Possessions" (Hepburn Board Rept), 3Jan39, *passim*.

lying sand islands within a fringing reef. Each atoll had at least one island big enough to contain an airstrip; Midway had two. The lagoons within the reefs were all large enough to permit the dredging and blasting of seaplane landing lanes and anchorages for small cargo ships; Midway's and Wake's were also slated for development as forward bases for the Pacific Fleet's submarines. Civilian contractors were hired to build the naval base installations, but until war actually broke out most of the work on the island defenses was done by the men who were to man them, Marines of the 1st, 3d, and 6th Defense Battalions.

The organization of the defense battalions varied according to time and place of employment, but by late 1941 the standard T/O called for a unit with more than 900 men assigned to a headquarters battery, three 5-inch coast defense gun batteries, three 3-inch antiaircraft batteries, a sound locator and searchlight battery, a battery of .50 caliber antiaircraft machine guns, and a battery of .30 caliber machine guns for beach defense. Midway was the only outpost that actually drew an entire battalion, although Wake originally was slated to be garrisoned by one. On Johnston and Palmyra the habitable area was so limited that it was impossible to accommodate more than a small defense detachment.

Some development work had been done on Wake and Midway, the two northern islands, before the arrival of the naval contractors' construction crews. In 1935 Pan American World Airways had set up way stations for its Clipper service to the Orient on both Midway and Wake and a relay station of the trans-Pacific cable had been in operation on Midway's Sand Island since 1903. Most construction, like the passenger hotel on Wake and the quarters for the airline's and cable company's personnel, was of little military value.

Midway, which had the most ambitious base plan, was also the first outpost scheduled to receive a Marine garrison—the 3d Defense Battalion which arrived at Pearl Harbor on 7 May 1940. The bulk of the battalion remained in Hawaii for the next eight months while reconnaissance details, followed by small advance parties, did the preliminary work on supply and defense installations.[12] On 27 January 1941, in the face of the threat posed by Japan's aggressive actions, the Chief of Naval Operations (CNO) directed that the rest of the 3d Defense Battalion be moved to Midway, that detachments of the 1st Defense Battalion be established at Johnston and Palmyra, and that the 6th Defense Battalion, then in training at San Diego, move to Pearl Harbor as a replacement and reserve unit for the outposts.[13]

On 15 February, the same day that the 3d Battalion began unloading its heavy equipment at Midway, an advance detachment of the 1st Defense Battalion left San Diego on the *Enterprise*. At Pearl Harbor the detachment left the carrier and transferred to a small cargo ship that steamed on to the southwest for 800 miles

---

[12] BriGen A. R. Pefley notes on draft manuscript, 14Jan57. Since all fresh water had to be distilled, the capacity of the distillers set the limit for the size of the island garrison. In terms of water consumption each contractor's workman took the place of a Marine. Adm C. C. Bloch ltr to ACofS, G–3, HQMC, 7Jan57.

[13] CNO Serial 0618, 17Jan41, "Establishment of Permanent Marine Defense Forces at Johnston, Midway, and Palmyra Islands."

to reach tiny Johnston where on 3 March two 5-inch guns, six Marines, and two naval corpsmen were set ashore. After a few days layover to help the caretaker detail get set up, the rest of the advance party (3 officers and 45 enlisted men) went on to Palmyra, approximately 1,100 miles south of Oahu.

After the remainder of the 1st Defense Battalion arrived at Pearl, small reinforcing detachments were gradually added to the southern outpost garrisons as the islands' supply and quartering facilities were expanded. On Johnston and Palmyra, as at Midway, the civilian contractors' crews and construction equipment were heavily committed to the naval air base program, and only occasionally could the Marines borrow a bulldozer, truck, or grader to help out in their own extensive schedule of defense construction. For the most part, the garrisons relied on pick and shovel to get their guns emplaced and to dig in the ammunition magazines, command posts, and fire direction centers necessary for island defense.

Duty on the small atolls was arduous and dull with little relief from the monotony of a steady round of work and training. When a few hours off was granted, there was no place to go and little to do; the visible world shrank to a few uninviting acres of dunes, scrub brush, and coral surrounded by seemingly endless stretches of ocean. The visits of patrol planes, supply ships, and even inspection parties were welcomed. Under the circumstances, morale at the isolated posts remained surprisingly high, helped perhaps by the prospect of action.

In so far as possible, the 14th Naval District attempted to follow a policy of rotation for the men at the outlying posts, replacing those that had been longest "in the field" with men from Pearl Harbor. In midsummer a group of 1st Defense Battalion personnel was sent to Midway to start the relief of the 3d Battalion and on 11 September the 6th Defense Battalion arrived to take over as the atoll's garrison. The 3d Battalion returned to Hawaii for a well-deserved break from the gruelling monotony and work of building defenses.

By August 1941 the work on the naval air base at Wake was well along and the need for a garrison there was imperative. An advance detachment of the 1st Defense Battalion arrived at the atoll on 19 August and immediately began the now familiar process of backbreaking work to dig in guns, dumps, aid stations, and command posts. Again the contractor's men and machines were largely devoted to work on the airfield and the lagoon, and the Marines had to get along with the hand tools organic to the unit. In late October reinforcements from the parent battalion made the 2,000-mile trip from Hawaii to bring the garrison up to a strength of nearly 400 men. The unit scheduled to be the permanent garrison on Wake, the 4th Defense Battalion, arrived at Pearl Harbor on 1 December, too late to reinforce or replace the Wake Detachment. A most important addition to the atoll's defenses did arrive, however, before war broke. Twelve Grumman Wildcats of Marine Fighter Squadron 211 flew in to the airstrip off the *Enterprise* on 4 December.

Just before the Japanese attacked, the strength of defense battalion personnel on outpost duty and at Pearl Harbor was:

	Pearl Harbor		Johnston		Palmyra		Midway		Wake	
	Off	Enl	Off	Enl	Off	Enl	Off	Enl	Off	Enl
1st DefBn	20	241	7	155	7	151			16	406
3d DefBn	40	823						1		
4th DefBn	38	780								
6th DefBn	4	17					33	810		

For armament the outposts relied mainly on the organic weapons of the defense battalions: 5-inch naval guns, 3-inch antiaircraft guns, and .30 and .50 caliber machine guns. Midway had, in addition, three 7-inch naval guns still to be mounted and a fourth gun at Pearl Harbor waiting to be shipped. The breakdown of weapon strength showed:[14]

	Midway	Johnston	Palmyra	Wake
5-inch guns	6	2	4	6
3-inch guns	12	4	4	12
.50 cal MGs	30	8	8	18
.30 cal MGs	30	8	8	30

Although the list of weapons was imposing, the garrisons were not strong enough to man them adequately; the standard defense battalion of 1941, moreover, included no infantry.

In contrast to the garrisons of the Pearl Harbor outposts, the 7th Defense Battalion slated for duty at Tutuila, main island of American Samoa, was a composite infantry-artillery unit. The battalion was organized at San Diego on 16 December 1940 with an initial strength of 25 officers and 392 enlisted men. Its T/O called for a headquarters company, an infantry company, and an artillery battery as well as a small detail which had the mission of organizing and training a battalion of Samoan reservists.

The islands of American Samoa had a native population of almost 10,000 which could be drawn upon as a labor force and for troops to back up a regular garrison. This was not the only significant difference between the outpost atolls and Samoa, however. The terrain of Tutuila, which was by far the largest and most heavily populated of the islands, was mountainous and heavily forested, and its 52 square miles contained a number of areas that could be converted into camps and supply depots. There was room for training areas and small arms ranges. The fine harbor at Pago Pago, site of the U. S. Naval Station and headquarters of the naval governor, could be used by large vessels. This combination of harbor, elbow room, and an indigenous labor force, plus its location along the shipping route to the Southwest Pacific, made Tutuila a vital strategic base. (See Map 3)

During the spring and early summer of 1940, Major Alfred R. Pefley of Colonel Pickett's staff made a thorough survey of Tutuila and prepared a detailed plan for its defense. On 29 November the CNO directed that defense plans based on Pefley's recommendations be implemented

---

[14] ComFourteen Rept of Status of DefBns assigned to the 14th ND, 1Dec41 (located at NRMC). Personnel figures include naval medical personnel assigned to the defense battalions.

immediately. The naval governor was authorized to begin construction of coast defense and antiaircraft gun positions. Most of the guns to be mounted were already in storage at the naval station and the Bureau of Ordnance was directed to provide the ammunition and additional weapons still needed.[15]

The primary purpose of raising the 7th Defense Battalion was the manning of the four 6-inch naval guns and six 3-inch antiaircraft guns provided for in initial defense plans. The wisdom of including infantry in the battalion and making provision for reinforcement by trained Samoan reserves can hardly be questioned. Tutuila was far too large an island to be adequately protected by a relatively few big guns, most of which were concentrated around Pago Pago harbor. Small beach defense garrisons were needed all around the island shorelines to check enemy raiding parties. It was intended that most of the Samoan reserves would be equipped and trained with rifles taken from naval stores and used in the beach defenses where their knowledge of the terrain would be invaluable.

An advance party of the 7th Defense Battalion, which left the States before the unit was formally activated, arrived at Pago Pago on 21 December 1940. The rest of the battalion made the 4,500-mile voyage from San Diego via Pearl Harbor in March, arriving on the 15th. The next months were busy ones as guns were emplaced and test fired, beach defenses were constructed, miles of communication lines were laid, and trails were cut which would enable quick reinforcement of threatened landing points.

It was midsummer before the first Samoan Marine was actually enlisted, but many natives voluntarily took weapons training on an unpaid status, continuing a practice begun by the naval governor in November 1940.[16] The first native recruit was enlisted on 16 August 1941 and the 1st Samoan Battalion, Marine Corps Reserve, was a going concern by the time war broke. The authorized strength of the battalion was 500 enlisted men, but this figure could never be reached because of the great number of men needed as laborers on essential base construction.

There was one factor of the defense picture at Tutuila that matched the situation at Midway, Johnston, and Palmyra. None of these islands had, at the onset of war, any land planes. The Marine air squadrons which were scheduled to join the defenders were either still in the States or else based on Oahu, waiting for the signal that the airfields were ready for use. That part of Marine Air which was in the Hawaiian Islands was based at Ewa Field, located approximately four air miles west of Pearl Harbor. Just prior to the Japanese attack, the units stationed at the field were Headquarters and Service Squadron of Marine Aircraft Group 21 (MAG–21); Marine Scout Bomber Squadron 232 (VMSB–232); Marine Utility Squadron 252 (VMJ–252); and the rear echelon of VMF–211, which had moved forward to Wake. Operational control of the Marine planes in the Hawaiian area was exercised by the Commander Aircraft, Battle Force, Pacific Fleet.[17]

---

[15] CNO serial 054430, 29Nov40, "Defense of American Samoa."

[16] Gov of AmerSamoa ltr to CNO, 13Feb41, "Establishment of Native Insular Force."

[17] 2dLt B. Hollingshead, "The Japanese Attack on 7 December 1941 on the Marine Corps Air

Aside from the Marine forces in the Western Pacific assigned to the Asiatic Fleet,[18] the only sizeable Marine units in the Pacific not already accounted for were guard detachments on Oahu and the 2d Engineer Battalion (less Companies C and D) which had been sent to Oahu to establish an advance amphibious training base for the 2d Marine Division. There was a 485-man Marine Barracks at the Pearl Harbor Navy Yard and 102 men assigned to the barracks at the Naval Air Station at Ford Island. Marines provided the guard (169 men) at the Naval Ammunition Depot at Lualualei in the hills northwest of Honolulu. The defense battalions which were quartered in or near the navy yard were under the operational control of the Commanding Officer, Marine Barracks, Colonel Pickett.

There were an additional 877 Marines present in Pearl Harbor on 7 December as members of the guard detachments of the battleships and cruisers of the Pacific Fleet.[19] In all, there were more than 4,500 Marines on Oahu that first day.

Station at Ewa, Oahu, Territory of Hawaii" (MS, HistDiv, HQMC, January 1945), 3–8, hereinafter cited as *Ewa Monograph*. The other squadrons assigned to MAG–21 were either at sea with the Navy's carriers or still in the U. S.

[18] See Part IV, "Marines in the Philippines," for the prewar situation in China and the Philippines.

[19] The strength of most Marine units on Oahu is listed in *Hearings Record*, Part 24, Exhibit No. 40. "Location of regularly assigned commanding officers of ships present during the Japanese attack of 7 December 1941."

CHAPTER 2

Japan Strikes

PEARL HARBOR [1]

Perhaps no action in American military history has been so thoroughly documented, examined, and dissected as the Pearl Harbor attack. Investigation has followed investigation; a host of books have been written on the subject, all in an effort to pin down the responsibility in the welter of charge and countercharge. The issue of what individuals or set of circumstances, if any, should bear the blame for the success of the Japanese raid has not been, and may never be, finally decided. On one point, however, there has been unanimous agreement—that the courage of the vast majority of defending troops was of a high order.

The first inkling of the Japanese attack came not from the air, but from the sea. At 0637 on 7 December, more than an hour before any enemy planes were sighted, an American patrol bomber and the destroyer *Ward* attacked and sank an unidentified submarine in the restricted waters close to the entrance to Pearl Harbor.[2] This vessel was one of five Japanese two-man submarines which had the extremely risky mission of penetrating the Pacific Fleet's stronghold. The midgets were transported to the target on board large long-range submarines, part of an undersea scouting and screening force which had fanned out ahead of the enemy carriers. Not one of the midget raiders achieved any success; four were sunk and one ran aground.

The Japanese attack schedule allowed the Americans little time to evaluate the significance of the submarine sighting. The first enemy strike group was airborne and winging its way toward Oahu before the *Ward* fired its initial spread of depth charges. The Japanese carrier force had turned in the night and steamed full ahead for its target, launching the first plane at 0600 when the ships were approximately 200 miles north of Pearl Harbor. A second strike group took off at 0745 when the carriers had reached a position 30 miles closer to the American base. Although a radar set on the island picked up the approaching planes in time to give warning, the report of the sighting was believed an error and disregarded, and the Japanese fighters and bombers appeared unannounced over their objectives.

The enemy plan of attack was simple. Dive bombers and fighter planes would

---

[1] Unless otherwise noted the material in this section is derived from *Pearl Harbor Rept; Hearings Record*, Part 13, Exhibits Nos. 8–8D, Japanese Records, and Parts 23 and 24, Hearings and Exhibits of the Roberts Commission; MarFor, 14th ND Jnl, December 1941; *Ewa Monograph;* Col H. K. Pickett ltr to BriGen C. D. Barrett, 22Dec41 (located at NRMC, Job 6608, Box 25); *Rising Sun in the Pacific.*

[2] "Unfortunately, the radio report sent to the 14th N. D. was not clear, and in view of many previous false reports, it was considered necessary to check the report. The air attack started before verification was received." Adm C. C. Block ltr, *op. cit.*

70

strafe and bomb the major Army and Navy airfields in an attempt to catch defending aircraft on the ground. Simultaneously, the battleships moored to pilings along the shore of Ford Island would be hit by high- and low-level bombing attacks. The shipping strike groups included large numbers of dive and horizontal bombers, since the Japanese anticipated that protective netting might prevent their lethal torpedo bombers from being fully effective. In all, 321 planes took part in the raid, while 39 fighters flew protective cover over the carriers to guard against a retaliatory attack that never materialized.

At 0755 the soft stillness of Sunday morning was broken by the screaming whine of dive bombers and the sharp chatter of machine guns. At half a dozen different bases around the island of Oahu Japanese planes signaled the outbreak of war with a torrent of sudden death. Patrol bombers were caught in the water at Kaneohe Naval Air Station, across the island from Honolulu; closely parked rows of planes, concentrated to protect them from sabotage, were transformed into smoking heaps of useless wreckage at the Army's Wheeler and Hickam Fields, the Marines' air base at Ewa, and the Navy's Ford Island air station. The attack on the airfields had barely started before the first bombs and torpedoes were loosed against the sitting targets of "battleship row." Within minutes most of the battleships at the Ford Island moorings had been hit by one or more torpedoes and bombs. If the Japanese had drawn off after the first fifteen minutes of their attacks, the damage done would have been terrific, but the enemy planes kept on strafing and bombing and the toll of ships, planes, and men soared.

The Americans did not take their beating lying down. The first scattered shots from sentries ashore and watch standers who manned antiaircraft guns on board ship flashed back at the enemy even before the bugles and boatswains' pipes sounded "Call to Arms" and "General Quarters." The ships of the Pacific Fleet were on partial alert even in port and most of the officers and men were on board. Crew members poured up the ladders and passages from their berthing compartments to battle stations. While damage control teams tried to put down fires and shore up weakened bulkheads, gun crews let loose everything they had against the oncoming planes. In many cases guns were fired from positions awash as ships settled to the bottom and crewmen were seared with flames from fuel and ammunition fires as they continued to serve their weapons even after receiving orders to abandon ship. On many vessels the first torpedoes and bombs trapped men below deck and snuffed out the lives of others before they were even aware that the attack was on.

The reaction to the Japanese raid was fully as rapid at shore bases as it was on board ship, but the men at the airfields and the navy yard had far less to fight with. There was no ready ammunition at any antiaircraft gun position on the island; muzzles impotently pointed skyward while trucks were hurried to munitions depots. Small arms were broken out of armories at every point under attack; individuals manned the machine guns of damaged aircraft. The rage to strike back at the Japanese was so strong that men even fired pistols at the enemy planes as they swooped low to strafe.

At Ewa every Marine plane was knocked out of action in the first attack.

JAPANESE PHOTOGRAPH *of the sneak attack at Pearl Harbor showing the line of American battleships caught at their mooring near Ford Island. (USN 30550)*

JAPANESE LANDING ON GUAM *depicted by a propaganda artist who shows a portion of the troops and transports of the South Seas Detached Force. (SC 301167)*

Two squadrons of Japanese fighters swept in from the northwest at 1,000 feet and dived down to rake the aircraft parked near the runways with machine-gun and cannon fire. Pilots and air crewmen ran to their planes in an attempt to get them into the air or drag them out of the line of fire, but the Japanese returned again and again to complete the job of destruction. When the enemy fighters drew off at about 0825 they left behind a field littered with burning and shot-up aircraft.

The men of MAG-21 recovered quickly from their initial surprise and shock and fought back with what few rifles and machine guns they had. Salvageable guns were stripped from damaged planes and set up on hastily improvised mounts; one scout-bomber rear machine gun was manned to swell the volume of antiaircraft fire. Although the group commander, Lieutenant Colonel Claude A. Larkin, had been wounded almost as soon as he arrived at the field that morning, he continued to coordinate the efforts to meet further enemy attacks.

Two Japanese dive bombers streaked over the field from the direction of Pearl Harbor at 0835, dropping light fragmentation bombs and strafing the Marine gun positions. A few minutes after the bombers left, the first of a steady procession of enemy fighters attacked Ewa as the Japanese began assembling a cover force at nearby Barber's Point to protect the withdrawl of their strike groups. The Marine machine guns accounted for at least one of the enemy planes and claimed another probable. Two and three plane sections of fighters orbited over the field, and occasionally dived to strafe the gunners, until the last elements of the Japanese attack force headed out to sea around 0945.

Three of the Marine airmen were killed during the attacks, a fourth died of wounds; 13 wounded men were treated in the group's aid station. Flames demolished 33 of the 47 planes at the field; all but two of the remainder suffered major damage. The sole bright note in the picture of destruction was the fact that 18 of VMSB-231's planes were on board the *Lexington*, scheduled for a fly-off to Midway, and thereby saved from the enemy guns.

Within the same half hour that witnessed the loss of Ewa's planes, the possibility of effective aerial resistance was canceled out by similar enemy attacks all over Oahu. Ford Island's seaplane ramps and runways were made a shambles of wrecked and burning aircraft in the opening stage of the Japanese assault. The Marines of the air station's guard detachment manned rifles and machine guns to beat off further enemy thrusts, but the dive bombers had done their job well. There was no need for them to return. The focus of all attacks became the larger ships in the harbor.

The raid drew automatic reactions from the few Marines in the navy yard who saw the first enemy planes diving on the ships. While the guard bugler broke the majority of the men of the barracks detachment and the 1st and 3d Defense Battalions out of their quarters, the early risers were already running for the armories and gun sheds. By 0801 when Colonel Pickett ordered the defense battalion machine-gun groups to man their weapons, eight of the guns had already been set up. More machine guns were hastily put in position and men were detailed to belt the ammunition needed to feed them, while rifle ammunition was issued to the hundreds of men assembled on the barracks' parade ground. Pickett ordered the 3-inch antiaircraft guns in the defense battalions' reserve supplies to be taken out of storage and emplaced on the parade. He dispatched trucks and working parties of the 2d Engineer Battalion to Lualualei, 27 miles up in the hills, to get the necessary 3-inch shells. The Marine engineers also sent their heavy earth-moving equipment to Hickam Field to help clear the runways.

Thirteen machine guns were in action by 0820 and the gunners had already accounted for their first enemy dive bomber. During the next hour and a half the fire of twenty-five more .30's and .50's was added to the yard's antiaircraft defenses, and two more planes, one claimed jointly with the ships, were shot down. The 3-inch guns were never able to get into action. The ammunition trucks did not return from the Lualualei depot until 1100, more than an hour after the last Japanese aircraft had headed back for their carriers. By that time the personnel of all Marine organizations in the navy yard area had been pooled to reinforce the guard and antiaircraft defense, to provide an infantry reserve, and to furnish the supporting transport and supply details needed to sustain them.

In the course of their attacks on battleship row and the ships in the navy yard's drydocks, the enemy planes had strafed and bombed the Marine barracks area, and nine men had been wounded. They were cared for in the dressing stations which Pickett had ordered set up at the beginning of the raid to accommodate the flow of wounded from the stricken ships in the harbor. Many of these casualties were members of the Marine ship detachments; 102 sea-going Marines had been killed during the raid, six later died of wounds, and 49 were wounded in action.[3]

The enemy pilots had scored heavily: four battleships, one mine layer, and a target ship sunk; four battleships, three cruisers, three destroyers, and three auxiliaries damaged. Most of the damaged ships required extensive repairs. American plane losses were equally high: 188 aircraft totally destroyed and 31 more damaged. The Navy and Marine Corps had 2,086 officers and men killed, the Army 194, as a result of the attack; 1,109 men of all the services survived their wounds.

Balanced against the staggering American totals was a fantastically light tally sheet of Japanese losses. The enemy carriers recovered all but 29 of the planes they had sent out; ship losses amounted to five midget submarines; and less than a hundred men were killed.

Despite extensive search missions flown from Oahu and from the *Enterprise*, which was less than 175 miles from port when the sneak attack occurred, the enemy striking force was able to withdraw undetected and unscathed. In one respect the Japanese were disappointed with the results of their raid; they had hoped to catch the Pacific Fleet's carriers berthed at Pearl Harbor. Fortunately, the urgent need for Marine planes to strengthen the outpost defenses had sent the *Lexington* and the *Enterprise* to sea on aircraft ferrying missions. The *Enterprise* was returning to Pearl on 7 December after having flown off VMF–211's fighters to Wake, and the *Lexington*, enroute to Midway with VMSB–231's planes, turned back when news of the attack was received. Had either or both of the carriers been sunk or damaged at Pearl Harbor, the outlook for the first months of the war would have been even more dismal. The Japanese success had the effect of delaying the schedule of retaliatory attacks and amphibious op-

---

[3] Casualty figures were compiled from records furnished by Statistics Unit, PersAcctSec, PersDept, HQMC.

JAPAN STRIKES

erations in the Central Pacific that had been outlined in Rainbow 5. A complete reevaluation of Pacific strategy was necessary.

The critical situation facing the outpost islands was clearly appreciated and an attempt was made to get reinforcements to Wake before the Japanese struck; it did not come in time. The tiny atoll was one of the first objectives on the enemy timetable of conquest.[4] Midway was more fortunate; when the *Lexington* returned to Pearl on 10 December with its undelivered load of Marine scout bombers, they were ordered to attempt an over-water flight to the atoll. On 17 December, ten days after the originally scheduled fly-off, 17 planes of VMSB–231, shepherded by a naval patrol bomber, successfully made the 1,137-mile flight from Oahu to Midway. It was the longest single-engine landplane massed flight on record, but more important it marked a vital addition to Midway's defensive potential.

The outpost islands needed men and materiel as well as planes. Rear Admiral Claude C. Bloch, Commandant of the 14th Naval District, gave the responsibility for organizing and equipping these reinforcements to Colonel Pickett. On 13 December, all Marine ground troops in the district were placed under Pickett as Commanding Officer, Marine Forces, 14th Naval District. The necessary reinforcements to be sent to Midway, Johnston, and Palmyra were drawn from the 1st, 3d, and 4th Defense Battalions. By the month's end the first substantial increments of men, guns, and equipment had been received at each of the outposts.[5] They were not safe from attacks by any means, but their positions were markedly stronger.

GUAM FALLS [6]

The Washington Naval Disarmament Treaty of 1922 provided for the maintenance of the *status quo* in regard to fortifications and naval bases in certain areas of the Pacific. American adherence to these terms through the 14-year life of the treaty had the practical effect of weakening the defenses of the Philippines and preventing the development of Guam as a naval stronghold. The Hepburn Board of 1938 recommended that Guam be heavily fortified and garrisoned,[7] but Congress failed to authorize the expenditure of the necessary funds. Unhappily, the planners of Rainbow 5 had to concede the capture of the island in the first stages of a war with the Japanese. It was almost as if they could look over enemy shoulders and see the terse direction to the commander of the Japanese Fourth Fleet to "invade Wake and Guam as quickly as possible"[8] at the onset of hostilities. (See Map 2)

Guam was a fueling station for naval vessels making the long run to and from the Orient, a relay point for the trans-Pacific cable, the site of a naval radio station, and a stop for Pan American clippers. Assigned to protect its 20,000 natives and its 228 square miles of rugged, jungled terrain was a token force of 153

---

[4] For the detailed story of the defense of Wake see Part III.

[5] CO, MarFor, 14th ND ltr to MGC, 5Jan42, Development of outpost garrisons.

[6] Unless otherwise noted the material in this section is derived from Maj O. R. Lodge, *The Recapture of Guam* (Washington: HistBr, G–3 Div, HQMC, 1954), 7–9; Capt G. J. McMillin, USN, OffRept to the CNO of the Surrender of Guam to the Japanese, 11Sep45; T. Wilds, "The Japanese Seizure of Guam," *MC Gazette*, July 1955.

[7] Hepburn Board Rept, *op. cit.*

[8] *Hearings Record*, Part 13, Exhibit No. 8–C, CombFlt OpOrd No. 1, 5Nov41, 475.

Marines. Backing them up was a Guamanian infantry unit, the 80-man Insular Force Guard, and a volunteer native naval militia with 246 ill-armed and ill-trained members.[9] The island's government departments and naval station activities were manned by 271 regular Navy personnel. A naval officer, Captain George J. McMillin, was both island governor and garrison commander.

The war threat was so real by October 1941 that all women and children of U. S. citizenship were evacuated from Guam. On 6 December the garrison destroyed all its classified papers and like other Pacific outposts awaited the outcome of the U. S.-Japanese negotiations in Washington. The word came at 0545 on 8 December (7 December, Pearl Harbor time). Captain McMillin was informed of the enemy attack by the Commander in Chief of the Asiatic Fleet. In less than three hours Saipan-based Japanese bombers were over the island.

The initial enemy target was the mine sweeper USS *Penguin* in Apra Harbor; this small ship's 3-inch and .50 caliber guns were the only weapons larger than .30 caliber machine guns available to the Guam garrison. Under repeated attacks, the *Penguin* went to the bottom, and her survivors joined the forces ashore. The attack continued throughout the daylight hours with flights of bombers hitting the various naval installations and strafing roads and villages. The island capital, Agana, was cleared of civilians, and the few local Japanese were rounded up and interned.

That night a native dugout landed near Ritidian Point on the northern cape of the island, and the three men in it were captured. They claimed to be Saipan natives sent over to be on hand as interpreters when the Japanese landed. These natives insisted that the Japanese intended to land the next morning (9 December) on beaches near Agana. Captain McMillin suspected a trick. He believed that by this ruse the Japanese sought to draw the Marines out of their prepared positions in the butts of the rifle range at Sumay on Orote Peninsula. He decided not to allow this information to cause a shift of his major defensive force from a position which guarded important Apra Harbor.

By guess or knowledge the Saipan natives had one of the landing sites located accurately, but they were off on their time. The 9th brought no landing, but the bombers came back to give Guam another pounding. The Insular Force Guard was posted to protect government buildings in Agana, but the rest of the island's garrison remained at their assigned posts. Lieutenant Colonel William K. McNulty's 122 Marines of the Sumay barracks continued to improve their rifle range defenses, and the 28 Marines who were assigned to the Insular Patrol, the island's police force, kept their stations in villages throughout Guam.

After the Japanese bombers finished for the day all was quiet until about 0400 on 10 December. At that time flares burst over Dungcas Beach north of Agana, and some 400 Japanese sailors of the *5th Defense Force* from Saipan came ashore. While the naval landing party moved into Agana where it clashed with the Insular Force Guard, elements of the Japanese

---

[9] The members of the Insular Force Guard were in the U. S. Government service and received 50 percent of the pay of corresponding ratings in the U. S. Navy. The native militia served without pay and had no arms except obsolete and condemned rifles. RAdm G. J. McMillin ltr to CMC, 3Nov52.

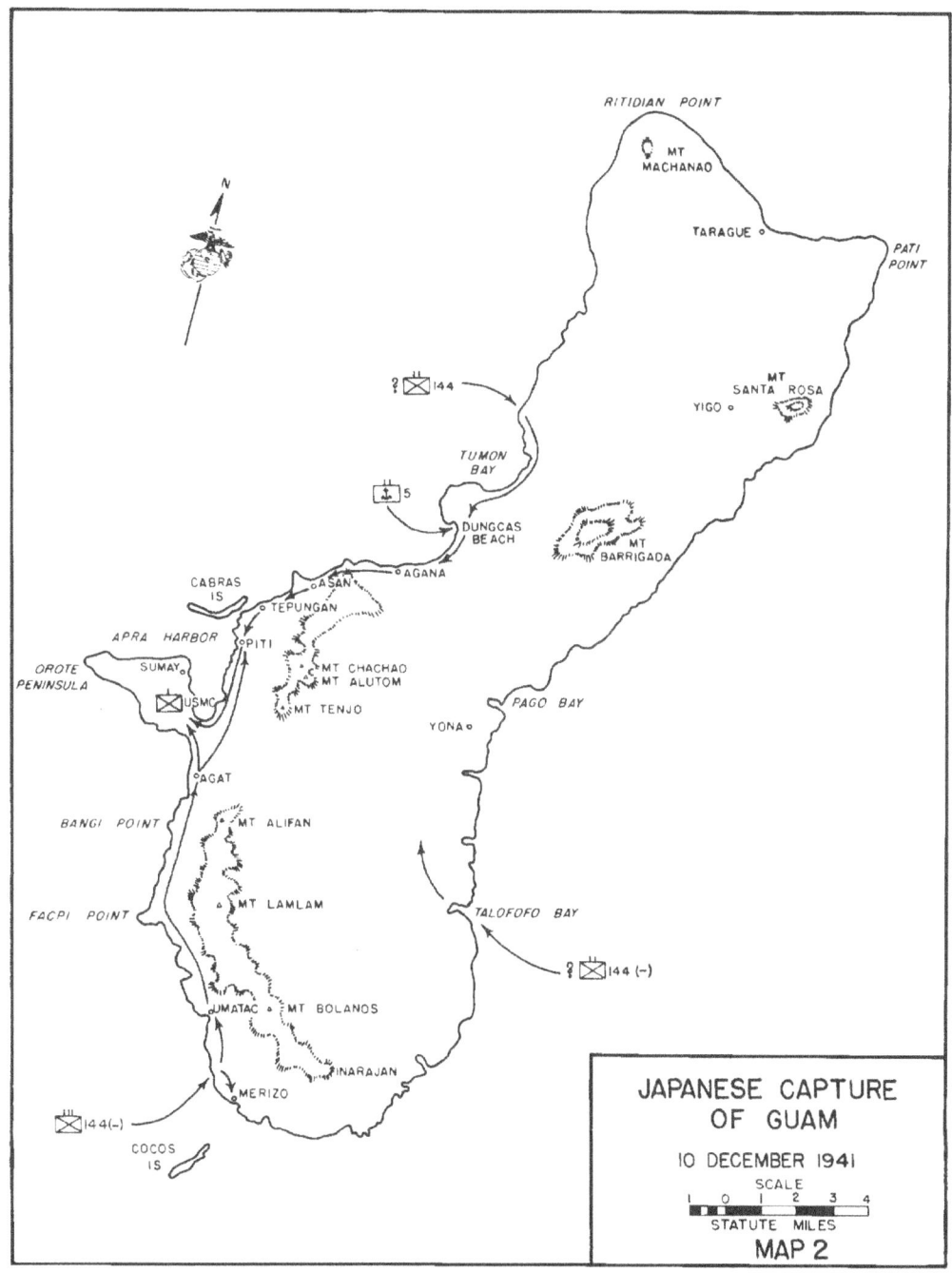

South Seas Detached Force (approximately 5,500 men)[10] made separate landings at Tumon Bay in the north, on the southwest coast near Merizo, and on the eastern shore of the island at Talafofo Bay.

At Agana's plaza the lightly-armed Guamanians, commanded by Marine First Lieutenant Charles S. Todd, stood off the early Japanese attacks, but their rifles and machine guns did not provide enough firepower to hold against a coordinated attack by the Dungcas Beach landing force. Captain McMillin, aware of the overwhelming superiority of the enemy, decided not to endanger the lives of the thousands of civilians in his charge by further and fruitless resistance. "The situation was simply hopeless," he later related.[11] He surrendered the island to the Japanese naval commander shortly after 0600, and sent orders to the Marines at Sumay not to resist. The word did not reach all defenders, however, and scattered fighting continued throughout the day as the enemy spread out to complete occupation of the island. But this amounted to only token resistance. There was no chance that the determined Japanese might be driven off by a force so small, even if the defenders could have regrouped. Guam had fallen, and it would be two and a half years before the United States was in a position to win it back.

During the two days of bombing and in the fighting on 10 December, the total garrison losses were 19 killed and 42 wounded including four Marines killed and 12 wounded.[12] The civilian population suffered comparable but undetermined casualties. The Japanese evacuated American members of the garrison to prison camps in Japan on 10 January 1942, and the enemy naval force that had been present at the surrender settled down to duty as occupation troops.

FIRST ATTACK ON MIDWAY [13]

Part of the Japanese striking force which raided Pearl Harbor was a task unit of two destroyers and a tanker which proceeded independently from Tokyo Bay to a separate target—Midway. The mission of the destroyers was implied in their designation as the Midway Neutralization Unit; they were to shell the atoll's air base on the night of 7 December while the Japanese carrier force retired from the Hawaiian area. (See Map 10, Map Section)

Dawn of 7 December found five seaplanes of Midway's patrol bomber squadron (VP–21) aloft on routine search missions; two other (Dutch) patrol bombers had just taken off for Wake, next leg of their journey to the Netherlands East Indies. On the Sand Island seaplane ramp two more PBYs (Catalina patrol

---

[10] This reinforced brigade, commanded by MajGen Tomitara Horii, had been organized in November 1941 to take part in the capture of Guam and to move on from there to seize Rabaul in the Bismarcks. It was built around the 144th InfRegt and reinforced by units of the Japanese 55th Division. MIDiv, WD, Order of Battle for Japanese Armed Forces, 1Mar45, 122.

[11] McMillin Surrender Rept, *op. cit.*

[12] Marine casualty figures were compiled from records furnished by the Statistics Unit. PersAcctSec, PersDept, HQMC.

[13] Unless otherwise noted the material in this section is derived from *Hearings Records*, Part 24, Exhibit No. 34, "History of Action Occurring at Midway 7–31Dec41 as Compiled from Official Dispatches and Correspondence," Exhibit No. 35, CO, NAS, Midway ltr to CinCPac, Action of 7Dec41, n. d., and Exhibit No. 36, CO, 6th DefBn ltr to ComFourteen, Rept of action on the night of 7Dec41, 12Dec41; *Marines at Midway*.

bombers) were warming up to guide in VMSB–231 which was scheduled to fly off the *Lexington* that day. At 0630 (0900 Pearl Harbor time) a Navy radio operator's signal from Oahu flashed the first news of the Pearl Harbor attack. A few minutes later a dispatch from Admiral Bloch confirmed this report and directed that current war plans be placed in effect.

Commander Cyril T. Simard, the Island Commander, recalled the Dutch PBYs (which were then put to use by VP–21), established additional air search sectors, and ordered Lieutenant Colonel Harold D. Shannon's 6th Defense Battalion to general quarters. The remainder of the day was spent in preparation for blackout, and in issuing ammunition, digging foxholes, and testing communications. All lights and navigational aids were extinguished after it was learned that the *Lexington*, with VMSB–231 still on board, had been diverted to seek the enemy's Pearl Harbor striking force.

Air searches returned late in the day without having sighted any signs of Japanese ships or planes, and the atoll buttoned up for the night with all defensive positions fully manned. At 1842, a Marine lookout saw a flashing light some distance southwest of Sand Island, but it quickly disappeared, and it was about 2130 before the one operational radar on Sand began picking up what seemed to be surface targets in the same general direction. Simultaneously two other observers, equipped with powerful 8x56 night glasses, reported seeing "shapes" to seaward.

Shannon's searchlight battery commander, First Lieutenant Alfred L. Booth, requested permission to illuminate, but his request was turned down. Senior officers did not want to risk premature disclosure of defensive positions. It was also erroneously believed that friendly ships were in the area, and there were strict orders against illuminating or firing without specific orders.[14]

The apprehension of these observers was justified. The Japanese destroyers *Akebono* and *Ushio* had left their tanker *Shiriya* at a rendezvous point some 15 miles away and made landfall on the atoll at about 2130. By the time Lieutenant Booth had been cautioned about his searchlights, the two enemy ships had their guns trained on Midway and were ready to make their first firing run. The firing began at 2135.

The first salvos fell short, but as the destroyers closed range on a northeast course the shells began to explode on Sand Island. The initial hits struck near Battery A's 5-inch seacoast guns at the south end of the island, and subsequent rounds bracketed the island's power plant, a reinforced concrete structure used also as the command post of a .50 caliber antiaircraft machine-gun platoon. One round came through an air vent and exploded inside the building. The Japanese ships then suspended fire while they closed on the atoll for a second firing run.

In the island's power plant First Lieutenant George H. Cannon, although severely wounded, directed the re-establishment of wrecked communications and the evacuation of other wounded. He refused evacuation for his own wounds until after Corporal Harold R. Hazelwood had put the switchboard back in operation. Cannon died a few minutes after reaching the

---

[14] LtCol A. L. Booth ltr to CMC, 27Jan48, hereinafter cited as *Booth;* LtCol L. S. Fraser ltr to CMC, hereinafter cited as *Fraser.*

aid station, but for this action he received posthumous award of the Medal of Honor. He was the first Marine so honored in World War II.

Meanwhile the enemy ships opened fire again, this time at closer range, and Commander Simard ordered Shannon to engage targets of opportunity. Japanese shells set the roof of the seaplane hangar on Sand ablaze, lighting up the target for the enemy gunners, and accurate salvos struck the Pan American radio installation, the island laundry, and adjacent shops. At 2153 the Marine searchlight crews got Shannon's orders to illuminate, but by then only the light on the south end of Sand could bear on the ships. This light silhouetted the *Akebono* about 2,500 yards south of the island, before a near miss from one of the destroyers put it out of commission. Crewmen reacted immediately to get the light back in action and on target, but Battery A's 5-inchers stayed silent because communication damage had prevented passing of Shannon's command to open fire.[15]

But Captain Jean H. Buckner, commanding Battery D's 3-inch antiaircraft guns, could now see the large Japanese battle flag on the *Akebono's* foremast, and he ordered his guns into action. Splashes could not be made out, although illumination was excellent, and Buckner's fire controlmen were positive that the shells were either passing through the ships' superstructures or into their hulls. Battery B (First Lieutenant Rodney M. Handley) on Eastern Island now added its 5-inch fire to the battle and .50 caliber machine guns opened up on the targets which were well within range. This firing from the Marine batteries kept up for five minutes before the Japanese succeeded in knocking out the searchlight. Although some observers believed that the *Ushio* had also been hulled, results of this Marine fire have never been determined.[16] Both Japanese ships retired soon after the light was shot out and a Pan American clipper captain flying overhead that night en route from Wake reported seeing an intense fire on the surface of the sea and the wakes of two ships on the logical retirement course of the destroyers. Both enemy ships, however, returned to Japan safely, despite any damage that might have been done by the Marine guns.

The enemy fire had cost the 6th Defense Battalion two killed and ten wounded;[17] two men from the naval air station were killed and nine wounded. Material damage on Midway was not too severe and was confined to Sand Island; the airfield on Eastern Island was not touched. The seaplane hangar had burned, although the frame was still intact, and one plane was lost in the flames. Another PBY was badly damaged by shell fragments, and fragments also caused minor damage to a number of buildings. The garrison had stood off its first Japanese attack, but there was little comfort in this. The defenders estimated—correctly—that the enemy would be back sooner or later with a much more serious threat.

With the outbreak of war, completion of the coastal and antiaircraft defenses of Midway took first priority and Marines were treated to the welcome and unusual

---

[15] *Booth; Fraser;* Col L. A Hohn ltr to CMC, 30Jan48.

[16] The *Ushio*, evidently a very lucky ship, was the only enemy vessel that took part in the Pearl Harbor attack that was still afloat on V–J Day.

[17] Casualty figures were compiled from records

[17] Casualty figures were compiled from records furnished by Statistics Unit, PersAcctSec,

sight of the civilian contractor's heavy equipment turned to on dugout and battery construction. Authorities at Pearl Harbor were determined to get reinforcements to the atoll and within a week after VMSB-231 made its historic long flight from Oahu, two batteries of the 4th Defense Battalion with additional naval 3-inch and 7-inch guns for coast defense were being unloaded. On Christmas, the Brewster Buffaloes of VMF-221 flew in from the *Saratoga* which had been rushed out to Pearl from San Diego after the Japanese attack. This carrier had taken part in the abortive attempt to relieve Wake. The next day the island received another contingent of 4th Defense Battalion men, the ground echelon of VMF-221, and much needed defense materiel when the seaplane tender *Tangier*, which had also been headed for Wake, unloaded at Midway instead. By the end of December the atoll, which was now Hawaii's most important outpost, had for its garrison a heavily reinforced defense battalion, a Marine scout-bomber and a fighter squadron, and VP-21's patrol bombers. Midway was in good shape to greet the Japanese if they came back, and the passage of every month in the new year made the atoll a tougher nut to crack.[18]

THE SOUTHERN OUTPOSTS [19]

Tiny Johnston Island, set off by itself in the open sea southwest of Hawaii, proved to be a favorite target of Japanese submarines in the first month of the war. It was too close to the Pacific Fleet base at Pearl and too limited in area to make it a prize worth risking an amphibious assault, but its strategic location, like an arrowhead pointing at the Japanese Marshalls, made damage to its air facilities well worth the risk of bombardment attempts. The airfield on the atoll's namesake, Johnston Island, was only partially completed on 7 December, but temporary seaplane handling facilities were in operation at Sand Islet, the only other land area within the fringing reef. There was no permanent patrol plane complement, but Johnston was an important refueling stop and a couple of PBYs were usually anchored in the lagoon.

The news of the outbreak of war created a flurry of activity on Johnston, and the civilian contractor's employees turned to at top speed to erect additional earthworks around the Marine guns and to prepare bomb shelters.[20] No Japanese ship or submarine made its appearance on 7 December, perhaps because the first day of war found the *Indianapolis* and five destroyer minesweepers at Johnston testing the performance of the Higgins landing boat on coral reefs.[21] These ships were

---

[18] See Part V, "The Battle of Midway" for the story of the events leading up to the decisive naval action which took place at Midway in June 1942.

[19] Unless otherwise noted the material in this section is derived from *Hearings Record*, Part 24, Exhibit No. 27, "History of Action Occurring at Palmyra Island 7-31Dec41, As Compiled from Official Dispatches and Correspondence," Exhibit No. 28, "History of the Action Occurring at Johnston Island 7-31Dec41, As Compiled from Official Dispatches and Correspondence," Exhibit No. 31, CO, NAS, PalmyraIs ltr to ComFourteen, 24Dec41,, and Exhibit No. 32, CO, NAS, JohnstonIs ltr to ComFourteen, 19Dec41; CO, NAS, JohnstonIs ltr to ComFourteen, 22Dec41; MarGarFor, Pac File C-1455-40-5, "Defense-Fortification Johnston Island," 12Sep41-13Jun43; MarGarFor, Pac File C-1455-40-15, "Defense-Fortification Palmyra Islands," 26Sep41-30Jun43.

[20] CO, NAS, JohnstonIs, Progress and Readiness Rept, 15Dec41.

[21] *Hearings Record*, Part 23, 758-759.

immediately recalled toward Pearl to form part of the extensive search pattern for the enemy carrier force, and Johnston's defense rested with its own slim garrison. Major Francis B. Loomis, Jr., Executive Officer of the 1st Defense Battalion, caught while returning to Pearl by air from an inspection of the western outposts, assumed command of the Johnston detachment as senior Marine officer present.

Shortly after dark on 12 December a submarine surfaced 8,000 yards off Sand Islet and began firing green star clusters which burst high over the island. The 5-inch battery could not pick up the vessel in its sights, but it fired one star shell in the general direction of the submarine. The submarine ceased firing immediately as she evidently was not seeking a duel.

The next enemy attack came at dusk three days later. The supply ship *Burrows* had delivered a barge load of supplies originally intended for the Wake garrison and picked up 77 civilian construction employees for return to Pearl when a sentry atop Johnston's water tower spotted a flash to seaward and sounded general quarters. The flash had been spotted by the batteries also, and the 5-inch control estimated the range at 9,000 yards. The 3-inch director and height finder made out two ships, one larger than the other. The first two enemy salvos bracketed Johnston and the third struck near the contractor's power house and set off a 1,200-gallon oil tank which immediately fired the building. A strong wind whipped up 50-foot flames from the oil fire, and "as observed from the Naval Air Station at Sand Islet, Johnston Island seemed doomed."[22] The Japanese continued to fire for ten minutes at this well-lighted target and they hit several other buildings. The 5-inch guns delivered searching fire, and just as the Marines were convinced they were hitting close aboard their targets, the enemy fire ceased abruptly.

The enemy vessels had fired from the obscuring mists of a small squall and spotters ashore never clearly saw their targets, but the defenders believed that they had engaged two surface vessels, probably a light cruiser and a destroyer. Later analysis indicated, however, that one or more submarines had made this attack. Fortunately no one in the garrison was hurt by the enemy fire, although flames and fragments caused considerable damage to the power house and water distilling machinery. The *Burrows*, although clearly outlined by the fire, was not harmed. The fact that its anchorage area was known to be studded with submerged coral heads probably discouraged the Japanese from attempting an underwater attack, and Johnston's 5-inch battery ruled out a surface approach.

During the exchange of fire one of the Marines' 5-inch guns went out of action. Its counter-recoil mechanism failed. After this the long-range defense of the island rested with one gun until 18 December when two patrol bombers from Pearl arrived to join the garrison. This gun was enough, however, to scare off an enemy submarine which fired star shells over Sand Islet after dark on 21 December. Again the simple expedient of firing in the probable direction of the enemy was enough to silence the submarine. The

---

[22] *Ibid.*, Part 24, Exhibit No. 32, CO, NAS, JohnstonIs ltr to ComFourteen, 19Dec41.

next night, just as the ready duty PBY landed in the lagoon, another submarine, perhaps the same one that had fired illumination over Sand, fired six shells at the islets. Both 5-inchers on Johnston now were back in action and each gun fired ten rounds before the submarine submerged. The patrol plane was just lifting from the water as the last enemy shot was fired. Only one shell hit Sand, but that one knocked down the CAA homing tower and slightly wounded one Marine.

Johnston Island was clearly a discouraging place to attack, and the shelling of 22 December marked the last enemy attempt at surface bombardment. It was just as well that the Japanese decided to avoid Johnston, because reinforcement from Pearl soon had the atoll bursting at its seams with men and guns. An additional 5-inch and a 3-inch battery, 16 more machine guns, and the men to man them arrived on 30 December. In January a provisional infantry company was sent and eventually the garrison included even light tanks. The expected permanent Marine fighter complement never got settled in at Johnston's airfield. The island became instead a ferrying and refueling stop for planes going between Pearl and the South and Southwest Pacific.

Palmyra, 900 miles southeast of Johnston, also figured in the early development of a safe plane route to the southern theater of war. But before the atoll faded from the action reports it too got a taste of the gunfire of a Japanese submarine. At dawn on 24 December an enemy raider surfaced 3,000 yards south of the main island and began firing on the dredge *Sacramento* which was anchored in the lagoon and clearly visible between two of Palmyra's numerous tiny islets. Only one hit was registered before the fire of the 5-inch battery drove the submarine under. Damage to the dredge was minor and no one was injured.

Colonel Pickett's command at Pearl Harbor had organized strong reinforcements for Palmyra and these arrived before the end of December. Lieutenant Colonel Bert A. Bone, Commanding Officer of the 1st Defense Battalion, arrived with the additional men, guns, and equipment to assume command of the defense force. On 1 March the official designation of the Marine garrison on Palmyra was changed to 1st Defense Battalion and former 1st Battalion men at other bases were absorbed by local commands. The Marine Detachment at Johnston became a separate unit.

After these submarine attacks of December, Palmyra and Johnston drop from the pages of an operational history. The atolls had served their purpose well; they guarded a vulnerable flank of the Hawaiian Islands at a time when such protection was a necessity. While the scene of active fighting shifted westward the garrisons remained alert, and when conditions permitted it many of the men who had served out the first hectic days of the war on these lonely specks in the ocean moved on to the beachheads of the South and Central Pacific.

CHAPTER 3

The Southern Lifeline

STRATEGIC REAPPRAISAL[1]

In December 1941 reverse followed reverse in the fortunes of the Allies in the Pacific. The Japanese seemed to be everywhere at once and everywhere successful. Setbacks to the enemy schedule of conquest were infrequent and temporary. On the Asian mainland Hong Kong fell and Japanese troops advanced steadily down the Malay Peninsula toward Singapore. In the Philippines Manila was evacuated and American-Filipino forces retreated to Bataan and Corregidor for a last-ditch stand. To the south the first Japanese landing had been made on Borneo, and superior enemy forces prepared to seize the Netherlands East Indies. The capture of Wake and Guam gave the Japanese effective control over the Central Pacific from the China coast to Midway and Johnston. (See Map 1, Map Section)

By the turn of the year only the sea area between the Hawaiian Islands and the United States and the supply route from the States through the South Pacific to New Zealand and Australia were still in Allied hands. The responsibility for holding open the lines of communication to the Anzac area[2] rested primarily with the U. S. Pacific Fleet. On 31 December that fleet came under the command of the man who was to direct its operations until Japan unconditionally surrendered—Admiral Chester W. Nimitz (CinCPac).

As soon as he arrived at Pearl Harbor, Nimitz was given a dispatch from Admiral Ernest J. King, the newly appointed Commander in Chief, United States Fleet (CinCUS, later abbreviated as CominCh). King's message outlined Nimitz's two primary tasks as CinCPac. He was to use his ships, planes, and men in:

(1) Covering and holding the Hawaii-Midway line and maintaining its communications with the west coast.

(2) Maintaining communications between the west coast and Australia, chiefly by covering, securing and holding the Hawaii-Samoa line, which should be extended to include Fiji at the earliest possible date.[3]

Although the Japanese had severely damaged the Pacific Fleet in their Pearl Harbor raid, they had concentrated on

---

[1] Unless otherwise noted the material in this section is derived from *The War Reports of General of the Army George C. Marshall—General of the Army H. H. Arnold—Fleet Admiral Ernest J. King* (Philadelphia & New York: J. B. Lippincott Company, 1947), hereinafter cited as *War Reports;* FAdm E. J. King and Cdr W. M. Whitehill, *Fleet Admiral King: A Naval Record* (New York: W. W. Norton & Company Inc., 1952) hereinafter cited as *King's Naval Record; Strategic Planning*.

[2] Anzac is actually the abbreviation for Australian and New Zealand Army Corps used in WW I, but the term was so understandable and easy to use in reference to the two Commonwealth nations that it was adopted in the Pacific War and applied frequently to the geographic area in which they lay.

[3] *King's Naval Record*, 353–354.

ships rather than installations, and the repair facilities of the navy yard were virtually untouched. Round-the-clock work promptly restored to operation many vessels which might otherwise have been lost for good or long delayed in their return to fleet service. But Nimitz's strength was not enough to hazard a large scale amphibious offensive, even with the addition of reinforcements sent from the Atlantic Fleet. In the first few months of 1942, Allied strategists had to be content with defensive operations. The few local attacks they mounted were hit-and-run raids which did little more than boost homefront and service morale at a time when most news dealt with defeat and surrender.

From 22 December to 14 January, the political and military leaders of the United States and Great Britain met in Washington (the ARCADIA Conference) to chart the course of Allied operations against the Axis powers. The Americans, despite the enormity of the Japanese attack, reaffirmed their decision of ABC-1 that Germany was the predominant enemy and its defeat would be decisive in the outcome of the war. The Pacific was hardly considered a secondary theater, but the main strength of the Allied war effort was to be applied in the European, African, and Middle Eastern areas. Sufficient men and materiel would be committed to the battle against Japan to allow the gradual assumption of the offensive.

One result of the ARCADIA meetings was the organization of the Combined Chiefs of Staff (CCS), a supreme military council whose members were the chiefs of services in Great Britain and the United States. The CCS was charged with the strategic direction of the war, subject only to the review of the political heads of state. The necessity of presenting a united American view in CCS discussions led directly to the formation of the United States Joint Chiefs of Staff (JCS) as the controlling agency of American military operations.

On 9 February 1942, the first formal meeting of General George C. Marshall (Chief of Staff, United States Army), Lieutenant General Henry H. Arnold (Chief of the Army Air Corps), Admiral Harold R. Stark (CNO), and Admiral King (CominCh) took place. Except for the combination of the offices of CominCh and CNO in the person of Admiral King which took effect on 26 March (Admiral Stark became Commander U. S. Naval Forces Europe) and the addition of Admiral William D. Leahy as Chief of Staff to the President on 20 July, the membership of the JCS remained constant for the duration of the war. As far as the Marine Corps was concerned their representative on the JCS was Admiral King, and he was consistently a champion of the use of Marines at their greatest potential—as specially trained and equipped amphibious assault troops.[4]

---

[4] On 13Apr51, before a subcommittee of the Senate Committee on Armed Services, Gen Holcomb stated that he was called in during the ARCADIA conferences and "sat as a member of that group." Later " . . . a formal organization occurred in which I was not included. However, because of my intercourse with Admiral Stark I was in on nearly all of the discussions that took place." This intimate relationship changed, however, when Stark was relieved as CNO on 26Mar42. An interesting sequel to this story of the "exclusion" of the Commandant from the JCS was revealed by Gen Holcomb when he further related how after a dinner party

On 10 January 1942, the CCS, acting with the approval of Prime Minister Churchill and President Roosevelt, set up a unified, inter-Allied command in the western Pacific to control defensive operations against the Japanese along a broad sweep of positions from Burma through Luzon to New Guinea. The commander of ABDA (American-British-Dutch-Australian) forces holding the barrier zone was the British Commander in Chief in India, General Sir Archibald P. Wavell; his ABDA air, naval, and ground commanders were respectively an Englishman, an American, and a Dutchman. But ABDA Command had no chance to stop the Japanese in the East Indies, Malaya, or the Philippines. Wavell's forces were beaten back, cut off, or defeated before he could be reached by reinforcements that could make a significant difference in the fighting. By the end of February Singapore had fallen and the ABDA area was split by an enemy thrust to Sumatra. Wavell returned to India to muster troops to block Japanese encroachment into Burma. On 1 March ABDA Command was formally dissolved.

Although this first attempt at unified Allied command was short-lived and unsuccessful, it set a pattern which governed operational control of the war through its remaining years. This pattern amounted to the selection as over-all commander of a theater of an officer from the nation having the most forces in that particular theater. His principal subordinates were appointed from other nations also having interests and forces there. Realistically, the CCS tried to equate theater responsibility with national interest. On 3 March the Combined Chiefs approved for the western Pacific a new dividing line which cut through the defunct ABDA area. Burma and all Southeast Asia west of a north-south line between Java and Sumatra were added to Wavell's Indian command and the British Chiefs of Staffs were charged with the strategic direction of this theater. The whole Pacific east of the new line was given over to American JCS control.

The Joint Chiefs divided the Pacific into two strategic entities, one in which the Navy would have paramount interests, the Pacific Ocean Area (POA), and the other in which the Army would be the dominant service, the Southwest Pacific Area (SWPA). (See Map 1, Map Section for boundary.) Naval planners had successfully insisted in JCS discussions that all positions such as New Caledonia, the New Hebrides, and New Zealand which guarded the line of communications from Pearl Harbor to Australia must be controlled by the Navy. In terms of the air age, the JCS division of the Pacific gave the Army operational responsibility for

---

at the White House in July 1943, the President, associating himself with the Marine Corps, had said to him confidentially: "You know, the first thing you know we are going to be left out of things. We are not represented on the Joint Chiefs of Staff . . . . how would you like to be a member of the Joint Chiefs of Staff?" Holcomb replied that he would like it very much but didn't know how the Joint Chiefs would feel about it. That was the last, however, that Holcomb ever heard of this matter directly or officially. Senate Committee on Armed Services, 82d Congress, Hearings on S. 667, "A Bill to Fix the Personnel Strength of the United States Marine Corps and to make the Commandant of the Marine Corps a Permanent Member of the Joint Chiefs of Staff" (Washington: GPO, 1951), 34–36.

an area of large land masses lying relatively close together where land power supported by shore-based air could be decisive. To the Navy the JCS assigned the direction of the war in a vast sea area with widely scattered island bases where the carrier plane reigned supreme.

The American commander in the Philippines, General Douglas MacArthur, was the Joint Chiefs' choice to take over direction of SWPA operations; Admiral Nimitz was selected to head POA activities. Formal announcement of the new set-up was not made until MacArthur had escaped from Corregidor and reached safety in Australia. On 18 March, with the consent of the Australian government, MacArthur was announced as Supreme Commander of the SWPA (CinCSWPA) The JCS directive outlining missions for both Pacific areas was issued on 30 March, and the confirmation of Nimitz as Commander in Chief of the POA (CinCPOA) followed on 3 April. By CCS and JCS agreement, both commanders were to have operational control over any force, regardless of service or nation, that was assigned to their respective theaters.

Nimitz still retained his command of the Pacific Fleet in addition to his duties as CinCPOA. The fleet's striking arm, its carriers and their supporting vessels, stayed under Nimitz as CinCPac no matter where they operated. In the final analysis, however, the major decisions on employment of troops, ships, and planes were made in Washington with the advice of the theater commanders. MacArthur was a subordinate of Marshall and reported through him to the JCS; an identical command relationship existed between Nimitz and King.

SAMOAN BASTION [5]

The concern felt in Washington for the security of the southern route to Australia was acute in the days and weeks immediately following the Pearl Harbor attack. Despite world-wide demands on the troops and equipment of a nation just entering the war, General Marshall and Admiral King gave special attention to the need for holding positions that would protect Australia's lifeline. Garrison forces, most of them provided by the Army, moved into the Pacific in substantial strength to guard what the Allies still held and to block further Japanese advances. Between January and April nearly 80,000 Army troops left the States for Pacific bases.

An infantry division was sent to Australia to take the place of Australian units committed to the fighting in the Middle East. At the other end of the lifeline, a new division was added to the Hawaiian Island garrison. Mixed forces of infantry, coast and antiaircraft artillery, and air corps units were established in early February at Canton and Christmas Islands, southwest and south of Pearl Harbor. At about the same time a New Zealand ground garrison reinforced by American pursuit planes moved into the Fiji Islands, and a small garrison was sent to the French-owned Society Islands to guard the eastern approaches to the supply route. In March a task force of

---

[5] Unless otherwise noted the material in this section is derived from HqDeFor Rept of SamoanGru AdvB Facilities, 10Oct42; 2d MarBrig AnRept, 16Jul42; 2d MarBrig Diary, 23Dec41–30Jun42; CG 3d MarBrig ltr to CMC, 10Sep43; 3d MarBrig Brief of Ops, 21Mar42–31Aug43; MAG–13 War Diary, 1Mar42–31May43; Hist of the 7th DefBn, 21Dec42; *Strategic Planning*.

almost division strength arrived in New Caledonia and the Joint Chiefs sent additional Army garrison forces to Tongatabu in the Tonga Islands, south of Samoa, and north to Efate in the New Hebrides. By the end of March 1942 the supply route to Australia ran through a corridor of burgeoning island strong points and the potential threat of major Japanese attacks had been substantially lessened. (See Map 1, Map Section and Map 3)

Actually the initial Japanese war plan contemplated no advances into the South Pacific to cut the line of communications to Australia. The Allied leaders, however, can be forgiven for not being clairvoyant on this point, for the enemy's chance to seize blocking positions along the lifeline was quite apparent. Samoa seemed to be one of the most inviting targets and its tiny garrison of Marines wholly inadequate to stand off anything but a minor raid. The necessity for building up Samoan defenses as a prelude for further moves to Fiji and New Caledonia had been recognized by Admiral King in his instructions to Nimitz to hold the Hawaiian-Samoa line,[6] and reinforcements from the States to back up those instructions were underway from San Diego by 6 January. These men, members of the 2d Marine Brigade, were the forerunners of a host of Marines who passed through the Samoan area and made it the major Marine base in the Pacific in the first year of the war.

Only two weeks' time was necessary to organize, assemble, and load out the 2d Brigade. Acting on orders from the Commandant, the 2d Marine Division activated the brigade on 24 December at Camp Elliott, outside of San Diego. The principal units assigned to the new command were the 8th Marines, the 2d Battalion, 10th Marines, and the 2d Defense Battalion (dispatched by rail from the east coast). Colonel (later Brigadier General) Henry L. Larsen was named brigade commander. A quick estimate was made of the special engineering equipment which the brigade would need to accomplish one of its most important missions—completion of the airfield at Tutuila. Permission was obtained to expend up to $200,000 in the commercial market for the purchase of such earthmoving equipment as could not be supplied from quartermaster stocks. When the first cargo ship arrived at San Diego on New Year's day, the brigade went on a round-the-clock loading schedule. Sixty-two hours later all assigned personnel and gear had been loaded and the 4,798 officers and men were on their way to Tutuila.

When the news of Pearl Harbor reached Samoa, Lieutenant Colonel Lester A. Dessez, commanding the 7th Defense Battalion, ordered his troops to man their positions. The Samoan Marine Reserve Battalion was called to active duty and assigned to reinforce the defenses. Despite a spate of rumors and false alarms, no sign of the Japanese was evident until the night of 11 January, when a submarine shelled the naval station for about seven minutes from a position 10,000–15,000 yards off the north shore where the coast defense guns could not bear. The station suffered only light damage from the shells, some of which fell harmlessly into the bay, and two men were wounded slightly by fragments. The Marines remained on alert but received no further visits from the enemy.

---

[6] *King's Naval Record*, 354.

On 19 January radar picked up signs of numerous ships, and observation stations on the island's headlands soon confirmed the arrival of the 2d Brigade.

While still at sea, General Larsen had received orders from the Navy Department appointing him Military Governor of American Samoa and giving him responsibility for the islands' defense as well as supervisory control over the civil government. As soon as the ships docked antiaircraft machine guns of the 2d Defense Battalion were promptly unloaded and set up in the hills around Pago Pago harbor. The 8th Marines took over beach defense positions occupied by the 7th Defense Battalion and immediately began improving and expanding them. The artillerymen of 2/10 and the 2d Defense set up their guns in temporary positions while they went to work on permanent emplacements. Navy scouting amphibians of a shore-based squadron (VS-1-D14) attached to the brigade soon were aloft on a busy schedule of antisubmarine and reconnaissance missions.

The airfield on Tutuila was only 10 per cent completed when Larsen arrived, but he directed that construction be pushed around the clock, work to go on through the night under lights. He also detailed the brigade's engineer company to assist the civilian contractors in getting the field in shape. For the 2d Brigade's first three months in Samoa, its days were filled with defense construction. There was little time for any combat training not intimately connected with the problems of Samoan defense. The work was arduous, exacting, and even frustrating, since the brigade had arrived during the rainy season and the frequent tropical rainstorms had a habit of destroying in minutes the results of hours of pick and shovel work.

General Larsen took immediate steps after his arrival in American Samoa to ascertain the status of the defenses in Western (British) Samoa, 40 or so miles northwest of Tutuila. On 26 January the brigade intelligence officer, Lieutenant Colonel William L. Bales, flew to Apia, the seat of government on the island of Upolu, to confer with the New Zealand authorities and make a reconnaissance of Upolu and Savaii, the two principal islands. The New Zealanders were quite anxious to cooperate with the Marines since they had a defense force of only 157 men to guard two large islands with a combined coastline of over 250 miles. Bales, whose investigation was aimed primarily at discovering the feasibility of developing either or both of the islands into a military base, reported back that Upolu's harbor facilities, road net, and several potential airfield sites made it readily susceptible to base development. He found, on the other hand, that Savaii had no safe major anchorages and that its lava-crusted surface did "not offer airfield sites that could be developed quickly by the Japanese or anyone else."[7] On his return to Tutuila, Lieutenant Colonel Bales reported to General Larsen that:

> In its present unprotected state, Western Samoa is a hazard of first magnitude for the defense of American Samoa. The conclusion is unescapable that if we don't occupy it the Japanese will and there may not be a great deal of time left.[8]

Naval authorities in Washington and Pearl Harbor recognized the desirability

---

[7] LtCol W. L. Bales ltr to CG, 2d MarBrig, 8Feb42, Rept on Recon in Western Samoa, 8.
[8] *Ibid.*, 10.

of occupying Western Samoa and extended their interest to include Wallis (Uea) Island, a small French possession 320 miles from Tutuila on the western approaches to Samoa. Negotiations were entered into with New Zealand regarding the defense of Western Samoa, and the Free French government in regard to the occupation of Wallis. In March warning orders were sent out to Larsen's brigade and both marine divisions to be prepared to furnish troops for the garrisoning of Western Samoa and Wallis.[9] Negotiations for the use of land and other facilities in Western Samoa were completed on 20 March when Larsen and a New Zealand representative signed an agreement giving the Americans responsibility for defense of all the Samoan islands. This group, together with Wallis, was now considered a tactical entity and a new Marine brigade was to be organized to occupy the western islands.

As an advance force of this new garrison, the 7th Defense Battalion was sent to Upolu on 28 March, and a small detachment was established on Savaii. In the States, the 1st Marine Division at New River, North Carolina, organized the 3d Marine Brigade on 21 March with Brigadier General Charles D. Barrett in command. Its principal units were the 7th Marines and the 1st Battalion, 11th Marines. The 7th's 3d Battalion and Battery C of 1/11 were detached on the 29th to move overland to the west coast for further transfer to Samoa as part of the garrison for Wallis. General Larsen meanwhile had been directed to organize the 8th Defense Battalion on Tutuila, as the major element of the Wallis garrison. To exercise overall authority, Headquarters Samoan Area Defense Force was established on Tutuila. Major General Charles F. B. Price, who was appointed to this command, arrived with his staff at Pago Pago on 28 April from the States. On 8 May the 3d Marine Brigade convoy arrived off Apia and General Barrett assumed military command of Western Samoa. At the end of the month, the 8th Defense Battalion (Reinforced) under Colonel Raphael Griffin moved into Wallis.

More than 10,000 Marine ground troops were stationed in the Samoan area by the beginning of June, and reinforcements arrived in a steady flow. Marine air was also well established. General Larsen's interest and pressure assured that Tutuila's airfield was ready for use on 17 March, two days before the advance echelon of MAG–13 arrived. The new air group, organized on 1 March at San Diego, was earmarked for Price's command. Initially the group commander, Lieutenant Colonel Thomas J. Walker, Jr., had only one tactical squadron, VMF–111, operating from Tutuila's airfield, but VMO–151, a scout-bomber squadron, joined in May with the arrival of the 3d Marine Brigade convoy. The amphibians of the Navy's VS–1–D14 squadron were also put under Walker's command and sent forward to operate from Upolu and Wallis while the airfields projected for those islands were rushed to completion by naval construction battalions.

Like the rest of the garrison forces in the South Pacific which were rushed out to plug a gaping hole in Allied defenses, General Price's defense force was never called upon to conduct the island defense for which it was organized. Samoa might

---

[9] CMC Serial 003A7842, 20Mar42, Defense of Western Samoa and Wallis Island.

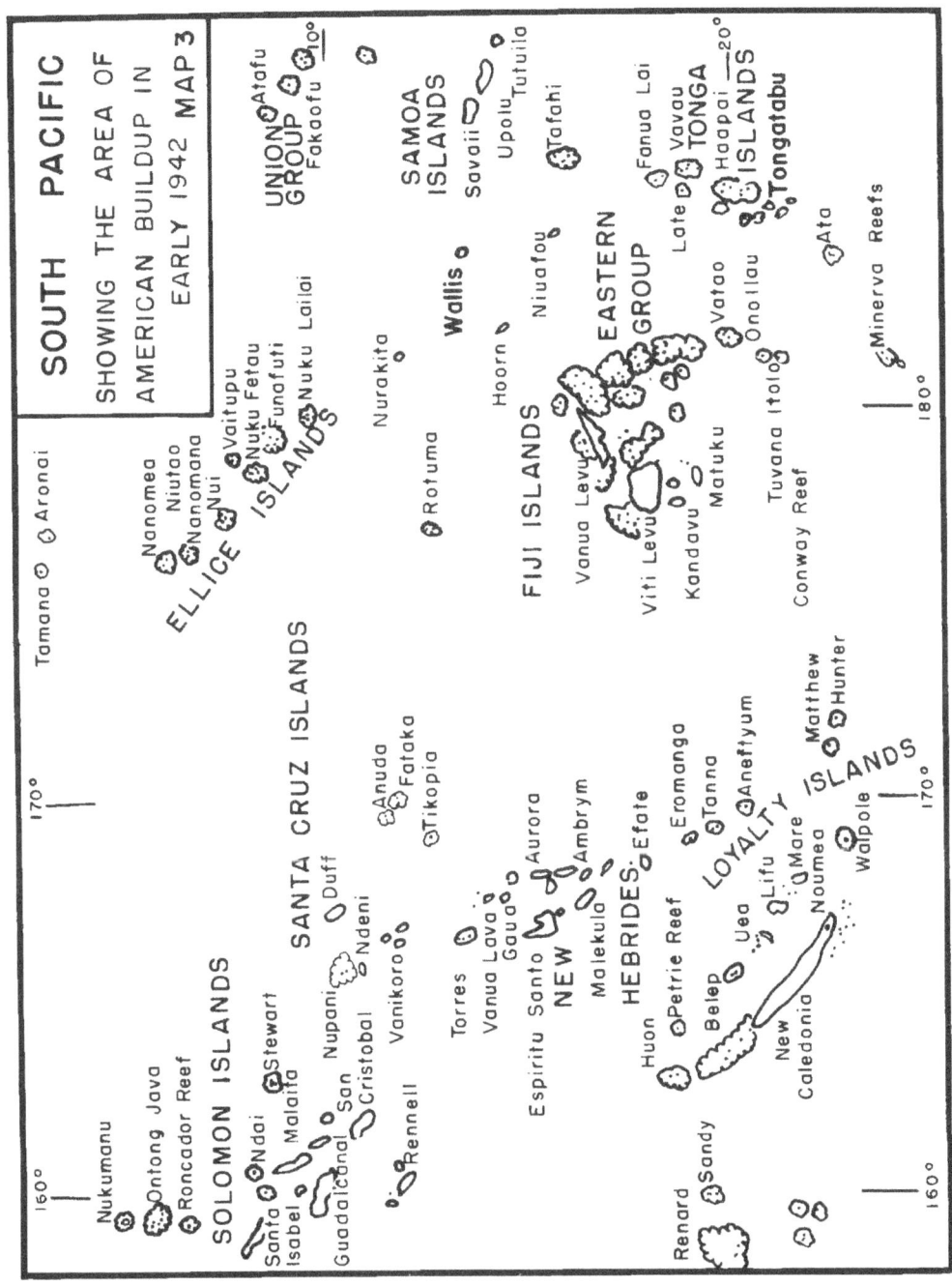

well have become a target for enemy attacks, but the decisive Battle of Midway forced the Japanese to curb their soaring ambition.[10] Samoa became a vast advanced combat training camp instead of a battleground. Most of the units coming there after the arrival of the 2d Brigade drew heavily on the recruit depots for their personnel,[11] and for these Marines Samoan duty was an opportunity for learning the fundamentals of teamwork in combat operations. As the need for defense construction was met and the danger of Japanese attacks lessened, Samoa became a staging area through which replacements and reinforcements were funnelled to the amphibious offensives in the Solomons.[12] Units and individuals paused for a while here and then moved on, more jungle-wise and combat ready, to meet the Japanese.

---

[10] *Campaigns of the Pacific War*, 3. See Part V, "Decision at Midway" and especially Chapter 1, "Setting the Stage—Early Naval Operations" for events leading up to the Midway battle.

[11] At least 40% of the 3d MarBrig initial complement was straight out of boot camp. 3d Mar Brig AnRept, 6Sept42, 9.

[12] From December 1942 to July 1943 Samoa was the training center for all Marine replacement battalions raised on the east coast of the U. S. K. W. Condit, G. Diamond, and E. T. Turnbladh, *Marine Corps Ground Training in World War II* (Washington: HistBr, G–3, HQMC, 1956), 181–186.

PART III

The Defense of Wake

CHAPTER 1

Wake in the Shadow of War[1]

In the strategic context of 1940 and 1941, the importance of Wake, both to the United States and Japan, was considerable. At this time the United States had not won its ocean-girdling net of Pacific bases, and, with the exceptions of Wake, Midway, and Guam, the islands between the Hawaiians and the Philippines were *terra incognita*. Wake, a prying outpost north of the Marshalls and on the flank of the Marianas, would be a strategic prize for Japan's ocean interests and a corresponding embarrassment while it was in the hands of the United States.

These factors had been noted by the U. S. in the Hepburn Report of 1938 which recommended a $7,500,000 three-year program to develop the atoll as an advanced air base and an intermediate station on the air route to the Far East. Acting on these recommendations, initial development of Wake began early in 1941.[2] Base construction was given first priority, and by the time the first military contingent arrived on the atoll a civilian contractor's crew of approximately 1,200 men, under supervision of Mr. Daniel Teters, was hard at work.

By 18 April 1941, Admiral Husband E. Kimmel, Commander in Chief, U. S. Pacific Fleet, became fearful that the defensive efforts had started too late. In a study sent to the Chief of Naval Operations, Kimmel stressed the importance of Wake and asked that work on defense be given a higher priority than base construction. He also requested that a Marine defense battalion be assigned to the atoll.[3]

In 1941 the strength of a typical defense battalion was 43 officers and 939 enlisted men, and its two most characteristic attributes were balanced structure and a high degree of strategic mobility. But mobility disappeared at the battalion's destination. Once its guns were in position, a defense battalion suffered from insufficient transportation and a shortage of men.[4]

The Pacific strategy of 1941 contemplated rendering our bases relatively secure against air raids, hit-and-run surface attacks, or even minor landings. Fleet Marine Force defense battalions, organized for defense against just such operations, could provide antiaircraft protection, could stand off light men-of-war and transports, and in extreme emergency could fight on the beaches with individual weapons in the tradition that every Ma-

---

[1] For a résumé of the previous history of Wake, see *Defense of Wake*, Appendix II, "Prewar History of Wake, 1586–1941." Col Heinl's monograph has been the principal source used in compiling this account; his version of the action has been followed closely.

[2] Capt R. A. Dierdorff, USN. "Pioneer Party— Wake Island," *USNI Proceedings*, April 1943, 502.

[3] CinCPac ltr to CNO, 18Apr41.

[4] USMC T/O's, D–133 through D–155–D inclusive, 27Feb41; MGC ltr, 28Aug41, "Employment of Defense Battalions."

rine, first and last, is an infantryman.[5] Within and about the structure of such lightly held but secure bases, the Pacific Fleet would ply, awaiting the moment when battle could be joined with enemy naval forces—"to get at naval forces with naval forces,"[6] as Admiral Kimmel put it—in decisive action for control of the sea.

As might be expected, the Japanese concept of strategy in the Central Pacific was to seize or neutralize the few advanced United States bases west of the Hawaiian Islands as quickly as possible after the outset of war. For this purpose Japanese forces in the Marshalls and Carolines (the *Fourth Fleet*) were organized along lines resembling an American amphibious force.[7] Commanded by Vice Admiral Nariyoshi Inouye, the *Fourth Fleet* was composed of amphibious shipping, a few old cruisers, destroyers, submarines, shore-based aircraft, and a Japanese version of our own Fleet Marine Force: the special naval landing force.[8] Fleet headquarters were at Truk, where Admiral Inouye's flag flew in the light cruiser *Kashima*.[9]

The war missions of Admiral Inouye and his fleet had been decided generally in 1938 when the basic East Asia war plans had been prepared in Tokyo.[10] But it was not until November 1941 that detailed instructions for commanders within the *Combined Fleet* were formulated and issued. In these instructions, Wake was dismissed in a single phrase:

> Forces of the Fourth Fleet:
> Defend the South Seas Islands, patrol, maintain surface communications, capture Wake . . . .[11]

Wake would be strictly a local operation. By Admiral Inouye's scheme, 450 special naval landing force troops could, in a pinch, turn the trick.[12]

FINAL PREPARATIONS, AUTUMN, 1941 [13]

On 23 June 1941 the Chief of Naval Operations directed that elements of the 1st Defense Battalion, FMF, be established at Wake "as soon as practicable." This directive (as eventually modified)

---

[5] *Ibid.*

[6] CinCPac ltr to CNO, 18Apr41, "Defense and Development of Wake Island."

[7] ATIS (SWPA) Doc No. 17895A, "Full translations of answers to questions concerning attack on Wake Island," hereinafter cited as *Wake Attack*.

[8] The special naval landing force (SNLF, sometimes contracted to SLF) were Japanese Navy personnel organized for service and duties in limited land operations similar to those performed by U. S. Marines. Throughout the war, they gave an outstanding account of themselves.

[9] *Wake Attack*.

---

[10] USSBS(Pac), NavAnalysisDiv, *Interrogations of Japanese Officials*, 2 vols (Washington: GPO, 1946), "Japanese Naval Planning," I, 176, hereinafter cited as *USSBS Interrogations* with subject or interviewee.

[11] *Campaigns of the Pacific War*, 47.

[12] *USSBS Interrogations*, "Japanese Capture of Wake Island," II, 371, hereinafter cited as *Capture of Wake*.

[13] Unless otherwise noted the material in this section is derived from CO 1st DefBnDet Wake, Rept to CMC, 18Mar46, hereinafter cited as *Devereux Rept*; Col P. A. Putnam Rept to CMC, 18Oct45, hereinafter cited as *Putnam Rept*; informal reports by key subordinates to Cols Devereux and Putnam on which the official reports are largely based, hereinafter cited as (*officer's name*) *Rept*; ships' logs of the U. S. naval vessels concerned; Col J. P. S. Devereux, *The Story of Wake Island* (Philadelphia: J. P. Lippincott Company, 1947), hereinafter cited as *Devereux Story*.

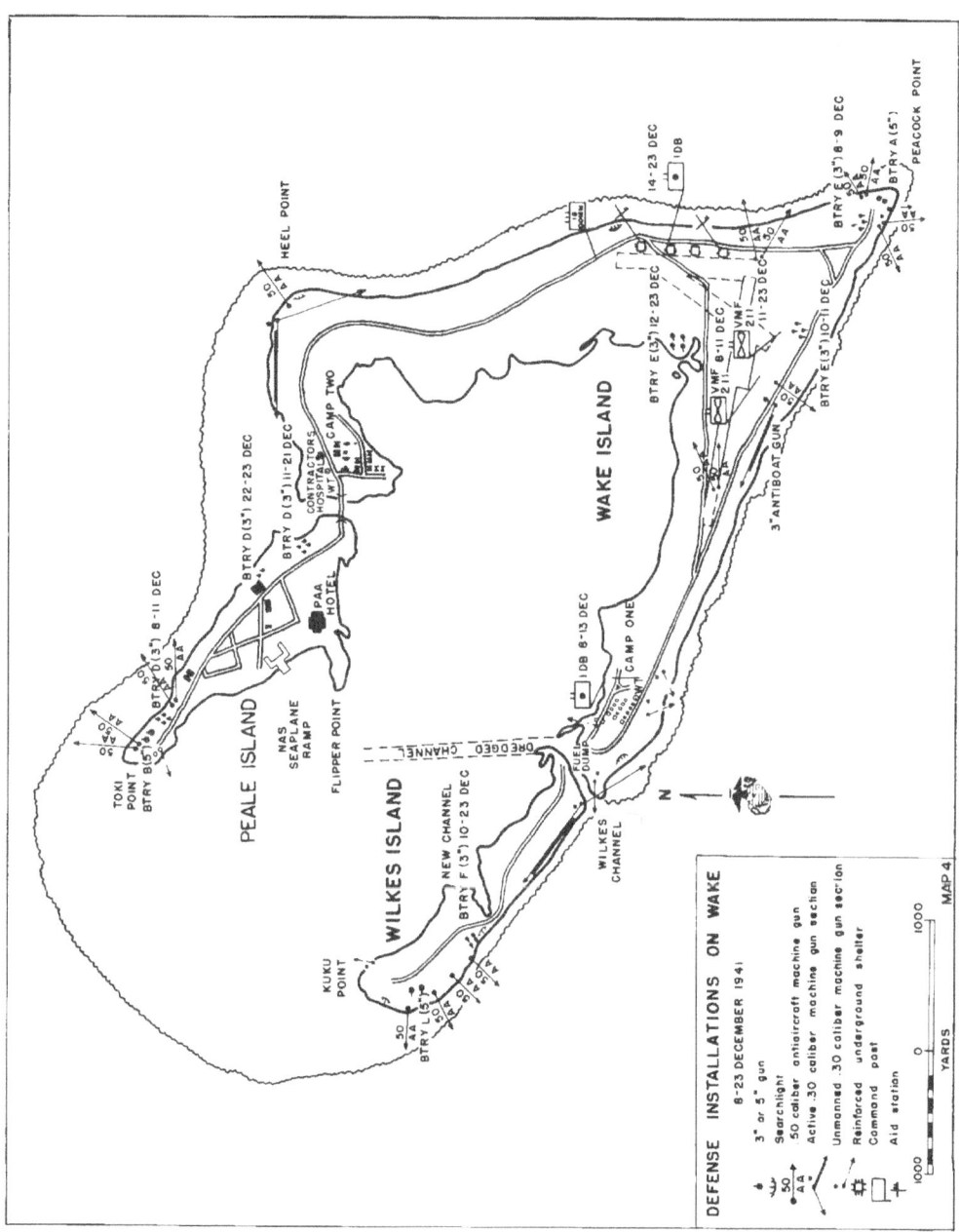

specified that the following units should compose the defensive garrison:

> Four 3-inch antiaircraft batteries
> Three 5-inch seacoast batteries
> Appropriate automatic weapons
> One SCR-268 fire-control radar, and one SCR-270B search radar.[14]

CNO's "as soon as practicable" was translated into immediate action by the Pacific Fleet. About 1 August Major Lewis A. Hohn with five officers and 173 enlisted Marines and sailors from the 1st Defense Battalion commenced loading the USS *Regulus*, a twenty-year-old "Hog Island" transport which would carry the battalion advance detail to Wake. *Regulus* sailed on 8 August, and arrived off Wake on 19 August. Weapons and camp equipment were lightered ashore, and by the time the *Regulus* departed on 22 August, a camp facing the lagoon had been set up on a site near the west end of Wake's west leg. To distinguish this camp from the one west of Heel Point housing the 1,200 Pacific Naval Air Base contract workmen, the Marine camp was designated as Camp One. The civilian establishment became known as Camp Two. (See Map 4)

Wake, as it appeared to the Marines of the 1st Defense Battalion, was a V-shaped atoll composed of three islands: Wake Island proper,[15] the body of the V; and Wilkes and Peale, the two tip-ends. Its land mass consisted of some 2,600 acres of sand and coral. Offshore, heavy surf roared continually against a coral reef which surrounded the whole atoll at distances varying from 30 to 1,000 yards. The beaches and much of the terrain inland were covered with coral boulders, some large enough to conceal several men. The interior lagoon, although affording sufficient surface and depth for seaplanes, was studded with coral heads and foul ground which had to be dredged before ships could enter the single channel between Wilkes and Wake Island. Despite Wake's limited land area, its coastline exceeded 21 miles. An excellent vignette of Wake in 1941 was given by Colonel Bayler:

> Wake is by no means the bare sandy spit one thinks of when atolls are mentioned. Considerable areas of it are covered by woods, and though the trees are small, their thick foliage and the scrubby tangled underbrush provided admirable cover . . . Walking in these jungles was difficult but not impossible . . .[16]

In August 1941, Wake was in rapid transition from its past solitude to the mechanized modernity of an outlying air base. Patrol plane facilities and a concrete ramp, the result of Pan American's pioneering, were already available on Peale.[17] Just inshore of Peacock Point along the west leg of Wake Island a narrow airstrip, 5,000 by 200 feet, had been chopped out of the dense growth. A main roadnet of packed coral was taking shape rapidly as the contractor's work-

---

[14] CNO ltr to CinCPac, 23Jun41, "Establishment of defensive garrison on Wake Island."

[15] To prevent confusion, Wake Island, as distinguished from the entire atoll, will hereinafter be entitled "Wake Island," whereas the single word, "Wake" will designate the atoll.

[16] LtCol W. L. J. Bayler, *Last Man off Wake Island* (Indianapolis, Bobbs-Merrill, 1943), 62, hereinafter cited as *Last Man off Wake Island*.

[17] In 1935, with Navy cooperation, Pan American Airways began development of a staging and refueling base on Peale to service its big clippers on the run to the Orient. At the time of this narrative major facilities included, in addition to those mentioned above, a powerful radio station, a pier, and a small but excellent hotel for overnight accommodation of passengers. Dierdorff, *op. cit.*, 501.

men blasted, slashed, and dozed the terrain of Wake.

In spite of the need for haste, rigid official separation existed between the construction efforts of Marines and those of the contractors.[18] Operating on a semi-private basis with their heavy equipment, supplies, and facilities the naval air base contract workers were concerned with building roads, shops, utilities, quarters, air base facilities, and the like. They built no defense installations. This construction fell solely to the Marines who had little engineering equipment except picks and shovels or the infrequent luxury of a borrowed civilian bulldozer. The Marines installed their heavy weapons by hand, hewed emplacements and foxholes from the coral, and erected their own living quarters. Understanding this basic difference in available means, the Navy's construction representative, Lieutenant Commander Elmer B. Greey,[19] and the civilian general superintendent, Mr. Daniel Teters, did their best to assist the shorthanded and meagerly equipped Marines. At no time, even after the outbreak of war, did the contractor's establishment or workmen come under full military control.

On 15 October Major Hohn was relieved as Marine detachment commander by Major James P. S. Devereux, who until this time had been executive officer of the 1st Defense Battalion. Major Devereux also became Island Commander, an additional duty which he would hold until relieved late in 1941 by a naval officer, Commander W. S. Cunningham, at this time still navigator of the USS Wright.

Major Devereux, as he saw Wake at this time, describes it as follows:

When I arrived on the island, the contractor's men working on the airfield near the toe of Wake proper had one airstrip in usable condition and were beginning the cross-runway. Five large magazines and three smaller detonator magazines, built of concrete and partly underground, were almost completed in the airfield area. A Marine barracks, quarters for the Navy fliers who would be stationed on the island, warehouses and shops also were going up on Wake. On Peale Island, work was progressing on a naval hospital, the seaplane ramp and parking areas. On Wilkes, there were only fuel storage tanks and the sites of proposed powder magazines, but a new deepwater channel was being cut through the island. In the lagoon, a dredge was removing coral heads from the runways for the seaplanes which were to be based at Wake. Some of these installations were nearly finished; some were partly completed; some were only in the blueprint stage.[20]

To bring Wake's defenses to the highest possible state of readiness in the shortest time, Major Devereux found much to be done. In addition, as senior representative of the armed forces on Wake, he was confronted by other demanding problems. To reinforce Army air strength in the Philippines, B-17 "Flying Fortresses" were being staged across the Pacific[21] through Wake, but no aviation ground crews were available there to service the big airplanes. Some 3,000 gallons of gasoline for each of these planes therefore had to be manhandled and hand-pumped

---

[18] Capt W. S. Cunningham, USN, transcript of recorded interview, "History of Wake Island Defense," 9Jan46, 3, hereinafter cited as *Cunningham Interview*.

[19] "Resident Officer-in-Charge" was LCdr Greey's official designation. With four enlisted Navy radiomen to maintain his communications, he was, until the arrival of Maj Hohn's detachment, sole naval representative on Wake.

[20] *Devereux Story*, 25.
[21] *War Reports*, 67.

by the Marines.²² This they did in addition to their normal duties, and the fueling tasks came at all hours of the day or night. It was ironic that many of these aircraft, which cost Wake so many man-hours of vital defensive preparations, would be trapped on the ground by the initial Japanese attacks on Clark and Nichols Fields in the Philippines.

Although this servicing of Army planes represented the heaviest single additional duty imposed upon the Marines, they were also required to act as stevedores in the time-consuming and exhausting process of unloading ships which arrived at the atoll. This work was required until the channel, berthing and turning facilities inside the lagoon could be completed. These additional duties hampered defense work during the autumn of 1941; but fortunately the detachment needed little combat training because it contained a number of "old Marines" of the best type.²³ On 2 November, two weeks after Major Devereux's arrival, the Wake garrison was augmented by a draft from the parent 1st Defense Battalion. This group included 9 officers and 200 enlisted men who arrived from Pearl on board the USS *Castor*. This brought the total Marine strength on Wake to 15 officers and 373 enlisted Marines.

During October and November progress on and about the airstrip, by now a going concern, indicated that there was room on Wake for the aviation component of fighters necessary to balance and round out the defense force. Commander, Aircraft Battle Force, had determined that this was to be Marine Fighter Squadron 211, supported in its independent role by a provisional service detachment drawn from Marine Air Group 21, to which VMF–211 was assigned. To establish the ground facilities required to maintain this squadron, Major Walter L. J. Bayler from the staff of MAG–21, together with a detachment of 49 Marines commanded by Second Lieutenant Robert J. Conderman,²⁴ were dispatched from Pearl on 19 November in USS *Wright*, an aircraft tender which was also bringing out the prospective Island Commander and commanding officer of the Naval Air Station.

While the *Wright* plowed westward bearing VMF–211's ground components, the air echelon of that squadron, consisting of the squadron commander, nine officers and two enlisted pilots,²⁵ had on the

---

²² Tankers would pump bulk aviation gas into tank storage ashore; Marine working parties would pump this gasoline into 50-gallon drums and transfer the drums to dispersed fuel dumps; finally, on arrival of planes the same gasoline would again be pumped by the same means into a lone tank-truck for delivery to the aircraft. When time pressed—as it usually did—Marines reinforced the truck by pumping directly from 50-gallon drums into the Fortresses.

²³ *Devereux Story*, 27.

²⁴ This detachment, like a similar one organized for the Marine air component at Midway, had been provisionally made up from key personnel representing each squadron in MAG–21, inasmuch as, at the time of organization, firm decision had not been made as to which squadrons from that group would be assigned to which islands. Wake aviation's ground detachment, therefore, included personnel not only from VMF–211 but from H&S Sq–21 and VMSB–231 and –232. CO MAG–21 Rept to CMC, 23Dec41.

²⁵ The pilots of VMF–211's Wake detachment were: Maj Paul A. Putnam (commanding), Capts Henry T. Elrod, Herbert C. Frueler, Frank C. Tharin; 1stLt George A. Graves; 2dLts Robert J. Conderman (in command of advance detail and ground maintenance, but also a pilot), Carl R. Davidson, Frank J. Holden, John

afternoon of 27 November received secret verbal warning orders to prepare for embarkation on board a carrier. Such orders had been expected by the squadron commander (though not by the pilots, virtually all of whom carried little more than toilet articles and a change of clothing), and few preparations were required. The squadron had only to fly the 12 new F4F-3 (Grumman Wildcat) fighters from Ewa Mooring Mast (as that air station was then designated) over to Ford Island, the naval air base in the middle of Pearl Harbor, for further transfer by air to the flight deck of the USS *Enterprise*. This was a routine operation for Marine pilots, and except for their unfamiliarity with the new aircraft, and the fact that one plane's starter misbehaved,[26] the morning flight of 28 November onto the *Enterprise* went off without incident.[27]

The best description of VMF-211's voyage to Wake is contained in a personal letter, composed on the eve of the squadron's debarkation, from Major Paul A. Putnam to Colonel Claude A. Larkin who commanded MAG-21. Excerpts are quoted:

AT SEA,
December 3, 1941.

DEAR COLONEL LARKIN:

It is expected that we will go ashore tomorrow morning. The extreme secrecy under which we sailed is still in effect and I understand is to remain so at least until this Force has returned to Hawaiian operating area. Therefore I am sending this first report via guard mail on this ship, rather than by air mail after landing . . .

You will recall that I left one plane at Ford Island. The Admiral at once gave me a plane to replace it, from VF-6; and he made it plain to me and to the whole ship that nothing should be overlooked nor any trouble spared in order to insure that I will get ashore with 12 airplanes in as near perfect condition as possible. Immediately I was given a full complement of mechs and all hands aboard have continually vied with each other to see who could do the most for me. I feel a bit like the fatted calf being groomed for whatever it is that happens to fatted calves, but it surely is nice while it lasts and the airplanes are pretty sleek and fat too. They have of course been checked and double checked from end to end, and they have also been painted so that all 12 are now of standard blue and gray . . .

The Admiral seems to be most determined to maintain secrecy regarding the position and activity of this Force. There has been a continuous inner air patrol during daylight, and a full squadron has made a long search to the front and flanks each morning and evening. They are armed to the teeth and the orders are to attack any Japanese vessel or aircraft on sight in order to prevent the discovery of this Force.

My orders, however, are not so direct. In fact I have no orders. I have been told informally by lesser members of Staff that I will be given orders only to fly off the ship and go to the land, and that there will be nothing in the way of instructions other than to do what seems appropriate at the moment. Of course I shall go and ask for orders and instructions, but it seems unlikely that I shall be given anything definite . .

This is written Wednesday forenoon. Should I receive any orders at variance with the foregoing, I will add a postscript. Otherwise I think of nothing further of importance or interest at this time. . . .

When the *Enterprise* had reached a point approximately 200 miles northeast of Wake, the squadron, from a materiel standpoint, was "as far as possible ready

---

F. Kinney, David D. Kliewer, Henry G. Webb; TSgt William J. Hamilton, and SSgt Robert O. Arthur.

[26] A hint as to the importance of the squadron's mission might have been drawn at this time from the fact that, when this starter trouble developed, the pilot of this defective plane was flown by a torpedo plane to the carrier where a brand-new F4F-3 from an *Enterprise* squadron was issued to him.

[27] Maj. P. A. Putnam ltr to CO MAG-21, 3Dec41.

for combat service," according to Major Putnam. However, he added, it was:

> ... seriously handicapped by lack of experience in the type of airplane then used. It is believed that the squadron was excellently trained and well qualified for war duty in a general sense, but it was unfortunate that the new type of airplane, so radically different from the type in which training had been conducted, had been received too recently to permit familiarization in tactical flying and gunnery.[28]

On the morning of 4 December this force was met by a Navy PBY sent out from Wake,[29] and the VMF-211 aircraft took off from the *Enterprise* and followed this plane to the atoll. Within less than two hours the last F4F-3 had pancaked on the narrow strip at Peacock Point.

Major Bayler had arrived on 29 November and already was busy setting up airbase communication facilities. Commander Cunningham had succeeded Major Devereux as Island Commander, and Lieutenant Conderman and his 49 headquarters and service personnel were waiting to greet the squadron, but the aircraft operating facilities at Wake were hardly in a finished stage. The landing strip, although sufficient in length, was too narrow to permit safe operation of more than one airplane at a time. Takeoffs or landings by section were thus impossible. Parking was extremely restricted, and all areas about the hardstand mat were in such rough and unfinished condition that passage of airplanes over them, even when pushed by hand, could cause serious plane damage. Fueling still depended on hand pumps and man power. No shelters or aircraft revetments existed, and the new planes were somewhat puzzling to pilots and mechanics who had no instruction manuals. Major Putnam began immediately to negotiate for the construction of revetments,[30] and he also began a training program to be carried on in conjunction with the daily dawn and dusk patrols which started on the morning after VMF-211 arrived.

These patrols, executed by four aircraft, circled the atoll approximately 50 miles out, and pilots combined this duty with navigation and instrument training. Instrument practice was particularly important because Wake had no electronic homing or navigational aids suitable for fighter operations, and the atoll was a small mark for pilots to locate through a floor of intermittent clouds.[31]

Other changes had taken place since the arrival of the *Wright*. Commander

---

[28] *Putnam Rept*, 13.

[29] On the day before, to the surprise of the men on Wake, a 12-plane squadron of PBY's had glided down onto the lagoon, anchored, and commenced a daily series of long-range air searches to the south of Wake. These seaplanes, however, were recalled from Wake on 5 December. The PBY which assisted VMF-211 with its navigation was from this squadron. *Last man off Wake Island*, 29.

[30] "Backed by a written request from the Commander, Aircraft Battle Force, a request was made through the Island Commander to the Civilian Contractor's superintendent on the morning of 5 December, asking for the immediate construction of bunkers for the protection of aircraft, and outlining various other works to follow. Great emphasis was put on the fact that speed, rather than neatly finished work, was required. However, an inspection that afternoon revealed a young civil engineer laboriously setting out stakes with a transit and three rodmen. It required an hour of frantic rushing about and some very strong language to replace the young engineer and his rodmen with a couple of Swedes and bulldozers." *Putnam Rpt*, 6.

[31] HistSec, HQMC interview with 1stLt J. F. Kinney, 23Jul45, 4, hereinafter cited as *Kinney Interview*.

Cunningham had brought with him Commander Campbell Keene, eight Navy officers, and 58 bluejackets who comprised the initial detachment of the Naval Air Station. All these personnel, like the Army Air Force communication detachment [32] of one officer and four soldiers, were without arms or field equipment. In spite of the efforts, men, and equipment consigned to Wake, the situation was still grim on 6 December 1941. The ground defenses, embodying the complete artillery of a defense battalion, had been emplaced during 12-hour working days, and some protective sandbagging and camouflage accomplished. But to man these weapons the 1st Defense Battalion detachment had only 15 officers and 373 enlisted men, although the 1941 T/O called for 43 officers and 939 men. This meant that one 3-inch antiaircraft battery [33] was entirely without personnel, and that each of the other two batteries could man only three of its four guns. Thus only six of the twelve 3-inch guns on the island could be utilized. Only Battery D had its full allowance of fire-control equipment. Battery E had a director but no height finder, and it had to get altitude data by telephone from Battery D. There were not half enough men to employ the ground and antiaircraft machine guns. There was no radar, despite plans for its eventual provision, and the searchlight battery did not have sound locators with which to detect approaching aircraft. Only the crews of the 5-inch seacoast batteries were at or near authorized strengths, and they also were devilled by unending minor shortages of tools, spare parts, and miscellaneous ordnance items.[34]

Peale Island's base development and defensive organization were the most advanced in the atoll. Although Battery B, the 5-inch seacoast unit at Toki Point, had been fully organized only after the arrival of personnel on 2 November, its position was in good shape. Much the same could be said of Battery D, 3-inch antiaircraft, set up near the southeast end of the island. All emplacements had not been completely sandbagged, but there were adequate personnel shelters plus underground stowage for 1,400 rounds of 3-inch ammunition. Telephone lines, although not buried, linked all positions with the island command post. Work on Wake Island was not far behind. Battery A, the 5-inch seacoast unit at Peacock Point, was completely emplaced and well camouflaged although it lacked individual shelters. Battery E, (3-inch antiaircraft), although working with only 43 Marines, had completely emplaced, sandbagged and camouflaged two guns and the director, and work on the third gun was nearly completed by 6 December. Telephone lines (with important trunks doubled or tripled) connected all units on Wake Island, but the wire was on the surface.

"Wilkes Island was the least developed," reported Captain Wesley McC. Platt, the local commander:

> ... At the outbreak of war, weapons ... had been set up. All were without camouflage or protection except the .50 caliber machine

---

[32] Commanded by Capt Henry S. Wilson, USA. This detachment manned an Army Airways Communication Service radio van to assist B-17's en route westward.

[33] This was Btry F. For this battery, however, the necessary fire control equipment had not yet arrived; so, even with full gun crews, its effectiveness would have been slight.

[34] File, dispatches received from Wake, 7-23 Dec 41, hereinafter cited as *Wake File*.

guns, which had been emplaced. All brush east of the new channel had been cleared. The remaining brush west of the new channel was thick and ... as a result of ... this [the] ... .50 caliber machine guns had been placed fairly close to the water line. The beach itself dropped abruptly from 2½ to 4 feet just above the high water mark.[35]

In addition to four .50 caliber AA and four .30 caliber machine guns, Platt had two searchlights and one 5-inch seacoast battery (L) which was set up at Kuku Point. The four 3-inch guns destined for Battery F were parked on Wilkes without personnel or fire control gear. Wire communications were in between the island command post and all units.[36]

Wake, intended primarily as a patrol plane base for PBY's, "the eyes of the Fleet," had no scouting aircraft after the PBY's departed on 5 December, and only the most primitive facilities for any type of aircraft operations. Its defending fighter squadron was learning while working, and these planes had neither armor nor self-sealing fuel tanks. In addition, their naval type bomb racks did not match the local supply of bombs.[37]

Exclusive of the 1,200 civilian contract employees, the military population of Wake (almost twenty per cent of whom were without arms or equipment) totalled 38 officers and 485 enlisted men:[38]

1st Defense Battalion detachment:	15 officers, 373 enlisted
VMF-211 and attachments:	12 officers, 49 enlisted
U. S. Naval Air Station:	10 officers, 58 enlisted (without arms).
Army Air Corps:	1 officer, 4 enlisted (without arms).
USS *Triton*:	1 enlisted (without arms, landed for medical attention).

Thus there were only 449 Marines on the atoll who were equipped and trained for combat.

Supplies on Wake, although aggravatingly short in many particular items, were generally adequate. The Marines had a 90-day supply of rations, and the civilian workers had a six-month supply. No natural water supply existed, but a sufficient number of evaporators were in service. Ammunition and aviation ordnance supplies initially could support limited operations, but would not withstand a protracted defense. Medical supplies were those normal for a remote, outlying station and could thus be considered adequate.[39] In addition to the naval medical equipment and personnel on Wake, the contractor's organization operated a fully-equipped hospital in Camp Two.[40]

But since November, when dispatches had warned that the international situation demanded alertness, the atoll was as ready for defense as time and material available permitted. When this warning arrived, Major Devereux, then the island commander, asked whether the civilian workers should be turned to tasks dealing more directly with military defense, but he was told not to revise work priorities. Small-arms ammunition was nevertheless

---

[35] LtCol W. McC. Platt reply to HistSec, HQMC questionnaire, 10Mar47.

[36] *Ibid.*, 2.

[37] Capt Frueler, squadron ordnance officer, at this moment was devising homemade modifications of the troublesome bomb lugs. By 8 December two 100-pound bombs could be precariously swung onto each aircraft, though hardly in any manner to inspire pilot confidence in clean release or assurance that return to base could be accomplished without dangling armed bombs.

[38] *Devereux Rept.*

[39] Maj. W. L. J. *Bayler Rept*, 9-10.

[40] *Cunningham Interview*, 3.

issued to individual Marines, and ready-service ammunition was stowed at every gun position. A common "J"-line (so-called) which augmented normal telephone circuits, joined all batteries, command posts, observation posts, and other installations with which the commander might need contact during battle,[41] and primitive "walky-talkies" formed a radio net established to parallel wire communications between command posts on Wake Island, Wilkes, and Peale. Atop the 50-foot steel water tank at Camp One, the highest point on Wake, Major Devereux had established a visual observation post linked by field telephone to the command post. This OP, with a seaward horizon of about nine miles, was the only substitute for radar.

On the morning of Saturday, 6 December, Major Devereux found time to hold the first general quarters drill for the entire defense battalion. "Call to Arms" was sounded, and all gun positions were manned (to the extent which personnel shortages permitted), communications tested, and simulated targets were "engaged."[42] The drill ran smoothly, and Major Devereux granted his men an almost unheard-of reward: Saturday afternoon off, and holiday routine for Sunday.

His timing of this "breather" was better than he knew.

---

[41] Maj W. L. J. Bayler Rept, 3.

[42] Prior to the outbreak of war, no opportunity had been found for test firings, calibration, or other gunnery exercises after emplacement of weapons on Wake. The first actual firing was in combat against the Japanese. *Cunningham Interview* 3.

CHAPTER 2

The Enemy Strikes[1]

The Pan American Airways *Philippine Clipper* which had spent the night of 7–8 December at Wake re-embarked passengers shortly after sunrise on Monday[2] 8 December, taxied into the calm lagoon, and soared toward Guam. Ashore breakfast was nearly over, and some Marines were squaring away their tents prior to falling out for the day's work. Major Devereux was shaving. In the Army Airways Communications Service radio van near the airstrip, an operator was coming up on frequency with Hickam Field on Oahu when at 0650 a frantic uncoded transmission cut through: Oahu was under enemy air attack.

Captain Henry S. Wilson snatched the message and rushed to Devereux's tent. The major tried unsuccessfully to reach Commander Cunningham by telephone, and then called the base communication shack. There, a coded priority[3] transmission from Pearl was being broken down. Devereux put down the telephone and ordered the field music to sound "Call to Arms.[4] Gunnery sergeants broke out their men and made sure that all had their ammunition. The Marines then piled into trucks which rushed them to the battery areas. By 0735 all positions were manned and ready, the planned watch was established atop the water tank in Camp One, and defense battalion officers had held a brief conference.

The dawn air patrol was up before the news came from Pearl,[5] but aviation personnel took hurried steps to safeguard the new Wildcats still on the ground. The *Philippine Clipper* was recalled ten minutes after its takeoff, and it circled back down to the lagoon. But in spite of these measures, things were not running smoothly at the airstrip. VMF–211 had been on Wake only four days and could hardly call itself well established. Aircraft revetments still being dozed would not be ready until 1400 that day, and suitable access roads to these revetments likewise were unfinished. Existing parking areas restricted plane dispersal to hazardously narrow limits. As Major Putnam stated it:

The Squadron Commander was faced with a choice between two major decisions, and inevitably he chose the wrong one. Work was

---

[1] Unless otherwise noted, the material in chap 2 is derived from *Devereux Rept; Putnam Rept; (officer's name) Repts; Bayler Rept; Devereux Story.*

[2] By east longitude date; this was the same as Sunday, 7 December east of the date line.

[3] At this time relative priorities in dispatch traffic were as follows: Urgent (to be used only for initial enemy contact reports), Priority, Routine, Deferred. Thus a priority dispatch presented a considerably more important transmission than it now would.

[4] Cdr Cunningham, who immediately recalled the *Philippine Clipper*, has since stated that it was he who ordered the defense battalion to general quarters, but it appears that this action had already been taken prior to his issuance of any order. *Cunningham Interview*, 4.

[5] *Kinney Interview*, 3.

THE ENEMY STRIKES

progressing simultaneously on six of the protective bunkers for the airplanes, and while none was available for immediate occupancy, all would be ready not later than 1400. Protection and camouflage for facilities were not available but could be made ready within 24 hours. Foxholes or other prepared positions for personnel did not exist but would be completed not later than 1400. To move the airplanes out of the regular parking area entailed grave risk of damage, and any damage meant the complete loss of an airplane because of the complete absence of spare parts ... The Squadron Commander decided to avoid certain damage to his airplanes by moving them across the rough ground, to delay movements of material until some place could be prepared to receive it, and to trust his personnel to take natural cover if attacked.[6]

Thus VMF-211's handful of pilots and mechanics spent the morning dispersing aircraft as widely as possible in the usable parking area, relocating the squadron radio installation from its temporary site to a covered one, and arming and servicing all aircraft for combat.

At 0800, only a few hours after the blazing and dying *Arizona* had broken out her colors under enemy fire at Pearl Harbor, Morning Colors sounded on Wake. Defensive preparations hummed. Trucks delivered full allowances of ammunition to each unit, the few spare individual weapons in Marine storerooms were spread as far as they would go to the unarmed Air Corps soldiers and Naval bluejackets, and gas masks and helmets of World War I vintage were distributed to the battery positions. Watches were set at fire control instruments and guns, while the balance of personnel worked on foxholes and filled the few remaining sandbags. The 3-inch antiaircraft batteries were specifically directed to keep one gun, plus all fire control instruments, fully manned. Marine units and the Island Commander hastily set up command posts. Commander Cunningham located his CP in Camp Two, and VMF-211's remained in the squadron office tent. Aviation personnel had to stick with their jobs of belting extra ammunition and transferring bulk fuel into more dispersable drums.

At 0900 the four-plane combat air patrol returned to base. The planes were refueled while the four pilots [7] took a smoking break, and then clambered back into F4F's 9 through 12 and took off again to scout the most likely sectors for enemy approach. Shortly after this the pilot of the *Philippine Clipper*, Captain J. H. Hamilton, reported for duty to Major Putnam at VMF-211's headquarters. He had orders from the Island Commander to make a long-range southward search with fighter escort. These orders, however, were later cancelled.[8]

While VMF-211's combat air patrol made a swing north of Wake at 12,000 feet, 36 twin-engined Japanese bombers were flying northward toward the atoll. This was *Air Attack Force No. 1* of the *Twenty-Fourth Air Flotilla*, based at Roi, 720 miles to the south.[9] As the enemy group leader signalled for a gliding let-

---

[6] *Putnam Rept*, 8.

[7] There were: Capt Elrod, who had relieved Maj Putnam on station, and 2dLt Davidson in one section, and 1stLt Kinney and TSgt Hamilton in the other.

[8] Orders were changed and the clipper took off for Midway at 1250 that afternoon to evacuate certain PAA personnel plus all passengers. Mr. H. P. Hevenor, a government official who missed the plane, was marooned on Wake and eventually ended up in Japanese hands. "It struck me as a rather drastic lesson in the wisdom of punctuality." commented Col Devereux. *Devereux Story*, 58.

[9] Notes on Enemy Interviews, n. d., hereinafter cited as *Enemy Notes*.

down in his 10,000-foot approach, he noted that the south coast of the atoll was masked by a drifting rain squall at about 2,000 feet. The three Japanese divisions, in 12-plane Vs, dropped rapidly down into the squall and emerged a few seconds later almost on top of the Wake airstrip. First Lieutenant William W. Lewis, commanding Battery E at Peacock Point, saw these planes at 1150, and he grabbed a "J"-line telephone to warn Devereux. Just as the major answered, a spray of bright sparks began to sail through the air ahead of the enemy formation. One civilian thought "the wheels dropped off the airplanes." But the planes had not come to lose their wheels. Japanese bombs were falling on Wake.

Lewis, an experienced antiaircraft artilleryman, had not only complied with the commanding officer's directive to keep one gun manned, but had added another for good measure. Within a matter of seconds he had two of Battery E's 3-inch guns firing at the Japanese,[10] and .50 caliber guns along the south shore of Wake quickly took up the fire. A tight pattern of 100-pound fragmentation bombs and 20mm incendiary bullets struck the entire VMF–211 area where eight Grummans were dispersed at approximately hundred-yard intervals. While two 12-plane enemy divisions continued to release bombs and to strafe Camp Two, one division broke off, and swung back over Camp One and the airstrip.

For a second time within less than ten minutes the airstrip was bombed and strafed. By 1210 the strike was over. The enemy planes turned away and commenced their climb to cruising altitude. "The pilots in every one of the planes were grinning widely. Everyone waggled his wings to signify 'Banzai'."[11]

The enemy attack burned or blasted seven of the eight F4F–3's from propeller to rudder, and the remaining Wildcat sustained serious but not irreparable damage to its reserve fuel tank. A direct bomb hit destroyed Major Bayler's air-ground radio installation, and the whole aviation area flamed in the blaze from the 25,000-gallon avgas tank which had been hit in the first strike. Fifty-gallon fuel drums burst into flame. VMF–211's tentage, containing the squadron's scanty stock of tools and spares, had been riddled and partially burned. Worst of all, 23 of the 55 aviation personnel then on the ground were killed outright or wounded so severely that they died before the following morning, eleven more were wounded but survived. At one stroke, VMF–211 had sustained nearly 60 per cent casualties. Nearly 50 per cent of the ground crewmen were dead. Three pilots (Lieutenants George A. Graves, Robert J. Conderman, and Frank J. Holden) were killed, and another, Lieutenant Henry G. Webb, was seriously wounded. Three more pilots, Major Putnam, Captain Frank C. Tharin, and Staff Sergeant Robert O. Arthur, had received minor wounds but remained on duty. In Camp

---

[10] Battery E, it will be recalled, had no height finder but was supposed to rely for this data on telephonic information from Battery D on Peale. Without waiting for word from Peale, Lt Lewis made a quick estimate of target altitude, cranked it onto his director, and had the battery in action within a matter of seconds.

[11] Account by Norio Tsuji, a Japanese observer during the raid. ATIS (SWPA), Enemy Publications No. 6, "Hawaii-Malaya Naval Operations," 27Mar43, 27–38, hereinafter cited as *Hawaii-Malaya NavOps*.

Two and the adjacent Pan American area, the hotel and other seaplane facilities were afire, the *Philippine Clipper* had received a few stray machine-gun bullets, and some ten civilian employees of PAA had been killed.[12] The enemy did not lose a single bomber although "several" were damaged by antiaircraft fire.[13] The Marine combat air patrol, well above the raid and momentarily scouting to the north, had not made contact. These pilots returned for landing shortly after the attack, and by a final stroke of ill fortune Captain Henry T. Elrod damaged his propeller seriously on a mass of bomb debris.

Wake's defenders were most concerned that this first raid had struck almost before they knew that enemy planes were overhead. The rain squall had helped the Japanese, but the atoll's lack of early-warning equipment was almost as beneficial to the enemy. The garrison needed radar, but none was available. Throughout the siege the Japanese planes continued to elude the most vigilant visual observation, and with the sound of their engines drowned by the booming surf they would often have their bombs away before they were spotted.

Damage control began at the airstrip as soon as the enemy departed. Casualties went to the one-story contractor's hospital which had been taken over as the island aid station,[14] the dead were placed in a reefer box at Camp Two, and able-bodied aviation personnel turned their attention to the airplanes and to the gasoline fires. The three planes still able to fly were sent up on combat air patrol. In the sky they would be safe from another surprise raid. Crews and officers reorganized and reallocated jobs. Second Lieutenant John F. Kinney became engineering officer to replace First Lieutenant Graves who had been killed.[15] Kinney's principal assistant was Technical Sergeant William J. Hamilton, an enlisted pilot, and these two men began salvaging tools and parts from burned planes. Their efforts immeasurably aided future operations of VMF–211. Captain Herbert C. Freuler reorganized the ordnance section, Lieutenant David D. Kliewer took over the radio section, and Captains Elrod and Tharin supervised construction of individual foxholes, shelters, and infantry defensive works in the VMF–211 area. Other work included mining the airstrip at 150-foot intervals with heavy dynamite charges to guard against airborne landings. Furrows were bulldozed throughout the open ground where such landings might take place, and heavy engineering equipment was placed to obstruct the runway at all times when friendly planes were not aloft. Plans called for continuation of the dawn and dusk reconnaissance flights, and for the initiation of a noon combat air patrol as well. It was hoped that these patrols could intercept subsequent enemy raids.

---

[12] *Cunningham Interview*, 5.

[13] JICPOA Item No 4986, Professional notebook of Ens T. Nakamura, IJN, 1941–1943, 25Feb44, hereinafter cited as *Nakamura Notebook*.

[14] The battalion surgeon of the 1st DefBnDet, Lt (jg) Gustave M. Kahn (MC), USN, was ably assisted by his civilian colleague, Dr. Lawton M. Shank, the contractor's surgeon, whose coolness and medical efficiency throughout the siege won high praise.

[15] *Kinney Interview*, 4.

Elsewhere on the atoll new defense work progressed just as rapidly.[16] Emplacements, foxholes, and camouflage were improved at all battery positions. A Navy lighter loaded with dynamite surrounded by concrete blocks was anchored in Wilkes channel to guard this dredged waterway. Telephone lines were repaired, key trunk lines were doubled wherever possible, and every possible attempt was made to bury the most important wires.[17] Construction of more durable and permanent command posts and shelters began before the day ended in a cold drizzle. Working that night under blackout restrictions, aviation Marines and volunteer civilians completed eight blast-proof aircraft revetments. The atoll's four operational planes were thus relatively safe within these revetments when 9 December dawned bright and clear, and Captain Elrod's plane also was in a bunker undergoing repairs to its propeller and engine.

General quarters sounded at 0500, 45 minutes before dawn, and the defense commander set Condition 1. This readiness condition required full manning of all phone circuits, weapons, fire control instruments, and lookout stations. The four F4F-3's warmed up and then took off at 0545 over Peacock Point. They rendezvoused in section over the field and then climbed upward to scout 60- to 80-mile sectors along the most probable routes of enemy approach. At 0700 the fighters finished their search without sighting any enemy planes and then turned back toward the atoll. There the defense detachment shifted to Condition 2 which required that only half the guns be manned, and that fewer men stood by the fire control instruments. This permitted Marines to get after other necessary work around their positions. At the airstrip Lieutenant Kinney continued work on Elrod's plane, and the squadron's engineering problem made it evident that hangar overhaul and blackout facilities had to be set up. Major Putnam decided to enlarge two of his new plane shelters for this purpose. Entrance ramps were cut below ground level, and the revetments were roofed with "I" beams, lumber, and lightproof tarpaulins. These expedients allowed extensive overhaul and maintenance at all hours, and provided maximum protection for planes and mechanics.

As the morning wore on, men began to work closer to their foxholes and to keep a wary eye skyward. A dawn takeoff from the nearby Japanese-mandated Marshalls could bring a second Japanese bomber raid over Wake at any time after 1100. This "clock-watching" was justified. Disgustingly prompt, enemy planes from the *Twenty-Fourth Air Flotilla* at Roi arrived at 1145.[18] Marine Gunner H. C. Borth spotted them first from the water tank OP, and he shouted the warning over the "J"-line circuit. Seconds later the air-ground radio (again in operation with makeshift equipment) passed

---

[16] Approximately ten per cent of the civilian workers volunteered for military or defensive duties, and some attempted to enlist. Many of these men served with heroism and efficiency throughout the operation.

[17] "Surface lines could not seem to stand up although they were all paralleled. We wanted to bury them, but we could not do so by hand . . . considering the scarcity of men to do the work. We could not obtain permission to use the ditch diggers of the contractors. . . ." LtCol C. A. Barninger reply to HistSec, HQMC questionnaire, 18Feb47, 8–9, hereinafter cited as *Barninger*.

[18] *Enemy Notes*, 1.

this alarm to the combat air patrol, and battery crewmen rushed to general quarters. Soon three bursts of antiaircraft fire, the new alarm signal,[19] were exploding from all sectors, and Wake stood by for its second attack of the war.

The leading Japanese planes approached from the southeast at 13,000 feet, and antiaircraft batteries on Peale Island and Peacock Point opened fire just before the first bombs were released. Minutes earlier the combat air patrol had made contact with one flank of the Japanese planes south of Wake, and Lieutenant Kliewer and Technical Sergeant Hamilton managed to cut off a straggler. They shot it down despite hot return fire from a top turret, and as the enemy plane spun away in flames the ground batteries' 3-inch shells began to burst among the Japanese. The Marine fighters broke contact and withdrew.

The first sticks of bombs exploded around Batteries E and A on Peacock Point and damaged a 3-inch gun in the E Battery position and a range finder at Battery A. Other bombs crashed along the east leg of Wake Island and into Camp Two. There direct hits destroyed the hospital, the civilian and Navy barracks buildings, the garage, blacksmith shop, a storehouse, and a machine shop. The falling bombs then straddled the channel at this tip of Wake and began to rain down on Peale Island. They made a shambles of the Naval Air Station which was still under construction, and scored a direct hit on the radio station. This destroyed most of the Navy's radio gear.[20] Meanwhile the antiaircraft guns continued to fire into the tight Japanese formation, and five bombers were smoking by the time Peale Island was hit. A moment later one of these planes burst into flames and blew up in the air. That was Wake's second certain kill. The others limped away still smoking.[21]

The hospital burned to the ground while the two surgeons saved first the patients and then as much medical supplies and equipment as they had time to salvage. Camp Two and the Naval Air Station were now as badly wrecked as the aviation area had been on the previous day, and four Marines and 55 civilians had been killed. But the defenders had learned some lessons, and the Japanese were not to have such an easy time hereafter. Major Putnam summed it up:

> The original raid . . . was tactically well conceived and skillfully executed, but thereafter their tactics were stupid, and the best that can be said of their skill is that they had excellent flight discipline. The hour and altitude of their arrival over the island was almost constant and their method of attack invariable, so that it was a simple matter to meet them, and they never, after that first day, got through unopposed. . . .[22]

Defenders spent that afternoon collecting wounded, salvaging useful items from blasted ruins, and moving undamaged installations to safer spots. These jobs were to become painfully familiar on succeeding afternoons.

---

[19] Wake did not have an air raid alarm, and this traditional three-shot signal was the only alternative. Defenders tried to make an alarm system with dismounted auto horns wired to storage batteries, but it never worked. *Last Man Off Wake Island*, 65, 122.

[20] CO NAS Wake Rpt to ComFourteen, 20-Dec41, 1–2.

[21] A Japanese report indicates that 14 of these bombers were damaged by antiacraft fire during this attack. *Nakamura Notebook*.

[22] *Putnam Rept*, 10.

The Japanese attack on Battery E at Peacock Point and along the island's east leg suggested to Major Devereux that the enemy would plan their raids in a logical sequence to pass over the atoll's long axis. On the previous day they had struck Wake's aviation, and now they had bombed not only the Naval Air Station but the 3-inch battery which had engaged them so promptly during that first raid. Thus Peacock Point was particularly vulnerable, and to protect his remaining antiaircraft weapons, Devereux ordered Battery E to shift to a new site some six hundred yards east and north. There the battery could manage its job equally well. And to make sure that its fire power did not suffer, the battery drew one of the unused 3-inch guns assigned to the "phantom" Battery F on Wilkes. This weapon replaced the one damaged by bombs.

To provide new hospital facilities, ammunition was cleared from the two most widely-separated reinforced concrete magazine igloos, and these were converted into underground medical centers. Each measured 20 by 40 feet and could accommodate 21 hospital cots. They met blackout requirements, and with lights furnished by two small generators could be operated efficiently at night. Medical supplies were divided between the two aid stations. Dr. Kahn was in charge of the Marine hospital in the southern shelter, and Dr. Shank maintained the Navy-civilian facility at the north end of the row of magazine igloos. Both were in use by nightfall that day.

During the night Battery E displaced to its new position. Aided by contractor's trucks and almost 100 civilian volunteers, Marines moved the guns, sandbags (too valuable and scarce to be left behind), fire control equipment, and ammunition. Emplacements were dug at the new site, sandbags refilled, and the guns readied for action. By 0500, just in time for dawn general quarters, the battery was in position and ready to fire.[23] Dummy guns were set up at the old position.

On 10 December the Japanese confirmed Devereux's theory that they would maintain certain patterns of approach and attack. At about 1045, 26 enemy bombers appeared, this time from the east. Again VMF-211 intercepted, and some of the bombers were hit before they reached the atoll. Captain Elrod, leading the fighters, shot down two enemy planes after the 3-inch guns began to fire. Bombs hit Battery E's abandoned position at Peacock Point, but the new site was not threatened. On Peale Island Battery D received two successive passes by one enemy flight division. The first pass scored a damaging hit on the battery's powerplant, but the guns continued to fire on barrage data. One plane burst into flames.

On Wilkes Island, undamaged from the earlier raids, one stick of bombs lit squarely on a construction dump where 125 tons of dynamite were cached west of the "New Channel."[24] The resultant explosion stripped most of the underbrush off Wilkes, detonated all 5- and 3-inch ready ammunition at battery positions,[25]

---

[23] LtCol W. W. Lewis reply to HistSec, HQMC questionnaire, 28Feb47, 1, hereinafter cited as *Lewis*.

[24] The "New Channel" was a partially-completed waterway through the center of Wilkes.

[25] By this time the Btry F position was being activated, but it was not as yet in full commission. Marine Gunner McKinstry, with naval personnel and volunteer civilians, had started that morning to form an antiboat battery with this unit's three guns and the damaged gun inherited from Btry E.

and swept Battery L's emplacement clean of accessories, light fittings and other movable objects. Fortunately only one Marine was killed. Four others were wounded, and one civilian sustained shock. But materiel-wise, Battery L was in serious shape. All fire control instruments except the telescopes on Gun 2 had been blasted away or damaged beyond repair, the gun tubes were dented, firing locks were torn off, and traversing and elevating racks were burred and distorted. Equipment loss at Battery F, organizing that morning, was less serious. One gun was damaged from blast and flying debris. In addition, the 60-inch searchlight on Wilkes had been knocked end over end. This seriously damaged the light's delicate arcs, bearings, and electronic fittings.

After this raid Major Devereux again ordered Battery E to displace. This time it would set up north of the airstrip and near the lagoon in the crotch of Wake. The dummy guns at Peacock Point, damaged by this third raid, were refurbished during the afternoon of 10 December, and Battery E's unmanned fourth gun was detached for antiboat emplacement elsewhere.[26] Battery E's new position would be most advantageous, the battery commander reasoned:

> Most all bombing runs were made from the east or west and the bombs were dropped along the length of the island. In this position the Japanese must make a run for the battery alone and most of the bombs would be lost in the lagoon.[27]

That night the battery personnel sweated through their second displacement, and by next morning they were in position and again ready to shoot.

GENESIS OF THE RELIEF EXPEDITION [28]

After the Pearl Harbor attack, President Roosevelt warned the American people to be prepared for the fall of Wake. Yet before the *Arizona's* hulk stopped burning, plans were underway to send relief to the atoll. But with much of the Pacific Fleet on the bottom of Pearl Harbor, little assistance could be provided. Wake, like other outer islands, would stand or fall on its own unless it could be augmented from the meager resources then at Pearl Harbor. Marine forces on Oahu included two defense battalions, the 3d and 4th,[29] elements of the 1st Defense Battalion, and miscellaneous barracks and ships' detachments. Any personnel sent to relieve Wake would have to come from these units, and that meant that other important jobs would have to be slighted. There was a limited source of equipment including radar and other supplies at Pearl Harbor in the hands of the Marine Defense Force quartermaster; and fighter

---

[26] This 3-inch gun, which figured conspicuously in the later defense, was located south of the airstrip and the VMF-211 area.

[27] *Lewis*, 2.

[28] Unless otherwise noted the material concerning the Relief Expedition is derived from a magazine article by LtCol R. D. Heinl, Jr., "We're Headed for Wake," *MC Gazette*, June 1946.

[29] This battalion, which during 1941–1943 executed more overseas displacements than any other defense battalion in the Fleet Marine Force, pulled out of Guantanamo Bay, Cuba, during late October 1941, moved secretly through the Panama Canal, and arrived at Pearl Harbor on Monday 1 December. On 7 December the battalion manned a 3-inch battery at the Navy Yard, and also served some antiaircraft machine guns. Since it had just completed this oversea movement, and had its equipment ready for service, the 4th was a logical choice for its eventual role in the attempt to relieve Wake.

aircraft, needed almost as much as radar, were already en route from San Diego on board the USS *Saratoga*.[30]

On 9 December [31] Admiral Kimmel's staff decided to send relief to Wake in a task force built around this carrier, Cruiser Division 6 (cruisers *Astoria*, *Minneapolis*, and *San Francisco*), the nine destroyers of Destroyer Squadron 4, the seaplane tender *Tangier*, which would carry troops and equipment, and the fleet oiler *Neches*. These ships would comprise Task Force 14. While it sailed for Wake, Task Force 11 built around the USS *Lexington*, would make diversionary strikes in the vicinity of Jaluit some 800 miles south of Wake. A third task force, commanded by Vice Admiral Halsey in the carrier *Enterprise*, would provide general support by conducting operations west of Johnston Island.[32]

Men and equipment to aid Wake would be drawn from the 4th Defense Battalion, and on 10 December this unit was alerted for immediate embarkation. The destination was not announced, but it did not require much imagination for rumor to cut through military secrecy. "We're going to Wake" was the word that circulated all day while the batteries prepared to mount out. By nightfall the personnel and equipment were squared away, and units groped about in the blackout to assemble their gear for loading. But in the midst of this work came orders to knock off and return to original battery positions. The CinCPac staff wanted to make a complete new study of the Pacific situation before it sent this relief off to Wake.[33] Besides, the task force had to await the arrival of the *Saratoga*.

CinCPac finally decided to make the attempt to reinforce Wake, and embarkation of certain units of the 4th Defense Battalion began two days later, on 12 December. By this time the Wake defenders had sent a partial list of their most critical needs, and Pearl Harbor supply activities filled this as best they could. These important items, which were loaded in the *Tangier* at pier 10 in the Navy Yard,[34] included an SCR-270 early-warning radar unit and an SCR-268 radar set for fire control. Also stowed on board were 9,000 rounds of 5-inch ammunition, 12,000 of the 3-inch shells with 30-second time fuzes, more than three million rounds of belted ammunition for .50 and .30 caliber machine guns, quantities of grenades, ammunition for small arms, barbed wire, antipersonnel mines, and additional engineering tools. Other equipment would enable the men at Wake to repair their bomb-damaged weapons. This included three complete fire control and data transmission systems for 3-inch batteries, needed replacement equipment for the atoll's 5-inch guns, electrical cable, ordnance tools, and spare parts.

Units of the 4th Defense Battalion embarked for this expedition included Battery F with 3-inch guns, Battery B with 5-inch guns, a provisional machine gun detachment drawn from Batteries H and I,

---

[30] These planes comprised VMF-221. The *Saratoga* had departed at maximum speed on 8 December (9 December on Wake). Ship's Log USS *Saratoga*, December 1941, hereinafter cited as *Saratoga* log.

[31] Throughout this section dealing with the relief attempt, west longitude dates and local times are used.

[32] CinCPac OPlan 39-41, 15Dec41, 2.

[33] Notes of interview by Capt S. E. Morison, USNR, with RAdm C. H. McMorris, 13Jan47, hereinafter cited as *McMorris Interview*.

[34] USS *Tangier* log, December 1941.

THE ENEMY STRIKES

and a headquarters section drawn from the Headquarters and Service Battery of the defense battalion. First Lieutenant Robert D. Heinl, Jr., commanded this force when it completed embarkation on 13 December, but the command passed to Colonel H. S. Fassett just prior to the departure of the task force two days later.[35] After loading, the *Tangier* moved to the upper harbor[36] where Rear Admiral Fletcher's Cruiser Division 6 waited for the *Saratoga*. The carrier came in to fuel on the 15th,[37] and the task force sortied late that day and set course for Wake.

ENEMY PLANS AND ACTIONS, 8–11 DECEMBER[38]

Admiral Inouye, commanding the Japanese *Fourth Fleet* at Truk, had set numerous projects and operations in motion on 8 December. Current war plans called for him to capture and develop Wake, Guam, and certain Gilbert islands including Makin and Tarawa. By 10 December, when Guam fell, Inouye could check off all these jobs except the one at Wake.[39] Despite its small size this atoll was giving the admiral and his people at Truk and Kwajalein some moments of worry. The other islands had fallen to them with little trouble, but they knew that Wake's defense was in better shape. They estimated that this atoll was defended by about 1,000 troops and 600 laborers. Wake's fighter planes were aggressive, and the flak from the island was at least prompt and determined. Between the Marine planes and this flak the *Twenty-Fourth Air Flotilla* surely had lost five of its planes, not counting four more "smokers" that the Wake defenders fervently hoped never made it back to Roi.

This *Twenty-Fourth Air Flotilla* was composed of *Air Attack Forces One* and *Three*. *Force One* flew shore-based bombers, and *Force Three* operated approximately 15 four-engined patrol bombers (probably Kawanishi 97s). *Force One* based on Roi, while *Force Three*, which was also bombing or scouting Baker, Howland, Nauru, and Ocean Islands, flew out of Majuro Atoll 840 miles south of Wake. The commander of this air flotilla had the mission of softening Wake for capture, and he was going about it in a creditable fashion. First he struck the airstrip to clear out the fighter planes, and then he figured to come back with the sky to himself and finish off his job. Subsequent targets had been the Naval Air Station, seaplane facilities, and other installations. With these missions accomplished, the pilots of the *Twenty-Fourth Air Flotilla* could settle down to the methodical business of taking out the antiaircraft and seacoast batteries. Thus the raid of 10 December concentrated on Peale where poor bombing and Battery D's fire held the Japanese to no gains, and on Wilkes where bombs set off the dynamite cache.

After those three strikes the Japanese decided Wake was ripe for a landing, and

---

[35] Col Fassett was to become Island Commander at Wake when the relief force arrived at the atoll. ComFourteen orders to Col Fassett, 15Dec41.

[36] *Tangier* log, op. cit.

[37] The *Saratoga* arrived in the Hawaiian area during the night of 14 December, but she could not enter the harbor until next day when the antisubmarine nets were opened. *Saratoga* log.

[38] Except as otherwise noted material in this section dealing with Japanese operations is derived from *Capture of Wake*; *Wake Attack*; *Nakamura Notebook*; *Enemy Notes*.

[39] *Campaigns of the Pacific War*, 47.

the job went to Rear Admiral Kajioka who commanded *Destroyer Squadron 6* in his new light cruiser *Yubari*. Kajioka planned to land 150 men on Wilkes Island to control the dredged channel, and 300 men on the south coast of Wake Island to capture the airfield. An alternate plan called for landings on the north and northeast coasts, but the admiral hoped to avoid these beaches unless unfavorable winds kept his men away from the south side of the atoll. The Japanese expected that a landing force of only 450 men would face a difficult battle at Wake, but this force was the largest that Admiral Kajioka could muster at this early date in the war. But if things hit a snag, destroyer crews could be used to help storm the beaches. The naval force at Admiral Kajioka's disposal included one light cruiser (the flagship), two obsolescent light cruisers for fire support and covering duties, six destroyers, two destroyer-transports, two new transports, and two submarines.[40] The *Twenty-Fourth Air Flotilla* would act as his air support. Wake was so small that the admiral did not consider carrier air necessary.

The 450 men of the landing force constituted Kajioka's share of the special naval landing force personnel assigned to the *Fourth Fleet*. It is probable that they were armed with the weapons typical to a Japanese infantry unit of company or battalion size, and that their weapons included light machine guns, grenade launchers, and possibly small infantry cannon. It is likely that assault troops were embarked in the two old destroyer-transports (*Patrol Craft 32 and 33*), while the garrison and base development echelon was assigned to the medium-size transports. The assault shipping from Truk arrived at Roi on 3 December, and on 9 December[41] the force sortied on a circuitous route for Wake.

The Japanese expected no American surface opposition, but they nonetheless screened their approach with customary caution. Two submarines scouted 75 miles ahead of the main body, and these boats were to reconnoiter Wake prior to the arrival of the task force.[42] Specifically they would try to find out whether the atoll defenders had any motor torpedo boats. Behind these submarines, and 10 miles forward of the main body, a picket destroyer maintained station from which it would make landfall and conduct a further reconnaissance. Ships of the task force neared Wake on the evening of 10 December. The weather was bad with high winds and heavy seas, but there was advantage even in this. The squalls provided a natural screen behind which the approach would surely remain undetected. Reports from the submarines and the screening destroyer indicated that Wake was not aware of the Japanese approach, and at 0300 on 11 December the

---

[40] *Yubari; Tatsuta* and *Tenryu* (2 old light cruisers, comprising Cruiser Division 18); *Oite, Hayate, Mutsuki, Kisaragi, Mochizuki* and *Yayoi* (6 older destroyers, comprising Destroyer Division 29 and 30); Patrol Boats 32 and 33, so-called (actually old destroyers converted into light troop-carrying craft with missions similar to the American APD); and *Kongo Maru* and *Konryu Maru*, both medium transports.

[41] *Capture of Wake*, II, 373 lists this date as 8 December, but other dates from this authority are consistently one day behind, and it is therefore probable that the date of 9 December is correct.

[42] The submarines were scheduled to arrive at Wake prior to dawn, and it is therefore not clear how they expected to make a visual reconnaissance that would be of much value.

THE ENEMY STRIKES

task force made landfall and prepared to disembark the landing force. From Kajioka's flagship Wake was barely visible while the admiral led his force to bombardment and debarkation stations five or six miles off the atoll's south shore.

THE ATTEMPTED LANDING, 11 DECEMBER

In spite of Wake's black silent appearance to the Japanese, the atoll defenders had spotted the enemy. Lookouts reported ships in sight just prior to 0300, and as the shadowy outlines drew closer Devereux decided they formed an enemy force which included cruisers, destroyers, and some auxiliaries. The garrison went to general quarters, and Devereux ordered Major Putnam to delay the takeoff of his four airplanes until after the shore batteries began to fire. And these batteries were ordered to hold their fire [43] until they received orders to open up. Major Devereux reasoned that the enemy force could outgun his defense force, and that premature firing would only reveal the location and strength of the seacoast batteries and rob them of a chance to surprise the enemy.

Meanwhile the enemy force was having trouble with the bad weather that had screened its approach. Assault troops found it difficult to make their transfer to sea-tossed landing craft, and some of these craft overturned or became swamped in the high waves. By dawn at 0500, the flagship *Yubari*, still in the van, reached a position approximately 8,000 yards south of Peacock Point. There she turned westward and commenced a broadside run parallel to the south shore of Wake. The other enemy ships followed generally along this course but kept approximately 1,000 yards further to seaward. Although the Japanese were not aware of it, the *Yubari* was being tracked along this course by the 5-inch guns of Battery B on Peacock Point. The camouflage had been removed from battery positions so that the guns could train.[44]

A few minutes later, the *Yubari* and the other two cruisers (*Tatsuta* and *Tenryu*) opened fire at area targets along the south shore of Wake. These salvos laddered the island from Peacock Point to the vicinity of Camp One. The high-velocity 6-inch shells which hit near Camp One ignited the diesel-oil tanks between the camp and Wilkes Channel, and only a repetition of Devereux's order to hold fire restrained Lieutenants Clarence A. Barninger and John A. McAlister, respectively commanding the 5-inch batteries at Peacock and Kuku Points, from returning fire. The other Japanese ships, following the cruiser and destroyer screen, maneuvered to take stations for their various missions.

After completing her initial firing run the *Yubari*, apparently accompanied by the two destroyer-transports, reversed course in a turn which closed the range on Wake. By this time it was daylight, and by 0600 these ships were some 3,500 yards south of Battery A on Peacock Point.[45]

---

[43] Cdr Cunningham's postwar report states that Maj Devereux wanted to illuminate the enemy force with searchlights and to open fire much sooner, but that this request was denied. *Cunningham Interview*, 7. Devereaux denies this, and he is supported by virtually all other records of the action.

[44] *Barninger*, 4.

[45] The range finders on the 5-inch guns of Btrys A and L had been rendered inoperative by previous bombings, and ranges therefore had to be estimated. This resulted in considerable variance among the later reports of this action. These discrepancies undoubtedly were aggra-

Battery A, with no range finder, had estimated the range to these ships, and the range section personnel were plotting the target while the gun section crews stood by to fire. The order to fire came from Devereux's command post at 0615, and the guns at Peacock Point opened fire on the *Yubari* and the ships with her while Battery L engaged the other enemy ships within range of Wilkes Island. Battery A's first salvo went over the Japanese flagship, and Lieutenant Barninger ordered the range dropped 500 yards. This fire from the beach caused the cruiser to veer away on a zig zag course, and to concentrate her fire on the Battery A guns. Her shots straddled the Marine positions as she pulled away rapidly. Barninger adjusted as best he could for the evasive tactics of the Japanese ship, and his guns soon scored two hits. Both shells entered the cruiser at the waterline amidships on her port side, and the ship belched steam and smoke as she slackened speed. Two more shells then caught her slightly aft of these first wounds, and she turned to starboard to hide in her own smoke. A destroyer then attempted to lay smoke between the troubled cruiser and the shore battery, but it was chased away by a lucky hit from a shell aimed at the cruiser. The *Yubari* continued to fire at Peacock Point until her 6-inch guns could no longer reach the island. Then, listing to port, she limped smoking over the horizon.[46]

Meanwhile Battery L had opened up from Wilkes on the three destroyers, two transports, and the light cruisers *Tatsuta* and *Tenryu* which had broken off from the *Yubari* at the west end of her first firing run. These cruisers and transports steamed north at a range of about 9,000 yards southwest of Kuku Point while the destroyers (probably Destroyer Division 29 consisting of the *Hayate*, *Oite*, and either the *Mutsuki* or *Mochizuki*)[47] headed directly for shore and opened fire. At about 4,000 yards from the island they executed a left (westward) turn, and the *Hayate* led them in a run close along the shore. At that point Battery L opened fire. At 0652, just after the third two-gun salvo, the *Hayate* erupted in a violent explosion, and as the smoke and spray drifted clear, the gunners on Wilkes could see that she had broken in two and was sinking rapidly. Within two minutes, at 0652, she had disappeared from sight.[48] This prompted such spontaneous celebrations in the Battery L positions that a veteran noncommissioned officer had to remind the gun crews that other targets remained.

Fire then shifted to *Oite*, next in line behind the *Hayate*. This destroyer was now so close to shore that Major Devereux had difficulty restraining his .30 caliber machine gun crews from firing at her. A 5-inch gun scored one hit before the onshore wind carried smoke in front of the target. With this concealment, the destroyers turned to seaward away from Battery L. Marines fired several more salvos into the smoke, but they could not spot the splashes. Some observers on Wilkes thought they saw the *Oite* transfer

---

vated by the long dispersion pattern characteristic of these flat trajectory naval weapons.

[46] The Btry A commander, whose comments are the source of this account of action against Adm Kajioka's flagship, believes that his guns scored two more hits on the cruiser before she got out of range. *Barninger*, 4–5.

[47] *Wake Attack*.

[48] Platt, *op cit.*, 3. The *Hayate* thus was the first Japanese surface craft sunk during the war by U. S. naval forces.

survivors and sink, but reliable enemy records indicate only that she sustained damage.[49]

Battery L now shifted fire to the transports *Kongo Maru* and *Konryu Maru* then steaming approximately 10,000 yards south of Wilkes. One shell hit the leading transport, and this ship also turned to seaward and retired behind a smoke screen which probably was provided by the two fleeing destroyers. Their course carried them past the transport area. By this time civilians on Wilkes had joined the defensive efforts as volunteer ammunition handlers, and the battery next engaged a cruiser steaming northward 9,000 yards off the west end of the island. This was either the *Tenryu* or the *Tatsuta;* but whatever her identity, she hurried away trailing smoke after one shell struck her near the stern. The departure of this ship, at about 0710, removed the last target from the range of Battery L. In a busy hour, this unit had fired 120 5-inch shells which sank one destroyer, damaged another, and inflicted damage to a transport and a light cruiser. Two Marines had sustained slight wounds.

Meanwhile the other half of the Japanese destroyer force (*Destroyer Division 30*) ran into its share of trouble as it moved west of Kuku Point on a northwesterly course. Led (probably) by the *Yayoi*, these three destroyers at 0600 steamed within range of Battery B's 5-inch guns on Peale. The Marines opened fire on the leading ship, and the Japanese promptly raked Peale with return salvos which scored hits in and about the positions of Batteries B and D. This shelling destroyed communications between Battery B's guns and the battery command post, and put Gun Two out of action with a disabled recoil cylinder. Lieutenant Woodrow W. Kessler, the battery commander, continued his duel with only one gun, and used personnel from Gun Two to help keep up the fire. Ten rounds later a shell caught the *Yayoi* in her stern and set her afire. Kessler then shifted his fire to the second ship which was maneuvering to lay a smoke screen for the injured *Yayoi*. Under this concealment all three destroyers reversed course and retired southward out of range.

The Japanese force was now in full retirement. At 0700 Admiral Kajioka ordered a withdrawal to Kwajalein. Bad weather and accurate Marine fire had completely wrecked the admiral's plan to take Wake with 450 men. But commanders on the atoll took immediate precautions to guard against a dangerous relaxation of defenses. They reasoned that the Japanese might have carrier aircraft ready to continue the attack which the ships had started, and Major Putnam was already aloft with Captains Elrod, Freuler, and Tharin to reconnoiter the area from 12,000 feet. When this search located no enemy aircraft or carriers, the Marine pilots turned southwest to overtake the retiring Japanese task force. The fliers found the enemy little more than an hour's sail from Wake, and they swept down to attack.

Captains Elrod and Tharin strafed and bombed two ships (probably the cruisers *Tenryu* and *Tatsuta*),[50] and got their planes damaged by heavy antiaircraft fire

---

[49] *Enemy Notes*, 1.

[50] The VMF pilots were not sure about the identification of their targets, but a consultation of all available sources of information seems to substantiate this account of the action.

from these two targets. But the *Tenryu* suffered bomb damage to her torpedo battery, and the *Tatsuta's* topside radio shack was hit. Captain Freuler landed a 100-pound bomb on the stern of the transport *Kongo Maru*, and saw his target flare up with gasoline fires. After dropping their two bombs each, the fliers hurried back to Wake to rearm.

Two fresh pilots, Lieutenant Kinney and Technical Sergeant Hamilton, substituted for two of the original fliers during one of these shuttles between the atoll and the enemy ships, and the air attacks continued for a total of 10 sorties during which the Marines dropped 20 bombs and fired approximately 20,000 rounds of .50 caliber ammunition.[51] The destroyer *Kisaragi*, probably hit earlier by Captain Elrod, finally blew up just as Lieutenant Kinney nosed over at her in an attack of his own. One of the destroyer-transports also sustained damage from the air strikes.

This action was not all "ducks in a barrel" to the Marine fliers, and any damage to the scanty Wake air force was a serious one. Japanese flak cut the main fuel line in Elrod's Grumman, and although he managed to get back to the atoll he demolished his plane in a crash landing amid the boulders along Wake's south beach. Antiaircraft fire pierced the oil cooler and one cylinder in Captain Freuler's plane. He returned to the field safely, but he finished his approach on a glide with a dead engine that could never be repaired.

Accurate assessment of enemy losses in this first landing attempt is not possible. Japanese records indicate, however, that the destroyer *Hayate* was sunk by shore batteries and the destroyer *Kisaragi* by the VMF-211 bombs. Two more destroyers, the *Oite* and the *Yayoi*, were damaged as was a destroyer-transport. The transport *Kongo Maru* was bombed and set afire. All three cruisers (*Yubari*, *Tatsuta*, and *Tenryu*) received injuries from air or surface attacks.[52]

Japanese personnel casualties can be fixed only approximately. Assuming that the two sunken destroyers were manned by crews comparable to those required by similar U. S. types (about 250 officers and men per ship), it would be logical to claim approximately 500 for these two losses with the fair assumption that few if any survivors escaped in either case. Personnel losses on the other seven ships damaged are not known, but it must be assumed that casualties did occur.[53]

---

[51] CO VMF-211 Rept to CO MAG-21, 20Dec41.

[52] The widely-credited claim, originated in good faith, that dive-bombing attacks sank a cruiser off Wake cannot be supported. All three cruisers returned to Wake less than two weeks later to support the final attack on the atoll. The officially established occasion of the loss of each is as follows: *Yubari* (Philippine Sea, 27 Apr44); *Tenryu* (Bismarck Sea, by submarine action, 18Dec42); *Tatsuta* (off Yokohama, by submarine action, 13May44). As indicated in the text the violent explosion and sinking of the *Kisaragi*, combined with recognition inexperience, probably accounts for the cruiser claimed. ONI StatisticalSec, "Naval Losses of All Nations," (located at NHD), 5Feb46, Table VIII.

[53] In a letter dated 22Nov51, Capt Tashikazu Ohnae, leading Japanese naval student of WW II, puts Japanese losses for this phase of the Wake operation at "nearly 500." Ohmae letter cited in Robert Sherrod, *History of Marine Corps Aviation in World War II* (Washington: Combat Forces Press, 1952), 41, hereinafter cited as *Marine Air History*.

CHAPTER 3

Wake Under Siege[1]

Scarcely had the VMF-211 planes returned to the field before it was time for Lieutenants Davidson and Kinney to fly the only two serviceable fighters on the early midday combat patrol. It was then nearly 1000, almost time for the Japanese bombers to arrive, and the Marines soon spotted 30 of these enemy planes coming out of the northwest at 18,000 feet. Davidson downed two of these aircraft, and Kinney turned a third homeward with smoke trailing behind it. Then the fliers pulled away as the enemy formation entered the range of the Wake guns.

This antiaircraft fire splashed one bomber in the water off Wilkes and damaged three others. Bombs hit close to Battery D on Peale, and others exploded on Wake. There were no Marine casualties, and damage was slight, but the pattern of the attack convinced Devereux that the Japanese had spotted the position of Battery D. As soon as the attack ended he ordered this unit to displace from the neck of Toki Point to the southeastern end of Peale.[2] Marines and civilians began this displacement after dark. Sandbags at the old position could not be reclaimed, and cement bags and empty ammunition boxes had to serve this purpose at the new location. The work was finished by 0445, and Battery D again was ready to fire.

On 12 December the Japanese came to work early. Two four-engine Kawanishi patrol bombers arrived from Majuro at about 0500 and bombed and strafed Wake and Peale Islands. Bombs hit the airstrip but caused little damage. Captain Tharin, who had just taken off on the morning reconnaissance patrol, intercepted one of the big flying boats and shot it down. After this raid the Wake defenders went on with their work. Beach defenses were improved on Wilkes, and the ordnance officer, Gunner Harold C. Borth, serviced Battery L's battered 5-inch guns. At the airfield Lieutenant Kinney managed to patch up one of VMF-221's cripples, and this brought the strength of the Wake air force up to three planes. Such work continued for the remainder of the day. To the surprise of everyone on the atoll, the

---

[1] Unless otherwise noted the material in Chap 3 is derived from *Devereux Rept; Putnam Rept; (officer's name) Repts*. especially 1stLt J. F. *Kinney Rept*, Major W. L. J. *Bayler Rept*, and LtCol B. D. *Godbold Rept; Devereux Story*.

[2] At 1700, just prior to Battery D's displacement, a smoke bomb and a chain-flare of three red balls was sighted about two miles northeast of Toki Point. This signal was repeated twice in the next 20 minutes. The significance of these signals has not been established. Japanese submarines were operating in the vicinity of Wake, however and it may be that the signals had something to do with rescue operations in which these boats were trying to aid survivors from a bombing raid or from the surface action.

enemy did not arrive for the usual noon raid.[3]

This freedom from attack was a welcome and profitable interlude for the garrison. Captain Freuler, who had been attempting since the opening of the war to devise some means of employing welder's oxygen to augment the dwindling supply for the fighter pilots, finally managed, at great personal hazard, to transfer the gas from commercial cylinders to the fliers' oxygen bottles. Without this new supply the pilots could not have flown many more high altitude missions.

Another important experiment failed. Marines tried to fashion a workable aircraft sound locator out of lumber. It was "a crude pyramidal box with four uncurved plywood sides," by Major Devereux's description. It was too crude to be of any value; it served only to magnify the roar of the surf.

That evening Lieutenants Kinney and Kliewer and Technical Sergeant Hamilton readied Wake's three planes for the final patrol of the day. Kliewer drew a plane that was always difficult to start,[4] and his takeoff was delayed for nearly fifteen minutes. While he was climbing to overtake the other fliers he spotted an enemy submarine on the surface some 25 miles southwest of the atoll. He climbed to 10,000 feet and maneuvered to attack with the sun behind him. He strafed the Japanese boat with his .50 caliber guns, and then dropped his two bombs as he pulled out of his glide. Neither bomb hit, but Kliewer estimated that they exploded within fifteen feet of the target. Bomb fragments punctured his wings and tail as he made his low pull-out, and while he climbed to cruising altitude he saw the enemy craft submerge in the midst of a large oil slick.[5]

After their various activities on 12 December, the atoll defenders ended the day with a solemn ceremony. A large grave had been dug approximately 100 yards southwest of the Marine aid station, and in this the dead received a common burial while a lay preacher from the contractor's crew read simple prayers.

Next day the Japanese did not bother Wake at all, and Marine officers thought it possible that Kliewer's attack on the enemy submarine had brought them this day of freedom. The tiny atoll, frequently concealed by clouds, was a diffi-

---

[3] From 12 December until about 20 December, another day on which the enemy did not raid Wake, the recollections of surviving defenders sometimes are confused beyond any possible reconciliation. This condition is acute for the period of 12-14 December inclusive. Sources reconstructing the events of those dates arrive at few compatible accounts. This volume attemps to draw the best possible compromise from these conflicts.

[4] *Last Man off Wake Island*, 120.

[5] The fate of this submarine is not known. Enemy records are not clear. But after the fall of Wake, Kinney and other pilots were questioned by a Japanese officer who asked them if they knew anything about a Japanese submarine that had disappeared in the vicinity of the atoll. This led Kliewer to believe that concussion from his bombs had finished off the submarine. The Japanese list two of their submarines (RO-66 and RO-62) sunk 25 miles southwest of Wake on 17 Dec 1941. RO-66 was lost not to enemy action but to disaster, the Japanese said. The cause of the loss of RO-62 is not known, and it therefore may be assumed that there was some confusion as to the date. And since the Wake Marines had trouble remembering exact dates in their postwar reconstruction of specific events, it may be that Kliewer's bombs sank the RO-62. MilHistSec, SS, GHQ, FEC, Japanese Studies in WWII No. 116, The IJN in WWII, February 1952 (located at OCMH).

cult place to find, and the Marines reasoned that the Japanese were using submarine radios as navigational homing aids. Accurate celestial navigation would have been possible at night, but the bombers had been making daylight runs of from 500 to 600 miles over water with no landmarks. By dead reckoning alone this would have been most difficult, yet the bombers hit at about the same time each day. This convinced some of the Marines, including Lieutenant Kinney, that the submarine had been leading them in.[6]

But even this quiet day[7] did not pass without loss. While taking off for the evening patrol, Captain Freuler's plane swerved toward a group of workmen and a large crane beside the runway. To avoid hitting the men or this crane, Freuler made a steep bank to the left. The plane lost lift and settled into the brush, a permanent wash-out. It was set up in the bone yard with other wrecks which were parked to draw bombs.

December 14 started explosively at 0330 when three four-engine Kawanishi 97 flying boats droned over from Wotje[8] and dropped bombs near the airstrip. They caused no damage, and the garrison made no attempt to return fire. But later that day the pilots of the *Twenty-Fourth Air Flotilla* resumed their bombing schedule. Thirty shore-based bombers arrived from Roi at 1100, and struck Camp One, the lagoon off Peale, and the west end of the airstrip. Two Marines from VMF-211 were killed and one wounded, and a direct bomb hit in an airplane revetment finished off another fighter plane, leaving the atoll's aviation unit only one plane that could fly.[9] Lieutenant Kinney, VMF-211's engineering officer, sprinted for the revetment where he was joined by Technical Sergeant Hamilton and Aviation Machinist's Mate First Class James F. Hesson, USN,[10] his two assistants. Despite the fire which engulfed the rear end of the plane, these men accomplished the unbelievable feat of removing the undamaged engine from the fuselage and dragging it clear.

During his morning patrol flight of 15 December, Major Putnam sighted another submarine southwest of Wake. But it appeared to have orange markings, and Putnam did not attack. He thought it might be a Netherlands boat because he had observed markings of that color on Dutch airplanes in Hawaii in late 1941. Putnam's examination of the craft caused it to submerge, however, and Marines later took significant notice of this when the regular bombing raid did not arrive that day. This seemed to add credence to the theory that submarines were providing navigational "beams" for the bombers.

But the Kawanishi flying boats kept the day from being completely free of Japanese harassment. Four to six of these four-motored planes came over at about 1800, and one civilian was killed when the planes made a strafing run along the atoll.

---

[6] *Kinney Interview*, 4.

[7] On this date hot rations cooked in the contractor's galley were delivered to all battery positions by a "chuck wagon." This service continued for as long as possible thereafter. It was one of Mr. Teters' many contributions to the defense.

[8] *Enemy Notes*, 1.

[9] *Wake File*.

[10] Hesson was a Navy aviation instrument repairman sent over to VMF-211 from the Naval Air Station after the first attack had played such havoc among the fighter squadron's ground personnel. He turned out to be an outstanding general aviation maintenance man.

Their bombing was less effective. They apparently tried to hit Battery D on Peale Island, but most of the bombs fell harmlessly into the lagoon and the others caused no damage.

Meanwhile defensive work continued during every daylight hour not interrupted by such bombing raids. Another aircraft was patched up, personnel shelters for all hands had been completed in the VMF-211 area, and at Peacock Point Battery A now had two deep underground shelters with rock cover three feet thick.[11] And before nightfall on 15 December the garrison completed its destruction of classified documents. This security work began on 8 December when the Commandant of the 14th Naval District ordered Commander Cunningham to destroy reserve codes and ciphers at the Naval Air Station,[12] but codes remained intact in the VMF-211 area. Now Major Bayler and Captain Tharin shredded these classified papers into an oil drum and burned them in a gasoline fire.[13]

On the 16th the Japanese made another daylight raid. Twenty-three bombers from Roi came out of the east at 18,000 feet in an attempt to bomb Peale Island and Camp Two. Lieutenants Kinney and Kliewer, up on air patrol, warned the garrison of this approach, but the Marine fliers had no luck attacking the enemy planes. They did radio altitude information for the antiaircraft gunners, however, and the 3-inch batteries knocked down one bomber and damaged four others. The Japanese spilled their bombs into the waters of the lagooon and turned for home.

But experience had taught the atoll defenders not to expect a rest after this daylight raid was over. The flying boats had become almost as persistent as the shore-based bombers, and at 1745 that afternoon one of the Kawanishis came down through a low ceiling to strafe Battery D on Peale Island. Poor visibility prevented the Marines from returning fire, but the attack had caused little damage. The plane dropped four heavy bombs, but these fell harmlessly into the lagoon. Marines who were keeping score—and most of them were—marked this down as Wake's 10th air raid.

After this attack Wake had an uneasy night. It was black with a heavy drizzle, and maybe this put sentinels on edge just enough to cause them to "see things"—although no one could blame them for this. At any rate lookouts on Wilkes passed an alarm at 0200 that they had sighted 12 ships, and everybody fell out for general quarters. Nothing came of this alarm and postwar Japanese and U. S. records indicate that there were no ships at all around Wake that night.

At 0600 on 17 December Lieutenant Kinney reported proudly that his engineering crew had patched up two more airplanes. This still left the atoll with a four-plane air force, but fliers and other aviation personnel could hardly have been more amazed if two new fighter squadrons had just arrived. Major Putnam called the work of Kinney, Hamilton, and Hesson "magical."[14]

> . . . With almost no tools and a complete lack of normal equipment, they performed all types of repair and replacement work. They changed engines and propellers from one airplane to another, and even completely built up new

---

[11] *Wake File.*
[12] *Cunningham Interview,* 4.
[13] *Last Man Off Wake Island,* 112.

[14] *Putnam Rept,* 15.

engines and propellers from scrap parts salvaged from wrecks. . . . all this in spite of the fact that they were working with new types [of aircraft] with which they had no previous experience and were without instruction manuals of any kind. . . . Their performance was the outstanding event of the whole campaign.[15]

"Engines have been traded from plane to plane, have been junked, stripped, rebuilt, and all but created," another report said of Kinney's engineering work.[16]

At 1317 that afternoon 27 Japanese bombers from Roi came out of the southwest at 19,000 feet. Their bombs ignited a diesel oil tank on Wilkes and destroyed the defense battalion messhall as well as much tentage and quartermaster gear at Camp One. A bomb explosion also damaged one of the evaporator units upon which Wake depended for its water supply. The 3-inch guns brought down one of these planes.

Later that day one of the Kinney-patched fighter planes washed out during take-off, and it had to be sent back to the boneyard. Then at 1750 came the heaviest raid the Kawanishi flying boats ever put into the air against Wake.[17] Eight of these planes bombed and strafed the atoll but inflicted little damage.

As if the Wake defenders did not already have their hands full, construction authorities in Pearl Harbor wanted to know how things were going with the lagoon dredging. They also asked for a specific date on which the atoll would have certain other improvements completed. The island commander prefaced his preliminary reply to this query with an account of the latest air raid, and followed this with a damage report which summarized his battle losses since the beginning of the war. He pointed out that half of his trucks and engineering equipment had been destroyed, that most of his diesel fuel and dynamite were gone, and that his garage, blacksmith shop, machine shop, and building supplies warehouse either had been blasted or burned to the ground.

In a supplementary report sent later, Commander Cunningham told the Pearl Harbor authorities that everybody on Wake had been busy defending the atoll and keeping themselves alive. They could not do construction work at night, he pointed out, and if they used too much heavy equipment during the day they could not hear the bombers approaching. Besides, he reiterated, much of his equipment had been destroyed by the bombing raids, and most of his repair facilities had met the same fate. On top of all this, he added, civilian morale was bad. Cunningham said he could not promise a completion date on anything unless the Japanese let up the pressure.[18] The originator of this Pearl Harbor query might have found a pointed hint in this reference to a let-up of pressure. But at any rate Cunningham never again was asked how his construction work was coming along.

The 18th of December was quiet.[19] One enemy plane was sighted in the vicinity of

---

[15] *Ibid.*

[16] CO VMF-211 Rept to CO MAG-21, 20Dec41, 2.

[17] As an example of how memories can grow dim, not a single defender remembered to mention this raid in accounts prepared after the war ended. Yet there is no doubt that the raid occurred, because the garrison reported it to Pearl Harbor that same afternoon. *Wake File.*

[18] *Ibid.*

[19] Likewise typical of the day-to-day confusion which exists in the Wake records and recollections is the fact that contemporary records—the Wake dispatches and Maj Bayler's official narrative report prepared in December 1941—

Wake, however, and the defenders considered its activity ominous. It was almost directly overhead at about 25,000 feet when first sighted. Well beyond antiaircraft or fighter range, it flew northwest along the axis of the atoll, and then turned south, presumably returning to Roi. Defenders believed this to be a photo-reconnaissance flight.

Next morning the defenders continued their routine work, trying to add to their defensive installations before the bombers were due. This was a routine now familiar to them. After being cleared from morning general quarters, the men went about their work until the midday raid sent them to gun positions or to cover. After that raid was over, the men cleaned up after the bombs or went ahead with their other duties. Then late in the afternoon they had to take time out to deal with the flying boats. At night they could usually sleep when they were not on sentry duty, or standing some other type of watch. Following this pattern, crew members of the various batteries had completed their sturdy emplacements, and everybody had contributed to the construction of primary and alternate positions for beach defense. They had built more beach positions than they could possibly man, but many of these were to be manned only under certain conditions.[20] The shortage of trained fighting men was so critical that a well coordinated Japanese landing attack would require them to be everywhere at once.

At 1050, 27 bombers from Roi came in from the northwest at about 18,000 feet. They worked over the VMF-211 area south of the airstrip, finished off the Marines' messhall and tentage at Camp One, and struck the PanAir area. Batteries D and E hit four of these bombers, and observers on the atoll saw one of them splash after its crew bailed out over the water. Bomb damage at Camp One was serious, but elsewhere it was slight, and there were no casualties.

December 20 dawned gloomily with heavy rain, and ceilings were low and visibility poor all day. This wide weather front apparently dissuaded the Japanese from attempting their usual noon visit, but it did not stop a U. S. Navy PBY which arrived that day and provided Wake with its first physical contact with the friendly outer world since the start of the war. This plane landed in the lagoon at 1530 to deliver detailed information about the planned relief and reinforcement of the atoll. These reports contained good news for nearly everyone. All civilians except high-priority workers were to be evacuated. A Marine fighter squadron (VMF-221) would fly in to reinforce VMF-211, which was again down to a single plane. And the units from the 4th Defense Battalion would arrive on the *Tangier* to reinforce the weakened detachment of the 1st Defense Battalion. The PBY fliers had a copy of the *Tangier's* loading plan,[21] and this list made the ship seem like some fabulous floating Christmas package that was headed for the atoll.

That night Commander Cunningham, Majors Devereux and Putnam, and Lieu-

---

indicate that the memories of the survivors have almost unanimously transposed the events of 17 and 18 December.

[20] LtCol A. A. Poindexter reply to HistSec, HQMC questionnaire, 8Apr47.

[21] Capt W. S. Cunningham, USN, ltr to Capt S. E. Morison, USNR, 7Feb47; *McMorris Interview*, 2; CinCPac OPlan 39-41, 15Dec41.

tenant Commander Greey prepared reports to send back to Pearl Harbor. Major Bayler, his mission long since completed, would carry the papers back as he complied with his orders directing him to return from Wake "by first available Government air transportation." Mr. Hevenor, the Bureau of the Budget official who had missed the *Philippine Clipper* on 8 December, also planned to leave on the PBY, but someone pointed out that he could not travel in a Naval aircraft without parachute and Mae West, neither of which was available. So Mr. Hevenor missed another plane.

At 0700 next morning, 21 December, the PBY departed. Within less than two hours, at 0850, 29 Japanese Navy attack bombers, covered by 18 fighters, lashed down at Wake through the overcast and bombed and strafed all battery positions. These were planes from *Carrier Division 2* (*Soryu* and *Hiryu*), called in by the Japanese to help soften Wake's unexpected toughness.[22] Due to the low ceiling, the attack was consummated before the 3-inch batteries could get into action, but the .50 caliber antiaircraft machine guns engaged the enemy. The attack caused little damage, but its implications were ominous.

Only three hours later, 33 of the shore-based Japanese bombers arrived from Roi, and again they concentrated on Peale Island and Camp Two. They approached from the east at 18,000 feet in two main formations, and the bombs from the second group plastered Battery D's position on Peale. This unit had fired 35 rounds in half a minute and had hit one bomber when a bomb fell squarely inside the director emplacement of the battery. This explosion killed the firing battery executive, Platoon Sergeant Johnalson E. Wright, and wounded the range officer and three other Marines.

Now there was only one firing director mechanism left on the atoll, and it belonged to Battery E located in the crotch of Wake Island. But Battery E had no height finder, although Battery D still had one of these. Thus the two 3-inch batteries had only enough fire control equipment for one battery. Because of Battery E's more desirable location, and because it had escaped damage since its move to this spot, Major Devereux decided to maintain it as his primary antiaircraft defense of the atoll. Thus by taking over Battery D's height finder, certain other fire control gear, one gun, and the necessary personnel, Battery E became a fully manned and fully equipped four-gun battery. Two other Battery D guns were shifted to a new position on Peale Island where they could assume beach-defense missions, and the fourth gun remained at the original battery position. Dummy guns also were mounted there to create the impression that the battery was still intact. As a further measure of deception, Battery F on Wilkes, also reduced to two guns, would open fire by local control methods whenever air raids occurred. Battery D was parceled out that night, and by next morning the garrison on Peale had been reduced to less than 100 Marines and a small group of civilians who had been trained by Marine noncommissioned officers to man one of Battery D's guns.[23]

---

[22] *Capture of Wake*, II, 372.

[23] Of these civilians the Peale Island commander, Capt. Godbold, later wrote: "The civilians who served with this battery were of inestimable value . . . under the capable leadership of Sergeant Bowsher, they soon were firing their gun in a manner comparable to the Marine-manned guns. Before the surrender of the is-

By 22 December VMF-211 again had two airplanes capable of flight, and Captain Freuler and Lieutenant Davidson took them up for morning patrol. Davidson had been out almost an hour and was covering the northern approaches to Wake at 12,000 feet when he spotted enemy planes coming in. He called Captain Freuler, who was then south of the atoll, and the Marines began independent approaches to close with the enemy. The Japanese flight consisted of 33 carrier attack planes (dive bombers) escorted by six fighters, all from the *Soryu-Hiryu* carrier division. The fighters were at 12,000 feet and the dive bombers at 18,000. The fighters were of a sleek new type, the first Zeros to be encountered over Wake.

Captain Freuler dived his patched-up F4F-3 into a division of six fighters, downing one and scattering the others. Coming around quickly in a difficult opposite approach, Freuler attacked another of the Zeros and saw it explode only 50 feet below. This explosion temporarily engulfed the Grumman in a cloud of flames and flying fragments. The Marine plane was badly scorched, its manifold-pressure dropped, and the controls reacted sluggishly. As the captain turned to look for the atoll, he saw Lieutenant Davidson attacking the dive bombers. The lieutenant was diving at a retreating bomber, but a Zero was behind him closing on the Marine Grumman. This enemy fighter probably downed Davidson, because the lieutenant did not return to the atoll.

Meanwhile a Zero got on Freuler's tail while he took in Davidson's plight, and fire from the Japanese plane wounded the Marine pilot in the back and shoulder. Freuler pushed his plane over into a steep dive, managed to shake off his pursuer, and dragged the shattered, scorched F4F into the field for a crash landing. In the words of Lieutenant Kinney, whose shoestring maintenance had kept VMF-211 flying for fifteen days: "This left us with no airplanes." In spite of the Marine squadron's last blaze of heroism, the enemy dive bombers came on in to strike at all battery positions. But the atoll pilots were not much impressed by the work of the Japanese naval aviators. "We who have been used to seeing only the propeller hub are a bit taken aback by their shallow dives and their inaccuracies," Lieutenant Barninger said. The Japanese bombs did not cause much damage, and there were no casualties on the ground.

But now that carrier air was being brought to bear against them, the Wake defenders concluded that it would not be long before the Japanese came back with a bigger task force and a better amphibious plan. Ground defense preparations intensified that afternoon. VMF-211's effectives—less than 20 officers and men—were added to the defense battalion as infantry, Peale Island completed its beach defense emplacements, and Captain Platt drew up final detailed orders for his defense of Wilkes. Platt ordered Marine Gunner McKinstry, who commanded Battery F, to fire on enemy landing boats as long as his guns could depress sufficiently, and then to fall back to designated positions from which his men would fight as riflemen. There these men from the 3-inch battery would be joined by the personnel from Battery L. After that it would be an infantry fight. "All that can be done

---

land, some of these men were slated to be evacuated to Honolulu; however, the entire gun crew offered to stay on the island and serve with the battery." LtCol B. D. *Godbold Rept*, 14.

is being done," noted one of the Wake officers, "but there is so little to do with."[24]

ENEMY PLANS AND ACTIONS, 11–21 DECEMBER [25]

Wake defenders were correct in assuming that the Japanese soon would be back with a stronger effort than the one which had failed for Rear Admiral Kajioka. The admiral began to mull a few plans for his next attack while he withdrew toward Kwajalein on 11 December, and he had his staff in conference on 13 December while his battered fleet still was anchoring in that Marshall atoll. Rear Admiral Kuniori Marushige, who had commanded *Cruiser Division 18* (including the light cruisers *Tatsuta* and *Tenryu* as well as the flagship *Yubari*), analyzed the causes of failure as follows: The landing attempt had failed, he said, because of the vigorous seacoast artillery defense, fighter opposition, adverse weather, and because of insufficient Japanese forces and means.

But Admiral Kajioka was more interested in the success of the next operation, and so was *Fourth Fleet* Commander Inouye at Truk. While the ships remaining in Kajioka's task force were being patched up at Kwajalein, Admiral Inouye sent destroyers *Asanagi* and *Yunagi* over to replace the destroyers lost in the Wake action. He also added the *Oboro*, a much more powerful and newer ship of destroyer-leader characteristic which was armed with six 5-inch guns.[26] The mine layer *Tsugaru* came over from Saipan with the *Maizaru Special Landing Force Number Two;* and the transport *Tenyo Maru* and the float-plane tender *Kiyokawa* also joined the force. Troop rehearsals began on 15 December, but Admiral Inouye still was not convinced that his force was large enough, and he asked the Commander in Chief of the *Combined Fleet* to send him more ships.

Inouye's superior officer, now apparently convinced that Wake would be hard to crack, sent to the *Fourth Fleet* admiral the fleet carriers *Soryu* and *Hiryu* of *Carrier Division 2*, heavy cruisers *Aoba, Furutaka, Kako,* and *Kinugasa* of *Cruiser Division 6*, heavy cruisers *Tone* and *Chikuma* of *Cruiser Division 8*, and a task force screen of six destroyers.[27] The commander of the *Combined Fleet* assigned over-all command of this Wake task force to Rear Admiral Koki Abe, commander of *Cruiser Division 8*. Rear Admiral Kajioka retained his command of the amphibious force.

Plans for the second attack against the American atoll called for more softening up than Wake had received previous to Kajioka's first attempt to land troops there. On 21 December, two days prior to the proposed landing, the aircraft of *Carrier Division 2* would work over the atoll's defenses to destroy first the U. S. air capability and then the shore batteries and the antiaircraft weapons. Then the amphibious force would move up for the landing, and in order that the atoll might be surprised [28] there would be no preliminary naval bombardment on 23 December.

To make sure that troops got ashore, the two destroyer-transports (*Patrol Craft*

---

[24] LtCol C. A. *Barninger Rept.*

[25] Unless otherwise noted the material in this section is derived from *Capture of Wake; Enemy Notes.*

[26] ONI 222–J, "A Statistical Summary of the Japanese Navy," 20Jul44, 56.

[27] *Ibid.*, 47, 49.

[28] *Capture of Wake*, II, 372.

32 and 33) would run aground on the south shore of the atoll near the airstrip, and the approximately 1,000 men of the special naval landing force [29] would then be carried to the beach in four to six landing barges. Two of these would land on Wilkes Island, two on Wake Island between the airstrip and Camp One, and the other two probably provided for would put their troops ashore just west of Peacock Point.[30] If these special landing force troops ran into serious trouble on the atoll, the naval force would send in 500 men organized from ships' landing forces. And if this combined force failed to subdue the atoll defenders, more help would be sent by means of an ultimate and desperate expedient. The destroyers of the task force would be beached, and their crews would swarm ashore. Admiral Inouye was determined that this second attack should not fail.

The possibility of U. S. naval surface intervention was taken into consideration. This possibility had been dismissed during planning for the attack of 11 December because the Japanese reasoned that the shock of Pearl Harbor would immobilize American surface operations for some time. But now the Japanese assumed that U. S. surface opposition was probable. To guard against such threat, the four heavy cruisers of *Cruiser Division 6* would act as a covering force east of Wake. If a major surface action developed, Rear Admiral Abe would enter the fight with *Cruiser Division 8* and conduct the battle. As on the first attempt, submarines would precede the invasion force to reconnoiter the island and to look out for U. S. surface forces.

With these final plans issued, the invasion force well rehearsed, and carriers *Soryu* and *Hiryu* on their way down from north of Midway, the operation against Wake was ready to go. At 0900 on 21 December Admiral Kajioka cleared Roi with the ships of his amphibious force and headed back up toward the American-held atoll.

THE RELIEF ATTEMPT, 15–23 DECEMBER [31]

Now the U. S. commanders taking help to Wake were in a race with Admiral Kajioka, even if they did not know it. Admiral Fletcher's Task Force 14 sortied from Pearl Harbor in two task groups on 15 and 16 December,[32] rendezvoused southwest of Oahu during the afternoon of this second day, and sailed westward toward Wake. Fletcher's force was to arrive at the atoll on 23 December (east longitude time). There the pilots of Major Verne J. McCaul's VMF–221 would fly in from the carrier *Saratoga* while the *Tangier* anchored off Wilkes channel to unload supplies, equipment, and the Marines from the 4th Defense Battalion.[33] After taking wounded men

---

[29] *Wake Attack*, 2.

[30] HistSec, HQMC interview with Col J. P. S. Devereux, 12Feb47, 8, hereinafter cited as *Devereux Interview*.

[31] Principal sources bearing on the Relief Expedition are: CinCPac OPlan 39–41, 15Dec47; *McMorris Interview; Saratoga* log; LtCol R. D. Heinl, Jr., "We're Headed for Wake," *MC Gazette*, June 1946.

[32] Dates in this section are either west or east longitude as applicable to the location of events identified by dates. Where confusion is possible the type of date will be indicated.

[33] Troops and equipment would be transported to the atoll on lighters, and if the *Tangier* were seriously damaged by enemy action she would be run aground so the cargo would not be lost.

and certain civilians on board, these ships then would return to Pearl Harbor.

But the advance was aggravatingly slow. The old fleet oiler *Neches*, in the train with the *Tangier*, could not manage more than 12 knots, and the fleet's zig-zag evasive tactics further slowed the rate of advance. To the Marines and seamen in this first westward sally of the war, the waters beyond Oahu seemed very lonely and ominous, and there was no contact, either friendly or enemy, to vary the tense monotony of the run. Each day on the *Tangier* began with general quarters and then lapsed into normal shipboard routine. Marines received such training and instruction as could be fitted into this schedule, and part of this educational program included lectures by the few radar technicians on board.

The few available maps and charts of Wake received intense study. In anticipation that Wake's 3-inch guns might have to deliver direct fire on ships or ground targets, improvised sights were designed and constructed in the ship's machine shops. The officer commanding the machine-gun detachment contrived with the ship's force to construct special slings with which his .50 caliber antiaircraft machine guns could be hoisted from ship to barges while remaining ready to ward off possible enemy attacks during unloading. The 5-inch seacoast men stayed in practice by standing their share of watches on the after 5-inch gun of the *Tangier*. All Marine antiaircraft machine guns were set up and manned on the superstructure.

On 18 December CinCPac ordered U. S. submarines which were patrolling in the vicinity of Wake to move south out of the area. These boats of Task Force 7 were to patrol around Rongelap in the Marshalls until the relief expedition reached Wake. CinCPac wanted to avoid any possibility of one U. S. force confusing another for the enemy.[34] Three days later, on the 21st, intelligence information which had been arriving at Pearl Harbor indicated that a large force of shore-based Japanese planes was building up in the Marshalls, and that enemy surface forces might be east of Wake where they could detect the approach of Fletcher's Task Force 14. Other reports indicated the presence of Japanese carriers, including possibly the *Soryu*, northwest of the atoll. Fletcher's mission, now about 650 miles east of Wake, appeared to be growing more hazardous with each hour. CinCPac ordered the carrier *Lexington* and other ships of Task Force 11 over from the southeast to give Fletcher closer support.[35]

By 0800 on 22 December, Task Force 14 was within 515 miles of Wake, and Admiral Fletcher in the cruiser *Astoria* kept up on the news about his race by monitoring the CinCPac radio nets. Ominous reports of Japanese surface operations around the atoll continued to filter in at Pearl Harbor, but conditions at Wake were unchanged. Fletcher decided to refuel. Although his destroyers still had a reasonable supply of oil, it might not be enough if they had to fight. But this very act of fueling, which took most of the day, kept them out of the fight. By the time the U. S. ships moved on toward Wake, Admiral Kajioka was only about 50 miles from the atoll with his amphibious force. Fletcher had lost the race.

---

[34] Paraphrased file of CinCPac dispatches concerning Wake relief, December 1941.
[35] *Ibid*.

The Fall of Wake[1]

At Wake, 23 December began with intermittent rain squalls, and shortly after 0100 the defenders saw a succession of vivid, irregular flashes beyond the horizon north of Peale Island. Men on the atoll could hear nothing above the rain and the boom of the surf, but it was obvious that the flashes were not signals or searchlights. They were too brilliant and irregular for that. Old fleet-duty hands were reminded of night battle practice at sea. Was there a naval battle, or were the Japanese coming back? The defenders could only guess.

By this time the Marines were used to seeing lights, even though these were unusual. But at 0145 came a more urgent alarm. The word over the "J"-line announced that the Japanese were landing at Toki Point on Peale. Major Devereux alerted all units and then telephoned Lieutenant Kessler at Toki Point for additional information. The Battery B commander told Devereux that he could see lights in the distance but that there was no landing in progress. The beach positions had been manned, Kessler added, because boats were "believed" to be somewhere offshore. By this time all units had sent their men to general quarters, and at Camp One, Second Lieutenant Poindexter loaded his scanty mobile reserve unit of eight Marines[2] and four .30 caliber machine guns into their truck, reported his actions to the command post, and moved out toward Peale Island. But the word from Kessler had convinced Devereux that if the enemy were landing, they were not doing it on Peale Island. He put a damper on the general alarm, and ordered that Poindexter be intercepted when his truck passed the command post. He held the mobile reserve there to await developments.

THE JAPANESE APPROACH

Developments were not long in coming. Admiral Kajioka's amphibious force had at last sighted the atoll's faint outline, and the ships were reducing speed. Moments later, in the words of a Japanese "combat correspondent" who was moved to poetry by this amphibious venture, "The honorable, first order of 'CHARGE' was given, and the daring officers and men, with white sashes, bravely went down to the surface of the sea."[3]

---

[1] Unless otherwise noted the material in Chap 4 is derived from *Devereux Rept*; *Putnam Rept*; *(Officer's name) Repts*, especially LtCol W. McC. Platt Rept, 1stLt J. A. McAlister Rept, MG C. B. McKinstry Rept; *Devereux Interview*; replies to HistSec questionaire by Col G. H. Potter, LtCol W. McC. Platt, LtCol A. A. Poindexter; *Capture of Wake*; *Wake Attack*; *Hawaii-Malaya NavOps*; *Devereux Story*.

[2] This unit, along with a few Marines from supply and administration sections and 15 Navy enlisted men commanded by BM 1stCl James E. Barnes, was also responsible for the defense of Camp One.

[3] This latter-day Masefield was Kayoshi Ibushi of the Japanese Naval Information Section.

Approximately 800 of the *SNLF* troops were distributed between the two destroyer-transports.[4] The other 200 presumably were embarked on board one or more of the transports or the float-plane tender *Kiyokawa*, and the 500 sailors of the provisional reserve force apparently were to remain at their normal duties unless called to reinforce the landing effort.[5] The *Maizuru Second Special Naval Landing Force*, now brought to full strength by reinforcements from Saipan, was essentially a Japanese version of the battalion landing team (BLT). Its three rifle companies had numerical designations but were more commonly identified by the names of their commanders. Thus the *1st Company*, commanded by Lieutenant Kinichi Uchida, was often called the *Uchida unit*. Similarly, the *2d* and *3d Companies* were styled respectively the *Takano unit* and the *Itaya unit*.

The *Uchida* and *Itaya companies* would assault Wake Island while 100 "picked men" of the *Takano unit* seized Wilkes.[6]

The balance of the *Takano company* presumably would back up the other two companies on Wake Island. At about the time the premature landing alarm was sounded on the atoll, the amphibious force was putting landing craft over the side. The weather was giving them trouble, but at about 0200 the *SNLF* troops clambered down into these craft. "The hardships encountered in lowering the landing barges were too severe even to imagine," reported correspondent Ibushi. "Now we, the Naval Landing Force, on the barges which we were in, must charge into enemy territory and carry out the final step of securing a landing point after touching the shore."[7]

As the landing craft pitched through the breakers, the destroyer-transports turned to make their final runs onto the reef south of the airstrip. These vessels, *Patrol Boats 32* and *33*, mounted the reef in a smother of breakers and foam, and went aground near the west end of the airstrip. Two of the landing barges scraped bottom as they approached the reef near Camp One, and still there was no sign that the atoll defenders were awake. But suddenly tracers pencilled from the beach at Wilkes Island and .50 caliber slugs splattered through the gunwales of one barge. Then a searchlight from Wilkes flared on to silhouette the picked men of the *Takano unit* landing on that island. It was then 0245, and the battle for Wake was on. (See Map 5, Map Section)

THE DEFENSE OF WAKE ISLAND

Since 0215 Marines had been confident that a landing against them was in prog-

---

"This reporter," as he later said of himself, ". . . was able to have the honor of taking the first step upon the Island as a man of letters . . . the capture of Wake Island . . . was so heroic that even the gods wept." *Hawaii-Malaya NavOps*, 32.

[4] One account says 500 men of this force were on the two destroyer-transports. At this time all SNLF units attached to the Fourth Fleet were concentrated for the seizure of Wake in much the same manner that U. S. Fleet Marine Force units would have been employed.

[5] The exact number of Japanese troops who fought on Wake has not been determined. Adm Morison cites Marine estimates that "at least 1,200 troops landed early on the 23rd," and that others came ashore after the surrender. *Rising Sun in the Pacific*, 245.

[6] Itaya's name and that of his company appears in one Japanese source as "Itatani." *Hawaii-Malaya NavOps*, 28.

[7] *Ibid.*

ress. Lights could be seen offshore north of Peale Island and all along the south coasts of Wake and Wilkes Island. At about 0230 Marines on Peacock Point thought they could see the outlines of two barges heading along the coast toward the airfield, but these evidently were the patrol craft heading in toward the reef. By now Major Devereux, Major Potter, his executive officer, a radioman, and a switchboard operator in the defense detachment command post were swamped by reports of sounds, lights, and shapes. As he collected this information and relayed reports to Commander Cunningham, Devereux saw that the greatest threat was developing along the south coast of the atoll, and he dispatched Lieutenant Poindexter's eight-man mobile reserve to defensive positions between Camp One and the airstrip.

Poindexter's men had not left the truck, and the lieutenant had them transported down the island and into position within 15 minutes. The area into which they moved was just west of the road junction near the west end of the airstrip. There this small force commanded the south shore road as well as the critical beach section south of the field. The lieutenant reported that this area was being bombarded when he reached his defensive positions, but there were no signs of a landing.

But at 0235 [8] defenders on Wilkes reported that they could hear barge engines above the surf, and Marine Gunner McKinstry opened fire with a .50 caliber machine gun at a dark shape near the beach below. Ten minutes later Captain Platt requested permission to illuminate the beach with his 60-inch searchlight, and the landing was discovered. Two barges could be seen on the beaches at Wilkes, the lights also revealed the patrol craft aground off Wake.

Neither of the 5-inch batteries which commanded the south approaches to Wake [9] could bear against the landings. Terrain masks likewise prevented them from firing at *Patrol Craft 32* and *33* on the reef.[10] The only weapon larger than a machine gun that could engage these destroyer-transports, already beginning to spew out their human cargo, was the 3-inch gun emplaced on the rise between the beach road and VMF-211's hard-stand parking area. But this gun was not manned. Realizing the importance of this weapon, Second Lieutenant Robert M. Hanna, in command of the antiaircraft machine guns about the field, gathered a scratch crew consisting of one Marine, Corporal Ralph J. Holewinski, and three civilians [11] and

---

[8] The Japanese list 0235 as the official time of their landing. Statements of Marine officers do not agree. Some say the landings came at about 0130, while others place the time almost an hour later. In his official report, Devereux gives the time of landing on Wilkes at 0215, but his published narrative says 0120. Yet a subsequent study convinced him that the time of 0235 was closer to the fact. Excepting the variances concerning events during these dark early hours of the battle, Marine accounts agree generally as to events after daylight.

[9] Btry A (Peacock Point) and Btry L (Wilkes).

[10] One of the advantages of the Navy 5"/51 for seacoast defense missions was that it had 360° train, as contrasted to the limited traverse of the 155mm field guns used by the Army for this role. In this instance, however, terrain masks, slight though they were, prevented either A or L from bearing.

[11] 1stLt R. M. *Hanna Rept* to CO, 1st DefBnDet, 11Oct45, 2. Of these three civilians, two (Paul Gay and Bob Bryan) were subsequently killed in action, and the third, Eric Lehtola, was wounded. Hanna states that they fought with "exceptional gallantry."

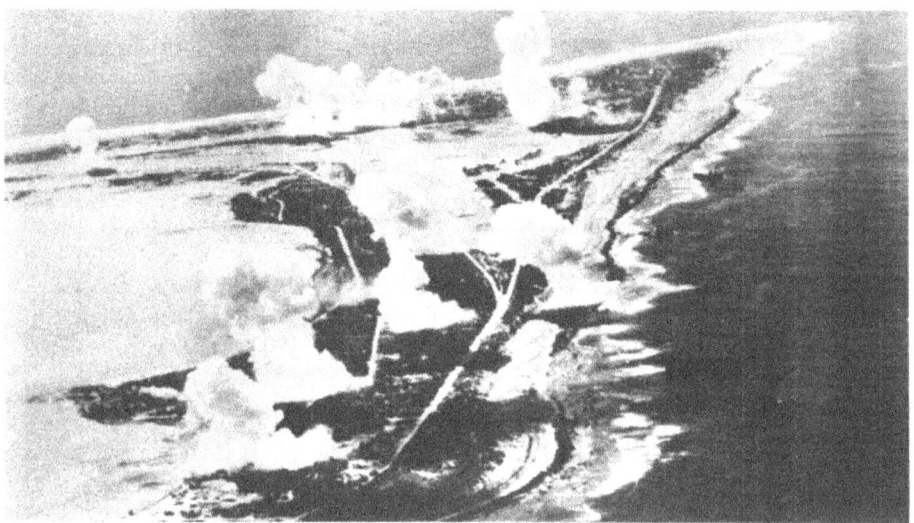

JAPANESE PATROL CRAFT *lost in the assault on Wake Island are silent witnesses to an American carrier raid during the last days of the war. (USN 495560)*

JAPANESE NAVAL TROOPS *who took Wake Atoll are shown in a contemporary propaganda painting taking their prisoners toward a collecting point. (SC 301066)*

raced to this gun. Major Devereux also realized the critical importance of holding this area, and he ordered Major Putnam and the 20 men of VMF–211 to form an infantry support between the 3–inch gun and the enemy landing.

All defense units on Wake Island were disposed to meet the enemy. Hanna and the VMF–211 "infantrymen" held the left flank south of the airfield parking area. To the west, and squarely in the path of the enemy's initial rush toward the west end of the field, were Second Lieutenant Kliewer and three aviation Marines. They guarded one of the generators which was wired to detonate the mines buried in the airstrip. At the road junction farther west Poindexter's mobile reserve was already firing its four machine guns eastward along the beach at *Patrol Craft 32* where the enemy troops had revealed themselves by injudicious use of pyrotechnic signals. At Camp One four .30 caliber machine guns were manned for beach defense by Battery I's gun shed crew and the Naval Air Station sailors who had been serving as lookouts on the water tank OP. Behind this general line, two .50 caliber machine-gun sections (each of two guns) guarded the airstrip. One section held the west end of the strip near Lieutenant Kliewer's generator, and the other section was located on the east end of the strip.[12] These two sections could command the length of the field, and could partially interdict movement across the field. Other machine guns were in the Peacock Point area. At the battery positions gun crews stood by their weapons and manned such local perimeter defenses as their meager strength permitted.

Lieutenant Hanna and his jury-rigged crew quickly got the 3–inch gun into action. They laid the weapon by estimate and "Kentucky windage",[13] and fired their first round at *Patrol Craft 33* which was less than 500 yards away. The shell hit the bridge of the destroyer-transport, and wounded the captain, the navigator, and five seamen. Two other sailors were killed. While men of the *Uchida* and *Itaya units* swarmed off the ship, Hanna and his crew fired 14 more rounds into the superstructure and hull of the craft. Finally it burst into flames, illuminating the landing area. "The scene was too beautiful to be a battlefield," reported a Japanese observer on board the cruiser *Yubari*.[14]

Flames from this ship lighted *Patrol Craft 32* farther west along the beach, and Hanna shifted his fire to this vessel. Three-inch shells hulled this transport-destroyer, and crews from both these ships joined the *SNLF* troops landing on the island. This added possibly 100 extra men to the battle ashore, and Hanna's gun already was seriously threatened by the *Uchida unit* which had made the beach assault. Major Putnam's aviators fought off these early attempts to silence the 3-inch gun, but the Japanese continued to attack. Alternating between creeping infiltration tactics and screaming rushes, the Uchida troops drove the Marines back on each side

---

[12] These two sections had been sited to provide antiaircraft fire as well as final protective fire along the airstrip. This conformed with defense battalion practice, but the light of hindsight prompted Devereux to wish that he had moved these sections closer to the beach where they could have been tied in with the general line.

[13] These 3-inch Army antiaircraft guns were equipped only for indirect fire at aerial targets, and they had no sights or other fire control equipment to facilitate direct sighting by local control.

[14] *Hawaii-Malaya NavOps*, 33.

of the gun until the defenders were in a position which Devereux later described as "a box-shaped thing." Here they continued to hold.

But farther west Japanese troops had reached the south shore road between the mine field generator and Lieutenant Poindexter's small mobile reserve, and by the light from the burning patrol craft Poindexter could see these enemy cross the road and disappear into the brush beyond. The lieutenant was directing machine-gun fire into this brush area when he heard other firing from the direction of Camp One. He left Gunnery Sergeant T. Q. Wade in charge of the reserve force and headed toward the camp. There he found that two large landing craft had grounded on the reef some 30 yards offshore southeast of the camp.[15] Four machine guns from Camp One fired at the barges, but the rounds ricocheted off. This fire evidently discouraged the craft from attempting a landing at this point, however, because they backed off the reef and nosed about as if seeking a better site.

While these two boats floundered about in the surf, Lieutenant Poindexter formed two teams of grenadiers to move down to the water's edge and lob hand grenades into the barges. One team consisted of himself and Boatswain's Mate First Class James E. Barnes, while the other consisted of Mess Sergeant Gerald Carr, and a civilian, R. R. Rutledge, who had served as an Army officer in France during World War I. The machine guns suspended fire, and the grenadiers attacked. By this time the Japanese had landed a short distance farther east, and Boatswain's Mate Barnes managed to throw at least one grenade inside a barge just as the enemy

---

[15] *Lewis.*

debarkation commenced. The explosion inflicted heavy casualties, but some 75 to 100 enemy splashed ashore and entered the underbrush east of Camp One. This heavy growth north of the road soon became a sort of no man's land into which the Japanese continued to infiltrate and expand their beachhead.

All this Poindexter managed to report back to Major Devereux in a final message from Camp One before wire communication was lost. But shortly after this a panicky civilian who had managed to pick his way through the brush from Camp One to Devereux's command post brought in reports—totally untrue—that Camp One was being overrun and that he had seen Japanese troops bayoneting the machine gunners of the mobile reserve.

The loss of communications was not localized at Camp One. Devereux's command post had lost contact with Lieutenant Hanna, the VMF-211 infantrymen, the CP of the .50 caliber machine-gun battery near the airstrip, and Battery A at Peacock Point. The tactical line to Wilkes Island also went out at this time, but the "J"-line, which lay north of the airfield, still linked the defense battalion CP with that of Captain Platt on Wilkes. Nobody knows exactly what caused this communications failure, but the nature of the trouble suggests that it might have been caused by a single break. The location of this major break, if there was one, must have been near the battalion command post where lines were close together. But all Wake survivors hold the opinion that the Japanese cut the lines; and they point out that the Wilkes "J"-line did not go out until some time after this failure of the line south of the field. Thus defenders believe that the lines were being cut as the enemy attack progressed inland. Devereux tried to contact his Wake Island positions by radio, but this inter-island net never had been reliable, and the sets characteristically failed to function that morning. There were no communications personnel in the command post to trouble-shoot lines,[16] and for the remainder of the battle Devereux had no communications with his defensive line along Wake's south coast.

It was now obvious to Devereux at his "blacked-out" CP that fights were in progress all along the west leg of Wake Island, and that he must sacrifice a defensive unit from some other area to reinforce his effort in the critical zone. Lieutenant Lewis' Battery E in the crotch of Wake Island could not be disbanded. It was the only completely equipped and up-to-strength[17] antiaircraft battery on the atoll. Battery B's 5-inch guns on Peale Island also should remain manned for possible missions against enemy ships. But Captain Godbold's Battery D might be used as infantry. This unit had two 3-inch guns, but no fire control equipment; and Peale Island did not appear to be threatened. Two officers and some 40 men from this battery became the atoll reserve, and at 0300 Major Devereux ordered Godbold to send one gun section (about nine men) from this reserve force to the aid of Hanna's untrained crew. Corporal Leon Graves brought these men around from Peale Island in a truck driven by one of the civilians, and Major Devereux directed them toward Hanna's position.

By this time the Japanese had made at least two penetrations through the Marine "line" along the south edge of Wake Island, and it is possible that the enemy was also landing inside the lagoon in rubber boats. Several defenders speak of seeing red flares rising from within the lagoon, and after the surrender Marine working parties found rubber boats on these interior beaches. If these landings were taking place, it is probable that they occurred on the north beaches of Wake Island's west leg.[18] From such sites the men landing in rubber boats could join up with those landing on the south beaches.

Captain Godbold on Peale Island was one of the defenders who saw these red flares inside the lagoon, and he had Battery B at Toki Point send a two-man patrol down the interior coast of that island to investigate. Godbold then sent a three-man patrol from his own battery down the outer coast of Peale. These two patrols met at the southeast end of the island without encountering any enemy. The captain then established a three-man outpost to cover the bridge between Peale and Wake Islands.

---

[16] MSgt R. M. June reply to HistSec, HQMC, questionnaire, 11Mar47, 2.

[17] "Up-to-strength" was a relative term on Wake. The 1941 tables of organization allowed such batteries two officers and 75 enlisted men. At this time Battery E had two officers and about 50 men.

[18] Although Japanese sources do not mention such interior landings the evidence to support them is generally convincing. The rubber boats did not enter the lagoon through the channel between Wilkes and Wake Island, because this narrow channel was covered throughout the battle. Devereux surmises that the boats entered the lagoon at the open end of the atoll between Kuku and Toki Points. Such landings would explain, without necessarily ruling out infiltration, the early presence of individual Japanese at various points along the lagoon shore. One Japanese source does mention that red rocket flares were to be used as a signal that "We have succeeded in landing." *Hawaii-Malaya NavOps*, 33.

THE FALL OF WAKE

But interior landings or no, the Wake defenders had their hands full. Japanese cruisers began to bombard the atoll's main island at about 0330. The landings continued in spite of the fact that Battery E now fired air bursts over the beaches, and enemy infantry continued to press closer to Hanna's 3-inch gun south of the airstrip. The VMF-211 troops still held, but their partial perimeter was being compressed tighter and tighter around the gun. This action was now little more than a battle for preservation of the weapon and the Marines involved. Major Putnam's men could not check the Japanese penetration farther to the west, nor could they prevent the enemy from moving behind them or into the island triangle above Peacock Point. And the Japanese wanted to concentrate in this triangle so they could launch an attack up the island's east leg. The VMF-211 troops could only hope to cling to the slight hillock of their position, and stay there as long as possible.[19]

Meanwhile Coporal Graves and his detached gun squad from Battery D were trying to reach Hanna's 3-inch gun. Devereux had told them to detruck at the road junction some 600 yards below the end of the strip and west of Peacock Point. From there they were to go through the underbrush to the gun position. But the squad detrucked considerably short of this junction—probably less than 200 yards below the strip. From there the men struck out through the brush in the general direction of the Hanna-VMF-211 area. They were soon stopped, however, by enemy machine-gun and small-arms fire which killed one Marine and pinned down the others.[20] After a time Graves withdrew his unit northward toward the command post where it later participated in defensive efforts commanded by Major Potter.

It is not clear what sort of an enemy force Corporal Graves encountered in the Peacock triangle, or how the Japanese got there. There are indications that a landing might have been made in that area, with barges coming in on the south coast between Battery A on Peacock Point and the Hanna-VMF-211 position. Devereux said after the war that he believed a landing took place at this point, but the matter never has been confirmed. Some Japanese accounts, including those of Captain Koyama and a correspondent,[21] mention a landing "near the southeast tip of Wake" to overrun Battery A, which must have been remembered from the action of 11 December—especially by men in the cruiser *Yubari*. But Captain Koyama also insisted that the Japanese made only two barge landings with a total of four barges. And these are accounted for by the landings near Camp One and at Wilkes Island. Discounting a third barge landing, this force must have been built up by the rubber boat landings within the lagoon, or by wholesale infiltration behind the position held by Putnam and Hanna.

But at any rate, Devereux soon learned from Corporal Graves that there was an

---

[19] *Kinney Interview.* At about this time Maj Putnam, already wounded, told his men, "This is as far as we go." Six hours later, when the island fell, they still held.

[20] Col Devereux suggests that some of the machine-gun fire which swept through the Peacock triangle might have come from friendly weapons. He points out that Marines had .30 or .50 caliber machine gun sections on virtually the entire perimeter of the triangle.

[21] *Capture of Wake*, II, 372.

enemy force in the triangle. And from there the Japanese threatened the entire eastern rim of the atoll. Battery E was now receiving light mortar and long-range machine-gun fire, and Battery A likewise began to receive enemy mortar fire.[22] In the face of this, Captain Barninger armed his range section with two .30 caliber machine guns and formed an infantry outpost line on the high ground behind his 5-inch guns.

The enemy fire against Battery E seemed to come from the thick brush on the other side of an inlet southwest of the battery position. Direct 3-inch fire into this area silenced one automatic weapon, but this did not seem to ease the pressure much. Lieutenant Lewis then sent a patrol of approximately 10 men under Sergeant Raymon Gragg to investigate. Gragg went out to the road north of the airstrip, and patrolled to the southwest along this road. Within 50 yards of the battery Gragg's patrol ran into heavy Japanese fire which forced the Marines to deploy. Answering the enemy fire, the patrol held here until the surrender.

At about 0430 the .50 caliber machine-gun section at the east end of the airstrip, still in communication with Devereux, reported that the Japanese were attacking in company strength up the road from Peacock Point. Corporal Winford J. McAnally, in charge of the six Marines and three civilian volunteers at this position, was trying to hold the Japanese south of the airstrip. Fire from the .50 caliber gun position had halted the enemy advance along the road, but the enemy now attempted to infiltrate around the strong point. McAnally contacted another machine gun position some 400 yards to the south on the atoll's east shore, and these two sections alternated in firing at the enemy.

This Japanese force probably was the *Itaya unit*. This reinforced company evidently infiltrated behind the Putnam-Hanna position at the 3-inch gun while the *Uchida company* remained near the beach to deal with that weapon which had fired on the patrol craft. The enemy at first had trouble locating McAnally's gun section, but before daylight they were all around the position. McAnally's men continued to hold, however, and the corporal's reports to Devereux gave the major his only link with the action south of the command post.

By 0500, a half hour before dawn, it was clear that the Japanese had a superior force firmly established on the atoll, and that the enemy was free to infiltrate almost at will around and between the isolated positions of the defenders. At this time Commander Cunningham sent his message, "Enemy on island issue in doubt."[23] But actually there was little doubt, although the defenders were far from admitting it at that point. The 500 defenders on the atoll were then outnumbered approximately two to one by the enemy; but what was worse, the Marines had their mission and their own atoll against them. "Little Wake" has a vulnerable shore line about 21 miles in length, and the defenders had insufficient men to man even a minimum of their antiaircraft and seacoast guns and at the same time the beach defenses. On Wake Island alone, nearly

---

[22] Barninger's report also speaks of occasional fire from "a small field piece." Lt Col C. A. *Barninger Rept*, 6. This may have been a 70mm howitzer of the type organic to Japanese infantry battalions.

[23] *Wake File*.

half of the 200 defenders had to remain at Batteries A and E, and another 15 Marines manned machine guns and searchlights at Heel Point where the island's east leg crooks toward Camp Two. Thus only about 85 men could oppose the enemy landing force, and half of these were machine-gun crewmen. Marines serving as riflemen against the enemy on Wake Island numbered between 40 and 45.

When Cunningham sent his message, Major Putnam still held the position around Hanna's gun, but the Japanese now had these Marines surrounded. Here the defenders had sustained a number of casualties, including the death of Captain Elrod.[24] Camp One also continued to hold, and Lieutenant Poindexter had rejoined his small mobile reserve force near the road junction west of the airstrip. There at first dawn the Marines were taken under heavy fire from the brush off their left (north) flank. Light mortar shells began to fall around the gun positions, and one of the .30 caliber weapons was put out of action. In danger of being outflanked here, Poindexter ordered a withdrawal to Camp One where he would consolidate for his final stand. The unit displaced by section in 150-yard bounds, and arrived at Camp One shortly after daybreak. There Poindexter organized his defenders along a semi-circular line facing seaward and to the southeast. In this line he had about 40 riflemen and 10 machine guns.

Lieutenant Kliewer and his three Marines had survived the night beside the mine field generator, but a heavy Japanese attack threatened them just before dawn.

---

[24] The Japanese sustained at least 62 casualties trying to take this gun position, and one of them was Lt Uchida, the company commander.

This was repulsed by close-in fighting with submachine guns and grenades, but the Japanese came back again at dawn. This time the enemy made a shouting bayonet charge against the Marines, but again Kliewer and his men, now aided by the .50 caliber machine guns at the west end of the airstrip, managed to halt the attack.

Enemy pressure against McAnally's machine-gun position east of the airstrip also increased during the hour before dawn. The Marine strong point now had been located, and the defenders were under heavy attack by small-arms fire and grenades. McAnally's gunners already had broken up a number of enemy rushes by holding their fire until it would be most effective, but these 10 men could not expect to hold out for long against the reinforced company opposing them.

This was clear also to Devereux at the command post, and at 0530 he directed Major Potter, who until now had assisted in the command post, to assemble every headquarters, service, supply, or casual Marine in the command post area, including Corporal Graves' detached squad from Battery D, and to form a final defensive line approximately 100 yards south of the command post. This force of approximately 40 men would take up positions astride the north-south main road. Devereux then telephoned Captain Godbold on Peale and directed him to truck his entire Battery D, plus the few .50 caliber gunners, to the battalion command post for immediate employment as infantry. With these orders, the atoll's final reserve, totalling approximately 30 officers and men, was committed.

By 0600 McAnally's position was nearly surrounded and under continual infantry [25] attack. Unless he was to lose these personnel, Major Devereux had no alternative but to pull them back. This he did shortly after 0600, when McAnally was ordered to withdraw northward and join Major Potter's line.

After Captain Godbold's reserve force left Peale Island, First Lieutenant Kessler became commander there since his Battery B was all that remained on the island. In the light of dawn Kessler could see on Wilkes a line of Japanese flags across the center of the island, and a large enemy flag waving from the approximate position of Marine Gunner McKinstry's provisional Battery F. This he reported to Major Devereux, who could only conclude that Wilkes, which had been silent since about 0300, had shared the fate which now appeared imminent for Wake Island.

Above the brush and slight rise of ground which topped the west leg of Wake Island, Kessler could also see the superstructure of *Patrol Craft 32*. Observing that the ship appeared intact, Kessler at 0600 requested Major Devereux's permission to fire on it. Although the line of fire and intervening partial mask [26] made this hazardous, the request was approved, and on the first salvo Battery B shot away the ship's mainmast. As a result of subsequent adjustment, the ship was hit about the superstructure and upper hull. It finally caught fire.

Meanwhile Second Lieutenant Robert W. Greeley had reached the command post with the first 20 men from Battery D. There Major Potter, trying to piece out and extend his sparse line to the right (west), directed that the reinforcements be placed on that flank around the edge of the clearing originally dozed out to prepare for the north-south leg of the airstrip. Captain Godbold arrived with other reinforcements at about 0700,[27] and these men joined those already emplaced by Greeley. This line now turned to the right (north) to refuse the flank along the edge of the clearing. Potter's line, now containing about the equivalent of a rifle platoon, thus extended from near the beach, across the two roads south of the CP, and to the airstrip clearing where it made a northward turn. Thus a gap of approximately 450 yards existed between the skirmish line and the shore of the lagoon. This gap the defenders would attempt to cover by fire.

By daylight the atoll defenders could make out the large task force which supported the landing operations. There were then 13 ships at various positions around the island (the four cruisers of *Cruiser Division 6* were out of sight east of Wake), and all of them were keeping a safe distance from the 5-inch shore batteries. "Due to the previous experience with the American shore batteries," a senior Japanese officer said later, "we did

---

[25] Among the Japanese killed before his position at about this time were two flame-thrower operators. Although use of flame is not recorded, this was perhaps the earliest tactical employment of this weapon in the Pacific island war.

[26] Kessler had to train the flat-trajectory 5"/51's so as to fire across Flipper Point and just clear the crest of Wake Island. The line of fire passed less than 250 yards to the west of Lt Kliewer's position at the generator.

[27] Like so many other questions as to exact times of events during the defense of Wake, this one is subject to conflicting testimony. Maj Potter states that Godbold reached the command post at 0600. Godbold gives 0715 as the time. Other sources, while not giving times, put the arrival of Battery D shortly after daybreak. Balancing all accounts against each other, 0700 or shortly before seems to be the best synthesis.

not want to come within range."[28] In spite of this caution, however, the destroyer *Mutsuki* began at 0654 to lead two other destroyers (probably the *Yayoi* and the *Mochizuki*) in toward Wilkes Island, possibly to fire shore bombardment missions. But fire from Battery B on Peale quickly hit the *Mutsuki*, and the formation turned and scurried away. Observers believed that Kessler's fire also hit the second destroyer in the formation after the ships turned, and that the *Mutsuki* later sank, but Japanese records do not confirm this.

Farther to the northwest the two Japanese carriers *Soryu* and *Hiryu* headed upwind with their cruiser and destroyer escort,[29] and at 0700 "the gallant Eagles of the Navy," as the Japanese Naval Information Service styled them, approached Wake at 6,000 feet. As the formation wheeled over Peacock Point, Battery E opened fire in what was the last antiaircraft action of the battle. The formation split into component groups according to mission, and commenced a methodical and unceasing series of air strikes in close support of the special landing force. Wilkes, Peale, and Wake Island were hit repeatedly.

Dive bombers now battered Kessler's 5-inch gun battery on Peale Island, and the air-supported enemy troops began to move rapidly against Major Potter's line south of the defense battalion command post. Battery E also was being attacked by the carrier planes, and Devereux believed that Wilkes Island and most of the west leg of Wake Island already had fallen to the Japanese. Shortly after 0700 the major called Commander Cunningham and told him that organized resistance could not last much longer. Was there a chance that the relief expedition might yet arrive? No chance at all, Cunningham said.

And there was no chance, although up until two and a half hours earlier than this the men in Task Force 14 thought there might be. During the night of 22–23 December (21–22 December at Hawaii) Vice Admiral William S. Pye, acting CinCPac pending the arrival of Admiral Nimitz from Washington, had been in conference about this relief force for Wake. The officers at Pearl Harbor knew that Admiral Fletcher was running a close race, and they were concerned that this task force would be lost, along with Wake, if the race ended in a dead heat. At one point they decided to order the *Tangier* to make a solitary dash for the atoll while the *Saratoga*, then some 425 miles short of Wake, launched Major McCaul's planes from that distance. But this order was countermanded before Fletcher could begin its execution; and finally at 0811 Hawaiian time (some two and a half hours before Wake was to surrender) Task Force 14 was recalled. The force spent most of the day refueling its cruisers, and that night retired toward Midway.

Commander Cunningham and Major Devereux decided that additional defense efforts would be hopeless, and the island commander made the decision to surrender. Acting on these orders, Devereux carried a white flag out of his CP at 0730 and walked south along the shore road to meet the Japanese.

---

[28] *Hawaii-Malaya NavOps*, 29.

[29] In addition to the two carriers, this task force was composed of the new 12,000-ton heavy cruisers *Chikuma* and *Tone*, and six destroyers, two of which were *Tanikaze* and *Urakaze*.

THE FIGHT ON WILKES ISLAND

"At this time," states a Japanese report, "Wilkes Island was the scene of a fierce and desperate battle."[30] Here at 0245 Gunner McKinstry fired the first shots in the battle of Wake when he saw barges approaching to land at a point just west of the new channel. After this first burst from gun 10 (see Wilkes map) a Marine searchlight flashed on to reveal the 100 men of the *Takano unit* coming through the surf and onto the beach. But by this time the Wilkes detachment was completely disposed to repel a landing, thanks to the earlier and erroneous report of a landing on Peale Island. (See Map 6)

When that false alarm sounded, Captain Platt ordered two Battery L gun sections (each about the size of a rifle squad) to positions on the lagoon side of the island, and pulled the remainder of Battery L personnel back to defensive positions along the road near the new channel. Extra ammunition and grenades were issued, and the Battery F personnel were instructed to fire against any landing for as long as they could, and then to pull back across the road to join the men of Battery L. Thus the Battery L position, commanded by Lieutenant McAlister, was well prepared when the Japanese barges hit the beach near that defensive site.

The searchlight beam lasted for only a minute in the face of the Japanese attack, but McKinstry continued to fire at the landing craft he could see on the beach, and McAlister sent two men down toward the beach to hurl grenades at the Japanese. Enemy fire killed one of these men and wounded the other. Battery F then began to fire into the landing area with their 3-inch shells cut for muzzle-burst, but the attack came on up the beach so rapidly that these guns soon were unable to depress sufficiently to engage the Japanese.

Gunner McKinstry had crossed to the 3-inch guns to direct this air-burst fire, but it soon became apparent to him that the position could not hold. The enemy continued to expand their beachhead, and a strong force near Battery F was throwing grenades in among the Americans. The gunner removed the firing locks from the 3-inch guns, and then directed his men to retire to their designated infantry position on the right flank of McAlister's line beyond the road. Japanese tried to pursue this withdrawal, but McKinstry's men drove them back.

McKinstry and McAlister now were in good position to protect themselves and to guard the road to Wake Island, but there was little to stop the Japanese from moving farther west and spreading out over all of Wilkes Island unless fire from machine-guns 9 and 10 could aid the main defense line to keep the enemy bottled up around the abandoned 3-inch guns. Gun 9 was already delivering flanking fire against these Japanese, and the enemy advance was temporarily checked. The Takano troops now turned their attacks to knock out this machine gun, but its position was well prepared and well camouflaged. Although nearly surrounded, the Marines on this gun continued to hold and to repel attacks which kept up until dawn.

Meanwhile Captain Platt, in his CP behind the former positions of Battery L, was having the same sort of communications trouble that plagued Major Devereux on Wake Island. By 0300 the captain had lost contact with every position except that

---

[30] *Hawaii-Malaya NavOps*, 29.

THE FALL OF WAKE   145

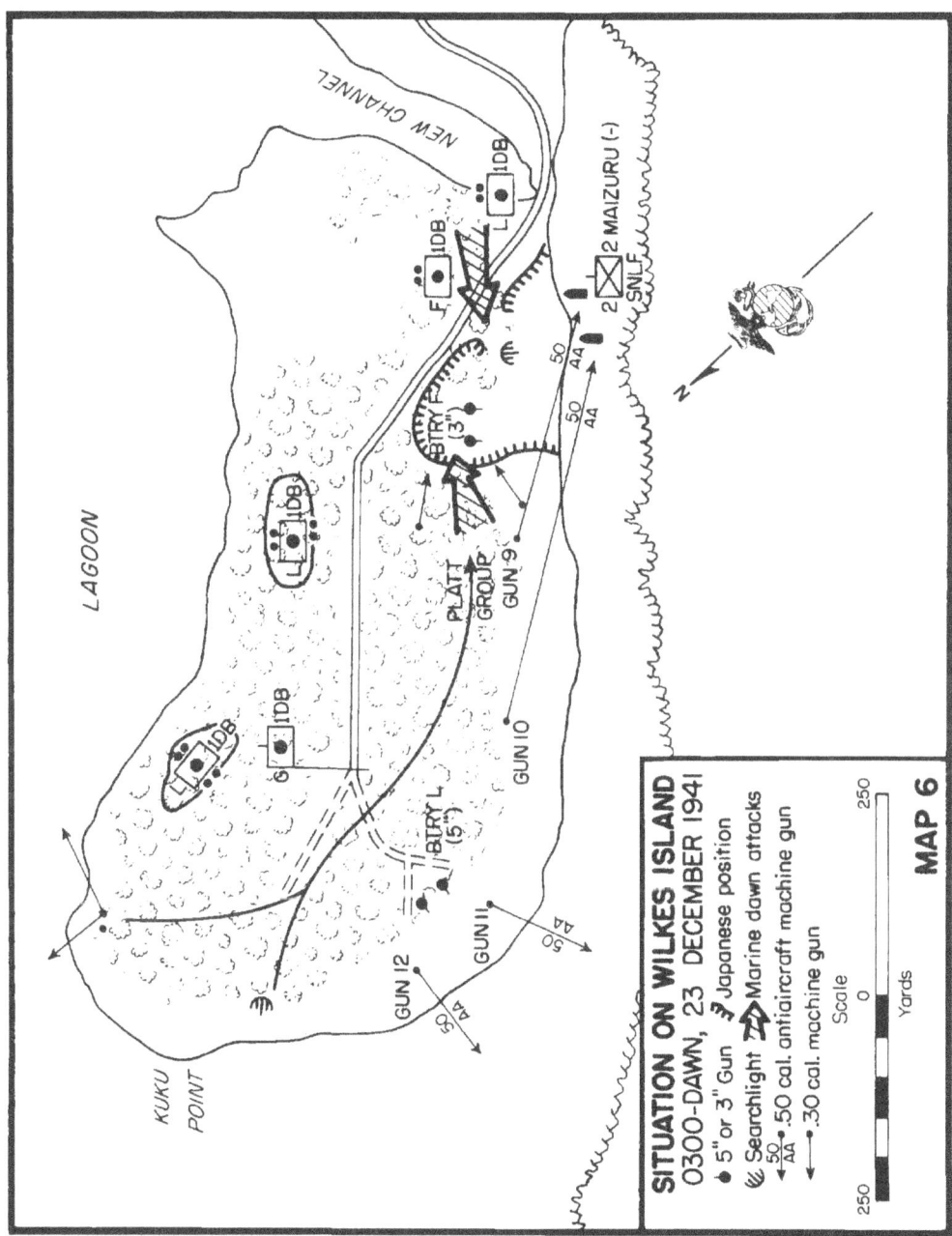

of the beleaguered men on Gun 9. From them he learned that the enemy were building up pressure to extend their beachhead farther inland. At about 0400 Captain Platt moved out to the Gun 11 position near the beach, and from there he crept through the brush to a vantage point east of Gun 10. It was now about 0500, and Platt decided quickly that he must mount a counterattack if the Japanese were to be prevented from staging daylight attacks which would enable them to overrun Gun 9 and spread out into the interior of the island.

He hurried back to Gun 10 and ordered Platoon Sergeant Raymond L. Coulson to round up the .30 caliber machine-gun crews and searchlight personnel from Kuku Point, plus anyone else he could lay hold of, and assemble them at Gun 10 for the counterattack. In 25 minutes Coulson was back with the two machine-gun crews and eight riflemen—about a squad in all. These men the captain led back through the underbrush toward the Japanese.

The Marines crept and crawled to within 50 yards of the Japanese. Platt then placed his two machine guns on each flank of his line of departure, and ordered the gunners to fire their short bursts close to the ground so this fire would not endanger the McAlister and McKinstry line farther to the east. By this time dawn was breaking, and Platt quickly drew up his skirmish line of eight Marines. He signalled the machine guns to open fire, and then he led his riflemen forward against the 100 men of the *Takano unit*.

At about this time on the other side of the Japanese position, Lieutenant McAlister had observed a six-man enemy patrol moving toward his Marines, and he ordered his line to open fire. One enemy was killed and the others sought cover behind a large coral rock near the beach. McAlister's men continued to fire into this area to keep the Japanese pinned down while Gunner McKinstry and Private First Class William C. Halstead worked their way out to this rock and finished off the rest of the patrol.

Meanwhile Platt's counterattack had surprised the other flank of the penetration, and the Japanese at that point were in trouble. Obviously they had expected no opposition from the west, and their light machine guns had been sighted for fire to the east against the McAlister-McKinstry line. Platt's attack carried the Marines into the former position of Battery F, and the Japanese were driven back toward the beach and toward the Marine defense line by the island road.

It was now daylight, and McAlister could see this Marine attack on the far side of the Japanese position. When his men finished mopping up the enemy around the rock near the beach, the lieutenant gathered 24 Marines into a skirmish line of his own and launched a counterattack from his side of the battlefield. The men of the *Takano landing force* panicked. Organized resistance evaporated in front of the two Marine attacks, and the forces of Platt and McAlister soon joined. About 30 Japanese fled to shelter around the Marine searchlight truck southeast of the Battery F guns, and there the Marines under Platt and McAlister flushed them out and killed them. The *Takano unit* on Wilkes had been destroyed.

McAlister counted four officer and 90 enlisted bodies while his men policed up the battlefield and removed the flags the Japanese had placed in the ground to mark their front lines. Two wounded Japanese were captured. The other four Japanese—if the *Takano unit* actually included an even 100—were not accounted for. Marines found several small maps of Wake in the effects of the dead Japanese, and Marine positions were marked accurately on these maps. The photographic missions over the atoll had obviously paid off well.

By 0800 Captain Platt had reorganized his Wilkes defenders, and he again tried to establish contact with Wake Island. He was able to contact the motor pool at Camp One where Poindexter's force had managed to hold throughout the night, but he could not get through to Devereux at the defense battalion CP. At about noon the men on Wilkes observed Japanese landing boats headed for Wake Island and several ships approaching toward Wilkes channel. Platt ordered McAlister to get his 5-inch guns into action against these vessels, but the gun crews found that the weapons were beyond use. The training mechanism on Gun 1 was wrecked, and the Gun 2 recoil cylinder had been riddled by bomb fragments.

Wilkes had been under attack by the dive bombers which had arrived over the atoll at about 0700, but sign language interrogation of the wounded prisoners indicated that the enemy planned no more landings against this section of the atoll. Platt decided to go find the enemy. He ordered McAlister, McKinstry, and Coulson to round up all the men and to strike out east toward the old channel. Dive bombers attacked this route column as it moved down the island, and a destroyer moved in to open up from 2,000 yards. One Marine, Private First Class Robert L. Stevens, was killed by this bombing, but the action against the Marines suddenly ceased.

Platt moved the men forward again in a dispersed formation, and near the old channel he saw three men advancing from the other direction. Two were obviously Marines, Platt decided, but the figure in the rear was a Japanese officer armed with a large sword. The captain moved forward and soon recognized Major Devereux who told him that the island had been surrendered. It was then shortly after 1330. Platt's force did not get a chance to help in the fighting on Wake Island, but it had given such a good account of itself in earlier action that a Japanese officer was prompted later to make this estimate of the Wilkes fighting: "In general, that part of the operation was not successful."[31]

THE SURRENDER AND AFTER

Prior to moving down the road toward the Japanese, who were still receiving determined small-arms fire from the few Marines south of the command post, Major Devereux passed word of the surrender to all units in communication with his command post. These were Batteries A and E on Wake Island, Battery B on Peale, and other small detachments including those at Heel Point, and some of the .50 caliber positions on Wake Island. Communications with Battery A had been restored at about daybreak. All units were ordered to destroy their materiel as best they could prior to actual surrender.

These instructions were carried out with all possible thoroughness. At Battery E an attempt was made to damage the 3-inch antiaircraft guns by stuffing blankets into the muzzles and then firing a round or two. When this failed to produce appreciable

---

[31] *Capture of Wake*, II, 372.

results, the firing locks were removed and smashed, and grenades were rolled down the muzzles to explode inside and damage the rifling. All electrical fire control data receivers were smashed, electric cables chopped up, and the battery commander fired twenty rounds of .45 caliber ammunition through the delicate optical and electro-mechanical parts of the height finder and director. After completing these measures, Lieutenant Lewis assembled the men of Battery E and marched them under a white flag to the battalion command post.

At Battery A, the 5-inch firing locks were broken and buried, and all gun telescopes smashed. The range keeper was damaged beyond repair. After that a white flag was run up, and Lieutenant Barninger ordered his men to eat as much as they could hold. He then held his men on the position to await arrival of the Japanese. Elsewhere, the hard-pressed riflemen stripped the bolts from their rifles and flung them into the brush.

It was after 0800 before all this had been attended to, and the rifle fire of Potter's line was still covering the final operations of the command post. Major Devereux then tried to contact the Marine aid station located some 300 yards south of the CP. He believed that the Japanese advance must have reached this point, and he wanted to instruct the battalion surgeon to contact the Japanese. But there was no response from the aid station, and it became apparent that a surrender party must go forward from the CP. Major Devereux and Sergeant Donald Malleck, who carried a white rag tied to a mop-handle, then made their way down the road toward the fighting. At the Marine line Devereux ordered Potter's men to hold their fire, and he and Malleck walked on toward the Japanese.

Near the hospital Devereux and the sergeant were halted by a Japanese rifleman who motioned for them to throw down their arms and helmets. Then the soldier took them to the hospital where the Japanese already were in charge. They had killed one patient and wounded another while capturing the hospital, and now they had all the patients outside trussed up with telephone wire. Commander Cunningham arrived by truck while Devereux was explaining his mission to an English-speaking Japanese officer, and the Marine major turned over his surrender duties to the island commander. A Japanese officer then escorted Devereux and Malleck forward to pass the surrender order to Marine units on the west leg of Wake Island and on Wilkes Island.

They found the VMF-211 riflemen and Hanna's unit still holding around the 3-inch gun in spite of continuing efforts by the Japanese. The Japanese, unable to advance, had taken up positions behind nearby plane revetments, and the fighting here was a deadlock. Captain Tharin was the only officer unwounded in the Marine position, and he was directing the action when Major Devereux contacted him at 0930. There were now but 10 Marines surviving, and nine of them were wounded.

At 1014 Devereux reached Lieutenant Kliewer and his three men beside the mine field generator. These men had been trying since 0900 to coax some life into the gasoline generator so they could blow up the airfield, but the rain during the night had given it a thorough soaking and it would not operate. "Don't surrender, lieutenant," one of the men told Kliewer. "Marines never surrender. It's a hoax."

"It was a difficult thing to do," Kliewer reported later, "but we tore down our guns and turned ourselves over."[32]

Shortly before 1115 the surrender party, now west of the airstrip, came upon the rear of a Japanese skirmish line facing westward and evidently engaged in a fire fight against Marines in the brush beyond the west end of the strip. After some confusion during which the Japanese fired on the surrender group, Major Devereux passed through the lines and made contact with Lieutenant Poindexter. The lieutenant's mobile reserves, in ignorance of the surrender, had retaken the ground between Camp One and the west end of the strip during the morning's fighting. When Devereux came upon Poindexter, the 30-odd Marines in this force had just completed a steady eastward advance from Camp One, fighting their way forward along the beach with the edge of the brush to their left. Special naval landing force troops were in the thick brush to the north, but they had not attempted to attack the Marines. Divided into three 10-man squads, Poindexter's improvised platoon had advanced with two squads in assault, one on the seaward side of the road and the other north of the road. The support squad protected the exposed left flank by advancing in rear of the left assault squad.

During the advance, particularly as he neared the airfield and retraced by daylight the scenes of his fighting during the night, Lieutenant Poindexter counted approximately 80 enemy dead.

After assuring the surrender of this force, Major Devereux led the Japanese toward Camp One, still held by machine-gun sections of Poindexter's group. There the Marine prisoners watched a Japanese climb up the water tank and cut down the American flag which had been flying there throughout the battle.

The surrender group, followed by approximately 30 Japanese, then crossed Wilkes channel by launch. No Marines were to be seen when Devereux landed at about 1300, and the party began walking cautiously westward. At this time the enemy destroyer began firing on the island, but this fire was soon checked by a Japanese signalman who flagged the ship to silence. At 1330, almost midway between the new and old channels on Wilkes, Major Devereux saw "a few grubby, dirty men who came out of the brush with their rifles ready . . ." These were Platt's Marines who had annihilated the *Takano landing party* on Wilkes and now were advancing eastward to repel what they thought was still another landing. Thus all resistance had been silenced, and Wake now was in Japanese hands.

---

[32] 1stLt D. D. *Kliewer Rept.*

CHAPTER 5

Conclusions

The defense of Wake was the first wartime operation conducted by the Marine Corps in defense of an advanced naval base. It was also the first combat test of the Marine defense battalion, although the strength of the Wake detachment was greatly reduced. The main reason for the fall of Wake seems obvious. The enemy in greatly superior strength, supported by ample surface and air forces, was able to effect a lodgement on the atoll and then to apply his ground superiority to overwhelm the dispersed defenders in detail. Had it been possible for U. S. surface forces to intervene, or for substantial reinforcements to reach Wake, the results might have been entirely different. But military lessons of some value still may be drawn by a survey of certain specific reasons why the defense was handicapped. These factors were interacting, of course. No single one of them can be clearly isolated within the framework of events which brought military defeat to the atoll.

Japanese procedure for the reduction and seizure of Wake, if not executed with the skill or standards that U. S. forces later attained, was nevertheless orthodox. It consisted essentially of two phases, the preliminary bombardment and the assault landing. The enemy's first landing plan underestimated the amount of preparation required, and he paid for this miscalculation in the defeat of 11 December. But this he corrected in his second attempt.

Lack of radar and other early-warning equipment severely handicapped Marines during preliminary aerial bombardment, and it would be difficult to overstate the seriousness of this shortage. It enabled the initial Japanese raid to destroy over half of VMF-211's fighters on the ground, and the same lack of early warning continued to hamper the effectiveness of those fighter planes which remained in operation. Thus the VMF-211 pilots never had a chance to plan effective fighter interception against the enemy bombers, and the Japanese could proceed quite methodically with their program for the aerial softening of Wake.

This lack of early warning and the shortage of aircraft can be lumped together as matters of air defense, and air defense depends upon coordinated employment of fighter aircraft, antiaircraft artillery, and the essential warning systems. But on Wake only the antiaircraft artillery—undermanned and partially operational though it was—could be considered fully and consistently effective, and nobody ever expected antiaircraft weapons alone to defend an advanced naval base against air attack. They were there to provide close-in protection to the aviation facilities; the planes were to be the important factor in keeping the enemy away from an island base. Determination and stubbornness of the fighter pilots could not avert the final outcome. The fliers could only exact from the enemy a maximum cost for every bomb dropped. This was

CONCLUSIONS

done until the last Grumman was destroyed by massed enemy fighters on 22 December. After that, landing operations against Wake could proceed.

Once the ground combat began, the fundamental weakness of the defense battalion concept as it then existed became starkly underlined. The unit had no infantry component to act as an effective mobile reserve. Most garrison personnel were tied to weapons and battery positions, and Major Devereux could muster only a fraction of his manpower against the invaders even after enemy intentions became apparent. On Wake Island, for example, only about 85 of 200 Marines were readily available to check the assault landing of a thousand Japanese. Militarily speaking, there is something pathetic in the spectacle of Lieutenant Poindexter and his "mobile reserve" of eight men and four machine guns dashing by truck from one threatened point to another in the face of such fantastic odds.

True, at that time trained infantry was almost as scarce as radar. But the fault lay in the defense battalion tables of organization. Later this omission was corrected, and Midway had both infantry and light tanks. Had even one Marine infantry company reinforced with tanks been on Wake, it is possible that the garrison might have thrown the Japanese back into the sea. This is borne out by what happened on Wilkes Island, where Captain Platt was able to annihilate twice his numbers of the enemy by shrewd, coordinated counter-attack. And after daylight on Wake Island, Poindexter, with the makeshift defenders of Camp One added to his "mobile reserve," had assumed the offensive, driven back the Japanese to his front, and regained most of the ground given up during the confused hours of darkness.

After the Japanese had landed in force on the south coast of Wake Island, it appears that the coast artillery and antiaircraft missions of Batteries B and D, respectively, had become of secondary importance in light of the serious enemy ground threat. The military reader might wonder why all available personnel from Batteries B and D, with whom Devereux was still in communication, were not early in the battle brought down to the vicinity of the airfield and employed, together with such few other available Marines, as a mobile reserve to counterattack the main Japanese beachhead. This was partially accomplished at 0530 on the final morning when Captain Godbold was directed to bring the personnel of his battery (D) to the command post for employment as infantry. By this time, however, it was too late for such a small number to influence the outcome of the battle. In this connection, Major Devereux later pointed out that because of the partial failure of communications he never had anything like a clear picture of the situation during the final Japanese attack. For several hours he was in doubt as to the location of the main enemy landing and hence did not consider himself justified in stripping Peale Island of all defenders.

As alluded to above, another major lesson to be derived from this phase of the operation was a re-emphasis of Admiral Mahan's famous dictum that "Communications dominate war." The partial failure of communications, which occurred shortly after the Japanese landing, isolated the defense detachment commander from most of his subordinate units then in action. As a result he not only lost control over much of the battle, but he also—and perhaps more important to this case—became unavoidably deceived as to the progress of the situation. In ignorance of what happened on Wilkes or at Camp One, he surmised that all was lost in those areas. Buried telephone lines and reliable field radios would have prevented this failure of communication, and the surrender decision would not have been made at that particular stage of the action. The Wake garrison, however, had neither the personnel to dig by hand, nor the machinery to dig by mechanical means, the many miles of ditches which would have been necessary to bury the telephone lines.

Perhaps one of the fundamental reasons for the state of the Wake defenses stemmed from the fact that base development had consistently received priority over defense preparations. That the defensive installations were in as good a condition as they were when the Japanese struck may be credited to the tremendous efforts of the small Marine garrison.

All things taken into account, however, the decision to surrender Wake was reasonable, especially when considered in light of the civilian situation and the fact that relief was no longer in prospect. Marines who fought through the Pacific campaigns would later see many examples of a totally unreasoning enemy who never surrendered but was always defeated. At the same time, insensibly, some might come to believe that unyielding refusal to surrender was the proper role of a defender. Of course this was neither true nor logical. Wake had exacted a full and more than honorable toll from the Japanese, but its defensive resources had been exhausted.

No fighter aircraft remained. Only one antiaircraft battery was effectively operational. Enemy dive bombers on 23 December had completely disabled one 5-inch battery (Wilkes) and largely destroyed the fire control instruments of the remaining two. Without airplanes, fire control instruments, radar, spare parts, and personnel to bring the defense to full strength Wake could not carry on. The only answer was surrender. This took place fifteen days after the initial attack, and it was eleven hours after the fighting commenced on shore before Wilkes Island surrendered.

During this period the Marines sustained almost 20 per cent casualties, but they exacted a heavy toll from the Japanese. Nearly 500 enemy had been lost in the abortive landing attempt of 11 December, the defenders on Wilkes Island accounted for nearly 100 in their defeat of the *Takano unit*, and Poindexter counted approximately 80 enemy bodies during his morning attack from Camp One. Give the Hanna–VMF–211 position credit for at least 20 more kills, and this would bring the Wake total to 700 enemy. Others must have lost their lives on Wake Island landing beaches and elsewhere on the island, although the figure probably would not be great. But in earlier action the atoll antiaircraft and fighter plane fire had downed 21 enemy aircraft and claimed credit for damaging another 11.[1]

Based on this record, Major Putnam's final VMF–211 report of 21 December would truthfully state that "All hands have behaved splendidly and held up in a manner of which the Marine Corps may well tell."

---

[1] A Japanese source says that 51 planes, in addition to those shot down, were damaged by flak over Wake. *Nakamura Notebook.*

PART IV

Marines in the Philippines

CHAPTER 1

China and Luzon

In the first few months after Pearl Harbor, it seemed that nothing could stop the Japanese. One by one, the western outposts in the Far East were overwhelmed. Allied ground troops, in desperately unequal contests, were forced to retreat, fight, and retreat again; at sea and in the air the pitifully few ships and planes which had survived the initial onslaught were hoarded against the surety of further enemy advances. A grim holding battle was joined along a line protecting Australia and New Zealand and their South Pacific lifeline to the States. Yet, despite its strategic importance, this vital defensive action gave first place in the news to the outcome of a hopeless struggle hundreds of miles behind the enemy's forward positions.

For almost five months, two names—Bataan and Corregidor—dominated the headlines, taking fire in the minds of the Allied peoples as symbols of courage and devotion to duty. To the Japanese, who realized that they could starve out the embattled defenders at little cost to themselves, it became imperative that the issue be decided forthwith in battle. On the eve of the all-out offensive that brought the end on Bataan, the Japanese commander, addressing his combat leaders, clearly stated the importance of the isolated strong points in the eyes of the world:

> The operations in the Bataan Peninsula and the Corregidor Fortress are not merely a local operation of the Great East Asia War. This battle has lasted for about three months as compared with our speedy victories in Malaya, Dutch East Indies, and other areas in the Philippines. As the Anti-Axis powers propagandize about this battle as being a uniquely hopeful battle and the first step toward eventual victory, the rest of the world has concentrated upon the progress of the battle tactics on this small peninsula. Hence, the victories of these operations do not only mean the suppression of the Philippines, but will also have a bearing upon the English and Americans and their attitude toward continuing the war.[1]

Lieutenant General Masaharu Homma was right: the outcome of the battle did have a direct bearing on the Allied attitude toward vigorous pursuit of the war. Perhaps in no instance since the defense of the Alamo stirred Americans in another century did an unsuccessful battle carry within its waging and its ending the source of so much national pride and dedication.

THE SHADOW OF WAR[2]

On 26 July 1941, shortly after Japan occupied military bases in Indo-China, President Roosevelt authorized the mobilization of the Philippine Army. The War

---

[1] HistSec, G–2, GHQ, FEC, Japanese Studies in WWII No. 1, 14th Army Ops, 2 vols., n. d. (located at OCMH), 141–142, hereinafter cited as *14th Army Rept*.

[2] Unless otherwise noted the material in this section is derived from Adm T. C. Hart, Narrative of Events, AsFlt Leading up to War and From 8Dec41 to 5Feb42, written before 11Jun42 (located at NHD), hereinafter cited as *Hart Narrative*; Adm T. C. Hart, Supplementary Narrative to *Hart Narrative*, 8Oct46 (located at NHD); Gen J. C. Wainwright, Rept of Ops of

Department, which had requested this move, followed through with a directive organizing a new command, USAFFE (United States Army Forces in the Far East), which included all American Army and Commonwealth troops in the Philippines. To head USAFFE the Army called out of retirement its former chief of staff, General MacArthur, who had served as Military Advisor to the Commonwealth Government since 1935. He was given rank as a lieutenant general and with characteristic energy tackled the enormous job of putting the Philippines into a state of readiness against attack.

The bulk of USAFFE's troop strength was drawn from the Philippine Army which was, in July 1941, an army in name only. It consisted of the islands' police force, the 6,000-man Philippine Constabulary, a token air force and inshore naval patrol, and ten territorial reserve divisions. Since the start of the Commonwealth's defense training program in 1936 about 110,000 Filipinos had received a few months of basic military instruction, but most of these reservists had no experience with crew-served weapons and only rudimentary knowledge of their own pieces.

The divisions had never operated as such in field maneuvers and were scantily provided with arms and equipment. In order to mold an effective fighting force from the Philippine Army, MacArthur needed just about everything in the military supply catalogs, but most of all he needed time—time for training, time for materiel and men to reach the Philippines from the United States.

The instructors and cadres needed for training the Philippine Army were drawn from the Constabulary and the regular Army units available to USAFFE. Most of the 22,000 U. S. Army troops in the islands were serving in Coast Artillery regiments, the Army Air Corps, or the Philippine Division, sole regular infantry division in the islands. Over half of these men were members of crack Philippine Scout units.[3] The regulars suffered, too, from a general lack of up-to-date weapons and equipment,[4] but they were well trained to use what they had.

The War Department supported MacArthur's requests for additional troops and supplies to the fullest extent possible in light of the country's world-wide commitments; USAFFE received priority in almost every man power and materiel category. More than 7,000 men, mostly members of service and air units, and the

---

USAFFE and USFIP in the Philippine Islands 1941–42, 10Aug46 (located at TAGO), hereinafter cited as *USAFFE-USFIP Rept;* Annex VIII to *USAFFE-USFIP Rept*, MajGen G. F. Moore, Rept of CA Comd and the Harbor Defenses of Manila and Subic Bay, 19Feb41–6May42, 15Dec45 (located at TAGO), hereinafter cited as *Moore Rept;* BriGen S. L. Howard, "Report of the operation, employment and supply of the old 4th Marines from September, 1941 to the surrender of Corregidor, May 6, 1942," 26Sep45, hereinafter cited as *Howard Rept; 14th Army Rept;* L. Morton, *The Fall of the Philippines—United States Army in World War II* (Washington: OCMH, DA, 1953), hereinafter cited as *Fall of the Philippines; Rising Sun in the Pacific.*

[3] The Philippine Scouts was a U. S. Army organization in which the enlisted men were native Filipinos and most of the officers were Americans. The Scouts had and merited a high reputation for fielding units with good morale, excellent discipline, and a consistently superior level of combat readiness.

[4] At the outbreak of the war, "the Philippine Division, less than two-thirds strength, had only three (3) new 37mm automatic firing cannon, three (3) 81mm mortars per infantry regiment and no (0) 60mm mortars..." *USAFFE-USFIP Rept*, 94.

major portion of the United States' heavy bomber strength reached the Philippines prior to the outbreak of war. Much more was promised and planned, but the Japanese surprise attack effectively cut off the flow of reinforcement. It also forced a revision of MacArthur's defensive strategy.

In view of his healthy reinforcement prospects, the USAFFE commander had adopted an aggressive defense plan that conceded the enemy nothing. He did not expect the Japanese to attack before April 1942 [5] and by that time he considered that his air and ground strength would be such that he could successfully hold his position against any attacking force. He was confident that the Philippine Army, when adequately trained and equipped, would be a match for the Japanese.

The Commander in Chief of the U. S. Navy's Asiatic Fleet (CinCAF), Admiral Thomas C. Hart, was in substantial agreement with MacArthur's philosophy of an aggressive defense. He recommended that in the event of war his fleet units remain based at Manila Bay and fight the Japanese in Philippine waters. The Navy Department, however, adhered to its long-established plan that the major ships of the fleet would retire to the south at the imminence of war, to a base of operations in the Netherlands East Indies or Malaya, where they could cooperate with Allied naval units.[6] Hart's slim collection of cruisers, destroyers, submarines, and auxiliaries, was certainly no match for the Japanese fleet, nor was it intended to be. The U. S. Pacific Fleet, based at Pearl Harbor, was the American striking force, and war plans envisaged its fighting advance to the Philippines if the Japanese attacked.

The Asiatic Fleet's major shore installations were located at Olongapo on Subic Bay and at Mariveles and Cavite within Manila Bay. Since denial of Manila Bay to the enemy was a key point in war planning, the activities of the 16th Naval District (Rear Admiral Francis W. Rockwell), the shore establishment supporting the Asiatic Fleet, were closely coordinated with USAFFE's defensive preparations. Contact mines were laid to connect with controlled mine fields of the Army's harbor defenses, completely closing Manila Bay. On Corregidor, site of the prospective command post for the defense of Luzon, protected installations for naval headquarters, a radio intercept station, and a torpedo replenishment depot were prepared and equipped. Large quantities of fuel and ammunition stored at Cavite were moved to dumps away from the naval base to lessen their vulnerability to bombing. (See Maps 7 and 8, Map Section)

If the Japanese attacked, the most dangerously exposed elements of the Asiatic Fleet were those stationed in China: seven Yangtze River gunboats; Colonel Samuel L. Howard's 4th Marine Regiment at Shanghai; and the Marine embassy guard detachments at Peiping and Tientsin.

---

[5] Gen J. C. Wainwright, *General Wainwright's Story*, R. Considine, ed. (Garden City, N. Y.: Doubleday and Company, Inc., 1946), 13, hereinafter cited as *Wainwright's Story*.

[6] After the war, in supplementary comments to his original report, Adm Hart agreed that the Navy Dept decision was the best that could have been made considering the situation at the time. He added, however, that if his original proposal of 27Oct41 to continue to base at Manila had been turned down sooner he might well have made a better disposition of his fleet units; he had acted on the assumption that his proposal would be accepted until it was disapproved in late November.

Admiral Hart had begun making informal proposals that his China forces be withdrawn early in 1941, and after July, when he was "entirely convinced that the war was coming,"[7] he followed up with emphatic official recommendations that his men be gotten out before it was too late. Japanese war preparations were so evident by 1 September that the American Consul-General at Shanghai, the commander of the Yangtze Patrol, and Colonel Howard jointly recommended that all naval forces in China be withdrawn. Hart naturally concurred and further recommended to the Navy Department that the troops be evacuated in late September when the transport *Henderson* made a routine call on Chinese ports to pick up short-timers and other returnees.

Hart's request was turned down as far as withdrawal on the *Henderson* was concerned. He was told, however, that joint State-Navy conferences would be held within a couple of weeks time to consider the problem of a withdrawal and its effect on negotiations for a settlement of Japanese-American differences. Despite CinCAF's protest that this "was not a question that could be delayed for weeks but must be acted upon immediately,"[8] he did not receive permission to withdraw the gunboats and the Marines until 10 November, "embarrassingly late" as he later noted.[9] Five of the gunboats were able to reach Manila without hinderance once clearance to leave was given.[10]

Two President liners, the *Madison* and the *Harrison*, were chartered to transport the Marines, attached naval personnel, and their supplies and equipment; provision was also made to evacuate some American civilians from Shanghai on the same ships. After it reached the Philippines and unloaded, the *Harrison* was to return to North China and pick up the embassy guards and their gear at Chinwangtao. All signs pointed to the necessity for haste in the withdrawal.

The Japanese were replacing their seasoned troops around Shanghai with recruits, and large numbers of special armored landing barges which had previously been seen near the city disappeared; intelligence pointed to movement southward of both veteran units and landing craft. Intelligence also indicated that the Japanese Army was eager to take over the International Settlement, by force if necessary, and that it was only being restrained by the Nipponese Navy's desire for an "incident" which would seem to justify such action. Several attempts were made to manufacture incidents, but the Marines refused to knuckle under to the pressure, and Colonel Howard initiated prompt action which kept the American defense sector clear. A copy of a Japanese warning order was obtained which stated that "in the event of war the 4th Marines would attempt to break through [our] lines;"[11] ample evidence of this belief was seen in the increase in size and number of the patrols in the city and in the construc-

---

[7] Adm T. C. Hart ltr to CMC, 10Oct56, hereinafter cited as *Hart Comments*.

[8] Quoted in *Howard Rept*, 1.

[9] *Hart Narrative*, 29.

[10] The smallest of the gunboats, the *Wake*, was stripped and left at Shanghai to be used as a station ship and radio outlet for the remaining

Americans; it was captured on 8 December. The *Tutuila* at Chungking was turned over to the Chinese Nationalist Government under lend-lease since it could not get downstream through the Japanese blockade.

[11] *Howard Rept*, 3.

tion of concrete blockhouses on all roads leading out of Shanghai.

Both the *Madison* and *Harrison* needed to be converted to troop use after their arrival at Shanghai, and the first ship was not ready until 27 November. By 1600 that date, the *Madison* with half the regiment and half its equipment on board sailed for Olongapo. While this forward echelon, the 2d Battalion and half of the Regimental Headquarters and Service Companies, was loading out, a message was received from CinCAF to expedite the evacuation. Even though the conversion work on the *Harrison* was three days short of completion, the decision was made to clear Shanghai the following day with the rest of the regiment and its remaining equipment.

Despite the short notice and the harassing tactics of the Japanese,[12] the Regimental R-4 and Quartermaster, Major Reginald H. Ridgely, Jr., was able to load all organizational gear, over 500 tons, by 1300 on the 28th. At 0900 that morning, the regiment assembled at the 1st Battalion's billet, formed up behind its band, and marched down Bubbling Well-Nanking Roads to the President Line's dock on the Bund. Thousands of cheering people lined the route of march, and the banks of the river were alive with flag-waving Chinese as a power lighter took the Marines downstream to their ship. At 1400 the *Harrison* weighed anchor and sailed for the Philippines, marking the end of a colorful era in Marine annals.

As soon as the *Harrison* cleared the Whangpoo River, machine guns were broken out and manned for antiaircraft defense, and blackout regulations were put into effect.[13] Flights of Japanese aircraft checked the liner regularly as it moved out into the China Sea, but there were no incidents, and contact was made on the 29th with submarine escorts dispatched by Admiral Hart. On 30 November and 1 December the two transports arrived at Olongapo where the troops disembarked. Only a few supplies were unloaded at the naval station, ostensively because CinCAF had issued orders that the ships must pass through the mine field into Manila Bay by nightfall on the day of arrival. Actually, Admiral Hart had given oral orders to his staff that the Marines were to be landed with field equipment only, because it was his intention that:

. . . they would get into the field, near Olongapo, as soon as they could. We [Hart and his staff] all knew that they had been cooped up in Shanghai through all those years where conditions for any sort of field training were very poor—and we thought that not much time remained.[14]

While the regiment's heavy equipment was unloaded at Manila and trucked to Olongapo, the *Harrison* was readied for a return voyage to pick up the Marines from Peiping and Tientsin. It was al-

---

[12] "All supplies had to pass through the Japanese Sector on the way to the Customs dock. About 3:00 p.m. November 27th they closed the Garden Bridge over Soochow Creek to traffic and our trucks were delayed nearly an hour before contact could be made with the Japanese Admiral to get this bridge reopened to traffic. Customs officials ostensibly at the instigation of the Japanese were insistent that our supplies pass through the Custom House, but we ignored such orders and loaded them on lighters. The Japanese instigated three strikes during the night by the laborers loading the lighters." *Ibid.*, 4.

[13] No special defensive arrangements were made by the 4th Mar elements on the *President Madison*. CWO C. R. Jackson ltr to CMC, 10Oct56, hereinafter cited as *Jackson*.

[14] *Hart Comments*.

ready too late, however, to rescue the North China Marines. The Japanese war plans had been activated, and the carrier task force that would strike Pearl Harbor was at sea en route to its target. The troops, ships, and planes that would be sent against the Philippines were concentrated at Formosa, the Ryukyus, and the Palaus with orders to begin their attack on X-Day—8 December 1941 (Manila Time).[15]

8 DECEMBER 1941[16]

When the dawn of the first day of the Pacific War reached the China Coast, the attack on Pearl Harbor was over and the troops in the Philippines had been alerted to their danger. At the Chinwangtao docks, Second Lieutenant Richard M. Huizenga was supervising the stockpiling of supplies for the expected arrival of the *President Harrison*. A truck driver brought him word that the radio at his railhead, Camp Holcomb, was full of news of Pearl Harbor. Although the Japanese made half-hearted attempts to stop him on his three-mile drive back to the camp, Huizenga was able to get through to his unit. He found the 21 Marines of the loading detail surrounded, at a respectful distance, by a cordon of Japanese troops. The men, under Chief Marine Gunner William A. Lee, were setting up a strong point amid the boxcars of supplies; two machine guns and several Tommy guns and BARs had already been broken out of their cosmoline packing. Despite their desperate situation the Marines were ready to fight.

Huizenga and a Japanese captain held an armed parley where the lieutenant was given time to communicate to his superior at Tientsin, Major Luther A. Brown, the enemy's demand that he surrender the detachment. Orders soon came back to offer no resistance and the Marines were stripped of their weapons. Later in the day they were returned under Japanese guard to the Marine barracks at Tientsin.[17]

The situation of the detachments at Tientsin and Peiping was similar to that of the one at Camp Holcomb; Japanese troops surrounded their barracks in strength and demanded their surrender. Since the embassy guard was not required to maintain a continuous watch on CinCAF's command radio circuit,[18] the first word that the senior Marine officer, Colonel William W. Ashurst, had of the outbreak of hostilities came from the Japanese. He was given till noon to make his decision whether to fight or not and was allowed to communicate by radio with CinCAF and by phone with Major Brown. In a sense Ashurst had been given a Hobson's choice: he could surrender or he could let his troops, fewer than 200 officers and men, be overwhelmed. If discipline and spirit would have won the day,

---

[15] *Campaigns of the Pacific War*, 26–27, 50.

[16] Unless otherwise noted the material in this section is derived from *Hart Narrative; USAFFE-USFIP Rept; 14th Army Rept; Howard Rept;* 4th Mar Jnl and Rec of Events, 8Dec41–2May42, hereinafter cited as *4th Mar Jnl;* Capt A. F. Metze Rept to CMC, "Surrender of U. S. Marine Forces in North China," 23Aug42; *Fall of the Philippines; Rising Sun in the Pacific*.

[17] MIS, G-2, WD, Escape Rept No. 665, Capt R. M. Huizenga, 12Jul45.

[18] LtCol W. T. Clement Rept to CMC, "Dispositions and employment of U. S. Marines on the Asiatic Station during the initial stages of the war," 6Apr42, hereinafter cited as *Clement Rept.*

Ashurst could have opened fire on the besiegers—his men had already demonstrated at Camp Holcomb that they were willing to take on hopeless odds. But there was no purpose in fighting if the end result could only be useless bloodshed.

In the absence of instructions to the contrary, Colonel Ashurst took the only sensible course open to him and ordered his men to lay down their arms. A strong possibility existed that if no resistance was offered the embassy guards would be considered part of the diplomatic entourage, entitled to repatriation. As the initial treatment of the Marines was relatively mild and they repeatedly received informal assurances from the Japanese that they would be exchanged, few attempted escape. When these rumors proved false, the opportunity had passed.[19]

By the time Ashurst's report of his decision to surrender reached Hart in Manila, the Philippines were in the thick of the war. The first news of the Japanese attack was picked up at 0257 by a radio operator at CinCAF Headquarters who, recognizing the technique of the sender, vouched for the reliability of the now famous message, "Air raid on Pearl Harbor. This is no drill."[20] The duty officer, Marine Lieutenant Colonel William T. Clement of Hart's staff, immediately notified the admiral who sent a war alert to all fleet units. Minutes later, by a combination of intercepted official and commercial broadcasts and the spreading of the word by the first agencies notified, the report had reached all major USAFFE headquarters.

A cacophony of sound broke the stillness at Olongapo when the alert reached the naval base at 0350; the bugler of the guard blew "Call to Arms;" the steam whistle at the power plant blasted a recall signal to PBY crewmen; and the ship's bell at the main gate clanged continuously.[21] Companies immediately mustered in front of their wooden barracks and in the streets of tent areas and were put to work setting up machine guns for antiaircraft defense and digging individual protective holes. Colonel Howard initiated the first moves in what was to be a hectic period of redisposing, reorganizing, and reinforcing the regiment which lasted throughout the month of December.

When the 4th Marines arrived from Shanghai its strength stood at 44 officers and warrant officers and 728 enlisted men; organic naval medical personnel raised the total strength to 804. The regiment "had been permitted to dwindle by attrition"[22] in China so that it consisted only of Headquarters Company, Service Company, and two battalions—the battalions short one of their rifle companies and the companies each short one of their three rifle platoons. By utilizing the members of the regimental band and absorbing the Marine Barracks Detachment, Olongapo, Howard was able to form some of the missing pla-

---

[19] Huizenga, *op. cit.*; MIS, G–2, WD, Escape Rept No. 666, Capt J. D. McBrayer, Jr., 12Jul45.

[20] *Clement Rept.*

[21] Capt F. W. Ferguson, Personal Experiences 8Dec41–6May42, n. d., hereinafter cited as *Ferguson*.

[22] *Howard Rept*, 8. As the threat of war with Japan increased, Adm Hart initiated a policy of withholding replacements from Marine units in China. Almost all of the men held back were assigned to the 1st SepMarBn at Cavite. Hart felt that if by some mischance he was unable to get the 4th Mar out of China he "could at least stop sending any more Marines there until someone bawled us out most vociferously. They never did." *Hart Comments.*

toons. In keeping with previous orders from Admiral Rockwell, he sent the 1st Battalion by tug, lighter, and truck to Mariveles to relieve the Marine detachment there. The men of the Mariveles guard had been taken from the other major Marine unit in the Philippines, the 1st Separate Marine Battalion at Cavite.

The battalion was organized to function either as an antiaircraft or an infantry unit, but its primary mission was the antiaircraft defense of the naval installations in the Cavite-Sangley Point area. Its firing batteries, 3-inch guns and .50 caliber machine guns, had been on partial alert since 14 October and as the threat of war grew stronger the guns and their crews had reached a high degree of readiness. On 4 December, the battalion's one long range radar set and the necessary operating personnel were assigned to USAFFE's control and moved to a position on the west coast where the radar could scan the approaches to Manila from the south;[23] the set was one of two operating in the Philippines on 8 December. When the battalion commander, Lieutenant Colonel John P. Adams, passed the word of the Pearl Harbor attack there was little left to be done but to "cut fuzes, going into the last stage of readiness."[24] But the Marine guns were not to see action. The Japanese reserved their first day of attack for their primary target, MacArthur's Far East Air Force (FEAF). And when that day was over, the Japanese figured that their "supremacy, at least in the air, was established conclusively."[25]

Except for 16 B–17's at Del Monte on Mindanao, the bulk of FEAF's strength in first-line planes was stationed at fields in central Luzon. Dawn of the 8th found most of these planes airborne, waiting to engage or evade Japanese attackers. But the land-based naval fighters and bombers of the Japanese *Eleventh Air Fleet*, charged with making the main air assault, did not appear at dawn. The enemy plan had called for such a surprise attack, timed to coincide with the start of operations in Malaya and at Pearl Harbor, but thick clouds and heavy fog delayed the take-off from Formosa of the major attack formations. It was noon before the enemy planes could reach their targets, Luzon's airfields, and the Japanese pilots very reasonably assumed that with the loss of surprise they would be met in force.[26]

But this was not to be, for "shortly after 1130 all American aircraft in the Philippines, with the exception of one or two planes, were on the ground."[27] The fighters were refueling after their fruitless morning patrols or awaiting a warning of imminent attack; the bombers were arming for an offensive mission against Formosa. By an incredible chain of circumstances, compounded by poor communications, a woefully inadequate air warning system, and a generous amount

---

[23] LtCol H. L. Davis ltr to CMC, 31Oct56.

[24] 1stLt W. F. Hogaboom, Personal Experiences 14Oct41–6May42, n. d., 1–2, hereinafter cited as *Hogaboom*. This narrative was published in the *MC Gazette*, April 1946, under the title, "Action Report—Bataan."

[25] HistSec, Japanese Research Div, GHQ, FEC, Japanese Studies in WWII No. 11, Philippines AirOpsRec, 1Feb52, 7, hereinafter cited as *Philippines AirOpsRec*.

[26] *Ibid*.

[27] W. S. Craven and J. L. Cate (eds.), *Plans and Early Operations, January 1939 to August 1942—The Army Air Forces in World War II* (Chicago: University of Chicago Press, 1948), 209.

of pure bad luck, the Japanese were given a sitting target. After a day of violent action, when all concerned tried to make up for what hindsight calls mistakes, the strength of the FEAF had been reduced by half. The way was open for the Japanese to begin landing operations.[28]

The enemy had in fact made his first landing by the time of the main air attacks. A small force came ashore at dawn on Batan Island midway between Luzon and Formosa and immediately began work to set up an air base on an already existing strip to accommodate the relatively short-ranged Army fighters. The next day elements of two fighter regiments of the Japanese *5th Air Group* were using the field and flying reconnaissance and strike missions over northern Luzon, site of the next planned landings.

THE FIRST DAYS [29]

On 9 December only a few enemy bombers attacked, but these planes filtering through the early morning darkness reached Nichols Field outside Manila unscathed where their bombs increased the damage and added to the toll of American planes. An all-out attack on the Manila Bay area had been planned for the second day of the war, but fog over Formosa prevented the take-off. Although the weather was again bad on the 10th, the enemy naval squadrons were on their way to their targets by midmorning.[30] Radar and ground observers spotted the incoming flights, but to no avail. When the outnumbered American interceptors rose to greet the raiders, the enemy fighters swarmed all over them, not giving as good as they got, but more than making up for their losses whenever they downed one of the few remaining planes of FEAF.

The Japanese bomber groups were heading for the best protected area in the Philippines; almost all of the antiaircraft units in USAFFE were concentrated near Manila. But the gunners below had an insoluble problem; they had plenty of ammunition, but very little of it was fused so that it could reach above 24,000 feet. After a few false starts the enemy learned that they could bomb from heights of 25,000 feet with relative impunity. There was a limited supply of mechanically-fused ammunition which could reach 30,000 feet, but there were not enough such rounds to materially increase antiaircraft defenses.

The gunners of the 1st Separate Marine Battalion at Cavite scored a kill on 10 December when they downed an over-eager dive bomber that strayed from the pack over Nichols Field, lured by the target of two PBY's taking off from Sangley Point. But that was the end of it. The three-inch batteries turned back the first flight of bombers, which came in too low, but all subsequent flights approaching the

---

[28] See Craven and Cate, *op. cit.*, 201–213 and *Fall of the Philippines*, 79–90 for an examination of the contradictory statements and chronology of misadventures that marked what may well have been the blackest day in the history of the Army Air Corps.

[29] Unless otherwise noted the material in this section is derived from *Hart Narrative; USAFFE-USFIP Rept; Moore Rept;* RAdm F. W. Rockwell, Narrative of Naval Activities in the Luzon Area, 1Dec41–19Mar42, 1Aug42 (located at NHD), hereinafter cited as *Rockwell Narrative; Howard Rept; 4th Mar Jnl; 14th Army Rept; Fall of the Philippines; Rising Sun in the Pacific.*

[30] HistSec, G–2, GHQ, FEC, Japanese Studies in WWII No. 13, NavOps in the Invasion of the Philippines, 15May46 (located at OCMH), 7.

naval base stayed well out of range and the gunners were helpless spectators to the destruction that followed.[31]

Stick after stick of bombs rained down on the naval base as successive flights of bombers criss-crossed the area laying a perceptible pattern. Fires sprang up everywhere as small dumps of ammunition and gasoline were hit and the old town of Cavite was soon a raging mass of flames. All the ships that could possibly get away from the yard headed out into the bay, but the bombers caught and fatally damaged a submarine and a mine sweeper. Everyone feared that the ammunition depot, which still had large quantities of powder and ammunition in it, would be hit, but the bombers missed their most promising target. Still, the fires being blown toward the depot from Cavite might touch it off,[32] and the rescue parties searching amid the flaming ruins for the hundreds of civilian casualties were in constant danger. Long after the raid was over, into the night and the early morning of the next day, the fires raged and Admiral Rockwell ordered all personnel to evacuate the base. Only a small group of men from Lieutenant Colonel Adams' battalion and a few Manila firemen remained. These volunteers localized the fire and were able to save the commissary stores; the ammunition depot soon was out of danger.[33]

Admiral Hart had watched the air attack from the roof of his headquarters building in Manila and had seen the end of Cavite as a base of operations. Rockwell's damage report confirmed his observations. On the night of the 10th Hart ordered most of the remaining ships of the Asiatic Fleet still in Manila Bay to sail south to comparative safety. The next day he advised the captains of all merchant ships in the bay to get their vessels out while they still could; fortunately, only one merchantman out of 40 was caught by enemy bombers.[34] The strongest element of Hart's fleet, his 29 submarines, continued to operate from the bay for a short while, until Japanese control of the air made this base untenable. By the year's end only the submarine tender *Canopus* and a small collection of yard craft, motor torpedo boats, and auxiliaries remained in Manila's waters.

In the judgment of a naval historian of this period the Asiatic Fleet was "sadly inadequate" and therefore "unable to prevent the enemy from landing wherever he chose, or even to delay his efficient timetable of conquest."[35] Nor were FEAF or the ground troops of USAFFE able to do the job. In some instances there was a temporary delay when planes hit the landing forces, but nowhere were the Japanese stopped and forced to turn back. On 10 December two combat teams from the *2d Formosa Regiment* of the *48th Division* came ashore at Aparri in northern Luzon and at Vigan on the northwest coast. Their mission, which was to secure airfields for use by Army planes, was successful. In a day the Japanese, despite the loss of several ships to American bombers, were firmly established ashore and in practical control of the northern tip of Luzon. The one Philippine Army division in the area, the 11th, was responsible for the de-

---

[31] *Hogaboom*, 3.
[32] LtCol J. V. Lyon ltr to CMC, 31Oct56.
[33] LtCol J. W. Keene, Narrative and tactical dispositions of the 1st SepMarBn at Cavite, 8–26Dec41, n.d.

[34] *Hart Comments*.
[35] *Rising Sun in the Pacific*, 181.

fense of the island north of Lingayen Gulf and was of necessity spread so thin that it could offer no effective resistance.

The same situation held true in southern Luzon where the defending forces, two Philippine Army divisions, were completely unable to cover all possible landing beaches. On 12 December, when a Japanese convoy carrying the advance assault detachment of the *16th Division*, staged from the Palaus, reached Legaspi in southeastern Luzon, there was nothing to oppose their landing. The troops were ashore, had taken their airfield objective, and were moving north by nightfall. In all there were less than 10,000 enemy troops ashore at this time, but they had behind them the rest of the *Fourteenth Army* and command of the sea and air to insure its arrival on schedule.

The heavy air attacks of the 8th and 10th were only harbingers of further aerial assaults. Reinforced by Army fighters and bombers operating from newly-seized airfields, the naval planes of the Formosa-based *Eleventh Air Fleet* spread out over Luzon seeking new targets. The first turn of Olongapo and the 4th Marines came on 12 December, the day that marked the end of effective U. S. air support.

A flight of Japanese fighters followed the PBY's based at Olongapo into their anchorage after the flying boats had made a fruitless search for a supposed enemy carrier task force. The enemy pilots caught the seaplanes at their moorings and destroyed them all. As the Japanese strafed the naval station Marine machine gunners attempted to bring them down; Colonel Howard noticed that the tracers of Company H's .30's seemed to be "bouncing off these planes indicating sufficient armor plate to prevent penetration." [36] The enemy attacked again on the 13th, this time bombing from altitudes beyond the range of the Marine automatic weapons. The few hits scored were all in the town of Olongapo; there was no damage to the naval station and only a few Marine casualties. The Filipinos who ignored the air raid warning suffered heavily; a bomb hit right in the midst of a large group of townspeople who were "standing under a tree watching the performance," [37] killing 22 and wounding at least as many more. Although alarms were frequent thereafter, the Japanese did not attack again until the 19th and then their aim was bad and they liberally plastered the bay with bombs.

During this period, while the original Japanese landing forces were advancing toward Manila, top-level discussions were held between Hart and MacArthur and their staffs regarding employment of the 4th Marines.[38] On 20 December, MacArthur formally requested that the regiment be assigned to his command "as developments of the Navy plan can make it available." [39] Admiral Hart concurred and directed Howard to report to USAFFE for such employment as Mac-

---

[36] *Howard Rept*, 9.

[37] *Jackson*.

[38] Although the war plan for the Philippines had long called for the available Marines to be assigned to the defending ground forces under Army control, USAFFE made no effort in the first few days of the war to contact CinCAF regarding his Marine forces. After a reminder from Hart, "there came back a request to send one battalion into Manila City to guard USAFFE Headquarters. Feeling that it would be a wrong use of the best infantry available, [Hart issued] no order to that effect." *Hart Comments*.

[39] Copy of CG, USAFFE ltr to CinCAF, 20Dec41, in *4th Mar Jnl*, 237; *Clement Rept*, 6.

Arthur might deem necessary in the defense of Luzon.[40] In a covering memo to Rockwell, he pointed out that the assignment of the 4th Marines was the sole commitment that he had made and that he had verbally made it clear that it was his policy that excess naval personnel be organized and equipped and then "fed up into the combat areas on shore with the Fourth Regiment of Marines. A command exercised over them by the Army would normally be via C. O. Fourth Marines."[41]

The Navy Department had directed Hart on his departure from the Philippines to place all naval personnel, munitions, and equipment at the disposal of USAFFE. Rockwell, who was to relieve Hart as senior naval officer in the Philippines, nominally retained independent status. He adhered firmly, however, to the principle of unity of command and cooperated closely with MacArthur's headquarters.

On 22 December, the reinforced Japanese *48th Division* landed in Lingayen Gulf. It was the logical landing point for any force whose objective was Manila, for the gulf stood at the head of a broad valley leading directly to the capital. The landing was expected and it was resisted, but the combined efforts of American air, submarine, and ground forces could not prevent the Japanese from putting their men ashore and effecting a juncture with Vigan-Aparri landing forces which had driven down from the north. Resistance, although sparked by the 26th Cavalry of the Philippine Scouts, was spotty and ineffectual, and the Japanese soon proved that the partially-trained men of the Philippine Army were not yet a match for their troops. Covered by the Scout cavalrymen, the Filipino reservists fell back in disorder to reorganize in positions below the Agno River.

The enemy was ready to drive on Manila from the north.

On the 24th, the last major assault element of the *Fourteenth Army*, the *16th Division* from the Ryukyus, landed at Lamon Bay only 60 miles cross-island from Manila. Here the story was much the same as Lingayen Gulf. The enemy overwhelmed scattered, ill-trained troops and made good his beachhead. The American South Luzon Force began to fight a delaying action along the roads leading to Manila. The decision, however, had already been made to declare the capital an "open city," and the troops were headed for the Bataan Peninsula.

Bataan, northern arm of Manila Bay, had long been considered the ultimate stronghold in a defense of Luzon. While it was held, and with it the fortified islands across the mouth of the bay, no enemy could use the harbor, and it was possible to gain succor from friendly naval forces which might break through a blockade. MacArthur had rejected the concept of a static, last-ditch defense when he took over USAFFE and had expected with the forces underway to him from the States and trained Philippine Army divisions to be able to repulse or contain enemy landing attempts. When the Japanese won

---

[40] According to the *Hart Narrative*, 45, one plan considered for the employment of the 4th Mar entailed the brigading of the regiment (reinforced by a naval battalion from Mariveles) and a constabulary regiment under a Marine brigade commander. The Marines were to furnish officers and NCO's to the Constabulary unit. Time did not permit the execution of this scheme.

[41] CinCAF memo to ComSixteen, 22Dec41, in *4th Mar Jnl*, 239.

control of the sea and air, however, he lost all chance for successful execution of his orders to "attack and destroy" [42] any landing force, and he was forced to adopt the only course of action that would save his army: a desperation withdrawal to Bataan. He made the fateful decision on 23 December and the following day preparations to effect it were begun.

Basically the withdrawal plan called for Major General Jonathan C. Wainwright's North Luzon Force to fight a series of delaying actions in the central island plain which would allow the South Luzon Force (Major General George M. Parker, Jr.) to reach the peninsula. Then Wainwright's units would pull back to Bataan, join forces with Parker, and stand off the enemy. In the time gained by the delaying actions, USAFFE would make every effort to augment the supplies already gathered in scattered dumps on Bataan with food, ammunition, weapons, and equipment from installations in the Manila area.

The role of the 4th Marines in this plan was laid out for Colonel Howard in a series of conferences which took place in Manila on 24 December. Admiral Hart, who was preparing to leave for Java the following day, informed the Marine commander that the 1st Separate Battalion would be added to his regiment as soon as it could clear Cavite and that he was to report immediately to MacArthur for duty. At USAFFE headquarters, amidst the bustle attendant on its move to Corregidor, Howard got a cordial welcome from his new chief and then received orders to move the 4th to Corregidor and take over its beach defenses. In a meeting with Admiral Rockwell, after he had made a final call on Hart, Howard was told to destroy the Olongapo Naval Station when he pulled out.

Mariveles at the southern tip of Bataan had been designated the assembly area and transshipment point for the Marine units and their supplies. The 1st Battalion had already spent two weeks in bivouac near the base weathering a series of air attacks and furnishing guard details, unloading parties, and dump construction crews. Two men were killed and three wounded on 24 December during a bombing raid that struck shipping in the harbor. It was an inauspicious portent for the reception of the forward echelon of the regiment which left for Mariveles at 2200 that night.

Shortly after the truck convoy had cleared Olongapo, Colonel Howard received warning from naval headquarters of an impending Japanese landing, and "sounds of motors could be distinctly heard from seaward" [43] in Subic Bay. All available men manned beach defense positions, but fortunately the report proved false and the motors turned out to be those of American torpedo boats. Early on Christmas morning a message from Rockwell's new headquarters on Corregidor ordered Howard to expedite evacuation and destruction lest the regiment be cut off by advancing Japanese troops. The Philippine Army's 31st Division had pulled back to Bataan from its coastal positions northwest of Olongapo on the 24th and the Marines' north flank was now open; a threat also existed to seaward, since the Army's coast defense troops were withdrawing from Fort Wint in Subic Bay. Motorcycle patrols ranging north of the base could find no sign of the enemy, however, and the movement of men and

---

[42] *Wainwright's Story*, 28.

[43] *Howard Rept*, 11.

supplies was completed without undue haste. At 1410 Howard's new CP opened outside Mariveles, and the fate of Olongapo was left in the hands of a demolition detail under Captain (later Major) Francis H. Williams.

Using charges improvised from 300-pound mines, "Williams set out with his demolition gang to do a good job of erasing the Naval Station from the face of the globe."[44] They sank the hull of the old armored cruiser *Rochester* in the bay and blew up or burned everything of value except the barracks which closely bordered the native town.[45] The last supplies were loaded early Christmas evening, and the rear echelon pulled out with darkness.

Christmas also saw the completion of destruction at Cavite where a Marine demolition party from the 1st Separate Battalion blew up or fired all remaining ammunition stocks and destroyed the submarine damaged in the 10 December air raid. The naval radio station near Sangley Point was already a shambles, for in a raid on 19 December enemy bombers leveled the buildings and set afire large quantities of gas and oil scattered in dumps throughout the surrounding area.[46] Lieutenant Colonel Adams received orders on 20 December to evacuate the Cavite area, and for the next few days men and supplies were trucked to Mariveles; the Christmas day demolition detail was the last element to leave.[47]

After darkness fell on 26 December, the first Marines to move to Corregidor, 14 officers and 397 men of Adams' battalion, made the seven and a half mile voyage from Mariveles' docks to North Dock on "The Rock."

THE FORTIFIED ISLANDS [48]

The four islands that guarded the mouth of Manila Bay were fortified in the decade prior to World War I before air power changed the concept of coastal defense. Most of the powerful 14- and 12-inch guns were sited in open emplacements for the purpose of repelling an invasion from the sea. Disarmament treaty obligations and drastically reduced defense expenditures in the period between the wars allowed little concession to be made to the threat of air attack. Some antiaircraft guns were added to the fort's defenses, however, and a start was made toward providing underground bombproof shelters, especially on Corregidor (Fort Mills).

Corregidor was at its closest point just a little over two miles from the tip of Bataan Peninsula. The island was tadpole-shaped, three and a half miles long and one and a half miles wide at its head. This wide area, called Topside, loomed high above the rest of the island, its 500-foot cliffs dropping sharply to a narrow beachline. Most of the coast defense batteries and permanent quarters were located here, and the only access routes to the top from the western shore were two ravines, James and Cheney. East of Topside, along the neck of land that connected the tadpole's head and tail, was Middleside, a plateau which held several more battery positions and permanent buildings. A

---

[44] *Ferguson*, 3.

[45] The town's natives later burned their own houses and the barracks was consumed in the resulting fire.

[46] *Hogaboom*, 4.

[47] *Keene, op. cit.*, 10.

[48] Unless otherwise noted the material in this section is derived from *Moore Rept; Howard Rept; 4th Mar Jnl; Philippine AirOpsRec; Fall of the Philippines*.

third ravine, Ramsay, which led from the southern beaches to Middleside, was a critical defensive point. (See Map 8, Map Section)

A logically-named third distinctive portion of the island, Bottomside, consisted of the low ground occupied by the industrial and dock area and the native town of San Jose. The nerve center of Luzon's defenses was an extensively-tunnelled hill, Malinta Hill, which rose directly east of San Jose. The headquarters of MacArthur, Rockwell, and Major General George F. Moore, commanding the fortified islands, were all eventually located in the tunnels and laterals that spread out beneath the hill. From Malinta the long, low, narrow tail of the island bent away to the east; a light plane landing strip, Kindley Field, had been built along the spine of the tail.

The other three island forts, Hughes, Drum, and Frank, complemented the defenses of Fort Mills, and Marines served as part of the beach defense troops on all but the last named. Caballo Island (Fort Hughes), a quarter-mile square in area, stood less than two miles from Corregidor; its low-lying eastern shore rose abruptly to a 380-foot height which contained most of the battery positions. Four miles south of Caballo was the "concrete battleship," Fort Drum. Tiny El Fraile Island had been razed to water level and on its foundation a steel-reinforced concrete fortress had been erected with sides 25- to 36-feet thick, and a top deck 20-feet deep. Two case-hardened steel gun turrets, each sporting a pair of 14-inch guns, were mounted on the deck and the sides of the fort boasted four 6-inch gun casements. Its garrison could be completely contained within its walls, and "the fort was considered impregnable to enemy attack."[49] The island which seemed most vulnerable to assault was Carabao (Fort Frank) which lay only 500 yards from the shore of Cavite Province. However, since some of its guns were capable of firing inland and most of its shoreline was ringed with precipitous cliffs, the job of taking Fort Frank promised to be quite a task.

General Moore later noted that "the fortresses were not designed to withstand a landing attack from adjacent shores supported by overwhelming artillery emplaced thereon;"[50] and that of his big guns only the turrets of Fort Drum, the 12-inch mortars, and two 12-inch long-range guns were capable of all-round fire. A tabulation of the major coast defense armament of the forts shows:

Type	Number of Guns			
	Mills	Hughes	Drum	Frank
14″ guns	—	2	4	2
12″ guns	8	—	—	—
12″ mortars	10	4	—	8
10″ guns	2	—	—	—
8″ guns	2	—	—	—
6″ guns	5	2	4	—
155mm guns	19	3	—	4
3″ guns	10	2	1	—

The forts had in addition a small number of 75mm beach defense guns. For antiaircraft defense, including tied-in batteries on southern Bataan, there were 17 searchlights, 40 3-inch guns, and 48 .50 caliber machine guns.[51]

Marines from the 1st Separate Battalion were able to add a few .50 caliber

---
[49] *Moore Rept*, 4.
[50] *Ibid.*, 9.
[51] *Ibid.*, Annex C.

machine guns and a battery of four 3-inch guns taken from Cavite to the antiaircraft defenses, but the primary function of the battalion was now that of infantry. It was reorganized and re-equipped at Mariveles to fill the role of the missing battalion of the 4th Marines; the formal change of title to 3d Battalion, 4th Marines came on 1 January.

With the exception of Batteries A and C and the radar detachment of Adams' battalion which remained on Bataan, the whole of the 4th Marines moved to Corregidor in successive echelons on the nights of 27 and 28 December. Enough rations for 2,000 men for six months, ten units of fire for all weapons, two years supply of summer khaki, and the medicines and equipment to outfit a 100-bed hospital accompanied the move. Fortunately, the Quartermaster, Major Ridgely, dispersed these supplies in small, scattered dumps as they arrived and they emerged relatively unscathed from the first Japanese air raid on Corregidor.

Many of the Marines in the bamboo jungles surrounding Mariveles, who had to shift camp constantly to avoid bombing and sleep "on the ground near a foxhole or some convenient ditch into which [they] could roll in the event of an air attack"[52] looked forward to moving to The Rock. They had "watched the Jap bombers steer clear of its antiaircraft barrages" and it had been pointed out to them "that Corregidor's antiaircraft was so good that the Japs had not even dared to bomb it—yet!"[53] An additional lure of the island to some men was the vision of a Gibraltar, and they talked knowingly of the (nonexistent) intricate underground system of defenses.[54]

At 0800 29 December, Colonel Howard reported to General Moore for orders as Fort Mills' beach defense commander and then started out to make a reconnaissance of the island. His men, temporarily quartered in Middleside Barracks, were startled to hear the air raid sirens sound shortly before noon. No one paid too much attention to them as Corregidor had never been bombed, but soon their trusting attitude changed. "All hell broke loose," and as one 1st Battalion officer described the scene, "there we were—the whole regiment flat on our bellies on the lower deck of Middleside Barracks."[55]

The Japanese planes, 40 bombers of the *5th Air Group* with 19 covering fighters, attacked at 1154. For the next hour a parade of Army aircraft flew the long axis of Corregidor dropping 200- and 500-pound bombs from 18,000 feet, and dive bombers attacked the antiaircraft batteries, strafing as they plunged down. At 1300, the Army planes gave way to the Navy and bombers of the *Eleventh Air Fleet* continued to attack until 1415. None of FEAF's few remaining fighters, which were being saved for vital reconnaissance missions, took to the air, but Corregidor's gunners exacted a good price from the enemy—13 medium bombers fell to the 3-inchers and the .50 calibers shot down four of the dive bombers in a vivid demonstration of the folly of flying within reach of these guns. But the damage done by the enemy was considerable.

---

[52] Statement of Lt(jg) R. G. Hetherneck in Cdr T. H. Hayes Rept on MedTactics, 4th Regt USMC, 7Dec41–6May42, 15Feb46, 79, hereinafter cited as *Hayes Rept*.

[53] LtCol R. F. Jenkins, Jr., Personal Experiences 28Dec41–6May42, n.d., 1, hereinafter cited as *Jenkins*.

[54] *Ibid.*
[55] *Ibid.*

Almost all of the barracks and headquarters buildings and a good half of the wooden structures on the island were battered, set afire, or destroyed. A thick pall of black smoke and clouds of dust obscured the island from observers on Bataan, and the detail left to load out Marine supplies wondered at the fate of the regiment in the center of this maelstrom.[56] The casualty score was miraculously low, only one man killed and four wounded. With a single exception, bombs used by the Japanese did not penetrate all the way through to the bottom deck of the concrete barracks, but the building, shaken repeatedly by hits and near misses, was a shambles. In all, the island's defenders suffered about 100 casualties, and 29 December marked the end of "normal" above ground living for The Rock's garrison.

As soon as the air raid was over, Howard assigned beach defense sectors to his battalions, and the troops moved out to their new bivouac areas before dark. The 1st Battalion, 20 officers and 367 enlisted men under Lieutenant Colonel Curtis T. Beecher, drew a possible enemy landing point—the East Sector which included Malinta Hill and the island's tail. The beaches of Bottomside and most of Middleside (Middle Sector) up to a line including Morrison Hill and Ramsay Ravine were occupied by Lieutenant Colonel Adams' battalion with 20 officers and 490 men. The defense of the rest of the shoreline of Corregidor was the responsibility of the 2d Battalion (Lieutenant Colonel Herman R. Anderson) which mustered 18 officers and 324 enlisted men. A general reserve of 8 officers and 183 men, formed from the Headquarters and Service Companies, commanded by Major Stuart W. King,[57] bivouacked in Government Ravine, on the southern shore of the island below Geary and Crockett Batteries.

Not all of Adams' battalion was assigned to the Middle Sector; besides the units left on Bataan, the 3d Battalion furnished most of the other special detachments. One platoon (1 officer and 28 men) with four .50 caliber machine guns and a second (1 officer and 46 men) with four .30's left for Fort Hughes on the 30th to bolster the antiaircraft and beach defenses; the 2d Battalion added ten men and four more .30 caliber machine guns to the beach defenses on 3 January.[58] Fort Drum got a section of 15 men and two .50's to augment its crew. A third antiaircraft platoon with six .50's (1 officer and 35 men) was directly assigned to Fort Mills' air defenses and attached to a similarly-equipped battery of the 60th Coast Artillery which was emplaced near the Topside parade ground.

By 1 January the pattern had been set for the Marines' duties on Corregidor. The men were digging in, stringing barbed wire, emplacing their 37mm's, mortars, and machine guns, and tying-in for a coordinated and protracted defense. Ahead lay more than four months of waiting and preparation for a battle, months in which more than one survivor likened life on Corregidor to existence in the center of a bull's eye.

---

[56] *Ferguson*, 6.

[57] *Howard Rept*, 14 lists Maj (then Capt) Max W. Schaeffer as commander of the regimental reserve at this point; however, the contemporary muster rolls at HQMC and survivors' comments indicate that Maj King held this position until 17Feb42 when Maj Schaeffer took over and King became ExO of the beach defense force at Fort Hughes.

[58] Lyon ltr, *op. cit.*

CHAPTER 2

Bataan Prelude

DRAWING THE BATTLE LINES[1]

The Japanese did not confine their operations in the Philippines to Luzon, but December landings on Mindanao and Jolo Islands were made primarily to secure bases for further attacks against Borneo. Here again the hastily mobilized Philippine Army reservists and Constabulary troopers were no match for the assault forces, and the enemy made good his lodgment. Offensive operations in the south, however, were limited by the fact that General Homma did not have sufficient troops to press a campaign on two fronts. The main strength of the *Fourteenth Army* remained on Luzon to win control of Manila Bay.

The original Japanese operation plan for Luzon had contemplated its occupation by the end of January and had provided for a mop-up force of one division and one brigade with a small air support unit. Shortly after Homma's troops entered Manila on 2 January, he received orders to expedite the withdrawal of the *48th Division* and the *5th Air Group* which were needed to reinforce stepped-up operations against Java and on the Asian mainland. In short return for these troop losses Homma got the *65th Brigade* from Formosa, originally assigned to mop-up and police duties. The brigade, which landed on Lingayen Gulf beaches on 1 January, was selected by Homma as his Bataan assault force and reinforced with an infantry regiment from the *16th Division* and tank, artillery, and service troops from army reserves. (See Map 7, Map Section)

The necessary reorganization of the *65th Brigade* for combat and its movement into jump-off positions gave MacArthur time to establish an initial defense line. On 7 January he reorganized his forces into two corps and a rear area service command. Wainwright was given I Philippine Corps with responsibility for holding the western front, and Parker became II Philippine Corps commander with his troops manning defenses on the Manila Bay side of Bataan. More than 80,000 men were now bottled up on the peninsula and some 50,000 held positions on or near the initial defense line. These were impressive figures, and in paper strength the Bataan defenders outnumbered the *Fourteenth Army* which had about 50,000 troops under its command.

Military superiority depends, however, on many other factors besides relative troop strength. The conglomerate American-Filipino forces, completely cut off from effective relief, had limited supplies of rations, medicines, weapons, ammunition, and equipment. By contrast, the enemy's control of the sea and air gave the Japanese an unmatchable resupply and reinforcement potential. Even when

---

[1] Unless otherwise noted the material in this section is derived from *USAFFE-USFIP Rept; 14th Army Rept; Fall of the Philippines.*

the *Fourteenth Army's* fortunes were at their lowest ebb, the enemy troops could reasonably expect rescue and relief.

On 5 January MacArthur, in a move to conserve dwindling food stocks, had cut all troops on Bataan and the fortified islands to half rations.[2] This order was undoubtedly the most significant given in the campaign. It prolonged the fighting for weeks, until Bataan's defenses eventually collapsed. Men sapped by malnutrition and its attendant diseases, for which there were no medicines, could resist no more.

In launching their initial attack on Bataan the Japanese did not expect that the reinforced *65th Brigade* would have much trouble defeating the American-Filipino forces. The enemy was flushed with his successes and "completely ignorant concerning the terrain of Bataan Peninsula."[3] Homma's intelligence officers had underestimated MacArthur's strength by half, had given their commander a distorted picture of Filipino morale, and had formulated an altogether incorrect estimate of the defensive situation on Bataan. The *Fourteenth Army* staff had:

... optimistically presumed that, considering its position relative to Corregidor Island, the enemy would offer serious resistance at the southern end of the Peninsula with Mariveles as a nucleus, withdrawing later to Corregidor Island. Taking this for granted, the threat of enemy resistance was taken lightly.[4]

Bataan Peninsula was an ideal position from the viewpoint of a force committed to a last-ditch stand. Thirty miles long at its deepest point and 25 miles wide at its base, the peninsula tapered to an average width of 15 miles. Numerous streams, ravines, and gullies cut up the interior and thick jungle growth blanketed everything. A spine of mountains running northwest to southeast split Bataan roughly in half. The dominant features in the north were Mt. Natib (4,222 feet) and its companion Mt. Silanganan (3,620 feet), and in the south, Mt. Bataan (4,700 feet), which commanded the Mariveles area. Although numerous trails crisscrossed the peninsula, only two motor roads existed, one running along the coast and the other over the saddle between the mountain masses. The western coast line was uneven with many promontories formed by mountain ridges; the eastern coast was more regular and open but became hilly and rugged in the south. (See Map 7, Map Section)

The final defense line selected by USAFFE was midway down the peninsula, anchored on the towns of Bagac and Orion, and generally along the trace of the cross-peninsula motor road. It was the necessity of covering the preparation of this area for defense and the need to use the road as a supply route as long as possible that dictated the occupation of the initial defense line. Stretching across the peninsula just above the point where it narrowed, this position had a grave natural weakness. The corps boundary ran along the Natib-Silanganan mountain mass which pierced the defenses and prevented liaison or even contact between Wainwright's and Parker's men. The Japanese attempt to crack this defense line eventually involved landings far behind the front and brought the Marines at Mariveles into action.

---

[2] "Actually, the troops on Bataan received about one-third ration." *USAFFE-USFIP Rept*, 42.

[3] *14th Army Rept*, 90.

[4] *Ibid.*, 91.

SYMBOLIC OF JAPANESE SUCCESSES *in the early stages of the war is this photograph taken on Mt. Limay on Bataan during the fighting in the Philippines. (SC 334265)*

THE NAVAL BATTALION[5]

Although the farthest distance from the rear boundaries of the corps areas to the southern shore of Bataan was only ten miles, the defensive problem facing Brigadier General Allan C. McBride's Service Command was acute. With a relatively few men McBride had to guard over 40 miles of rough, jungle-covered coast line against enemy attack. A successful amphibious thrust which cut the vital coastal supply road could mean the prompt end of the battle for Bataan. To protect the east coast he had the newly-organized 2d (Constabulary) Division; on the west coast he had a motley composite force of service troops and planeless pursuit squadrons converted to infantry, backed up by a few elements of the 71st Division and a Constabulary regiment. Responsibility for the security of the naval reservation at Mariveles remained with the Navy.

In order to provide protection for Mariveles and support the Army in the defense of the west coast, Admiral Rockwell on 9 January directed Captain John H. S. Dessez, commander of the section base, to form a naval battalion for ground combat. The senior naval aviator remaining in the Philippines, Commander Francis J. Bridget, was appointed battalion commander and he immediately set about organizing his force. For troops he had about 480 bluejackets including 150 of his own men from Air, Asiatic Fleet, 130 crewmen from the submarine tender *Canopus*, 80 sailors from the Cavite Naval Ammunition Depot, and 120 general duty men from Cavite and Mariveles. He was also assigned approximately 120 Marines, members of Batteries A and C which had remained behind on Bataan under naval control when the rest of the 1st Separate Battalion (now 3/4) had moved to Corregidor.

The men of First Lieutenant William F. Hogaboom's Battery A had originally been slated to provide replacement and relief gun crews for Battery C (First Lieutenant Willard C. Holdredge) whose 3-inch guns were set up in a rice paddy between the town of Mariveles and the section base. But on 5 January Hogaboom had received instructions from a USAFFE staff officer, "approved by naval authorities on the 'Rock',"[6] to move his unit to the site of MacArthur's advance CP on Bataan where the Marines were to furnish the interior guard. This assignment was short-lived, however, since Commander Bridget needed the men to serve as tactical instructors and cadres for the naval battalion, and on 14 January he directed Hogaboom to report back to Mariveles. To replace Battery A, USAFFE detached two officers and 47 men from the 4th Marines[7] and sent them from Corregidor to Bataan where they guarded the advance headquarters until the end of the campaign.

The most serious problem Bridget faced in forming his battalion was the lack of ground combat training of his bluejackets. As the commander of the *Canopus*, naturally an interested spectator, noted:

---

[5] Unless otherwise noted the material in this section is derived from *Rockwell Narrative;* 16th NavDist War Diary, 8Dec41–19Feb42 (located at NHD); *Clement Rept;* Cdr F. J. Bridget Rept to ComSixteen, Action at Longoskawayan Point, 9Feb42 (located at NHD), hereinafter cited as *Bridget Rept;* Capt E. L. Sackett, USN, "History of the USS Canopus," 28Apr47 (located at NHD), hereinafter cited as *Canopus Hist; Hogaboom.*

[6] *Hogaboom,* 5.
[7] *4th Mar Jnl,* 268.

... perhaps two-thirds of the sailors knew which end of the rifle should be presented to the enemy, and had even practiced on a target range, but field training was practically a closed book to them. The experienced Marines were spread thinly throughout each company in hope that through precept and example, their qualities would be assimilated by the rest.[8]

Even after the formation of the naval battalion, the primary responsibility for antiaircraft defense of Mariveles still rested with the Marine batteries and only a relatively few men, mostly NCO's, could be spared to help train the bluejacket companies. Holdredge's 3-inchers required at least skeleton crews and Hogaboom's unit, after its return from USAFFE control, was directed to mount and man nine .50 caliber machine-gun posts in the hills around the harbor. Therefore, in both batteries the majority of men available for ground combat were sailors; Battery A joined one officer and 65 bluejackets on 16-17 January and a Navy officer and 40 men joined Holdredge's battery on the 18th and 19th.[9] Throughout the naval battalion, training was confined to fundamentals as Bridget strove to qualify his men as infantry. As was the case so often in the Philippines, the time for testing the combat readiness of the jury-rigged battalion came all too soon.

LONGOSKAWAYAN POINT [10]

In opening his atack on Bataan, General Homma committed the main strength of the *65th Brigade* along the front of Parker's II Corps, figuring that the more open terrain along the east coast gave him a greater opportunity to exploit successes. By 11 January the Japanese had developed and fixed Parker's defenses and were probing for weak spots preparatory to an all-out assault. It was inevitable that they found the open and highly vulnerable left flank. By 22 January Parker's position along the slopes of Mt. Natib had been turned and all reserves with the exception of one regiment had been committed to contain the penetration. In order to prevent the defending forces from being cut off, USAFFE ordered a general withdrawal to the Bagac-Orion defense line, to be completed by the 26th.

The enemy advancing along the mountainous west coast did not contact General Wainwright's forward positions until 15 January. By that date, Homma, impressed by the lack of resistance in this sector, had already ordered the *20th Infantry* of the *16th Division* to reinforce and exploit the drive, strike through to the Bagac road junction, and gain the rear of Parker's corps. Although I Corps had been stripped of reserves to back up the sagging eastern defense line, Wainwright's front-line troops were able to stand off the initial Japanese assaults. When Homma's fresh troops attacked on the 21st, however, they effected a lodgment behind the front which eventually made withdrawal toward Bagac mandatory. The local Japanese commander, encouraged by his success, de-

---

[8] *Canopus Hist*, 14.

[9] Col W. F. Prickett ltr to CMC, October 1956.

[10] Unless otherwise noted the material in this section is taken from *USAFFE-USFIP Rept; 14th Army Rept; 4th Mar Jnl; Clement Rept; Bridget Rept; Hogaboom;* Btry A, US NavBn, Narrative of events, 2Feb42; 2dLt M. E. Peshek ltr to CO, 2/4, "Report of operation of Marine Detachment sent to Bataan on 25 January 1942," 2Feb42; GunSgt H. M. Ferrell ltr to CO, 1/4, "Temporary Duty of Mortar Platoon, vicinity of Mariveles, Bataan, Philippine Islands, from January 25, 1942, to January 30, 1942, inclusive," 31Jan42; *Fall of the Philippines*.

cided on a shore-to-shore amphibious assault which would hit the Bataan coastal road about four miles below Bagac.

Embarking after dark on the night of 22–23 January, the enemy's 900-man landing force (*2d Battalion, 20th Infantry*) started out for its objective. It never arrived. En route two launches of the battalion's boat group were discovered and sunk by an American torpedo boat [11] and it is possible that these attacks were instrumental in scattering the remainder of the landing force. In any event, the enemy boats lost their bearings completely in the darkness. Instead of landing on the objective, two-thirds of the unit landed at Quinauan Point, eight miles south of Bagac. The remainder of the battalion, 7 officers and 294 men, came ashore at Longoskawayan Point, a finger-like promontory only 2,000 yards west of Mariveles. (See Map 7, Map Section)

The Longoskawayan landing force was not discovered immediately, and the enemy had time to advance along jungle-matted cliffs and reach Lapiay Point, the next promontory to the north. The Japanese patrols headed inland from Lapiay for Mt. Pucot, a 617-foot hill which commanded both the west coast road and the landing site. The first word of the presence of the enemy in his defense sector reached Commander Bridget at 0840 on 23 January when the small lookout detachment he had posted on Pucot was driven from its position by enemy machine-gun fire.

Bridget immediately phoned Hogaboom and Holdredge, directing both officers to send out patrols. Hogaboom, closest to the scene of action, sent one bluejacket platoon under Lieutenant (junior grade) Leslie A. Pew directly to Pucot while he led a second platoon himself in a sweep through the ridges south of the hill. Pew's platoon deployed as it approached the hilltop, attacked through scattered rifle and machine-gun fire, and secured the high ground without difficulty. The Japanese offered only slight resistance and then faded out of contact.

South of the hill Hogaboom ran into a platoon from Battery C which had had a brush with the Japanese and taken a couple of casualties, but again the enemy had disappeared. The story of light firing and no firm resistance was much the same from the rest of the probing patrols which Bridget ordered out on the 23d; the Japanese evidently were still feeling out the situation and were not as yet disposed to make a stand or an attack. At dusk the patrols assembled on the mountain and set up a defense line along its crest and the ridges to the south facing Lapiay and Longoskawayan Points.

During the day Bridget had called on the Service Command for reinforcements but few men could be spared as most reserves already had been committed to contain the larger landing force at Quinauan Point. For infantry he got the 3d Pursuit Squadron and 60 men from the 301st Chemical Company whom he put into a holding line above Lapiay Point and on the north slope of Pucot; for fire support he received one 2.95-inch mountain pack howitzer and crew from the 71st Division. By nightfall the chemical company had tied in with the pursuit squadron on its right and with Battery A atop Pucot on its left; platoons from Battery C, the Air, Asiatic Fleet Company, and the Naval

---

[11] ComMTBron-3, Rept of Act of USS PT-34 on the night of 22–23Jan42, 27Feb42 (located at NHD), 1.

Ammunition Depot Company held the rest of Pucot's crest and the southern ridges which blocked off the landing area from Mariveles.[12] None of the naval battalion units was at full strength and none of the platoons strung out along the ridges was strictly a Navy or a Marine outfit. Sailors predominated but Marines were present all along the line, mostly as squad leaders and platoon sergeants. The composition of that part of the battalion which got into action became even more varied as the battle shaped up, and eventually about a third of the men on the front-line were drawn from the Marine batteries.

Bridget's men got their first real taste of the blind fighting of jungle warfare on the 24th. Hogaboom led a patrol down the bluff above Lapiay Point and ran head-on into an enemy machine gun firing from heavy cover. Grenades thrown at the gun exploded harmlessly in a tangle of lush vegetation which screened it from view; the men were being fired upon and they were replying, but sound rather than sight was the key to targets. When reinforcements arrived later in the day an attempt was made to establish a holding line across the point, but the Japanese opened up with a second machine gun and steady rifle fire. Then they began dropping mortar and howitzer shells among Hogaboom's group.

The Marine officer ordered a withdrawal to the previous night's positions.

The source of the mortar and howitzer fire was Longoskawayan Point where a patrol led by Lieutenant Holdredge had encountered the main body of Japanese. His two-man point had surprised an enemy group setting up a field piece in a clearing and opened up with a rifle and a BAR, dropping about a dozen men around the gun. The Japanese reaction was swift, agreeing with the BAR-man's evaluation that the surprise fire "ought to make them madder'n hell."[13] The patrol fell back, fighting a rear guard action until it cleared the area of the point's tip, and then it retired to the ridges. After the day's action Hogaboom and Holdredge compared notes and estimated that they faced at least 200 well-equipped enemy troops in strong positions; they informed Bridget of their conclusion that it would take a fully-organized battalion with supporting weapons to dislodge them.

On the morning of 25 January, USAFFE augmented Bridget's force by sending him a machine-gun platoon and an 81mm mortar platoon from the 4th Marines on The Rock. The two mortars immediately set up on a saddle northwest of Pucot and, with Hogaboom spotting for them, worked over the whole of Lapiay and Longoskawayan Points; direct hits were scored on the positions where the Japanese had been encountered the day before. A midafternoon patrol discovered that the enemy had evacuated Lapiay, but it was soon evident where they had gone. Holdredge led a combined force of several platoons against Longoskawayan Point and ran into a hornet's nest. He himself was among those wounded before the pla-

---

[12] An officer of 3/4 who knew many of the survivors of this action, later wrote an article describing the battle. He maintained that the Army detachments mentioned never joined, although they may have been assigned, and that the purely naval companies were not used as such. Instead the sailors who could be spared joined one of the Marine units. While this story is quite credible, in this instance the contemporary *Bridget Rept* has been used as a guide. See LtCol W. F. Prickett, "Naval Battalion at Mariveles," *MC Gazette*, June 1950, 40–43.

[13] Quoted in *Hogaboom*, 10.

toons could extricate themselves. Again the naval battalion occupied blocking positions on the ridges east of the points for night defense.

During the action of the 25th, USAFFE had changed the command structure in the rear service area and given the corps commanders responsibility for beach defense throughout Bataan. In addition, MacArthur had granted permission for the 12-inch mortars on Corregidor to support Bridget's battalion. Shortly after midnight, the giant mortars, spotted in by an observer on Mt. Pucot, laid several rounds on Longoskawayan Point. The daylight hours were spent in light patrol action while the battalion was readied for a full-scale attack on the 27th. General Wainwright sent a battery of Philippine Scout 75mm guns to support the drive.

At 0700 on 27 January the mountain howitzer, the Marine mortars, the Scout 75's, and Corregidor's 12-inch mortars fired a preparation on Longoskawayan, and a skirmish line of about 200 men, some 60–75 of them Marines, started to advance. The enemy reoccupied his positions as soon as the supporting fire lifted, and the jungle came alive with bullets and shell fragments. The right and center of the line made little progress in the face of heavy machine-gun fire. On the left where the going was a little easier a gap soon opened through which Japanese infiltrating groups were able to reach the reserve's positions.

During the resulting hectic fighting, the enemy opened up with mortar fire to herald a counterattack; fortunately, the 4th Marines' 81's were able to silence this fire, but it was soon obvious that the naval battalion was in no shape to advance farther or even to hold its lines on Longoskawayan. Bridget again authorized a withdrawal to the night defense lines on the eastern ridges.

The solution to the problem of eliminating the Japanese beachhead arrived late that afternoon. Colonel Clement, who had come over from Corregidor to advise Bridget on the conduct of the Longoskawayan action, had requested reinforcements from I Corps. Wainwright sent in the regular troops needed and the 2d Battalion of the 57th Philippine Scout Regiment relieved the naval battalion, which went into reserve. The 4th Marines' mortars and machine guns were assigned to the Scouts to support their operations. The oddly-assorted platoons of Bridget's battalion were not committed to action again, but they had done their job in containing the Japanese though outnumbered and outgunned.

The Scouts spent 28 January in developing the Longoskawayan position. On the 29th they attacked in full strength with all the support they could muster. The mine sweeper *Quail*, risking an encounter with Japanese destroyers, came out from Mariveles and cruised offshore while Commander Bridget spotted for the 12-inch mortars and the 75mm guns. The ship closed from 2,200 to 1,300 yards firing point-blank at Japanese soldiers trying to hide out in the caves and undergrowth along the shores of the point.[14] Ashore the Scouts, supported by machine-gun and mortar fire from the landing flanking the point, did the job expected of them and smashed through the enemy lines. By nightfall organized resistance had ended and the cost of taking Lapiay and Long-

[14] CO USS *Quail* Rept of Act at Longoskawayan Pt morning of 29Jan42, 30Jan42 (located at NHD), 1.

oskawayan had been counted. Bridget's unit had lost 11 killed and 26 wounded in action; the Scout casualties were 11 dead and 27 wounded; and the Japanese had lost their entire landing force.

During the next few days patrols, aided by ship's launches armored and manned by crewmen from the *Canopus*, mopped up the area, killing stragglers and taking a few prisoners, but the threat to Mariveles was ended. Similar action by adequately supported Scout units wiped out the Quinauan Point landing force by 7 February. The major Japanese attempt to reinforce the beleaguered troops on Quinauan was beaten back by the combined fire of artillery, naval guns, and the strafing of the four P–40's remaining on Bataan. Elements of an enemy battalion which did get ashore on a point of land just above Quinauan on 27 January and 2 February were also finished off by the Scouts.

By 13 February the last survivors of the amphibious attempts had been killed or captured. The make-shift beach defense forces which had initially contained the landings had barely managed to hold their own against the Japanese. They had had to overreach themselves to keep the enemy off balance and prevent a breakthrough while the troops of I and II Corps were falling back to the Bagac-Orion position. Once that line was occupied and Wainwright could commit some of his best troops in sufficient numbers and with adequate support, the Japanese were finished. Discouraged by their amphibious fiasco, the enemy never again attempted to hit the coastal flanks of the American-Filipino positions.

At the same time the survivors of the landing attempts were being hunted down, the Japanese offensive sputtered to a halt in front of the Bagac-Orion line. The initial enemy advance on Bataan had not been made without cost, and the casualty rate now soared so high that the attacking troops were rendered ineffective. On 13 February Homma found it necessary to break contact, pull back to a line of blocking positions, and to regroup his battered forces. The lull in the *Fourteenth Army's* attack was only temporary, however, as Homma was promised replacements and reinforcements. When the second phase of the battle for Bataan opened, the scales were heavily tipped in favor of the Japanese.

The detachment of *Canopus* crewmen, the sailors from the Cavite Naval Ammunition Depot, and the majority of the general duty men, nine officers and 327 enlisted men in all, were transferred to the 4th Marines on Corregidor on 17–18 February. Commander Bridget and his naval aviation contingent moved to Fort Hughes on the 30th where Bridget became beach defense commander with Major Stuart W. King of the 4th Marines as his executive officer. Battery C of 3/4 remained at Mariveles to man its antiaircraft guns, but Battery A rejoined the regiment, with most of its men going to Headquarters Company to augment the regimental reserve.

The assignment of the sailors of the naval battalion to Colonel Howard's command accentuated the growing joint-service character of the Marine regiment. Small contingents of crewmen from damaged or sunken boats of the Inshore Patrol also had been joined and over 700 Philippine Army air cadets and their officers were now included in the 4th's ranks. These men, most of whom had never had any infantry training, were distributed throughout the companies on beach defense and in reserve where the experienced Marines could best train them by example and close individual instruction. No company in the regiment retained an all-Marine complexion.

The arrival of reinforcements on Corregidor and Caballo came at a time when the Japanese had stepped up their campaign against the fortified islands. On 6 February, the first enemy shells, fired by 105mm guns emplaced along the shore of Cavite Province, exploded amidst the American positions on all the islands. The reaction was swift and the forts replied with the guns that could bear. The counterbattery exchange continued throughout February and early March, occasionally waning as the Japanese were forced to shift to new firing positions by gunners on Forts Frank and Drum. The limited number of planes available to Homma made enemy bombers infrequent visitors during this period, and the Japanese concentrated on reducing the island defenses with artillery fire. In the first week of March, the American commander on Fort Frank received a demand for its surrender with a boast that the Cavite coast was lined with artillery and that:

... Carabao will be reduced by our mighty artillery fire, likewise Drum; after reduction of Carabao and Drum our invincible artillery will pound Corregidor into submission, batter it, weaken it, preparatory to a final assault by crack Japanese landing troops.[16]

The surrender note was unproductive for the enemy, but it was prophetic regarding the fate of Corregidor.

Until the Japanese were ready to renew their assault on Bataan in late March, the severity of the enemy shellings from Cavite was not great enough to be effective in halting the construction and improvement of beach defenses on Corregidor. Trenches and gun positions lined the shores of Bottomside and the ravines leading to Topside and Middleside from the beaches. Barbed wire entanglements and mine fields improvised from aerial bombs were laid across all possible approaches. The ordnance stores of the island were searched to provide increased firepower for the 4th Marines,[17] and guns were sited to insure that any landing force would be caught in a murderous crossfire if it attempted to reach shore.

The thoroughness of the regiment's preparations was indicative of its high state of morale. The men manning the beach defenses, and to a lesser extent their comrades in the jungles of Bataan, never completely abandoned hope of rescue and relief until the very last days of their ordeal.[18] Even when General MacArthur was ordered to leave the Philippines to take over a new Allied command in the Southwest Pacific, many men thought that he would return, leading a strong relief force. The senior commanders in the Philippines and the Allied leaders knew the truth, however, and realized that barring a miracle, Luzon was doomed to fall. Only a few key men could be taken out of the trap by submarine, torpedo boat, or

---

[16] Quoted in *USAFFE-USFIP Rept*, 40–41.

[17] One source of beach defense guns was the sub-caliber 37mm's which were used for practice firing by Corregidor's big guns. These were dismounted from the gun tubes and turned over to the Marines. LtGen S. L. Howard interview by HistBr, G–3, HQMC, 26Oct56, hereinafter cited as *Howard Interview*.

[18] Maj T. E. Pulos ltr to CMC, 30Oct56.

plane; the rest had to be left to accept their fate.

On 11 March, the day before MacArthur and his party started the first leg of their journey to Australia, he created a new headquarters, Luzon Force, to control the operations on Bataan and appointed General Wainwright to its command. On 20 March, the War Department notified Wainwright of his promotion to lieutenant general and of the fact that he was to be commander of all forces remaining in the Philippines. To take the place of USAFFE, an area headquarters, United States Forces in the Philippines (USFIP), was created.

To take his place on Bataan, Wainwright appointed the USAFFE Artillery Officer, Major General Edward P. King, Jr. King drew an unenviable task when he took over Luzon Force, for the volume of Japanese preparatory fire on Bataan and on the island forts indicated the start of a major effort. To meet this attack, King had troops who had already spent two weeks on a diet of 3/8 of a ration on top of two months of half rations; they were ready to fight but "with not enough food in their bellies to sustain a dog."[19] The USAFFE Surgeon General, on 18 February, had accounted Bataan's defenders as being only 55% combat efficient as a result of "debilities due to malaria, dysentery, and general malnutrition."[20] These same men were now a month further along on the road to exhaustion and collapse and were destined to meet a fresh and vigorous enemy assault.

[19] *Wainwright's Story*, 76. The ration was cut to 3/8 on 2 March according to *USAFFE–USFIP Rept* entry for that date.

[20] Quoted in Diary of Maj A. C. Tisdelle, Aide to MajGen King, entry of 18Feb42.

THE FALL OF BATAAN [21]

The *Fourteenth Army* set 3 April as D-day for its renewed offensive on Bataan, and General Homma foresaw "no reason why this attack should not succeed."[22] He could well be confident since he had received the infantry replacements needed to rebuild the *16th Division* and the *65th Brigade*, and he had been sent the *4th Division* from Shanghai. In addition, *Imperial Headquarters* had allotted him a strongly reinforced infantry regiment from the *21st Division*, originally slated for duty in Indo-China. His artillery strength had been more than doubled and now included far-ranging 240mm howitzers. Two heavy bomber regiments had been flown up from Malaya to increase materially his mastery of the air.

Once the enemy attack was launched, the pressure on Bataan's defenders was relentless. In less than a week the issue had been decided. The physically weakened Americans and Filipinos tried desperately to stem the Japanese advance, but to no avail. By 7 April the last reserves had been committed. A growing stream of dazed, disorganized men, seeking to escape the incessant bombardment at the front and the onrushing enemy, crowded the roads and trails leading to Mariveles. Only isolated groups of soldiers still fought to hold the Japanese back from the tip of the peninsula. Under these circumstances, General King decided to seek surrender terms. His aide recorded the situation in his diary:

8th [April]. Wednesday. The army can not attack. It is impossible. Area is congested with stragglers . . . General King has ordered all

[21] Unless otherwise noted the material in this section is derived from *USAFFE–USFIP Rept; 14th Army Rept; Fall of the Philippines*.

[22] *14th Army Rept*, Appendix 4, 17.

tanks thrown [blown?] and arms destroyed, and is going forward to contact the Japanese and try to avert a massacre.[23]

Near midnight on the 8th a severe earthquake tremor was felt on Corregidor and Bataan, and soon thereafter the Mariveles harbor was shaking violently from manmade explosions, as King's orders to destroy all munitions dumps were carried out. To an observer on The Rock it seemed that:

> ... the southern end of Bataan was a huge conflagration which resembled more than anything else a volcano in violent eruption ... white hot pieces of metal from exploded shells and bombs shot skyward by the thousands in every conceivable direction. Various colored flares exploded in great numbers and charged off on crazy courses much the same as a sky rocket which has run wild on the ground.[24]

All night long the water between Bataan and Corregidor was lashed with falling debris and fragments from the explosions. Through this deadly shower a procession of small craft dodged its way to the north dock of Bottomside. Everything that could float was pressed into use by frantic refugees. Some of the arrivals, however, such as the nurses from Bataan's hospitals, were under orders to report to Corregidor. Specific units that could strengthen The Rock's garrison, antiaircraft batteries and the 45th Philippine Scout Regiment, had also been called for. Only the AAA gunners from the Mariveles area, including the 4th Marines' Battery C, managed to escape. The Scout regiment was prevented from reaching the harbor in time by the jammed condition of the roads.

By noon on 9 April, General King had found out that no terms would be given him; the Japanese demanded unconditional surrender. With thousands of his men lying wounded and sick in open air general hospitals and all hope of successful resistance gone, King accepted the inevitable and surrendered, asking only that his men be given fair treatment. The battle for Bataan had ended, and more than 75,000 gallant men began the first of more than a thousand days of brutal captivity.

---

[23] Tisdelle, *op. cit.*

[24] LCdr T. C. Parker, "The Epic of Corregidor-Bataan, December 24, 1941–May 4, 1942," *USNI Proceedings*, January 1943, 18, hereinafter cited as *Parker*.

CHAPTER 8

The Siege and Capture of Corregidor

THE JAPANESE PLANS[1]

On 9 April the victorious *Fourteenth Army* paused on the shore of Bataan with its next target—Corregidor—dead center in its sights. Many enemy staff officers, both in Tokyo and on Luzon, wanted to launch an immediate amphibious attack, taking advantage of the army's success on Bataan. The dearth of landing craft in Manila Bay, however, effectively served to postpone the operation. Most of the Japanese landing barges and boats were located in Lingayen Gulf or Subic Bay and had to be moved past Corregidor's guns to the designated staging areas on the eastern coast of Bataan. (See Map 8, Map Section)

On the night of 14 April the first small group of boats slipped by The Rock, hugging Bataan's shore while the enemy shelled and bombed the island's north coast to prevent their discovery.[2] Because they were forced to follow this method of moving a few boats at a time and these only at night and behind a curtain of protective fire, the Japanese took more than three weeks to assemble the necessary assault craft.

The need for extreme caution in making the risky passage into Manila Bay was not the only factor which acted against rapid execution of the Japanese assault plan. In mid-April a severe outbreak of malaria in the ranks of the *4th Division*, Homma's chosen landing force, severely hampered attack preparations, but amphibious training and rehearsals continued despite the temporary decrease in the division's effective strength. Emergency supplies of quinine tablets were flown to Luzon in time to check the spread of the disease and restore fighting trim.

The *Fourteenth Army* was obsessed, with the need for deception and secrecy and stringent security measures were taken to conceal the preparations for the attack on Corregidor. A consistent effort was made to create the impression that Cavite Province was the Japanese amphibious base and that Forts Frank and Drum were the targets. Landing craft maneuvered off Cavite's shores while the army's air and artillery pounded the defenses of the southern islands. Two battalions of the *16th Division* feigned preparations for an attack on Frank and Drum, but there was little doubt at USFIP Headquarters that Corregidor was the primary Japanese objective.

Every day in April, starting with the day Bataan fell, an increasingly heavier concentration of enemy artillery pieces found firing positions in the peninsula's jungled hills. At least thirty-seven batteries, whose weapons ranged from 75mm mountain guns to 240mm howitzers, covered Corregidor with a continuous pattern of fire that reached every position and knocked out the major portion of the

---

[1] Unless otherwise noted the material in this section is derived from *14th Army Rept; Philippine AirOpsRec; Fall of the Philippines.*

[2] *4th Mar Jnl,* 374.

island's defenses.[3] Nine Japanese bombing squadrons, capitalizing on the gradual weakening of antiaircraft fire, were overhead to add their bombardment to the attack preparation.

The enemy *4th Division* was reinforced for the assault with two independent engineer regiments to man the transport and support landing craft as well as a tank regiment and three mortar battalions to provide additional firepower. The actual landing operation was to be made in two stages with Colonel Gempachi Sato's *61st Infantry Regiment* (two infantry battalions, a tank company, a mountain artillery battery, and mortar units) designated the initial assault force. Sato was to land his unit in successive waves, battalions a b r e a s t along the beaches between Infantry and Cavalry Points on the night of 5 May. After establishing a beachhead, he was to send most of his men against Malinta Hill while the remainder of the regiment drove across the tail of the island to isolate and contain the defenders east of Infantry Point. The plan called for the *61st Regiment* to be in possession of Malinta Hill by dawn, ready to support a second landing.

Twenty-four hours after Sato's force landed, the division's main assault effort would strike beaches between Morrison and Battery Points, near James Ravine, and at the neck of the island. This second landing force, four heavily reinforced infantry battalions, would have the assistance of Sato's unit which was scheduled to make a concurrent attack against Ramsay Battery hill. Throughout the whole operation the artillery on Bataan, operating under army control, was to deliver preparatory and supporting fires, and in daylight hours the army's air squadrons were to fly close support missions.

The *4th Division* had three infantry battalions in reserve for its attack but did not expect that they would be needed. The Japanese were confident that their preparatory bombardment had knocked most of the fight out of Corregidor. Every terrain feature on the island was plotted and registered on artillery target maps and any signal for support from the assault forces would call down a smother of accurate fire on the defenders. The enemy felt certain that dusk of 7 May would see their assault troops in control of Corregidor.

LIFE ON A BULL'S EYE [4]

During the 27 days between the fall of Bataan and the assault on Corregidor, life on The Rock became a living hell. The men in the open gun pits and exposed beach defenses were subjected to an increasing rain of shells and bombs. It became virtually impossible to move about the

---

[3] Many survivors and a number of accounts of this siege credit the Japanese with having as many as 400 artillery pieces firing on the fortified islands by 5 May. The figure of 37 batteries (approximately 150 pieces) represents only the enemy artillery units listed in *14th Army Rept*, 187 as part of the Corregidor attack organization.

[4] Unless otherwise noted the material in this section is derived from *USAFFE-USFIP Rept; Moore Rept; 4th Mar Jnl; Hayes Rept;* Capt C. B. Brook, USN, Personal Experiences 8Apr–6 May 56, n.d., hereinafter cited as *Brook;* Maj H. E. Dalness, USA, "The Operations of the 4th Battalion (Provisional) 4th Marine Regiment in the Final Counterattack in the Defense of Corregidor 5–6 May 1942," AdvInfOff Course 1949–50, The InfSch, Ft. Benning, Ga., hereinafter cited as *Dalness; Ferguson; Jenkins;* 1stLt O. E. Saalman, USA, Personal Experiences 12Apr–6May42, n.d., hereinafter cited as *Saalman.*

AERIAL VIEW OF CORREGIDOR ISLAND *showing in the foreground the area of the battle between the Japanese landing force and the 4th Marines.* (SC 200883-S)

EFFECT OF JAPANESE BOMBARDMENT OF CORREGIDOR *is shown in this photograph taken the day after the surrender near the main entrance to Malinta Hill.* (SC 282343)

island by daylight; enemy artillery spotters aloft in observation balloons on Bataan and in planes overhead had a clear view of their targets. The dense vegetation which had once covered most of Corregidor was stripped away by blast and fragmentation to reveal the dispositions of Howard's command. The tunnels through Malinta Hill, their laterals crowded with headquarters installations and hospital beds, offered refuge for only a fraction of the 11,000-man garrison and the rest of the defenders had to stick it out with little hope of protection from the deadly downpour.

Most of the escapees from Bataan were ordered to join the 4th Marines, thus adding 72 officers and 1,173 enlisted men to its strength between 9 and 12 April.[5] The majority of the Army combat veterans, however, "were in such poor physical condition that they were incapable of even light work,"[6] and had to be hospitalized. The mixed collection of infantry, artillery, aviation, and service personnel from both American and Philippine units assigned to the beach defense battalions was in little better shape than the men who had been committed to the hospital under Malinta Hill. The commander of 1/4's reserve, First Lieutenant Robert F. Jenkins, Jr., who received a typical contingent of Bataan men to augment his small force commented that he:

... had never seen men in such poor physical condition. Their clothing was ragged and stained from perspiration and dirt. Their gaunt, unshaven faces were strained and emaciated. Some of them were already suffering from beriberi as a result of a starvation diet of rice for weeks. We did what we could for them and then put them to work on the beach defenses.[7]

The sailors from Mariveles, mostly crewmen from the now-scuttled *Canopus*, were kept together and formed into a new 275-man reserve battalion for the regiment, the 4th Battalion, 4th Marines.[8] Not only was the designation of 4/4 unusual, but so was its makeup and its personnel. Only six Marines served in the battalion: its commander, **Major Francis H. Williams**, and five NCOs. The staff, company commanders, and platoon leaders were drawn from the nine Army and 18 Navy officers assigned to assist Williams.[9] The four rifle companies were designated Q, R, S, and T, the highest lettered companies the men had ever heard of. Another boast of the bluejackets turned Marines was that they were "the highest paid battalion in the world, as most of the men

---

[5] The former sergeant major of 2/4 believes that the regiment joined substantially more men than this figure which appears in the regimental journal. He recalls that the 2d Bn "picked up for rations, and on the crudest rolls, at least 600 men" and believes that the other battalions did the same. *Jackson*.

[6] *Wainwright's Story*, 87.

[7] *Jenkins*, 13.

[8] Most survivors of 4/4 refer to the battalion as having had approximately 500 men in its ranks. Strength breakdowns of the 4th Mar exist up through 1May42, however, and nowhere do they support the larger figure. The S-3 of 4/4 is certain that the total strength of the battalion on 6 May was no more than 350 men. Maj O. E. Saalman ltr to CMC, 22Oct56, hereinafter cited as *Saalman 1956*.

[9] Survivors of 4/4 are unable to agree on the identity of the man who served as ExO of the battalion; at least five Army or Navy officers have been mentioned. In addition, the possibility that a Marine who was closely connected with 4/4 was *de facto* ExO was brought out by one of the NCOs who recalls that "Major Williams always considered Gunner Joe Reardon [QMClk Joseph J. Reardon] as his Executive Officer and Adjutant." MSgt K. W. Mize ltr to CMC, 1Nov56.

were petty officers of the upper pay grades." [10]

The new organization went into bivouac in Government Ravine as part of the regimental reserve. The reserve had heretofore consisted of men from the Headquarters and Service Companies, reinforced by Philippine Air cadets and Marines from Bataan. Major Max W. Schaeffer, who had replaced Major King as reserve commander, had organized this force of approximately 250 men into two tactical companies, O and P. Company O was commanded by Captain Robert Chambers, Jr. and Company P by Lieutenant Hogaboom; the platoons were led by Marine warrant officers and senior NCOs.

A good part of Schaeffer's men had primary duties connected with regimental supply and administration, but each afternoon the companies assembled in the bivouac area where the troops were instructed in basic infantry tactics and the employment of their weapons. Despite the constant interruptions of air raids and shellings, the Marines and Filipinos had a chance "to get acquainted with each other, familiarize themselves with each others' voices, and to learn [the] teamwork" [11] so essential to effective combat operations. Frequently, Major Schaeffer conducted his company and platoon commanders on reconnaissance of beach defenses so that the reserve leaders would be familiar with routes of approach and terrain in each sector in which they might fight.

While Schaeffer's unit had had some time to train before the Japanese stepped up their bombardment of the island in late March, Williams' battalion was organized at the inception of the period of heaviest enemy fire and spent part of every day huddled in foxholes dug along the trail between Geary Point and Government Ravine. [12] Any let-up in the bombardment would be the signal for small groups of men to gather around the Army officers and Marine NCOs for instruction in the use of their weapons and the tactics of small units. Rifles were zeroed in on floating debris in the bay and for most of the men this markmanship training was their first since Navy boot camp. When darkness limited Japanese shelling to harassment and interdiction fires, the sailors formed eager audiences for the Army Bataan veterans who gave them a resumé of enemy battle tactics. Every man was dead serious, knowing that his chances for survival depended to a large extent upon how much he learned. "The chips were down; there was no horseplay." [13]

To a very great extent the record of the 4th Battalion in the fighting on Corregidor was a tribute to the inspirational leadership of its commander. During the trying period under enemy shellfire and bombing when the battalion's character was molded, Major Williams seemed to be omnipresent; wherever the bombardment was heaviest, he showed up to see how his men were weathering the storm. When on separate occasions Battery Crockett and then Battery Geary were hit and set afire, he led rescue parties from 4/4 into the resulting holocausts of flame, choking smoke, and exploding ammunition to rescue the wounded. He seemed to have

---

[10] *Brook*, 1.
[11] *Ferguson*, 10.

[12] Dr. C. E. Chunn ltr to CMC, 12Nov56, hereinafter cited as *Chunn*.
[13] *Dalness*, 7.

an utter disregard for his own safety in the face of any need for his presence. Survivors of his battalion agree with startling unanimity that he was a giant among men at a time when courage was commonplace.

Raw courage was a necessity on the fortified islands after Bataan's fall, since there was no defiladed position that could not be reached by Japanese 240mm howitzers firing from Cavite and Bataan. The bombers overhead, increasingly bold as gun after gun of the antiaircraft defenses was knocked out, came down lower to pinpoint targets. Counterbattery and antiaircraft fire silenced some enemy guns and accounted for a number of planes, but nothing seemed to halt the buildup of preparatory fires.

On 28 April Howard issued a warning to his battalions that the next day would be a rough one. It was the Emperor's birthday and the Japanese could be expected to "celebrate by unusual aerial and artillery bombardment."[14] The colonel's prophecy proved to be a true one, and on the 29th one observer noted that even "the kitchen sink came over."[15] The birthday celebration marked the beginning of a period when the enemy bombarded the islands without letup, day and night. The men manning the beach defenses of Corregidor's East Sector found it:

... practically impossible to get any rest or to repair any damage to our positions and barbed wire. Our field telephone system was knocked out; our water supply was ruined (drinking water had to be hauled from the other end of the island in large powder cans) ... Corregidor was enveloped in a cloud of smoke, dust, and the continuous roar of bursting shells and bombs.

There were many more casualties than we had suffered in the previous five months.[16]

About three days prior to the Japanese landing, Lieutenant Colonel Beecher reported to Colonel Howard that defensive installations in the 1st Battalion's sector were:

... practically destroyed. Very little defensive wire remained, tank traps constructed with great difficulty had been rendered useless, and all my weapons were in temporary emplacements as the original emplacements had been destroyed. I told Colonel Howard at this time that I was very dubious as to my ability to withstand a landing attack in force. Colonel Howard reported the facts to General Wainwright, who, according to Colonel Howard, said that he would never surrender. I pointed out to Colonel Howard that I had said nothing about surrender but that I was merely reporting the facts as it was my duty to do.[17]

The increase in the fury of the Japanese bombardment with the coming of May, coupled with the frequent sightings of landing craft along the eastern shore of Bataan, clearly pointed to the imminence of an enemy landing attempt. The last successful effort to evacuate personnel from the island forts was made on the night of 3 May. The submarine *Spearfish* surfaced after dark outside the mine fields off Corregidor and took on a party of officers and nurses who had been ordered out, as well as a load of important USFIP records and a roster of every person still alive on the islands.[18] The 4th Marines

---

[14] *4th Mar Jnl*, 392.
[15] *Parker*, 20.

[16] *Jenkins*, 15–16.
[17] BriGen C. T. Beecher ltr to Mr. G. J. Berry, 17Mar50 (deposited by Capt G. J. Berry, USMCR, in the USMC Archives, 30Oct56).
[18] Submarines were the beleaguered garrison's only contact with Allied bases outside the Philippines during most of the siege. Although the subs brought in rations, antiaircraft ammunition, and medical supplies on scattered occasions, the

sent out their regimental journal, its last entry, dated 2 May, the list of the five men who had been killed and the nine who had been wounded during the day's bombardment.

To one of the lucky few who got orders to leave on the *Spearfish* the receding island looked "beaten and burnt to a crisp." [19] In one day, 2 May, USFIP estimated that 12 240mm shells a minute had fallen on Corregidor during a five-hour period. On the same day the Japanese flew 55 sorties over the islands dropping 12 1,000-pound, 45 500-pound, and 159 200-pound bombs.[20] The damage was extensive. Battery Geary's eight 12-inch mortars were completely destroyed as was one of Battery Crockett's two 12-inch guns. The enemy fire also knocked out of action two more 12-inch mortars, a 3-inch gun, three searchlights, five 3-inch and three .50 caliber antiaircraft guns, and a height finder. Data transmission cables to the guns were cut in many places and all communication lines were damaged. The beach defenses lost four machine guns, a 37mm, and a pillbox; barbed wire, mine fields, and antiboat obstacles were torn apart.

The logical landing points for an assault against Corregidor, the entire East Sector and the ravines that gave access to Topside and Middleside, received a special working over so steady and deadly that the effectiveness of the beach defenses was sharply reduced. Casualties mounted as the men's foxholes, trenches, and shelters crumbled under the fire. Unit leaders checking the state of the defenses were especially vulnerable to the fragments of steel which swept the ground bare. By the Japanese-appointed X-Day (5 May) the 1st Battalion had lost the commander of Company A, Major Harry C. Lang, and Captain Paul A. Brown, commanding Company B, had been hospitalized as a result of severe concussion suffered during an enemy bombing attack.[21] Three Army officers attached to the Reserve Company, an officer of Company B, and another of Company D had all been severely wounded.

Despite the damage to defenses it had so laboriously constructed, the 4th Marines was ready, indeed almost eager, to meet a Japanese assault after days and weeks of absorbing punishment without a chance to strike back. On the eve of a battle which no one doubted was coming, the regiment was perhaps the most unusual Marine unit ever to take the field. From an understrength two-battalion regiment of less than 800 Marine regulars it had grown until it mustered almost 4,000 officers and men drawn from all the services and 142 different organizations.[22] Its ranks contained 72 Marine officers and 1,368 enlisted

---

amount that they could carry was only enough for stop-gap relief. For the interesting story of the diversified submarine actions in support of USAFFE-USFIP see, T. Roscoe, *United States Submarine Operations in World War II* (Annapolis: U. S. Naval Institute, 1949), 23–39.

[19] *Parker*, 22.

[20] *Philippine AirOpsRec*, Plate 8.

[21] Beecher ltr to Berry, *op. cit.*

[22] The last complete contemporary breakdown of strength of the 4th Mar by component units is contained in *4th Mar Jnl*, 390. It was corrected through 1 May. A slightly earlier list dated 28Apr42, detached from the journal book but unmistakably once part of it, has an interesting appendix which gives the units from which attached personnel originated. It shows that 26 Navy, 104 American and Philippine Army, 9 Philippine Scout, and 3 Philippine Constabulary organizations furnished men to the 4th Mar.

Marines, 37 Navy officers [23] and 848 bluejackets, and 111 American and Philippine Air Corps, Army, Scout, and Constabulary officers with 1,455 of their men.

The units that actually met the Japanese at the beaches—1/4, 4/4, and the regimental reserve—had such a varied makeup that it deserves to be recorded: [24]

Service component	HqCo		SerCo		1st Bn		4th Bn	
	Off	Enl	Off	Enl	Off	Enl	Off	Enl
USMC & USMCR	14	80	6	63	16	344	1	5
USN (MC & DC)	3	7		1	3	13	2	6
USN	1	16		1	1	78	16	262
USNR		21				30		
USA	1		1		26	286	9	2
Philippine Insular Navy		4						
Philippine Army Air Corps	6	83			7	217		
Philippine Scouts						33		
Philippine Army						22		
Philippine Constabulary					1	1		
Totals	25	211	7	65	53	1,024	28	275

THE JAPANESE LANDING [25]

The area chosen by the Japanese for their initial assault, the 4th Marines' East Sector, was a shambles by nightfall on 5 May. Two days earlier the regimental intelligence journal had noted that:

> There has been a distinct shifting of enemy artillery fire from inland targets to our beach defenses on the north side of Corregidor the past 24 hours.[26]

This concentration of fire continued and intensified, smashing the last vestiges of a coordinated and cohesive defensive zone and shaping 1/4's beach positions into an irregular series of strong points where a few machine guns and 37mm's were still in firing order. A pair of Philippine Scout-manned 75mm guns, located just

---

[23] The five Marine officers, two Navy doctors, and 96 Marine enlisted men previously captured in China and on Bataan have been omitted from these figures.

[24] The 1May42 listing of regimental strength does not indicate the tactical breakdown of Hq and SerCos into Cos O and P. The figures shown, therefore, include a number of regimental staff officers, probably two-thirds of the total, and a few enlisted men who did not serve in Maj Schaeffer's command. One officer and five enlisted men have been deducted from SerCo's USMC Strength and added to that of 4/4.

[25] Unless otherwise noted the material in this section is derived from *USAFFE-USFIP Rept; Moore Rept; 14th Army Rept; Howard Rept;* MG H. M. Ferrell, Personal Experiences 5-6 May42, n. d., hereinafter cited as *Ferrell; Jenkins;* H. W. Baldwin, "The Fourth Marines at Corregidor," *MC Gazette,* in 4 parts November 1946–February 1947, hereinafter cited as *Baldwin Narrative; Fall of the Philippines;* K. Uno, *Corregidor: Isle of Delusion* (China: Press Bureau, Imperial Japanese Army Headquarters, September 1942) (located at OCMH), hereinafter cited as *Isle of Delusion.*

[26] 4th Mar R-2 Jnl, 8Dec41–3May42, last entry.

east of North Point, which had never revealed their position, also escaped the destructive fires. Wire lines to command posts were ripped apart and could not be repaired; "command could be exercised and intelligence obtained only by use of foot messengers, which medium was uncertain under the heavy and continuous artillery and air bombardment."[27]

Along the northern side of the hogback ridge that traced its course from Malinta Hill to the bend in Corregidor's tail, Company A and the reserves of 1/4 waited doggedly for the Japanese to come. There was no sharp division between unit defense sectors, and the men of the various units intermingled as the bombardment demolished prepared positions. Along the battered base and sides of Malinta Hill, a special target for enemy fire, were the men of Lieutenant Jenkins' Reserve Company. Next to them, holding the shoreline up to Infantry Point, was a rifle platoon organized from 1/4's Headquarters Company; Captain Lewis H. Pickup, the company commander, held concurrent command of Company A, having taken over on the death of Major Lang. The 1st Platoon under First Lieutenant William F. Harris defended the beaches from Infantry to Cavalry Points, the landing site selected in Japanese pre-assault plans. Master Gunnery Sergeant John Mercurio's 2d Platoon's positions rimmed the gentle curve of land from Cavalry to North Point. Extending from North Point to the tip of the island's tail were the foxholes and machine-gun emplacements of First Sergeant Noble W. Well's 3d Platoon.

Positions along the top of the steep southern face of the East Sector's dominant ridge were occupied by the platoons of Company B under First Lieutenant Alan S. Manning, who had taken over when Captain Brown was wounded.[28] The machine guns and 37mm's of Captain Noel O. Castle's Company D were emplaced in commanding positions along the beaches on both sides of the island; the company's mortars were in firing positions near Malinta Hill.

At about 2100 on 5 May, sensitive sound locators on Corregidor picked up the noise of many barges warming up their motors near Limay on Bataan's east coast. Warning of an impending landing was flashed to responsible higher headquarters, but the lack of wire communication kept the word from reaching the men in the foxholes along the beaches of the East Sector. They did not need any additional advice of enemy intentions anyway, since the whole regiment had been on an all-out alert every night for a month, momentarily expecting Japanese landing barges to loom out of the darkness. The men of 1/4 had withstood some pretty stiff shellings, too, as they waited, but nothing to compare with the barrage that began falling on the beach defenses manned by Harris' 1st Platoon at about 2245.

The Japanese had begun to deliver the short preparatory bombardment designed to cover the approach of Colonel Sato's assault waves which was called for in their operation plan. If Sato's boat groups adhered to their schedule they would rendezvous and head in for the beaches just as the artillery fire lifted and shifted to the west, walling off the landing area from American reinforcement efforts. The regiment would be ashore before the moon rose near midnight to give Corregidor's gunners a clear target. In two respects the

---

[27] *USAFFE-USFIP Rept*, 77.

[28] LtCol R. F. Jenkins ltr to CMC, 30Oct56.

plan miscarried, and for a while it was touch and go for the assault troops.

The artillery shoot went off on schedule, but Sato's first waves, transporting most of his *1st Battalion*, were carried by an unexpectedly strong incoming tide hundreds of yards to the east of the designated landing beaches. Guides in the oncoming craft were unable to recognize landmarks in the darkness, and from water level the tail of the island looked markedly uniform as smoke and dust raised by the shelling obscured the shoreline. The *61st Regiment's 2d Battalion*, slated to follow close on the heels of the *1st*, was delayed and disrupted by faulty boat handling and tide currents until it came in well out of position and under the full light of the moon.

When the Japanese preparatory fires lifted shortly after 2300, the troops along the East Sector beaches spotted the scattered landing craft of the *1st Battalion, 61st* heading in for the beaches at North Point. The few remaining searchlights illuminated the barges, and the island's tail erupted with fire. Enemy artillery knocked out the searchlights almost as soon as they showed themselves; but it made little difference, since streams of tracer bullets from beach defense machine guns furnished enough light for the Scout 75's near North Point and 1/4's 37's to find targets. A Japanese observer on Bataan described the resulting scene as "sheer massacre,"[29] but the enemy *1st Battalion* came in close enough behind its preparation to get a good portion of its men ashore. Although the Japanese infantrymen overwhelmed Mercurio's 2d Platoon, the fighting was fierce and the enemy casualties in the water and on the beach were heavy. Colonel Sato, who landed with the first waves, sorely needed his *2d Battalion's* strength.

This straggling battalion which began heading shoreward about midnight suffered much more damage than the first waves. The remaining coast defense guns and mortars on Corregidor, backed up by the fire of Forts Hughes and Drum, churned the channel between Bataan and Corregidor into a surging froth, whipped by shell fragments and explosions. The moon's steady light revealed many direct hits on barges and showed heavily burdened enemy soldiers struggling in the water and sinking under the weight of their packs and equipment. Still, some men reached shore and Colonel Sato was able to organize a drive toward his objective, Malinta Hill.

Individual enemy soldiers and machinegun crews infiltrated across Kindley Field and through the rubble of torn barbed wire, blasted trees, and crater-pocked ground to Denver Battery, a sandbagged antiaircraft gun position which stood on relatively high ground south of Cavalry Point. The American gunners, whose weapons were out of action as a result of the bombardment, were unable to beat back the encroaching Japanese who established themselves in a commanding position with fields of fire over the whole approach route to the landing beaches. Captain Pickup's first word that the Japanese had seized Denver Battery came when he sent one of Company D's weapons platoon leaders, Marine Gunner Harold M. Ferrell, to establish contact with the battery's defenders. Ferrell and one of his men found the battery alive with enemy soldiers digging in and setting up automatic weapons. Ferrell immediately went back to his defense area west of Infantry Point and

---

[29] Quoted in *Isle of Delusion*, 17.

brought up some men to establish a line "along the hogsback to prevent the enemy from coming down on the backs of the men on the beaches." [30]

Pickup came up shortly after Gunner Ferrell got his men into position and considered pulling Lieutenant Harris' platoon out of its beach defenses to launch an attack against the enemy. After a conference with Harris the company commander decided to leave the 1st Platoon in position. Japanese landing craft were still coming in, and the platoon's withdrawal would leave several hundred yards of beach open. The fact that enemy troops were ashore had been communicated to Lieutenant Colonel Beecher's CP just inside Malinta Tunnel's east entrance, and small groups of men, a squad or so at a time, were coming up to build on the line in front of Denver Battery. The enemy now fired his machine guns steadily, and intermittent but heavy shellfire struck all along the roads from Malinta to Denver. Casualties were severe throughout the area.

By 0130 surviving elements of 1/4 on the eastern tip of the island were cut off completely from the rest of the battalion. Beecher was forced to leave men in position on both shores west of Denver Battery to prevent the enemy landing behind his lines. All the men who could be spared from the beaches were being sent up to the defensive position astride the ridgeline just west of Denver, but the strength that could be assembled there amounted to little more than two platoons including a few Philippine Scouts from the silenced antiboat guns in 1/4's sector. No exact figures reveal how many Japanese were ashore at this time or how many casualties the *61st Infantry*'s assault companies had suffered, but it was plain that the enemy at Denver Battery outnumbered the small force trying to contain them, and Japanese snipers and infiltrating groups soon began to crop up in the rear of Pickup's position.

The situation clearly called for the commitment of additional men in the East Sector. Colonel Howard had made provision for this soon after getting word of the landing attempt. He alerted Schaeffer's command of two companies first, but held off committing Williams' battalion until the situation clarified itself. There was no guarantee that the Japanese would accommodate the 4th Marines by landing all their troops in the East Sector; in fact, there was a general belief among the men manning the defenses which commanded the ravines leading to Topside that the East Sector landing was not the main effort and that the enemy would be coming in against West and Middle Sector beaches.[31] Complicating the entire problem of command in the confused situation during the early morning hours of 6 May was the fact that only runners could get word of battle progress to Beecher's and Howard's CP. And any runner, or for that matter any man, who tried to make the 1,000-yard journey from the Denver line to the mouth of Malinta Tunnel stood a good chance of never completing his mission. The area east of Malinta Hill was a killing ground as Schaeffer's men soon found out when they made their bid to reach Denver Battery.

---

[30] *Ferrell*, 1.

[31] *Hayes Rept*, Statement of LCdr E. M. Wade, 65. The *general* existence of this belief was questioned by one survivor. *Jackson*.

THE COMMITMENT OF THE RESERVE [32]

In Government Ravine the 4th Marines' reserve companies saw and heard the machine guns along the East Sector beaches hammering at the Japanese landing craft. Major Schaeffer's command was already standing by to move out, and near 2400 Companies O and P filed down the trail and started for Malinta. There was little confusion, for the men had rehearsed their movements often. Crossing Bottomside by means of a tank trap which protected them from enemy shellfire, they moved into Malinta Tunnel where company and platoon commanders supervised the distribution of machine-gun ammunition and grenades cached there for just such an emergency. Volunteers from the Navy and Marine headquarters installations joined the companies to serve as ammunition carriers "although they were neither officially or morally obligated to do so." [33]

Major Schaeffer reported to Colonel Howard and received his instructions; he was to take his men out into the East Sector and counterattack the Japanese posision. At 0200 the companies began to move out of the oppressive heat and foul air of the crowded main tunnel onto the deeply cratered roads which led to Denver.[34] Lieutenant Hogaboom's Company P was in the lead, following the left fork of the road behind its guide, Captain Golland L. Clark, Jr., the 1st Battalion Adjutant. As the last platoon of the company cleared the tunnel it was diverted to a vicious fire fight raging on the right of the Marine line by an officer who had come back seeking reinforcements. Several enemy machine guns had been set up near the base of a stone water tower forward of Denver Battery and to the right front of the Marine positions. The platoon, in common with most of the rest of the units that tried to reduce this strong point, was chopped to pieces by interlocking bands of machine-gun fire.

On Clark's order, Hogaboom deployed his remaining two platoons in line of skirmishers once they were well clear of the tunnel. The advancing line made contact with Lieutenant Harris and the remnants of Company A's 1st Platoon holding the left of the Denver defensive position and tied in with them. Hogaboom found that his right flank was open; Captain Chambers' Company O which was to have followed him out of the tunnel and come up on his right was not to be found.

Chambers' men had left the tunnel all right, but almost immediately after the company column cleared the entrance bright flares were seen going up over the Japanese position. Chambers and his 1st Platoon leader, Quartermaster Clerk Frank W. Ferguson, concluding that the flares were a signal to the artillery on Bataan, passed the word along the line to look for the nearest shelter. The guess on

---

[32] Unless otherwise noted the material in this section is derived from *USAFFE-USFIP Rept; 14th Army Rept; Howard Rept; Ferguson; Ferrell; Hogaboom; Jenkins; Baldwin Narrative; Isle of Delusion; Fall of the Philippines.*

[33] *Ferguson,* 14.

[34] By the time the Japanese landed, the only road into the East Sector was that which led through Malinta Tunnel. The road cut out of the side of the hill on the north had been completely demolished, and Col Howard, looking for an alternate route of approach, had discovered shortly before the landing that enemy artillery had blown a deep, ravine-like depression in the southern circling road that rendered it impassable to organized troop movement. *Howard Interview.*

the flares was right, and Ferguson's platoon was fortunate in taking its shelling in an area where the Japanese had provided deep bomb craters. The platoon came through with only eight casualties. As soon as the bombardment lifted, Ferguson moved toward Denver until he was forced to deploy by heavy machine-gun and mortar fire. He looked for the 3d Platoon to come up on his right according to plan, but only its commander, Quartermaster Sergeant John E. Haskin, and five men appeared, the rest had been lost in the shelling. Captain Chambers sent up the reserve platoon, which was in even worse shape, having been caught in the open near the tunnel entrance. Quartermaster Clerk Herman L. Snellings had only four survivors alive and unwounded.

Company O now contained but one platoon and had not yet made its attack.

Major Schaeffer established control over the scattered groups of men from the 1st Battalion and the reserve and launched three separate counterattacks on the dug-in Japanese. Sometimes the men would get up the slopes leading to the battery gun pits, but they were always driven back, fewer in number each time. On the right flank, Sergeant Major John H. Sweeney and Sergeant Haskin took advantage of the water tower's battered elevation to hurl grenades down on the machine guns that were holding up the advance; Haskin was killed trying to get more grenades up to Sweeney, and Sweeney was picked off after he had knocked out at least one of the guns. Ferguson, who knew and had served with both these long-time regulars, wrote their simple epitaph:

> They were very close friends in life and it was most fitting that they should go out together.[35]

Many close friends died that morning in the darkness and choking dust as the Japanese and the Americans and Filipinos faced each other from positions less than forty yards apart. Some men cut off behind the enemy lines still kept firing at occasional landing craft that were coming in to reinforce Sato. Hogaboom could see the tracers of a single .50 caliber and felt that "the bullets smacking into the armor of the barges sounded like rivet hammers rattling away."[36] Every movement of the Japanese boats which stood in number offshore was counted as an attempt at landing, although many of them were improvised gunboats whose mission was protecting and supporting the landing craft. But detachments of Sato's force kept coming in all night, and one enemy lieutenant, probably a member of one of the *61st's* supporting units, gave a vivid description of the helpless feeling of the men in the barges as they were caught in Corregidor's fire:

> American high powered machine guns poured a stream of bullets on us from all directions. Rifle fire added to the hail of death. Our men who were huddled in the center of the boat were all either killed or wounded. Those who clung to the sides were hit by shells that pierced the steel plating. The boat had already sprung several leaks when we finally came within landing distance of Corregidor. Desperately I gave the signal and led the charge against the shore defenses. I don't remember how many men responded. I know I heard only a small chorus. In that mad dash for shore many were drowned as they dropped into the water mortally wounded. Many were killed outright . . . . If it had not been for the fact that it was the dark hour before the dawn, pitch black, I doubt if any of us would be alive today to tell the story.[37]

However heavy the Japanese casualties were, they did not measurably weaken the

---

[35] *Ferguson*, 18.

[36] *Hogaboom*, 16.
[37] Quoted in *Isle of Delusion*, 34.

firepower of the Denver position. Each attack by Schaeffer's men thinned the Marine line still more. Lost were officers and NCOs whose leadership was vital to the operations of mixed units such as those which held the Japanese at bay. Captain Castle of Company D was killed trying to silence a machine gun, and many small unit leaders who still held their place in line were badly wounded. The situation was so desperate that Colonel Howard could no longer hold his last reserves out of the action. He ordered the 4th Battalion to move into the East Sector and join the embattled defense line.

THE 4TH BATTALION IN ACTION [38]

Major Williams' 4th Battalion had been alerted early in the night's action, and he had ordered the issue of extra ammunition and grenades. At about 0100 he got the word to move the battalion into Malinta Tunnel and stand by. The sailors proceeded cautiously down the south shore road, waited for an enemy barrage which was hitting in the dock area to lift, and then dashed across to the tunnel entrance. In the sweltering corridor the men pressed back against the walls as hundreds of casualties, walking wounded and litter cases, streamed in from the East Sector fighting. The hospital laterals were filled to overflowing, and the doctors, nurses, and corpsmen tended to the stricken men wherever they could find room to lay a man down. At 0430, Colonel Howard ordered Williams to take his battalion out of the tunnel and attack the Japanese at Denver Battery.

The companies moved out in column. About 500 yards out from Malinta they were caught in a heavy shelling that sharply reduced their strength and temporarily scattered the men. The survivors reassembled and moved toward the fighting in line of skirmishers. Companies Q and R, commanded by two Army officers, Captains Paul C. Moore and Harold E. Dalness, respectively, moved in on the left to reinforce the scattered groups of riflemen from Companies A and P who were trying to contain the Japanese in the broken ground north of Denver Battery. The battery position itself was assigned to Company T (Lieutenant Bethel B. Otter, USN), and two platoons of Company S,[39] originally designated the battalion reserve, were brought up on the extreme right where Lieutenant Edward N. Little, USN, was to try to silence the enemy machine guns near the water tower. The bluejackets filled in the gaps along the line—wide gaps, for there was little that could be called a firm defensive line left—and joined the fire fight.

The lack of adequate communications prevented Colonel Howard from exercising active tactical direction of the battle in the East Sector. The unit commanders on the ground, first Captain Pickup, then Major Schaeffer, and finally Major Williams made the minute-to-minute decisions that close combat demanded. By the time Williams' battalion had reorganized and moved up into the Marine forward positions, Schaeffer's command was

---

[38] Unless otherwise noted the material in this section is derived from *USAFFE-USFIP Rept; 14th Army Rept; Howard Rept; Brook; Dalness;* SSgt C. E. Downing, Personal Experiences 5–6– May 42, n. d.; *Ferguson; Ferrell; Hogaboom; Jenkins; Baldwin Narrative; Isle of Delusion; Fall of the Philippines.*

[39] *Saalman 1956.*

practically nonexistent. Williams, by mutual consent (Schaeffer was senior), took over command of the fighting since he was in a far better position to get the best effort out of his bluejackets when they attacked.[40]

At dawn Major Williams moved along the front, telling his officers to be ready to jump off at 0615. The company and platoon command posts were right up on the firing line and there were no reserves left; every officer and man still able to stand took part in the attack. On the left the Japanese were driven back 200–300 yards before Williams sent a runner to check the advance of Moore and Dalness; the right of the line had been unable to make more than a few yards before the withering fire of the Denver and water tower defenses drove the men to the deck. The left companies shifted toward Denver to close the gap that had opened while the men on the right tried to knock out the Japanese machine guns and mortars. Lieutenant Otter was killed while leading an attack, and his executive, Captain Calvin E. Chunn, took over; Chunn was wounded soon after as Company T charged a Japanese unit which was setting up a field piece near the water tower.[41] Lieutenant Little was hit in the chest and Williams sent a Philippine Scout officer, First Lieutenant Otis E. Saalman, to take over Company S.

The Marine mortars of 1/4, 3-inch Stokes without sights, were not accurate enough to support Williams' attack. He had to order them to cease fire when stray rounds fell among his own men, who had closed to within grenade range of the Japanese. Robbed of the last supporting weapons that might have opened a breach in the Denver position, the attack stalled completely. Major Schaeffer sent Warrant Officer Ferguson, who had succeeded to command of Company O when Captain Chambers was wounded, to Colonel Howard's CP to report the situation and request reinforcements. Ferguson, like Schaeffer and many of the survivors of 1/4 and the reserve, was a walking wounded case himself. By the time Ferguson got back through the enemy shelling to Malinta at 0900, Williams had received what few reinforcements Howard could muster. Captain Herman H. Hauck and 60 men of the 59th Coast Artillery, assigned by General Moore to the 4th Marines, had come up and Williams sent them to the left flank to block Japanese snipers and machine-gun crews infiltrating along the beaches into the rear areas.

At about 0930 men on the north flank of the Marine line saw a couple of Japanese tanks coming off barges near Cavalry Point, a move that spelled the end on Corregidor. The tanks were in position to advance within a half hour, and, just as the men in front of Denver Battery spotted them, enemy flares went up again and artillery salvoes crashed down just forward of the Japanese position. Some men began to fall back, and though Williams and the surviving leaders tried to halt the withdrawal, the shellfire prevented them from regaining control. At 1030 Williams sent a message to the units on the left flank to fall back to the ruins of a concrete trench which stood just forward of the entrance to Malinta Tunnel. The next thirty minutes witnessed a scene of utter confusion as the Japanese opened up on the retreating men with rifles, mortars, machine guns, and mountain howitzers. Flares signalled

---

[40] Mize ltr, *op. cit.*
[41] *Chunn.*

the artillery on Bataan to increase its fire, and a rolling barrage swung back and forth between Malinta and Denver, demolishing any semblance of order in the ranks of the men straining to reach the dubious shelter of the trench. "Dirt, rocks, trees, bodies, and debris literally filled the air," [42] and pitifully few men made it back to Malinta.

Williams, who was wounded, and roughly 150 officers and men, many of them also casualties, gathered in the trench ruins to make a stand. The Japanese were less than three hundred yards from their position and enemy tanks could be seen moving up to outflank their line on the right. The Marine major, who had been a tower of strength throughout the hopeless fight, went into the tunnel at 1130 to ask Howard for antitank guns and more men. But the battle was over: General Wainwright had made the decision to surrender.

SURRENDER [43]

Colonel Howard had personally reported the landing of the Japanese tanks to General Wainwright at 1000. The USFIP commander, who had kept current on the situation in the East Sector throughout the night's fighting, made the fateful decision to surrender. He later related that "it was the terror that is vested in a tank that was the deciding factor," for he "thought of the havoc that even one of these could wreak if it nosed into the tunnel, where lay our helpless wounded . . ." [44] He did not believe, nor did any other officer he consulted, that the defenses outside Malinta could last more than the remaining hours of the day, and he set the hour of surrender for noon in order "to avoid the horrors which would have accrued had I let the fight go on until dark." [45]

The order to surrender was passed to the troops on Topside and Middleside along with instructions to destroy all weapons larger than .45 caliber. The sickened men of the 4th Marines' 2d and 3d Battalions, who had been forced to stand by helplessly as they heard and watched the battle to the east, carried the order even further, smashing their rifles against the rocks. Veterans of fighting in World War I and a dozen "banana wars" stood unashamedly crying as they were told they would have to surrender. Inside Malinta, Colonel Howard ordered the regimental and national colors of the 4th Marines burned to prevent their falling into enemy hands. Two 1st Battalion officers, Captain Clark and Lieutenant Manning, a field music, and an interpreter were selected to carry Wainwright's flag of truce to the Japanese. As the white flag was carried out of the tunnel, Major Williams ordered survivors of the East Sector fighting to move inside the hill and take shelter from the Japanese bombardment which still was falling.

Captain Clark's party passed the last American outpost; the music sounded off and Manning waved a pole which bore a piece of sheeting. The enemy infantrymen, who had been given special instructions regarding the reception of flags of truce, did not fire, and Clark was taken to the senior Japanese officer on the island who contacted Bataan and arranged for a parley on the peninsula with General Homma. When Wainwright, accompa-

---

[42] *Dalness*, 18.

[43] Unless otherwise noted the material in this section is derived from *USAFFE-USFIP Rept; 14th Army Rept; Howard Rept; Baldwin Narrative; Fall of the Philippines; Wainwright's Story.*

[44] *Wainwright's Story*, 119.

[45] *Ibid.*, 186.

denied by a few senior officers and aides, walked out of the tunnel and up the long slope toward Kindley Field, he saw dead and dying men on every hand, a grim record of the ferocity of the fighting in the past 12 hours.

No complete figures exist for the casualties suffered by either side on 5–6 May; estimates of the Japanese losses range from 900 to 4,000.[46] The strait between Bataan and Corregidor was heavily dotted with enemy bodies, and American prisoners on Corregidor estimated that they helped collect and cremate the remains of hundreds of Japanese soldiers.[47] The detailed losses of the 4th Marines will probably never be known because of the joint-service nature of the regiment at the time of battle and the scarcity of contemporary records. The casualties of Marines alone are known, however, and they may be considered indicative of the fate of soldiers and sailors who served with them. In the whole Philippine campaign the regiment had 315 officers and men killed, 15 missing in action presumed dead, and 357 men wounded;[48] the great majority of these casualties occurred during the battle for Corregidor.

The bloody battle for the island fortress did not end with Wainwright's decision to surrender. The Japanese went right ahead with their assault plan and preparatory bombardments, paying no heed to the white flags displayed on all the islands in the bay. Eighty-eight tons of bombs were dropped on 6 May, a good part of them after the surrender.[49] Wainwright, who had released his southern Philippine commanders to MacArthur's control before he attempted to meet the enemy commander, tried to surrender only the fortified islands to the Japanese. He was rebuffed coldly by Homma's emissary and told that the Japanese knew that he was commander of all the forces in the Philippines and that they would not accept his surrender unless it meant the capitulation of every man in his command, everywhere in the islands. The American general, convinced that the Japanese would treat the men on the fortified islands as hostages, perhaps even massacre them if the fighting continued in the south, finally acceded to the enemy demand and broadcast a surrender message at midnight on 6 May to all his commanding officers. There was considerable dissension regarding this order, especially on islands where the Japanese had not made much effort to subdue the Philippine Army troops, but eventually most of the organized units of USFIP came out of the hills to lay down their arms. Wainwright felt, as did most of his advisors at the time, that the Japanese were quite capable of slaughtering the men surrendered on the fortified

---

[46] Most American survivors of the battle mention that they heard from the Japanese later in prison camp that the enemy had suffered almost 4,000 casualties in trying to take Corregidor. However, Japanese officers commenting on Dr. Morton's draft manuscript of *The Fall of the Philippines* wrote that the total casualties of the Japanese in the Corregidor operation between 14Apr–7May42 were 903. MilHistSec, SS, GHQ, FEC, Comments of Former Japanese Officers Regarding "The Fall of the Philippines," 19Apr42 (located at OCMH), Chap XXXI, 3.

[47] *Saalman 1956.* Saalman recalls having remarked to Maj Williams shortly after daybreak on 6 May, "I believe we could walk from Corregidor to Bataan over dead bodies." In light of the number of bodies that were collected and cremated, Saalman is convinced that the 903 figure supplied by the Japanese in commenting on the draft of *The Fall of the Philippines* reflects only enemy dead rather than total casualties.

[48] See Appendix D for Marine casualties.

[49] *Philippine AirOpsRec*, Plate 8.

islands if he did not insure a complete surrender of all his forces.

The struggle for control of Manila Bay finally ended on 7 May when the Japanese occupied the last of the island forts, but for most of the captured men "the fight for life had just begun."[50] Thousands succumbed in the next three years to brutal mistreatment, malnutrition, and disease in Japanese prison camps in the Philippines, in the enemy home islands, and in Manchuria. Two hundred and thirty-nine officers and men of the 4th Marine Regiment died in enemy hands.

CONCLUSION

The battle for Corregidor was bitter and confused; relatively few men survive who fought in the East Sector through the night and morning of 5–6 May 1942. Hundreds of well-trained infantrymen in positions within a mile or so of Malinta Hill were only spectators and auditors of the fighting. The poorest-trained elements of the 4th Marines constituted the vital mobile reserve. On the surface and in hasty consideration it would seem that the tactics of the beach defense left much to be desired.

Corregidor, however, was not a fortress with only one entrance. The beaches fronting the ravines defended by 2/4 and 3/4 led directly to the island's major defensive installations. The threat of amphibious assault existed all around the island's perimeter, but especially along the northern and western shores. The Japanese laid down preparatory fires all along the north side of the island, devoting as much attention to James Ravine and Bottomside west of Malinta as they did the eastern beaches. Until the night of 5 May there was no compelling reason to believe that the East Sector would draw the first assault. And even after the enemy landed at North Point the very present threat to western Corregidor existed and could not be ignored. To meet it, a number of Army units were alerted to back up the positions of 2/4 and 3/4.[51]

The problem which Colonel Howard faced of when, where, and in what strength to commit the reserves available to him was a classic one for commanders at all troop levels. If he committed all his reserve at one time and in the area of greatest existing threat, he distinctly increased the vulnerability of other sectors to enemy attack. If he committed only part of his reserve and retained the capability of reinforcing against further attacks, he stood the chance of not using enough men to have a decisive effect in any sector. The decision to commit the reserve piecemeal reflected the regiment's estimate of the enemy's capabilities and intentions in light of their actions.[52] The Japanese, although opposed by a relatively small force, did not or could not vigorously pursue their advance after reaching the Denver position. The continued presence of numerous small craft off Corregidor's north shore indicated a possible, even probable, early attempt at a second landing. Under these circumstances the East Sector assault might well be a secondary effort which had stalled, with the enemy's main attack still to come. Actually this was the Japanese plan, with the difference that the second landing was to follow the first after a day's interval

---

[50] *Jenkins*, 19.

[51] Col F. P. Pyzick ltr to CMC, 30Oct56.
[52] *Howard Interview*.

rather than as soon as the Marines expected.

In large part the 4th Marines' reserve strength was already committed on 5 May. The Japanese preparatory fires, especially those which were laid on areas in plain sight of Bataan, made movement by any body of troops extremely difficult—witness the fate of Company O. The bombardment had the effect of tying the regiment to its defenses. The trained infantrymen in its ranks were kept where they could do the most to bolster the crucial beach positions.[53] If any sizable number of these men had been withdrawn from the beaches to form a reserve, it is questionable whether the remaining men could have withstood any enemy assault. Once the Japanese began to bombard Corregidor in earnest there was no such thing as a strong beach defense position; the very fury of the bombardment, destroying as it did most of the prepared defenses and demolishing the major supporting weapons, placed a high premium on having the best infantrymen at the point where their value would be greatest—the beaches.

The fall of Corregidor was inevitable; the garrison simply did not have enough food to hold out until relief could arrive. Although the enemy, primarily for prestige and propaganda reasons, choose to assault the island, they could easily have starved its defenders into submission. When the Japanese did make their attack they paid a high price for their haste, but extracted as great a one from the defenders. In the immediate tactical sense, however, the enemy artillery was the victor in the siege and fall of Corregidor; no defending force could have withstood its devastatingly accurate bombardment.

Although it was a defeat, the battle of Corregidor is marked down in the annals of the 4th Marines as a fight to be proud of. Those who fought and died in its ranks, whatever their service of origin, were, if only for a brief moment, Corregidor Marines.

---

[53] *Ibid.*

PART V

Decision at Midway

CHAPTER 1

Setting the Stage: Early Naval Operations[1]

Early in January 1942 the U. S. Pacific Fleet was looking for a way to strike back at the Japanese; and advocates of the fast carrier force, believing their case ironically had been proven by the Japanese at Pearl Harbor, were ready to test their theories.[2] But first there were some fences to mend. The all-important communications chain to Australia and New Zealand was rather tenuous, and the bulk of the Navy had to be used for escort duty until reinforcements could be put ashore to bolster some of the stations along the route.

One of the most important links in this communication chain was Samoa. The worst was feared for this area when the Pago Pago naval station was shelled by a Japanese submarine on 11 January while the 2d Marine Brigade (composed for the most part of the 8th Marines and the 2d Defense Battalion) still was en route to the islands from San Diego. But on 23 January after the Marines' four transports and one fleet cargo vessel were delivered safely to Samoa, Vice Admiral William F. Halsey's *Enterprise* force, together with a new fast carrier force commanded by Rear Admiral Frank Jack Fletcher and formed around the *Yorktown*, were released for the raiding actions that the fleet was anxious to launch.

While the 2d Marine Brigade unloaded at Samoa on 23 January, the Japanese landed far to the west at Rabaul where the small Australian garrison was quickly overrun. Although the importance of Rabaul to the Japanese was not realized at once, it was soon clear that from the Bismarcks the enemy could launch an attack through the Coral Sea toward Australia and New Zealand. This threat tended to increase rather than diminish the danger to Samoa. It was reasoned that a Japanese attack there would precede a strike at Australia or New Zealand to block U. S. assistance to the Anzac areas. Japanese occupation of Makin Island in the Gilberts seemed to point toward Samoa, and naval commanders held that the best insurance against subsequent

---

[1] Unless otherwise noted the material in Part V is derived from *Rising Sun in the Pacific*; S. E. Morison, *Coral Sea, Midway and Submarine Actions, May 1942–August 1942: History of United States Naval Operations in World War II* (Boston: Little, Brown and Company, 1949), hereinafter cited as *Coral Sea and Midway*; *U. S. & Sea Power*; M. Fuchida and M. Okumiya, *Midway: The Battle That Doomed Japan* (Annapolis: U. S. Naval Institute, 1955), hereinafter cited as *Battle That Doomed Japan*; *Marines at Midway*; "The Japanese Story of the Battle of Midway," *ONI Review*, May 1947, hereinafter cited as *ONI Review*.

[2] "There was still much difference of opinion [about the effectiveness of the carrier striking force] until 7 Dec 1941 when the Japanese attack took the controversy out of the laboratory class . . . Japan knifed us with our own invention." Capt Miles R. Browning, USN, "The Fast Carrier Force," *MC Gazette*, June 1946, 19.

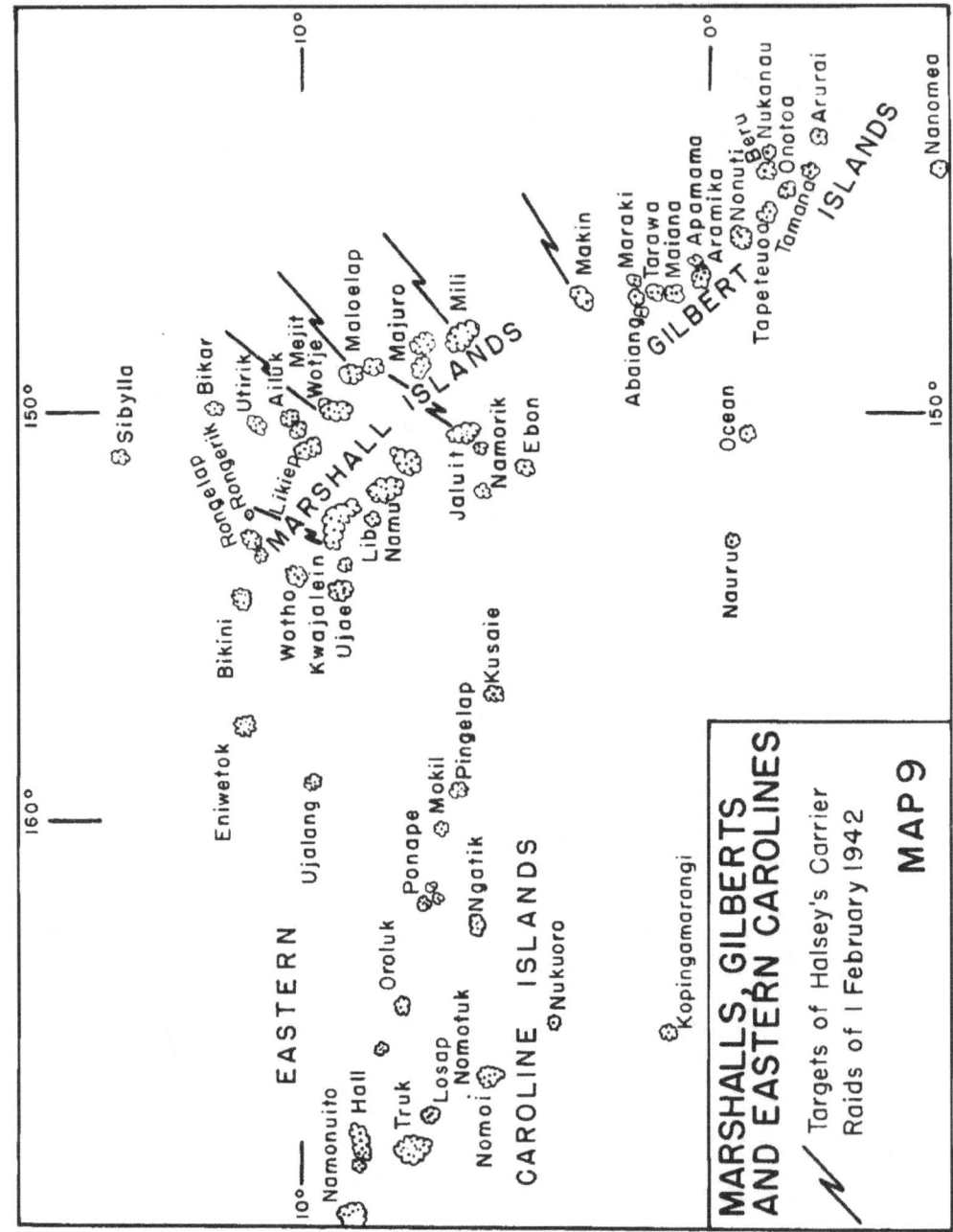

moves would be a raid against the Marshalls, from which much of this Japanese action was mounted. Halsey's *Enterprise* force therefore set out to strike Wotje and Maleolap, seaplane bases in the Marshalls, while Fletcher prepared to attack Mili and Jaluit (also in the Marshalls) plus Makin with his *Yorktown* group. (See Map 9)

A submarine reconnaissance found the Marshalls lightly defended and spotted the largest concentration of Japanese planes and ships at Kwajalein Atoll in the center of the island group. Halsey decided to add this choice target to his list, and for the missions he divided Task Force 8 into three groups. The *Enterprise* with three destroyers would strike Wotje, Maloelap, and Kwajalein; Rear Admiral Raymond A. Spruance with the cruisers *Northampton* and *Salt Lake City* plus one destroyer would bombard Wotje; and Captain Thomas M. Shock in USS *Chester*, and with two destroyers, would shell Maloelap. The three southern atolls in the Marshalls group and Makin in the northern Gilberts would be attended to by Fletcher in the *Yorktown* with his independent command (TF 17) made up of the cruisers *Louisville* and *St. Louis* and four destroyers.

The twin attacks struck on 1 February. Halsey began launching at 0443 under a full moon when his carrier was just 36 miles from Wotje. Kwajalein, the main objective was 155 miles away. Nine torpedo bombers and 37 dive bombers led off the attack, the SBD's striking Roi air base on the northern end of the atoll and the torpedo bombers hitting Kwajalein Island across the lagoon.

At Kwajalein the hunting was better; but in spite of the fact that there was no fighter opposition, and that the reports brought back by pilots were enthusiastic, damage to the Japanese installations and shipping was slight. Five Wildcats shot down two Japanese planes over Maloelap, and nine SBD's that returned from Roi later sortied again and damaged some airfield installations. The surface bombardment, too, was disappointing, and the bombardment flagship, *Chester*, took a light bomb through her main deck and lost eight men killed and eleven wounded.

To the south, Fletcher had bad luck over Jaluit when his fliers found their targets concealed by thunder showers. Two Japanese ships off Jabor Town were hit, but not sunk, and the damage ashore was slight. A mine layer was hit at Makin, and damage at Mili was also slight.

Similar actions were continued in other areas of the Pacific to harass the Japanese and to provide at least one outlet for efforts to fight back at the enemy when the news from all other fronts was gloomy. Most notable were strikes in early March against Wake and Marcus Island, and the daring raid by planes of Admiral Wilson Brown's task force over New Guinea's 15,000-foot Owen Stanley Mountains to hit the Japanese newly moved into Lae and Salamaua. But in all cases actual damage to the enemy still failed to measure up to expectations, much less to the reports turned in by overenthusiastic aviators.

Most audacious and unorthodox of the attacks, of course, was that which launched Lieutenant Colonel James H. Doolittle and his Army raiders from the *Hornet's* deck to the 18 April Tokyo raid. Planned as "something really spectacular"—a proper retaliation for Pearl Harbor—the raid was designed more for its dramatic impact upon morale than for any other purpose. In that it was highly successful.

AN ARMY B-25, *one of Doolittle's Raiders, takes off from the deck of the carrier* Hornet *to participate in the first U. S. air raid on Japan.* *(USN 41197)*

JAPANESE CARRIER SHOHO, *dead in the water and smoking from repeated bomb and torpedo hits, was sunk by carrier planes in the Coral Sea Battle.* *(USN 17026)*

SETTING THE STAGE: EARLY NAVAL OPERATIONS

After security-shrouded planning and training, Doolittle's 16 B-25's left San Francisco on 2 April 1942 on board the *Hornet* which was escorted by cruisers *Vincennes* and *Nashville*, four destroyers, and an oiler. After a 13 April rendezvous with the *Enterprise* of Halsey's TF 16, the raiding party continued along the northern route toward the Japanese home islands.[3] Enemy picket boats sighted the convoy when it was more than 100 miles short of the intended launching range, and, with Doolittle's concurrence, Halsey launched the fliers at 0725 on 18 April while the *Hornet* bucked in a heavy sea 668 miles from the Imperial Palace in central Tokyo.[4]

Much of the raid's anticipated shock effect on Tokyo was lost by the coincidence of Doolittle's arrival over the city at about noon just as a Japanese air raid drill was completed. The Japanese, confused by the attack which followed their own maneuvers, offered only light opposition to the B-25's which skimmed the city at treetop level to drop their bombs on military targets. One plane which struck Kobe received no opposition, although two others over Nagoya and Osaka drew heavy fire from antiaircraft batteries; but none was lost over Japan.

Halsey managed to retire from the launching area with little difficulty, and both carriers returned to Pearl Harbor on 25 April. Although the raid did more to boost American morale than it did to damage Japanese military installations, more practical results came later. It allowed a Japanese military group which favored a further expansion of their territorial gains to begin execution of these ambitious plans, and this expansion effort led directly to the Battle of Midway which ". . . alone was well worth the effort put into this operation by . . . [those] . . . who had volunteered to help even the score."[5]

The first of Japan's planned expansion moves in the spring of 1942 aimed for control of the Coral Sea through seizure of the Southern Solomon Islands and Port Moresby on New Guinea as bases from which to knock out growing Allied air power in northeastern Australia. Seizure of New Caledonia, planned as part of the third step in the second major series of offensives, would complete encirclement of the Coral Sea. This would leave the U. S. communications route to the Anzac area dangling useless at the Samoan Islands; and later Japanese advances would push the U. S. Pacific Fleet back to Pearl Harbor and perhaps even to the west coast.

Characteristically, the Japanese plan called for an almost impossible degree of timing and coordination. It depended for success largely on surprise and on the U. S. forces behaving just as the Japanese hoped that they would. But this second element was largely corollary to the first, and, when surprise failed, the Japanese were shocked to discover that the U. S. fleet did not follow the script.

---

[3] Plans called for the bombers to land on friendly Chinese fields some 1,093 miles from Tokyo, and completion of this trip for the planes loaded initially with four 500-pound bombs and 1,140 gallons of gasoline required that they be launched within 500 miles of Tokyo.

[4] Although the picket boats were prompt with a warning, Japanese interception attempts were tardy. It was assumed that Navy planes, with a shorter range than B-25's, were on the carrier, and that the force could not strike Japan until the ships steamed for another day.

[5] *Rising Sun in the Pacific*, 398.

The Japanese anticipated resistance from a U. S. carrier task force known to be lurking somewhere to the south or southeast, but they expected to corner this force in the eastern Coral Sea with a pincers movement of carrier task forces of their own. Vice Admiral Takeo Takagi would skirt to the east of the Solomons with his *Striking Force* of heavy carriers *Shokaku* and *Zuikaku* and move in on the U. S. ships from that direction, while Rear Admiral Aritomo Goto's *Covering Force* built around the light carrier *Shoho* would close in from the northwest. Destruction of the northeast Australian airfields would follow this fatal pinch of the U. S. fleet, and then the *Port Moresby Invasion Group* could ply the southeastern coast of New Guinea with impunity.

But Japanese overconfidence enabled U. S. intelligence to diagnose this operation in advance, and Fletcher's Task Force 17 had steamed into the Coral Sea where he all but completed refueling before the first Japanese elements sortied from Rabaul. On 4 May Fletcher's *Lexington*, *Yorktown*, screening ships, and support vessels were joined by the combined Australian-American surface force under Rear Admiral J. C. Crace of the Royal Navy.

On the previous day the Japanese had started their operation (which they called "Mo") like any other routine land grab. A suitable invasion force, adequately supported, moved into the Southern Solomons, seized Tulagi without opposition[6] and promptly began setting up a seaplane base. There Fletcher's planes startled them next day with several powerful air strikes on the new garrison and on the Japanese ships still in the area. The U. S. carrier planes struck virtually unopposed,[7] but they caused little damage in proportion to the energy and ammunition they expended. This startling deviation from the "Mo" script caused the Japanese to initiate the remaining steps of the operation without further delay.

The Battle of the Coral Sea proved the first major naval engagement in history where opposing surface forces neither saw nor fired at each other.[8] Although both were eager to join battle, combat intelligence was so poor and aerial reconnaissance so hampered by shifting weather fronts that three days passed before the main forces found each other. But other things they did find led to a series of events on the 7th that might be described as a comedy of errors, although there was nothing particularly comical about them to those involved.

Early that morning an over-enthusiastic Japanese search pilot brought Takagi's entire striking air power down on the U. S. fleet tanker *Neosho* and her lone convoying destroyer, the USS *Sims*, by reporting them as a carrier and heavy cruiser respectively. This overwhelming attack sank the *Sims* and so damaged the *Neosho*

---

[6] Tulagi, with which U. S. forces were to get better acquainted, was the capital of the British Solomon Islands Protectorate. Officials and such garrison as existed had been amply forewarned and evacuated several days earlier. See Part VI of this volume.

[7] Experience to date had indicated to the Japanese that one of their landings constituted a *fait accompli* which no enemy would dare dispute, and the naval force supporting the landing had departed in order to get on with the war. Takagi's powerful Carrier Striking Force at this time lay north of Bougainville to keep beyond the range of Allied air search.

[8] "So many mistakes were made on both sides in this new mode of fighting that it might be called the Battle of Naval Errors." *Coral Sea and Midway*, 63.

that she had to be destroyed four days later.

Not to be outdone, the Americans reacted similarly a short time later to a scout plane's report of two Japanese carriers and four cruisers north of the Louisiades. Actually these craft were a subordinate enemy task group consisting of two old light cruisers and three converted gunboats. But more by good luck than good management, the attacking planes investigating the report sighted the Japanese *Covering Force*, then protecting the left flank of the *Port Moresby Invasion Group*, and concentrated on the *Shoho* to the virtual exclusion of her consorts. Against 93 aircraft of all types, the lone light carrier had no more chance than Task Force *Neosho-Sims* had against the Japanese, and her demise prompted the morale-boosting phrase, "Scratch one flattop!" [9]

As a result of these alarms and excursions, both commanding admirals had missed each other once again. By mid-afternoon, however, Takagi had a pretty good idea of the U. S. carriers' location and, shortly before nightfall, dispatched a bomber-torpedo strike against Fletcher. Thanks to a heavy weather front, these planes failed to find their target, and American combat air patrol intercepted them on their attempted return. In the confusion of dogfights, several Japanese pilots lost direction in the gathering darkness and made the error of attempting to land on the *Yorktown*.[10]

Early the following morning, U. S. search planes finally located the Japanese carriers at about the time the Japanese rediscovered the U. S. flattops. At last the stage was set for the big show.

Loss of the *Shoho* had cut the Japanese down to size. The opponents who slugged it out on 8 May 1942 were evenly matched, physically and morally, to a degree rarely found in warfare, afloat or ashore.[11] However, at the time the battle developed, the Japanese enjoyed the great tactical advantage of having their position shrouded by the same heavy weather front that had covered the U. S. carriers the previous afternoon, while Fletcher's force lay in clear tropical sunlight where it could be seen for many miles from aloft.

The attacking aircraft of both parties struck their enemy at nearly the same time (approximately 1100), passing each other en route.[12] The two Japanese carriers and their respective escorts lay about ten miles apart. As the *Yorktown's* planes orbited over the target preparatory to the attack, the *Zuikaku* and her screening force disappeared into a rain squall and were seen

---

[9] "Scratch one flattop! Dixon to Carrier, Scratch one flattop!" Voice radio report LCdr R. E. Dixon to USS *Lexington*, quoted in *Coral Sea and Midway*, 42. Action against the *Shoho* was U. S. Navy Air's first attack on an enemy carrier.

[10] Six planes in two groups of three each. Although they were recognized and fired on, all but one escaped. In this action the Japanese lost 9 planes in combat and 11 attempting night landings without benefit of homing devices, against U. S. loss of 2 fighters.

[11] A lucid summary of the several factors involved occurs in *Coral Sea and Midway*, 48. Fletcher's potential marked advantage in surface screening strength had been dissipated when, early on 7 May, he had dispatched Crace's force of cruisers and destroyers on a dash westward to intercept the enemy transport convoy expected to round the southeastern tip of New Guinea the next morning en route to attack Port Moresby. For analysis of this perhaps ill-judged move and its results, see *Ibid.*, 37-39.

[12] "The story current shortly after the battle, that the Japanese and American planes sighted but paid no attention to each other when passing on opposite courses, is not true." *Ibid.*, 52n.

no more during the brief action that followed, thereby escaping damage. So all U. S. planes that reached the scene concentrated on the *Shokaku*, but with disappointing results.

The *Yorktown's* torpedo bombers went in first, low and covered by fighters. But faulty technique and the wretched quality of U. S. torpedoes at this stage of the war combined to make this attack wholly ineffective: hits (if any) proved to be duds, the pilots launched at excessive ranges, and the torpedoes traveled so slowly that vessels unable to dodge had only to outrun them. The dive bombers, following closely, scored only two direct hits. But one of these so damaged the *Shokaku's* flight deck that she could no longer launch planes, although she still was capable of recovering them. Many of the *Lexington* planes, taking off ten minutes after those from *Yorktown*, got lost in the overcast and never found their targets. Those that did attack made the same mistakes the *Yorktown* fliers committed. The torpedoes proved wholly ineffective, and the damaging bomb hit on the *Shokaku* was something less than lethal despite the pilot's enthusiastic report that she was "settling fast."[13]

The Japanese did considerably better, thanks to vastly superior torpedoes and launching techniques. Two of these powerful "fish" ripped great holes in the *Lexington's* port side, and she sustained two direct bomb hits plus numerous near misses that sprang plates. The more maneuverable *Yorktown* dodged all of the torpedoes aimed at her and escaped all but one of the bombs. But this was an 800-pounder, and it exploded with such a spectacular display of flame and smoke that the Japanese pilots may be excused their claim that they had sunk her.

These events made up the Battle of the Coral Sea. It was all over by 1140.

Preoccupation of both forces with the flattops left opposing escort vessels unscathed, although the Japanese claimed to have left burning "one battleship or cruiser."[14] The Americans had sustained far the heavier damage and casualties, but had inflicted the greater tactical blow in knocking the *Shokaku* out of further offensive action while both U. S. carriers still were operational. Even the crippled *Lexington* had put out fires, shored up torpedo damage, and was capable of sustaining 25-knot speed and conducting nearly normal flight operations an hour after the battle ended.

The Japanese had lost the greater number of planes: 43 from all causes against 33 for the Americans. Their command, accepting at face value the ecstatic reports of their pilots that they had sunk both U. S. carriers, started the beat-up *Shokaku* for home, and in the afternoon commenced withdrawal from the area on orders from Rabaul. Admiral Takagi concurred with higher authority that it would be unwise to risk the vulnerable transport convoy in the narrowing waters of the western Coral Sea in face of the Allies' Australian airfields under cover of the whittled-down air complement of the single operational carrier. So the *Port Moresby Invasion Group* was ordered back to Rabaul.

But the final, tragic act of the drama remained. The gallant old *Lexington*, her wounds patched up and apparently fit to return to Pearl Harbor for permanent repairs, was suddenly racked by a terrible

---

[13] *Ibid.*, 51.

[14] *Ibid.*, 56.

explosion. This resulted only indirectly from enemy action: released gasoline fumes were ignited by sparks from a generator someone had carelessly left running. This set off what amounted to a chain reaction. The best efforts of her crew availed nothing, and at 1707 her skipper gave the order to abandon ship. This movement was carried out in the best order, without the loss of a man. At about 2000, nearly nine hours after the Japanese had withdrawn from the battle, torpedoes of her own escort put her under the waves forever.

Loss of the *Lexington* gave tactical victory to the Japanese. But by thwarting the invasion of Port Moresby, principal objective of the entire operation, the United States won strategic victory. At the time the enemy regarded this merely a postponement of their invasion plans; but events would prove that no Japanese seaborne invasion ever would near Port Moresby again.

CHAPTER 2

Japanese Plans: Toward Midway and the North Pacific

Apparently ignoring this setback in the Coral Sea, Japan next turned toward the Central and North Pacific to launch the second complicated operation on her schedule. Admiral Yamamoto's two-pronged thrust at Midway and the Aleutians would automatically wipe clean the Coral Sea reverses and extend the outer perimeter of defense a safer distance from the home islands. And in the bargain, Yamamoto hoped, these attacks would lure forth the remainder of the U. S. fleet so that he could finish off the job he started on 7 December.[1]

The admiral accepted his aviators' reports that they had destroyed both U. S. carriers in the Coral Sea, and he therefore reasoned that the U. S. could bring no more than two flattops against him anywhere in the Pacific. Actually the Pearl Harbor yard had put the *Yorktown* back into operation in less than 48 hours so that the U. S. had three carriers, including the *Enterprise* and the *Hornet*. But against these Yamamoto had seven, and four seaplane carriers as well. His force also contained 11 battleships, including three of the latest type.[2] The U. S. had no battleships—or at least none in position for this upcoming battle.[3] And Yamamoto also had a substantial edge over the U. S. in cruisers, destroyers, and submarines. But the Japanese admiral squandered this lopsided advantage by dispersing his armada in widely scattered groups and opened himself for defeat in detail by the inferior U. S. Pacific Fleet.[4]

This Japanese fleet, divided for the complicated plan into five major forces, with some of these split into smaller groups, steamed eastward independently to carry out the various phases of the second step in this strategy for 1942. Planes from two light carriers in the *Second Mobile Force* would strike Dutch Harbor, Alaska on 3 June to confuse the U. S. com-

---

[1] *Battle That Doomed Japan*, Chaps 4 and 5, *passim*. The Aleutians phase was intended only as a diversion and to protect the northern flank of the Midway thrust, the plan being to withdraw the landing troops in September. *Ibid.*, 79.

[2] Adm Yamamoto flew his flag in the *Yamato*, the largest, fastest, and most heavily armed (18″ guns) ship in the world.

[3] Although some of the battleships knocked out at Pearl Harbor had been put back in service, and three others had been brought around from the Atlantic, these ships were operating from the west coast as a final defense for the U. S.

[4] In view of subsequent developments, Morison describes Yamamoto's disposition as "cockeyed." *Coral Sea and Midway*, 77–79. See also *Battle That Doomed Japan*, 73–78. These Japanese authors, although sometimes carefully kind to Yamamoto (who was killed later in a Solomon Islands air action), are most often highly critical of the Japanese Navy and of war plans in general. Although the work is valuable and serious (*n. b.* the final two paragraphs of the book, at pages 247–248), the authors sometimes sound like men on the morning after, ruefully surveying the night before.

mand and to cover diversionary Japanese landings in the western Aleutians by the *Occupation Forces* for Adak-Attu and Kiska. Next the *Carrier Striking Force*, commanded by Vice Admiral Chuichi Nagumo, would soften Midway with the planes from the big fleet carriers *Akagi*, *Kaga*, *Hiryu*, and *Soryu*,[5] and would then move on to strike the first blow at the U. S. Pacific Fleet if it challenged in a sortie from Pearl Harbor.

Admiral Yamamoto's *Main Body*, including three battleships and a light cruiser of his force plus the *Aleutian Screening Force* of four battleships and two light cruisers, then would go in for the kill against the U. S. Fleet. This engagement would be followed, after darkness on 5 June, by Vice Admiral Nobutake Kondo moving in to shell the U. S. base for two days. Then Kondo's convoyed *Transport Group* would approach to land the *Midway Occupation Force* of 5,000 ground troops. While crossing the Pacific, Yamamoto remained some hundreds of miles to the rear with his *Main Body*, awaiting word from the *Advance Expeditionary Force* of large fleet submarines already manning stations on the approaches to Pearl Harbor to warn about sorties of the American ships.

This ambitious plan might have worked, even though it was over-intricate. But again the Japanese had allowed their optimism and overconfidence to cast the U. S. Pacific Fleet in the role of a timid character actor cued for a vulnerable "walk-on" part. They begged the question of tactics before their plan moved to the operational stage. The U. S. Fleet, according to Japanese plans, would be steaming for the *Second Mobile Force* in the Aleutians, or would be vacillating in Hawaiian waters, until the strong *Carrier Striking Force* hit Midway and revealed the target of the main effort.[6] In either event nothing but the small Marine garrison force would stand in the way of the occupation of Midway, and the Japanese would have an air base of their own there before the U. S. Fleet could reach them.

But, as at the Coral Sea encounter, the U. S. Fleet already had sortied to await the Japanese. For more than a month Nimitz had been aware that something like this was in the wind, and he bet nearly everything he had that the strike would hit Midway. The weakened Pacific Fleet stood some 300 miles northeast of Midway, there to refuel, before the Japanese picket submarines took position. As a result, these boats sighted no U. S. ships and radioed no reports, and Admiral Nagumo discovered the presence of the U. S. carriers in a most unpleasant manner.

---

[5] Absent members of the original Pearl Harbor striking force were the *Shokaku* and the *Zuikaku*, the former undergoing Coral Sea damage repairs, and the latter reforming its air groups battered in that same action. Presence of these big carriers at Midway might well have been decisive.

[6] Fuchida and Okumiya state that Japanese plans "calculated that the enemy naval forces would be lured out by the strike on Midway Island and not before." *Battle That Doomed Japan*, 128. But in this calculation their overconfidence must have been tempered somewhat, else why the diversion into the Aleutians? Morison discusses this faulty Japanese strategy, probably more realistically. *Coral Sea and Midway*, 74–79.

CHAPTER 3

Midway Girds for Battle[1]

Even before these Japanese plans were made, and long before Admiral Yamamoto sortied eastward, all U. S. military planners recognized the vulnerable position of the Midway Atoll.[2] Especially was this position clear in the light of early Japanese successes elsewhere in the Pacific, and none was more keenly aware of the grim situation than the atoll's small garrison force. The 12 PBY's of VP-21 were soon withdrawn, and little help was expected from the crippled fleet. But on 17 December, while the 6th Marine Defense Battalion worked to improve existing defense installations, 17 SB2U-3's (Vindicators) of Marine Scout-Bomber Squadron 231 (VMSB-231) flew in unexpectedly from Hawaii. Led by Major Clarence J. Chappell, Jr., and assisted in over-water navigation by a PBY, the obsolescent craft made the 1,137-mile hop in nine hours and twenty minutes.[3] Other reinforcements, including about 100 officers and men of Batteries A and C of the 4th Defense Battalion, left Pearl Harbor on 19 December with the old Navy 7-inch[4] and the 3-inch guns which had been shipped to Pearl Harbor for Midway prior to the outset of war. (See Map 10, Map Section)

This force, on board the USS *Wright*, arrived on Christmas Eve, and Lieutenant Colonel Harold D. Shannon, who commanded Marine defense forces on the atoll, turned over to Battery A (Captain Custis Burton, Jr.) the mission of installing and manning the 7-inch and 3-inch batteries to be emplaced on Eastern Island. Battery C (First Lieutenant Lewis A. Jones) was assigned the job of setting up its 3-inch battery on Sand Island.[5]

Next day Midway received another Christmas present: 14 Brewster F2A-3's, the air echelon of Marine Fighter Squadron 221 (VMF-221), flew in from the USS *Saratoga* which was retiring from the abortive attempt to relieve Wake Island. This squadron immediately began a daily schedule of air search and patrolling. On 26 December the USS *Tangier* brought in

---

[1] Editor's Note: Material contained in Chapters 3 and 4 is derived mainly from Chapters III and IV of the historical monograph *Marines at Midway* by Lieutenant Colonel Robert D. Heinl, Jr., published by Headquarters, U. S. Marine Corps, in 1948. This has been extensively rewritten and checked against sources subsequently brought to light.

[2] See Part II for a description of the geography and history of Midway.

[3] This was then the longest massed flight of single engine landplanes on record, and it had been carried out with no surface rescue craft available. CO MAG-21 serial 1173 to MGC, 19Dec41. The flight took off from Hickam since Ewa's runways were too short for the heavily-laden planes to use with complete safety.

[4] These 7-inch weapons had been removed from pre-World War I battleships and stored in reserve at naval yards. K. J. Bauer, "Ships of the Navy, 1775–1945," (MS available from the author).

[5] Interview with LtCol C. Burton, Jr., 26Sep47, hereinafter cited as *Burton*. The two Eastern Island batteries were located side by side on the south shore of the island, near the western tip, and the Sand Island battery was set up along the north shore of Sand Island.

Battery B of the 4th Defense Battalion (First Lieutenant Frank G. Umstead); additional machine gunners and 12 antiaircraft machine guns from the Special Weapons Group of that same battalion; an aviation contingent of three officers and 110 enlisted Marines constituting the ground echelon of VMF-221; aviation supplies; additional radar; and much-needed base-defense artillery material. Umstead's 5-inch battery, along with the island's other 7-inch battery, were set up south of the radio station on Sand Island. By New Year's Day of 1942 Midway was garrisoned by a strongly-reinforced defense battalion, and one fighter and one scout-bomber squadron.

A major air base took shape on Eastern Island under the direction of Lieutenant Colonel William J. Wallace who on 9 January became commanding officer of the Marine Aviation Detachment. Individual aircraft bunkers and underground personnel shelters were built, emergency fueling expedients devised, radars calibrated, and inexperienced operators trained to use them properly. Colonel Wallace was assisted by Major Walter L. J. Bayler, the Marine aviation officer who had been sent back from Wake with that atoll's last reports.[6]

The first test of this defense came on 25 January during twilight general quarters when a Japanese submarine surfaced abruptly and opened fire on Sand Island, apparently trying to knock out the radio station. Battery D opened up with its 3-inch guns and forced the enemy craft to crash-dive three minutes after it had surfaced. Sand Island and the adjacent lagoon had received from 10 to 15 indiscriminate hits, and Captain Buckner's Battery D had expended 24 rounds.

The next action against the atoll came two weeks later, on 8 February, when another submarine appeared less than 1,000 yards south of Sand Island and opened fire on the radio towers. Captain Loren S. Fraser's Battery A opened fire on this boat, and it submerged after Marines had returned two rounds. The enemy had hit a concrete ammunition magazine, but fortunately the small arms ammunition was not detonated. Two days later another submarine—or the same one—surfaced almost directly below two Marine fighter planes flying the sunset antisubmarine patrol. The submarine got off two rounds before First Lieutenant John F. Carey and Second Lieutenant Philip R. White, the fliers, could launch a diving attack. Both rounds from the submarine splashed in the lagoon, and then the boat was driven under water by the air attack just as the batteries of the 6th Defense Battalion were going into action. This was the last time for a number of months that Midway was troubled by enemy submarines.

As the winter wore on, Midway's air arm began to profit from the general expansion of Marine Corps aviation, and the two squadrons and their small provisional headquarters on 1 March became Marine Aircraft Group 22 (MAG-22). On 20 April Lieutenant Colonel Wallace was succeeded in command by Major Ira L. Kimes, and at the same time Major Lofton R. Henderson took command of VMSB-241, (the new designation of former VMSB-231). This was a busy time for MAG-22, which was then converting Eastern Island from a small advanced air base to a major installation capable of handling as many squadrons and aircraft types as could

---

[6] LtCol W. J. Wallace ltr to Col C. A. Larkin, 18Jan42.

physically be accommodated and protected there.

On 10 March, during the work and reorganization, the Marine fliers got their first test against enemy aircraft. Radar picked up a Japanese four-engined "Mavis" (Kawanishi 97) approximately 45 miles west of Midway, and 12 fighters under Captain Robert M. Haynes vectored out to intercept. They made contact with the enemy flying boat at 10,000 feet and shot it down.

Although the enemy plane did as well as it could to fight off this attack, this contact was more important as intelligence for Nimitz' staff in Pearl Harbor than as a test for the Marine fliers. Two aircraft of this type had tumbled four bombs into the hills behind Honolulu on the night of 3–4 March, and Nimitz already believed that this portended an offensive toward Hawaii. Now this new sighting near Midway gave added weight to his estimate, and this information went into the CinCPac intelligence "hopper" which shortly thereafter reached the considered opinion that the Japanese attack would strike Midway. By this time the Japanese code had been broken, also.[7] Thus were the fragments pieced together into Nimitz's May 1942 decision which caused him to wager nearly every ship he had in an early sortie from Pearl Harbor to the position 300 miles northeast of Midway from which the Japanese could be intercepted.

It was a bold, even though well-calculated, wager. The many ships on South Pacific convoy duty had to be left on their important jobs; Halsey's *Enterprise* and *Hornet* had rushed from the Doolittle launching area part way to the Carol Sea and back again to Pearl Harbor where they were placed under a new commander, Rear Admiral Raymond A. Spruance; Fletcher's *Yorktown* had just limped in from the Coral Sea needing an estimated 90 days of repair work; and all the Fleet's battleships were on the west coast where they could not be used (partly because Nimitz felt he did not have enough air strength to protect them, anyway). But Nimitz was convinced that his intelligence estimate was correct, and that the stand had to be made.

For the engagement Nimitz gave Fletcher, in over-all tactical charge,[8] direct command of Task Force 17 which included the *Yorktown* (rushed into shape in two days rather than 90), two cruisers, and six destroyers. Spruance commanded Task Force 16 which included the *Enterprise* and *Hornet*, six cruisers, and nine destroyers. Four oilers and 19 submarines also were assigned to the area, and, in addition, a North Pacific Force was formed of five cruisers and ten destroyers to screen the Aleutians. The Japanese had him outnumbered on all counts, and Nimitz knew that the enemy would be gunning for the three U. S. carriers. But his carriers likewise were his only hope, and the admiral ordered his subordinates to apply the rule of calculated risk when they went in with their air groups to stop the Japanese.

While Nimitz readied this reception committee, the Japanese completed their Midway plans and polished the rough operational edges with carrier training and

---

[7] *Battle That Doomed Japan*, 131; *U. S. & Sea Power*, 686.

[8] Fletcher was senior to Spruance, and thus became Officer in Tactical Command. But as it turned out, Spruance exercised practically an independent command during the critical days of 4–6 June, and this probably was fortunate because Fletcher had no aviation staff while Spruance had inherited Halsey's.

rehearsals. By the last week of May, all Japanese fleet elements were underway, and on decks Imperial sailors sunbathed and sang songs—vocal eruptions of what has been described as the "Victory Disease."[9]

Meanwhile on Midway, the focal point for these vast efforts, Marines got their first inkling of all this attention when Nimitz flew in on 2 May to see their senior officer, Lieutenant Colonel Shannon, and the atoll commander, Commander Cyril T. Simard. The admiral inspected the installations, and then directed Shannon to submit a detailed list of all supplies and equipment he would need to defend the atoll against a strong attack. Nimitz promised that all available items requested would be forwarded immediately, and within less than a week men and material were being embarked in Hawaii to bolster the island strength.

Three more 3-inch antiaircraft batteries totaling 12 guns, a 37mm antiaircraft battery of eight guns, and a 20mm antiaircraft battery of 18 guns were temporarily detached from the 3d Defense Battalion at Pearl Harbor; and two rifle companies of the 2d Marine Raider Battalion, together with a platoon of five light tanks, also were sent along to Midway. For MAG-22, still flying Brewster fighters and Vought Vindicator dive bombers, there would be 16 SBD-2 dive bombers and seven relatively new Grumman F4F-3 fighters.

Shortly after his return from Midway to Pearl Harbor, Nimitz arranged "spot" promotions to captain and colonel respectively for Simard and Shannon, and described to them in a joint personal letter the steps being taken to reinforce their atoll against the anticipated attack. Japanese D-Day, the admiral predicted, would be about 28 May. On the day they received this letter, Simard and Shannon conferred on their final plans for defense, and that evening Colonel Shannon assembled his key subordinates and warned them of the impending enemy attack. Additional defensive measures and priorities of final efforts were outlined, and all recreational activities suspended. May 25 was set as the deadline for completion of the measures ordered.

On the 25th, however, came two welcomed changes for the picture. First, Nimitz passed the word that the Japanese attack was not expected until early June, and, second, the first reinforcements arrived. On this date the USS *St. Louis* came in with the 37mm antiaircraft battery of the 3d Defense Battalion plus the two companies of raiders. Four of the 37's were emplaced on each island while Raider Company C (Captain Donald H. Hastie) went to Sand Island, and Company D (First Lieutenant John Apergis) to Eastern Island.

Next day the aircraft tender *Kittyhawk* arrived with the 3d Defense Battalion's 3-inch antiaircraft group commanded by Major Chandler W. Johnson, the light tank platoon for the mobile reserve, and the SBD-2's and the F4F-3's. In the following week additional Army and Navy planes arrived, and by 31 May there were 107 aircraft on the island.[10]

---

[9] *Battle That Doomed Japan*, 245. ". . . the spread of the virus was so great," the authors say, "that its effect may be found on every level of the planning and execution of the Midway operation."

[10] By this date the daily aviation gasoline consumption of planes based on Eastern Island was 65,000 gallons, and the following numbers of planes were based there: U. S. Army—four B-26's and 17 B-17's; U. S. Navy—16 PBY-5A's and six TBF's; U. S. Marine Corps—19 SBD-2's, 17 SB2U-3's, 21 F2A-3's, and seven F4F-3's.

For the ground forces and key civilian workers who had remained behind to help defend the island, the week was equally busy. Reinforcing weapons were installed, tanks tested in the sand, all defensive concentrations registered in, and the emplacing of an extensive system of obstacles, mines and demolitions completed. Sand Island now was surrounded with two double-apron barbed wire barriers, and all installations on both islands were ringed by protective wire. Antiboat mines of sealed sewer pipe, and obstacles of reinforcing steel lay offshore; the beaches were sown with homemade mines of ammunition boxes filled with dynamite and 20-penny nails; cigar box antitank mines covered likely beach exits; and bottles of molotov cocktail stood ready at every position. A decoy mockup airplane (a JFU—Japanese fouler-upper) was spotted prominently on the seaplane apron, and all underground fuel storage areas on Sand Island were prepared for emergency destruction by demolition.[11]

---

[11] The demolition system worked, too. On 22 May a sailor threw the wrong switch and blew up a good portion of the aviation gasoline. The supply was so critical after this that the pilots who arrived on the *Kittyhawk* did not get a prebattle chance to check out in their SBD-2's. Pipe lines also were wrecked in the blast, and MAG-22 thereafter had to refuel all planes by hand from 55-gallon drums.

Midway Versus the Japanese
4–5 June 1942

CHAPTER 4

A Midway PBY spotted the approaching Japanese first, at about 0900 on June 3,[1] and tracked them long enough to report eleven ships making 19 knots eastward. These vessels were probably the transport and seaplane groups of the *Occupation Force*, and they were attacked at 1624 by nine B-17's which Captain Simard sent out following the PBY's contact report. The pilots reported having hit "two battleships or heavy cruisers" and two transports in the group then 570 miles away from Midway, but the fliers were mistaken in both ship identification and in calling their shots, for they actually hit nothing. A Catalina scored on one of these oilers later that night in a moonlight torpedo run.

This was enough to convince Fletcher that the battle would soon be on, and he changed course from his station 300 miles east-northeast of Midway to gain a new position about 200 miles north. From there he could launch his planes the following morning against the Japanese carrier force which was expected to come in from the northwest. U. S. intelligence still was good. Nagumo continued to steam in from the northwest while his transports were under attack, and near daybreak on 4 June, when the *Yorktown* launched an early-morning search and while 11 PBY's

---

[1] Midway (Zone plus 12) time and West Longitude date.

were going up to patrol from Midway, he had reached a position approximately 250 miles northwest of the atoll. There at 0430 the Japanese admiral launched 36 "Kate" torpedo planes and 36 "Val" dive bombers, plus 36 escorting Zeros, for the first strike against the atoll.

At 0545 one of the Midway PBY's sighted these planes about 150 miles out from the island, and a short time later another PBY reported visual contact with two enemy carriers and the balance of the Japanese *Carrier Striking Force* some 200 miles from Midway. *Enterprise* intercepted this report, but Fletcher wanted to recover his search planes and sift further intelligence before launching his strike, and so he ordered Spruance to take the van southwesterly and lead off the attack against the enemy carriers.

Meanwhile the Midway Marines were ready for the first shock of attack. Ground force defenders at general quarters manned every weapon and warning device, and MAG-22, which already had fighters up to cover the sortie of the PBY's stood by for orders. At 0555, shortly after the second PBY report had fixed the position of the Japanese *Striking Force*, the 6th Defense Battalion radar logged a report of "many planes," and the Naval Air Station raised similar blips almost simultaneously. Air raid sirens began to wail, Condition One was set, and the MAG-22 pilots manned their planes. Both squadrons were in the

CAMOUFLAGED LOOKOUT TOWER AT SAND ISLAND *stands amidst the damage caused by Japanese dive bombers which attacked Midway Atoll on 4 June 1942.* (USN 17057)

JAPANESE CRUISER MIKUMA, *sunk at the Battle of Midway, lies battered and smoking from the attacks of pilots of MAG-22 and the American carriers.* (USN 11528)

air in less than 10 minutes, VMF-221 heading to intercept the enemy planes and VMSB-241 off to rendezvous station 20 miles east where the dive bomber pilots would receive further instructions.

The VMF fliers under Major Floyd B. Parks sighted the Zero-escorted Val dive bombers at 0616 about 30 miles out from Midway, and Captain John F. Carey, leading one of Parks' divisions in an F4F-3, launched the attack from 17,000 feet. The Marine fliers were hopelessly outnumbered, and they found that the Zero fighters could "fly rings around them." They had time for only one pass at the bombers, and then had to turn their attention to the swarm of Zeros, from one to five of which got on the tail of each Marine fighter. Only three of the original 12 Marine pilots survived this brawl, and although the damage they inflicted on the enemy has never been assessed, it is believed that they splashed a number of the bombers and some of the Zeros. Other Zeros were led into the Midway antiaircraft fire.

Meanwhile another group of 13 Midway fighters under Captain Kirk Armistead came in for an attack against the enemy air formation. Again the damage inflicted upon the enemy was undetermined, but fewer Marine pilots were lost. For better or for worse, however, the fighter defense of Midway had been expended, and the problem now passed to the antiaircraft guns on the atoll.

The first Japanese formation attacked at about 0630 from 14,000 feet. Antiaircraft fire knocked down two of these horizontal bombers before they could unload, but 22 came on through to drop their bombs. And just as these initial explosions rocked the two islands, 18 planes of the enemy's second wave came over for their strike. Since each of these Japanese formations had left the carriers with 36 planes, it is possible that the Marine fliers scored some kills.[2]

The *Kaga* aircraft group in the first wave, assigned to attack the patrol plane facilities on Sand Island, dropped nine 242-kilogram bombs on and about the seaplane hangars, setting them aflame and starting a large fire in the fuel oil tanks 500 yards to the north. The *Akagi* planes plastered the north shore of Eastern Island to destroy the Marine mess hall, galley, and post exchange. These the returning enemy fliers described as hangars.[3] Other targets of the Japanese dive bombers included the already-flaming fuel storage at the north end of Sand Island, the Sand Island dispensary, and the Eastern Island powerhouse which suffered direct hits from two 805-kilogram bombs. These hits virtually destroyed the entire plant. And at the very end of the strike, the 6th Defense Battalion's Eastern Island command post received a direct hit which killed the Marine sector commander, Major William W. Benson, and wounded several other men. After these bombers completed their runs, the Zeros came in for strafing attacks. This one and only air strike on Midway was over shortly after 0700.

[2] Maj W. S. McCormick, an experienced antiaircraft officer, counted the 22; and Capt M. A. Tyler, a VMSB-241 pilot with a grounded plane, counted the 18. CO, VMF-221 Rept to CO, MAG-22, 6Jun42, 1. However, *Battle That Doomed Japan*, 155, reports that "not a single hit" was sustained by the Japanese bombers until they struck in two waves of 36 planes each. This seems highly improbable in view of eyewitness accounts and damage sustained.

[3] *ONI Review*, 45-48. Information on ground defense from CO, 6th DefBn Rept to CO, NAS, Midway on action of 4-5Jun42, 13Jun42, 1-8.

Marine defense batteries fired throughout these attacks, and one source credited this antiaircraft fire with 10 kills.[4] Reports from Marine flyers would appear to require an increase of this estimate, however, since returning Midway pilots described enemy planes falling out of formation and others floundering into the water.[5] But Japanese authorities claim that only six of their planes—three level bombers, two dive bombers, and a fighter—failed to make it back to the carriers.[6] This controversy probably will never be resolved, for regardless of how many of these Japanese planes made it back to their carrier decks, Fletcher and Spruance—with a certain unintentional assistance from Nagumo—initiated action which resulted in the destruction of all these planes, anyway.

Nagumo's mistake was a natural one for a commander who believed himself to be unopposed on a "field" of battle of his own choice. Lieutenant Joichi Tomonaga, the flight officer who had commanded the first attack wave against Midway, radioed during his return flight that "There is need for a second attack wave." Meanwhile, with Nagumo still ignorant of the U. S. fleet's presence in the vicinity, six American TBF's and four B-26's from Midway came in to attack his ships. This convinced the Japanese admiral that Tomonaga was right, and he sent below to hangar spaces the 93 planes he had kept spotted for strikes against possible surface opposition. These planes were to be re-armed with bombs for the second strike. Then Nagumo called in the returning planes to arm them for the new attack of the atoll. While his men were involved in this work on the flight deck and in hangar spaces, Nagumo got the belated word from a *Tone* search plane that U. S. ships, including at least one carrier, were in the area. This caused another change of mind, and the admiral ordered the planes' ordnance changed again, from bombs back to torpedoes with which to attack the surface ships. But this decision was just tardy enough to allow Spruance to catch him with his planes down, and with torpedoes and bombs strewn in great confusion about the hangar deck.[7]

Meanwhile, as Nagumo vacillated, Admiral Nimitz's orders for Captain Simard to "go all out for the carriers," while Marine antiaircraft batteries worried about Midway, were under execution. VMSB–241, like the fighter squadron, had divided into two striking units, the first composed of 16 SBD–2's led by Major Lofton Henderson, and the second of 11 SB2U–3's commanded by Major Benjamin W. Norris. Henderson's group climbed to 9,000 feet to locate the enemy carriers, which were then undergoing the attack from the TBF's and the B–26's. Fliers of this group sighted the Japanese ships at 0744, but as the SBD's spiralled down they were set upon by swarms of Nakajima 97's and Zeros flying air cover, which were soon reinforced by more fighters from the carriers below. Henderson and several others were shot down (only eight of these planes got back to Midway) and the strike scored no hits although some were claimed.[8]

---

[4] *ONI Review*, 72.

[5] CinCPac Rept to ComInCh on the Battle of Midway, 8.

[6] *Battle That Doomed Japan*, 156.

[7] *ONI Review*, 17–19, 44–45.

[8] Statement of Capt E. G. Glidden, 7Jun42, 1. Japanese sources disclose, however, that no hits were scored in this attack. The Guadalcanal

Next came an attack by 15 B–17's led by Lieutenant Colonel Walter C. Sweeney, USA, but again claims of hits were optimistic. And as these Flying Fortresses pulled away, Major Norris came in with his 11 Vindicators which had taken off with Henderson. Beset by the Zeros, Norris turned to the nearest target at hand, and the Marines crowded their ancient planes into a standard glide run almost on top of the Japanese battleship *Haruna*—previously claimed as an Army B–17's victim off Luzon. Some of the fliers also went after the *Kirishima*, which was nearby, but neither attack managed any hits. Three Marines were shot down, and the group was credited with splashing two enemy fighters, plus two probables.[9]

By 1100 all surviving Marine aircraft had made their way back to the atoll where all hands grimly assessed the battle's damage and prepared for subsequent action. Of the VMF–221 fighters which had gone in against the attacking Japanese planes, only 10 returned, and of this number only two were in shape to leave the ground again. Thirteen F2A–3's and two F4F's were missing, along with the eight craft lost from the Henderson group and the three shot away from the Norris force. Slick black smoke from oil fires billowed up from the islands, and ruptured fuel lines left more than two-thirds of the aviation fuel temporarily unavailable. Gasoline had to be sent to the field from Sand Island, and hand-pumped from drums. The Marine ground defense force had sustained 24 casualties, and four ordnancemen of VMF–221 had been lost to a direct bomb hit.

At 1700 a burning enemy carrier was reported 200 miles northwest of Midway, and Major Norris prepared VMSB–241's six operational SBD–2's and five SB2U–3's for a night attack. The planes took off at 1900, but could not find the carrier. Major Norris failed to return from this mission, although the other pilots managed to home by the light of oil fires and the antiaircraft searchlights which were turned up as beacons.[10] Meanwhile, the Battle of Midway had been decided at sea in a fight of carrier aircraft.

---

airfield, captured two months later, was named in Maj Henderson's honor. Rear gunners of this strike group are credited with four enemy kills plus two additional probables.

[9] *ONI Review*, 19; *USSBS Interrogations*, Nav No 2, Capt Susumu Kawaguchi, IJN,I,6. See also *Coral Sea and Midway*, 111, for Adm Morison's dismissal of damage claims by land-based fliers.

[10] VMSB–241 Rept of Combat, 7Jun42, 3.

Battle of the Carrier Planes
4 June 1942

While the land-based fliers had their morning go at the Japanese *Striking Force*, and while Nagumo juggled his planes and decisions, Spruance steamed southeast to lead off the attack against the enemy. The American admiral intended to hold his planes until he drew within about 100 miles of the Japanese. But when he heard of the strike on Midway, Spruance launched two hours before this intended range would have been reached. By this calculated risk he hoped to catch the Japanese planes back on their carriers rearming for a second attack of the atoll. And about twenty minutes later Nagumo made the decision which set up himself and his planes as exactly the target Spruance hoped his pilots would find.[1]

Enterprise and *Hornet* began launching at about 0700, sending off every operational plane they carried, except a few to cover the task force. The strike was led by 29 Devastator (TBD-1) torpedo bombers, and these were followed by 67 Dauntless dive bombers and 20 Wildcat fighters. Eighteen other Wildcats, plus a like number withheld to relieve them later, patrolled overhead. *Yorktown* held back its planes for about two hours; Fletcher considered that the aircraft from his carrier might be needed against other enemy carriers not yet located, but by 0838 there had been no enemy sightings, and he decided to launch half his dive bombers and all his torpedo planes, along with escorting fighters. By shortly after 0900 the *Yorktown* had 17 SBD's, 12 TBD's, and six F4F-3's in the air, and other planes ready for takeoff.

As Spruance had hoped, Nagumo continued for more than an hour to steam toward Midway, and the first U. S. planes found the Japanese *Carrier Striking Force* with its flattops in the center of a larger formation consisting of two battleships, three cruisers, and 11 destroyers. By 0917, Nagumo had recovered his Midway attack planes, and at that time he made a 90-degree change of course to east-northeast. This course change caused 35 of the *Hornet's* SBD's and escorting fighters to miss the battle, but *Hornet's* torpedo planes found the enemy and went in low without fighter cover.

The 15 obsolete Devastators met heavy antiaircraft fire from the Japanese *Strik-*

---

[1] In his introduction to *Battle That Doomed Japan*, Spruance writes: "In reading the account of what happened on 4 June, I am more than ever impressed with the part that good or bad fortune sometimes plays in tactical engagements. The authors give us credit, where no credit is due, for being able to choose the exact time for our attack on the Japanese carriers when they were at the greatest disadvantage—flight decks full of aircraft fueled, armed and ready to go. All that I can claim credit for, myself, is a very keen sense of the urgent need for surprise and a strong desire to hit the enemy carriers with our full strength as early as we could reach them."

ing Force, and pulled down upon themselves the bulk of the Zeroes patrolling overhead. Against this combined fire, few of the planes got close enough to Japanese ships to launch torpedoes, and again, as in the Coral Sea battle, any hits scored by the slow unreliable torpedoes of that period proved duds. This antiaircraft and fighter opposition started while the planes had yet eight miles to go to reach the Japanese ships, and only one Devastator pilot lived to pull up from this attack.[2]

The 14 TBD's from the *Enterprise* fared only a little better. Four of these planes, likewise striking without fighter escort, survived their torpedo runs against the Japanese ships, although they scored no hits. But these two Devastator attacks, costly as they were, served to pull down the Zero canopy to such a low altitude that the following SBD's from *Enterprise* and *Yorktown* had an easier time of it.

These Dauntless dive bombers came in at about 1020 while Nagumo's ships still were dodging the Devastators. The *Akagi* took two hits which set her afire, and Admiral Nagumo transferred his flag to the light cruiser *Nagara*.[3] The *Kaga* sustained four hits, and at 1925 she blew up and sank. The *Soryu* was hit three times by the planes and also struck by three torpedoes from the submarine *Nautilus* which arrived on the scene between 1359 and 1495.[4] Finally the *Soryu's* gasoline stowage exploded and broke the ship in half.

By 1030, Nagumo had lost the services of three carriers, and in all three cases, as Spruance had hoped, the American attack had caught the ships in process of refueling and rearming the planes of their Midway strike. But even with these ships and their planes gone, Nagumo still was determined to fight back with his surviving carrier, the *Hiryu*, which had escaped damage by getting far out of position in some of the earlier evasive actions to escape the torpedo planes. "Although defeat now stared the Japanese starkly in the face, they felt that the battle had to be continued as long as we retained even a small part of our striking power."[5]

When the *Akagi* was shot from under Nagumo, the Japanese *Striking Force* commander temporarily passed his command to Rear Admiral Hiroaki Abe on board the heavy cruiser *Tone*, and command of air operations simultaneously passed to Rear Admiral Tamon Yamaguchi in the *Hiryu*. At about 1050 two float planes from the cruiser *Chikuma* sighted the *Yorktown* task group and guided to it a strike of 18 dive bombers and six fighters up from the *Hiryu*. The U. S. air patrol and antiaircraft fire knocked down or turned back most of these enemy planes which arrived

---

[2] Ensign George H. Gay was this sole survivor. His plane splashed shortly after he had pulled up from his run which had skimmed a carrier deck at about 10 feet. Gay's gunner had been killed, but Gay was rescued from his life raft next day by a Catalina.

[3] Although the *Akagi* remained afloat, she was abandoned at 1915 and later scuttled by a torpedo from one of her screening destroyers.

[4] *Battle That Doomed Japan*, 185, 189–191, presents strong evidence to indicate that this was not the *Soryu* but the *Kaga*, and that the one torpedo which actually hit proved a dud.

[5] *Battle That Doomed Japan*, 191. In *Coral Sea and Midway*, at page 132, Adm Morison points out that the Japanese at this time assumed from scout plane reports that the U. S. force had no more than two carriers, and possibly only one. The Japanese authors in *Battle That Doomed Japan* point out on page 174, however, that while the torpedo planes were yet approaching for their first strike against Nagumo, "Reports of enemy planes increased until it was quite evident that they were not from a single carrier."

at about noon, but those that got through scored three hits which started fires. Within 20 minutes the big carrier was dead in the water.

Her crew got her underway again in about an hour, but a second strike from the *Hiryu* appeared early in the afternoon. Although the Japanese lost half of the 10 Kate torpedo bombers and six Zero fighters of this attack, four of the Kates came in to attack the *Yorktown* at masthead level. Launching at a range of about 500 yards, two of the torpedo planes scored hits which left the carrier not only dead in the water but listing so badly that she was abandoned a few minutes later.[6]

Meanwhile, one of *Yorktown's* search planes (one of 10 scout bombers sent out before the first attack on the ship) spotted the *Hiryu*, two battleships, three cruisers, and four destroyers at 1445, and reported the position of these enemy ships. At 1530 Spruance had 24 SBD's[7] up from the *Enterprise*, and they found the *Hiryu* and her screening ships at 1700. Using the same tactics which had paid off in their morning attacks, the dive bombers scored four hits which finished operations for Nagumo's fourth and last flattop.[8] The bombing cost three SBD's and their crews.

During all this action Admiral Yamamoto, still miles to the rear, considered himself fortunate to have drawn out the U. S. Pacific Fleet. Shortly after noon, when he heard of the *Hiryu's* first strike against the *Yorktown*, the Japanese commander ordered the *Aleutian Screening Group* and Admiral Kondo's *Second Fleet* to join his *Main Body* by noon the next day to finish off the U. S. ships and complete the occupation of Midway. And a full hour and twenty minutes after he heard of the fate of Nagumo's final carrier, Admiral Yamamoto sent out a message in which he reported the U. S. fleet "practically destroyed and . . . retiring eastward," and he called on Nagumo, the *Invasion Force* (less *Cruiser Division 7*) and the *Submarine Force* to "immediately contact and attack the enemy." A stimulating message, but "In the light of the whole situation . . . so strangely optimistic as to suggest that Commander in Chief was deliberately trying to prevent the morale of our forces from collapsing."[9]

Nagumo's morale obviously needed to be stimulated by stronger stuff; at 2130 he reported: "Total enemy strength is 5 carriers, 6 heavy cruisers, and 15 destroyers. They are steaming westward. We are retiring to the northwest escorting *Hiryu*. Speed, 18 knots."[10] Yamamoto's answer

---

[6] The speed with which her crew had put *Yorktown* in shape after the first attack led the Japanese to believe that this second strike was against a different carrier. They had by now spotted all three U. S. carriers, but at this point they thought they had destroyed two of them. This second strike still did not finish the battered carrier, however. She remained afloat and regained some degree of equilibrium without human aid. Salvage parties went on board the following day, and the ship was taken under tow. But one of Nagumo's float planes spotted her early on 5 June, and a submarine was sent out to finish her off. The sub found the carrier on the 6th, put two torpedoes in her, and she finally went down early on 7 June.

[7] Ten of these were refugees from *Yorktown*, and the others veterans of the earlier strikes.

[8] The *Hiryu* floated in flames until, as in the case of the *Akagi*, one of the ships of her screening force put her to death with torpedoes at 0510 next morning. *ONI Review*, 13.

[9] *Battle That Doomed Japan*, 213.

[10] *Ibid*. To which message the authors quote a response by one of Yamamoto's staff officers, who, they say, "voiced the dejection of the entire Combined Fleet staff. . . ." Made by Rear Admiral Matome Ugaki, Yamamoto's chief of staff,

relieved Nagumo of command in favor of Rear Admiral Kondo; but later messages told the commander in chief that there was little chance of finding the U. S. Fleet until after dawn next day. At 0255 on 5 June the admiral changed his mind, abandoned the Midway venture, and ordered a general withdrawal.

Admiral Spruance, now more on his own than ever, following Fletcher's move from the damaged *Yorktown* to the *Astoria*,[11] of course did not know of Yamamoto's decision; but he did know that vastly more powerful enemy surface forces could well be nearby, quite possibly with additional carriers that had come in with the *Main Body* or with another enemy force. His problem, as he saw it, was to avoid combat in which he could be hopelessly outclassed, especially at night, and yet at the same time keep within air support distance of Midway in case the Japanese should persist in their assault plans. This he succeeded in doing, but in the process lost contact with the enemy fleet. He did not regain contact until 6 June.

In the early morning hours of 5 June, however, a retiring Japanese column of four cruisers and two destroyers was sighted by U. S. submarine *Tambor;* and when the Japanese sighted the *Tambor*, evasive action resulted in a collision of their cruisers, *Mogami* and *Mikuma*. While the other Japanese cruisers retired at full speed, these two lagged behind with the destroyers to screen them, the *Mogami* with a damaged bow and the *Mikuma* trailing oil. The submarine continued to stalk these four ships, did not manage to gain a firing position, but at break of day reported their position.

Captain Simard sent 12 B–17's out from Midway to attack these ships, but the Flying Fortresses had trouble locating their targets, and Simard then ordered a Marine bombing squadron off on this mission. Captain M. A. Tyler with six SBD–2's and Captain Richard E. Fleming with six SB2U–3's took off at about 0700 to attack the ships which were then reported to be 170 miles west of the atoll. They located the ships at about 0800, and Tyler led his division out of the sun toward the stern of the *Mogami* while Fleming and the other Vindicator pilots went down at the *Mikuma*.

Both divisions met heavy antiaircraft fire, but Tyler and his fliers bracketed their target with six near misses which caused some topside damage to the *Mogami*.[12] Fleming's plane was hit, but the pilot stayed on course at the head of his attack formation and crashed his plane into the *Mikuma's* after gun turret.[13] This additional damage further slowed the

---

the statement must likewise be considered a classic of understatement: "The Nagumo Force has no stomach for a night engagement!"

[11] Shortly after 1300 on 4 June, Spruance radioed his disposition and course to Fletcher on board the *Astoria*, and asked if Fletcher had instructions for him. Fletcher replied: "None. Will conform to your movements." *Coral Sea and Midway*, 141n.

[12] *USSBS Interrogations*, Nav No 83, RAdm Akira Soji, I, 363. Adm (then Capt) Soji had command of the *Mogami* during this action.

[13] Fleming's dive ". . . crashed into the after turret, spreading fire over the air intake of the starboard engine room. This caused an explosion of gas fumes below, killing all hands working in the engine room. This was a damaging blow to the cruiser, hitherto unscathed except for the slight hull damage received in the collision with *Mogami*. Both cruisers were now hurt, and they continued their westward withdrawal with darkening prospects of escaping the enemy's fury." *Battle That Doomed Japan*, 226.

cruisers, and Admiral Spruance's carrier planes found the cripples the following day, the 6th. The attack of these planes sank the *Mikuma* and inflicted enough additional damage on the *Mogami* to keep her out of the war for the next two years.

The Battle of Midway—which many historians and military experts consider the decisive naval engagement of the Pacific War—was over, and all actions following those of 4 June were anti-climactic. The U. S. had lost 98 carrier planes of all types, and would lose the *Yorktown*, then under tow. The Japanese carriers sustained total losses of about 322 planes of all types.[14] And with the four carriers had gone the cream of their experienced naval pilots. This, along with later losses in air battles over Guadalcanal, was a blow from which the Japanese never fully recovered.[15]

Although the carrier planes had decided the large issue, the contribution of Marines to the defense of Midway had been considerable, from the inception of base development to the end of the action. Not only had the 3d and 6th Defense Battalions contributed their share of labor, vigilance, and flak, but the aviation personnel of MAG-22, at a cost rarely surpassed in the history of U. S. naval aviation, had faced a superior enemy and exacted serious damage. At a cost of 49 Marines killed and 53 wounded, Midway had destroyed some 43 enemy aircraft (25 dive bombers and 18 Zeros) in air action, plus another 10 shot down by antiaircraft guns.[16]

In another air-air action, similar to that at Coral Sea, Fletcher and Spruance had sent the proud *Imperial Fleet* scurrying home to Japan without firing a shot from its superior naval rifles. Yamamoto could gain little consolation from the fact that the northern operation had secured two Aleutian bases: what good the bowl if the rice is gone? For ". . . unlike most of the Nipponese war lords, [Yamamoto] appreciated American strength and resources." [17] He knew that destruction of the U. S. Fleet early in 1942 was a necessary prerequisite to the year's plans for control of the Coral Sea and the American sea lanes to Australia and New Zealand, and, in the final analysis, the necessary prerequisite to the success of Japan's entire war effort.[18]

But now that the Japanese clearly were defeated at Midway, they no longer could overlook the setback they had received at Coral Sea in phase one of their 1942 plans, and phase three—occupation of the Fijis, Samoa and New Caledonia—soon was scrapped. "The catastrophe of Midway definitely marked the turning of the tide in the Pacific War . . ." [19] and from arrogant offense the Japanese soon turned to chagrined defense and ultimate defeat. U. S. plans for a first offensive already were well advanced, and the rest of 1942 was destined to be a most gloomy period for the Japanese.

In *Battle That Doomed Japan*, Fuchida and Okumiya devote their final chapter to a scholarly and complete analysis of this

---

[14] *Ibid.*, 250. This figure may be suspect. It exceeds considerably the regular complement of the four carriers.

[15] For a discussion of the "crack-man policy" of the Japanese Navy Air Force, see *Battle That Doomed Japan*, 242-243.

[16] These are reported figures based on the soundest possible estimates. The Japanese account in

---

Battle That Doomed Japan does not bear them out. The authors list only six planes lost in the Midway strike and 12 in combat air patrol.

[17] *Coral Sea and Midway*, 75.

[18] *Ibid.* See also *Battle That Doomed Japan*, 60.

[19] *Battle That Doomed Japan*, 231.

defeat, and they end on an introspective note:

In the final analysis, the root cause of Japan's defeat, not alone in the Battle of Midway but in the entire war, lies deep in the Japanese national character. There is an irrationality and impulsiveness about our people which results in actions that are haphazard and often contradictory. A tradition of provincialism makes us narrow-minded and dogmatic, reluctant to discard prejudices and slow to adopt even necessary improvements if they require a new concept. Indecisive and vacillating, we succumb readily to deceit, which in turn makes us disdainful of others. Opportunistic but lacking a spirit of daring and independence, we are wont to place reliance on others and to truckle to superiors. Our want of rationality often leads us to confuse desire with reality, and thus to do things without careful planning. Only when our hasty action has ended in failure do we begin to think rationally about it, usually for the purpose of finding excuses for the failure. In short, as a nation, we lack maturity of mind and the necessary conditioning to enable us to know when and what to sacrifice for the sake of our main goal.

Such are the weaknesses of the Japanese national character. These weaknesses were reflected in the defeat we suffered in the Battle of Midway, which rendered fruitless all the valiant deeds and precious sacrifices of the men who fought there. In these weaknesses lies the cause of Japan's misfortunes.[20]

---

[20] *Ibid.*, 247–248.

PART VI

The Turning Point: Guadalcanal

CHAPTER 1

Background and Preparations[1]

Scarcely had Admiral Yamamoto pulled his *Combined Fleet* away from its defeat at Midway before the U. S. Joint Chiefs of Staff began reconsidering basic Pacific policy. They wanted an offensive which would aid containment of the Japanese advances toward Australia and safeguard the U. S. communication lines to the Anzac area. As early as 18 February, Admiral Ernest J. King, Commander in Chief of the U. S. Fleet and Chief of Naval Operations, told Chief of Staff George C. Marshall that he considered it necessary to garrison certain South and Southwest Pacific islands with Army troops [2] in preparation for launching U. S. Marines on an early offensive against the enemy.[3] And shortly after the Battle of the Coral Sea, General MacArthur advanced plans for an attack against the Japanese at Rabaul. For this move he requested aircraft carriers, additional troops, and more planes.[4] But Nimitz rejected this plan. His carriers were too precious for commitment in waters so restricted as the Solomon Sea, he told the general. Besides, the admiral had a plan of his own. He wanted to capture Tulagi with one Marine raider battalion.[5] Admiral King's reaction to this plan was initially favorable, but on 1 June he sided with Marshall and MacArthur that the job could not be done by one battalion. (See Map 11)

---

[1] Unless otherwise noted the material used in Part VI is derived from 1st MarDiv FinalRept on the Guadalcanal Operation, Phases I through V, issued June-August 1943, hereinafter cited as *FinalRept* (with Phase No); action reports, war diaries, and journals of the various units which served with or as part of the 1st MarDiv; *Marine Air History; Strategic Planning;* W. F. Craven and J. L. Cate (eds.), *The Pacific: Guadalcanal to Saipan—The Army Air Forces in World War II* (Chicago: University of Chicago Press, 1950); J. Miller, Jr., *Guadalcanal: The First Offensive—United States Army in World War II* (Washington: HistDiv, DA 1949), hereinafter cited as *Miller, Guadalcanal;* S. E. Morison, *The Struggle for Guadalcanal—History of United States Naval Operations in World War II* (Boston: Little, Brown and Company, 1950), hereinafter cited as *Struggle for Guadalcanal;* Capt H. L. Merillat, *The Island* (Boston: Houghton Mifflin Company, 1944), hereinafter cited as *The Island;* Maj J. L. Zimmerman, *The Guadalcanal Operation* (Washington: HistDiv, HQMC, 1949); VAdm R. Tanaka with R. Pineau, "Japan's Losing Struggle for Guadalcanal," two parts, *USNI Proceedings*, July and August 1956, Copyright 1956 by the U. S. Naval Institute, hereinafter cited as *Tanaka Article.* Specific citations of material, in addition to direct quotations, taken from *FinalRept* have been noted where the information presented may be of special interest.

[2] CominCh ltr to CofSA, 18Feb42 (located at NHD).

[3] Specific mention of Marines for assault work came after Marshall questioned King's plans and asked why these FMF troops could not perform the garrison duty. CofSA ltr to CominCh, 24Feb42; CominCh ltr to CofSA, 2Mar42 (located at NHD).

[4] CinCSWPA msg to CofSA, 8May42 (located at OCMH).

[5] CinCPac ltr to CinCSWPA, 28May42 (located at NHD).

But now time and the victory at Midway had improved the U. S. position in the Pacific, and on 25 June Admiral King advised Nimitz and Vice Admiral Robert L. Ghormley, Commander of South Pacific Forces,[6] to prepare for an offensive against the Lower Solomons. Santa Cruz Island, Tulagi, and adjacent areas would be seized and occupied by Marines under CinCPac, and Army troops from Australia then would form the permanent occupation garrison.[7] D-Day would be about 1 August.

The task seemed almost impossible. Ghormley had just taken over his Pacific job after a hurried trip from London where he had been Special Naval Observer and Commander of U. S. Naval Forces in Europe; the 1st Marine Division, slated for the Solomon landing, was making an administrative move from the United States to New Zealand; and Marshall and King continued to debate matters of command. The general contested the Navy's right to command the operation. The area lay in the Southwest Pacific, Marshall pointed out, and so MacArthur ought to be in charge.[8]

Never mind arbitrary geography, King's reply seemed to say. The forces involved would not come from MacArthur, but from the South Pacific; and King doubted that MacArthur could help the operation much even if he wanted to. The Southwest Pacific's nearest land-based bomber field was 975 miles from Tulagi. The command setup must be made with a view toward success, King said, but the primary consideration was that the operation be begun at once. He stated unequivocally that it must be under Nimitz, and that it could not be conducted in any other way.[9]

The Joint Chiefs resolved this conflict on 2 July with issuance of the "Joint Directive for Offensive Operations in the Southwest Pacific Area Agreed on by the United States Chiefs of Staff." The directive set the seizure of the New Britain-New Ireland-New Guinea area as the objective of these operations, but it broke this goal down into three phases designed to resolve the dispute between MacArthur and Nimitz. Phase One would be the seizure of the islands of Santa Cruz and Tulagi, along with positions on adjacent islands. Nimitz would command this operation, with MacArthur concentrating on interdiction of enemy air and naval activity to the west. And to remove MacArthur's geographic claim on the Phase One target area, the Joint Chiefs shifted the boundary between the general and Admiral Nimitz to place the Lower Solomons in the admiral's South Pacific area. MacArthur then would take command of Phase Two, seizure of other Solomon Islands plus positions on New Guinea, and of Phase Three, the capture of Rabaul and adjacent bases in New Britain and New Ireland. Questions of timing, establishment of task organizations, and arrangements for command changes from one area to another would be governed by the Joint Chiefs.

Preparation of this directive in Washington had prompted King's warning

---

[6] Two days earlier a message from Nimitz gave Ghormley the Midway victory tally and suggested that the carriers now might be made available for support of an operation against the Solomon Islands. ComSoPac War Diary, June 1942 (located at NHD).

[7] ComInCh disp to CinCPac and ComSoWesPacFor, 25Jun42 (located at NHD).

[8] CofSA ltr to ComInCh, 26Jun42 (located at NHD).

[9] ComInCh ltr to CofSA, 26Jun42 (located at NHD).

BACKGROUND AND PREPARATIONS

order which Ghormley received on 25 June; and when the directive arrived in the South Pacific the force commander there already was making his plans for Phase One, which Washington labeled Operation WATCHTOWER. But, valid as was the Chiefs' of Staff determination to lose no time in launching this first offensive, problems facing Ghormley and Nimitz were so grim that the pseudo code name for the undertaking soon became "Operation Shoestring."

JAPANESE SITUATION

Since Pearl Harbor the Japanese had expanded through East Asia, the Indies, and much of Melanesia to a gigantic line of departure which menaced Australia from the Indian Ocean to the Coral Sea. Lae, Salamaua, and Finschhafen on New Guinea's north coast had been occupied, and a force for the capture of Port Moresby—a New Guinea town just across the north tip of the Coral Sea from Australia's Cape York Peninsula—stood poised at Rabaul in the Bismarcks, a position taken by the Japanese on 23 January 1942.

A month later the Japanese took Bougainville Island in the Northern Solomons, and on 4 May they took a 300-mile step down this island chain to capture Tulagi, which lay between the larger islands of Florida and Guadalcanal. This started the Japanese encirclement of the Coral Sea, a move that was thwarted by Admiral Fletcher in the naval battle that preceded the fight at Midway (see Part V, Chapter 1).

Defeat of their fleet at Midway forced the Japanese to alter many of their ambitious plans, and on 11 July they gave up the idea of taking New Caledonia, Fiji, and Samoa. But if Admiral Yamamoto realized that the failure of his fleet at Midway spelled the doom of Japanese ambitions in the Pacific, U. S. fighting men were to meet a number of his countrymen who did not get the word, or who were bent on convincing Yamamoto that he was wrong. Rabaul and Solomons positions grew stronger after the Battle of Midway, and reduction of Fortress Rabaul would occupy efforts of the Allied South Pacific forces for nearly two years. Operation WATCHTOWER, which turned out to be the landing against Tulagi and Guadalcanal, was the first Allied step toward Rabaul.

In 1942 the Australian garrison at Tulagi consisted of a few riflemen of the Australian Imperial Force, some members of the Royal Australian Air Force, a member of the Australian Naval Intelligence, the Resident Commissioner, the civil staff, and a few planters and missionaries. Most of these people evacuated the area after a heavy Japanese air raid of 1 May, and the subsequent sighting by coastwatchers of enemy ships en route toward the Southern Solomons. Among those who remained in the Solomon area were the coastwatchers, courageous old island hands who now retired into the bush and hills from which they would observe Japanese movements and report regularly by radio to their intelligence center in Australia.[11]

The *3d Kure Special Landing Force* made the Tulagi landing from the cruiser-mine layer *Okinoshima* which flew the flag of Rear Admiral Kiyohide Shima. One group of these Japanese "marines"—a machine gun company, two antitank gun

---

[11] For an excellent account of the work of these men see Cdr E. A. Feldt, RAN, *The Coastwatchers* (New York and Melbourne: Oxford University Press, 1946), hereinafter cited as *Coastwatchers*.

platoons, and some laborers—occupied Tulagi while a similar task organization from the *3d Kure Force* went ashore on Gavutu, a smaller island nearby. They met no opposition, except that from Admiral Fletcher's planes in the action ancillary to the Battle of the Coral Sea, and defensive installations were set up immediately to protect the base construction and improvement work which soon got underway. The Japanese set up coastwatcher stations on Savo Island at the northwest end of the channel between Florida and Guadalcanal, and on both tips as well as the south coast of Guadalcanal.

Tulagi has an excellent harbor,[12] and initial efforts of the Japanese landing force improved this and developed a seaplane base there. The enemy took no immediate steps to develop airfields, and a full month passed before surveying parties and patrols crossed the 20-mile channel to Guadalcanal where they staked out an air strip site on the plains of the Lunga River. They finished this survey late in June and began to grade a runway early in July.

With a scrapping of the plans to occupy Samoa, Fiji, and New Caledonia, and with the importance of Rabaul thus increased, Japanese holdings in the Lower Solomons had gained in value. Tulagi with its excellent harbor, and Guadalcanal with its broad plains suitable for airstrips, would be an important outwork to Rabaul. A new offensive likewise could be mounted from the Bismarck-Solomon positions, to erase the Coral Sea and Midway setbacks.

Japan still had her eye on Port Moresby. The troops slated for that occupation already waited at Rabaul, and now a new fleet, the *Eighth*, under Vice Admiral Gunichi Mikawa, was created to help look after this southern end of the Japanese conquest string. This fleet, with the help of aircraft from Rabaul and the Lower Solomons, would protect the ferrying of troops to Buna, and the subsequent overland march of these troops across New Guinea's Owen Stanley Mountains to capture Port Moresby. Thus Australia would be well blocked if not completely isolated; and maybe if the Japanese did not think about the defeat at Midway the sting would just go away and everything would be all right again.[13]

U. S. PREPARATIONS

After reinforcing the Anzac lifeline (see Part II, Chapter 3), the U. S. began edging toward its Solomon Islands target area. Near the end of March some 500 Army troops from Major General Alexander M. Patch's America Division in New Caledonia went up to garrison Efate in the lower New Hebrides. On 29 March the 4th Marine Defense Battalion and Marine Fighter Squadron 212, diverted from their deployment from Hawaii to Tongatabu, also landed on this island. These Marines and Army personnel built an airstrip for the fighter squadron. Naval forces also began to arrive during this time, and in April other elements of Marine Air Group 23, parent organization of Squadron 212, came to the island. The prewar seaplane base at Vila, Efate's larg-

---

[12] Earl Jellicoe, the British admiral who commanded at Jutland, recommended after a South Pacific inspection trip following World War I that the Tulagi harbor be developed as a major fleet base.

[13] For an idea of the pains taken by official Japan to hide the facts of the Midway defeat, see the preface of Mitsuo Fuchida in *Battle That Doomed Japan*, xiii–xv.

est town, was improved, and another such base was built in Havannah Harbor on the island's northwest coast.

This was a hazardous and rather unnerving extension of defensive lines for the meager American force of that period. The Japanese were just 700 miles to the north in the Lower Solomons, and this fact gave these New Hebrides islands and waters that same hostile, "creepy" feeling that members of the unsuccessful Wake relief expedition had sensed while on that venture deep into the enemy zone. The Japanese made a few air raids into this area, but the greatest opposition came from the anopheles mosquito.

In the New Hebrides American troops of World War II had their first wholesale encounter with this carrier of malaria, and the field medical units were not prepared to cope with the disease in such proportions. Atabrine tablets were not yet available, and even quinine was in short supply. By the end of April there were 133 cases of malaria among the 947 officers and men of the 4th Defense Battalion, and by the time of the Guadalcanal landing early in August the entire New Hebrides force reported the disease in even greater proportions. Medical units were dispatching requests for "an enormous amount of quinine."[14]

In May both General Patch and Admiral Ghormley recommended that a force be sent even farther north, to Espiritu Santo. An airfield there would put the Allied planes 150 miles closer to the Solomons, and the force there would be a protective outwork for Efate until that first offensive started. Admiral Ghormley also recommended that the Ellice Islands, between the Samoan group and the Gilberts, be occupied as an additional outpost of the communication lines to Australia. This move was postponed, however, and it was not until October that Marines landed at Funafuti in the Ellice group. Espiritu Santo was immediately important to the Solomons operation, however, and on 28 May a force of about 500 Army troops moved from Efate to the larger New Hebrides island farther north. The first attempt of these troops to build an airfield there bogged down in a stretch of swamp and new outbreaks of malaria.

By this time, plans for the WATCHTOWER landings were firming up, and the effort at Espiritu Santo was reinforced so that the airfield would be completed in time. On 15 July a detachment from the 4th Marine Defense Battalion went up to Santo with a heavy antiaircraft battery and an automatic weapons battery. The airfield was completed in time, but the Army troops and Marines were mostly walking cases of malaria by then. However, important islands had been reinforced, new garrisons formed to protect the communication lines, and these displacements toward enemy bases had been accomplished. The time had come to strike back at the Japanese.

PLANS FOR BATTLE

When Admiral Ghormley received the WATCHTOWER warning order on 25 June, the 1st Marine Division, commanded by Major General Alexander Archer Vandegrift, was en route from the United States to Wellington, New Zealand. The advance echelon had arrived on 14 June, and the rear was at sea. It would land on 11 July. Until 26 June when information of the operation reached the division staff, Vandegrift had planned to continue

---

[14] MedRept, 4th DefBn, March–August 1942.

training his division in New Zealand.[15] The division, the Marine Corps' major unit available for employment on such short notice, was understrength by about one third because of detachment of the reinforced 7th Marines to Samoan duty.

Army troops in the area, originally under Ghormley's command, could provide little more than moral support to the landings. This shoestring venture would not remove the need for garrison forces elsewhere in the South Pacific. Besides, Ghormley lost his direct control of these troops on 1 July when Major General Millard F. Harmon, USA, became Commanding General, South Pacific Area, to head all Army forces in the theater. Even though Harmon would be under Ghormley's command, the admiral at first disliked this command setup. But he later came to regard Harmon as one of the finest administrators and coordinators he had ever met.[16]

Admiral Ghormley's job in the South Pacific seemed almost to resemble that of a traffic director more than it did the role of a commander. According to plans, Nimitz would order task force commanders, with their missions already assigned them, to report to Ghormley when they were going to carry out missions in his area. Ghormley then would direct these commanders to execute the missions Nimitz had assigned them, and he could not interfere in these missions except when tasks were opposed by circumstances of which Nimitz was not aware.[17]

To complete the picture of command for WATCHTOWER, Rear Admiral Richmond K. Turner arrived from Washington on 18 July and reported to Ghormley as commander of the amphibious force. Ghormley, under Nimitz, was in over-all strategic command, but he would remain at his headquarters in Noumea. Admiral Fletcher would command the joint expeditionary force. But in practice Fletcher confined himself almost completely to providing air cover from his carriers, and this left Turner, in addition to commanding Vandegrift and his division, in charge of almost everything else as well.

This command setup which placed Vandegrift under the Navy's amphibious force commander rankled until nearly the time of the withdrawal of the 1st Marine Division from Guadalcanal fighting. It was not a case of small jealousy about control or any sort of petty peevishness on the part of either Vandegrift or Turner. Rather it was a clash of serious opposing convictions about how such an operation should be conducted. Turner and many other Naval authorities looked upon the landing force as just a detachment from the force afloat, and still connected to the Navy's amphibious force by firm command lines. That was a traditional view from an earlier age.

But this was the beginning of a big new war, and Marines had experience and thinking time enough in amphibious matters to have definite studied opinions about how these intricate over-the-beach operations should be conducted when they reached the proportions which would be

---

[15] Gen Vandegrift was under the impression that his division would not be called for combat duty prior to early 1943.

[16] Adm R. L. Ghormley personal notes, n. d., hereinafter cited as *Ghormley MS*; Maj J. L. Zimmerman interview with Adm R. L. Ghormley, January 1949.

[17] ComSoPac War Diary, 9May42 (located at NHD).

necessary in the Pacific. Vandegrift, faced with the task of putting these studied opinions and experiments into practice, wanted a clear-cut command right, free from any vestige of divided responsibility shared with the commander afloat. Once firmly established ashore, Marine opinion held, the landing force commander should command his own land operation. His training and position on the battleground made him more qualified for this job than was the amphibious force commander. It took some arguing, and this matter finally had to be taken to the top of military hierarchy, but the Navy eventually saw the point and agreed with it.

Turner's second in command was Rear Admiral V. A. C. Crutchley, RN, whose covering force would include eight cruisers (three Australian and five U. S.) and fifteen destroyers (all U. S.). These ships were to provide naval gunfire support and antiaircraft protection. In all, the naval contingent included three aircraft carriers with a strength of 250 planes; a number of light and heavy cruisers; two new battleships; and the available screening vessels and auxiliary craft. Transports and cargo vessels were at a premium, and would continue so for some time.

In addition to the approximately 250 carrier aircraft, Ghormley could muster only 166 Navy and Marine Corps planes (including two Marine squadrons—VMF-212 and VMO-251), 95 Army planes, and 30 planes from the Royal New Zealand Air Force. These 291 aircraft—all unfortunately based beyond striking range of the target area—were under the command of Rear Admiral John S. McCain whose title was Commander Aircraft South Pacific.

He was instrumental in bringing about the construction of the Espiritu Santo airfield and seeing that it was available for aircraft on 28 July, in spite of all the troubles which befell the force in the New Hebrides.

VMO-251 came in to Noumea on 12 July on board the USS *Heywood*. The outfit barely had time to set up camp at Tontouta and uncrate its aircraft before it got the word to go up to that new field at Santo and back up the landing. On 2 August the unit began to arrive at this northern New Hebrides field, and within nine days Lieutenant Colonel John N. Hart had his squadron installed there with its sixteen F4F-3P long-range photographic planes. Hart still was short his wing tanks for long-range flying, however. These were finally flown out from Pearl Harbor and arrived on 20 August.

MacArthur's contribution to the Guadalcanal operation consisted of about sixteen B-17's which flew reconnaissance over the area west of the 158th meridian east (the boundary between the South and Southwest Pacific Areas for air search) and attempted to put a stopper on the enemy air from Rabaul.

Thus Ghormley could rely only on the services of a small, highly trained striking force of fluctuating but never overwhelming power. He had no assurances of reserve ground troops, although plans were under way to release both the 7th and 8th Marines from their Samoan defense missions,[18] and he had been advised that garrison forces would have to come from the troops already within his area on base de-

---

[18] Relief for 7th Mar. was to leave the U. S. on 20 July and that for the 8th Mar on 1 September. ComSoPac War Diary, June 1942 (located at NHD).

fense duty.[19] The 1st Base Depot had set up an advance echelon in Wellington on 21 June, and other supply bases were to be established later at Noumea and Espiritu Santo.

The general structure organized to employ these resources against the Japanese was laid down in Nimitz' order to Ghormley of 9 July, and Ghormley's Operation Plan 1-42 of 17 July 1942.[20]

Ghormley, exercising strategic command, set up his organization in three main groups:

Carrier Forces (Task Force 61.1), commanded by Rear Admiral Leigh Noyes, was composed of elements of three task forces from Nimitz's area—11, 16, and 18. It would include three carriers, *Saratoga*, *Enterprise*, and *Wasp*, the fast new battleship *North Carolina*, five heavy cruisers, one so-called antiaircraft cruiser, and 16 destroyers.

Amphibious Force (Task Force 61.2), commanded by Rear Admiral Richmond K. Turner, included the Marine landing force carried in 13 attack transports, four destroyer transports, and six cargo ships; a fire support group of one antiaircraft and three heavy cruisers plus six destroyers; a screening group of one light and three heavy cruisers as well as nine destroyers; and a small mine-sweeping group.

Shore-Based Aircraft (Task Force 63), under Rear Admiral J. S. McCain (ComAirSoPac), included all aircraft in the area except those on carriers.

Complicating this symmetrical structure was the tactical command role played by Vice Admiral Fletcher. He was in overall command of TF 61 which included the forces of Noyes and Turner.

Ghormley called for a rehearsal in the Fiji area and directed that all task force commanders arrange to hold a conference near the rehearsal area. He himself would move from Auckland to Noumea about 1 August in order to comply with his orders to exercise strategic command within the operating area.[21]

By this time the plans and orders were formed, the target selected, the forces organized, and the Navy given leeway to operate without poaching in the territory of the Southwest Pacific. Only the detail of a landing date remained unsettled. Vandegrift pointed out to Ghormley that the late arrival of his second echelon, and a stretch of bad weather, had so complicated his loading problem as to make it impossible to meet the date of 1 August. Ghormley and Nimitz agreed that an additional week was needed, and King consented to postpone the landing until 7 August. King warned, however, that this was the latest date permissible and that every effort should be made to advance it.

ACCUMULATION OF INTELLIGENCE

From an intelligence point of view, the Guadalcanal-Tulagi landings can hardly

---

[19] Adm King's effort to secure quick release for the assault troops was not successful. The Army's commitments to the European Theater were such that no units were available for such missions. Initially assured that air support and air replacements would be available, King was advised on 27 July by LtGen Joseph C. McNarney, acting Chief of Staff, that commitments in other areas would not permit further air reinforcements of the South Pacific—a dictum which King protested strongly. ComInCh memo to CofSA, 1Aug42 (located at NHD).

[20] *Ghormley MS*, 54, 58.

[21] *Ibid.*, 59.

BACKGROUND AND PREPARATIONS   243

be described as more than a stab in the dark. When General Vandegrift received his initial warning order on 26 June 1942, neither his staff nor the local New Zealand authorities had more than the most general and sketchy knowledge of the objective area or the enemy's strength and disposition, and there was but a month available before the scheduled date of mounting out, 22 July.

As in the case with most tropical backwaters, the charting and hydrographic information was scanty and out of date. Lieutenant Colonel Frank B. Goettge, Intelligence Officer of the 1st Marine Division, therefore set out to locate traders, planters, shipmasters, and a few miners who had visited or lived at Guadalcanal or Tulagi. A number of likely sources resided in Australia, and while his subordinates tabulated the formal data available, Goettge left for Australia on 2 July. He returned to New Zealand on the 13th.

Long after the conclusion of the campaign, it was learned that Colonel Goettge's efforts deserved better success than they had enjoyed. During his hurried trip to Australia, he arranged with the Southwest Pacific Area for maps to be made from a strip of aerial photographs and to be delivered prior to the sortie of the 1st Marine Division. The maps were made, but were not received because of certain oversights and confusion in mounting out the division.

From Buka and Bougainville in the north, the Solomons form a double column of islands streaming southeast between latitudes five and twelve degrees south. Looking northwest toward Bougainville, the large islands on the right are Choiseul, Santa Isabel, and Malaita. In the column to the left are the islands of the New Georgia group, the Russells, Guadalcanal, and San Cristobal. Buka and Bougainville at outbreak of the war were part of the Australian Mandated Territory of New Guinea; the remainder of the double chain formed the British Solomon Islands Protectorate. In all, the islands number several hundred, with some 18,600 square miles of land area. (See Map 11)

Florida, the largest island of the Nggela Groan, lies between Malaita and Guadalcanal; and between the northern tips of Guadalcanal and Florida is the small, nearly-conical island of Savo. Indispensable Strait separates Florida from neighboring Malaita to the east, and the twenty-mile-wide strait between Florida and Guadalcanal to the south is known generally as Sealark Channel. (See Map 13, Map Section)

Nestled into the northwest rim of a jagged bight in Florida's south coast lies Tulagi, seat of the British Resident Commissioner. Tulagi Harbor, the water between the two islands, is the best anchorage in the Southern Solomons.

In the middle of Florida's bight, generally east southeast of Tulagi, lie the smaller causeway-connected islands of Gavutu and Tanambogo. Gavutu was the local headquarters of Lever Brothers which operated coconut plantations in the area, and this island, as well as Tanambogo and Tulagi, possessed some docks, jetties, and other developments for shipping, management, and copra processing.

Mostly volcanic in origin and lying within the world's wettest area, the Solomons are jagged, jungle-covered, and steamy with humid tropical heat. Lofty peaks and ridges cross-faulted by volcanic action and dramatic erosion cuts from swift rivers chop the islands into conflict-

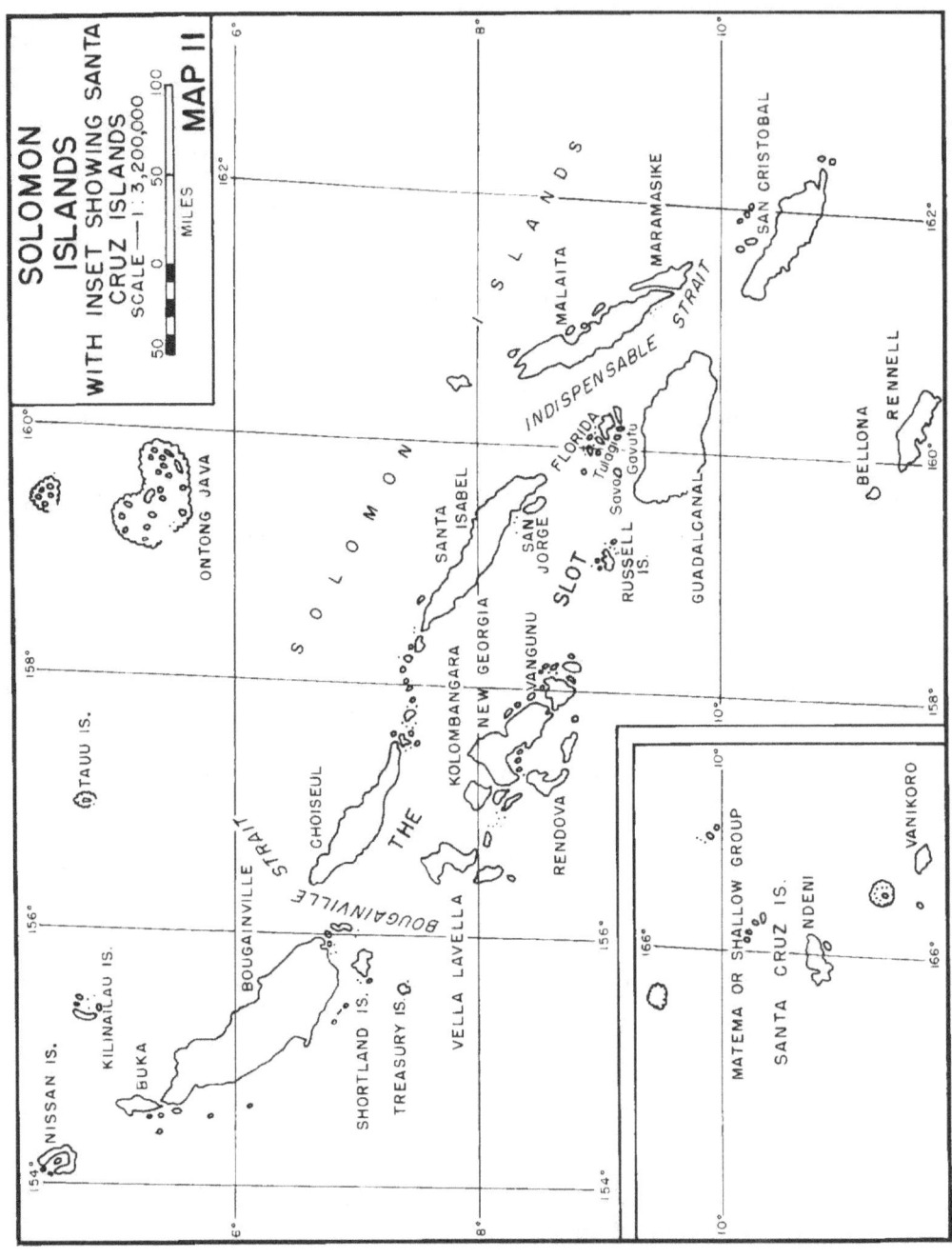

ing terrain that became a nightmare for military operations.

Guadalcanal, some 90 miles in length and about 25 miles wide, presents a varied topography ranging from plains and foothills along the north coast to a mountain backbone dropping rapidly to the south coast. Rainfall is extremely heavy, and changes in season are marked only by changes in intensity of precipitation. This, together with an average temperature in the high 80's, results in an unhealthy climate. Malaria, dengue, and other fevers, as well as fungus infections, afflict the population.

Rivers are numerous and from the military point of view may be divided arbitrarily into two classes. The first of these is the long, swift, relatively shallow river that may be forded at numerous points. Generally deep only for a short distance from its mouth, it presents few problems in the matter of crossing. Examples of this type on Guadalcanal are the Tenaru, the Lunga, and the Balesuna. The second type is that of the slow and deep lagoon. Such streams are sometimes short, as in the case of the Ilu River, and some lagoons are merely the delta streams of rivers of considerable size, as in the case of the Matanikau. This type, because of depth and marshy banks, became a military obstacle.

Although such accumulation of data afforded much enlightenment beyond the little previously known, it included corresponding minor misinformation and many aggravating gaps, for detailed information in a form suitable for military operations was mainly lacking.

In spite of the number of years which had elapsed since initiation of the systematic economic development of the islands by the British, not a single accurate or complete map of Guadalcanal or Tulagi existed in the summer of 1942. The hydrographic charts, containing just sufficient data to enable trading schooners to keep from grounding, were little better, although these did locate a few outstanding terrain features of some use for making a landfall or conducting triangulation. Such locations were not always accurate. Mount Austen, for example, was assigned as an early landing objective, but the landing force discovered that instead of being but a few hundred yards away from the beaches, the mountain actually lay several miles across almost impassable jungle.[22]

Aerial photographs would have been a profitable source of up-to-date information, but the shortage of long-range aircraft and suitably located bases, and the short period available for planning, combined to restrict availability of aerial photos in the quantity and quality normally considered necessary.

Perhaps the most useful photographic sortie carried out prior to the Guadalcanal-Tulagi landings was that undertaken on 17 July by an Army B-17 aircraft in which Lieutenant Colonel Merrill B. Twining, assistant operations officer of

---

[22] This was the so-called "Grassy Knoll" assigned to the 1st Marines. Guadalcanal residents described it as lying virtually within the perimeter area ultimately occupied and defended by Gen Vandegrift, whereas its true location was six miles to the southwest. This discrepancy, unexplained for years, has given much cause for speculation to historians of the Guadalcanal campaign, some of whom have raised the question whether Mount Austen was really the "Grassy Knoll" which Goettege's informants had in mind. This school of thought suggests that a feature within the described limits which might answer that description would have been the high ground later to become known as Edson's Ridge.

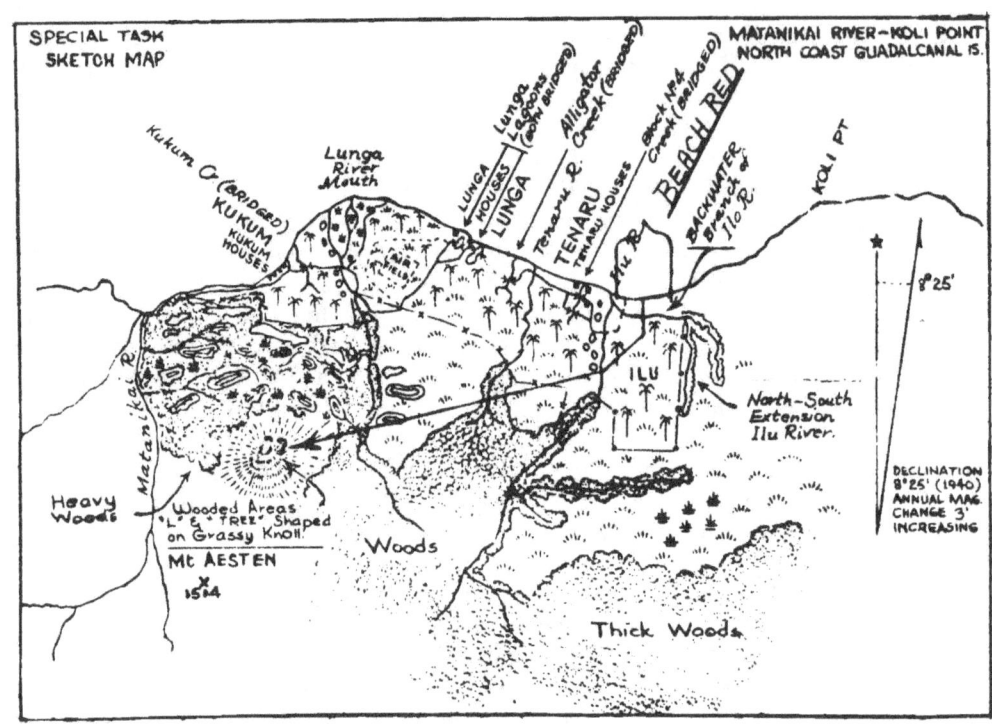

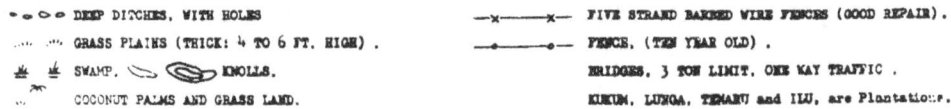

CRUDE SKETCH MAP *used in the planning and early operational phases of the Guadalcanal campaign by units of the 5th Combat Team; it is an adaptation of a map prepared by the D-2 Section and typifies the scarcity of reliable terrain information available to the 1st Marine Division when it left New Zealand.*

BACKGROUND AND PREPARATIONS

the 1st Marine Division, and Major William B. McKean, member of the staff of Transport Squadron 26, conducted a personal reconnaissance of the landing areas. They assured General Vandegrift that the Lunga beaches appeared suitable for landing.[23]

The coastal map of Guadalcanal finally adopted by the 1st Marine Division (and employed, with such corrections as could later be developed, through the entire campaign) was traced from an aerial strip-map obtained by Colonel Goettge on his mission to Australia. It was reasonably accurate in general outline, but contained no usable indications of ground forms or elevations. The Goettge map was supplemented by aerial photos of Tulagi, Gavutu, and Tanambogo Islands, and these constituted the sum of the Marines knowledge of Tulagi and Guadalcanal prior to the landings.[24]

Information concerning the enemy's strength, dispositions, and activities was collected by the U. S. planners from coastwatcher reports.[25] Strength figures were by no means as definite or convincing as were the factual accounts of the defenses. Various intelligence estimates, prepared during July, gave figures as high as 8,400. Admiral Turner's Operation Plan A3-42, issued at the Koro Island rehearsals in the Fijis on 30 July, estimated that 1,850 enemy would be found on Tulagi and Gavutu-Tanambogo, and 5,275 on Guadalcanal. 130th figures were high. A count of enemy dead in the Tulagi and Gavutu area placed the number of defenders at about 1,500 (including 600 laborers), while study of positions, interrogation of prisoners, and translation of enemy documents on Guadalcanal proper indicated that about 2,230 troops and laborers had been in the Lunga area at the time of the Marines landing.

Close and determined combat was anticipated with these forces; and on 17 July, Admiral Nimitz notified Admiral King that it would be unsafe to assume that the enemy would not attempt to retake the area to be attacked, and that, if insufficient forces were assigned, the Marines might not, be able to hold on.[26]

PLANNING AND MOUNTING OUT

For the dual landing operation, General Vandegrift divided his organization into two forces. The units landing on the Florida side of Sealark Channel (**Group Yoke**) were to be commanded by Brigadier General William H. Rupertus, the assistant division commander (ADC), while Vandegrift himself would exercise command over Group X-Ray landing at Lunga Point. (See Map 13, Map Section)

It was expected that the Florida-side landings would be more severely contested by the Japanese, and to that landing group the general assigned his best-trained units: the 1st Marine Raider Battalion, com-

---

[23] HistSec, HQMC interview with Col W. B. McKean, 18Feb48.

[24] Two aerial photos, taken on 2 August by a ComAirSoPac R-1 i and developed aboard the USS *Enterprise*, were forwarded to Division Headquarters. They showed Tulagi defensive positions in sharp detail, and verified the reports of coastwatchers about the rapidly approaching completion of the airstrip in the Lunga plains.

[25] "The invaluable service of the Solomon Islands coastwatching system . . . cannot be too highly commended." *FinalRept*, Phase I, Annex E, 2.

[26] CinCPac disp to CominCh, 17Jul42 (located at NHD).

manded by Lieutenant Colonel Merritt A. Edson; the 1st Parachute Battalion of Major Robert H. Williams; and the 2d Battalion, 5th Marines under Lieutenant Colonel Harold E. Rosecrans, all with their reinforcing units attached. Edson would be the commander of the Tulagi landing force ; Williams the commander at Gavutu-Tanambogo. The Guadalcanal group included Colonel Clifton B. Cates' 1st Marines and Colonel Leroy P. Hunt's 5th Marines (less 2/5), both reinforced, plus the balance of the division special and service troops.[27]

The Tulagi plan called for the 1st Raider Battalion and 2d Battalion, 5th Marines to land in column on the island's south coast, turn east, and attack down the long axis of the island. This would be followed by 1st Parachute Battalion landings on Gavutu and Tanambogo, and a two-company sweep along Florida Island's coast line fronting Tulagi Bay. (See Map 15, Map Section)

The Guadalcanal scheme envisaged landing the 5th Marines (less 2d Bn) across a beach some few hundred yards east of the Lunga Point area where the Japanese were expected to be concentrated, and there to establish 'a beachhead. The 1st Marines then would come ashore in a column of battalions and pass through this perimeter to take Mount Austen. The primary goal was to establish a beachhead in an area not strongly defended."[28]

To make up for the division's manpower shortage caused by the detached duty of the 7th Marines in Samoa, Admiral King on 27 June had proposed that Vandegrift be allotted the 2d Marines of the 2d Marine Division. Accordingly this unit (reinforced) sailed combat loaded from San Diego on 1 July.[29] The regiment would be the landing force reserve.[30]

While staff planners contemplated a target area nearly as unfamiliar to them as the back side of the moon, other members of the landing force wrestled the monumental chore of preparing for the movement to combat. "Seldom," General Vandegrift said later, "has an operation been begun under more disadvantageous circumstances." [31]

When the decision to land on enemy beaches reached the 1st Marine Division, the command post and the 5th Marine Regiment were in Wellington, New Zealand; the 1st Marines and the 11th Marines, less two of its battalions, were at sea en route to New Zealand; service and special troops were split between the forward and rear echelons ; the 2d Regiment was on

---

[27] At this time, the later-used phrase "regimental combat team" (RCT) had not come into uniform use. This we would currently style a "regimental landing team" (RLT). What Guadalcanal Marines labeled a "combat group" included a rifle regiment with its direct-support artillery battalion, engineers, signal, medical, and other supporting elements. Within the so-called combat groups, similar battalion-sized aggregations were designated combat teams. This usage will be followed throughout this narrative.

[28] 1st MarDiv OpOrd T-12, 20Jul42. See Appendix E.

[29] Original plans called for this unit to carry out projected landings at Ndeni in the Santa Cruz Islands. Needless to say, these were never made, although occupation plans for that island, always involving Marine forces, continue to appear in Adm Turner's record until October 1942.

[30] "It is most desirable that 2d Marines be reinforced and combat unit loaded and ready upon arrival this area for employment in landing operations as a reinforced regimental combat team." ComSoPac War Diary, 27Jun42 (located at NHD).

[31] *FinalRept*, Phase V, 1.

the way from San Diego to the South Pacific; the 1st Raider Battalion was in Samoa, and the 3d Defense Battalion was in Hawaii. Preliminary plans and moves had to assemble these widely scattered units into a fighting force which could make an amphibious landing, one of the most intricate of military maneuvers. From the understanding that it would be the nucleus for the buildup of a force which would be trained for operations which might come late in 1942, the 1st Marine Division had to shift at once into hurried preparations to mount out for action.

Most of the ships transporting units of the division had been loaded organizationally for the voyage to New Zealand, but for the proposed amphibious assault the supplies had to be reshuffled and ships combat loaded so that items first needed in the fighting would be readily at hand in the holds. The reloading and re-embarking of Combat Group A (5th Marines, reinforced) went smoothly, uncomplicated by the necessity for simultaneous unloading and reloading which plagued the rear echelon. The group began embarkation on 2 July and remained on board its transport to await the arrival of the rear echelon.

This second echelon arrived on 11 July, and had eleven days to empty and reload its ships. No troops were disembarked except those who were to remain in New Zealand as rear echelon personnel. All others, who already had been in cramped quarters during the long trip across the Pacific, were put to work in eight-hour shifts, and parties of 300 men were assigned to each ship.[32]

Aotea Quay at Wellington was the scene of this squaring away. It was inadequate in all ways save that it could accommodate five ships at a time. Labor difficulties with the highly unionized stevedores resulted in the entire task being undertaken and carried through by Marines. Because of security regulations, no appeal to patriotism could be made to the regular dock workers since care was taken to have civilians believe that all the flurry was merely preparation for a training exercise. Dockside equipment was meager, and there was no shelter close at hand.

As the gear began to be juggled from ship to dock and back again, a cold, wet "southerly" settled down to lash New Zealand. But in spite of the weather, work had to continue around the clock. Carton-packed food and other supplies "deteriorated rapidly," the division later reported by way of an understatement, and the morale of troops followed the direction of the down-slanting rain.

On the dock, cereal, sugar, and other rations mushed together with globs of brown pulp that once had been cardboard boxes. A great number of wet cartons that were rushed to the hopeful safety of wool warehouses later gave way under the weight of stacking. Lieutenant Colonel Randolph McC. Pate and his logistics section had a herculean task in managing this unloading

---

[32] The passage from the United States to New Zealand had been particularly trying for the officers and men on board the *Ericsson*, a commercial ship under charter. Lack of proper food, and use of oil substitutes for shortening, resulted in loss of weight of as high as 23 pounds per man. Two meals only were served during the greater part of the passage, and one of these often consisted of soup or soup and bread. Medical officers estimated the daily calorie content of meals at less than 1,500. The ship's personnel enjoyed a full and well balanced diet during the same period. *Ibid.*, Phase I, Annex M. 1.

and reloading. Transport quartermasters of the various ships supervised work on board while a relay of officers from the division took charge of the eight-hour shifts dockside. The New Zealand Army furnished 30 flatbed lorries and 18 ten-wheelers to transfer fuel, small-arms ammunition and explosives to dumps several miles away.

There was not enough hold space for all the division motor transport. Most of the quarter- and one-ton trucks were put on board, but 75 percent of the heavier rolling stock was set aside to stay with the rear echelon that would be left behind when the division sailed for the Solomons.

Engineers loaded what little dirt-moving equipment they owned, but it was so meager that they hoped the Japanese would have most of the airfield built by the time it was captured. The engineer battalion also loaded bridging material, demolitions, and all available water supply equipment. No major construction was contemplated in early phases of the operation, however, and equipment and supplies for such work were not taken.

With the D-4 or an assistant in constant touch with the dockmaster, order began to appear from the chaos of strewn gear, swelling cereal, wilting cardboard cartons, and frayed tempers. But there were still serious problems. Supplies and equipment piled on docks often made it difficult for trucks to negotiate the narrow passages to reach all areas of the stacked gear, and during this mounting out certain modifications of the logistical plan became necessary. As finally loaded, the Marines carried 60 days supplies, 10 units of fire for all weapons, the minimum individual baggage actually required to live and fight, and less than half the organic motor transport authorized.

Regardless of the difficulties, however, the force sailed as scheduled at 0900 on 22 July, under escort of cruisers of Admiral Turner's Task Force 62.[33] General Vandegrift, despite his request for a vessel better suited in communications and accommodations, had been directed to embark his command post in the USS *McCawley*.

REHEARSALS AND MOVEMENT TO THE OBJECTIVE

In accordance with orders received from Nimitz on 1 July,[34] Ghormley had directed that all forces involved in the assault make rendezvous at a position south of Fiji, out of sight of land so that there would be no chance of observation by enemy agents and no chance that an inadvertent tip-off would be made by friendly observers.[35] At that point there would be a conference between the commanding officers who had not as yet been able to discuss in person the various aspects of the operation.

The components of the assault force not previously in New Zealand with the division were converging upon the rendezvous point from many directions. Colonel John M. Arthur's 2d Marines (reinforced), embarked in the *Crescent City*, *President Adams*, *President Hayes*, *President Jackson*, and *Alhena*, steamed south under escort of the carrier *Wasp* and a destroyer

---

[33] Adm Turner assumed the title of Commander, Amphibious Force South Pacific on his arrival in the South Pacific on 24 July.

[34] CinCPac OpOrd 34-42, cited in CinCPac War Diary, July 1942. By terms of this order also, Fletcher, CTF 11, had been ordered to assume command of the combined task forces at the rendezvous, and Ghormley had been put in command of the operation.

[35] *Ghormley MS*, 64.

EQUIPMENT FOR THE 1ST MARINE DIVISION, *including tanks and amphibian tractors, is unloaded in New Zealand preparatory to the Guadalcanal operation.* (USN 11526)

MARINE RAIDERS *and the crew of the submarine* Argonaut *line the deck of the vessel as it returns to Pearl Harbor after the Makin Island raid.* (USN 13859)

screen.[36] The 1st Raider Battalion, in the four destroyer transports of Transport Division 12, had been picked up at Noumea.

The 3d Defense Battalion (Colonel Robert H. Pepper) on board the USS *Betelgeuse* and *Zeilin* was en route from Pearl Harbor where it had been stationed since the outbreak of the war. It would meet the remainder of the force on 2 August. The Carrier Force, built around the *Saratoga* and the *Enterprise*, with Fletcher flying his flag in the former, likewise was on its way from Pearl Harbor. Rendezvous was made as planned, at 1400 on 26 July, some 400 miles south of Fiji. The conference convened at once on board the *Saratoga*. Ghormley, unable to attend, was represented by his Chief of Staff, Rear Admiral Daniel J. Callaghan and his Communications Officer, Lieutenant Commander L. M. LeHardy.

The conference pointed up several serious problems. General Vandegrift learned he would not have adequate air and surface support for the completion of the unloading phase of the operation. Fletcher wanted to retire within two days after the landing, and this meant that transport shipping would have to clear out within an unreasonably short period. The Marine general also learned that the 2d Marines, counted as his reserve, actually would be used for the proposed operation at Ndeni in the Santa Cruz islands. Admiral Callaghan reported Fletcher's retirement plans to Ghormley: "This sounds too sanguine to me," Callaghan reported, "but they believe it can be done. . . . AKs [cargo ships] may not be unloaded for three or four days."[37] Ghormley, too, believed that the ships could not be pulled out that soon.

Landing rehearsals at the island of Koro in the Fijis were conducted from 28 through 30 July, but Vandegrift labeled them a waste of time and effort. "A complete bust," he observed later.[38] Necessity for conserving landing craft made it impossible to conduct the practice landings in a realistic way, although the men involved were given additional training in debarkation,[39] and attack force ships were able to practice their gunfire support.

On 31 July, as night was falling, the ships weighed anchor and departed from Koro. The carrier task force proceeded north and west while the transports and their screen plodded steadily toward the Solomons. Almost 19,000 Marines were embarked in the 19 transports and four destroyer-transports.[40]

All circumstances favored the advancing convoy. Weather conditions during the final two days were extremely favorable: sky topped by a low ceiling and winds gusty with intermittent rain squalls. There was no sign of enemy aircraft or submarines, and no indication that the approach was observed. In fact, enemy

---

[36] The regiment had been on board since 1 June, lying in the harbor of San Diego.

[37] *Ghormley MS*, 67.

[38] Statement at Princeton, N. J., 12Mar48.

[39] Gen Vandegrift noted at the time that the precious landing craft were not in the best of condition in any event—12 of them were inoperative on one ship alone. Gen A. A. Vandegrift ltr to CMC, 4Feb49.

[40] A seemingly irreconcilable discrepancy of figures between those of the Amphibious Force, South Pacific, and the 1st Marine Division prevents a wholly accurate statement as to the number of troops embarked then or landed subsequently. The amphibious force lists a figure of 18,722, while the division records list, variously, 19,546 or 19,105.

BACKGROUND AND PREPARATIONS

patrol planes were grounded at Rabaul on 5 and 6 August because of bad weather.[41]

The convoy headed generally west from Fiji and well to the south of the Solomons chain. The course gradually shifted to the northward, and the night of 6–7 August found the entire group of ships due west of the western extremity of Guadalcanal.

Task Force 62, commanded by Admiral Turner, was divided into two Transport Groups. Transport Group X-Ray (62.1) commanded by Captain Lawrence F. Reifsnider, with the Guadalcanal forces embarked, consisted of four subgroups, as follows:

Transdiv A: *Fuller, American Legion, Bellatrix.*
Transdiv B: *McCawley, Barnett, Elliot, Libra.*
Transdiv C: *Hunter Liggett, Alchiba, Fomalhaut, Betelgeuse.*
Transdiv D: *Crescent City, President Hayes, President Adams, Alhena.*

Transport Group Yoke (62.2) commanded by Captain George B. Ashe, and carrying the assault troops for the Tulagi landing, consisted of the following subgroups:

Transdiv E: *Neville, Zeilin, Heywood, President Jackson.*
Transdiv 12: *Calhoun, Gregory, Little, McKean.* (the destroyer transport group).[42]

At 0310, 7 August, the force was directly west of Cape Esperance with an interval of six miles between groups and a speed of 12 knots. Transport Group X-Ray steamed in two parallel columns of eight and seven ships each with a distance of 750 yards between ships and an interval of 1,000 yards between columns. The rugged outline of the Guadalcanal hills was just visible to starboard when the course was shifted to 040°, and a few minutes later the two groups separated for the completion of their missions. X-Ray, shifting still further to starboard, settled on course 075°, which took it along the Guadalcanal coast, while Yoke, on course 058°, crossed outside Savo Island, toward Florida. The final approach to the transport area was made without incident, and there was no sound until, at 0614, the supporting ships opened fire on the island.[43]

There are some indications that the Guadalcanal operation on D-Day morning was something of a minor Pearl Harbor in reverse for the Japanese. A recent study of Japanese wartime messages indicates the enemy was aware that a U. S. force had sortied from Hawaii. Warnings were issued to Central Pacific outposts; Rabaul and points south were to be notified for information only. Commander of the Japanese *Twenty-Fourth Air Flotilla* (Marshall-Gilbert-Wake area) relayed his warning message south the next morning—at 0430 on 7 August. It was too late. Less than an hour later he received Tulagi's report that the U. S. striking force had been sighted in Sealark Channel at 0425.[44]

---

[41] Cdr J. Shaw ltr to Maj J. L. Zimmerman, February 1949.
[42] CTF 62 OPlan A3–42, 30Jul42.
[43] CTG 62.1 ActRept 7–9Aug42, 3.
[44] Capt. E. T. Layton, USN, ltr to HistBr, G–3, HQMC, June 1955.

CHAPTER 2

Guadalcanal, 7–9 August 1942

THE LANDING

When Task Groups X-Ray and Yoke separated northwest of Cape Esperance at 0240, the former group made for the Red Beach transport area off Guadalcanal in a double column at 12 knots. No enemy activity was observed, and the preliminary naval bombardment of the coastal area, which began at 0613, aroused no response. The X-Ray shipping reached its transport area at 0645 and began to lower the landing craft. Across the channel, Group Yoke likewise arrived at its assigned area off Tulagi without incident at 0630 and straightaway got the word from Captain Ashe that H-hour would be 0800. The units slated for Florida Island would hit their beaches first, as will be described in the next chapter.

The division's command post in the *McCawley* broke radio silence at 0519, and eight minutes later General Vandegrift set the H-hour for his side of the landing at 0910. The bombardment ships worked through their fire plans, and then as news of the successful landings on Florida and Tulagi reached Vandegrift, the first waves of assault troops moved toward the beach. (See Map 14, Map Section)

Three planes from the *Astoria* flew liaison missions in the Guadalcanal area while three from the *Vincennes* performed the same duty above Tulagi. An additional three aircraft, from the *Quincy*, were available for artillery spotting over Guadalcanal. During the ship to shore phase, these aircraft marked the beach flanks with smoke to assist naval gunfire and to guide the landing boats. Vandegrift and his division air officer held this use to be unwarranted and unnecessary.

But Admiral Turner considered it necessary to "accurately mark the extremities of the landing beaches" as directed by the operation order, and he marked them for twenty minutes. The planes made eight runs at extremely low altitudes, four runs on each beach extremity. Vandegrift pointed out that this would result in a serious if not complete loss of planes if the beaches were defended—this loss at a time when aircraft are critically needed as "eyes" to gain information about the progress of a landing.

Actually the liaison planes over Guadalcanal's random clouds and splotchy jungle furnished Vandegrift precious little information. It was not the fault of the pilots, however, since there was very little to see anyway. In the tense period of this first landing on a hostile beach, the sins were more often those of commission rather than omission. One pilot reported "many enemy troops" only to admit, under questioning for more explicit information, that his "troops" were, in fact, cows.

Other than the cows there still were no signs of activity around Lunga at 0859, 11 minutes before H-hour, when an observation plane from the *Astoria* reported that no Japanese could be seen in that area. But 15 minutes later the same pilot spotted some trucks moving on the Lunga

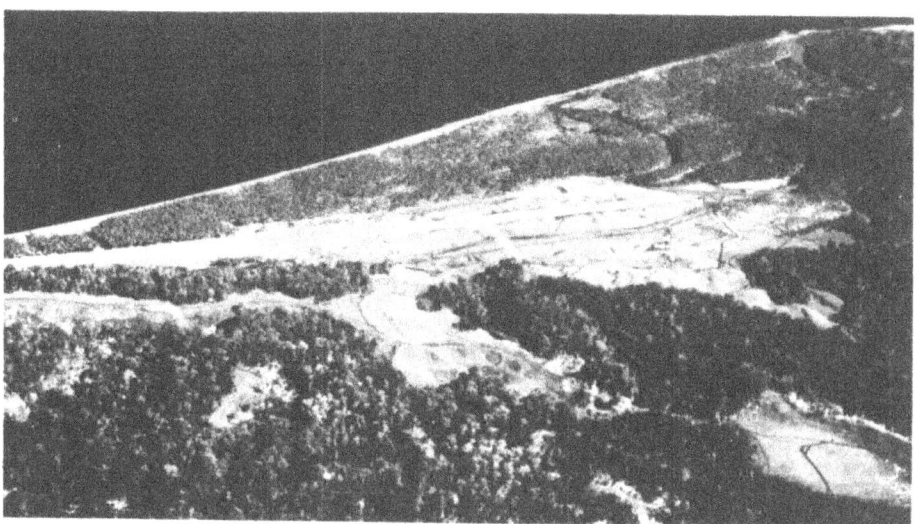

THE ORIGINAL HENDERSON FIELD, *target of the 1st Marine Division's assault at Guadalcanal, as it appeared shortly after its capture.* (USMC 108547)

TRANSPORTS AND CARGO SHIPS STAND OFFSHORE *as vitally needed supplies for the 1st Marine Division are manhandled by members of the Shore Party.* (USMC 51369)

airfield several thousand yards west of the landing beach.

Meanwhile the 5th Marines (less 2d Battalion) had crossed its line of departure and moved into the 5,000-yard approach to the beach. Naval gunfire lifted inland as the craft neared the shore, and minutes later, at 0910, the assault wave hit the beach on a 1,600 yard front and pushed into the sparse jungle growth beyond. With Lieutenant Colonel William E. Maxwell's 1st Battalion on the right (west) and Lieutenant Colonel Frederick C. Biebush's 3d Battalion on the left, the beachhead expanded rapidly against no opposition. A perimeter some 600 yards inland soon established a hasty defense. The line anchored on the west at the Tenaru River, on the east at the Tenavatu River, and reached on the south an east-west branch of the Tenaru.[1]

Regimental headquarters came ashore at 0938 to be followed two minutes later by heavy weapons troops. Landing of the reserve regiment, Colonel Cates' reinforced 1st Marines, already was underway. Beginning at 0930, this regiment came ashore in a column of battalions with 2/1 in the the van followed by the 3d and 1st Battalions in that order.

Artillery came next, and the units partially bogged down. The howitzer men admitted later that they had taken too much gear ashore with them. Prime movers for the 105mm howitzers did not get ashore initially because there were not enough ramp boats for this work, and one-ton trucks proved too light to handle the field pieces. Needed were two-and-a-half-ton six by sixes and ramp boats to put these vehicles on the beach simultaneously with the howitzers. Such prime movers were authorized, but so were a lot of other things the Marines did not have.

In spite of these troubles, the artillery units reached their assigned firing positions by making overland prime movers out of amphibian tractors that began to wallow ashore heavy with cargo.[2] Once in position, however, the gunners found the amphibian was a creature of mixed virtues: tracked vehicles tore up the communications wire, creating early the pattern of combat events that became too familiar to plagued wiremen.

Meanwhile the light 75mm pack howitzers had made it ashore with little trouble, and the advance toward the airfield got underway. At 1115 the 1st Marines moved through the hasty perimeter of the 5th Marines and struck out southwest toward Mount Austen, the "Grassy Knoll." Cates put his regiment across the Tenaru at an engineer bridge supported by an amphibian tractor, and the 1st Marines progressed slowly into the thickening jungle. Behind, to extend the beachhead, 1/5 crossed the mouth of the Tenaru at 1330 and moved toward the Ilu. Neither advance encountered enemy resistance.

---

[1] In early maps the names of the Tenaru and Ilu Rivers were incorrectly transposed. In this account the names will be applied to the correct rivers, but the name, "Battle of the Tenaru," will be retained to identify the August battle at the mouth of the Ilu.

[2] The amphibian, later to be used to transport assault troops from ship to shore, started its war career here in a modest manner. Its "usefulness exceeded all expectations,'" the Marines reported, but at the time nobody considered the strange craft capable of much more than amphibious drayage. The following day (D-plus one) on Gavutu an amphibian would create rather dramatic history by attacking a hostile cave, but such bravery was never recommended, even later when these craft entered the heyday of their more important role.

Colonel Cates realized almost at once that it would be impossible to reach Mount Austen as his day's objective. The so-called Grassy Knoll, visible from the ships, could not be seen from the beach. It commanded the Lunga area, but it lay much farther inland than reports of former planters and schooner pilots had indicated.

Under heavy packs, sometimes excessive loads of ammunition, and with insufficient water and salt tablets,[3] the 1st Marines by late afternoon had struggled but a mile when General Vandegrift ordered the regiment to halt, reorient, and establish internal contact. The men dug in a perimeter in the jungle, some 3,500 yards south of the Ilu's mouth where 1/5 had ended its advance, to set up for the night.

In spite of the breakneck pace with which the shoestring operation had mounted out and thrown itself in the path of the Japanese advance along the Solomon chain, the landing was a success. Although the lack of opposition (on the Guadalcanal side only) gave it somewhat the characteristics of a training maneuver, the need for additional training that Vandegrift had hoped to give his men in New Zealand became apparent. The general criticized the "uniform and lamentable"[4] failure of all units to patrol properly their fronts and flanks.

Logistical difficulties were worse. Movement of supplies from the landing craft to the beaches and then to supply dumps soon began to snarl. Admiral Turner blamed this on the Marines' failure to understand the number of troops required for such work, failure to extend the beach limits promptly enough and, to some extent, a lack of control and direction over troops in the beach area. But the trouble and its causes were neither as clear-cut nor as damning as that. Marine planners had foreseen a dangerous shortage of man power at this critical point, but under the uncertain circumstances on this hostile beach they felt they could allot no more men to the job than the 500 from Colonel George R. Rowan's 1st Pioneer Battalion. Vandegrift did not want working parties to cut the strength of his fighting units to a level which might risk getting them defeated.

Hindsight now makes it clear that the supplies mounting up as a juicy beach target jeopardized the operation more than a call for additional working parties would have done. There were hardly enough Japanese fighting men ashore on the island to bother the Vandegrift force, but if enemy planes from Rabaul had concentrated on hitting the congested beach they would have played havoc with this whole venture. Marines were aware of this risk, but they also expected to run into a sizable Japanese force somewhere in the thickening jungle. The people in the shore party would just have to work harder.

Sailors joined the pioneers but the beach remained cluttered in spite of this help. Needed, division officers reported later, were "additional personnel in the proportion of at least 100 men for each vessel discharging cargo across the beach."[5] It was not that this problem had never been thought out and planned for in fleet exercises over the years. It was just that this was "Operation Shoestring." The situation became so bad during the night of 7–8

---

[3] Medically speaking, the weight of individual equipment was excessive in most cases for men who had been cooped so long in steamy holds of ships and fed short, and sometimes inferior, rations. *FinalRept*, Phase II, 6.

[4] *Ibid.*, 10.

[5] *Ibid.*, Phase V, 7.

August that the landing force had to ask the ships to stop unloading. There had been air attacks that afternoon, and more were expected on the 8th. The exhausted workers needed time to clear the beaches and spread out the gear so it would be less of a target.

Fortunately the air attacks during the day had concentrated on the shipping. At about 1100 on the 7th a coastwatcher in the Upper Solomons passed the word on the watchers' network that about 18 bombers were on the way to Guadalcanal. This warning was relayed to Guadalcanal through Brisbane within 25 minutes, and the planes arrived at 1320. The destroyer *Mugford* suffered 20 casualties under a 250-pound bomb hit, but it was the only ship struck by the attack. Antiaircraft fire downed two of the twin-engined Type 97's. Later in the afternoon, at about 1500, 10 Aichi dive bombers had no luck at all, but fire from the ships scratched another two Japanese planes. Other planes from both these attacks were downed by Fletcher's carrier aircraft.

At 2200 on 7 August, Vandegrift issued his attack order for the following day. Plans had been changed. Since Mount Austen was out of reach, and because only 10,000 troops were available in the Lunga area, he ordered an occupation of the airfield and establishment of a defensive line along the Lunga River. Positions east and southeast of Red Beach would be maintained temporarily to protect supplies and unloading until shore party activities could be established within the new perimeter.

At 0930 on 8 August the 1st Battalion, 5th Marines and Company A, 1st Tank Battalion crossed the Ilu River at its mouth and advanced cautiously westward along the beach toward the Lunga. At the same time the 1st Marines moved from its night perimeter. Contact between units within this regiment was faulty, but by nightfall Lieutenant Colonel Lenard B. Cresswell's 1st Battalion had overrun the field and reached the Lunga. The other two battalions, slowed by difficult terrain, advanced about 500 yards an hour and bivouacked for the night south of the airfield.

Along the beach, 1/5 and the tanks met the first scattered resistance as they passed through the area in which the main Japanese force had been located. A few prisoners were taken, and intelligence indicated that the enemy was in no position to attack the superior Marine landing force. Continued lack of resistance elsewhere seemed to confirm this, and at 1430 the Marines contracted their front, crossed the Lunga by a bridge immediately north of the airfield, and advanced more rapidly toward the Kukum River, a stream in the western fan of the Lunga delta.

With Company D leading, this advance came upon the main Japanese encampment area at 1500. The enemy force, obviously smaller than anticipated, had retreated in evident haste and confusion. Large quantities of undamaged food, ammunition, engineering material, electrical gear, and radio equipment had been left behind. Although some improperly indoctrinated Marines began to destroy this gear, that tendency soon was halted, and in the next few weeks these men would lose their contempt for this windfall of material.

Except for token resistance from some of the straggling Japanese attempting to flee west, air action constituted the enemy's only effort to hamper the Marines. At about 1100 Coastwatcher Cecil John Mason, Pilot Officer, RAAF, warned from his Bougainville hide-out that a large number of planes were winging toward Guadalcanal. In another hour some 40 twin-engine torpedo planes appeared over the area to find the task force, alerted by the warning, maneuvering at top speed while employing evasive tactics.

A torpedo sent the destroyer *Jarvis* limping southeast for the New Hebrides. She was sunk next day by an enemy air attack. The transport *Elliott*, set afire when an enemy plane crashed aboard, had to be beached and destroyed by her sister ships. Survivors went on board the *Hunter Liggett*.

Ship antiaircraft fire and fighter planes from Admiral Noyes' carriers shot down 12 Japanese planes, and shore-based antiaircraft accounted for two more. Still others were splashed by carrier-based fighters west of the transport area. A total of seven American planes were lost.[6]

THE JAPANESE RETALIATE

These early attacks hampered Marine operations and unloading, but the beachhead continued to grow. The Japanese had no intentions of giving up their positions in the Southern Solomons without a fierce fight, however, and early on 8 August a task force of five heavy and two light cruisers and a destroyer made ready to strike American shipping in Sealark Channel.

After rendezvousing at St. George's Channel off Rabaul, this force steamed south along Bougainville's east coast until it sighted an Allied patrol plane observing its course. Reversing, the ships made back up the island coast until the plane departed. Then turning again, they sailed between Bougainville and Choiseul northeast of the Shortlands and set course down "The Slot" toward Guadalcanal.

Word of this approaching force reached Admiral Turner at 1800, and, when Admiral Fletcher notified him shortly thereafter that the carrier force was to be withdrawn, Turner called Vandegrift to the flagship *McCawley* and informed the general that, deprived of carrier protection, the transports must leave at 0600 the next day.

As early as 2 August Admiral Ghormley had known of Fletcher's intentions to retire the carriers before D-Day plus three.[7] At 1807 on 8 August Fletcher cited fuel shortage and plane losses that had reduced his fighter craft from 99 to 78 and again requested permission to withdraw until sufficient land-based aircraft and fuel were available to support shipping.[8] It seems that Ghormley had not really expected this problem to come up, in spite of Fletcher's announcement about this matter at the Fiji rehearsals. But now that Fletcher was making the request, Ghormley gave his approval. Ghormley explained later:

> When Fletcher, the man on the spot, informed me he had to withdraw for fuel, I approved. He knew the situation in detail; I did not. This resulted in my directing Turner to withdraw his surface forces to prevent their destruction. I was without detailed information as to Turner's situation, but I knew that his forces had landed and that our major problem would become one of giving every support possible to Vandegrift.[9]

---

[6] CinCPac, "Preliminary Report, Solomon Islands Operation," August 1942, 4.

[7] ComSoPac War Diary, 2Aug42 (located at NHD).

[8] *Ibid.*, 9Aug42. For a detailed discussion of Adm Fletcher's withdrawal of his carriers see also *Struggle for Guadalcanal*, 27–28, 117.

[9] *Ghormley MS*, 93.

Vandegrift held that retirement of the ships would leave him in a "most alarming" position.[10] Division plans assumed the ships would remain in the target area four days, and even then all available supplies would prove scanty enough, such was the haste with which the assault mounted out with less than the normal minimum in basic allowances. But a withdrawal early on 9 August would take much of the supplies and equipment away in the holds of ships and leave beach dumps in a state of chaos. The "shoestring" of this first Allied offensive seemed to be pulling apart. This was the first of the operation's many dark hours. (See Map 14, Map Section)

While Vandegrift conferred with Turner, the Japanese ships, elements of the enemy's *Eighth Fleet*, approached Savo Island undetected by destroyers *Ralph Talbot* and *Blue* on picket duty northwest of that small island. They slipped past these ships toward the two Allied cruisers, HMAS *Canberra* and the USS *Chicago*, and destroyers USS *Bagley* and *Patterson* which patrolled the waters between Savo and Cape Esperance. Farther north cruisers USS *Vincennes*, *Astoria*, and *Quincy* and destroyers *Helm* and *Wilson* patrolled between Savo and Florida. Down the channel two cruisers with screening destroyers covered the transports.

With seaplanes up from his cruisers to scout for the Allied ships, *Eighth Fleet* Commander Rear Admiral Gunichi Mikawa steamed southeast until he sighted his enemy at about the same time Allied ships in Sealark Channel received reports of one or more unidentified planes. But Admiral Mikawa's surface force still was undetected at 2313 when these reports came in. Admiral Turner had estimated that the Japanese ships would hole up in Rekata Bay on Santa Isabel Island and strike at the amphibious force with torpedo-carrying floatplanes.

At 0316 Mikawa ordered independent firing, and torpedoes leaped from their tubes two minutes later. Japanese floatplanes illuminated briefly. The *Canberra* caught two torpedoes in her starboard side, the *Chicago* lost part of her bow, and then the Japanese turned toward the Allied ships between Savo and Florida.

The resulting melee was one of the worst defeats ever suffered by the U. S. Navy. The *Vincennes* and the *Quincy* were lost; the Australian *Canberra* burned all night and had to be abandoned and sunk; destroyer *Ralph Talbot* was damaged, and *Astoria* went down at noon the next day. Fortunately Mikawa retired without pressing his advantage in an attack on the amphibious shipping farther down the channel, and Admiral Turner, delaying his departure, ordered unloading to continue. Late in the afternoon the transports got underway for Noumea, leaving the Marines on their own with four units of fire and 37 days' supply of food.

Even when loaded in Wellington the level of supplies and ammunition had been considered slim. That original loading of 60 days' supplies and 10 units of fire was respectively 33 and 50 per cent below the 90-day and 20-unit levels then considered normal for operations of this kind.[11] Now the ships had taken part of these loads

---

[10] *FinalRept*, Phase II, 13.

[11] Division staff officers admitted later that supplies for 60 days represented more gear than their slim fighting outfit could handle logistically at the beach. They recommended that levels should be pegged at 30 days for general supplies, 50 days for rations. The lower level

away, leaving a most inadequate fraction behind. And with air support so sketchy, there was no way to know when the transports could come back again. The stacks of captured Japanese rations began to gain in importance if not in palatability.

According to the war diary of the Commander, Task Force 62, the following troops were left in the Guadalcanal-Tulagi area when the transports and supply ships withdrew:

At Guadalcanal:
  Division Headquarters Company (less detachments)
  Division Signal Company (less detachments)
  5th Marines (less 2d Battalion)
  1st Marines
  11th Marines (less Battery E, 1st and 4th Battalions)
  1st Tank Battalion (less detachments)
  1st Engineer Battalion (less detachments)
  1st Pioneer Battalion (less detachments)
  1st Amphibian Tractor Battalion (less detachments)
  1st Service Battalion (less detachments)
  1st Medical Battalion (less detachments)
  1st Military Police Company
  2d Platoon, 1st Scout Company
  Units, 3d Defense Battalion
  Local Naval Defense Force
  Total on Guadalcanal, about 10,000

At Tulagi:
  1st Raider Battalion
  1st Parachute Battalion
  2d Battalion, 5th Marines (2d Platoon, Company A, 1st Pioneers attached)
  1st, 2d, and 3d Battalions, 2d Marines
  Batteries H and I, 3d Battalion, 10th Marines
  Detachment, Division Headquarters Company
  Detachment, 2d Signal Company
  3d Defense Battalion (less detachments)
  Company A, 1st Medical Battalion
  Company A, 2d Engineer Battalion (2d Platoon, Company A, 1st Engineer Battalion attached)
  Company C, 2d Tank Battalion
  Company A, 2d Amphibian Tractor Battalion (2d Platoon, Company A, 1st Amphibian Tractor Battalion attached)
  Company D, 2d Medical Battalion
  Company A, 2d Pioneer Battalion (2d Platoon, Company A, 1st Pioneer Battalion attached)
  Battery E, 11th Marines
  Company C, 2d Service Battalion
  Local Naval Defense Force
  Total on Tulagi, 6,075
  Total personnel left in area, about 16,075

The 2d Marines under Colonel John M. Arthur had formed the division reserve and was originally slated for the occupation of Ndeni, but all its battalions now were in action in the Tulagi area. The regimental headquarters remained afloat, however, as did working parties from all companies, most of the Headquarters and Service Company, Regimental Weapons Company, administrative units from the various battalions, and G and Headquarters and Service Batteries of 3/10.

The sudden withdrawal of the transports carried these units, which totaled about 1,400 officers and men, back to Espiritu Santo where they were used to "reinforce the garrison there," according to the reports of Admiral Turner. On 14 August, Turner ordered Colonel Arthur to report for duty with the Commanding General, Espiritu Santo. But a few days later Colonel Arthur and a small number of his officers and men got back up to Tulagi.[12]

There seemed no question in Turner's mind about his unrestricted claim of "possession" of the Marines in his area. If his handling of Colonel Arthur was a rather ungenerous bypass of General Vandegrift's command territory, the admiral's plan for those Marines who remained at Espiritu Santo was an even

---

of 10 units of fire was just right, they added; no attempt should be made to carry 20 units into future landings. *FinalRept*. Phase II, 17.

[12] CTF 62 War Diary, September and October 1942.

more glaring example of his theory of personal command possession. He ordered those "idle" 2d Marines to form a "2d Provisional Raider Battalion." Then he wrote to Admiral Ghormley recommending an overhaul of all Marine regiments in the Amphibious Force, South Pacific. All regiments then would contain raider battalions which could be sent out on special missions. Turner said he did not think Marine regiments would be suited to operations in the Pacific. "The employment of a division seems less likely," the admiral added. He would use raider battalions like building blocks, and fit the landing force to the special problem. Obviously, he expected the Pacific war to be small and tidy.

Admiral Ghormley answered that Turner ought to hold up such reorganization until he found out what the Commandant of the Marine Corps thought of all this. Admiral Ghormley then sent this letter and his endorsement to the Commandant via Admiral Nimitz at Pearl Harbor. Nimitz agreed with Ghormley, and he stressed that "extemporized organization of Marine Forces should be made only in case of dire necessity." Nimitz then forwarded this correspondence on to Lieutenant General Thomas Holcomb, Marine Commandant.

General Holcomb responded to Nimitz that the latter's objections had surely stopped Turner's plan without the need for the Commandant to add other objections, but Holcomb noted "with regret" that Turner had not seen fit to ask General Vandegrift about this plan to reorganize his troops.

This reaction from Nimitz, and the arrival at about that time in the New Hebrides of the "authentic" 2d Raider Battalion of Lieutenant Colonel Evans F. Carlson, caused Turner to halt his plan to turn all Amphibious Force Marines into raiders. But it took the admiral much longer than this to abandon his theory that these Marines were direct "possessions" of his.[13]

---

[13] ComPhibForSoPac ltr to ComSoPacFor, 29Aug42; ComSoPacFor ltr to CinCPOA, 6Sep42; CinCPOA ltr to CMC, 24Sep42; CMC ltr to CinCPOA, 3Oct42.

CHAPTER 3

Tulagi and Gavutu-Tanambogo

TULAGI: THE FIRST DAY

After Task Group Yoke separated from the larger body of ships at 0240 on D-Day, its approach to Tulagi was accomplished without incident. All elements of the group arrived in position at about 0630[1] and made ready for the landing.

As the ships approached the transport area, 15 fighters and 15 dive bombers from *Wasp* strafed and bombed the target area,[2] setting fire to seaplanes that were caught in the harbor.[3] (See Map 15, Map Section)

Five-inch naval gunfire from the destroyer *Monssen*, opened up at a promontory of Florida Island, west of Tulagi, and 60 rounds were expended on the target between 0727 and 0732. In the meantime, both the *Buchanan* and *San Juan* (an antiaircraft cruiser) pumped 100 rounds each into nearby targets. *Buchanan* concentrated on a point of land east of Haleta, on Florida, while the *San Juan* blasted a small island south of the same point of land.[4]

At 0740, 20 minutes before H-hour, Company B (reinforced) of the 1st Battalion, 2d Marines, under command of Captain Edward J. Crane, landed on Florida near Haleta to protect the left flank of the Tulagi Force. The landing was unopposed, although enemy troops had been reported in position there on 25 July.[5] Crane, his company reinforced by the 4th platoon of Company D and 21 men from Headquarters Company, reached his objective within 40 minutes. The 252 officers and men went ashore in eight landing boats and were guided to their objective by one of the several Australians on duty with the division.[6]

While this covering force deployed inland from its Florida beach, the remainder of the 1st Battalion, 2d Marines (Lieutenant Colonel Robert E. Hill) made a similar security landing at Florida's Halavo Peninsula near Gavutu and Tanambogo. The craft drew some fire from Gavutu but there were no casualties, and no enemy forces were encountered on the peninsula. These Marines later returned to their ships.

At Tulagi not a single landing craft of the first wave was able to set its passengers directly ashore. All of them hung up on

---

[1] At 0625, Tulagi sent its message to Japanese stations to the north that an enemy surface force had entered the channel. Tulagi CommB msg of 7Aug42 in 25th AirFlot War Dairy, August–September 1942, hereinafter cited as *25th Air Flot Diary*.

[2] Com*Wasp*AirGru Rept to CO *Wasp*, 10Aug42. In general, during the first day *Wasp* planes operated over the Tulagi area while *Saratoga* planes gave comparable support to the main landing off Beach Red at Guadalcanal. *Enterprise* planes gave protection to the carriers and flew patrol missions.

[3] "0630—All flying boats have been set afire by the bombardment." CTF 18 ActRept, 6–10Aug42, 1, hereinafter cited as *CTF 18 AR*.

[4] *Ibid.*, 2.

[5] ComSoPac War Diary, 25Jul42 (located at NHD).

[6] LtCol H. R. Thorpe ltr to CMC, 19Jan49.

coral formations at distances varying from 30 to well over 100 yards from the beach line, and the assault personnel of raider Companies B and D waded ashore against no opposition, through water initially from waist to armpit deep.[7]

Meanwhile the enemy defense forces, concentrated in the southeastern third of the island, realized that an all-out assault was underway. Between 0725 and 0749, the *Tulagi Communication Base* notified the Commanding Officer of the *Twenty-Fifth Air Flotilla* at Rabaul that Tulagi was under bombardment, that the landings had begun, and that the senders were destroying all equipment immediately. At 0800 the Japanese messages said shells were falling near the radio installation. Ten minutes later, the final message went out: "Enemy troop strength is overwhelming. We will defend to the last man."[8]

Companies B and D had reached the beach, and the landing craft carrying raider Companies A and C now began to hang upon the coral. The Weapons Company (Captain George W. Herring) of the raider battalion, whose 60mm mortars had been attached to the assault companies,[9] headed ashore to assume responsibility for beachhead security.

Assaulting Marines crossed the beach and moved up the face of a steep, heavily-wooded coral slope, the southwestern portion of the 350-foot ridge that forms an almost unbroken wall along the island's entire length. Major Lloyd Nickerson's Company B pushed on to the far coast of the island where it captured, without opposition, the native village of Sasapi. This company then swung to the right and, tying in with Major Justice Chambers' Company D which had gained the high ground, began moving southeast. The advance of these two companies was steady and without opposition until Company B reached Carpenter's Wharf, halfway down the east shore of the island, where it encountered a series of enemy outposts.

Meanwhile additional raiders had landed. Captain Lewis W. Walt's Company A, landing to follow the leading companies, swung right atop the ridge spine, and tied in on the left with Company D. Major Kenneth Bailey's Company C also swung right, tied its left flank to Company A, and echeloned itself to the right rear to the beach. Spread out across the island, the raiders swept southeast against little opposition until Phase Line A, from the high ground northwest of Hill 281 to Carpenter's Wharf, was reached at 1120. Here Major Chambers was wounded by mortar fire, and Captain William E. Sperling assumed command of Company D.

By this time Colonel Edson, commanding the 1st Raider Battalion, was ashore and ready to begin a coordinated attack to the southeast. Confronting him was the more thickly settled portion of the island where the British governmental activities had centered. This area is a saddle between the ridge first swept by the raiders and a smaller hill mass at the island's southeastern end.[10]

After directing a preparatory fire of infantry weapons into the area to their front,

---

[7] Maj J. C. Erskine interview in HistDiv, HQMC, 15Mar49.

[8] *25th AirFlot Diary*.

[9] Majs J. B. Sweeney, H. Stiff, W. E. Sperling interview in HistDiv, HQMC, 4Feb49, hereinafter cited as *Sweeney Interview*.

[10] The raiders had been well briefed on the terrain of the island by Lt H. E. Josselyn, RANR, a former resident of the area who had intimate knowledge of it. *Ibid.*

the raiders moved out toward the high ground beyond the saddle. Company C, on the right flank of the attack, drew fire almost immediately from Hill 208, a knob forward of the ridge that had just been cleared. The bulk of the Japanese resistance concentrated in the seaward face of the high ground, and Company C was caught by fire from enemy infantry weapons as it tried to pass between the hill and the beach. The raider company then turned its attack toward the hill and fought for nearly an hour before the Japanese positions were silenced.

Radio communications between Edson and General Rupertus deteriorated rapidly after this attack was launched, but the raider commander remained in contact with his fire support ships. Operation orders called for the various fire support sections to provide the landing force with naval gunfire liaison parties, and two of these were in Edson's CP with their radios.[11] When the other raider companies came under fire from Hill 281 while Company C fought against Hill 208, Edson put these naval gunfire teams to work. The *San Juan* fired a seven-minute, 280-round concentration of 6-inch shells onto Hill 281. When it lifted the raiders advanced with a steady pressure against the enemy.

Four hours later, at 1625, Edson notified Rupertus that 500 enemy had broken contact with his force and had withdrawn into the southeastern ridge.

The advance continued slowly until dusk. At that time Company E (raiders), relieved of the beach defense mission by 2/5 which had landed at 0916, reported to its parent organization. Company D, now on the extreme left flank, had met little opposition since midmorning, when the first enemy encountered were flushed near Carpenter's Wharf by Company B. After this contact Company D pushed south along the eastern beach and at dusk reached the crest of Hill 281. Meanwhile Company B moved up again, now on the right of Company D, and gained high ground overlooking the cut of a cross-island roadway through the saddle between Hills 281 and 230. Company D, on the far side of the road and to the left of B, took up night defensive positions with its right flank resting on the southern brink of the cut. Company B, augmented by elements of Headquarters Company, rested its left flank on the cut and extended its lines generally westward along the brink.[12] Both companies put listening posts forward of the lines.

Companies A and C (less one platoon) meanwhile encountered the terrain feature which harbored the island's most serious resistance. In the forward slope of Hill 281, a deep ravine lay almost parallel to the raider advance and debouched several hundred yards southeast of Hill 208. Its sides were precipitous, and within it the enemy held strong positions which made assault hazardous. Maps which had been captured and translated during the day confirmed that this ravine would contain the core of enemy resistance.

With further action against the pocket impossible at the time, all battalion elements went into position for the night. Company E was placed on Company B's right, while Companies A and C (less one platoon) respectively tied in from the right of Company E. The positions extended along high ground facing the ra-

---

[11] *CTF 18 AR*, 2; Lt A. L. Moon ltr to LtCol R. D. Heinl, Jr., 13Feb49.

[12] *Sweeney Interview*.

vine's long axis, and listening posts were established.[13]

During Edson's sweep down the island, the 2d Battalion, 5th Marines (Rosecrans), had landed 1,085 officers and men and committed its units to various tasks. Company F scouted the northwest section of the island but met no opposition. At 1000 Company E was ordered to operate generally in support of Company B (raiders), and one hour later the 3d Platoon of Company H (weapons) went forward to assist Company C (raiders) in the latter's attack against Hill 208. By 1300, when the raider battalion began its attack from Phase Line A, Company G moved down the trail along the ridge line and supported the raider battalion. Rosecrans' command post later displaced southeast from near Beach Blue toward the scene of this action.

TULAGI—THE FIRST NIGHT AND SUCCEEDING DAY

The first night on Tulagi set the pattern for many future nights in the Pacific war. During darkness, four separate attacks struck the raider lines, and, although minor penetrations occurred, the enemy made no attempt to consolidate or exploit his gains. The first attack, which met with some initial success, hit between Companies C and A. Outposts fell back to the main line of resistance (MLR), and the two companies were forced apart. The attack isolated Company C from the rest of the battalion, but the company was not molested again. Company A refused its right flank and awaited developments.

They were not long in coming. Shifting the direction of his attack toward his right front, the enemy attempted to roll back Walt's men from the refused flank. But the flank held, killing 26 Japanese within 20 yards of the MLR.

That ended the concerted attacks of the night. Thereafter, enemy efforts consisted entirely of attempts at quiet infiltration of the Marine positions. Individuals and small groups worked from the ravine through the raider lines and launched five separate small-scale attacks against the command post between 0030 and 0530. These were repulsed, and efforts on the part of two other enemy groups to skirt the beach flanks of Companies D and C likewise were turned back.

On the morning of 8 August, two companies of the 2d Battalion, 5th Marines, moved up to assist in the sweep of the southeastern part of the island. Companies E and F, 5th Marines, passed through Company D raiders, attacked down the forward slope of Hill 281, and swung right toward the enemy pocket in the ravine.

Now flanking this troublesome terrain feature on three sides, Marines laid down a heavy mortar concentration from the 60mm weapons of the raiders and 2/5's 81s. By midafternoon the preparation was complete, and at 1500 the raiders and Company G, 5th Marines, pushed through the ravine to wipe out remaining resistance. This ended organized opposition on the island, and by nightfall of 8 August Tulagi was labeled secure. For several days, however, individual Japanese and small groups continued to be flushed from hiding places and hunted down by patrolling Marines.

THE LANDINGS ON GAVUTU—TANAMBOGO

These islets, each dominated by a low, precipitous central hill of coral, are joined

---
[13] *Ibid.*

by a 500-yard causeway. Gavutu's hill, 148 feet in height, stands some 25 to 30 feet higher than Tanambogo's highest point, and Gavutu thus became the main objective of the landing which aimed at the higher ground.

The plans [14] called for the landing to strike the northeast coast after an approach from the east, and since Tanambogo lies approximately northwest of Gavutu the assault force faced the possibility of flanking fire from that island as well as frontal resistance from the main objective. Opposition from both islands was expected from the terrain dominating the flat beach.

Naval gunfire and close air support by SBD's from the *Wasp* were expected to neutralize most enemy emplacements on these hills, but the fire plan did not reckon with the coral cave. Caves of this type began to appear as serious obstacles for the parachute battalion on Gavutu at about the same time the raiders began to encounter them on Tulagi.

Surprise was impossible. There were not sufficient craft for simultaneous landings, and the hour of assault was established in General Vandegrift's Operation Order Number 7-42 as H-plus four hours. So four hours after the raider landing on Tulagi, the parachute battalion made its frontal assault in the face of fire from an alerted garrison which was supported by fires from a flanking position.

The battalion went ashore in three waves, one company per wave. The thoroughness with which the antiaircraft cruiser *San Juan* had carried out her fire support mission—280 rounds of 6-inch fire against Gavutu in four minutes [15]—and the intensity of the *Wasp's* dive-bombers' preparation caused heavy damage to the enemy installations, but this destruction actually worked to the disadvantage of the parachute battalion in one instance. The unit intended to land on a seaplane ramp from which the beach could be easily reached, but the ramp had been reduced to an unusable mass of rubble. Observing this, the landing wave commanders altered course slightly to the north where craft became even more vulnerable to flanking fire. Part of the troops, scrambling over a concrete pier that jutted four feet out of the water, were exposed to fire from both islands. General Vandegrift estimated that troops landing in this area suffered ten per cent casualties.

Company A, the first wave, got ashore without casualties to work inland against no serious opposition. The four boats carrying Company B and the final wave, with Company C and miscellaneous attachments, came under fire as they neared the island. The landing succeeded, however, and Company B, moving left and working toward Gavutu's southern end, gained some protection from enemy fire and continued to attack.

Pinned down on the beach under heavy fire, the other companies made no advances until Company B gained high ground from which its fire assisted in getting the attack off the beach. Hill 148, Gavutu's high ground, was plastered by naval guns and assaulted on the east and southeast. By 1430, Major Charles A. Miller, who had succeeded the wounded Major Robert H.

---

[14] 1st Mar Div OpOrd No. 7-42, 20Jul42. See *FinalRept*, Phase II, Annex E, 2. Gavutu's importance stemmed from the islet's numerous installations which included machine shops, jetties, and a radio station. USN ND Hydro, *Vol. I—Sailing Directions For the Pacific Islands*, (Washington: GPO, 1938, 4th ed.), 323.

[15] *CTF 18 AR*, 2.

Williams in command, controlled most of the island. Partially defiladed positions on Hill 148's west-southwestern slopes, however, still were active, and enemy emplacements there and on Tanambogo threatened further advance. Miller requested reinforcements to complete the capture of both islands.

In anticipation of their arrival, Miller also requested an air strike and naval gunfire on Tanambogo, and *Wasp* planes furnished a 10-minute strike while *Buchanan* and *Monssen*, in position south of Gavutu, fired over that island and subjected the exposed faces of the hill on Tanambogo to an intense concentration of 5-inch shells.

By this time all forces available to General Rupertus had been committed, but since Captain Edward Crane's Company B (1/2) had met no opposition on Florida near Tulagi, this unit was ordered to report to Miller. The message reached the company just as landing craft arrived to withdraw the Marines from their Florida beach.[16]

Embarked in six landing craft, the company arrived at Gavutu at about 1800, and Miller directed Crane to land on Tanambogo and seize that island. Told that only a few snipers held the island, Crane guided his overcrowded craft around the east shore of Tanambogo according to directions provided by Flight Lieutenant Spencer, RAAF, and under cover of darkness attempted a landing on a small pier on the northeastern tip of the island. (One boat, containing the 2d Platoon, hung up on a coral reef at Gavutu and took no part in the Tanambogo assault.)

The first boat landed without incident, and the men deployed along the beach; but as the second boat discharged its men, a shell from one of the fire support ships ignited a nearby fuel dump, and the resulting glare lighted the landing area and exposed the Marines. The enemy opened up immediately, taking all boats under rifle and machine-gun fire. Casualties mounted among the Marines ashore and still afloat, but the boat crews, being exposed, suffered most heavily. One crew was completely wiped out and a Marine assumed control of the craft.

The reinforcing machine-gun platoon (4th Platoon, Company D) in the second boat managed to set up two of its weapons on the pier, but intense enemy fire forced a withdrawal.

In the meantime, Crane and about 30 men had gone ashore. The intensity of resistance, however, made withdrawal inevitable, and Crane succeeded in reembarking all wounded and all but 12 of the able survivors. The boats withdrew, some to Gavutu where they reported the event, and others direct to ships where the wounded were put aboard. Two of the men left ashore managed to return to Gavutu at about 2200 in a rowboat, while Crane and Lieutenant John J. Smith, leader of the 2d Platoon, and the remainder of the dozen men made their way around the beach and over the causeway to arrive at Miller's Gavutu command post about midnight.

At 2200, having been informed of the abortive attack on Tanambogo, General Rupertus requested the release of an additional combat team. This request reached Vandegrift during his conference with Admiral Turner on board the USS *McCawley*, and Vandegrift, Turner concurring, released the remaining two battalions of the Division Reserve. At 0330, 8 August, the USS *President Hayes* and *President Adams*, with the 1st and 3d Bat-

---

[16] LtCol W. B. Kyle ltr to CMC, 10Feb49.

talions, 2d Marines (reinforced) embarked, were ordered to cross from the transport area off Guadalcanal's Beach Red to the Tulagi transport area. Simultaneously battalion commanders received orders to land their troops at Beach Blue on Tulagi and report to General Rupertus.[17]

Upon arrival at the transport area off Beach Blue at 0730, the 3d Battalion was directed to pass to Gavutu, reinforce the troops engaged there, and seize Tanambogo. Orders for the 1st Battalion were cancelled and this unit did not land.

The 3d Battalion, under Lieutenant Colonel Robert G. Hunt, landed on Gavutu in a succession of boat waves, with companies in the following order: Company L, with 5th Platoon, Company M attached, at 1000; Company K, with 4th Platoon, Company M attached, at 1025; Company I, with 3d Platoon, Company M attached, at 1050; Company M, less 3d, 4th, and 5th Platoons, with Headquarters Company, at 1120.

Troops deployed initially to eliminate Gavutu opposition and to take Tanambogo under fire. Company L, for example, assumed positions generally around the base of Hill 148 facing Tanambogo, while Company K moved up the hill to relieve parachute battalion elements in positions there. At 1330 Company K had just accomplished its mission when an SBD pilot dropped a bomb within company positions on the northwest nose of the hill. Three men were killed and nine wounded.

---

[17] CWO T. W. Huston ltr to CMC, 28Dec48. Orders to report to Rupertus did not go through Col J. M. Arthur, CO 2dMar. Each battalion commander was notified direct, and it was not until he reached Espiritu Santo that Arthur knew which of his troops had been committed. Col R. E. Hill interview at HistDiv, 18Apr49.

Eight of the casualties were men of the supporting platoon of Company M.

At 1225, Captain W. B. Tinsley, commanding Company I, was ordered to prepare for a landing on Tanambogo. He would have the support of two tanks from Company C of the 2d Tank Battalion (one of the reinforcing units of the 2d Marines), and his attack would be preceded by a 10-minute naval gunfire preparation by the *Buchanan*. The company would not be accompanied by its supporting machine-gun platoon, which was to stay in position on Gavutu and lay down supporting fires from there.

At 1315 the tanks landed on Gavutu. Lieutenant E. J. Sweeney, commanding them, was ordered to land at 1615 on Tanambogo, using one tank to cover the south side of the hill on that island and the other to cover the eastern slope.

The naval gunfire preparation began at 1600. Twenty minutes later the assault company, following the tanks, made its landing. Lieutenant Sweeney was killed, but his tank rendered valuable support to the riflemen. The other tank, getting too far ahead of the assault troops, was disabled by an iron bar and set afire by oil-soaked rags employed by Japanese riflemen. The entire enemy group was wiped out; 42 bodies were piled up around the disabled tank.

At 1620 Company I landed and formed two attack groups. One worked up the southern slope of the Tanambogo hill while the other, moving to the right and then inland, attacked up the eastern slope. Japanese fought fiercely from caves and dugouts, and the eastern group drew fire from a few enemy riflemen and machine gunners on Gaomi, a tiny islet a few hundred yards east of Tanambogo. Naval gunfire from USS *Gridley* was directed upon Gaomi at 1700 and positions on the small island were silenced. At this time the 1st platoon of Company K attacked across the causeway from Gavutu, secured the Tanambogo end of the causeway, and took up positions for the night.

By 2100, the southeastern two-thirds of the island had been secured, and at 2300 a light machine-gun platoon from Company M reported to Company I for support against enemy counterattacks. Considerable close-in fighting took place during the night between the Marines and Japanese who sallied from foxholes and dugouts. No change in position occurred, however, and by late the next day continued attacks had secured the island.

While Gavutu and Tanambogo were mopped up, the 1st and 2d Battalions, 2d Marines unloaded at Tulagi. The 1st Battalion, unengaged since its 7 August landing on Florida, went ashore at Beach Blue at 0900 on 9 August. The 2d Battalion (Major Orin K. Pressley) followed an hour later.

Here, as at Guadalcanal, the amphibian tractor emerged as a versatile piece of equipment whose importance and utility could hardly be overestimated. From noon of 8 August throughout the following night, five of these vehicles of the 3d Platoon, Company A, 2d Amphibian Tractor Battalion (one of the reinforcing elements of the 2d Marines) operated between Gavutu and the *President Adams*. They carried water, supplies, ammunition, and personnel to shore and evacuated wounded on the return trips. On one occasion a tractor moved some distance inland to attack a Japanese position that had pinned down and wounded a number of Marines. Using their two machine guns, one .30 and one .50 caliber, the tractor's crew neutralized the enemy fire and then evacuated the wounded Marines.[18] The five tractors of the platoon were taken back on board the *Adams* before sundown on 9 August.

With the fall of Tanambogo, the last effective resistance in the Nggela island group ceased. Subsequent operations consisted of mopping up, consolidating defenses, and occupying several small peripheral islands including Makambo, Mbangai, Kokomtumbu, and Songonangona.[19]

The mission of clearing out these small islands fell to various units of the 2d Battalion, 2d Marines. Makambo was taken by Company E, Mbangai by Company F, and Kokomtambu and Songonangona, by Company G. Occupation of all these smaller islands was completed during the morning of 9 August. In all cases, opposition was slight.

Occupation of the entire island group and destruction of the Japanese garrison had been accomplished in three days. The few prisoners taken were questioned and sent to rear areas. Most of them finally were placed in a prisoner of war camp near Featherstone, New Zealand.

Comparatively, the American losses were not excessive. An early report by Rupertus to the effect that the parachute

---

[18] ". . . this was an emergency undertaking only as it is not considered that the tractor is a tactical combat vehicle." *Final Rept*, Phase II, 16.

[19] Spelling of place names are those which appear in *Sailing Directions for the Pacific Islands*, op. cit. The versions given there differ in numerous cases from those used in official reports of the campaign. Kokomtambu, for instance, appears in at least three different guises, while Songonangona surrendered its musical name to emerge as "Singsong" Island.

battalion had suffered 50–60 per cent casualties can only be explained in terms of inadequate communications between him and his troops ashore.

The exact number of Japanese casualties will never be known. An estimated 750–800 enemy were present in the Tulagi-Gavutu-Tanambogo area at the time of the landings. Twenty-three prisoners were taken, and an intelligence summary gives 70 as the approximate number of survivors who escaped to Florida.

Immediately after organized resistance ceased and the isolated defending groups were rounded up or wiped out, Tulagi and its satellite islands were organized for defense against counterattack. The 1st Parachute Battalion, depleted by its experience on Gavutu, moved from that island at 1700 on 9 August to Tulagi, where it went into position in the Government building area. The 2d Battalion, 5th Marines occupied the southeastern sector of the island, while two battalions of the 2d Marines took over the defensive mission in the northwest. The 1st Battalion occupied the extreme end of the island while the 2d Battalion established positions at Sasapi. Third Battalion, 2d Marines, took over the occupation and defense of Gavutu, Tanambogo, and Makambo.[20]

The logistic problem on Tulagi was a miniature of that encountered on Guadalcanal, although certain details were peculiar to Tulagi. The beachhead, for instance, was severely restricted by the abrupt ridge and, there were no usable roads. Only after noon of the second day was it possible to move supplies ashore at the piers on the eastern coast. Both Gavutu and Tanambogo were so small that only ammunition and water were landed until the islands were secured.

Naval gunfire on this side of the Solomon Islands operation had more of a workout than it had received across the channel at Guadalcanal where opposition was at first light, but it was not an unqualified success. As a matter of fact it was "very poor," according to naval headquarters in Washington.[21] But this failing was caused mostly by lack of intelligence and time for planning and coordinated training. Improper ordnance made for another failing. Only armor-piercing shells could have blasted the Japanese from their caves, but the ships repeatedly fired high-capacity bombardment projectiles. Although many Naval officers were still of the opinion that a ship was a "fool to fight a fort," some began to agree with the Marine Corps that naval gunfire properly employed could be a big help in an amphibious assault. It was a case of the gunfire ships needing to move in closer for their fire missions. The commander of one ship reported:

> It was observed that the enemy had not been driven from the beach at Gavutu by the shelling and bombing preceding the landing. Furthermore Tanambogo withstood two days of intermittent bombing and strafing and was not taken until a destroyer closed in to point blank range and shelled it for several minutes. It was evident that this fire was necessary to insure the capture of Tanambogo without further heavy casualties.[22]

Taking into account the indications that these shortcomings would be corrected in

---

[20] Col C. P. Van Ness ltr to CMC, 12Jan49. Defense initially was oriented against an anticipated attack from Florida and artillery positions were selected with this, as well as the possibility of a sea-borne attack, in view. LtCol M. L. Curry interview at HistDiv, 28Jan49.

[21] CominCh, "Battle Experiences, Solomons Island Action," *Information Bulletin No. 2* (located at NHD), Chap X, 10.

[22] USS *Heywood* Rept. 12Aug42, 3.

TULAGI ISLAND, *framed against the background of the larger Florida Island, is fire-swept from the hits scored by American carrier dive bombers.* (USN 11649)

TANAMBOGO AND GAVUTU ISLANDS *photographed immediately after a pre-landing strike by USS* Enterprise *planes; Gavutu is at the left across the causeway.* (USN 11034)

later operations, the Marine Corps was generally satisfied with the ships' fire. "The operation did not involve a real test . . . [but] nothing developed during the operation to indicate the need for any fundamental change in doctrine."[23]

After these three days of fighting in the Tulagi area, this side of the operation remained quiet. Enemy planes bypassed it to strike at the more tempting Guadalcanal airfield and perimeter. Surface craft shelled Tulagi occasionally, but never was it subjected to the kind of bombardment that struck Guadalcanal in October. There is no record that enemy reinforcements landed either on Tulagi or on Florida Island. With this sharp fighting out of the way, the division could give all its attention to things on the larger island of Guadalcanal. There the picture was not a bright one.

---

[23] *Final Rept*, Phase V, 6.

CHAPTER 4

The Battle of the Tenaru

With naval support gone, about the only hope was the airfield. Shipping would need air cover before regular runs could bolster the Marines' slim supply levels, and time was of the essence. If the Japanese struck hard while the landing force was abandoned and without air support, the precarious first step toward Rabaul might well have to be taken all over again. Vandegrift centered his defense at the field and gave completion of the strip top priority equal to the task of building the perimeter's MLR.

On 8 August, almost as soon as the field was captured, Lieutenant Colonel Frank Geraci, the Division Engineer Officer, and Major Kenneth H. Weir, Division Air Officer, had made an inspection of the Japanese project and estimated the work still needed. They told Admiral Turner that 2,600 feet of the strip would be ready in two days, that the remaining 1,178 feet would be operational in about two weeks. Turner said he would have aircraft sent in on 11 August. But the engineer officer had made his estimate before the transports took off with his bulldozers, power shovels, and dump trucks.[1]

Again, however, the Marines gained from the Japanese failure to destroy their equipment before fleeing into the jungle.

Already the U. S. forces were indebted to the enemy for part of their daily two meals, and now they would finish the airfield largely through the use of enemy tools. This equipment included nine road rollers (only six of which would work), two gas locomotives with hopper cars on a narrow-gauge railroad, six small generators (two were damaged beyond repair), one winch with a gasoline engine, about 50 hand carts for dirt, some 75 hand shovels, and 280 pieces of explosives.

In spite of this unintentional assistance from the Japanese, the Marine engineers did not waste any affection on the previous owners of the equipment. The machinery evidently had been used continuously for some time with no thought of maintenance. Keeping it running proved almost as big a job as finishing the airfield, and one of the tasks had to be done practically by hand, anyway. The Japanese had started at each end of the airstrip to work toward the middle, and the landing had interrupted these efforts some 180 to 200 feet short of a meeting. Assisted by a few trucks and the narrow gauge hopper cars (which had to be loaded by hand), engineers, pioneers, and others who could be spared moved some 100,000 cubic feet of fill and spread it on this low spot at midfield. A steel girder the Japanese had intended to use in a hangar served as a drag, and a Japanese road roller flattened and packed the fill after it had been spread.

---

[1] "The failure to land engineer equipment and machinery severely handicapped our efforts to complete the airfield and its defenses. Construction equipment and personnel are not a luxury but an absolute necessity in modern warfare." *Final Rept*, Phase III, 12–13.

Problems facing the infantry troops were just as great. There had been no impressive ground action on Guadalcanal since the landing, but intelligence in the immediate vicinity as well as in the South Pacific in general was not yet able to indicate when, how, and where Japanese reaction would strike. Estimating a counterlanding to be the most probable course of Japanese action, General Vandegrift placed his MLR at the beach. There the Marines built a 9,600-yard defense from the mouth of the Ilu River west around Lunga Point to the village of Kukum. The Ilu flank was refused 600 yards inland on the river's west bank, and at Kukum the left flank turned inland across the flat land between the beach and the first high ground of the coastal hills. The 5th Marines (less one battalion) held the left sector of the line from Kukum to the west bank of the Lunga, and the remainder of the line (inclusive of the Lunga) was held by the 1st Marines. (See Map 16)

The line was thin. The bulk of the combat forces remained in assembly areas inland as a ready reserve to check attacks or penetrations from any sector. Inland (south) of the airfield, a 9,000-yard stretch of rugged jungle terrain was outposted by men from the artillery, pioneer, engineer, and amphibian tractor battalions. These men worked during the day and stood watch on the lines at night.

The workers on the airfield as well as those on the thin perimeter were under almost constant enemy observation. Submarines and destroyers shelled the area at will day or night. Large flights of high-level bombers attacked the airfield daily, and observation planes were continually intruding with light bombs and strafing attacks. At night the enemy patrols became increasingly bold, and troops on the MLR mounted a continuous alert during the hours of darkness. South of the airfield the outpost line had to be supplemented by roving patrols.

In spite of this harassment, the perimeter shaped up. The 1st Special Weapons Battalion dug in its 75mm tank destroyers (half-tracks) in positions inland from the beach, but kept them ready to move into prepared positions near the water. Howitzers of the 11th Marines were situated to deliver fire in all sectors. The 2d and 3d Battalions of the artillery regiment had 75mm pack howitzers and the 5th Battalion had 105mm howitzers. There were no 155mm howitzers or guns for counterbattery, there was no sound-flash equipment for the location of enemy batteries, and the 3d Defense Battalion had not had a chance to unload its 5-inch seacoast guns or radar units prior to the departure of the amphibious shipping. Air defense within the perimeter also was inadequate. There were 90mm antiaircraft guns ashore, but the restricted size of the perimeter kept them too close to the field for best employment.

It was a hazardous and remote toe-hold which the Marines occupied, and within the Pacific high command there were some grave doubts whether they could hang on. Major General Millard F. Harmon said to General Marshall in a letter on 11 August:

> The thing that impresses me more than anything else in connection with the Solomon action is that we are not prepared to follow up. . . . We have seized a strategic position from which future operations in the Bismarcks can be strongly supported. Can the Marines hold it? There is considerable room for doubt.[2]

---

[2] CGSoPac ltr to CofSA, 11Aug42 (located at OCMH).

Admiral Ghormley, also concerned about the precarious Marine position,[3] on 12 August ordered Admiral McCain's TF 63 to employ all available transport shipping to take aviation gasoline, lubricants, ammunition, bombs, and ground crews to Guadalcanal. To avoid Japanese air attacks, the ships were to leave Espiritu Santo in time to reach Sealark Channel late in the day, unload under cover of darkness, and depart early the following day.

For the "blockade run" to Guadalcanal, Admiral McCain readied four destroyer transports of TransDiv 12. They were loaded with 400 drums of aviation gasoline, 32 drums of lubricant, 282 bombs from 100- to 500-pounders, belted ammunition, tools, and spare parts. Also on board were five officers and 118 Navy enlisted men from a Navy construction base (Seabee) unit, Cub–1. Under the command of Major C. H. Hayes, executive officer of VMO–251, this unit was to aid the Marine engineers in work at the field and to serve as ground crews for fighters and dive bombers scheduled to arrive within a few days.

McCain's ships arrived off Guadalcanal during the night of 15 August, and the equipment and men were taken ashore. By this time the Marine engineers had filled the gap in the center of the landing strip and now labored to increase the length of the field from 2,600 feet to nearly 4,000 feet. Work quickened after the Seabees landed, but there was no steel matting and the field's surface turned to sticky mud after each of the frequent tropical rains.

General Harmon blamed a faulty planning concept for the serious shortages of tools, equipment, and supplies. The campaign, he said, ". . . had been viewed by its planners as [an] amphibious operation supported by air, not as a means of establishing strong land based air action."[4]

But in spite of these shortages at the airfield and elsewhere, the Lunga Point perimeter was taking on an orderly routine of improvement and defense. Motor transport personnel had put their meager pool of trucks into operation shortly after the landing, and they had added some 35 Japanese trucks to the available list. Pioneers had built a road from the airfield to the Lunga River where they erected a bridge to the far side of the perimeter. Supply dumps also had been put in order. The pioneers cleared the landing beach, moving gear west to the Lunga-Kukum area, and sorted and moved Japanese supplies. The old Japanese beach at Kukum was cleaned up and reconditioned to receive U. S. material.

Most of the work of moving the beach dumps to permanent sites was completed in four days. There was a great amount of tonnage to handle in spite of the fact that only a small portion of the supplies had been landed. Amphibian tractors and all available trucks, including the Japanese, were used. The Government Track (the coastal road to Lunga) was improved and streams and rivers bridged to speed truck traffic. The amphibians carried their loads just offshore through shallow surf, and farther out to sea the lighters moved from old beach to new and back

---

[3] He warned Adms King and Nimitz that Guadalcanal might again fall to the Japanese if carrier support and reinforcements were not made available. ComSoPac msgs to CinCPac and CominCh, 16 and 17Aug42, in SoPac War Diary (located at NHD).

[4] CGSoPac ltr to CGAAF, 23Aug42 (located at OCMH).

again. The amount of supplies at each of the new classified dumps was kept low to avoid excessive loss from bombardment.

Captured material included almost every type item used by a military force—arms, ammunition, equipment, food, clothing, fuel, tools, and building materials:

> As the division was acutely short of everything needed for its operation, the captured material represented an important if unforeseen factor in the development of the airfield and beach defenses and the subsistence of the garrison.[5]

The landing force was particularly short of fuel, but in this case the supply left behind by the Japanese garrison was not as helpful as it might have been. Marines found some 800 to 900 drums of Japanese aviation gasoline on Guadalcanal, but this 90-octane fuel was not quite good enough for our aircraft, and it was too "hot" and produced too much carbon in trucks and Higgins boats unless mixed evenly with U. S. 72-octane motor fuel. Likewise some 150,000 gallons of Japanese motor fuel of 60 or 65 octane proved unreliable in our vehicles although some of it was mixed with our fuel and used in emergency in noncombat vehicles.

So critical was the supply of gasoline and diesel fuel that the division soon adopted an elaborate routine of "official scrounging" from ships that came into the channel. Rows of drums were lined bung up on old artillery lighters, and these craft would wallow alongside ships where Marines would ask that a hose from the ships' bulk stores be passed over so they could fill the drums one at a time. This method helped the Marines' fuel supply, but not relations with the Navy. Small boats taking off supplies had difficulty negotiating their passes alongside with the unwieldy lighters in the way, and ships officers quite frequently took a dim view of dragging along such bulky parasites when they had to take evasive action during the sudden air raids. But the system often worked well when early preparations were made with particularly friendly ships.

This over-water work in Sealark Channel, maintaining contact between Tulagi and Guadalcanal as well as meeting the supply ships which began to sneak in more frequently, pointed to another serious deficiency: there was no organized boat pool available to the division. More often than not the personnel and craft that the division used in those early days had merely been abandoned when the attack force departed, and there was no semblance of organization among them. Even the creation of order did not solve all the problems. A high percentage of the boats were damaged and crewmen had no repair facilities. The situation was gradually improved but was never satisfactory.

At last, on 18 August, the engineers and Seabees had a chance to stand back and admire their work. The airfield was completed. On 12 August it had been declared fit for fighters and dive bombers, but none were immediately available to send up. A Navy PBY had landed briefly on the strip on that date, but this was before Admiral McCain made his initial blockade run, and there was very little fuel for other planes anyway. But by the 18th the fill in the middle had been well packed, a grove of banyan trees at the end of the strip had been blasted away to make the approach less steep, and newly-arrived gasoline and ordnance were ready and waiting for the first customers. In the South Pacific during that period of shoestring existence,

---

[5] *FinalRept*, Phase III, 4.

MARINE COMMANDERS ON GUADALCANAL appear in a picture taken four days after the landing which includes almost all the senior officers who led the 1st Marine Division ashore. Left to right, front row: Col George R. Rowan, Col Pedro A. del Valle, Col William C. James, MajGen Alexander A. Vandegrift, Col Gerald C. Thomas, Col Clifton B. Cates, LtCol Randolph McC. Pate, and Cdr Warwick T. Brown, USN. Second row: Col William J. Whaling, Col Frank B. Goettge, Col LeRoy P. Hunt, LtCol Frederick C. Biebush, LtCol Edwin A. Pollock, LtCol Edmund J. Buckley, LtCol Walter W. Barr, and LtCol Raymond P. Coffman. Third row: LtCol Francis R. Geraci, LtCol William E. Maxwell, Col Edward G. Hagen, LtCol William N. McKelvy, LtCol Julian N. Frisbee, Maj Milton V. O'Connell, Maj William Chalfont, III, Capt Horace W. Fuller, and Maj Forest C. Thompson. Fourth row: Maj Robert G. Ballance, Maj Henry W. Buse, Jr., Maj James G. Frazer, Maj Henry H. Crockett, LtCol Leonard B. Cresswell, LtCol John A. Bemis, Maj Robert B. Luckey, LtCol Samuel G. Taxis, and LtCol Eugene H. Price. Last row: Maj Robert O. Bowen, LtCol Merrill B. Twining, Maj Kenneth W. Benner (behind Bemis), LtCol Walker A. Reeves, LtCol John DeW. Macklin, LtCol Hawley C. Waterman, and Maj James C. Murray. Many of these men went on to become general officers and three of them (Vandegrift, Cates, and Pate) later became Commandants of the Marine Corps. (USMC 50509)

however, "readiness" was a comparative thing. There were no bomb handling trucks, carts or hoists, no gas trucks, and no power pumps.

The state of readiness had a way of fluctuating rapidly, too, and the breathing spell for the workers did not last long. With most sadistic timing, a large flight of Japanese planes came over and scored 17 hits on the runway. One engineer was killed, nine were wounded, and the field "was a mess."[6]

The runway damage was disquieting but not altogether a surprise. Air raids had been frequent, shelling from offshore submarines likewise was common, and planes droned overhead frequently during the hours of darkness to drop small bombs here and there at well-spaced intervals. After the big raid on the 18th, the well-practiced repair teams merely went to work again. In filling the craters, the engineers and Seabees first squared the holes with hand shovels and then air hammered the new dirt solid by tamping every foot and a half of fill. They had found that this system kept settling to a minimum and prevented dangerous pot holes.

Two days later Henderson Field, named after Major Lofton Henderson, a Marine aviator killed at Midway, was again ready. And this time the planes arrived. The forward echelon of Marine Aircraft Group 23, the first arrivals, numbered 19 F4F's and 12 SBD-3's. The units were under the command of Lieutenant Colonel Charles L. Fike, executive officer of the air group. The F4F's, a part of Marine Fighter Squadron 223, were commanded by Major John L. Smith, and the 12 Douglas dive bombers from Marine Scout-Bomber Squadron 232 were led by Lieutenant Colonel Richard D. Mangrum.

Arrival of planes ended an era for the Guadalcanal defenders—the hazardous period from 9 to 20 August when the landing force operated entirely without air or surface support. During this period lines of communications were most uncertain. Nothing was known of the general naval situation or the extent of losses at sea, and little information was received from aerial reconnaissance from rear areas. Ashore, patrolling was constant, but the terrain was such that much could be missed. Short rations, continuous hard work, and lack of sleep reflected in the physical condition of the troops. Morale, however, remained high.

Formed in March of 1942 at Ewa, Oahu, MAG-23 remained in training there, with much shifting of personnel and units, until this two-squadron forward echelon sailed to the South Pacific on 2 August on board the escort carrier *Long Island*. Smith's men had just been issued new F4F's with two-stage superchargers, and Mangrum's unit had turned in its old SBD-2's for the newer 3's with self-sealing gasoline tanks and armor plate. The remaining two squadrons of the group, Captain Robert E. Galer's VMF-224 and Major Leo R. Smith's VMSB-231, would sail from the Hawaiian area on 15 August.

John Smith's VMF-223 and Mangrum's VMSB-232 came down by way of Suva in the Fijis and Efate in the New Hebrides. At Efate, Smith traded some of his young, less-experienced pilots to Major Harold W. Bauer's VMF-212 for some fliers with more experience. On the afternoon of 20 August, the *Long Island* stood 200 miles southeast of Guadalcanal and launched the planes.

---

[6] *Ibid.*, Annex C, 2.

Two days later, on 22 August, the first Army Air Force planes, five P-400's [7] of the 67th Fighter Squadron, landed on the island. On 24 August, 11 Navy dive bombers from the battle-damaged *Enterprise* moved to Henderson Field to operate for three months, and on 27 August nine more Army P-400's came in. Performance of these Army planes was disappointing. Their ceiling was 12,000 feet because they had no equipment for the British high-pressure oxygen system with which they were fitted, and they could not reach the high-flying enemy planes. Along with the Marine SBD's, the P-400's spent their time during Japanese air raids off strafing and bombing ground targets, and they returned to Henderson after the hostile planes departed.

A short while later—early in September—supply and evacuation flights were initiated by two-engined R4D's (C-47's) of Marine Aircraft Group 25. Flying daily from Espiritu Santo and Efate, the cargo planes each brought in some 3,000 pounds of supplies and were capable of evacuating 16 stretcher patients.

Although this increased air activity at Henderson Field was of great importance to the operation in general and the combat Marines in particular, the field still was not capable of supporting bombers which could carry attacks to Japanese positions farther to the north. On 20 August General Harmon voiced the opinion that it would be too risky to base B-17's at Henderson until more fighter and antiaircraft protection were available. [8]

Early in September he suggested that heavy bombers stage through the Guadalcanal field from the New Hebrides and thus strike Rabaul and other Japanese bases,[9] but a closer investigation pointed up the impracticality of this plan. It would have meant hand-pumping more than 3,500 gallons of gasoline into each bomber landing at Guadalcanal on the 1,800-mile round trip from the New Hebrides to the Northern Solomons; and although this manual labor was not too great a price to pay for an opportunity to strike at the Japanese, it was impossible to maintain a fuel stock of that proportion at Henderson Field.

GROUND ACTION

Combat troops meanwhile probed the jungles with patrols, and early reconnaissance indicated that the bulk of Japanese troops was somewhere between the Matanikau River, about 7,000 yards west of the Lunga, and Kokumbona, a native village some 7,500 yards west of the Matanikau. General Vandegrift wanted to pursue the enemy and destroy him before the Japanese could reinforce this small, disorganized garrison, but no substantial force could be spared from the work of building the MLR and the airfield.

Minor patrol clashes occurred almost daily, but many of these meeting engagements were with wandering bands of uniformed laborers who only confused attempts to locate the main enemy force. This patrolling gradually revealed that the area between the Matanikau and Kokumbona was the main stronghold, however. Stiff resistance continued there with each attempt to probe the area, and this

---

[7] Early P-39 "klunkers" converted for export to the British. They could carry one bomb, were armed with a 20mm cannon, two .50 caliber, and four .30 caliber machine guns.

[8] CGSoPac Summary of Situation, 20Aug42 (located at NHD).

[9] CGSoPac ltr to CofSA, 9Sep42 (located at NHD).

pattern had started as early as 9 August when one officer and several enlisted men were wounded while trying to cross the river. This patrol had reported the west bank of the river well organized for defense. The enemy kept shifting his position, though, to maneuver for an advantage against the patrols which came to seek him out. Final confirmation of the enemy location came on 12 August when a Japanese warrant officer captured behind the 1st Battalion, 5th Marines said that his unit was between the Matanikau and Kokumbona.

Under questioning, the prisoner admitted that possibly some of his fellow garrison mates were wandering aimlessly through the jungle without food and that some of them might surrender. First Sergeant Stephen A. Custer of the division intelligence section made plans to lead an amphibious patrol to the area. Meanwhile, a Marine patrol reported seeing what it took to be a white flag west of the river. Hearing these reports, Lieutenant Colonel Frank Goettge, division intelligence officer, decided to lead the patrol himself.

The original plan had called for an early start so that a daylight landing could be made. The patrol then would work inland along the west bank of the Matanikau and bivouac for the night far back in the hills. The second day was to be spent in a cross-country return to the perimeter. The primary mission of the patrol would be that of reconnaissance, but it was to be strong enough for combat if it ran into a fight.

Colonel Goettge's new plans delayed departure of the patrol about 12 hours and cut down its combat potential by including among its 25-man strength Lieutenant Commander Malcolm L. Pratt, assistant division surgeon, Lieutenant Ralph Cory, a Japanese linguist, and several members of the 5th Marines intelligence section. The boat got away from the perimeter at about 1800 and landed after dark at 2200 at an undetermined point west of the Matanikau. The Japanese, instead of surrendering, attacked the patrol and cut off from the beach all but three men who escaped back into the surf to swim and wade to safety.

One of these men, Sergeant Charles C. Arndt, arrived in the perimeter at about 0530 on 13 August to report that the patrol had encountered enemy resistance. Company A, 5th Marines set off immediately as a relief patrol to be reinforced later by two platoons of Company L and a light machine-gun section. Meanwhile, the other two escaped patrol members, Corporal Joseph Spaulding and Platoon Sergeant Frank L. Few, came back at 0725 and 0800 respectively and revealed that the remainder of the Goettge patrol had been wiped out.

The relief patrol landed west of Point Cruz, a coastal projection a short distance west of the Matanikau's mouth. Company A moved east along the coastal road back toward the perimeter while the reinforced platoons of Company L traveled over the difficult terrain inland from the beach. Company A met brief Japanese resistance near the mouth of the river, but neither force found a trace of the Goettge patrol.[10]

This action was followed a week later by a planned double envelopment against the village of Matanikau. Companies B and L of the 5th Marines would carry out

---

[10] Goettge's position as Division G-2 was filled on 14 August by LtCol E. J. Buckley, formerly of the 11th Marines. *FinalRept*, Phase III, Annex F, 5.

MARINE ENGINEERS *erected this bridge across the Tenaru River to speed the flow of troops and supplies from the beaches to the perimeter.* (*USMC 50468-A*)

SOLOMONS NATIVES, *recruited by Captain W. F. Martin Clemens, BSIDF, guide a patrol up the winding course of the Tenaru River in search of Japanese.* (*USMC 53325*)

this attack while Company I of the same regiment made an amphibious raid farther west, at Kokumbona, where it was hoped that any Japanese retreating from Matanikau could be cut off. On 18 August Company L moved inland, crossed the Matanikau some 1,000 yards from the coast, and prepared to attack north into the village the next day. Company B, to attack west, moved along the coastal road to the east bank of the river.

Next day, after preparation fire was laid down by the 2d, 3d, and 5th Battalions of the 11th Marines, Company L launched its attack. Shortly after jumping off, scouts discovered a line of emplacements along a ridge some 1,000 yards to the left flank of the company front. The platoon on this flank engaged the small enemy force in these emplacements while the remainder of the company moved on toward the village. In this action off the left flank, Sergeant John H. Branic, the acting platoon leader, was killed. The company executive officer, Lieutenant George H. Mead, Jr. next took command. When he was killed a short time later Marine Gunner Edward S. Rust, a liaison officer from the 5th Marines headquarters took command. This platoon continued to cover the advance of the remainder of the company.

Company B, thwarted in its attempt to cross the river because of intense Japanese fire from the west bank, could only support the attack of its sister company by fire. Company L managed to reach the outskirts of the native village at about 1400, however, and one platoon entered the settlement. This platoon lost contact with the remainder of the company, and when the other platoons attempted to enter the village they were met by a strong Japanese counterattack which caused the separated platoon to withdraw to company lines. The Marines were nearly enveloped and succeeded in repulsing the attack only after close-range fighting. Defending in depth, the Japanese drew up on a line which extended from the river some 200 yards west through the village. While the Marines maneuvered for an attack, the Japanese fire became more sporadic, and an assault at about 1600 revealed that the enemy pocket had dispersed.

Meanwhile the amphibious raid of Company I also aroused opposition. Two enemy destroyers and a cruiser lobbed shells at the landing craft while they swung from the Marine perimeter to Kokumbona, and the raiding party escaped this threat only to be met at the beach by Japanese machine-gun fire. The landing succeeded, however, and the enemy resistance began to melt. By the time a Marine attack swept through the village, the defenders had retired into the jungle to avoid a conclusive engagement. The three companies killed 65 Japanese while suffering the loss of four Marines killed and 11 wounded.

Although these actions served only to locate the general area into which the original Japanese garrison of Guadalcanal had withdrawn in the face of the Marine landing, another patrol on 19 August indicated the pattern of things to come on the island.

The patrol and reconnaissance area assigned to the 1st Marines lay east and southeast of the perimeter where the plains of the Lunga fan into a grassy tableland which is nearly eight miles wide near the coastal village of Tetere. Some thought had been given to the construction of an airfield there, and on 12 August a survey party went out with a platoon-sized security force under Second Lieutenant John J. Jachym. Passing through a native village on 13 August, this group encountered Father Arthur C. Duhamel, a young Cath-

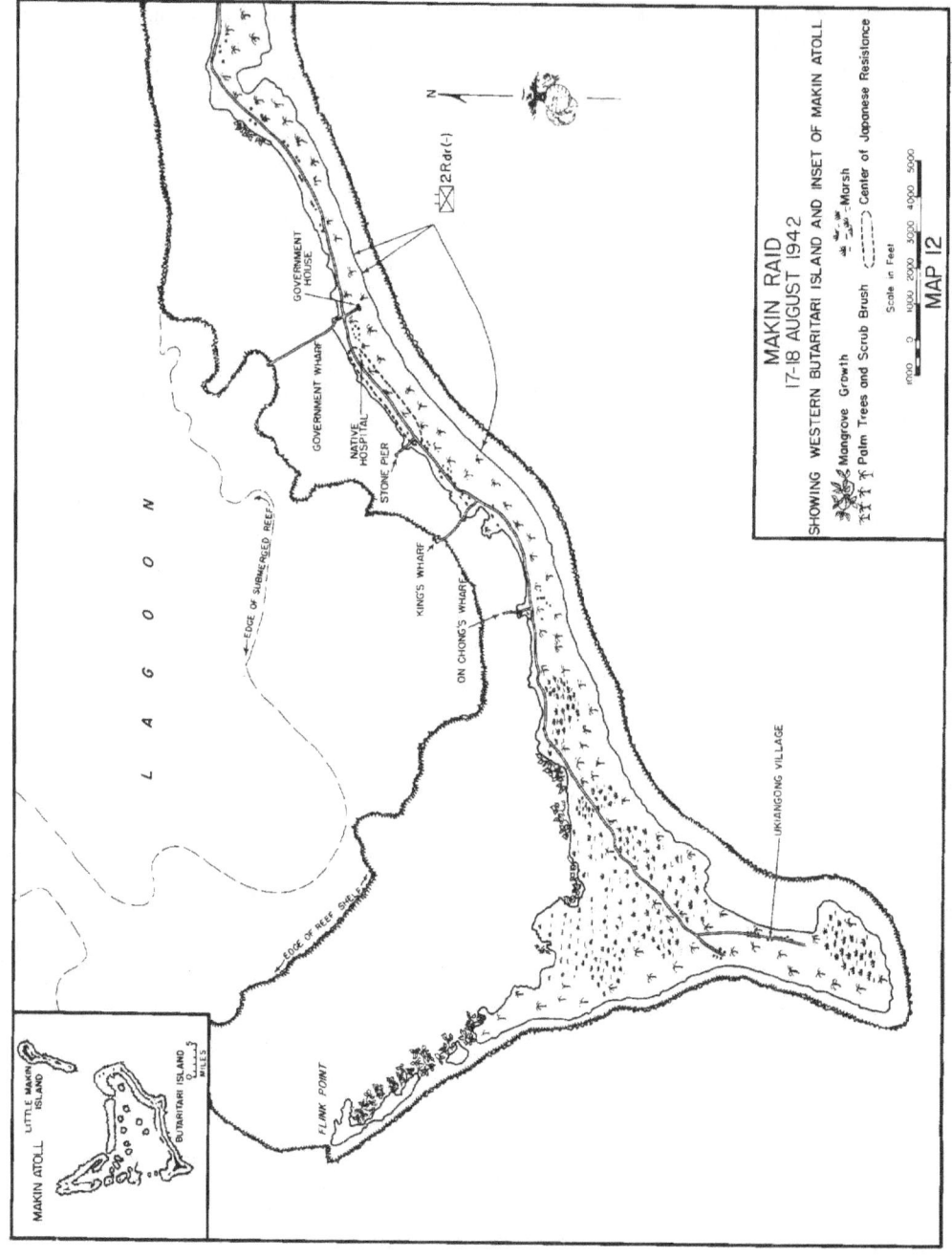

olic priest from Methuen, Massachusetts,[11] who related native rumors of an enemy force along the coast to the east.

Two days later a partial verification of the priest's information was made by Captain (of the British Solomon Islands Defense Force) W. F. M. (Martin) Clemens, the district officer who had withdrawn into the hills to become a coastwatcher when the Japanese entered his island. On 14 August Clemens left his watching station near Aola Bay with his 60 native scouts[12] and entered the Marine perimeter. Clemens and his scouts reported seeing signs of a new Japanese force. And on the heels of Clemens' reports came word from Admiral Turner that naval intelligence indicated a Japanese attack in force.

To investigate, Captain Charles H. Brush, Jr. took a part of his Company A of the 1st Marines and at 0700 on 19 August began a patrol eastward along the coastal track toward Koli Point and Tetere. At about noon near Koli Point the patrol spotted a group of four Japanese officers and 30 men moving, with no security to front or flanks, between the road and the beach. Captain Brush struck frontally with a part of his unit while Lieutenant Jachym led an envelopment around the enemy left flank. In 55 minutes of fighting, 31 of the Japanese were killed. The remaining three escaped into the jungle. Three Marines were killed and three wounded.

It was clear that these troops were not wandering laborers or even members of the original garrison. Helmets of the dead soldiers bore the Japanese Army star rather than the anchor and chrysanthemum device of the special landing force. A code for ship-to-shore communications to be used for a landing operation also was found among the effects, and the appearance of the uniforms indicated that the troops were recent arrivals to Guadalcanal. There appeared little doubt that the Japanese were preparing an attempt to recapture their lost airfield. And Brush found they had already completed some excellent advance work:

With a complete lack of knowledge of Japanese on my part, the maps the Japanese had of our positions were so clear as to startle me. They showed our weak spots all too clearly.[13]

While these patrols searched for the enemy on Guadalcanal, another force of approximately 200 Marines moved into enemy waters farther north and raided a Japanese atoll in the Gilbert Islands. Companies A and B of Lieutenant Colonel Evans F. Carlson's 2d Raider Battalion went from Oahu to Makin atoll on board submarines *Argonaut* and *Nautilus* and landed on the hostile beach early on 17 August. The raid was planned to destroy enemy installations, gather intelligence data, test raiding tactics, boost homefront morale, and possibly to divert some Japanese attention from Guadalcanal. It was partially successful on all of these counts, but its greatest asset was to home-front morale. At a cost to themselves of 30 men lost, the raiders wiped out the Japanese garrison of about 85 men, destroyed radio

---

[11] Father Duhamel, as well as Father Henry Oude-Engberink and Sister Sylvia of France, and Sister Odilia of Italy, were later tortured and killed by the Japanese.

[12] Including Vouza, a retired sergeant major of police and native of the Tetere area who previously had volunteered additional service to the Crown and Capt Clemens. A veteran of 25 years in the native constabulary, the "reactivated" Vouza provided valuable assistance to the coastwatchers and to the Marines.

[13] Maj C. H. Brush, Jr. ltr to CMC, 15Jan49.

stations, fuel, and other supplies and installations, and went back on board their submarines on 18 August for the return to Pearl Harbor. This raid attracted much attention in the stateside press but its military significance was negligible. Guadalcanal still held the center of the stage in the Pacific and attention quickly turned back to that theater.[14] (See Map 12)

BATTLE OF THE TENARU [15]

The picture that began to take shape as these bits of intelligence fitted together provided an early warning of Japanese plans that already were well underway. On 13 August, Tokyo ordered Lieutenant General Haruyoshi Hyakutake's *Seventeenth Army* at Rabaul to take over the ground action on Guadalcanal and salvage the situation. The naval side of this reinforcement effort would be conducted by Rear Admiral Raizo Tanaka, a wily Imperial sea dog who was a veteran of early landings in the Philippines and Indonesia and of the battles of Coral Sea and Midway. With no clear picture of his opponent's strength, Hyakutake decided to retake the Lunga airfield immediately with a force of about 6,000 men. On the evening of the 15th of August, while Tanaka's ships of the reinforcement force were loading supplies at Truk, the admiral got orders to hurry down to Rabaul and take 900 officers and men to Guadalcanal at once. Hyakutake had decided that the attack would begin with a part of the *7th Division's 28th Infantry Regiment* and the *Yokosuka Special Naval Landing Force.* These units would be followed by the *35th Brigade.*

Admiral Tanaka thought he was being pressed a little too hard, considering that the *Eighth Fleet* under which he operated had just been formed at Rabaul on 14 July, and that the admiral himself had hardly been given time to catch his breath after hurrying away from Yokosuka for his new job on 11 August. The admiral reported later:

> With no regard for my opinion . . . this order called for the most difficult operation in war—landing in the face of the enemy—to be carried out by mixed units which had no opportunity for rehearsal or even preliminary study. . . . In military strategy expedience sometimes takes precedence over prudence, but this order was utterly unreasonable.
>
> I could see that there must be great confusion in the headquarters of Eighth Fleet. Yet the operation was ordained and underway, and so there was no time to argue about it.[16]

Backbone of the initial effort would consist of the reinforced *2d Battalion, 28th Infantry*, a 2,000-man force of infantry, artillery, and engineers under the command of Colonel Kiyono Ichiki. This force had been en route to Midway when the defeat of the Japanese carriers caused a change to Guam.[17] Later the *Ichiki Force* was en route back to the home islands when the Marine landing in the Solomons brought another change of

---

[14] CTF 7.15 Rept, 24Aug42; 2dRdrBn Rept of Ops on MakinIs, 19Aug42; WDC Japanese Documents No. 161,013, 161,110, and NA 12053, "Records of Various Base Forces" and "Base Force Guard Units and Defense Unit Records," 17–22-Aug42 (located at NHD).

[15] Actually the Ilu. But as previously explained, Marines of the division identified these rivers incorrectly throughout the campaign and the action to be described has thus become known historically and to the participants as the Battle of the Tenaru.

[16] *Tanaka Article,* I, 690. Excerpts from this account are quoted in this volume with the permission of the U. S. Naval Institute.

[17] See Part V of this volume.

THE BATTLE OF THE TENARU

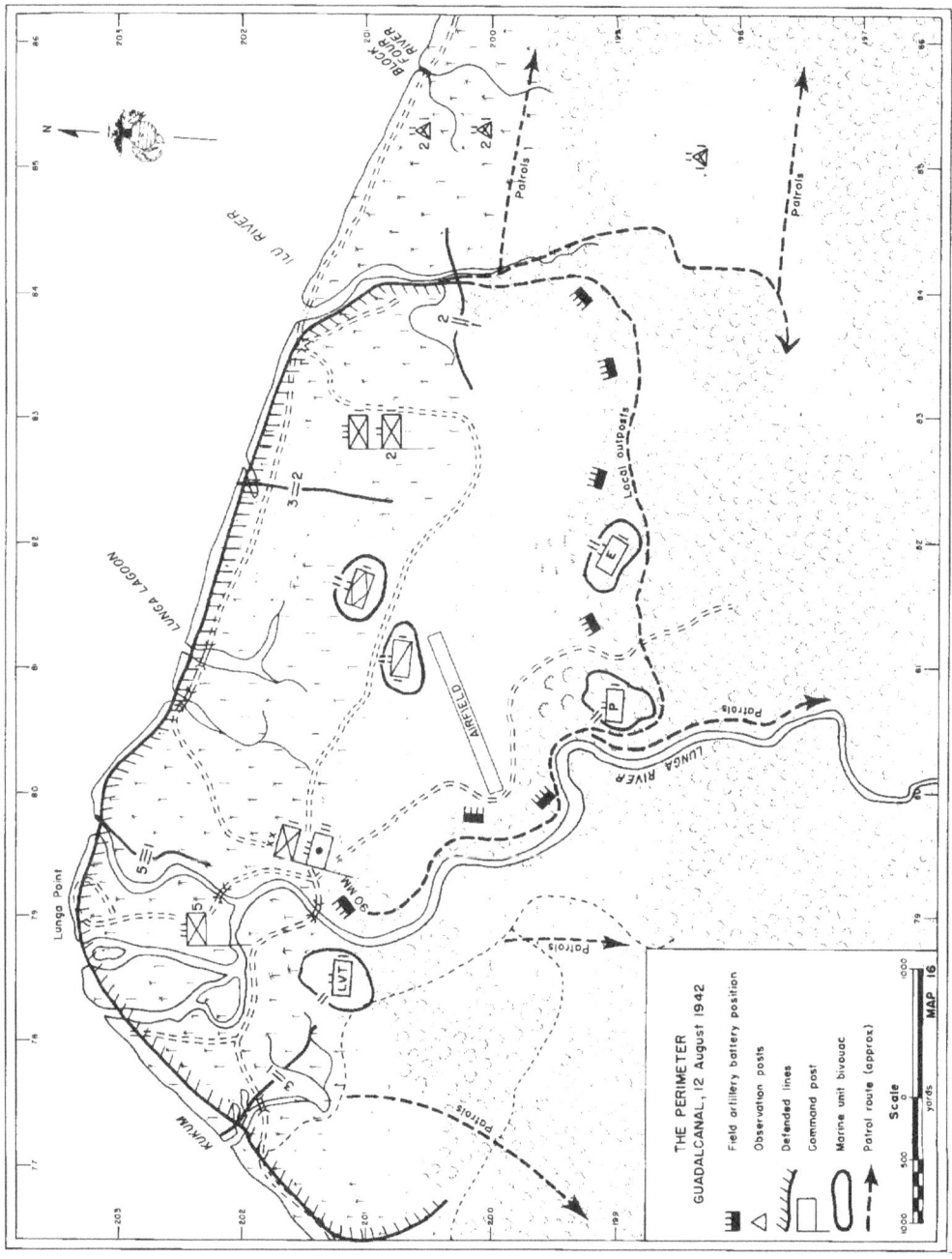

Japanese plans. The unit was diverted to Truk where it landed on 12 August and was attached to the *35th Brigade* which then garrisoned the Palau Islands. The brigade's commander was Major General Kiyotake Kawaguchi. The 900 or 1,000 men which Admiral Tanaka loaded for his first reinforcement run to Guadalcanal were from this Ichiki unit.

The reinforcement ships landed Colonel Ichiki and this forward echelon at Taivu Point on Guadalcanal during the night of 18 August. While this force landed at this point some 22 air miles east of the Lunga, some 500 men of the *Yokosuka Fifth Special Naval Landing Force* arrived at Kokumbona. This was the first of many runs of the Tokyo Express, as Marines called the Japanese destroyers and cruisers which shuttled supplies and reinforcements up and down The Slot in high-speed night runs. Brush's patrol had encountered part of Ichiki's forward echelon, and the Japanese commander, shaken by the fact that he had been discovered, decided to attack at once.

At that time the Marines had five infantry battalions available for defense of Lunga Point. Four battalions were committed to beach defense, one was withheld in division reserve. On 15 August work had begun on a new extension of the right flank by refusing it inland along the west bank of the Ilu River (then called the Tenaru) for a distance of 3,200 yards. This plan involved road and bridge construction as well as extensive clearing before field fortifications could be built. As of 18 August little progress had been made. (See Map 17)

In the face of the threats pointed out by intelligence sources, the division considered two courses of action: first, to send the division reserve across the Ilu to locate and destroy the enemy, or, second, to continue work on defensive positions while limiting actions to the east to strong patrols and outposts. The first course, General Vandegrift realized, involved accepting the premise that the main Japanese force had landed to the east and that it could be dealt with by one Marine battalion. But if Brush's patrol had encountered only a small part of the new enemy unit while the bulk of the force stood poised to strike from another direction, or from the sea, absence of the reserve battalion would become a serious manpower shortage in the perimeter. The intelligence Vandegrift had gleaned from all sources was good, but there wasn't enough of it. So the division sat tight to await developments. Work continued on field fortifications, native scouts worked far to the east, and Marines maintained a strong watch on the perimeter each night.

The Marines did not have long to wait. Colonel Ichiki had wasted no time preparing his attack, and during the night of 20–21 August Marine listening posts on the east bank of the Ilu detected enemy troops moving through the jungle to their front. A light rattle of rifle fire was exchanged, both sides sent up flares, and the Marines withdrew across the river mouth to the lines of their battalion, Lieutenant Colonel Edwin A. Pollock's 2d Battalion, 1st Marines. They reported that a strong enemy force appeared to be building up across the river.[18]

---

[18] At about the same time the native scout Vouza entered the command post of 2/1 to warn LtCol Pollock about the Japanese buildup. Badly wounded, Vouza had been captured by the Ichiki Force, knifed about the face, throat, and chest when he wouldn't talk, and then left for dead by the Japanese. This report to Pollock was one of the many services for which Vouza later was cited by the Americans and British.

THE BATTLE OF THE TENARU

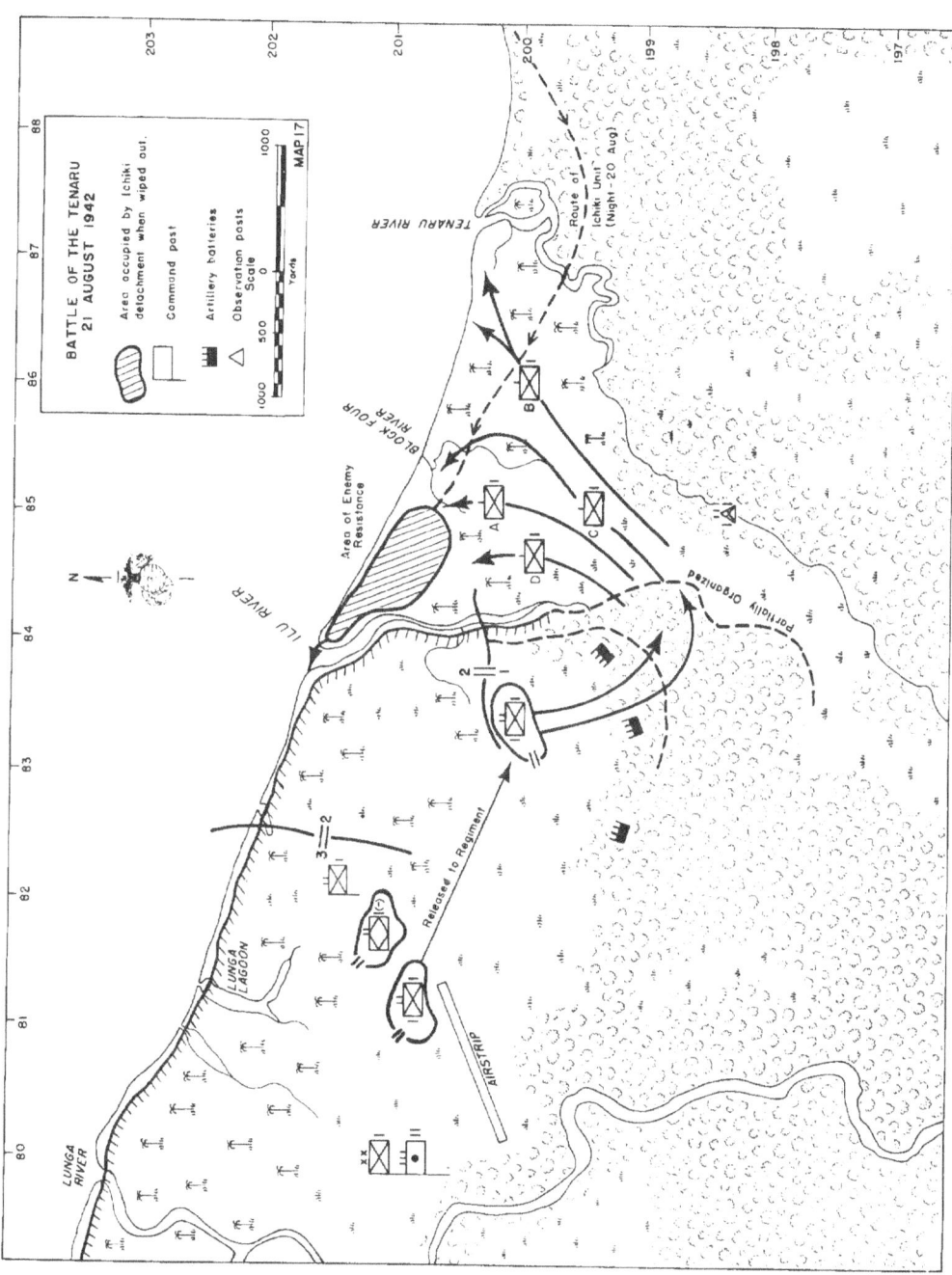

By this time Ichiki had assembled his force on the brush-covered point of land on the east bank of the river, and all was quiet until 0310 on 21 August when a column of some 200 Japanese rushed the exposed sandspit at the river mouth. Most of them were stopped by Marine small-arms fire and by a canister-firing 37mm antitank gun of the 1st Special Weapons Battalion. But the Marine position was not wired in, and the weight of the rushing attack got a few enemy soldiers into Pollock's lines where they captured some of his emplacements. The remainder of the line held, however, and fire from these secure positions kept the penetration in check until the battalion reserve could get up to the fight. This reserve, Company G, launched a counterattack that wiped out the Japanese or drove them back across the river.

Ichiki was ready with another blow. Although his force on the east bank had not directly supported this first attack, it now opened up with a barrage of mortar and 70mm fire, and this was followed by another assault. A second enemy company had circled the river's mouth by wading beyond the breakers, and when the fire lifted it charged splashing through the surf against the 2d Battalion's beach positions a little west of the river mouth.

The Marines opened up with everything they had. Machine-gun fire sliced along the beach as the enemy sloshed ashore, canister from the 37mm ripped gaping holes in the attack, and 75mm pack howitzers of the 3d Battalion, 11th Marines chewed into the enemy. Again the attack broke up, and daylight revealed a sandy battlefield littered with the bodies of the Japanese troops who had launched Guadalcanal's first important ground action.

Although outnumbered at the actual point of contact, Pollock assessed the situation at daybreak and reported that he could hold. His battalion had fire superiority because of the excellent artillery support and because the course of the river gave part of his line enfilade fire against the enemy concentration in the point of ground funneling into the sandspit. In view of this, General Vandegrift ordered Pollock to hold at the river mouth while the division reserve, the 1st Battalion, 1st Marines enveloped Ichiki. While this battalion prepared for its attack, Company C of the 1st Engineer Battalion went forward to Pollock's command to help bolster defensive positions. During the morning the engineers built antitank obstacles, laid a mine field across the sandspit, and helped the 2/1 Marines string tactical wire and improve field fortifications. They were under intermittent rifle fire during most of this work.

Meanwhile, Lieutenant Colonel Lenard B. Cresswell's division reserve battalion had reverted to parent control and reported to Colonel Cates to receive the attack plan for the envelopment. Before 0700, Cresswell crossed the Ilu upstream, posted elements of his Company D (weapons) to cover a possible Japanese escape route to the south, and then turned north toward the *Ichiki Force*. By 0900 his companies crossed their lines of departure in the attack against the Japanese left and rear.

Company C on the right along the coast met one platoon of the enemy near the village at the mouth of the Block Four River, and the Marines moved to encircle this force and isolate it from the remainder of Ichiki's unit farther west. The other companies moved north with little opposition, A on the right and B on the left. As the advance continued, the enemy was forced into the point of land on the Ilu's east bank. By 1400 the enemy was confined completely by the river, the beach, and the envelopment from the left and rear. Some of the Japanese made unsuccessful attempts to escape through the surf and along the beach; another group burst out temporarily to the east but ran head-on into Company C moving up from its battle at the mouth of the Block Four.

The fight continued, with Cresswell tightening his encirclement, and more of the Japanese attempted to strike through to the east. These breakout attempts gave the new Guadalcanal fliers, on the island less than 24 hours, a chance to fire their first shots in anger, and the F4F pilots from VMF-223 gave Cresswell's Marines a hand with strafing attacks that destroyed the Japanese or turned them back into the infantry trap.

To conclude the action by nightfall, Vandegrift ordered a tank attack across the sandspit and into what now had become the rear of the *Ichiki Force*. The platoon of light tanks struck at 1500, firing at the enemy with canister and machine guns. Two tanks were disabled, one by an antitank mine, but the crews were rescued by the close supporting action of other tanks and the attack rolled on into the Japanese positions. It was over by 1700. Nearly 800 Japanese had been killed and 15 were taken prisoner while only a few escaped into the jungle. Disgraced by the debacle, Colonel Ichiki committed suicide.

The action cost the Marines 34 dead and 75 wounded. A policing of the Japanese battlefield gleaned the division ten heavy and 20 light machine guns, 20 grenade throwers, 700 rifles, 20 pistols, an undetermined number of sabers and grenades, three 70mm guns, large quantities of explosive charges, and 12 flame throwers. The flame throwers were not used in the action.

Admiral Tanaka later had this to say about the disaster:

I knew Colonel Ichiki from the Midway operation and was well aware of his magnificent leadership and indomitable fighting spirit. But this episode made it abundantly clear that infantrymen armed with rifles and bayonets had no chance against an enemy equipped with modern heavy arms. This tragedy should have taught us the hopelessness of 'bamboo-spear' tactics.[19]

BATTLE OF THE EASTERN SOLOMONS

While Colonel Ichiki prepared for his ill-fated attack, Rear Admiral Tanaka and Vice Admiral Gunichi Mikawa, the *Eighth Fleet* commander, worked to get the colonel's second echelon ashore for what they hoped would be an orderly, well-coordinated effort against the Marines. These troops were on board the *Kinryu Maru* and four destroyer transports, and they were escorted by the seaplane carrier *Chitose* with her 22 floatplanes and by Tanaka's *Destroyer Squadron 2*, which Tanaka led in light cruiser *Jintsu*. A larger naval force operated farther to the east outside the Solomons chain. In all, the Japanese task forces included three aircraft carriers, eight battleships, four heavy cruisers, two light cruisers, and 22 destroyers in addition to the five transport vessels.

At this time Admiral Fletcher's force of two carriers, one battleship, four cruisers, and ten destroyers operated to the southeast of the Lower Solomons conduct-

---

[19] *Tanaka Article*, I, 691.

ing routine searches to the northwest. Fletcher believed the area to be temporarily safe from Japanese naval trespass, and he had sent the carrier *Wasp* off to refuel. This left him only the *Enterprise* and the *Saratoga* for his air support.

On 23 August, two days after the Battle of the Tenaru, American patrol planes first sighted the Japanese transports and the Tanaka escort some 350 miles north of Guadalcanal. Marine planes from Henderson Field attempted to attack the troop carriers, but a heavy overcast forced them back to Lunga. The fliers had a better day on the 24th, however. At 1420 the F4F pilots intercepted 15 Japanese bombers being escorted toward Guadalcanal by 12 fighters from the carrier *Ryujo*. Marines broke this raid up before it got close. They downed six of the Zeros and ten bombers in what was VMF–223's first big success of the war. Captain Marion Carl splashed two bombers and a Zero, and two planes each were downed by Lieutenants Zennith A. Pond and Kenneth D. Frazier, and Marine Gunner Henry B. Hamilton:

> This was a good day's work by the fighter pilots of VMF–223. It is necessary to remember that the Japanese Zero at this stage of the war was regarded with some of the awe in which the atomic bomb came to be held later. . . . The Cactus [Guadalcanal] fighters made a great contribution to the war by exploding the theory that the Zero was invincible; the Marines started the explosion on 24 August.[20]

Three Marine pilots did not return from the action, and a fourth was shot down but managed to save himself by getting ashore at Tulagi. In plane strength, however, the Cactus Air Force (as the Guadalcanal fliers called their composite outfit) gained. This was the day, as mentioned earlier in this chapter, that the 11 SBD's came in from the damaged *Enterprise*. At the time the ship was struck, Lieutenant Turner Caldwell, USN, was up with his "Flight 300," and, low on gas, he led his fliers to Guadalcanal where they more than paid for their keep until 27 September.

Meanwhile Admiral Fletcher's carrier planes located the enemy task force in the Eastern Solomons at about the same time Japanese planes spotted Fletcher. Like the Battle of Midway, the resulting action was an air-surface and air-air contest. Surface vessels neither sighted nor fired at each other.

The *Ryujo*, whose Zeros had fared so poorly with John Smith's F4F pilots, took repeated hits that finally put her out of control and left her hopelessly aflame. One enemy cruiser and a destroyer were sunk; a second cruiser was damaged; the *Chitose* sustained severe wounds but managed to limp away; and 90 Japanese planes were shot down. On the American side, 20 planes were lost and the damaged *Enterprise* lurched away to seek repair.

This action turned back the larger Japanese attack force, and Fletcher likewise withdrew. He expected to return next day and resume the attack, but by then the Japanese had moved out of range. The escorted transports with reinforcements for the late Colonel Ichiki continued to close the range, however, and early on 25 August SBD's from VMSB–232 and the *Enterprise* Flight 300 went up to find them. The Battle of the Eastern Solomons had postponed Tanaka's delivery of these reinforcements, but after that carrier battle was over the admiral headed his ships south again late on 24 August.

At 0600 on 25 August, Tanaka's force was some 150 miles north of Guadalcanal, and there the SBD's from Henderson

---

[20] *Marine Air History*, 81.

Field found him. The *Jintsu* shook under an exploding bomb that Lieutenant Lawrence Baldinus dropped just forward of her bridge, and Ensign Christian Fink of the *Enterprise* scored a hit on the transport *Kinryu Maru* amidships. Admiral Tanaka was knocked unconscious by the explosion on his flagship, and a number of crewmen were killed or injured. The ship did not list under the bow damage, however, and she still was seaworthy. When Tanaka recovered he transferred his flag to the destroyer *Kagero* and sent the *Jintsu* to Truk alone.[21]

Flames broke out on the *Kinryu Maru* which carried approximately 1,000 troops of the *Yokosuka 5th SNLF*, and the destroyer *Muzuki* went alongside to rescue survivors. At just that moment this ship became "one of the first Japanese warships to be hit by a B-17 since the war began"[22] when these big planes from the 11th Bombardment Group at Espiritu Santo arrived to lend a hand to the Cactus fliers. The *Muzuki* sank at once. Another ship then moved in to rescue the survivors from this destroyer while two destroyer transports went to the rescue of the men from the *Kinryu Maru*. These men were picked up just as the *Maru* also went to the bottom. Meanwhile another pass at the ships had resulted in light damage to the destroyer *Uzuki*, and Admiral Tanaka turned back for Rabaul. Many of the *SNLF* men had been lost, and his force was badly shaken and disordered:

> My worst fear for this operation had come to be realized. Without the main combat unit, the Yokosuka 5th Special Naval Landing Force, it was clear that the remaining auxiliary unit of about 300 men would be of no use even if it did reach Guadalcanal without further mishap.[23]

Thus had the 1st Marine Division gained some valuable time to prepare for the next Japanese attempt to dislodge its Lunga defense. With air support on Henderson Field and with a tenuous supply route established to the New Hebrides, the division's grip on Guadalcanal was much improved at month's end. But it still was a long way from being completely secure, especially now that Ichiki's act of *harakiri* had pointed up for the Japanese the impropriety of trying to dislodge the landing force with only 900 or 1,000 men.

---

[21] *Tanaka Article*, I, 693.

[22] *Marine Air History* 81. See also *Tanaka Article*, I, 694; *Struggle for Guadalcanal*, 105.

---

[23] *Tanaka Article*, I, 694.

CHAPTER 5

The Battle of the Ridge

General Vandegrift and his staff were aware that the defeat of the *Ichiki Force* left the division's position on the island only temporarily improved. Obviously the Japanese could be expected to mount larger and better planned attacks against the small Marine perimeter; air and naval activity at Guadalcanal indicated no waning enemy interest in the South Solomons area. A noon-hour visit from Rabaul bombers was an almost daily occurrence, and enemy warships and submarines entered Sealark Channel nearly every night to shell Henderson Field.

Although the Battle of the Eastern Solomons gave Allied shipping from Espiritu Santo an opportunity to increase the flow of supplies to the beleaguered Marines, the Lunga defenders still operated on a hand-to-mouth basis.

The Cactus Air Force performed beyond all proportion to its facilities and equipment, and the 3d Defense Battalion finally was able late in August to bring in the 5-inch guns of its two seacoast batteries; but there were not enough Marines on the island to enlarge the perimeter for an adequate defense. General Vandegrift believed that positions along 45 miles of Guadalcanal's north coast would have to be held before the Japanese could be restrained from landing and attacking Henderson Field and before air defenses would have sufficient room for deployment. The general did not have that kind of manpower.

Since Major John Smith and Lieutenant Colonel Mangrum arrived with their F4F's and SBD's on 20 August, the airfield had taken on a more proficient and permanent look. By the end of August a daily routine of scheduled patrol flights had been initiated. Four-plane fighter patrols flew from 0545 to 0830 each morning and from 1400 to 1830 each afternoon, and mixed fighter-bomber squadrons frequently made night searches for enemy shipping to the northwest. Cactus aviators flew cover for the Allied shipping to the island, and went up on intercept during the Japanese raids.

The U. S. fighters did well against the enemy bombers, but their only chance against the highly maneuverable Zero was to pair up in mutual support. In this way they could protect themselves when the Zeros came down to drive them away from the bombers. They found that the Grumman did have certain advantages over the Zero, however. It had great fire power, and it could stay in the air with more holes in it than the more flimsy Japanese fighter could endure. During the first ten days of Cactus operations, U. S. fliers shot down 56 Japanese planes at a cost of 11 of their own craft.

Marine engineers rigged a system of lights from captured Japanese equipment to outline the field for emergency night landings, and, when dump trucks and pneumatic tampers came in later, workers could fill a 500-kilogram-bomb crater in 30 minutes. Dump trucks were kept loaded with gravel and sand, and "flying squads" of engineers rushed out to repair any damage immediately after the departure of Japanese bombers.

But not even counting enemy action, Henderson personnel still had plenty of problems. An early method of fueling employed drums strung up in the rafters of partially built Japanese hangars, and even when gasoline trucks arrived later the fuel had to be hand pumped from drums to the trucks. There was no steel matting, and the field was completely at the mercy of the whimsical tropical weather:

> Henderson Field was a bowl of black dust which fouled airplane engines or it was a quagmire of black mud which made the take-off resemble nothing more than a fly trying to rise from a runway of molasses.[1]

When engineers and Seabees had no bomb craters to patch, they still had to fix up the field in the wake of the early SBD's which had hard-rubber tail wheels designed for landing on the sturdy decks of carriers. On the Henderson earth these wheels ". . . chewed up the runway like a plowshare."[2] The sorry condition of the field added serious operational losses to the troubles of the small Cactus force which was nearly always outnumbered in the air. Occasionally a plane was gripped so persistently by the mud that it failed to take off and crashed at the end of the runway; ruts and the beginnings of potholes were hazards on dry days, and on one foggy wet afternoon in early September a landing F4F crashed into a bulldozer.

But in spite of everything the installation grew and slowly improved, and this was a period when American fighting men were thankful for small favors. On 20 August the transport *William Ward Burrows* came up from the New Hebrides with the forward echelon of MAG-23. All the men and some of the gear were put ashore, but then the ship scurried across Sealark Channel for Tulagi when the word came in that a Japanese cruiser force was expected that night. Near Tulagi the transport went aground and much of the equipment still on board had to be jettisoned to float her free.

Next day Colonel William J. Wallace, group commander, came up to Henderson with more planes: 19 F4F's of Major Robert E. Galer's VMF-224, and 12 SBD-3's of VMSB-231 commanded by Major Leo R. Smith. That brought the Cactus strength to 86 pilots and 64 planes, 10 of them Navy and three Army.

On 1 September the ground crews got more help. Five officers and 387 men of the 6th Naval Construction Battalion (Seabees) landed with two bulldozers. They would ". . . help make an airfield out of Henderson and . . . clear a short grassy strip a mile to the east called Fighter 1."[3] But next day came one of the infamous Henderson disasters that always loomed as a threat to much of the backbreaking effort that had gone before.

With the frequent raids, fire was always a dangerous possibility, and a field fire brigade had been organized around two Japanese trucks which had been repaired by the 1st Marines. They got their baptism on 2 September when a bomb from a heavy Japanese raid hit an armed SBD parked at the edge of a coconut grove where ammunition was stored. The bomb could not be removed from the burning

---

[1] *Marine Air History*, 82.
[2] *Ibid.*, 83.

[3] *Ibid.*, 84.

90MM ANTIAIRCRAFT GUNS *of the 3d Defense Battalion point skyward at Henderson Field on alert against the attacks of Japanese bombers. (USMC 61608)*

105MM HOWITZER *of the 11th Marines nestles beneath the slope of a protecting ridge on Guadalcanal ready to go into action against the Japanese. (USMC 51832)*

SBD, and when it exploded it spewed flaming gasoline in all directions. One 90mm shell dump was ignited, and the fire brigade could not do its best work with all the explosions that resulted. Several of the fire-fighters were injured, and the trucks seemed to be making little headway since they had to take turns dashing off to the Lunga River, the closest supply of water. If the fire expanded much more it would set off a chain reaction and all the ammunition in the area would be lost.

Had not the situation been so grim, some old hands might have been reminded of the Chinese fire drill of ancient Marine legend. The blaze was eventually brought under control, however, and the loss was serious but not critical. After this, large water tanks from coconut plantations were spotted around the ammunition dumps; but this fire proved to be the most serious of the campaign. Subsequent losses occurred in division dumps as a result of naval shelling at night. These losses were negligible since the ammunition by that time had been buried.

This bombing raid had arrived at 1135, and while the fire department below worked to save the ammunition dumps, Cactus fliers were up among the bombers. They shot down three of the twin-engined craft and four Zeroes without a single loss of their own.

On 3 September the command echelon of the 1st Marine Aircraft Wing arrived. This group included Brigadier General Roy S. Geiger, commanding general of the wing; his chief of staff, Colonel Louis E. Woods; and Lieutenant Colonel John C. Munn, wing intelligence officer. Using the MAG-23 staff as his wing staff, Geiger established his command post near that of General Vandegrift. Liaison in the form of daily conferences between the two generals was established, and Kenneth H. Weir, now a lieutenant colonel, at last had a well-organized air headquarters with which to deal as division air officer.[4]

Fueling and arming of the planes continued in a make-shift manner for some time, and as late as November bombs had to be manhandled. Radio communications likewise posed problems. Army and Navy receiving channels did not mesh, and the Army planes of the Cactus Force could not receive Navy traffic. Operations resolved this by employing the radio from a grounded Army P-400 alongside the Navy set and thereafter making simultaneous broadcasts over twin microphones. This was a big help, but communications still were far from satisfactory. Beyond 20 miles the planes could not depend on receiving the field, but the field could normally read the planes' messages from as far as 100 miles.

Since the fight against Ichiki, there had been little opportunity for close air support of ground troops, but Marines continued to plan for this sort of air-ground teamwork. Communications was the big problem here, too. At that stage of operations only visual signals were used, consisting mainly of colored panels which the ground troops had, but they left much to be desired. Planes now flew higher and faster than they had in the banana wars and maneuvers, and this made it more difficult for pilots to read the panel messages, even if they could catch a glimpse of the colored markings. And more often than not in Guadalcanal's thick jungle and tall grass, they could not even see them. Guadalcanal Marines had heard about colored smoke grenades which were being tested back in the States, and they thought these

---

[4] As mentioned in the previous chapter, Weir's first look at the field had come on 8 August when he and the division engineer officer had estimated how much work they would have to add to the early Japanese efforts to make the strip usable.

might be helpful for air-ground signals. But what they really had their eyes out for were some radio sets. That seemed to be the only promising solution for air-ground coordination. Radios initially available to the division would not serve the purpose, and it would not be until October that Vandegrift could detail an officer and suitable radio equipment and personnel to train as "air forward observers" from each infantry regiment and thereby pioneer in what later became an important phase of Marine combat operations.

While Geiger built up his air arm, Vandegrift likewise added strength to the Lunga perimeter. With Tulagi quiet, he brought some of General Rupertus' troops across the channel to Guadalcanal. The 2d Battalion, 5th Marines made the move on 21 August, and the 1st Raider Battalion and the 1st Parachute Battalion crossed to the Guadalcanal side on 31 August. In early September, when a detachment of the 5th Defense Battalion came ashore at Tulagi, a 90mm battery of the 3d Defense Battalion joined its parent organization in the Henderson Field area.

From all indications these additional troops would be needed. Aerial observation and native scouts piled up reports of Japanese landings on both sides of the perimeter, and staff officers estimated a build-up of some 200 or 300 well-equipped enemy troops near the village of Tasimboko some 18 miles east of Lunga Point. Native scouts placed the enemy strength much higher, but Marines suspected such counts to be exaggerated.

Patrolling continued in all sectors, and on 27 August the 1st Battalion, 5th Marines under Lieutenant Colonel William E. Maxwell met a strong body of troops near the village of Kokumbona, west of the perimeter. The battalion had made an amphibious landing without incident at about 0730, but later ran into the Japanese force dug into positions throughout a narrow coastal gorge. Maxwell was beyond artillery range of the perimeter, and although the 2d and 5th Battalions of the 11th Marines fired diversionary missions east of him in Matanikau village, the Japanese facing the infantry Marines seemed inclined for once to make a strong stand rather than to slink off into the brush as they had frequently done in other such engagements.

Faulty communications and other difficulties bogged the Marine attack, and Lieutenant Colonel Maxwell withdrew his force to comply with a portion of his patrol order which required him to return to the perimeter by nightfall. But the regimental commander, Colonel Hunt, ordered the battalion back into the fight, relieved Maxwell of command, and soon thereafter arrived on the scene himself. Major Milton V. O'Connell succeeded to command of the battalion, but the attack was not resumed until the predawn hours of the following morning. A few Japanese were killed, but most of them had withdrawn. The Marines retired to Matanikau village and later returned by water to the perimeter.

On 2 September two companies of the raider battalion patrolled Savo Island but found no enemy. Following this the raiders and parachutists, consolidated into a provisional battalion, moved into defensive positions on the south rim of the perimeter, inland from the airfield. While they dug in, Colonel Edson and his staff made plans for an amphibious raid to the east where the enemy build-up was reported around the Tasimboko area.

The landing was made just east of Tasimboko before dawn on 8 September, and the raiders[5] advanced west into the rear of the reported Japanese positions. At about 0630 planes of MAG-23 bombed and strafed the suspected strong point, and two destroyer transports, *Manley* and *Mc-Kean*, opened up on the area. At 0830 Edson made contact against light resistance, and his advance overran two artillery pieces. He still could not determine the strength of the enemy, but the force appeared to be withdrawing toward the village, and he requested that supporting dive bombers remain on station in the event that the enemy pocket could be localized for an air strike. General Vandegrift ordered ten planes to remain in continuous support and placed another squadron on call to Edson.

By 1045 the resistance had stiffened, and the raiders requested that more troops land to the west of the village and support their attack. Not wanting to weaken the perimeter, division replied that such a move was not feasible. Vandegrift suggested that the raiding force reembark and return to the perimeter if the Japanese proved too strong to handle. Edson remained, however, and 45 minutes later had overrun more artillery pieces as the battalion advanced slowly against a heavy volume of fire. The colonel estimated the enemy as about 1,000 well-armed and well-equipped troops, and the force now seemed inclined to make a stand. Portions of Edson's advance drew fire from field artillery at point-blank range.

Some of the raider units had lost internal contact during the stiffening battle, but these faults were corrected at about 1100, approximately the same time that the parachute battalion reported to Edson, and the commander decided to make a coordinated attack against the firm opposition. The colonel called in a P-400 strafing attack and then followed this with an envelopment inland by his raiders while the parachutists protected his flank and rear. The assault carried the village, but again the Japanese had elected to break contact and prepare for an attack at a time and place of their own choosing.

The village was deserted, but the appearance of the abandoned encampment indicated that reports of native scouts had been most accurate. Edson estimated that some 4,000 Japanese had been in the vicinity until shortly before his attack, that his force had met only outposts and rear guards of a newly arrived unit which obviously was preparing a strong attack on Henderson Field. Twenty-seven Japanese had been killed. Marine casualties numbered two dead and six wounded.

Edson's estimate of the Japanese strength was a little low, but he was right about the enemy's intentions. Just as the 1st Marines had previously scouted elements of the *Ichiki Force* it later met at the mouth of the Ilu River, so Colonel Edson had located the gathering *Kawaguchi Force* his men would meet later in a bitter stand before the airfield.

Rabaul had kept Admiral Tanaka's reinforcement ships busy. The admiral had taken over the cruiser *Kinugasa* to replace his damaged *Jintsu*, and early on 29 August Admiral Mikawa had ordered Tanaka to begin transporting reinforcements by destroyer. The remnants of Ichiki's rear echelon would be taken down to Guadalcanal as would the *Kawaguchi Force*, due to arrive later that day from Truk on board the transport *Sado Maru*. Tanaka loaded supplies on board the ships of *De-*

---

[5] There was a shortage of landing craft and the parachute battalion would not leave the perimeter until shortly after 0800.

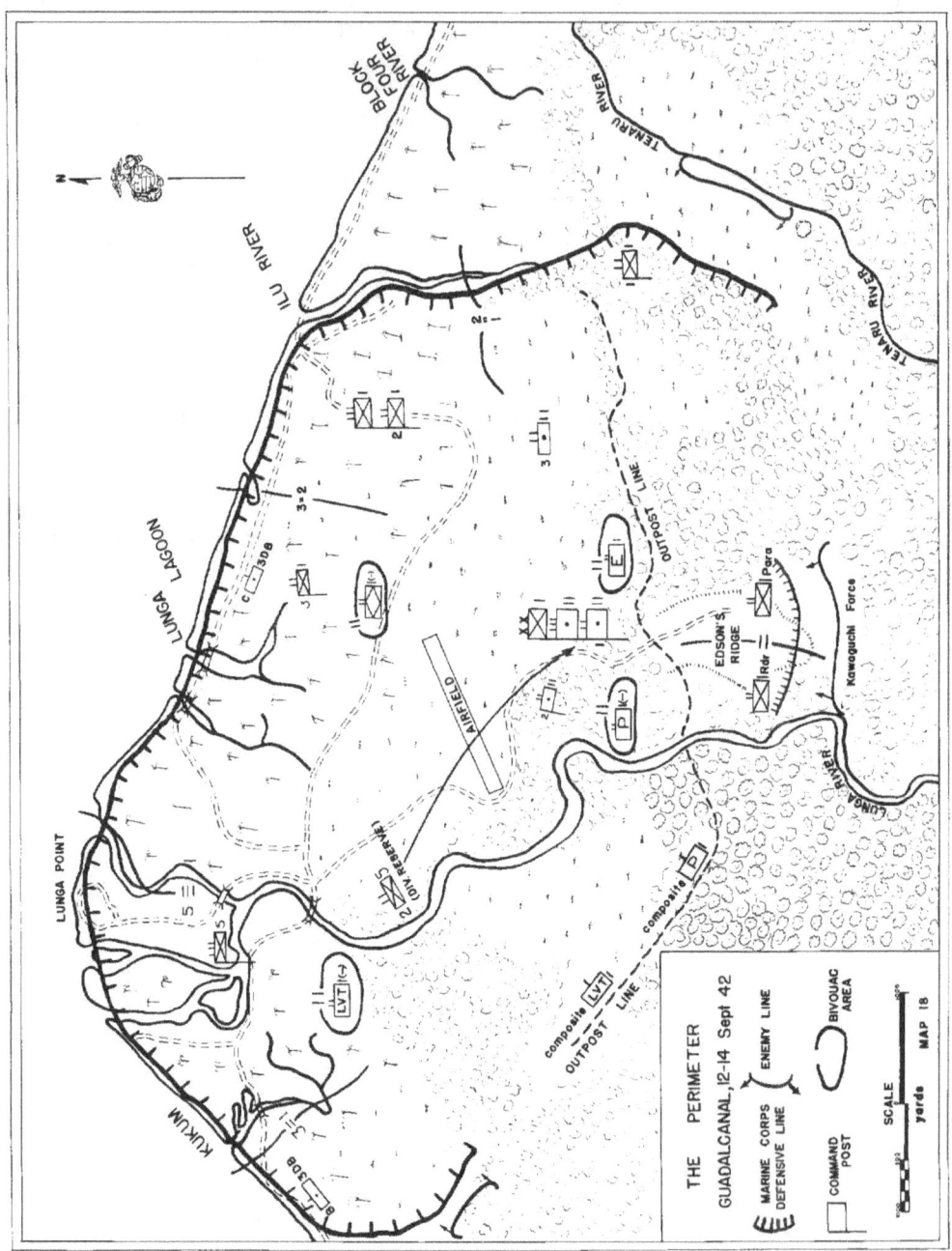

stroyer Division 24, and put the troops of Ichiki's rear echelon on board two destroyer transports. Then he stood by for the arrival of Kawaguchi.

Kawaguchi's *35th Brigade*, a part of the *18th Division* in China, was built around Colonel Akinosuka Oka's *124th Infantry Regiment*. From China the unit had moved in December 1941 to Borneo. In March 1942 it moved to Cebu in the Philippines, in April to Mindanao, and in June to Palau. Alerted for a New Guinea operation that never came off, the force remained in the Palau Islands until late in August when it began to stage in echelons through Truk for the Rabaul area. When it arrived for this new mission it was formed up to include the rear echelon of the *2d Battalion, 28th Infantry (Ichiki Force)*, the *124th Infantry*, the *2d Battalion, 4th Infantry*, and units of artillery, engineer, signal, and antitank troops. In that form the *Kawaguchi Force* numbered more than 6,000 men.[6]

Admiral Tanaka had his destroyers all ready when Kawaguchi arrived. The admiral met immediately with the general to hurry things along, but he ran into difficulty at once. Kawaguchi was a barge man, and he did not care much for this idea of going down to Guadalcanal in destroyers. He had once moved his unit 500 miles by barges to make a distinguished landing on Borneo. Now he wanted to know how it would be if he went on down to Gizo Harbor just north of New Georgia on board his *Sado Maru*, and then transferred to barges for the remainder of the trip and for the landing at Guadalcanal. Kawaguchi's subordinate officers nodded agreement to this idea. They were barge men, too. The impatient Tanaka referred this dispute to Mikawa of the *Eighth Fleet* and Hyakutake of the *Seventeenth Army*. These officers prevailed upon Kawaguchi to temporarily curb his warm regard for barges. He would make all of the trip on Tanaka's destroyers, and land on Guadalcanal from them, besides.[7]

For the build-up on Guadalcanal, Kawaguchi split his command. The general would land in the Tasimboko area with the Ichiki rear echelon and the *1st* and *3d Battalions, 124th Infantry Regiment*. Colonel Oka would land with the remainder of the force—the *2d Battalion, 124th Infantry*—west of Lunga Point near Kokumbona. Each of the two forces was reinforced by a share of the artillery, engineers, and other special troops. There was only one hitch in the reinforcement efforts, even if Kawaguchi might have been uneasy without a barge under him, but this bobble had no serious over-all results. Captain Yonosuke Murakami, commanding *Destroyer Squadron 24*, was to clear the way for the landings by going down The Slot on the night of 29 August to attack a U. S. task force which was reported to be off Lunga Point. Instead, Murakami came steaming back up The Slot for the comfort of the Shortlands. The night sky around Guadalcanal, he explained, was too full of a bright moon and U. S. aircraft. "He was transferred shortly to the homeland," Tanaka reported later.[8] The elements of the *Kawaguchi Force* landed during the nights of 30 and 31 August, at about midnight in both cases.

In spite of the fact that the commanders were separated by a distance of some 30 miles, Kawaguchi planned a difficult

---

[6] 17th Army Ops, I, cited in *Miller, Guadalcanal*, 114.

[7] *Tanaka Article*, I, 695, 697.

[8] *Ibid.*, 696.

maneuver that proposed to strike the Lunga perimeter in a three-jawed envelopment from the west, south, and southeast. It was to be a coordinated attack with air and naval support. To the normal problems inherent in such an involved plan, Kawaguchi imposed upon his force the additional task of cutting a trail over the steep jungle-covered ridges and gorges from the Tasimboko area to a point south of Henderson Field. The jungle trail, planned as a route which would enable the Japanese to escape observation, was begun about 2 September by Kawaguchi's engineers. Infantry, artillery, and other units followed the engineers along this hand-hewn jungle route toward their lines of departure for the attack against the Marines.

THE BATTLE OF THE RIDGE

Kawaguchi's fade-out into the jungle was successful. He was not spotted by Marines again until he was ready to attack, but it soon became apparent to the Lunga defenders that he would have imposing support from Rabaul. Far-ranging intelligence sources reported a Japanese naval build-up in the Truk and Palau areas and greatly increased air activity around the Bismarck Archipelago.

"The situation as I view it is very critical," Admiral Ghormley messaged Nimitz.[9] "Our transportation problem increases steadily as Japs perfect their blockade methods." Japanese pounding of Guadalcanal picked up; the defenders clearly were being softened up for a big attack, and while the South Pacific scurried to get them more planes the men at Lunga hoped that the field would stay dry for the important day.

[9] Quoted in *Marine Air History*, 88–89.

On 11 September, the pace of the attacks quickened. Twenty-six bombers and eight Zeros came over at 1210 to pock the field, kill 11 Marines, and wound 17 others, and destroy one P–400 parked beside the strip; and a heavy cruiser and two destroyers were spotted steaming south about 100 miles to the northeast. But on the same day the Cactus Air Force added to its strength. At 1620 a flight of 24 F4F's that had been idle since their carrier *Saratoga* had been torpedoed on 31 August came up to Henderson from Espiritu Santo under the command of Lieutenant Commander Leroy C. Simpler. Before noon the next day (12 September) Simpler's men got their chance to learn Cactus operations. Twenty-one of them went up with 11 "old" Cactus fliers to shoot down 12 bombers and three fighters out of a 42-plane Japanese strike that came over at 1100.

Meanwhile patrols from the 2d Battalion, 1st Marines began to encounter frequent opposition east and southeast of the perimeter. Native scouts brought word of large bodies of troops that clearly were not wandering remnants of Ichiki's action. The troops had an air of purpose and direction apparent even to the local natives who began to flee from their villages to the Marine perimeter. By 10 September native reports indicated that the enemy was less than five miles east of the perimeter and that he was cutting a road to the south.

The perimeter by this time had been improved and strengthened. The 1st Marines right (east) flank was refused for some 4,000 yards inland from the mouth of the Ilu, and on the west the 5th Marines, with a strong reserve in the form of its 2d Battalion just over from Tulagi, refused its flank inland for approximately half that distance. The space inland between these flanks still posed a serious problem, but it had been partially solved by the establishment of well-prepared strong points and outposts. (See Map 18)

Troops from the 1st Amphibian Tractor and Pioneer Battalions maintained positions south (inland) of the 5th Marines sector west of the Lunga, while east of the Lunga a 4,000-yard outpost line was maintained by the 1st Marines, artillerymen, the engineer battalion, the bulk of the pioneer battalion, and the raider-parachute battalion. General Vandegrift had ordered the raiders and parachutists out of division reserve to augment this line by preparing positions on a long low ridge that extended south of Henderson Field and parallel to the Lunga River. The thousand-yard-long ridge was but a mile south of the airfield and, unless well defended, offered the Japanese an inviting avenue of approach to the field.

The pioneer battalion (minus its company west of the Lunga) held positions just south of Henderson Field between the Lunga and the north spur of the ridge occupied by Edson's force. Farther to the east—and across the ridge spur from the pioneers—was the area of the engineer battalion. Between the two positions was the division command post which recently had been moved from its former, bomb-pocked position near the airfield.

On the 12th, the same day the *Saratoga* fliers went into business with the Cactus circus, Edson and his executive officers walked out on their ridge to decide on a location for defenses. The officers drew small-arms fire from the jungles to the south, and Edson called up his troops to dig in across the southernmost knoll on the ridge. This was forward of the flanks of engineers on his left (east) and the pioneers on his right, but Edson wanted to hold all the ground he could and to launch an attack against the enemy the next day.

At about 2100 that night a Japanese light cruiser and three destroyers entered Sealark Channel to shell the airfield, and at about the same time the enemy ground force probed lightly at the raider-parachute force on the ridge. Fighting was sporadic all along the line, and although one desultory Japanese attack actually made a slight penetration of the Marine line, the enemy made no attempt to consolidate or expand this gain.

Early the next morning (the 13th) Edson launched his counteroffensive, but he found the enemy too strong and well-prepared to be thrown back. In the afternoon the Marine officer withdrew his exhausted men north of the positions they had held the previous night and established a stronger line on a higher portion of the ridge closer to the engineers and pioneers to his left and right rear. On the right, in the jungle between the ridge and the Lunga, a sketchy contact was made with the pioneer battalion; on the left (east) the raider-parachute flank dangled open. (See Map 19)

While Edson's force sweated under the hot sun on the grassy ridge, Henderson Field was having more than its share of action. The Japanese raids started at 0950, came back at 1300 and again at 1730. The mixed Guadalcanal force shot down 11 of the enemy planes during the day while losing five of their own number. But again the U. S. air strength grew.

Navy pilots from the *Hornet* and *Wasp* brought in 18 F4F's, and in the afternoon more *Saratoga* fliers and planes came up

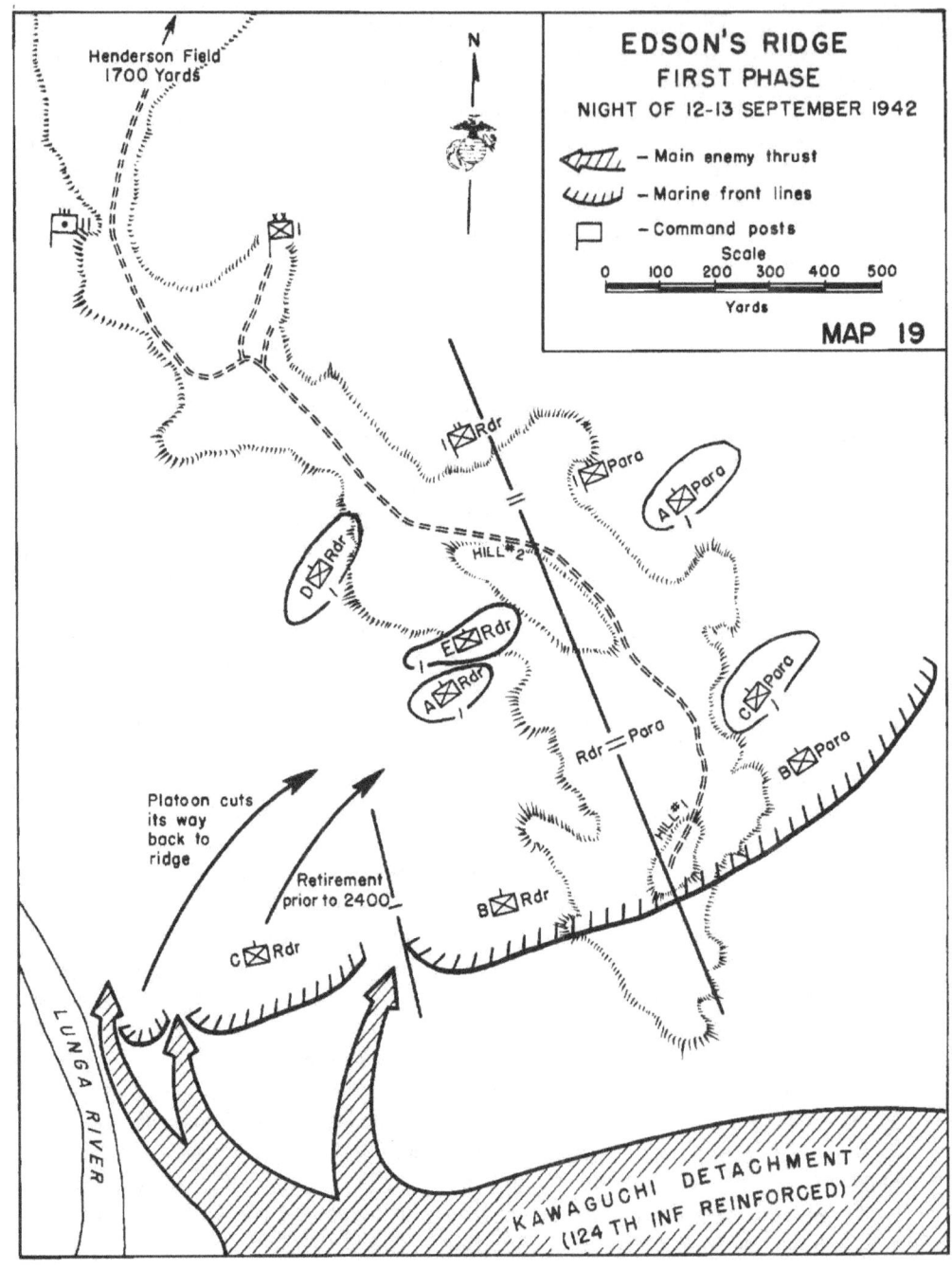

from Espiritu Santo. Nimitz and Ghormley were doing all they could to bolster the Solomons toe hold against the Japanese attack that was coming. Later in the day Lieutenant Commander Louis J. Kirn brought in a flight of 12 SBD's of VS-3 and the field also got its first torpedo planes when Lieutenant Harold H. Larsen, USN, flew in leading six TBF's of VT-8.[10] But while the Henderson flying force gained by 60 planes during the period of 11–13 September, Rabaul's air power jumped an additional 140 planes on 12 September alone.

Taking periodic cover from sniping and bombing raids, Edson's men continued to dig in for one more night on the ridge; on the morning of the 14th they were to be relieved by the 2d Battalion, 5th Marines. But it looked as if the night would be the worst they had seen yet; scouting planes spotted seven destroyers coming down The Slot, evidently to add their bombardment to the ground attack that appeared shaping up in the jungle to the south.

During the afternoon the reserve battalion (2/5) moved to an assembly area east of the Lunga and between the airfield and Edson's Ridge, and officers of this battalion had gone forward to Edson's lines to look over the area they would control the following day. The 105mm howitzers of the 5th Battalion, 11th Marines lay in direct support of the Edson force, and elements of the special weapons battalion had an observation post on the ridge. The Guadalcanal defense was as ready as it could get.

Edson's disposition placed his two parachute companies on the exposed left flank and tied them in on the right with raider Company B which held the ridge knoll in the center of the Marine line. Company A of the raiders extended down the west slope of the ridge toward the Lunga and to the makeshift contact with the pioneers. Raider Company C, on a high knoll to the north (rear) of Company B, was Edson's reserve.

At sunset units were organized in small combat groups of about platoon strength disposed at intervals along the main line of resistance. There were open fields of fire only in the center of the position where the MLR crossed the grassy ridge, but even here the abrupt slopes and broken ground made coordination of fires difficult. In the last hours of daylight the troops improved their foxholes and the fields of fire, but the resulting positions were neither continuous nor complete.

In the first hours of darkness, Louie the Louse, or Washing-Machine Charley,[11] chugged over to drop his inconsistent scattering of bombs, and about 2100 he let go a flare that hung over the field as a registration point for the destroyer task force that now opened up from Sealark Channel.

As if in answer, a flare went up from the troops south of Edson, and without artillery preparation Kawaguchi drove a two-battalion attack against the center and right of the raider-parachute line. Com-

---

[10] After this day account-keeping pretty well broke down. Records defy determination of who flew from Cactus on any given day. In the press of fighting, often with "staff" officers in the air as much as anybody else, administration and office work were marked by extreme casualness.

[11] Familiar but unaffectionate names by which Guadalcanal defenders identified the nuisance raiders that droned around almost nightly. Technically, "Charlie" was a twin-engine night bomber from Rabaul, "Louie" a cruiser float plane who signalled to the bombardment ships. But the harassed Marines used the names interchangeably.

pany B's central sector on the high knoll caught most of this first assault and turned it back, but the other attack column found an opening to the west and came through to cut off and envelop Company B's right platoon. While the Japanese drove through this gap between Companies A and B, the isolated platoon fought its way back along 250 yards of the ridge to join Company C on the knoll to the north. Still engaged and nearly overpowered, Company B refused its right flank along the ridge's west slopes. (See Map 20)

Edson had been calling in fire from 5/11's howitzers since the beginning of the attack, and as the Japanese continued to hammer at his men the colonel directed the artillery closer and closer until it was falling within 200 yards of the Company B lines. But still the Japanese came on, and by 2200 Edson estimated that the two understrength parachute companies and Company B (less the withdrawn platoon) were opposed by at least two enemy battalions attacking in full force.

Japanese infiltration parties were taking over some of the Company B foxholes, communication lines were cut throughout the area, and the Japanese now began to drum the ridge with heavy mortar fire. Following a violent barrage at 2230, the Japanese attack shifted to the east where it struck the thin flank held by the parachute troops. Screaming in English, "Gas attack! Gas attack!", the Japanese came out of the jungle through a smoke screen and drove the parachutists back along the ridge to expose the left flank of Company B.

This left the B Company raiders, now cut to approximately 60 men, exposed on both flanks as well as their front, and Edson called for them to pull back to a last-ditch stand with Company C. Company A would join the force there, and Edson ordered his men to hold at all costs. It was the last dominating terrain feature south of the airfield.

Screening the withdrawal of the two companies with artillery fire, Edson collected his men as they filtered back and built them up in what he hoped would be a line strong enough to make the final stand. The colonel and his officers ironed out the confusion of setting in the new defense in darkness and under fire while holding off repeated Japanese assaults. In all, the enemy struck more than a dozen times throughout the night, the Kawaguchi men grinding themselves into the fire from Marine artillery, mortars, machine guns, and rifles in vain attempts to dislodge Edson from his final knoll of Bloody Ridge.[12] Japanese flares "telegraphed" each attack, providing the 11th Marines gunners with reference points for their all-night firing in which they expended 1,992 rounds of 105mm projectiles, some at ranges as short at 1,600 yards.

At 0400, with the Japanese attacks still in progress, companies of reserve battalion 2/5 began to move singly through the darkness and into positions on the raider-parachute left flank. Darkness and uncertainty about Edson's new location brought confusion to this reinforcement effort, but the companies succeeded in gaining positions from which they aided in standing off the final Japanese attacks.

While the action on the ridge was in progress, another Japanese unit (possibly the Ichiki rear echelon) struck farther to the east where the right flank of the 3d Battalion, 1st Marines lay exposed near the Ilu River inland. Striking with a

---

[12] The name, used interchangeably with "Edson's Ridge," was employed after the battle, to identify this terrain feature.

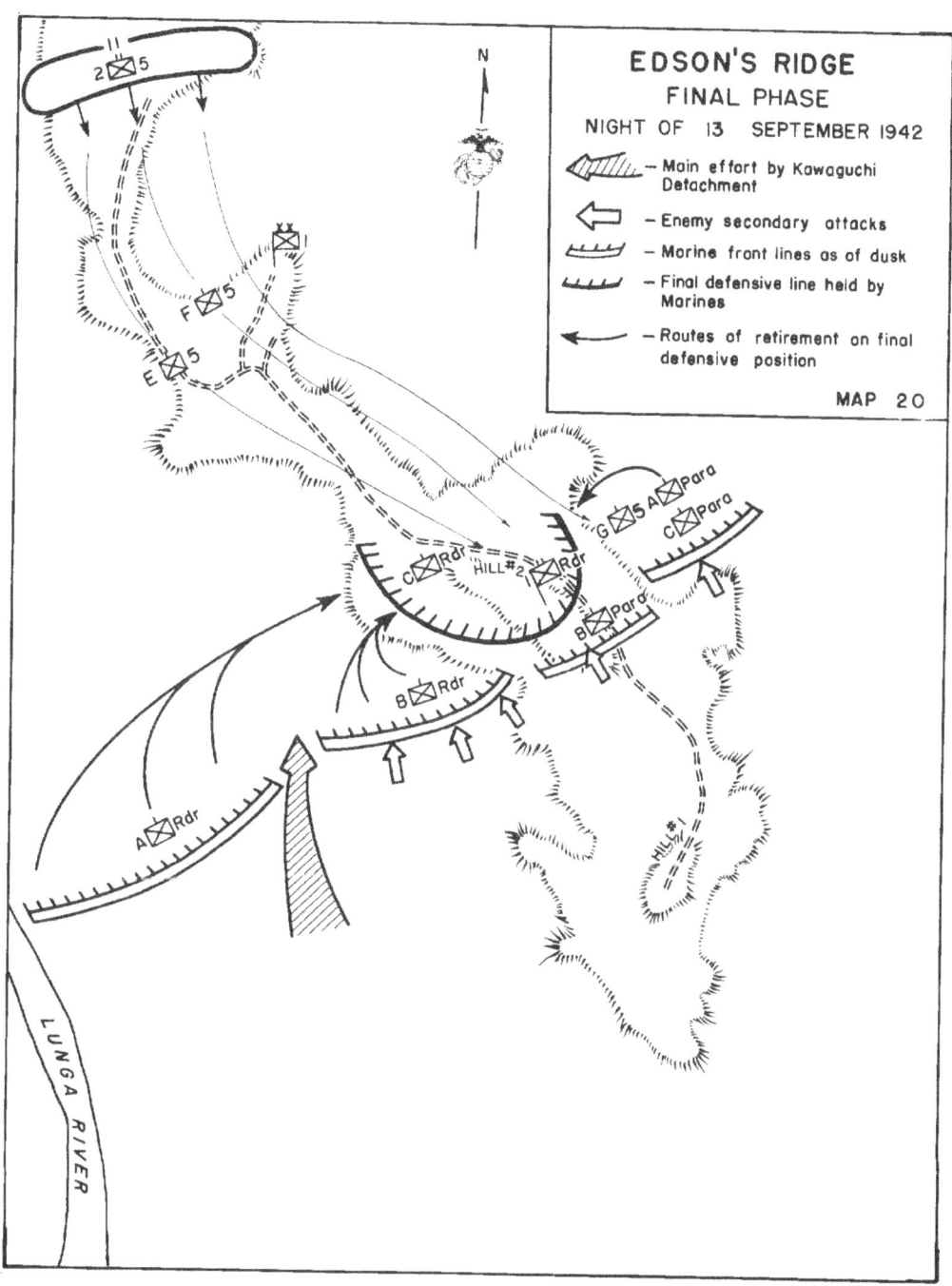

force of about two reinforced companies, the Japanese engaged the Marines in a night-long fire fight but failed to penetrate the line.

In another, lesser action of the night a patrol of some 30 Japanese, evidently from the force that penetrated Edson, wandered into a thin line of Company C, 1st Engineers in the area east of the division CP and near 5/11's Headquarters and Service Battery south of the airfield. The line had been thinned earlier in the night when Company A of the engineers had been called back to aid the CP defense, and the Japanese patrol which struck at 0530 succeeded in taking two left flank machine-gun positions before headquarters and service artillerymen came up to bolster the line and help evacuate wounded. The Japanese heckled the line for the short time remaining until daylight, then retired into the jungle. Four engineers were killed and 14 were wounded. Ten Japanese bodies were buried in the area.

Also by daylight (14 September) the attacks on Edson's Ridge and the 3/1 line had dwindled to sporadic sniping, and in the Edson Ridge sector the disorganized Japanese were bombed and strafed into retreat by three P-400's from Henderson Field. Survivors remaining near the ridge were hunted down and killed.

After this the only enemy still in action was a force of about battalion strength which fired across the Ilu plain some distance east of Bloody Ridge and harassed the Marines of 3/1 (Lieutenant Colonel William N. McKelvy, Jr.) who held that portion of the Marine line. Tanks were called up against this enemy force, and after a hasty reconnaissance six of these vehicles moved forward without infantry support toward the Japanese line in the fringe of jungle by the Tenaru. Two tanks were hit almost at once by a Japanese antitank gun. Another tank charged across the plain and over a grass hut only to plunge down a 30-foot bank into the Tenaru; all four crew members were killed. A fourth tank was hit by this antitank gun shortly after this, the fifth tank returned to the infantry lines, and the sixth tank was stopped by a wrecked track 50 yards in front of the Japanese gun. The men in this tank bailed out and returned to the infantry position. The tank attack had to be chalked off as a costly failure, but the Japanese caused little trouble in the area after this. A desultory fire fight continued across the plain until 16 September when the enemy withdrew.

Tactically the entire *Kawaguchi Force* could be scratched. About 400 of the Ichiki rear echelon subsequently reached Koli Point as did some troops of the *2d Battalion, 4th Infantry*, but these were hardly more than stragglers. The remainder of the force—the larger element which had struck Edson's Ridge—reduced itself to a rabble while cutting a tortuous jungle trail over the southern slopes of Mount Austen, across the up-country Matanikau territory, and finally to Kokumbona. Wounded died along the route and equipment was abandoned by the weakened, exhausted survivors.

The Marines had turned back a serious threat to their precarious Guadalcanal position, but again a part of the thanks could go to Japanese bungling—on the battlefield as well as in planning at higher echelons. Although Kawaguchi salvaged enough pride to spare himself the *hara-kiri* fate of Colonel Ichiki, he still was only a slightly stronger boy whom Tokyo and Rabaul hopefully had sent away on a man's job.

RAIDERS' RIDGE *looks calm in this after-action shot, but it was the scene of a violent and bloody fight crucial to the defense of the perimeter.* (USMC 50007)

MARINES OF THE 2D RAIDER BATTALION *land at Aola Bay, starting point of their month-long operations behind the enemy lines east of the perimeter.* (USMC 51359)

CHAPTER 6

Action Along the Matanikau

Retreat of the *Kawaguchi Force* promised the Marines of the Lunga perimeter another breathing spell from ground attacks, but there was no time for relaxation or relief from concern about the future. Air and naval strikes continued to pound the Henderson Field defenders, and aerial reports of a continued Japanese build-up at Rabaul forecast additional attempts to retake the Guadalcanal area. Patrolling schedules were stepped up; it was disquieting to know that both the *Ichiki* and *Kawaguchi Forces* had landed on the island and moved into attack positions without the Marines once being completely sure of their exact locations.

At the conclusion of the Battle of the Ridge on 14 September, the Marines had been ashore for 38 days without receiving either reinforcements or additional ammunition. For most of this period the men could be fed only two meals a day, and part of this food came from captured Japanese supplies. Malaria was beginning to add its toll to battle casualties, and although defensive emplacements were continually improved, the Marine force was wearing itself down while the Japanese ground strength continued to mount in staging areas in the Bismarcks.

In these lean early days in the Pacific, the problem of new strength for the Guadalcanal effort was a thorny one. The Solomon Islands position was merely a salient, and still not a strong one, which made a questionable contribution to the safety of other Allied positions farther to the south. So these areas could not be stripped of defenders, and even if some spare troops could be found there still was another operation slated. From the first, the plan for this initial Allied offensive in the Pacific had included an occupation of Ndeni Island in the Santa Cruz group southeast of the Solomons.

The 2d Marines first had been scheduled for this job, but Vandegrift had been allowed to keep this regiment when the opposition became so bitter on Tulagi. Later the general requested that his division's third organic infantry regiment, the 7th Marines, come over from its Samoan garrison duty with its supporting artillery, the 1st Battalion, 11th Marines. But Admiral Turner demurred; he still saw a need for the Ndeni operation, and the reinforced 7th Marines was the only amphibious force readily available for such an undertaking. On 20 August the admiral published his Ndeni plan, and on 4 September the 7th Marines with its artillery and part of the 5th Defense Battalion sailed from Samoa for Espiritu Santo.[1]

---

[1] Turner and Vandegrift often disagreed on conduct of the Guadalcanal operation ashore and on progress of the Solomon Islands action in general. Turner found fault with Vandegrift's perimeter concept of defense. His idea was to disperse the Marines along the Guadalcanal coast and set them upon the task of mopping up the remaining Japanese.

But by 9 September, with the 7th Marines' convoy still en route, Turner agreed with Vandegrift's August request for control of this infantry regiment, and he requested Admiral Ghormley's permission to divert the regiment from the Ndeni operation. The issue still was not won for the Marine general, however. Turner believed this fresh unit should set up coastal strong points outside the Lunga perimeter, while Vandegrift held that a reinforcement of his perimeter was the more pressing need. Turner relayed this question to Ghormley on 12 September, the same day the 7th Marines arrived in the New Hebrides, and Ghormley next day ordered the reinforced regiment to move as soon as possible to the Guadalcanal perimeter.

After unloading the 5th Defense Battalion units at Espiritu Santo, the ships bearing the infantry regiment and the artillery battalion departed for Guadalcanal on 14 September, the same day that the 3d Battalion, 2d Marines was brought across Sealark Channel from Tulagi. Operating with three cruisers plus the destroyers and mine sweepers of the newly-formed Task Force 65, the transports spent four days at sea skirting enemy naval forces in the Solomons waters. The convoy finally anchored off Kukum early in the morning of 18 September.

The trip cost the Navy dearly. Carriers *Hornet* and *Wasp*, then the only flattops operational in the entire South Pacific (both the *Saratoga* and the *Enterprise* were under repair) ranged southeast of the Solomons with other escort support for the convoy, and the Japanese had just sown the area with a division of submarines. The *Wasp* caught two torpedoes, burned and sank; the battleship *North Carolina* was damaged as was the destroyer *O'Brien*, which later broke in two and went down while heading back to the U. S. following temporary repairs.

But for Henderson Field there was advantage even from such grim disasters as this; pilots and planes that otherwise would have been flying from their carriers could now come up to give the Cactus Force a hand. On 18 September six Navy TBF's arrived in the Lunga area, and on 28 September 10 more planes, some SBD's and the other TBF's, flew in. Although enemy raids dropped off somewhat after the defeat of the *Kawaguchi Force*, operational losses still drained Geiger's air power, and such reinforcement managed only to keep the Cactus Force at a 50-to-70-plane level, but for this Lunga was most thankful.

September 18th was a red-letter day for the Guadalcanal defenders. While the reinforced 7th Marines unloaded its 4,262 men, three other transports which were not part of TF 65 entered the channel with an emergency shipment of aviation gasoline. In all, this shipping put ashore 3,823 drums of fuel, 147 vehicles, 1,012 tons of rations, 90 per cent of the 7th Marines supplies of engineering equipment, 82.5 per cent of the organizational equipment, and nearly all of the ammunition.[2] Turner's force then took on board the 1st Parachute Battalion, 162 American wounded, and eight Japanese prisoners and departed for Espiritu Santo at 1800.

After this successful unloading, men on Guadalcanal began to draw more adequate

---

[2] This was the first ammunition Marines had received since the landing. It included about 10 units of fire with additional hand grenades and 81mm mortar shells. *FinalRept*, Phase V, Annex Z, 10.

THE PAGODA AT HENDERSON FIELD, *headquarters of Cactus Air Force flyers throughout the first months of operations from the captured airfield.* (USMC 50921)

CACTUS AIR FORCE *spreads in all its variety across Henderson Field during a lull in the battle; in the foreground are Marine scout-bombers.* (USMC 108580)

rations, and General Vandegrift was able to adopt new defensive concepts for his force of some 19,200 men now at Lunga. Local air power made a counterlanding less likely, and the attack pattern set by Ichiki and Kawaguchi indicated that more attention should be given to the inland rim of the perimeter. On 19 September, Vandegrift's Operational Plan 11-42 provided for this new concept by dividing the defenses into new sectors with increased all-around strength.

Relieving special troops such as the engineers and pioneers, infantry battalions filled the yawning gaps that previously had existed south of the airfield and along the southern portions of the new inland sectors. The pioneers, engineers, and the amphibian tractor personnel now were able to perform their normal functions during the daylight hours and at night bolster the beach defenses where fewer men were needed. Each infantry regiment maintained a one-battalion reserve, one or all of which could be made available as a division reserve if necessary.[3]

Gaps still existed in the perimeter. Generally the lines followed the high ground of the ridges, but intervening stretches of low jungle often could not be occupied in mutually supporting positions. Barbed wire had become available in increasing quantity, and in most sectors double apron fences stretched across the ground in front of infantry positions of foxholes and logged and sand-bagged machine-gun emplacements. Colonel Robert H. Pepper's 3d Defense Battalion, with the 1st Special Weapons Battalion attached, retained responsibility for antiaircraft and beach defense, and Colonel Pedro A. del Valle's 11th Marines, bolstered by its 1st Battalion, remained in a central position supporting all sectors.

The 1st Marines retained responsibility for the east side of the perimeter, from an area near the mouth of the Ilu River inland to a point beyond the former right flank where McKelvy's battalion had fought the Japanese across the grassy plain. The fresh troops of the 7th Marines joined the 1st Marines at that point and extended across Edson's Ridge to the Lunga River. Beyond that river the 3d Battalion, 2d Marines built up a line that tied in on the right to the positions of the 5th Marines, and this latter regiment closed the perimeter with its right flank which connected with the left flank of the 3d Defense Battalion at the beach.

Tentative plans in the reorganization also included extending the perimeter with strong points of one- or two-battalion strength to the mouth of the Matanikau on the west and the Tenaru on the east. Such positions would take advantage of the natural defensive potential of the two rivers and aid the Marines in blocking Japanese movements in strength toward the main battle positions. These strong outposts were not established at this time, however. (See Map 21)

The first order of business seemed to require aggressive attention to the west.

---

[3] All large trucks were called in to a division pool each night to stand by in case a division reserve had to be trucked quickly into action. Although many additional vehicles had been landed on the day the 7th Marines arrived, the division still was critically short of motor transport. The supply of large trucks never topped a bare 30 per cent of the allowance. In rear areas there was a mistaken idea that one-and-a-half ton and larger trucks could not be used on Guadalcanal. *Ibid.*, 1.

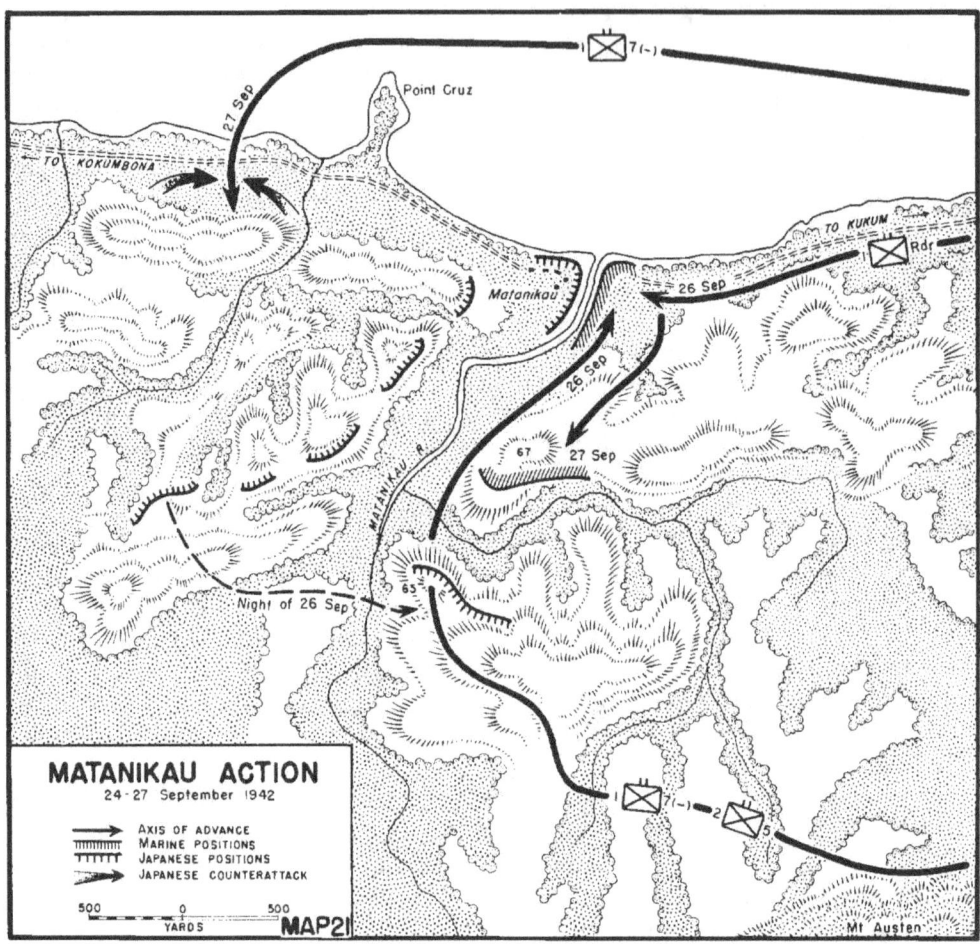

Patrol actions had confirmed intelligence estimates that a strong enemy force was operating from the Matanikau village area on the west bank of the river, but that from the southeast or east there seemed little danger of an attack. With the Henderson Field side of the Lunga perimeter thus reasonably safe from an attack in force, the division planned a series of actions to clear the Matanikau sector. Japanese troops there included elements from the *4th Infantry Regiment* of the *2d Division*, and other personnel of the *Kawaguchi Force*. The *4th Infantry* had been reinforced by new Japanese landings of mid-September.

The first action against this enemy force sent Lieutenant Colonel Lewis B. Puller's 1st Battalion, 7th Marines into the Mount Austen area on 23 September. The Marines were to cross the Matanikau upstream and patrol between that river and the village of Kokumbona. The action was to be completed by 26 September at which time the 1st Raider Battalion [4] was to advance along the coast to Kokumbona where a permanent patrol base was to be established.

After passing through the perimeter on 23 September, Puller's battalion next day surprised a Japanese force bivouacked on the Mount Austen slopes, and scattered the enemy in a brief clash that ended shortly after nightfall. The action cost Puller 7 killed and 25 wounded, and the commander requested air support for a continuation of his attack the next day (25 September) and stretchers for 18 of his wounded men.

Realizing that a prompt evacuation of 18 stretcher cases over the rugged terrain would take at least 100 able-bodied men, General Vandegrift sent Lieutenant Colonel Rosecrans' 2d Battalion, 5th Marines out to reinforce Puller. With this new strength to back him up, Puller sent a two-company carrying and security force back with the wounded and pushed on toward the Matanikau.

The general's 24 September communications with Puller also gave the colonel the prerogative of altering the original patrol plan so that he could conform to the termination date of 26 September. Accordingly, when 1/7 and 2/5 reached the Matanikau on 26 September they did not cross but patrolled northward along the east bank toward the coast.

At about 1400 the two battalions reached the mouth of the river and there began to draw fire from strong Japanese positions in ridges on the west bank. Companies E and G of 2/5 attempted to force a crossing but were repulsed, and soon were pinned down by fire from automatic weapons. Puller called in artillery and air, but the enemy positions remained active. By 1600 the combined forces of Puller and Rosecrans had sustained 25 casualties, and the action was broken off while the Marines strengthened their positions for the night.

Meanwhile the raider battalion, on its way to establish the patrol base at Kokumbona, had reached the vicinity of the fire fight, and division directed Griffith to join with 1/7 and 2/5 and to prepare for a renewal of the attack next day. With this large provisional group now formed, Vandegrift sent Colonel Edson up to take command. Puller would act as executive officer. Edson's plan for the coordinated attack next day (27 September) called for the raiders to move some 2,000 yards inland, cross the Matanikau, and envelop the enemy right and rear while 1/7 supported by fire and 2/5 struck frontally across the river near its mouth.

The attack began early on 27 September, but failed to gain. Marines of 2/5 could not force a crossing, and the raiders' inland maneuver stopped short when Griffith's battalion encountered a Japanese force which had crossed the river during the night to set up strong positions on high ground some 1,500 yards south of the beach. First fire from mortars and automatic weapons wounded Griffith and killed his executive officer, Major Kenneth D. Bailey, one of the heroes of the Battle of the Ridge.

A raider message reporting this action unfortunately was confusing, and from it Edson concluded that the battalion had succeeded in gaining the enemy right flank beyond the river and that the fight was in progress there. Thus misinformed, the colonel ordered the raider battalion and

---

[4] Now commanded by LtCol Samuel B. Griffith, II. Edson, the former commander, had recently advanced to the rank of colonel to take over the 5th Marines on 21 September. Edson succeeded Col Leroy P. Hunt who had departed for the U. S.

2/5 to resume their attacks at 1330 while the 1st Battalion, 7th Marines (less Company C) made an amphibious envelopment west of Point Cruz to strike the Japanese Matanikau line from the rear.

Under the command of Major Otho Rogers, the 1/7 troops left Kukum in landing craft just as a strong bombing raid came over from Rabaul. The division command post took heavy hits which wrecked communications, and the destroyer *Ballard*, supporting the landing, had to slight her mission while taking evasive action. The landing at 1300 was unopposed, however, and the companies pushed rapidly inland toward a high grassy ridge about 500 yards from the beach.

But as the leading elements reached the top of this ridge, they were taken under mortar and small-arms fire. Major Rogers was killed by a mortar round and Captain Zach D. Cox, Company B commander, was wounded. Captain Charles W. Kelly, Jr., acting second in command, took charge of the battalion just as the enemy cut the Marines off from the beach. Kelly found that he could not communicate with the perimeter, and the close-in fight with the surrounding enemy grew rapidly more desperate. The Company D mortar platoon had only one of its weapons and about 50 rounds of ammunition, and to bring this weapon to bear on the pressing Japanese a mortarman had to lie on his back with his feet supporting the nearly-perpendicular tube from the rear while Master Sergeant Roy Fowel called the range down to 200 yards.

Fortunately, Second Lieutenant Dale M. Leslie flew over at about that time in his SBD. As pilot of a plane incapable of dogfighting in the bomber pack, Leslie was hunting likely targets while staying clear of the field and air engagements. As he circled overhead, the Marines below spelled out the word "Help" in white undershirts laid on the hillside, and Leslie managed to make radio contact with Edson at the mouth of the Matanikau and relay this distress signal.

That was summons aplenty for Puller, chafing in Edson's provisional command post while his battalion went off to battle without him. The combined attack at the river mouth and inland clearly had miscarried, and his men in 1/7 stood exposed to the full wrath of the Japanese west of the river. With characteristic directness, the lieutenant colonel collected the landing craft and churned out to board the *Ballard*. The ship and her skipper, soon under the Puller spell, steamed to the rescue close ashore, the landing craft in the wake ready to be used for a withdrawal.

It was a day for heroic action. When the force trapped ashore saw the ship coming down the coast, Sergeant Robert D. Raysbrook stood out on a hillock of the ridge and semaphored for attention. From the bridge of the *Ballard* Puller ordered his men to pull out to the beach. Raysbrook, still exposed to the enemy fire, flagged back the information that their withdrawal had been cut off. The ship then asked for fire orders, and with Captain Kelly relaying his signals through the sergeant, batteries on the *Ballard* began to blast out a path to the beach.

Supporting fire from the ship was a deciding factor in the action, but the companies still had a fight ahead of them. Japanese artillery began to take casualties as the Marines withdrew fighting through the enemy infantry still pressing from the flanks and rear. Platoon Sergeant Anthony P. Malanowski, Jr. took a Browning automatic rifle from a man dropped in action and covered the withdrawal of Company A until he himself was overrun and killed by the Japanese. But by then his company had reached the beach where it set up a hasty defense into which Company B and elements of Company D drew shortly thereafter.

With the Marines fighting off the enemy at their rear, the landing craft now moved shoreward to begin their evacuation, and thereby exposed themselves to heavy Japanese fire from the high ground above the Marines on the beach and from the projecting terrain of Point Cruz to the east. The Japanese were determined not to allow a thwarting of their trap, and the stiffening crossfire drove the craft back offshore where they bobbed in ground swells and indecision.

This was observed by Lieutenant Leslie, still keeping a watchful eye on the action from his SBD, and he came down again to lend a hand. The pilot strafed the Japanese positions and then turned to make a few swooping passes over the landing craft to herd them on their way. Thus heartened and hurried along, the coxswains went back in to the beach.

The fire from the beach, although dampened by the strafing SBD, still was heavy, but Signalman First Class Douglas A. Munro of the Coast Guard, coxswain of the craft, led the other coxswains through it and maneuvered his Higgins boat to shield the others. The Marines loaded on board with their wounded while Munro covered them with the light machine guns on his boat. He ordered his boat away when the other craft were clear, and still firing, was making his own withdrawal when he was killed by fire from the beach.

The miniature flotilla returned to the perimeter landing site at Kukum by nightfall. The action had cost this battalion 24 killed and 23 wounded. The raiders and 2/5 likewise withdrew after 1/7 got safely clear of the Point Cruz area, and their casualties added another 36 dead and 77 wounded to the tally for the operation.

ACTION OF 7–9 OCTOBER

Costly as this action at the Matanikau had been, it confirmed the data being collected by intelligence agencies, and these facts over-all were as important as they were disquieting. Japanese ships still entered Guadalcanal waters nearly every night, barges beached along the coast indicated many new landings, air attacks had picked up again since a comparative lull following the Battle of the Ridge, and now it was clear that the Japanese troops assembling on the island were concentrating just beyond the Matanikau. Another and a stronger Japanese counteroffensive loomed, and although defeat of the *Ichiki* and *Kawaguchi Forces* gave the Marines a new confidence in their ability to hold the perimeter, there was yet another factor. Late in September the Japanese began to land 150mm howitzers, and these weapons would be capable of firing on Henderson Field from the Kokumbona area.

Cactus fliers continued to hold their own against enemy air attacks of the field; Japanese gunfire ships had to come late and leave early to avoid the U. S. planes in daylight encounter, and the frequent night raids of Washing-Machine Charlie were more damned than damaging. But big howitzers were something else. The Marines had no weapon that could reach a 150mm in counterbattery, and they had no sound-flash equipment to locate such firing positions, anyway. If the Japanese could

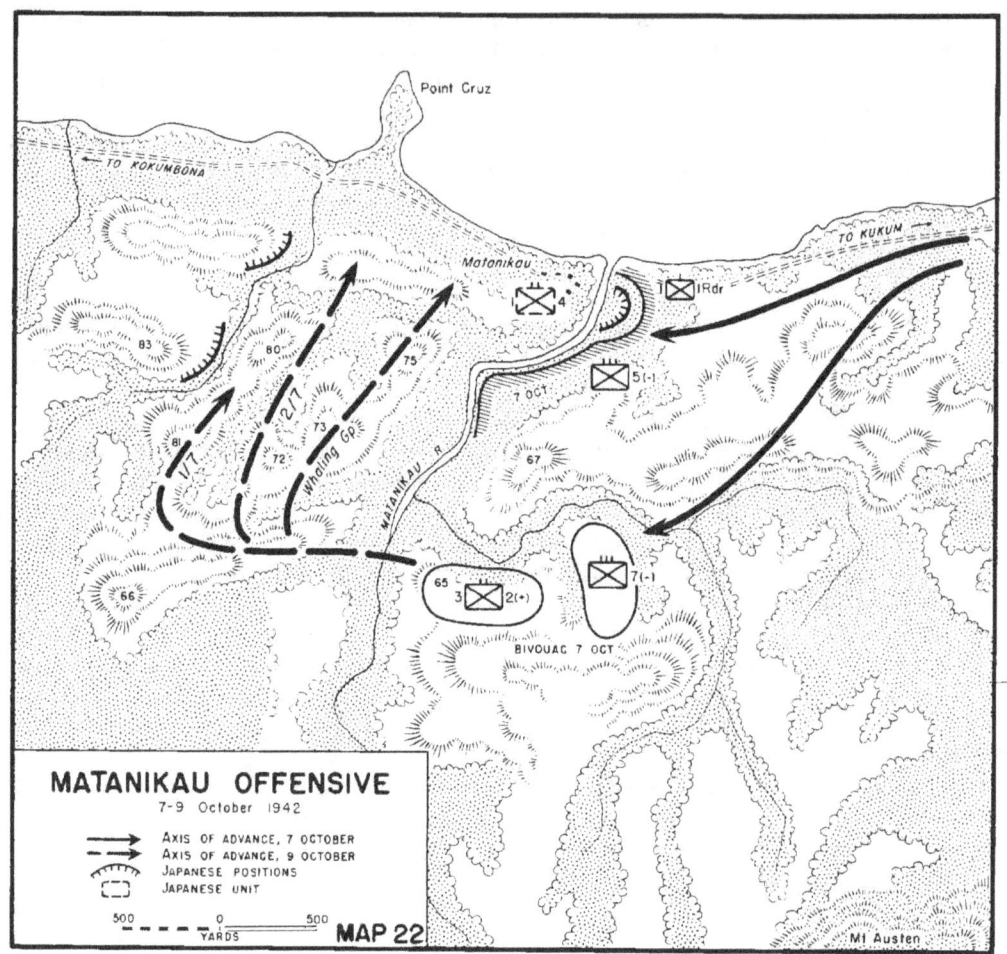

add the effective fires of these weapons to air raids and naval shelling, it might be just enough tip of balance in their favor to hold down the Cactus fliers while a large force mounted to dislodge the Americans from the Lunga.

Accordingly, an attack was scheduled to trap the enemy force and drive survivors beyond artillery range, and a success in this would be followed by establishment of a permanent patrol base at Kokumbona which could make sure the long-range field pieces stayed out of range. The plan of attack was similar to that of the operation which had just failed, but this new effort would be made in greater strength. The 5th Marines (less one battalion) would engage the enemy at the river mouth while the 7th Marines (also less one battalion) and the 3d Battalion, 2d Marines, reinforced by the division scout-sniper detachment, would cross the river inland and then attack north toward Point Cruz and Matanikau Village. (See Map 22)

Colonel William J. Whaling,[5] who commanded 3/2 and the scout-snipers on this special mission, was to lead to envelopment by crossing the Matanikau some 2,000 yards upstream and then attacking north into the village on the first ridge west of the river. Whaling would be followed by the 7th Marines battalions which would also attack north abreast and to the left of the Whaling group.

The 1st Marine Aircraft Wing, with its composite Cactus Force, was to provide planes for infantry liaison, close air support, and artillery spotting. In the artillery plan, 1/11 would support the 7th Marines; 2/11, the 5th Marines; 5/11, the Whaling Group; and 3/11 would be in general support of the Lunga perimeter. If all went well, Whaling's assault of Japanese positions near the coast would be followed by a 5th Marines river crossing, a passage of Whaling's lines, and a pursuit of the enemy toward Point Cruz where the 7th Marines on Whaling's left would close the trap in front to the withdrawing enemy. The 3d Battalion, 1st Marines provided the division reserve for the operation,[6] and Vandegrift's command post would coordinate the entire operation. Movements of the forces were to get underway on 7 October, and the coordinated attack would jump off on 8 October.

From recent experience with this growing Japanese force, the Marines expected a stiff fight with all the usual and unusual obstacles encountered in battle. But in this case there was to be one large factor they had no reason to suspect. By an unfortunate coincidence the Japanese also had set 8 October as the date for an attack of their own, and their scheme could hardly have been a better counter against the Marines had they been looking over the shoulders of Vandegrift's staff. Rabaul had ordered Colonel Tadamasu Nakaguma to cross the Matanikau on 8 October with his *4th Infantry* and establish artillery positions which could support the new counterattack then in planning. To accomplish this mission, Nakaguma sent an enveloping force inland across the Matanikau on 6 October while he slipped the cautious first echelon of a bridgehead across the river near the coast. There the Japanese forces met the Marines who moved from the Lunga perimeter at 0700 on 7 October.

Whaling's Group scrapped for several hours with the inland Japanese force which confined its opposition to sniping and harassment, but by the middle of the afternoon Whaling decided to bypass the enemy. At nightfall the envelopment force bivouacked on high ground south of the Matanikau's fork, the designated assembly area for the 8 October attack, and the Japanese did not pursue. Meanwhile the 5th Marines met with greater difficulty from Nakaguma's men near the river mouth.

---

[5] Whaling had been promoted to the rank of colonel shortly after the Guadalcanal landing, and although there was no billet for an additional colonel in the division, he stayed on to train scouts and snipers in practical, combat skills. Graduates of the course returned to their outfits to pass on their knowledge and thus increase the division's general proficiency in patrolling; others replaced these graduates and Whaling's schooling continued. As a unit, the scout-snipers normally operated independently, but sometimes, as in this case, joined other commands during a special mission.

[6] There was an indication that this unit might be employed in an amphibious envelopment. Arrangements had been made for a boat group, and McKelvy's battalion was on a 30-minute standby. *FinalRept*, Phase V, Annex D.

The advance guard of the 3d Battalion, 5th Marines came under fire from this enemy at about 1000, and the battalion deployed forward in an attack while the 2d Battalion swung to the left around the action and reached the river without opposition. The Japanese gave ground to previously prepared positions, but 3/5 was unable to push them beyond this line in spite of flanking assistance from 2/5. Vandegrift reinforced Edson with an understrength raider company, but the Japanese continued to hold their confined bridgehead some 400 yards inland from the beach, and the Marines drew up for the night. They held a 1,500-yard front which extended inland from the coast and bowed around the Japanese pocket on the river's east bank. During the night the 5th Marines and some amphibian tractors simulated noisy preparations for a tank-supported river crossing to divert Japanese attention from the Whaling-7th Marines envelopment force.

Heavy rains which began that night, and continued into the 8th, made trails and hills slick, muddy, and treacherous, and grounded the Cactus fliers. The attack had to be postponed, but the 5th Marines and raiders continued to reduce the Japanese positions on the east bank. At about 1830 the Japanese, under pressure all day from the Marines, made a final effort to break out of their nearly surrounded bridgehead and retreat across the river mouth. Running abreast, the enemy troops charged from their foxholes against the thinly-held Marine right flank where the raiders faced them. Front rank attackers engaged the Marines with small-arms fire while succeeding ranks pitched hand grenades into the raider positions. Some hand-to-hand fighting resulted, and casualties were high on both sides. Twelve raiders were killed and 22 wounded, while counted enemy dead numbered 59. Some of the surviving Japanese managed to escape across the river, and the bridgehead was completely reduced.

While the coordinated Marine attack waited out the rain, division was warned by higher intelligence sources that the expected strong Japanese counteroffensive appeared close at hand; aerial observers and coastwatchers to the north reported increased troop activity and a shipping concentration around Rabaul. General Vandegrift accordingly scaled down his planned attack to merely a raid in force so that no major troop strength would be beyond a day's march of the perimeter.

This decision did not alter the basic envelopment maneuver, however, and on 9 October Whaling and the 7th Marines moved across the Matanikau and attacked rapidly northward to raid the Point Cruz and Matanikau village areas. Whaling's Group moved along the first high ground west of the river; Lieutenant Colonel Herman H. Hanneken's 2/7 moved north on a ridge some 1,000 yards off Whaling's left flank, and Puller with 1/7 attacked along another ridge west of Hanneken.

Whaling and Hanneken reached the coast without serious opposition while 1/7 on the extreme left encountered a strong force of Japanese in a deep ravine about 1,500 yards inland from Point Cruz. Puller brought artillery and mortar fire down on the Japanese, and his men picked off the enemy with rifle and machine-gun fire as they climbed the far side of the ravine to escape the indirect fire. A few enemy escaped up the steep slope, but most of them were either killed by small-arms fire or driven back down the hill into the mortar and artillery concentration.

It was a most effective arrangement for methodical extermination, and Puller and his men kept it up until mortar ammunition ran low. Then they withdrew to join the Whaling Group and Hanneken, and by 1400 the combined raiding force had retired east of the Matanikau through the covering positions of the 5th Marines and the raiders.[7] The three-day operation had cost the Marines 65 dead and 125 wounded. A Japanese diary found later by Marines placed the *4th Infantry* losses at 700 men.

---

[7] Positions at the river mouth were retained to guard against a new Japanese crossing.

Rain and the threat of a new counteroffensive had thwarted the Marines' attack plans, but the action could still go down in the gain column. The raid had tripped up the attack Colonel Nakaguma had planned for the same period, and it had done away with a great number of his men. And in the short time that men of the 7th Marines had been ashore on the island, they had earned a right to identification as veteran troops. So with a completely combat-wise division on hand— and Army reinforcements on the way— Vandegrift and his staff now made plans to meet the strong Japanese attack that was bearing down upon them.

CHAPTER 7

Japanese Counteroffensive

In spite of the miscarriage of Nakaguma's effort to establish a bridgehead across the Matanikau, the Japanese *Seventeenth Army* continued preparations for its big push. On 9 October, the same day that Lieutenant Colonel Puller caught a major portion of Nakaguma's *4th Infantry* between the devil of small-arms and the deep sea of artillery and mortar concentrations, *Seventeenth Army* General Haruyoshi Hyakutake landed on Guadalcanal to take personal charge of the Japanese campaign.

Things were serious but not desperate. Although Ichiki and Kawaguchi had allowed unfounded optimism and overconfidence to swamp their missions against the Marines, Hyakutake still had a strong force and a proud confidence that he could wipe out the Lunga positions in one blow. And with Guadalcanal safely back in Japanese hands, Imperial troops then would retake Tulagi and occupy Rennell and San Cristobal. At the same time *Seventeenth Army* reserves and the Japanese Navy could renew attacks in New Guinea and take Port Moresby by late November. The *Bushido* spirit would be back at full strength.

By early October the Japanese had brought troops in from the Philippines, the East Indies, China, and Truk to place within the *Seventeenth Army* command in Rabaul and the Solomons two divisions, a brigade, and a reinforced battalion. Support forces included six antiaircraft battalions plus one other AAA battery; a heavy regiment and an independent tank company; one regiment and one battalion of mountain artillery; an engineer regiment, and other troops including a mortar battalion and a unit of reconnaissance aircraft. Included in this general listing were the *Kawaguchi brigade*, the *Ichiki reinforced battalion* and other battalions of the *4th* and *124th Infantry Regiments* (Nakaguma) already defeated or weakened by the Lunga defenders.

By reason of the odd impasse in which both the Japanese and the Allied navies chose to avoid decisive battle to conserve their fleets, the Solomons waters changed hands every twelve hours, and thus each side kept an important trickle of aid going to its small combat force which represented the single point of ground contact between the belligerent powers. In daylight when Cactus could fly cover, the Allied ships came in from Espiritu Santo and other southern areas with reinforcements and supplies for the Marines. Barges, landing craft, and YP's shuttled errands across Sealark Channel. By nightfall the larger ships departed, and most of the others still in the Sealark area withdrew to safety in the Tulagi anchorage. Until dawn the Japanese took over.

The destroyers and cruisers of the Tokyo Express habitually lurked in the Shortlands below Bougainville Island until the afternoon when they would start steaming south to be within 200 miles of

Guadalcanal by about 1800. This was just inside the range of SBD's and TBF's from Henderson Field, but the maneuvering ships made poor targets, and the late hour gave the American planes time for only one crack at them before turning back for Lunga. After that the Express had an open line all the way to Sealark.

While transport destroyers unloaded on either side of the Marine perimeter, Japanese warships stood close in at Lunga and went to work with their guns. Louie the Louse dropped flares to aid the naval gunners, and Washing-Machine Charlie lurked overhead to fritter out his bombs during lulls in surface firing. Under such attacks there was little the Marines could do but crouch in their foxholes and pray— or swear. Lunga defenders could estimate 150 new enemy ground soldiers for every destroyer transport—often five or six a night—that made the Express run, and by early October these troops began to land insultingly close, just across the Matanikau eight to ten miles from Henderson Field. The Allied turn to use the waters came at daylight, but U. S. forces did not have the man power to match the Japanese rate of reinforcement.

Fortunately, the Japanese started slowly. Still thinking in terms of their operation against New Guinea, and miscalculating Allied strength in the Solomons, Imperial planners only dribbled reinforcements to Guadalcanal in August when the Marine position was particularly vulnerable. Not until after the Ichiki and Kawaguchi defeats did Japan begin to take serious stock of Vandegrift and his Marines.

But now the Tokyo Express had stepped up its schedule, and by mid-October Hyakutake had landed his *2d Division*, two battalions of the *38th Division*, one regiment and three batteries of heavy artillery, a battalion and a battery of mountain artillery, a mortar battalion, a tank company, and three rapid-fire gun battalions. Special troops including engineers and medical personnel, and remnants of earlier attacks brought the Japanese force to about 20,000 men.

Facing this mounting Japanese strength was a Marine force of about the same size. Arrival of the 7th Marines and the transfer of other troops from Tulagi bolstered General Vandegrift's Lunga positions, but until 7 October there was little hope that more reinforcements would be forthcoming. Rear areas in the South Pacific had gained little strength since Vandegrift had argued for control of his 7th Marines, and the plan for the occupation of Ndeni still was in the pending basket. Marine strength thus promised to deteriorate while Japanese strength continued to mount. More than 800 Marine battle casualties had been evacuated by early October, and malaria continued to take its toll.[1]

The Cactus fliers were not doing much more than holding their own, either. By 1 October, Lieutenant Colonel Mangrum's original VMSB-232 and Lieutenant Commander Caldwell's Flight 300 were done for,[2] Army pilots from the 67th Fighter Squadron had only about six or eight of their P-400's in shape to fly, John Smith's VMF-223 had lost an even dozen pilots— six killed and six wounded—and other units, although stronger, still piled up

---

[1] In October 1,960 malaria patients were hospitalized.

[2] Mangrum was the only member of his outfit able to leave Henderson Field under his own power. He was evacuated on 12 October. Caldwell, who arrived at Lunga from the carrier *Saratoga* as a lieutenant, had been promoted.

their share of losses. On the first day of October General Geiger had 58 planes; two days later the count stood at 49.

If the Japanese had failed to win, place, or show with Ichiki, Kawaguchi, and Nakaguma, the Allies likewise had been unable to improve their odds by any comfortable margin. To General Harmon the situation looked about as grim as it had on 11 August when he expressed doubt that the Marines could hold their perimeter, and on 6 October he wrote to Admiral Ghormley that the Ndeni operation should be quashed until the situation improved. He questioned the logic of holding troops idle for a new operation when things were going so poorly in a battle already joined. He admitted certain factors favoring the Ndeni occupation, but he added that, "... in the final analysis they are individually or cumulatively vital to the success of main offensive operation or . . . maintaining security of South Pacific bases and lines of communications." [3]

Specifically, Harmon recommended abandoning the Ndeni operation until the Guadalcanal situation improved; reinforcements of Cactus (Guadalcanal) by at least one regimental combat team; the maximum possible intensification of naval surface action in South Solomons waters; and the prompt buildup of airdrome facilities and supplies at Henderson Field. Ghormley agreed that Vandegrift needed another regiment and that Henderson Field needed facilities and supplies, but the admiral retained for the time his plan to occupy Ndeni and build an airfield there. For the Guadalcanal reinforcement, Ghormley ordered Harmon to prepare a regiment of the New Caledonia garrison, and on 8 October he ordered Admiral Turner to embark the 164th Infantry of the Americal Division, Harmon's choice for the job, and depart Noumea for Guadalcanal on 9 October.

It was to be a blockade run in force. Transports *Zeilin* and *McCawley*, carrying supplies, 210 men of the 1st Marine Aircraft Wing and 85 Marine casuals as well as the 2,850 men of the Army regiment, sailed under escort of three destroyers and three mine layers while a larger force of four cruisers and five destroyers steamed off the convoy's left flank. These cruisers, *San Francisco*, *Salt Lake City*, *Helena*, and *Boise* and destroyers *Buchanan*, *Duncan*, *Farenholt*, *Laffey*, and *McCalla* were commanded by Rear Admiral Norman Scott. Other U. S. Naval forces in the surrounding waters included Rear Admiral George D. Murray's *Hornet* carrier group some 180 miles southwest of Guadalcanal, and Rear Admiral Willis Augustus Lee's battleship *Washington* group about 50 miles east of Maliata. Scott's screening station for the unloading was near Rennell Island.

THE BATTLE OF CAPE ESPERANCE

On 11 October, while the *Zeilin* and the *McCawley* made for their 13 October anchorage schedule in Lunga Roads, Admiral Scott learned from aerial observers that two Japanese cruisers and six destroyers were bearing down The Slot. It was the night's Tokyo Express, Scott decided, and at 1600 he started toward Guadalcanal at 29 knots to intercept the run. His orders charged him to protect the transports, and to search for and destroy enemy ships and landing craft; he rushed eagerly to work.

---

[3] CGSoPac ltr to ComSoPac, 6Oct42 (located at OCMH).

Actually Scott headed to intercept a force stronger than reports had indicated. Observers failed to spot three heavy cruisers, two seaplane carriers, and eight destroyers steaming some distance away outside of The Slot. Japanese Vice Admiral Gunichi Mikawa, commander of the *Eighth Fleet* and the *Outer Sea Forces*, and Vice Admiral Jinichi Kusaka, *Eleventh Air Fleet* commander, had teamed up to strike the strongest blow yet against the bothersome Cactus fliers. In the afternoon of the 11th, Kusaka had 30 fighters and 35 bombers up to occupy Henderson fliers while Mikawa's bombardment and reinforcing groups steamed south outside the normal Japanese transport route. Heavy cruisers *Aoba*, *Kinugasa*, and *Furutaka* with destroyers *Hatsuyuki* and *Fubuki* made up the bombardment group while the reinforcing fleet included seaplane carriers *Chitose* and *Nisshin*, and destroyers *Akizuki*, *Asagumo*, *Natsugumo*, *Yamagumo*, *Murakumo*, and *Shirayuki*.

By about 2200, while Scott maneuvered in the waters of Iron Bottom Sound between Savo Island and Cape Esperance, the Japanese bombardment group came into The Slot and steamed south in a double column at 26 knots. At 2330 a spotting plane from USS *San Francisco* reported Japanese ships 16 miles from Savo and off Cape Esperance,[4] but Scott's ships still were unaware of the serious trouble facing them. Gunnery radar failed to pick up the enemy then approximately 35 degrees forward of the port beam, and although the *Helena* earlier had spotted a Japanese ship bearing 315 degrees and at a distance of 27,700 yards, she didn't report this contact for 15 minutes.

[4] These ships were from the reinforcement group.

Flagship *San Francisco*, with rudimentary radar of that early period, had no contacts, and Scott continued to steam toward Savo with his ships in column. He counted this the best area for intercepting the Express he hoped to derail, and at about 2340 he had reversed course to head back toward the Cape when the *Helena*, at last confident about the blips from her better radar equipment, announced her fix of a target six miles away. Fortunately, since the U. S. fleet was having "eye" trouble, the Japanese ships were completely blind, and even though certain communications misunderstandings[5] further delayed American fire, first salvos from the *Helena* at 2346 caught the enemy by complete surprise. Scott's ships had usurped Tokyo's turn in Sealark Channel.

The *Salt Lake City*, *Boise*, and *Farenholt* quickly added their fire to that of the *Helena*, and shortly thereafter the U. S. fleet crossed the Japanese "T" (sailed ahead of the Japanese column and at right angles to it) so that a majority of the American guns could bear on each Japanese ship as it came forward. The Japanese destroyer *Fubuki* sank almost at once, the cruiser *Furutaka* took such a mauling that she limped away to sink later, and the *Aoba* caught fire. The only sound survivors, cruiser *Kinugasa* and destroyer *Hatsuyuki*, withdrew. On the American side, the *Boise*, *Salt Lake City*, *Farenholt*, and *Duncan* suffered damage, and the *Duncan* sank the following day.[6]

[5] For an account of these misunderstandings and for other descriptions of the Cape Esperance Battle see *Struggle for Guadalcanal*, Chap VIII.

[6] Also on 12 October Cactus fliers found the Japanese destroyers *Murakumo* and *Natsugumo* north of the Russell Islands, and their attack sank both of these ships.

Scott could count the engagement a victory, but it did not resolve the seesawing for power in the Solomons waters or skies. The Japanese only stepped up their air attacks on Henderson Field and continued preparations for the big push.

PREPARATION FOR BATTLE

Transports *McCawley* and *Zeilen* arrived at Kukum with the Army reinforcements early on 13 October, but this was one of the few bright spots of the day. Both radar and the Northern Solomons coastwatchers missed an air attack that came over at 1202, and the F4F's couldn't get up in time to hamper the 22 fighter-escorted bombers that rained down their bombs from 30,000 feet. Both Henderson Field and Fighter 1 were damaged, and fires from the attack burned 5,000 gallons of aviation fuel.

Between 1330 and 1400 a second strike of 15 Japanese bombers caught most of the American planes back on their fields refueling. Some planes were damaged, and the strike undid the repair work that had been started by the 6th Seabees following the earlier raid. A few Cactus planes got up to pursue the Japanese, but the only American kill was scored by Captain Joseph J. Foss who had arrived on 9 October with Major Leonard K. Davis' VMF-121 of MAG-14. The field was not completely out of action, but big bombers were advised to avoid it except for emergencies.

In spite of these interruptions, Colonel Bryant E. Moore managed to get his 164th Infantry ashore, along with other men and supplies from the transports, but trouble for the perimeter was not over. As the second bomber strike droned away, the 150mm howitzers near Kokumbona were finally heard from. Safely beyond counterbattery range, these weapons began a slow methodical registration on the field and the perimeter. The fire was a brand of damage and destruction the men at Lunga had to live with, and so to have a pinpoint target for their anger if not their weapons they named this new entrant in their war Pistol Pete.

Pete, as was most often the case with Louie the Louse and Washing-Machine Charlie, was plural. Hyakutake had landed 15 of these howitzers. But for the Marines and soldiers it was difficult to imagine batteries getting that personal, and Pete's particular brand of hell was a most personal and singular thing. So Pete became one enemy, the devil himself—the devil and one big gun acting as Tojo's personal Nimrod.

And after he thumped away at the perimeter all that day, an enemy task force built around battleships *Haruna* and *Kongo* came into Sealark Channel after nightfall to launch an 80-minute bombardment.[7] This was the Japanese *Combat Division 3*, commanded by Vice Admiral Takeo Kurita, and it also included light cruiser *Isuzu* and three ships of *Destroyer Division 31* as a screen, plus a rear guard of four ships from *Destroyer Division 15*. The battleships had on board some new bombardment shells which had just arrived from the home islands. These had a greater bursting radius than former Japanese bombardment shells, and there were enough of them for battleships *Haruna* and *Kongo* to have 500 each.

This was the first time that battleships had been used to bombard Henderson Field, and the Japanese hoped these big guns and the improved ammunition would

---

[7] The unloaded American transports had departed late in the afternoon.

completely knock out the Marine air and clear the way for a coordinated infantry attack. Louie the Louse illuminated the field, and the big guns cut loose. Coconut trees splintered, buildings and huts ripped open and crashed down, fragments and wreckage tore into planes and men, and more gasoline went up in bright fires which helped Japanese gunners stay on target for their systematic coverage of the field with more than 900 rounds of the high explosive shells.

As Admiral Tanaka described it later:

> The scene was topped off by flare bombs from our observation planes flying over the field, the whole spectacle making the Ryogoku fireworks display seem like mere child's play. The night's pitch dark was transformed by fire into the brightness of day. Spontaneous cries and shouts of excitement ran throughout our ships.[8]

Then, as the ships became silent and withdrew east of Savo Island, the planes came back. Night bombers continued their strikes intermittently until daybreak, and by dawn of 14 October the Cactus Air Force could fly only 42 of the 90 planes that had been operational 24 hours earlier. Forty-one men had been killed and many more wounded, and the airfield was a complete shambles. Among the dead were Major Gordon A. Bell, whose VMSB-141 had finally built up to 21 planes and fliers on 6 October, and four of his pilots: Captains Edward F. Miller and Robert A. Abbott and Lieutenants Henry F. Chaney, Jr. and George L. Haley.

Operations, sorely restricted by the loss of gasoline in the fire, moved to Fighter 1 which was left in better condition than Henderson; and a few B-17's which had been operating temporarily from Guadalcanal managed to bounce aloft from a 2,000 yard stretch of Henderson that still was usable and fly back to Espiritu Santo. The Japanese "Pagoda," air headquarters since the early days, had been partially wrecked, and General Geiger had it bulldozed away. It had proved too good a registration point for bombers, anyway.

For the rest of the day the Japanese ships maintained their control of the waters around Guadalcanal, and planes continued to press their advantage in the air. Between the bombings and the shellings, Pistol Pete's effective interdiction prevented repair or use of the main airstrip, and by midafternoon Henderson had to be chalked off as completely unfit for use. By late afternoon fliers of the Army's 67th Fighter Squadron and 13 dive bomber pilots used Fighter 1—and nearly all of Henderson's remaining supply of fuel—to strike back finally at the Japanese by attacking an early run of the Tokyo Express then only 70 miles north of Guadalcanal. One ship was sunk and another damaged, but the Express did not turn back.

That night (14 October) the Japanese cruisers *Chokai* and *Kinugasa* moved down the channel to bombard Henderson Field while the express brought the six transports carrying General Maruyama's *2d Division* on down to Tassafaronga. The cruisers fired 752 eight-inch shells at the men around Lunga, and by dawn on 15 October five of the enemy transports were clearly visible from the perimeter as they lay off Tassafaronga smugly unloading troops, supplies, and ammunition.

Cactus fliers, smarting from the two-day hammering, d r a i n e d gasoline from wrecked planes, searched the surrounding jungle for undamaged drums, and finally collected enough aviation fuel to mount an attack with the three SBD's that could still

---

[8] *Tanaka Article*, II, 815.

fly. But one of these planes had to be scratched when it tumbled into a crater on the way to the strip, and Lieutenant Robert M. Patterson lost SBD number two when the plane hit a shell hole while he raced for his takeoff. Patterson tried it again with the last dive bomber, and this time he made it. His single-plane attack did not hamper the Japanese much, but while he was flying, the ground crews quickly patched other planes. It resembled an informal neighborhood boxkite club, with members hardly able to wait for work to be completed before they tested their craftsmanship. One at a time the first four planes were taken up to have a chance at the cocky Japanese transports. Two minor hits were scored, but General Geiger stopped the assembly line combat action until he could muster more strength.[9]

At 1000 Cactus was ready with 12 SBD's, and they went up to drop 500- and 1,000-pound bombs on the transports and then strafe their decks. That attack sank one of the transports. Next came attacks from P-39's and the relic P-400's, and fires broke out on two of the ships. After that, fliers from Espiritu Santo began to show up, and B-17's and SBD's from the south sank another transport. The Tokyo Express was in most serious trouble, in spite of 30 Zeros overhead to provide cover, and General Hyakutake might well have considered that the admirals and senior pilots in Rabaul had been somewhat overconfident in this daring daylight delivery of his reinforcements.

Even General Geiger's own pilot, Major Jack Cram, had his turn during that day of desperation when he made a run on the transports with two torpedoes slung under the wings of the general's *Blue Goose*, a bulbous and gouty PBY-5A. Cram got the torpedoes off, but then he was chased back to Fighter 1 by a clutch of Zeros, like sparrows around a ponderous hawk, and one determined enemy fighter had to be shot away from the smoking *Goose* as Cram came in for his landing.

By day's end three bombed transports of 7,000 to 8,000 tons each were beached and burning off Tassafaronga, and the other two had fled back up Sealark Channel and The Slot. But in spite of this, the Japanese had managed to unload 3,000 to 4,000 men of the *230th* and *16th Infantry Regiments* as well as 80 per cent of the ships' cargo. These troops, the last the Japanese were able to land prior to their concentrated effort against the airfield, brought General Hyakutake's strength on the island to about 20,000 men.

General Vandegrift now had approximately 23,000 men, but the Marine force suffered severely from malnutrition, malaria, the exhaustive defensive actions, patrols, and field engineering work they had accomplished. Most of them were veterans, but in the unhealthy tropics that fact did not necessarily mean an advantage in the long run. Only the 164th Infantry of the Americal Division contained fresh troops.

With this additional regiment ashore, the division again reorganized the perimeter, this time into five new defensive sectors. Clockwise from the Kukum area they were: Sector One—The 3d Defense

---

[9] While this action was in progress, Army and Marine C-47's (R4D's) flew in with aviation gasoline, and seaplane tender *MacFarland* brought in additional supplies of the much-needed fuel. Japanese planes next day (16 October) damaged the tender, but she was repaired by her crew in an inlet of Florida Island.

Battalion with elements of the 1st Special Weapons Battalion, amphibian tractormen, pioneers, and engineers who held 7,100 yards of beach that straddled the Lunga River. (See Map 23, Map Section)

Sector Two—The 164th Infantry and elements of special weapons units with control of a 6,600-yard line from the beach inland along the Ilu River and thence west to a point near the east slope of Bloody Ridge.

Sector Three—The 7th Marines (less 3d Battalion), a 2,500-yard front of inland jungle from Bloody Ridge west to the Lunga River.

Sector Four—The 1st Marines (less 3d Battalion), 3,500 yards of jungle from the Lunga west to the inland flank of the final sector.

Sector Five—The 5th Marines holding the northwest curve of the main perimeter from the flank of the 1st Marines north to the sea and then east along the beach to the west flank of the 3d Defense Battalion.

Since the Japanese attack was expected from the west across the Matanikau, the greatest strength was concentrated on that side of the perimeter. Forward of the 5th Marines' lines the 3d Battalions of both the 1st and 7th Marines held a strong outpost line from the beach at the mouth of the river inland to Hill 67. This line was supported by a battalion of the 11th Marines and elements of the 1st Special Weapons Battalion. The 3d Battalion, 2d Marines and 1st Tank Battalion units constituted the division reserve, and each regimental sector commander was directed to keep a third of his infantry strength in reserve also.

Against these Marine and Army positions, General Hyakutake prepared to launch his attack for the recapture of the airfield. On 15 October in Kokumbona he issued his attack order to Lieutenant General Masao Maruyama's *2d Division*. Date for the assault was set tentatively for 18 October. The *2d Division* would swing far inland to hit the Marines from the south with a night attack in two columns of battalions while the *Seventeenth Army* artillery commander, General Sumiyoshi, would shell the perimeter and then launch a diversionary strike with infantry units near the mouth of the Matanikau. For this coastal attack Sumiyoshi had a force of some 2,900 men comprising the battalions of the *4th Infantry* plus a tank company, seven light field artillery pieces, fifteen of the 150mm howitzers, and three 100mm guns.

For his inland attack, Maruyama had some eight or nine infantry battalions totaling 5,600 men, plus artillery and supporting troops. General Kawaguchi, who had tried his hand in the same area before, would command the right arm of the assault with two battalions of the *230th Infantry*, one battalion of the *124th Infantry*, and elements of the *3d Light Trench Mortar Battalion, 6th* and *7th Independent Rapid Gun Battalions*, the *20th Independent Mountain Artillery*, engineers, and medical troops. The left attacking column would be under command of Major General Yumio Nasu and would include the *29th Infantry*, the remainder of the *3d Light Trench Mortar Battalion*, a rapid fire gun battalion, a mountain artillery battalion, and engineers. The *16th Infantry* and some engineers—a part of Nasu's command—would be in reserve behind the *29th Infantry*.

General Hyakutake was confident of success. He had left the bulk of his *38th Division* at Rabaul. *Banzai* was to be

Maruyama's signal of victory at the airfield, and his attack from the south was ordered to press unrelenting destruction upon the enemy until General Vandegrift himself came forth to surrender.

Thus charged, General Maruyama struck out through the jungle wilderness on 16 October.

THE GROUND ACTION

Transportation was pedestrian, cargo moved on bended backs, and hand power drove the engineering tools. Thus the column of enveloping Japanese inched single file across the tortuous Guadalcanal back country like a segmented serpent crawling through the perpetual wet shadows of the tropical forest.

The so-called Maruyama Trail, begun by engineers in September, scratched its thin scar along the floor of the jungle southward from Kokumbona, east across the Matanikau and the Lunga inland from Mount Austen, and then north to an assembly area south of Bloody Ridge. Safely beyond range of Marine patrols and hidden from aerial view by the vine-laced tops of giant hardwoods, the Japanese soldier moved with an artillery or mortar shell lashed to his already heavy load of normal equipment, frequently used ropes to scale the rough ridges and steep valleys, and by turns tugged a line or hunched his shoulder to the common effort of manhandling artillery, mortars, and machine guns.

Heavy rain fell almost every day. The van of the single-file advance often had completed its day's march and bivouacked for the night before the rear elements were able to move. Troops weakened on their half ration of rice. Heavy artillery pieces had to be abandoned along the route, and mortars also became too burdensome to manage. Frequently unsure of their exact location in the jungle, the Japanese by 19 October still had not crossed the upper Lunga, and Maruyama postponed his assault until the 22d. Meanwhile General Sumiyoshi's fifteen Pistol Petes pounded the Lunga perimeter, air attacks continued, and Imperial warships steamed brazenly into Sealark Channel nearly every night to shell the airfield, beaches, and Marine positions.

The tempo of action obviously was building up for the counteroffensive, and Marines and soldiers worked constantly to improve their field fortifications and keep up an aggressive patrol schedule. Patrols did not go far enough afield, however, to discover Maruyama's wide-swinging enveloping force, and reconnaissance to the east found no indications of a Japanese build-up on that flank. Thus General Vandegrift and his staff were aware only of Sumiyoshi's threat along the coast from the west.

There the first probe came on 20 October. A Japanese combat patrol, augmented by two tanks, ventured into view on the west bank of the Matanikau but turned back after one tank was knocked out by 37mm fire from the lines of the 3d Battalion, 1st Marines. Sporadic artillery fire was the only Japanese answer to this checkmate, and it continued until sunset the next day. Then the artillery fire intensified briefly, and nine infantry-supported tanks debouched from the west bank jungle and drove eastward for the sandspit at the mouth of the river. But again the fire from a 37mm stopped one of the tanks, and the attack turned back without seriously threatening the river-mouth positions of Company I, 3/1. The Marine

FIVE BLASTED JAPANESE TANKS *knocked out by Marine 37mm guns during the abortive attempt to force the perimeter along the mouth of the Matanikau.* (USMC 54898)

MARINE LIGHT TANKS, *mounting machine guns and 37mm cannon, were severely hampered in their operations by the jungle terrain of Guadalcanal.* (USN 18525)

battalion had taken a few casualties from artillery and mortar fire, but neither of these first two attacks had posed a serious threat.

At the Matanikau positions on 22 October Sumiyoshi continued firing his mortars and artillery but mounted no new assault. Inland, General Maruyama struggled with the jungle some distance from his lines of departure, and he was forced to postpone his proposed assault to 23 October. But on that day he still was unprepared to attack and again he set back his plans another 24 hours.

At about 1800 on the 23d, however, Sumiyoshi once more intensified his artillery and mortar fire to lay down an orthodox preparation pattern on the Marine east bank positions and along the coastal route from the Lunga Perimeter. Near the end of evening nautical twilight the artillery fire ceased, and a column of nine 18-ton medium tanks churned across the sandspit in an attempt to force a penetration. In assembly areas to the rear infantry troops stood by to assault in the wake of the tanks.

Slim-barreled 37's again blasted at the Japanese tanks while infantry mortars and howitzers of the 11th Marines dumped prearranged concentrations farther west to break up the pending infantry assault. The enemy ground troops never got started, and the tank charge miscarried when eight of the vehicles were hammered to a standstill by the 37's. One tank managed the crossing but staggered out of control when a Marine pitched a grenade in its track as it lumbered by his foxhole. Pursued by a half-track 75, the beset machine wallowed into the surf where it stalled to form a sitting duck target for the tank destroyer.

The other eight hulks remained strewn along the sand bar across the river mouth, and artillery fire knocked out three more tanks that never got to attack. Hundreds of the enemy soldiers who had been waiting to follow the tanks were killed. The action was over by 2200, although at about midnight the Japanese made a half-hearted attempt to cross the river farther upstream. This thrust was turned back with little trouble.

From his study of interrogations of the Japanese generals involved, Dr. John Miller, Jr., sums up:

Sumiyoshi had sent one tank company and one infantry regiment forward to attack a prepared position over an obvious approach route while the Americans were otherwise unengaged. The Maruyama force, still moving inland, had not reached its line of departure. In 1946, the responsible commanders gave different reasons for the lack of co-ordination and blamed each other. According to Hyakutake, this piecemeal attack had been a mistake. The coastal attack was to have been delivered at the same time as Maruyama's forces struck against the southern perimeter line. Maruyama, according to Hyakutake, was to have notified the *4th Infantry* when he reached his line of departure on 23 October, and he so notified the *4th Infantry*. The regiment then proceeded with its attack.

Maruyama disclaimed responsibility for the blunder, and blamed *17th Army Headquarters*. His forces, delayed in their difficult march, had not reached their line of departure on 23 October. The *17th Army*, he asserted, overestimated the rate of progress on the south flank and ordered the coast forces to attack on 23 October to guarantee success on the south flank.

Sumiyoshi was vague. He claimed that throughout the counteroffensive he had been so weakened by malaria that he found it difficult to make decisions. Despite an earlier statement that he did not know why the attack of 23 October had been ordered, he declared that he had attacked ahead of Maruyama to divert the Americans. Communication between the two forces, he claimed, had been very poor. Radio sets gave off too much light, and thus had been used only in daylight hours. Telephone communication had been frequently disrupted. As a result the coast force had been one day behind in its knowledge of Maruyama's movement.[10]

Meanwhile the Marine division[11] had started a shift of manpower within the perimeter. In the face of Sumiyoshi's attacks, and with no patrol contacts to the south or east, the 2d Battalion, 7th Marines on 23 October pulled out of its southern lines east of the Lunga and moved west to relieve the 3d Battalion, 1st Marines at the mouth of the Matanikau. This left the 1st Battalion, 7th Marines (Puller) with a responsibility for the defense of all of Sector Five, the 2,500-yard defense line from the inland flank of the 164th Infantry west across the southern slopes of Bloody Ridge to the Lunga River. Puller's extended lines were thin, but there appeared very little danger from the south.

Hanneken's 2/7 did not effect its intended relief, however, because of the heavy Japanese artillery fire that engaged 3/1 on the 23d, and on the following day a new assignment was given to the 7th Marines battalion. On the 24th the Marines of 3/7 on Hill 67 south of the Matanikau mouth had spotted a Japanese column, obviously a flanking force,[12] moving east across Mount Austen's foothills. Artillery and air was called in on this enemy movement, but the Japanese disappeared into jungle ravines about 1,000 yards south of Hill 67 before they could be engaged. In the face of this threat apparently headed for the 4,000-yard gap between the Matanikau outpost and the Lunga perimeter, 2/7 was assigned to plug this hole, and the 3d Battalion, 1st Marines retained its positions overlooking the beach and the Matanikau.

Later the same day came other indications that the Sumiyoshi action would not be the only Japanese effort against the perimeter. Late in the afternoon of 24 October an observer in the 1/7 lines south of the airfield saw a Japanese officer studying Bloody Ridge through field glasses, and a scout-sniper patrol reported seeing the smoke from "many rice fires" in the Lunga valley about two miles south of Puller's positions on the Ridge. By this time twilight was settling over Guadalcanal, and there was little the Marines could do but wait out developments from existing positions. The only troops not in front lines were those in reserve in the various defensive sectors and the 3d Battalion, 2d Marines, the division reserve, then bivouacked north of Henderson Field.

The rice fires and the officer with field glasses undoubtedly were signs—and the first the Marines had—of the reinforced *2d Division* that finally had negotiated the grueling advance from Kokumbona over the Maruyama Trail. With all his artillery and mortars strewn along the route behind him, Maruyama at last had crossed the Lunga into his assembly areas south of Bloody Ridge. There the force stood at twilight on 24 October ready to attack with only infantry weapons against the dug-in Marines who were backed up by artillery and mortars.

Hoping for bright moonlight to aid coordination (the night actually went black

---

[10] *Miller, Guadalcanal,* 157–159, quoted by permission of the author.

[11] BriGen Rupertus, ADC, became acting CG of the 1st MarDiv on 23 October. MajGen Vandegrift left at dawn that day for conferences at Noumea, flying out with LtGen Thomas Holcomb, Marine Corps Commandant, whose Pacific tour had brought him to Guadalcanal on 21 October.

[12] This force, never positively identified in reconstructions of battle events, is thought to have been that of Col Oka which appears later in night attacks of 25–26 October. *FinalRept,* Phase V, 22.

with heavy rain), the Japanese general ordered a narrow attack over the ground Kawaguchi's force had assaulted in mid-September. The main effort was assigned to the *29th Infantry*, with the *16th Infantry* in reserve, while farther to the east the Kawaguchi command—now led by Colonel Toshinari Shoji [13]—was to make a parallel assault.

At about 2130 a Japanese unit clashed briefly with a 46-man outpost Puller had stationed forward of his tactical wire, but after a short fire fight the enemy bypassed the position, and the battlefield was quiet. Platoon Sergeant Ralph Briggs, Jr., in charge of the outpost, notified Puller that a large force of Japanese were moving about the outpost hill toward the battalion lines, but Puller ordered his men to hold fire so that Briggs could infiltrate to safety. But the outpost already was flanked by the Japanese moving around the hill, and Briggs led his men to the east while the enemy moved closer to Puller's battalion and began to cut the tactical wire in front of the 1/7 positions.[14]

While Puller's men strained to hear the approaching enemy above the sound of drumming rain which lashed the night, the Japanese prepared their routes through the Marine barbed wire and formed up for their attack. Then at 0030 on 25 October, Nasu's men came out of the jungle screaming their *banzais*, throwing grenades, and firing rifles and machine guns to strike the left center of 1/7's line with an assault in depth on a narrow front. Puller called in mortar and artillery concentrations, his riflemen took up a steady fire, and the machine guns rattled almost endless bursts down their final protective lines.

From Puller's left, troops of the 2d Battalion, 164th Infantry added their fire to that of the Marines, but still the Japanese assaulted, trying to rush across the fields of fire toward the Ridge. The attack kept up for 10 or 15 minutes, but finally ground itself to a halt against the combined arms of the U. S. force. Then there was a lull while the Japanese regrouped and came back again, trying to clear a penetration with their grenades and small arms. The Marine commander assessed correctly that his men were standing off the main attack of Rabaul's big counteroffensive, and that the force in the jungle to his front obviously was strong enough to keep such attacks going most of the night. He called for reinforcements, and division headquarters ordered Lieutenant Colonel Robert K. Hall to take his 3d Battalion of the 164th Infantry down the Ridge to bolster Puller's thin line.

But the reinforcements had a mile of muddy ridge to cover before they could be of any help, and in the meantime the Japanese continued to assault out of the jungle and up the slopes. A small group forced a salient in the Marine line to fall upon a mortar position, and farther to the front Nasu's soldiers worked close to a water-cooled machine gun and knocked out all but two of its crew. Marines near

---

[13] Gen Kawaguchi, possibly with a justifiable dislike for this ridge terrain, had advocated an attack farther to the southeast, had thereby fallen from favor and had been relieved by Maruyama. Miller, *Guadalcanal*, citing Sumiyoshi and Tamaki (2d Div CofS), 160.

[14] Thirty-three members of this outpost managed to reach the lines of the 164th Inf the next day, but 13 men remained lost and hunted by the Japanese. Nine of these finally returned to safety after many harrowing adventures with the jungle and enemy, although one of the nine was gone for two weeks. Four of the wanderers were killed by the Japanese.

the mortar position won back the tube from the enemy, and in the machine-gun section Sergeant John Basilone took rescue matters into his own hands. For this action and later heroism in braving Japanese fire to bring up ammunition, Basilone became the first enlisted Marine of World War II to win the Medal of Honor.[15]

As these attacks continued, Colonel Hall's soldiers began to arrive in small detachments. Puller made no attempt to give this battalion a line of its own on his threatened front, but instead had his men lead these fresh troops into his line where they were most needed at the moment. The fighting was too brisk and the night too rainy for any major reshuffling of lines. By 0330 the reinforcement was complete, and the Japanese attacks were becoming less intense. Infantry and supporting fires had cut down the Nasu force so that each new assault was made with fewer and fewer men.

Fortunately, all had not gone well for the Japanese plans. Nasu bore the brunt of the effort without assistance to his right where the second assaulting column was to have struck. Colonel Shoji, with Kawaguchi's former command, had strayed out of position in the difficult terrain and poor weather and got in behind General Nasu's *29th Infantry*. Shoji was unable to correct this error in time for his battalions to participate in the action.

But Maruyama was true to his orders to press unrelenting attacks upon the Americans. With characteristic resolution, the Japanese struck at the Marines again and again throughout the night. The *Bushido* spirit was unswerving, but the flesh could not endure the concentrated fire from the combined U. S. infantry battalions, the artillery, and 37mm's from the neighboring 2d Battalion, 164th infantry. By dawn Maruyama called back his men to regroup for later attacks, and Puller and Hall began to reorganize their intermingled battalions and readjust their lines. The first strong effort of the counteroffensive had been turned back, but the remainder of 25 October, Sunday in the Solomons, was not a restful day.

Heavy rains on the 23d and 24th had turned Fighter 1 into a mud bog, and at 0800 Pistol Pete opened up again on Henderson to fire at ten-minute intervals until 1100. With Cactus fliers thus effectively grounded, enemy planes from Rabaul took advantage of this, and the first fair weather in three days, by attempting to give the Japanese counteroffensive some semblance of the coordination that Generals Sumiyoshi and Maruyama had muffed. Likewise strong enemy naval forces, to be engaged next day in the Battle of Santa Cruz, were known to be approaching, and early in the morning three Japanese destroyers, as bold as the Zeros overhead, cavorted into Sealark Channel to chase off two American destroyer-transports, sink a tug, set fire to two harbor patrol craft, and harass the beach positions of the 3d Defense Battalion. Finally venturing too close to shore, one of the enemy destroyers was chastised by three hits from 5-inch guns of the defense battalion, and the Japanese ships then withdrew. In all, the day earned its name of "Dugout Sunday."

But the name "was a misnomer in a sense."[16] Although the lurking Zeros kept "Condition Red" alerts in effect most of the day, bombing raids came over only

---

[15] Basilone was killed in 1945 during the Marine assault of Iwo Jima.

[16] *The Island*, 178.

twice,[17] and Lunga defenders not connected with Cactus operations climbed out of their foxholes to watch the dogfights which began after Fighter 1 dried enough to support takeoffs. These American planes were able to go up at 1430 to meet a 16-bomber strike from Rabaul and hamper this attack; and a nine-plane bombing raid at 1500 dumped its explosives on General Geiger's boneyard of discarded wrecks. It was 1730 before Condition Red lifted, but after getting airborne the Cactus fliers had given a good account of themselves.

For the second time in three days Captain Foss shot down four Japanese fighters, and all other members of the Guadalcanal flying force worked so well to make up for time lost during the wet morning that 22 enemy planes had been downed by late afternoon. Three American planes, but no fliers, were lost in the actions. And while the F4F's were battling the Zeros, SBD's and P-39's went off to the north to attack a lurking Japanese naval force. They sank a destroyer and put a cruiser out of action.

Meanwhile, in the reorganization of lines south of Bloody Ridge, Lieutenant Colonel Puller's 1st Battalion, 7th Marines held ground from the Lunga east across the southern slopes of the ridge, and Lieutenant Colonel Hall's 3/164 tied in at that point around four 37mm guns and extended across low jungle country to the right flank of the 2d Battalion, 164th. In the sector west of the Lunga the 5th Marines swung a line into the jungle about a half mile in from the beach and made visual contact with the left (east) flank of Colonel Hanneken's 2d Battalion, 7th Marines which extended from 3/7's dangling flank near the Matanikau back toward the Lunga perimeter. It was clear that Maruyama waited in the jungle to launch another attack in the big counteroffensive, and the Lunga defenders were determined to have stronger positions ready to meet him this time.

In spite of his losses the previous night, Maruyama still had manpower sufficient to build a better attack against the Marines and soldiers, but he somehow gained some faulty intelligence which kept the *Shoji (Kawaguchi) Force* idle for a second night. The intelligence caused Maruyama to expect a U. S. counterattack on his right (east) flank, and he sent Shoji, who had gotten lost in the wet darkness of the first assault, to screen the flank while Nasu's *29th Infantry* and the *16th Infantry* (previously the Maruyama reserve) made ready to carry the new assault.

After dark (on 25 October), the Japanese repeated the pattern of attack used the previous night. With only machine guns to augment their hand-carried weapons, groups of from 20 to 200 soldiers shouted out of the darkness to assault the entire length of the Puller-Hall line. The strongest of these attacks sent two machine-gun companies with supporting riflemen against the junction of the Marine and Army battalions where a jungle trail led north to the airfield. Artillery, mortars, small arms, and the four cannister-firing 37's cut down the repeated Japanese assaults. A company from the 1st Marine Division reserve, as well as an Army platoon, came forward to reinforce, and the lines held.

Taking staggering losses, the Japanese continued hammering against the Ameri-

---

[17] *Ibid.* The final action reports of the 3d DefBn mention seven attacks, but these included also strafing attacks from fighters. The *FinalRept*, Phase V, 25–26, mentions only that enemy fighters were overhead "at irregular intervals throughout the daylight hours."

can lines throughout the night while farther to the west Colonel Oka (whose troops probably had been those spotted on Mount Austen's slopes on 23 October) sent his force against the thin line of 2/7. This Marine battalion had been under artillery fire (from the Kokumbona area) throughout the day, snipers also had scored some American casualties, and now from 2130 to 2300 it was jarred by three strong attacks which Oka made in battalion strength. The weight of the attacks fell mostly heavily on Company F on the left flank of Hanneken's line.

Until midnight these thrusts were thrown back, but at 0300 an assault swept over the Marine company. Enfilading fire from nearby foxholes of Company G failed to dislodge the Japanese, and they took over Company F's high ground. In the haze of morning some 150 Japanese could be observed in F/2/7 foxholes firing American machine guns at adjacent Marine emplacements.

Major Odell M. Conoley, 2/7 executive officer, led a jury-rigged counterattack force of headquarters troops against these Japanese, and he was joined by a platoon from Company C, 5th Marines and by personnel from the 7th Marines regimental CP. Surprising the Japanese, this force killed and drove off the enemy penetration, while a mortar barrage prevented Oka's soldiers from reinforcing.

This was the end of the Japanese October counteroffensive. The Marines, this time with the valuable assistance of the Army regiment, had driven off the *17th Army's* strongest attempt to recapture the Henderson Field area. And again part of the Japanese failure could be laid to faulty intelligence, combined with an over-optimistic evaluation of their own capabilities, and a contemptuous evaluation of the American fighting man. Had the enveloping Japanese successfully negotiated the Maruyama Trail with their mortars and artillery, and had the Japanese managed over-all coordination, the battle might well have had a different outcome. At least the Japanese would have taken a heavier toll of Americans and might well have effected serious penetration of the perimeter. But these errors formed the foundation of a grisly monument of failure: some 3,500 Japanese soldiers dead, including General Nasu and his regimental commanders—Colonel Furumiya (*29th Infantry*) and Colonel Hiroyasu (*16th Infantry*). It was a beaten and disorganized Japanese force which began withdrawing inland during the morning of 26 October.[18]

By contrast, although records are sketchy or nonexistent, American losses were far less: probably around 300 dead and wounded, including those hit by shelling and bombing. The 164th Infantry sustained 26 killed and 52 wounded (during all of October), and the 2d Battalion, 7th Marines lost 30 dead in its action against Oka's Japanese. No figures are available on losses of 1/7, but evidence indicates that these probably did not much exceed 100 dead and wounded.[19]

THE BATTLE OF SANTA CRUZ

As Maruyama's assaults were weakening on the south slopes of Bloody Ridge

---

[18] A general withdrawal of the force began about 29 October, but there were no more attacks after the morning of 26 October when Maruyama broke contact with U. S. troops and pulled back into the jungle.

[19] Another source lists 7th Marine dead as 182, and total casualties for the 164th Infantry as 166 killed and wounded. *Struggle for Guadalcanal*, 198. Adm Morison's totals apparently are too high, and he lists no sources.

JAPANESE TORPEDO PLANE *ignores two American cruisers as it heads for the crippled carrier* Hornet *which was sunk during the Battle of Santa Cruz.* *(U.S.N 20447)*

NAVAL GUNFIRE SUPPORT *for the Army-Marine advance up the north coast of Guadalcanal is provided by the 5-inch guns of an American destroyer.* *(USN53439)*

and while Colonel Oka's brief penetration of 2/7's line still was two hours away, an American patrol plane southeast of Guadalcanal reported sighting elements of a large Japanese fleet in the waters near the Santa Cruz Islands. These ships comprised another part of the "coordinated" Japanese counteroffensive. Admiral Kondo of the *Second Fleet* and Admiral Nagumo of the *Third Fleet* had teamed up with four carriers and four battleships, eight cruisers, 28 destroyers, and supporting vessels; and they were standing by to steam into Sealark Channel when they got the "*Banzai*" signal that Henderson Field had been recaptured.[20] Meanwhile they guarded against American reinforcements or countermeasures from the south.

Rear Admiral Thomas C. Kinkaid, then northeast of the New Hebrides with the *Enterprise* and *Hornet* carrier groups, moved to attack. At 0650 on 26 October two more observation planes spotted Japanese carriers 200 miles northeast of the American force at about the same time Japanese planes were sighting the U. S. ships.

Air action began almost at once. Japanese carrier *Zuiho* was hit in her stern by two of the scouting U. S. dive bombers. A hole in *Zuiho's* flight deck prevented flight operations, but the undamaged carriers *Junyo*, *Shokaku*, and *Zuikaku* mounted air strikes against the American ships.

Twenty minutes later the *Hornet* sent up 15 SBD's, six Avenger torpedo planes, and eight Wildcats, and a short time after that the *Enterprise* got her first 19 planes into the air. By 0830, 73 American planes were airborne to meet the approximately 125 Japanese aircraft. Other flights followed from both forces.

Like some of the previous Pacific naval battles, it was an air-air and air-surface affair. The opposing ships did not close for surface fighting. Twenty U. S. planes were lost to enemy action and 54 to other causes. The Japanese lost 100 planes.

The fate of USS *Hornet* is an example of the desperate fighting which took place during the Santa Cruz battle. Lamed by a starboard bomb hit, the carrier next caught a spectacular suicide crash as the Japanese squadron leader's wounded plane glanced off her stack and burst through the flight deck where two of the plane's bombs exploded. Japanese "Kates" then bore in on the carrier to launch their torpedoes from low astern. Two exploded in engineering spaces, and the ship, clouded by thick smoke and steam, lurched to starboard. Dead in the water, she then took three more bomb hits. One exploded on the flight deck, another at the fourth deck, and the third below the fourth deck in a forward messing compartment.

As if that were not enough, a blazing "Kate" deliberately crashed through the port forward gun gallery and exploded near the forward elevator shaft. Salvage and towing operations got underway almost at once and continued, amid repeated Japanese attacks, until dark when the ship was abandoned and later sunk. The *Hornet* lost 111 killed and another 108 wounded.

Meanwhile the destroyer *Porter* had sustained fatal damage, and the *Enterprise*, *South Dakota*, light antiaircraft cruiser *San Juan*, and destroyer *Smith* were damaged but not sunk. The Japanese lost no ships, but three carriers and two destroyers were damaged. One carrier, the *Shokaku*,

---

[20] For an account of an over-optimistic Japanese "*banzai*" in this connection see *Struggle for Guadalcanal*, 201.

was so badly mauled that she saw no more action for nine months.

Not defeated, but hearing of the Army's failure on Guadalcanal, the Japanese naval force withdrew at the end of the day. Although control of South Pacific waters still had not been resolved, the loss of planes was a serious blow to Japan, and one that was to aid the Allied fleet within a few weeks. A bigger naval battle was brewing.

Critical November

If Tokyo by now realized that one of her long tentacles of conquest had been all but permanently pinched off unless the Solomons invaders were at last taken in all seriousness, the critical Guadalcanal situation likewise was getting more active attention in Washington. On 18 October Admiral Ghormley had been relieved of South Pacific Area command by the aggressive Admiral William F. Halsey, Jr., and almost immediately the new commander was allotted more fighting muscle to back his aggressiveness.[1]

Ten days after Halsey assumed his new command, the Marine Corps established a supra-echelon staff for coordination of all Fleet Marine Force units in the South Pacific. Major General Clayton B. Vogel headed this newly organized I Marine Amphibious Corps with headquarters at Noumea. He exercised no tactical control over the Guadalcanal operation; his staff was concerned only with administrative matters. And it would not be until later that the amphibious corps would have many troops with which to augment divisions for landing operations.

At a Noumea conference on 23–25 October, General Vandegrift assured Admiral Halsey that Guadalcanal could be held if reinforcements and support were stepped up. Some thought also had to be given to relief of the reinforced 1st Marine Division, weakened by strenuous combat and the unhealthy tropics. Halsey promised Vandegrift all the support he could muster in his area, and the admiral also requested additional help from Nimitz and from Washington.

Shortly after this conference the Marine Commandant, General Holcomb, who had concluded his observations of the Marine units in action on Guadalcanal, sought to clear up the command controversy between General Vandegrift and Admiral Turner. Holcomb prepared for Admiral King, the Chief of Naval Operations, a dispatch in which he set forth the principle that the landing force commander should be on the same command level as the naval task force commander and should have unrestricted authority over operations ashore. Holcomb then used his good offices to get Admiral Halsey to sign this dispatch. The Marine Commandant then started back to the States, and at Nimitz' office in Pearl Harbor he again crossed the path of the dispatch he had prepared for Halsey's signature. Holcomb assured Nimitz that he concurred with this message, and the admiral endorsed it on its way to King. It was waiting when Holcomb returned to Washington, and King asked the Commandant whether he agreed with this suggestion for clearing up the question of how a landing operation should be commanded. Holcomb said he did agree with it, and this led eventually to the establishment of firm lines of command for future operations in the Pacific. Holcomb had

---

[1] For a discussion of this command change see *Struggle For Guadalcanal*, 182–183.

shepherded Marine Corps thinking on this important matter across the Pacific to its first serious consideration by the top military hierarchy.[2]

Aside from the general policy that directed America's major war effort toward Nazi Germany during this period, the South Pacific was not intentionally slighted. But as Rear Admiral Samuel E. Morison points out, Washington at this time had its hands full:

> Our predicament in the Solomons was more than matched by that caused by the German submarines, which, during the month of October, sank 88 ships and 585,510 tons in the Atlantic. The North African venture was already at sea; British forces in Egypt still had to be supplied by the Cape of Good Hope and Suez route. Guadalcanal had to be fitted by the Joint Chiefs of Staff into a worldwide strategic panorama, but Guadalcanal could be reinforced only by drawing on forces originally committed to the build-up in the United Kingdom (Operation "Bolero") for a cross-channel operation in 1943. General Arnold wished to concentrate air forces in Europe for the strategic bombing of Germany; Admiral King and General MacArthur argued against risking disaster in the Solomons and New Guinea in order to provide for the eventuality of a future operation in Europe. President Roosevelt broke the deadlock on 24 October by sending a strong message to each member of the Joint Chiefs of Staff, insisting that Guadalcanal must be reinforced, and quickly.[3]

Immediate results of the Roosevelt order were particularly cheering to Halsey and Vandegrift. Admiral Nimitz ordered the new battleship *Indiana* and her task group to the South Pacific; the 25th Army Division in the Hawaiian area was alerted for a move south; the repaired USS *Enterprise*, damaged in the August Battle of the Eastern Solomons, headed back into the fighting. The Ndeni operation, much dog-eared from perpetual shuffling in the pending file, finally was scrapped by Halsey, and the 1st Battalion, 147th Infantry, the latest outfit to start the Ndeni job, was called off its course to the Santa Cruz Islands and diverted to Guadalcanal. Other battalions of the 147th regiment followed.

Also scheduled to reinforce the general Guadalcanal effort were Colonel Richard H. Jeschke's 8th Marines from American Samoa, two companies (C and E) of Colonel Evans F. Carlson's 2d Raider Battalion,[4] a detachment of the 5th Defense Battalion, Provisional Battery K (with British 25-pounders) of the Americal Division's 246th Field Artillery Battalion, 500 Seabees, two batteries of 155mm guns, additional Army artillery units, and detachments of the 9th Defense Battalion. The old Guadalcanal shoestring from which the operation had dangled for three critical months was being braided into a strong cord.

The two 155mm gun batteries—one Marine and the other Army[5]—landed in the Lunga perimeter on 2 November to provide the first effective weapons for answering the Japanese 150mm howitzers. On 4 and 5 November the 8th Marines landed with its supporting 1st Battalion of the 10th Marines (75mm pack howitzers), but the other reinforcements commenced a distinctly separate operation on the island. These units included the 1st Battalion of the 147th Infantry, Carlson's Raiders, the 246th Field Artillery's Provisional Battery K, and the Seabees. Joined under

---

[2] LtCol R. D. Heinl, Jr., interview with Gen. T. Holcomb, 12Apr49.

[3] *Struggle for Guadalcanal*, 184–185.

[4] Elements of this battalion conducted the Makin Island raid.

[5] Btry A of the Marine 5th DefBn and Btry F of the Army 244th CA Bn.

the command of Colonel W. B. Tuttle, commander of the 147th Infantry, this force landed on 4 November at Aola Bay about 40 miles east of the Lunga. There, over the objections of Vandegrift and others, Tuttle's command was to construct a new airfield.[6]

Geiger's Cactus Air Force also grew while Vandegrift added to his man power on the ground. Japanese pounding under the October counteroffensive had all but put the Guadalcanal fliers out of action; on 26 October, after Dugout Sunday, Cactus had only 30 planes capable of getting into the air.[7] But in the lull of action following the defeat of General Hyakutake and the withdrawal of the Japanese naval force from the Battle of Santa Cruz, Cactus ground crews had a chance to do some repairs, and more planes began to arrive at Henderson Field.

Lieutenant Colonel William O. Brice brought his MAG-11 to New Caledonia on 30 October, and in the next two days parts of Major Joseph Sailer, Jr.'s. VMSB-132 and Major Paul Fontana's VMF-211 reported up to Guadalcanal. On 7 November Brigadier General Louis E. Woods assumed command at Cactus, and General Geiger went down to his wing headquarters at Espiritu Santo. By 12 November MAG-11 completed a move to Espiritu Santo where it would be close to Henderson, and more of the units were able to operate from the Solomons field. "In mid-November there were 1,748 men in Guadalcanal's aviation units, 1,557 of them Marines."[8]

As these fresh troops and fliers came ashore, the veterans of Guadalcanal's dark early days were off on an expedition to the west. With the Japanese reeling back from their defeat of late October, the Marines sought to dislodge the enemy completely from the Kokumbona-Poha River area some five and a half miles west of the Matanikau. Once cleared from this area, where the island's north coast bends sharply northwest toward Cape Esperance, the Japanese Pistol Petes would be beyond range of Henderson Field, and the Marines and soldiers could possibly meet Japanese reinforcements from the Tokyo Express before another buildup could muster strength for a new major effort against the perimeter. Under Colonel Edson, the force on this operation included the colonel's 5th Marines, the 2d Marines (less 3/2), and a new Whaling Group consisting of the scout-snipers and the 3d Battalion, 7th Marines. The 11th Marines and Army artillery battalions, Cactus fliers, engineers, and bombardment ships were in support. (See Map 24)

The plan: At 0630 on 1 November attack west across the Matanikau on engineer footbridges; move on a 1,500-yard front along the coast behind supporting artillery and naval shelling; assault the Japanese with the 5th Marines in the van, the 2d Marines in reserve, and with the Whaling Group screening the inland flank. By 31 October preliminary deployment had taken place. The 5th Marines had relieved battalions of the 7th west of the Lunga; the 1st and 2d Battalions, 2d Ma-

---

[6] Vandegrift's objection to the Aola Bay airfield harked back to the old dispute between him and Adm Turner. Turner continually wanted to spread out along the Guadalcanal coast; Vandegrift objected to the establishment of additional perimeters before the first one became strong.

[7] These included 12 F4F's, 11 SBD's, 3 P-400's, 3 P-39's, and one F4F-7 photographic plane.

448777 O—58——23

[8] *Marine Air History*, 111.

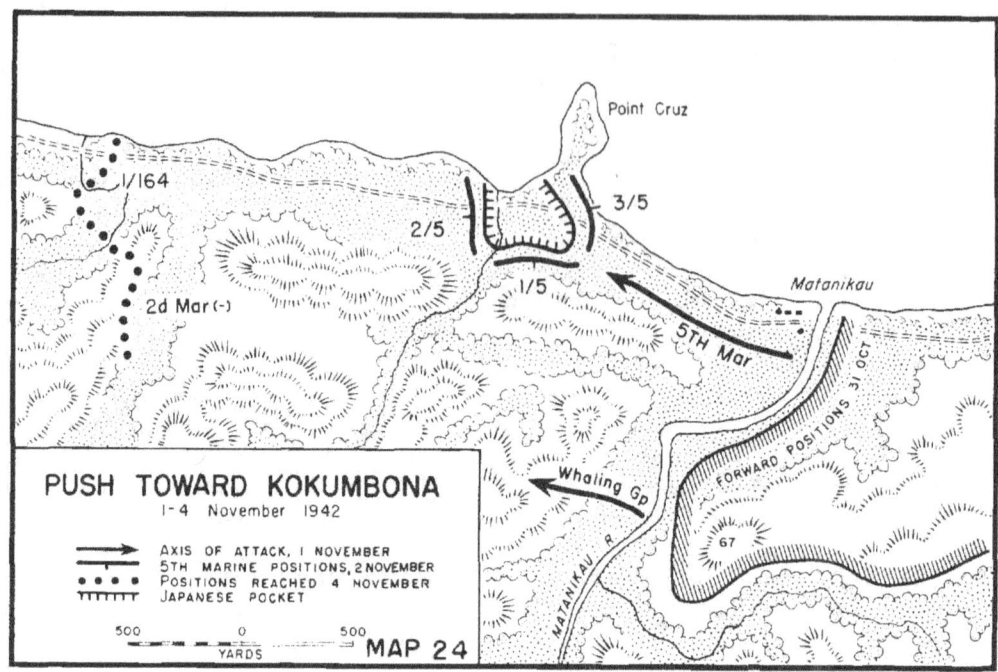

rines had come across from Tulagi;[9] and the engineers were ready with their fuel-drum floats and other bridging material for the crossing sites.

Companies A, C, and D of the 1st Engineer Battalion constructed the bridges during the night of 31 October, and by dawn of 1 November, Company E of 2/5 had crossed the river in rubber boats to cover the crossing of the other units on the bridges. The 1st and 2d Battalions of the 5th Marines reached their assembly areas on the Matanikau's west bank by 0700 and moved out in the attack with 1/5 on the right along the coast and 2/5 on high ground farther inland. The 3d Battalion was Edson's regimental reserve, and battalions of the 2d Marines followed as force reserve. The area around Point Cruz was shelled by cruisers *San Francisco* and *Helena* and destroyer *Sterrett* while P-39's and SBD's from Henderson Field and B-17's from Espiritu Santo strafed and bombed Japanese positions around Kokumbona.

Marines of 2/5 advanced against little opposition along the high ground to reach their first phase line by 1000 and their second phase line by 1440. But near the coast 1/5 met strong resistance, and as it held up to attack Japanese dug in along a deep ravine near the base of Point Cruz, the two 5th Marines battalions lost contact. Farther inland, Whaling screened the flank with no significant enemy contacts. It seemed clear that 1/5 had located the major Japanese force in the area.

While Companies A and C of 1/5 (Major William K. Enright) engaged the enemy, Company B was ordered up to fill

---

[9] The 3d Bn, 2d Mar, long the division's mobile reserve, was sent to rest on Tulagi.

a gap which opened between these attacking companies. The opposition held firm, however, and Company C, hardest hit in the first clash with the entrenched Japanese, had to withdraw. The Company B commander, trying to flank positions which had plagued the withdrawn unit, led a 10-man patrol in an enveloping maneuver which skirted behind Company C, but this patrol also suffered heavy casualties and it, too, was forced to withdraw. Edson then committed his reserve, and Companies I and K of 3/5 (Major Robert O. Bowen) came up to the base of Point Cruz on a line between 1/5 and the coast. This put a Marine front to the east and south of the Japanese pocket; but the enemy held, and the Marines halted for the night.

Next morning (2 November) Edson's 2d Battalion (Major Lewis W. Walt) came to the assistance of the regiment's other two battalions, and the enemy was thus backed to the beach just west of Point Cruz and engaged on the east, west, and south. The Marines pounded the Japanese with a heavy artillery and mortar preparation, and late in the afternoon launched an attack to compress the enemy pocket. Companies I and K stopped short against an isolated enemy force distinct from the main Japanese position, but this resistance broke up under the campaign's only authenticated bayonet charge, an assault led by Captain Erskine Wells, Company I commander.

Elsewhere the going also was slow, and advances less spectacular. A Marine attempt to use 75mm half-tracks failed when rough terrain stopped the vehicles. The 3/5 attack gained approximately 1,500 yards but the main pocket of resistance held, and the regiment halted for another night.

Final reduction of the Japanese stronghold began at 0800 on 3 November. Companies E and G of 2/5 first assaulted to compress the enemy into the northeast corner of the pocket, and this attack was followed by advances of Company F of 2/5 and Companies I and K of 3/5. Japanese resistance ended shortly after noon. At least 300 enemy were killed; 12 antitank 37mm's, a field piece, and 34 machine guns were captured.

It seemed that this success should at last help pave the way for pushing on to Kokumbona, the constant thorn in the side of Lunga defenders and long a military objective of the perimeter-restricted Marines. From there the enemy would be driven across the Poha River, Henderson Field would be beyond reach of Pistol Pete, and the Japanese would have one less weapon able to bear on their efforts to ground the Cactus fliers. But the frustrating Tokyo Express again quashed Marine ambitions. The Express had shifted its terminal back to the east of the perimeter, and another buildup was taking place around Koli Point.

The 8th Marines was not due in Sealark Channel until the next day (and there was always a chance that Japanese surface action would delay this arrival) so Vandegrift again pulled in his western attack to keep the perimeter strong. Division decided to hold its gain, however, and it left Colonel Arthur's 2d Marines (less 3d Battalion) and the 1st Battalion, 164th Infantry on the defense near Point Cruz while Edson and Whaling led their forces back to Lunga.

ACTION AT KOLI POINT

With their October counteroffensive completely wrecked, the Japanese faced an important decision, and on 26 October Captain Toshikazu Ohmae, Chief of Staff of the *Southeastern Fleet*, came down to Guadalcanal from Rabaul to see what General Hyakutake proposed to do about it. And while Hyakutake had been proud and confident when he reached Guadalcanal on 9 October, Ohmae reflected Rabaul's current mood which had been much dampened during the month. The counteroffensive failed, Ohmae believed, because Hyakutake bungled by not carrying out attacks according to schedule and because the Army did not understand problems facing the fleet. "The Navy lost ships, airplanes and pilots while trying to give support to the land assault which was continually delayed," Ohmae said later in response to interrogations.[10]

On 9 October Hyakutake's appetite had been set for Port Moresby; Guadalcanal was but a bothersome bit of foliage to be brushed aside along the way, and the general had the bulk of his 38th Division and other reserves, plus quantities of supplies, in Rabaul and the Shortlands ready to plunge south when the airfield at Lunga was plucked from the Solomons vine like a ripe grape. But now "the situation was becoming very serious,"[11] Ohmae was here to point out, and either Guadalcanal or Port Moresby had to be scratched off the conquest list, at least temporarily. In the conference with the naval captain, Hyakutake agreed that the U. S. advance in the Solomons was more serious than the one through New Guinea,[12] and he agreed to divert his reserves to a new assault against Vandegrift and the Henderson fliers on the banks of the Lunga.

This time, though, things would be conducted differently. Rather than lurking in wait of successes ashore, the *Imperial Fleet* would run the show. Ohmae's chief, Admiral Isoroku Yamamoto, commander of the *Combined Fleet*, wanted Hyakutake's uncommitted troops of the *38th Division*[13] to land at Koli Point so the Americans would be worried and split by forces on both sides of them. High-speed army vessels would transport these Japanese troops down The Slot under escort of the Tokyo Express. Then Yamamoto's bombardment ships and Japanese fliers would knock out Henderson Field once and for all, and Hyakutake could land more troops and finish off a battered defensive garrison which would have no air support.

It was a bold plan, but there were some Japanese officers who thought that it was not particularly wise. Admiral Tanaka, that veteran of many distressing hours in The Slot, was one of these. He had suggested after the October defeat that defenses should be pulled back closer to Rabaul so that they would have a better chance to stand off the Allies while Japan gained more strength in the Solomons. "To our regret," he reported later, "the Supreme Command stuck persistently to reinforcing Guadalcanal and never modified this goal until the time came when the island had to be abandoned."[14]

---

[10] Combined statements of Capt Ohmae and Cdr Tadashi Yamamoto, *USSBS Interrogations*, II, 468, hereinafter cited separately as *Ohmae Interrogation* and *Yamamoto Interrogation*.

[11] *Ohmae Interrogation*, 468.

[12] *Ibid*. By autumn of 1942 the Japanese garrisons on New Guinea, all but abandoned because of the press of things at Guadalcanal, had been handed their first setback by Australian troops who were beginning to take the offensive against them.

[13] Two battalions of this division already were ashore on Guadalcanal.

[14] *Tanaka Article*, II, 818.

Colonel Shoji already was at Koli Point with his veterans of the October assault against Bloody Ridge, and other Japanese troops now made ready to join him there. Hyakutake planned to build an airfield there so Japanese planes could be more effective during the November attacks. But while Edson and Whaling fought their action to the west around Point Cruz, a Marine battalion marched out to the east and stepped into the middle of Hyakutake's plans there.

On 1 November, the same day Edson and Whaling crossed their foot bridges westward over the Matanikau, division sent Lieutenant Colonel Herman H. Hanneken's 2d Battalion, 7th Marines out to investigate reports of Japanese activities to the east. Hanneken trucked his men to the Tenaru River that day, and on 2 November the battalion made a forced march across the base of Koli Point to the Metapona River, about 13 miles east of the perimeter. Intelligence had it that the Japanese had not yet been able to build up much strength here, and Hanneken's mission was to keep things that way. On the night of 2 November he deployed his battalion along the coast east of the Metapona and dug in for the night. (See Map 25, Map Section)

While 2/7 Marines strained to see and hear into the black rainy night, six Japanese ships came down Sealark Channel, lay to offshore about a mile east of the American battalion, and began to unload troops. This force was made up of about 1,500 men from the *230th Infantry*,[15] and they were carrying out initial plans of the Imperial Army and Navy for the buildup to the east.

Rain had put Colonel Hanneken's radio out of commission, and he could not contact division with information of this landing. The Marines held their positions that night but moved to attack next morning after an eight-man Japanese patrol approached their line by the Metapona. Marines killed four members of this patrol, and the battalion then moved up to fire 81mm mortars into the enemy's landing site. This brought no immediate response, but as Hanneken's infantrymen prepared to follow this mortar preparation a large force of Imperial soldiers maneuvered to flank the Marines who began also to draw mortar and artillery fire. In the face of this coordinated attack by the Japanese, 2/7 withdrew, fighting a rear guard action as it pulled back to take up stronger positions on the west bank of the Nalimbiu River, some 5,000 yards west of the Metapona.

During the withdrawal, Hanneken managed to make radio contact with the CP at Lunga. He reported his situation, and called for air attacks against the enemy and for landing craft to meet him at Koli Point and evacuate his wounded. This message reached division at 1445, and Vandegrift immediately dispatched the requested air support and also relayed the situation to gunfire ships which had supported the Koli Point operation.

---

[15] CG 1st MarDiv msg to ComSoPac, 17Nov42, in SoPac War Diary (located at NHD). Another source says no Japanese troops landed that night; only supplies were put ashore, and the force Hanneken's battalion met next day was only Shoji and his veterans of the October counteroffensive. *Miller, Guadalcanal,* citing interrogation of MajGen Takeo Ito, former CG of the 38th Division, 196n. Dr. Miller's text recognizes the landing, however, and lists the above message from the SoPac War Diary as the source. *Ibid.,* 196.

Cruisers *San Francisco* and *Helena* and destroyers *Sterrett* and *Lansdowne* shelled likely target areas east of the Marine battalion, and planes ranged overhead in vain searches for signs of the enemy. Communications still were none too good, however, and elements of 2/7 were accidentally strafed and bombed by some of the first planes that came out from Cactus.

Meanwhile, division had made the decision to concentrate more force against the evident buildup to the east. The western attack then in progress would be called back while General Rupertus, due to come across Sealark Channel from Tulagi, went to Koli Point with Colonel Sims of the 7th Marines, and Sims' 1st Battalion (Puller). And to the efforts of this regiment (less its 3d Battalion), Vandegrift added the 164th Infantry (less 1st Battalion) which would march overland to envelop the Koli Point enemy from the south. Artillery batteries of the 1st Battalion, 10th Marines would be in general support.

By dusk of 3 November the 2d Battalion, 7th Marines reached the west bank of the Nalimbiu River near the beach at Koli Point, and there General Rupertus met Hanneken next morning with Colonel Sims and Puller's 1st Battalion, 7th Marines. At 0600 on 4 November Brigadier General Edmund B. Sebree, American Division ADC who had just arrived on the island to prepare for the arrival of other Americal troops (which included the 132d and 182d Infantry regiments, in addition to the 164th Infantry already in the Solomons action), marched out of the perimeter in command of the 164th Infantry. Thus General Vandegrift, with two field forces commanded by general officers, operated his CP like a small corps headquarters.[16] And to add even more troops to this concentration of effort to the east, Vandegrift obtained release of Carlson's 2d Raider Battalion from Colonel Tuttle's command at Aola Bay, and ordered it to march overland toward Koli Point and cut off any Japanese who might flee east from the envelopment of the 7th Marines and the 164th Infantry.

On 4 November the Japanese on the east bank of the Nalimbiu did not seriously threaten the Marines on the west, but General Rupertus held defensive positions while awaiting the arrival of the 164th Infantry. The soldiers, weighted down by their heavy packs, weapons, and ammunition, reached their first assembly area on the west bank of the Nalimbiu inland at about noon. There the regimental CP bivouacked for the night with the 3d Battalion while the 2d Battalion pushed on some 2,000 yards downstream toward Koli Point.

Next day the 3d Battalion, 164th crossed the river about 3,500 yards upstream and advanced along the east bank toward the Japanese. The 2d Battalion likewise crossed the river and followed its sister battalion to cover the right rear of the advance. As the soldiers neared the Japanese force they began to draw scattered small-arms fire, and two platoons of Company G were halted temporarily by automatic weapons fire This opposition was silenced by U. S. artillery and mortars, however, and when the Army units halted for the night there still was no firm contact with the enemy.

---

[16] On 4 Nov the Lunga perimeter had been reorganized, this time in two sectors. Gen Rupertus took the sector east of the Lunga, Gen Sebree the sector west of the river.

Action on 6 November likewise failed to fix the Japanese in solid opposition, although the 7th Marines crossed the Nalimbiu and moved eastward along the coast, and the 164th Infantry found an abandoned enemy bivouac farther inland. Meanwhile, Company B of the 8th Marines, just ashore on the island, moved east to join the attacking forces as did regimental headquarters and the Antitank and C Companies of the 164th Infantry. The combined force then advanced to positions a mile west of the Metapona River and there dug in for the night, the Marines near the beach to guard against an expected Japanese landing that did not materialize.

Unknown to Marines and Army commanders, the situation was shifting because of new changes in the Japanese plans. During the night of 5-6 November the enemy began to retire eastward from positions facing the Marines across the Nalimbiu, and when the U. S. force stopped west of the Metapona the Japanese were east of the river preparing rear guard defensive positions that would aid a general withdrawal. General Hyakutake and Admiral Yamamoto on 3 or 4 November had changed their plans about hitting the Lunga perimeter from two sides, and the idea of an airfield at Koli Point was abandoned. Shoji was to return overland to Kokumbona where he would join the main elements of the *Seventeenth Army's* buildup on the west.[17]

After remaining in positions to guard against the expected landing throughout 7 November, the U. S. forces under Generals Rupertus and Sebree advanced eastward again on the 8th. Patrols had located the Japanese near the coast just east of Gavaga Creek, a stream some 2,000 yards east of the Metapona River. The 2d Battalion, 164th Infantry was attached to the 7th Marines as regimental reserve, and the combined forces moved rapidly to surround the Japanese. During the advance General Rupertus retired from the action with an attack of dengue fever, and Vandegrift placed General Sebree in command of the entire operation. The 1st Battalion, 7th Marines met stiff resistance, and four Marines were killed while 31, including Lieutenant Colonel Puller, were wounded. Major John E. Weber next day succeeded to command of this battalion.

Hanneken's 2/7 moved around the Japanese to take up positions east of the creek with its right flank on the beach. The 2d Battalion of the 164th Infantry, committed from reserve, tied in on 2/7's left (inland) flank, straddled Gavaga Creek south of the Japanese, and tied in with the right flank of the 1st Battalion 7th Marines. From this point 1/7 extended north to the beach along the west side of the Japanese positions, and the ring was closed on the enemy. With this action to the east thus stabilized, division called for the return of the 164th Infantry (less 2d Battalion) and Company B of the 8th Marines. Vandegrift planned to resume the western action toward Kokumbona.

On 9 November the 7th Marines and 2/164 began attacks to reduce the Gavaga Creek pocket. Supported by 155mm guns, two pack howitzer batteries, and aircraft, the two Marine battalions closed in from east and west while the soldiers of the Army battalion moved north to compress the Japanese into the beach area. The Japanese fought bitterly to break out of the trap, especially to the south through a gap where Companies E (on the right)

---

[17] *Yamamoto Interrogation*, 470.

and F of the 164th Infantry were unable to make contact across the swampy creek. This action continued through 10 November, with repeated orders by General Sebree for 2/164 to close the gap across the creek. This was not done, however, and the commander of 2/164 was relieved on 10 November.

During the night of 11–12 November most of the enemy escaped along the creek to the south. On 12 November the three battalions swept through the area where the Japanese had been trapped, met little opposition, and withdrew that afternoon across the Metapona River. Marines estimated that the action had cost the enemy approximately 450 dead. About 40 Americans were killed and 120 wounded.

Meanwhile, Colonel Carlson and his raiders, traveling cross-country to Koli Point, encountered the rear elements of the retiring Japanese. Joined by his Companies B and F, as well as elements of Company D, Carlson concentrated his battalion inland near the native village of Binu and patrolled the surrounding area. During the afternoon of 12 November the raiders beat off five attacks by two Japanese companies. Scattered actions took place for the next five days, and on 17 November the main Japanese force began withdrawing into the inland hills to skirt south of Henderson Field to Kokumbona. Carlson pursued, was augmented by the arrival of his Company A and by native bearers, and remained in the jungle and ridges until 4 December. His combat and reconnaissance patrol covered 150 miles, fought more than a dozen actions and killed nearly 500 enemy soldiers. Raiders lost 16 killed and 18 wounded.

Admiral Tanaka had now been placed in charge of a larger Japanese reinforcement fleet, and Admiral Mikawa of the *Eighth Fleet* had stepped up his plans for the buildup on the west side of the Marine perimeter. On the night of 7 November Tanaka sent Captain Torajiro Sato and his *Destroyer Division 15* down The Slot with an advance unit of some 1,300 troops. After evading a U. S. bomber attack in the afternoon, these ships landed the troops at Tassafaronga shortly after midnight and then sped back north to the safety of the Shortlands. While these ships came north, the second shuttle went south from Rabaul to the Shortlands with the main body of the *38th Division*. Two days later (on 10 November) 600 of these troops under Lieutenant General Tadayoshi Sano made the move from the Shortlands to Guadalcanal. The convoy was heckled by U. S. planes and PT boats, but the troops were landed safely, and the ships made it back to the Shortlands on 11 November.[18]

BRIEF RENEWAL OF WESTERN ATTACK

Meanwhile Colonel Arthur's 2d Marines (less 3/2), augmented by the 8th Marines and the 164th Infantry (less 2/164), pushed west from Point Cruz toward Kokumbona on 10 November. The force advanced against ragged opposition from infantry weapons and by 11 November had regained most of the ground that had been given up when Vandegrift shifted his attacks to the east earlier in the month.

General Hyakutake, to thwart this thrust at his Guadalcanal command post, assigned Major General Takeo Ito (formerly CO of the *228th Infantry* and now infantry group commander of the *38th*

---

[18] *Tanaka Article*, II, 820.

Division) to maneuver inland and flank the American advance.

But before Ito could strike—and before the Americans were aware of his threat—General Vandegrift again had to call off the western attack. On 11 November the troops pulled back across the Matanikau, destroyed their bridges, and resumed positions around the Lunga perimeter. Intelligence sources had become aware of the plans of Hyakutake and Yamamoto to mount another strong counteroffensive, and Vandegrift wanted all hands available.

DECISION AT SEA

It did indeed appear that the Lunga perimeter would need all the strength it could muster. Rabaul was nearly ready for a showdown, winner take all, and the time was now or never. The Japanese were losing their best pilots in this Solomons action, and shipping casualties likewise were beginning to tell. At the same time Allied strength in the South Pacific was slowly growing. It was becoming an awkward battle, and Japan was spending altogether too much time and material on this minor outpost which never had borne much intrinsic value. This needless loss had to be stopped, and Admiral Yamamoto was determined that the new counteroffensive would not be botched.

At 1800 on 12 November Admiral Tanaka's flagship, the destroyer *Hayashio*, headed out of the Shortlands leading the convoy which carried the main body of the *38th Division*.[19] Elsewhere in these Solomon waters two Japanese bombardment forces also made for Guadalcanal. Admiral Yamamoto had ordered them to hammer Henderson Field while Tanaka landed the soldiers. Yet a third Japanese flotilla ranged the Solomons in general support. Nothing was to prevent the *38th Division* from landing with its heavy equipment and weapons. The troops would be put ashore between Cape Esperance and Tassafaronga.[20]

On 23 November the 8th Marines passed through the 164th Infantry to attack the Japanese positions steadily throughout the day. Again there was no gain, and the American force dug in to hold the line confronting the strong Japanese positions. There the action halted for the time with the forces facing each other at close quarters. The 1st Marine Division was due for relief from the Guadalcanal area, and more troops could not be allotted for the western action.

On 29 November Admiral King approved the relief of Vandegrift's division by the 25th Infantry Division then en route from Hawaii to Australia. This division was to be short-stopped at Guadalcanal and the Marines would go to Australia.

During the period that preceded the withdrawal of the 1st Division, the last naval action of the campaign was fought off Tassafaronga. Shortly after midnight of 29 November the Japanese attempted to supply their troops in that area, and an American task force of five cruisers and six destroyers moved to block the attempt.

The American force, under the command of Rear Admiral Carleton H. Wright, surprised the Japanese force of eight destroyers, but the enemy ships loosed a spread of torpedoes before retiring. One Japanese destroyer was sunk,

---

[19] *Ibid.*

[20] *Yamamoto Interrogation*, 470.

but the U. S. lost the cruiser *Northampton*, and three others, the *Minneapolis*, *New Orleans*, and *Pensacola*, were seriously damaged.

But Japan's day of smooth sailing in The Slot was over. With a reinforced submarine fleet of 24 boats, Admiral Halsey's command had been prowling the route of the Tokyo Express to destroy or damage several enemy transports. The Japanese edge in fighting ships also was becoming less impressive. In addition to the carrier *Enterprise*, Halsey had available two battleships, three heavy and one light cruisers, a light antiaircraft cruiser, and 22 destroyers organized in two task forces.

The strength of the Lunga perimeter was likewise much improved since the Japanese attacks of late October. Arrival of fresh troops enabled an extension of defensive positions west to the Matanikau and the establishment of a stronger line along the southern (inland) portions of the infantry ring around Henderson Field. These new positions plus the shooting by the 155mm guns kept Pistol Pete from carefree hammering at the airfield and beach areas.

And the perimeter was to grow even stronger. More planes were becoming available to Henderson fliers, bombers from the south were able to provide more support for the Solomons area, and another regiment from the Americal Division was ready to move in from New Caledonia. Colonel Daniel W. Hogan's 182d Infantry (less 3d Battalion) sailed from Noumea in the afternoon of 8 November on board Admiral Turner's four transports. Admiral Kinkaid with the *Enterprise*, two battleships, two cruisers, and eight destroyers would protect the transports, and all available aircraft in the area would cover the troop movement. A day later (9 November) Admiral Scott sailed from Espiritu Santo with a supply run for Guadalcanal, and a day after that Admiral Callaghan followed with his five cruisers and ten destroyers.

Early on 11 November (the day Vandegrift called off his western advance) Scott's transports arrived off Lunga Road to begin unloading. Enemy bombers twice interrupted the operations, and damaged the *Betelgeuse*, *Libra*, and *Zeilin*. Damage to the latter ship was serious, and she was mothered back to Espiritu Santo by a destroyer. The other two transports retired at 1800 to Indispensable Strait between Guadalcanal and Malaita, and later joined Turner's transports. During the night Admiral Callaghan patrolled the waters of Sealark Channel.

Turner's transports with the 182d Infantry arrived at dawn on 12 November to begin unloading troops and cargo. During the morning the *Betelgeuse* and *Libra* drew fire from near Kokumbona. The two ships escaped damage, however, and American counterbattery and naval gunfire silenced the Japanese. Unloading ceased in the afternoon, and the ships were flushed into dispersion by an attack of about 31 torpedo bombers. The transports escaped unscathed, but Callaghan's flagship *San Francisco* and the destroyer *Buchanan* were damaged. Only one Japanese bomber survived the American antiaircraft fire and air action, and unloading resumed two hours later.

Meanwhile, intelligence reports plotted the Japanese fleet closing in on the Guadalcanal area. During the morning American patrol planes north of Malaita had spotted a Japanese force of two battleships, one cruiser, and six destroyers. Later five destroyers were observed 200 miles north-northwest. By midafternoon another sighting placed two carriers and a brace of destroyers some 250 miles to the west.[21] Coastwatchers in the upper Solomons logged other sightings. Turner appraised the various reports at two battleships, two to four heavy cruisers, and ten to twelve destroyers. Callaghan was heavily outweighed. But Halsey's orders were to get the naval support of Guadalcanal out of the dark back alleys of the South Pacific; and after he shepherded the unloaded transports south to open water, Callaghan turned back to engage the enemy.

Japanese battleships *Hiei* and *Kirishima*, light cruiser *Nagara*, and 15 destroyers steamed south to deliver Admiral Yamamoto's first blow of the new counteroffensive. This bombardment group was to enter Sealark Channel and hammer Henderson Field and the fighter strip to uselessness so that Cactus air could not bother General Hyakutake's reinforcements en route. This Japanese mission gave Callaghan one slight advantage. For shore bombardment, the Imperial battleships carried high explosive projectiles for their 14-inch guns, not armor-piercing shells which would have been much more effective against the hulls of U. S. cruisers.

Near Savo Island at 0124 on 13 November, cruiser *Helena* raised the Japanese in radar blips at a range of 27,000 yards, and she warned the flagship that the enemy was approaching between Savo and Cape Esperance. But radar on the *San Francisco* was inadequate, and Callaghan could not determine the exact positions of his own or the enemy ships. The

---

[21] A faulty report. Carriers were not in the area. *Struggle for Guadalcanal*, 235.

admiral therefore delayed action until he was sure of the situation. By that time the range had closed to about 2,500 yards, and the van destroyer of the American force was nearly within the Japanese formation. When they maneuvered to launch torpedoes, the American ships disorganized their formation, and they took up independent firing. Some swerved off course to avoid collision, and in the melee both American and Japanese ships fired at their sister craft.

The *San Francisco* caught 15 solid hits from big Japanese guns and was forced to withdraw with Admiral Callaghan killed and others, including Captain Cassin Young, her skipper, dead or fatally wounded. A cruiser hit on the *Atlanta* killed Admiral Scott and set fire to the ship. But the small American force held in spite of heavy losses, and by 0300 the Japanese group retired without being able to attempt its bombardment mission. The Imperial bombardment force had lost two destroyers and four others were damaged. The battleship *Hiei* limped away damaged by more than 80 American hits.

For the American ships it was a costly victory. Henderson Field had been protected, but the antiaircraft cruisers *Atlanta* and *Juneau* sank in the channel along with destroyers *Barton*, *Cushing*, *Monssen*, and *Laffey*. In addition to Callaghan's flagship, heavy cruiser *Portland* also was seriously damaged as were destroyers *Sterrett* and *Aaron Ward*. Destroyer *O'Bannon* sustained minor concussion to her sound gear. These ships struggled back to the New Hebrides after daybreak on 13 November. Of the 13 American ships in the action only destroyer *Fletcher* escaped damage.

Planes from Henderson Field took off at first light on 13 November to nip the heels of the retiring Japanese ships. They found the crippled battleship *Hiei* afire near Savo, and bombed and strafed her throughout the day. The Japanese fought a losing battle to salvage their hapless ship, but they had to scuttle her next day (14 November).

During the night battle off Guadalcanal, Admiral Tanaka had been ordered to lead his convoy back to the Shortlands. He headed south again from there during the afternoon of 13 November at about the same time that Admiral Halsey ordered Kinkaid to withdraw the carrier *Enterprise* south with the remnants of Callaghan's force. Halsey wanted this carrier—the South Pacific's sole operational flattop—safely out of Japanese aircraft range. To guard Henderson Field, Admiral Lee would steam on north with his battleships *Washington* and *South Dakota* and four destroyers from Kinkaid's task force. The distance was too great for Lee to make that night, however, and only the Tulagi PT boats were available to protect Sealark Channel. Shortly after midnight Japanese cruisers and destroyers entered the channel and shelled the Cactus airfield for about half an hour. There was no serious damage, however. At dawn on 14 November the Henderson fliers found their field still operational.

Early search flights found Admiral Tanaka's convoy heading down The Slot some 150 miles away and the bombardment cruisers and destroyers retiring north. In spite of the fact that the shelling of Henderson Field had been ineffective, Tanaka was coming on down to Guadalcanal with the 10,000 troops of the *38th Division's 229th* and *230th Regiments*, artillery personnel, engineers, other replacements, and some 10,000 tons of supplies.

First Cactus attacks struck the retiring warships which had shelled Henderson during the night. Ground crews on the field hand-loaded their planes and visiting craft from the *Enterprise* with fuel and ordnance, and the planes mounted from the muddy runways in attack. They damaged Japanese heavy cruiser *Kinugasa* and the light *Isuzu*. Planes still on the *Enterprise*, now 200 miles southeast of Guadalcanal, also attacked the Japanese warships. They added to the troubles of the *Kinugasa* and *Isuzu*, and also damaged heavy cruisers *Chokai* and *Maya* and destroyer *Michishio*.

Meanwhile, the 11 troop transports steamed on down The Slot until by about 1130 they were north of the Russells and near Savo. A previous light attack by *Enterprise* fliers had inflicted little damage to this convoy, but at 1150 seven torpedo bombers and 18 dive bombers from Henderson were refueled, rearmed, and boring in for an attack. This strike hulled several of the transports. About an hour later 17 fighter-escorted dive bombers delivered the second concentrated American attack on the transports and sank one of them. Next turn went to 15 B-17's that had left Espiritu Santo at 1018. They struck at 1430 from an altitude of 16,000 feet and scored one hit and several near misses with their 15 tons of explosives.

These attacks continued all day as the Henderson fliers scurried back and forth from their field. Nine transports were hit, and seven of them sunk. But from these sinking ships, some 5,000 men were rescued by destroyers. As Admiral Tanaka described the day:

The toll of my force was extremely heavy. Steaming at high speed the destroyers had laid smoke screens almost continuously and delivered a tremendous volume of antiaircraft fire. Crews were near exhaustion. The remaining transports had spent most of the day in evasive action, zigzagging at high speed, and were now scattered in all directions.

In detail the picture is now vague, but the general effect is indelible in my mind of bombs wobbling down from high-flying B-17's, of carrier bombers roaring toward targets as though to plunge full into the water, releasing bombs and pulling out barely in time; each miss sending up towering columns of mist and spray; every hit raising clouds of smoke and fire as transports burst into flame and take the sickening list that spells their doom. Attacks depart, smoke screens lift and reveal the tragic scene of men jumping overboard from burning, sinking ships. Ships regrouped each time the enemy withdrew, but precious time was wasted and the advance delayed.[22]

In spite of this disastrous day, Tanaka steamed on south in his flagship, doggedly leading transports *Kinugawa Maru*, *Yamatsuki Maru*, *Hirokawa Maru*, and *Yamaura Maru* on toward Guadalcanal. These ships and three destroyers from *Destroyer Division 15* which continued to escort him were the only sound vessels Tanaka had at sundown that day—". . . a sorry remnant of the force that had sortied from Shortland."[23] But what was worse, Tanaka then got the word that a strong U. S. task force appeared to be waiting for him at Guadalcanal. This was Admiral Lee's force, then some 100 miles southwest of Guadalcanal, but Japanese intelligence reported these ships to Tanaka as four cruisers and four destroyers. To counter this threat, headquarters at Rabaul ordered Vice Admiral Nobutake Kondo to hurry down and run interference for Tanaka with a fighting force which included the battleship *Kirishima*, heavy cruisers *Atoga* and *Takao*, light cruisers *Sendai* and *Nagara*, and an entire destroyer squadron. Kondo was to complete the Henderson Field knockout which Admiral Callaghan's force had thwarted two nights earlier.

Throughout the day Admiral Lee likewise sifted intelligence reports which funneled into his flagship, the battleship *Washington*. Then he moved against this powerful Tokyo Express which was headed his way.[23] Lee entered Sealark Channel at about 2100 on 14 November and patrolled the waters around Savo. An hour before midnight, radar indicated a Japanese ship (the cruiser *Sendai*) nine miles to the north. About 12 minutes later the target was visible by main battery director telescopes and Lee ordered captains of the *Washington* and the *South Dakota* to fire when ready. Their first salvos prompted the *Sendai* to turn out of range.

Shortly before this Admiral Tanaka, still leading his four transports south toward Guadalcanal, had been much relieved to see Admiral Kondo's *Second Fleet* in front of him in The Slot. But when the cruiser *Sendai* scurried back from this first brief brush with the American ships, the Japanese officers found that for the first time in the Pacific war they were up against U. S. battleships, and not just cruisers as they had expected.

Tanaka immediately ordered his three escorting destroyers—the *Destroyer Division 15* ships commanded by Captain

---

[22] *Tanaka Article*, II, 822.
[23] *Ibid*.

[23] The American admiral also moved against some powerful naval thinking. Many officers at ComSoPac headquarters "doubted the wisdom of committing two new 16-inch battleships to waters so restricted as those around Savo Island, but Admiral Halsey felt he must throw in everything at this crisis. And he granted Lee complete freedom of action upon reaching Guadalcanal." *Struggle for Guadalcanal*, 272.

Torajiro Sato—into the fight, and the admiral then turned his transports north and shepherded them beyond range of the impending action. Meanwhile Admiral Kondo's fleet closed for the fight, and soon the American destroyers leading Admiral Lee's formation came within visual range of some of these ships. The U. S. destroyers got the worst of the bargain. By 2330 all four of them were out of action: the *Walke* afire and sinking, the *Benham* limping away, the *Preston* gutted by fire that caused her abandonment later, and the *Gwin* damaged by a shell in her engine room. Only one Japanese destroyer, the *Ayarami*, had been damaged.

The two U. S. battleships continued northwest between Savo and Cape Esperance. The *South Dakota*, turning to avoid the burning destroyer *Preston*, came within range of the Japanese ships which had just scuffled with the American destroyers, and the word passed by these Japanese ships brought their "big brothers" out from the shelter of Savo's northwest coast.

Admiral Kondo steamed into the fight with destroyers *Asagumo* and *Teruzuki* in the van followed by heavy cruisers *Atago* and *Takao*, and the battleship *Kirishima* in the wake.

The *South Dakota*, partially blind because of a power failure that hampered her radar, soon came within 5,000 yards of the Japanese who illuminated her with their searchlights and opened fire. Almost at once the *Washington* blasted her 16-inch main batteries at the enemy battleship about 8,000 yards away.

The *Kirishima* took nine 16-inch hits and nearly half a hundred 5-inch wounds in less than ten minutes, and she staggered away in flames. Japanese cruisers *Atago* and *Takao*, revealed by their own searchlights, also were damaged. But the original Japanese onslaught had caused enough serious damage to the *South Dakota* to force her to retire, also.

Admiral Lee continued on a northwesterly course to divert the Japanese, then bore away to the southwest near the Russells, and finally retired from the area when he noted the Japanese likewise withdrawing. The enemy battleship *Kirishima* was abandoned as was the destroyer *Ayanami*. American destroyer *Benham* likewise had to be abandoned later.

With his escorting destroyers dispersed by this battle and its aftermath, Admiral Tanaka now was alone in his flagship *Hayashio* with the four transports. He made full speed for Tassafaronga, but it was clear to him that the transports would not be able to unload before daylight. After that the U. S. planes would attack them like they had those six transports which tried to unload during daylight in October. But these men were critically needed on Guadalcanal, Tanaka knew. He sent a message to Admiral Mikawa at *Eighth Fleet* headquarters and asked if he could run the transports aground on the beach to insure prompt unloading. Admiral Mikawa said "No." But Admiral Kondo, disengaging his *Second Fleet* from the battle with Lee's battleships, contacted Tanaka and told him to go ahead with this plan.

By now the early light of dawn was turning Sealark Channel a slick gray, and Tanaka followed Admiral Kondo's message of approval. He ordered the four transports to run aground off the landing beaches, and after he watched them head for shore the admiral turned north, gathered up his destroyers again and sailed through the waters east of Savo Island.[24]

The admiral wrote later:

> Daylight brought the expected aerial assaults on our grounded transports which were soon in flames from direct bomb hits. I later learned that all troops, light arms, ammunition, and part of the provisions were landed successfully.[25]

Two guns of the 244th Coast Artillery Battalion and the 5-inch guns of the 3d Defense Battalion also contributed to the damage of the grounded transports. This fire hit two of the ships, and then the American destroyer *Meade* came over from Tulagi to enter the fight. Planes from Henderson Field and Espiritu Santo soon joined this grisly "Buzzard Patrol," and the Japanese transports were reduced to useless hulks engulfed in flames. Japanese plans for a big November counteroffensive had met disaster, and Imperial headquarters now began to think seriously about the more cautious plan to pull the line back closer to Rabaul. There now were some 10,000 new Japanese troops on Guadalcanal, but these recent sea and air actions made it clear to the Japanese that these troops could not be supplied or reinforced on a regular basis. The shipping score against the Japanese scratched two battleships, a cruiser, three destroyers, and 11 transports. Nine other ships had been damaged.

American losses numbered one light cruiser, two light antiaircraft cruisers, and seven destroyers. Seven other U. S. ships were damaged. But the Tokyo Express had been derailed. Never again was Japan able to reinforce significantly with night runs from Rabaul. From this point the Imperial force on the island began to dwindle [26] while the American command continued to grow. Critical November had turned into decisive November, in the Pacific War as well as the Guadalcanal Battle. The Japanese never again advanced and the Allies never stopped.

Admiral Tanaka, whose skillful conduct of the convoy and aggressiveness in throwing his four escorting destroyers into the battle against Admiral Lee's force near Savo had contributed most to what limited success the Japanese had had during this harrowing month, summed it up this way:

> The last large-scale effort to reinforce Guadalcanal had ended. My concern and trepidation about the entire venture had been proven well founded. As convoy commander I felt a heavy responsibility.[27]

BACK TOWARD KOKUMBONA

With this Japanese attempt to reinforce General Hyakutake decisively stopped, the American ground advance to the west was resumed. General Sebree, western sector commander, would be in command. With the troops of his sector—the 164th Infantry, the 8th Marines, and two battalions of the 182d Infantry—the general planned to secure a line of departure extending from Point Cruz inland for about 1,700 yards. From this line the attack would press on to Kokumbona and the Poha River where the main Japanese force was concentrated.

---

[24] *Tanaka Article*, II, 823–824.

[25] *Ibid.*, 824.

[26] Capt Ohmae said later: "Following the [naval] battle, it was decided to do as much as we could by reinforcing the Guadalcanal Garrison by destroyers, while a sufficient supporting force of aircraft was built up in Rabaul. This plan was not too successful." *Ohmae Interrogation*, 471.

[27] *Tanaka Article*, II, 824.

The 2d Battalion of the 182d Infantry crossed the Matanikau on 18 November and took up positions on the south (inland) flank of the proposed line of departure. On the following day the 1st Battalion of the same regiment moved west to take up the right flank position at the base of Point Cruz. Company B of the 8th Marines screened the left flank of 1/182's advance, and these two units met sporadic infantry opposition. About noon the Army battalion halted, dug in, and refused its inland flank. The screening Marine company withdrew to rejoin its regiment east of the Matanikau. A gap of more than 1,000 yards separated the two battalions of the 182d Infantry.

Meanwhile, the Japanese deployed for a local offensive action of their own. With the *38th Division* troops who had been on the island, plus those few brought ashore from the ill-fated transports, the Japanese moved east to force a Matanikau bridgehead from which a new attack at the Lunga perimeter could be launched. Other elements of the *38th Division* moved inland to occupy the Mount Austen area. Remnants of the battered *2d Division* were held in Kokumbona.

On the night of 19–20 November, the Japanese took up positions facing the two Army battalions west of the river and engaged the Americans with artillery and mortar fire. At dawn (20 November) the Japanese struck the inland flank of 1/182. The Army troops gave ground for approximately 400 yards, but this was regained later in the morning with air and artillery support. This U. S. attack continued to the beach just west of Point Cruz, but halted there in the face of increased enemy artillery and mortar fire.

During the night the 1st and 3d Battalions of the 164th Infantry moved into the gap between the two battalions of the 182d, and a general American attack jumped off on the morning of 21 November. Strong Japanese positions fronting the 164th held the attempt to no gain, however, and a second attack on the morning of 22 November likewise was halted.

CHAPTER 9

Final Period, 9 December 1942 to 9 February 1943

CHANGE OF COMMAND

At the Noumea conference with Admiral Halsey in October, General Vandegrift stressed the need for getting the 1st Marine Division to a healthier climate. But at that time the Japanese counteroffensive was underway, and another enemy effort against the Lunga perimeter began shortly after this October attack was turned back. Troops could not be spared from Guadalcanal during that period, and sea lanes to the area were too hazardous for a rapid buildup of the island garrison. It was not until after the important naval actions of November that sufficient reinforcements could be brought in to relieve the 1st Marine Division. By that time it was clear to all that these veterans needed to be taken out of the jungle.

Compared to later actions in the Pacific, casualties in the division had not been excessive. From the landing early in August 1942 until relief in December, the division lost 605 officers and men killed in action, 45 who died of wounds, 31 listed as missing and presumed dead, and 1,278 wounded in action.[1] But unhealthy conditions in the jungle were, statistically, a greater hazard than the enemy. While 1,959 Marines of the division became casualties to enemy action, 8,580 fell prey at one time or another to malaria and other tropical diseases.

Records make it impossible to separate these two totals. Many men with malaria were hospitalized more than once and thus added to the total as cases rather than as individuals. Some of these later were killed or wounded in action. But on the other hand many suffered from a milder form of malaria or other illness and did not turn in at the hospital at all. It became a rule of thumb in front-line units that unless one had a temperature of more than 103 degrees there would be no light duty or excuse from a patrol mission. The tropics weakened nearly everyone. Food had been in short supply during the early weeks of the campaign, much of the fare had been substandard, and most of the long-time veterans of the fighting suffered some form of malnutrition.

On 7 and 8 December, men in one of the division's regiments were examined by Navy doctors who thus sought to assess the physical condition of the division. The doctors concluded that 34 per cent of the regiment was unfit for any duty which might involve combat. This percentage would have been higher but for the recent inclusion within the regiment of 400 replacements.

Plans for the operation called for the Marines to be relieved early and reorganized for a new assault mission else-

---

[1] These figures refer to organic units only; such reinforcing attachments as the 3DefBn, 1st RdrBn, and the 1st PrchtBn are not included in these statistics.

where. This could not be, however, and the Marines who held out in the Lunga perimeter during the dark early days deserved a break. They had taken America's first offensive step against long odds, and they had held out against strong Japanese attacks when Guadalcanal was all but cut off from Allied support. For this they were awarded a Presidential Unit Citation and—what was to be immediately more satisfying to the survivors—a rehabilitation and training period in Australia. The 2d Marines, also on hand for the original landing, was to be sent to New Zealand.

On 9 December 1942, command of the troops ashore on Guadalcanal passed from General Vandegrift to Major General Alexander M. Patch, commanding general of the Americal Division and senior Army officer present. On the same day the 1st Marine Division began to embark for Australia. The 5th Marines sailed that day, followed at intervals of a few days by division headquarters personnel, the 1st Marines and, after a longer interval, by the 7th Marines. The command of General Patch included Henderson Field, the fighter strip, the Tulagi area and seaplane base there, as well as the Guadalcanal perimeter. Although withdrawal of the 1st Marine Division meant that strong actions against the Japanese had to be temporarily suspended, reinforcements began to arrive concurrently with the departure of the Marines.

The third infantry regiment of General Patch's division, the 132d Regimental Combat Team (less 1st Battalion and Battery A, 247th Field Artillery Battalion) arrived on 8 December.[2] With this arrival the Army division numbered 13,169 men—more than 3,000 short of full strength. The 164th Infantry, in action since the October fighting on Bloody Ridge, was in little better shape than the 1st Marine Division regiments. Both this regiment and the 182d Infantry were each understrength by about 860 men.

Major General J. Lawton Collins' 25th Division, bound from Hawaii to New Caledonia, was diverted directly to Guadalcanal where its 35th Infantry Regiment landed on 17 December, the 27th Infantry on 1 January, and the 161st Infantry on 4 January. Also on 4 January, the 6th Marines (Colonel Gilder T. Jackson) and division headquarters of the 2d Marine Division landed from New Zealand to join their other regiments, the 2d and 8th Marines. Brigadier General Alphonse De Carre, the ADC, acted as division commander while this division was on Guadalcanal, and also served as commander of all other Marine ground units. Major General John Marston, commanding general of the 2d Marine Division, remained in New Zealand because he was senior to General Patch, the Army officer who now was in command at Guadalcanal.[3]

---

[1] This division's other infantry regiments, the 164th and the 182d, already were on Guadalcanal as were other elements of the division. Widely separated in their New Caledonia camps, the units operated together as a division for the first time on Guadalcanal. Other divisional units included the 221st, 245th, and 247th FA Bns; the 57th EngCBn; the 101st QM Regt; the 101st Med Regt; the 26th SigCo and the Mobile CReconSqn.

[3] LtGen Holcomb, Marine Commandant, later expressed the opinion that Marston should have had the opportunity to command his division in spite of his seniority over Patch. CMC ltr to MajGen C. B. Vogel, 12Feb43. Marston said he was never apprised of the Commandant's attitude, however. MajGen J. Marston ltr to CMC, 30Dec48.

FINAL PERIOD, 9 DECEMBER 1942 TO 9 FEBRUARY 1943

37MM GUNS *of Americal Division antitank units are landed on the beach at Guadalcanal as Army troops arrive to relieve 1st Division Marines.* (SC 164902)

SHOVING OFF *as relieving troops arrive, weary men of the 1st Marine Division file on board landing craft and leave the Guadalcanal battle behind.* (USMC 52978)

By 7 January arrival of additional replacements had placed Guadalcanal's combined air, ground, and naval forces at about 50,000. The 2d Marine Division now had a strength of 14,733; the Americal Division, 16,000; the 25th Division, 12,629. This was a manpower level beyond even the dreams of the early Lunga defenders, and, with the South Pacific air and naval power also growing, the Allies at last were able to lay plans for attacks that would defeat the Japanese on the island and keep reinforcement landings to a minimum.

With Guadalcanal clearly out of the shoestring category at last, General Harmon on 2 January designated the Guadalcanal-Tulagi command as XIV Corps. General Patch became corps commander and General Sebree, former Americal ADC, assumed command of that division.[4]

A month and a half earlier than this, on 15 November, installations of the Cactus Air Force also had gained a more dignified title. On that date Rear Admiral Aubrey W. Fitch, who had relieved Admiral McCain as ComAirSoPac, designated Henderson Field and Fighter 1 a Marine Corps Air Base, and Colonel William J. Fox became base commander. On 1 December and 30 January two new engineering units came in to improve the air facilities on Guadalcanal. On the earlier date, Major Thomas F. Riley's 1st Marine Aviation Engineer Battalion relieved the 6th Seabees, and on the January date Major Chester Clark's 2d Marine Aviation Engineer Battalion arrived. These were the only units of their kind within the Marine Corps, and, together with the remaining Seabees plus the organic engineer battalions of the 1st and 2d Marine Divisions, they kept the airfields in shape.

Part of this work included construction of a new strip, Fighter 2, closer to the beach near Kukum. Fighter 1, always unusually slow to dry adequately after tropical rains, was abandoned when this new strip became operational, about the middle of December. Both Henderson and Fighter 2 then were built up with coral for better drainage, and steel Marston mats, now becoming available, also were laid on the runways. Tools still were scarce, however, and the old Japanese road rollers, for example, continued to be used.

Brigadier General Louis E. Woods, who had relieved General Geiger at Cactus on 7 November so the wing commander could return to his headquarters at Espiritu Santo, stayed on as Commander Aircraft, Cactus Air Force until 26 December when he in turn was relieved by Brigadier General Francis P. Mulcahy, commanding general of the 2d Marine Aircraft Wing. Colonel William O. Brice succeeded Colonel Albert D. Cooley as strike commander, and Lieutenant Colonel Samuel S. Jack became fighter commander after Lieutenant Colonel Harold W. Bauer was lost to enemy action on 15 November.

By 20 November there were 100 planes on the Guadalcanal fields. This figure included 35 F4F–4's, 24 SBD's, 17 P–38's, 16 P–39's, 8 TBF's, and one lone and battle-scarred P–400. At about this time also, B–17's from two merged Army Air Force

---

[4] "The XIV Corps's staff section chiefs assumed their duties on 5 January 1943, but most of the posts at XIV Corps headquarters were manned by Americal Division staff officers . . . [who]. . . . acted simultaneously . . . as assistant staff section chiefs for the Corps. As late as 1 February 1943 XIV Corps headquarters consisted of only eleven officers and two enlisted men." *Miller, Guadalcanal,* 218–219.

Bomber Groups (the 11th and the 5th) began to operate through Guadalcanal on long-range reconnaissance missions. On 23 November six OS2U's came in to run antisubmarine patrols; on 26 November the 3d Reconnaissance Squadron of the Royal New Zealand Air Force arrived with its Lockheed Hudsons, and during the period 15 to 25 December night patrolling PBY's of VP-12 arrived. Also during December the Army sent in the 12th, 68th, and 70th Fighter Squadrons and the 69th Bombardment Squadron of B-26's.

This additional air strength enabled the Allies to maintain the upper hand they had gained over the Tokyo Express and Rabaul fliers. Japanese commanders pointed up their loss of pilots as the most serious trouble resulting from the fighting around Guadalcanal, and several Japanese officers, including Captain Ohmae, list this loss as the turning point at Guadalcanal and therefore the turning point in the Pacific war.[5] Ohmae said later:

> We were able to land a number of troops and supplies [on Guadalcanal], but our air losses were too great. Almost all of the Navy's first class pilots and a few of the Army's were lost in the Solomon Operations. The greatest portion of these were lost against Guadalcanal. At one time, we had three or four squadrons at Rabaul, but they were sent down one at a time. The constant attrition was very expensive. The 21st, 24th, 25th and 26th Air Groups were lost. This loss was keenly felt in the defense of the empire during the Marshall-Gilbert campaign.
>
> In 1943, our training program began to be restricted, so we were never able to replace these losses, although we still had a number of carriers. In January 1943, due to your increased strength and our difficulty in supplying Guadalcanal, it was necessary for us to withdraw.[6]

[5] *Ohmae Interrogation*, 471.
[6] *Ibid*.

GENERAL SITUATION

The U. S. forces had not been idle during December. The perimeter now extended west along the beach to Point Cruz, south to Hill 66 (nearly 2,000 yards inland from the beach at Point Cruz) where it was refused east to the Matanikau to join the former Lunga perimeter outpost line east of that river. There was little expansion to the east, but a separate American force held Koli Point outside the main perimeter.

The Aola Bay force, finally giving up airfield construction there because of swampy, unsuitable terrain, moved early in December to Koli Point where a field later was built. This force, still under the command of Colonel Tuttle, now included the colonel's 147th Infantry, the 9th Marine Defense Battalion, the 18th Naval Construction Battalion (Seabees), and elements of the 246th Field Artillery Battalion.

The limited offensive toward Kokumbona was halted late in November when the Japanese tried to mount a second strong counteroffensive against the perimeter, and at that time a Japanese movement to build up forces in the Mount Austen area was noted. Now, early in December, it seemed advisable to concentrate on this important piece of terrain as a prelude to a general corps offensive which would be launched when more troops became available.[7] The high ground just to

[7] Mount Austen was the "Grassy Knoll" the 1st Marine Division (planning at New Zealand with faulty maps) hoped to take early in the landing phase of the campaign. The importance of this terrain feature as a key to the security of Henderson Field had been recognized throughout the Guadalcanal planning and fighting. Gen Vandegrift's Marines patrolled the area repeatedly, but never had enough manpower to hold the ground permanently.

the south above Henderson Field had to be cleared before many troops went west along the north coast to drive the Japanese beyond Kokumbona. The enemy line from Point Cruz inland was dug in for a determined stand, and Japanese strength was again mounting in the Bismarcks.

On 2 December, General Hitoshi Imamura, commander of the Japanese *Eighth Area Army*, arrived in Rabaul to assume command of the enemy's South Pacific area and what was left of General Hyakutake's *Seventeenth Army*. Imamura had been ordered down from Japan to retake Guadalcanal, and for this job he brought along 50,000 men for his *Eighth Area Army*. Hyakutake remained on Guadalcanal where his troops were disposed generally from Point Cruz inland to Mount Austen, facing the American line west of the Matanikau. The rear areas, and the bulk of Hyakutake's support troops, extended from the Point Cruz line west to Cape Esperance. This Japanese force included remnants of the *2d Division* (General Maruyama), *38th Division* (General Sano), and the *Kawaguchi* and *Ichicki Forces*. (See Map 26, Map Section)

Confronting the Americans on his left flank from Point Cruz inland to Hill 66, General Hyakutake had troops of Maruyama's *2d Division* composed of the *4th, 16th,* and *29th Regiments*. From this division's right (inland) flank were the *1st* and *3rd Battalions* of the *228th Infantry* on high ground west of the Matanikau. The *124th Infantry* and other units extended from the Matanikau to Mount Austen. Remaining elements of the *38th Division* (including the *230th, 228th,* and *229th Regiments*) plus detachments of the *124th Infantry* were deployed in the Mount Austen area.

At this time the total Japanese strength on the island stood at about 25,000 men. But they were incapable of concentrated offensive action, and they had dug in for a defensive stand while awaiting General Imamura's *Eighth Area Army* reinforcements. Rations were low, malaria now was more prevalent in Japanese ranks than in American, ammunition stocks were nearly exhausted, preventive and corrective medical capabilities were practically nonexistent, and the Tokyo Express was hard pressed to maintain even a starvation-level of supplies. Admiral Tanaka still was in charge of this supply operation down The Slot, and the measures now being taken were desperate ones. Destroyers tried to supply these Imperial troops by making high-speed runs to Guadalcanal and dropping off strings of lashed-together drums into which supplies had been sealed. Barges from the island then were to tow these drums ashore. This procedure was not too successful, however, and the troops managed to retrieve only about 30 per cent of these supplies that Tanaka's destroyers cast upon the water.

Tanaka's first run with the drums occurred on the night of 29 November, and his force was the one engaged by American ships in the Battle of Tassafaronga. With the same sort of aggressive naval action which had characterized the sending of his four destroyers into the fight against Admiral Lee's battleship force earlier in the month, Admiral Tanaka made a creditable show in this action. But this did not get the troops supplied, and that was still the big problem.

With new action shaping up, the Japanese attempts to supply their force by floating drums continued. The force dug in to face the Americans could not even hold defensive positions unless they could be fed and cared for. Tanaka's destroyers raced down The Slot on 3 December and dropped strings of 1,500 drums. But the island troops managed to haul in only about 300 of these from the waters off Tassafaronga and Segilau. "Our troubles," Tanaka said, "were still with us."[8]

On 7 December Captain Sato led 10 destroyers to Guadalcanal for the third Japanese attempt to supply the troops. Fourteen U. S. bomber and fighter planes located this force in The Slot at about nightfall, however, and one Japanese ship was hit and had to start back north under tow by another destroyer. Two other ships escorted this aided cripple. Admiral Tanaka went south to the scene in his new flagship, the newly-built destroyer *Teruzuki*, an improved 2,500-ton model capable of 39 knots. The other destroyers which had been on the drum run went on south toward Guadalcanal but had to turn back when they encountered PT boats and U. S. planes. Thus the third supply run failed completely.

The fourth of these supply runs came on 11 December, and Tanaka himself led this one in his speedy *Teruzuki*. A flight of 21 U. S. bombers attacked these ships at about sunset but scored no hits. Tanaka's destroyers managed to shoot down two of six fighters which were covering for the bombers, and the Japanese steamed on south. The *Teruzuki* patrolled beyond Savo Island while the other destroyers dropped some 1,200 drums of supplies off Cape Esperance and then headed north again. Admiral Tanaka sighted some U. S. PT boats, and his new destroyer went to the attack. The Japanese ship chased the PT boats away but in the process got hit in its port side aft by a torpedo. The ship caught fire and became unnavigable almost at once, and the destroyer *Naganami* hurried alongside to rescue survivors. Tanaka, who had been wounded and knocked unconscious, plus others from the officers and crew were transferred to this other destroyer, and the destroyer *Arashi* also came up to help. But the heartened U. S. PT boats chased these sound ships away from the sinking *Teruzuki*, and the Japanese could only drop life rafts to crew members who were still in the water. Some of the drums were recovered by the troops ashore, but with the loss of such ships as the *Teruzuki*, this sort of supply operation was becoming very costly. And now the moon was entering a phase which caused other such attempts to be temporarily postponed. Japanese defenses had received very little help for the actions which now shaped up against them.

The 132d Infantry of the American Division began the offensive against Mount Austen on 17 December, and by early January troops of this regiment had the major Japanese force in the area surrounded in a strong point called the Gifu. Although this pocket was not completely reduced until 23 January, the enemy was sufficiently restricted to preclude any threat to the perimeter or the rear of the general corps attack.

Meanwhile, in other preliminaries of the corps offensive, the 1st Battalion, 2d Marines had taken Hills 54 and 55 west of the Matanikau, and the Americal Division Reconnaissance Squadron had seized Hill 56. These positions which were southeast of the southern anchor of the line extend-

---

[8] *Tanaka Article*, II, 828.

ing inland from Point Cruz served to extend the American positions farther into Japanese territory west of Mount Austen. (See Map 27, Map Section)

THE CORPS OFFENSIVE

With the Japanese in the Mount Austen area localized in the Gifu, the drive to the west could get underway. General Patch planned to extend his Point Cruz-Hill 66 line farther inland and then to push west, destroying the Japanese or driving them from the island. General Collins' 25th Division (with 3/182, Marines of 1/2 and the Americal Reconnaissance Squadron attached) would advance west of Mount Austen on the extended flank inland, and at the same time assume responsibility for the Gifu Pocket which now would be behind the XIV Corps line. (See Map 27, Map Section).

The 2d Marine Division (less 1/2) would provide the corps' right element from the 25th Division's north flank to the beach. The Americal Division (minus the 182d Infantry, division artillery, and 2/132) would hold the main perimeter.

Since the 25th Division apparently would have some fighting to do before it could come abreast of the Point Cruz-Hill 66 line, its phase of the offensive was the first ordered into action. Colonel Robert B. McClure's 35th Infantry, with the Division Reconnaissance Troop and 3/182 attached, was ordered to relieve the 132d Infantry at the Gifu and then advance to the west on the division's inland flank. The 27th Infantry (Colonel William A. McCulloch) would capture the high ground south of Hill 66 between the northwest and southwest forks of the Matanikau. The 161st Infantry (Colonel Clarence A. Orndorff) would be the division reserve.

The ground thus assigned to the 27th Infantry consisted of a jumble of hills (dubbed the Galloping Horse because of their appearance on aerial photographs) which lie some 1,500 yards south of Hill 66. Army units began their attacks against this terrain on 10 January, and, during the final actions here three days later, Marines on the right flank of the corps line began their forward movement.

Launching its attack with the 8th Marines on the right and the 2d on the left, the 2d Division immediately encountered a series of cross compartments in which the Japanese had established very effective defensive positions. Using a minimum of men and weapons, the enemy fired down the long axis of these valleys which were perpendicular to the Marine advance, and thus engaged the attackers in a cross fire in each terrain compartment.

Enemy positions of this type held up the 8th Marines throughout the day, but two battalions of the 2d Marines advanced about 1,000 yards on the inland flank. The 6th Marines then moved up to relieve the 2d Marines which was long overdue for withdrawal from the Guadalcanal area. Lines were adjusted at this time. The 8th Marines now was on the left and the 6th along the coast. This relief was completed by 15 January, and the 2d Marines sailed for New Zealand.

The 8th Marines hammered at the ravine defenses of the Japanese, and operations along the coast during this phase of the campaign as well as during actions later in January provided the first opportunity for Marines to test, in a rudimentary way, their principles of naval gunfire in support of a continuing attack against an enemy.[9] The four destroyers in action fired only deep support missions in this phase of the advance, however, and close-in fighting of the Japanese held the 8th Marines to insignificant gains until the afternoon of 15 January when flame throwers were put in action for the first time on this front. Three Japanese emplacements were burned out that day, and the attack, supported by tanks, began to move forward. By the end of 17 January the 8th Marines had advanced to positions abreast the 6th Marines.

The naval gunfire during this period indicated that both Marines and ships had much to learn. The Navy's peacetime training had not stressed this type of support, and likewise the Marine division had no naval gunfire organization or practice. There was no JASCO (Joint Assault Signal Company) such as appeared later, and no organic shore fire control parties or naval gunfire liaison teams in the infantry battalions and regiments.

But here along Guadalcanal's coast, Marines and ships took advantage of their new freedom from air and surface attacks to develop some gunfire procedures. Each direct support artillery battalion had two naval officers trained in naval gunfire principles, and these officers were sent out with FO (forward observer) teams to train them in shore fire control party (SFCP) duties. And while the naval officers ashore schooled Marine forward observers, artillery officers from the division went on board the support ships to inform commanders and gunnery officers of the missions desired by the division.[10]

In addition to establishing some sound naval gunfire practices which would be most helpful in later Pacific assaults, the Marine action since 13 January had gained approximately 1,500 yards, killed over 600 Japanese, and captured two prisoners and a variety of enemy weapons and ammunition.

While the Marines fought along the coast, the 35th Infantry (reinforced) battled about 3,000 yards through the twisted ridges of an area southeast of the 25th Division's inland flank to take the Sea Horse complex (so called because it looked like one on an aerial photograph), and finally cleared Colonel Oka's defenders out of the Gifu Pocket.

The western line of XIV Corps now extended from Hill 53, the head of the Galloping Horse, north to a coastal flank some 1,500 yards west to Point Cruz. With elements of the 35th Infantry south of the Galloping Horse to guard against a flanking attack from that direction, the Americans at last were poised on a line of departure from which an attack could be launched to Kokumbona and beyond.

DRIVE TO THE WEST

Hoping to trap the Japanese at Kokumbona, General Patch in early January had sent a reinforced company (I) of the 147th Infantry around Cape Esperance in LCT's to Beaufort Bay on the island's southwest coast, and from there the force advanced up the overland trail toward Kokumbona to block the mountain passes against a possible Japanese escape to the

---

[9] Although the 1st MarDiv landing was supported by naval gunfire, subsequent support fire from ships had been infrequent and on a catch-as-catch-can basis. Col F. P. Henderson, "Naval Gunfire in the Solomons—Part I: Guadalcanal," *MCGazette*, March 1956, 44–51.

[10] *Ibid.*

south.[11] With this unit in place, the XIV Corps attack jumped off with the 25th Division on the left to envelop the enemy south flank, and the CAM Division (Composite Army-Marine) to advance west along the coast. The CAM Division consisted of the 6th Marines, the 182d and 147th Infantry regiments, and artillery of the Americal and 2d Marine Division.[12] (See Map 28, Map Section)

The 25th Division began its flanking movement on 20 January, swinging in toward Kokumbona and taking Hills 90 and 98 by 21 January. This high ground, immediately south of Kokumbona, was in front of the CAM Division and dominated the coastal area around the Japanese base. The enemy troops facing the CAM Division thus were outflanked and partially surrounded by the two forces. The attack continued on 23 January when the 27th Infantry occupied Kokumbona, but by this time most of the enemy already had slipped away along the coast.

Meanwhile, the CAM Division on 22 January had opened a full-scale attack with the 6th Marines on the right by the beach, the 147th Infantry in the center, and the 182d Infantry on the left. Again the Marines had called on naval gunfire, and this time four destroyers provided close support to CAM troops who faced more cross compartments forward of Kokumbona.

---

[11] The Japanese did not attempt to escape by this route.

[12] The "Composite Division" was merely a convenient term for the force formed by Marine and Army units during the January drive to the west. The 2d Marine Division staff served as the CAM Division staff. The name first appears in a field order from the XIV Corps on 25 January, but the "division" itself had no administrative identity.

A radio spotting frequency was assigned the four SFCPs serving with the assault battalions of the 6th Marines and the 182d Infantry, and on this frequency the shore spotters called in fire missions from the destroyers. Another frequency was established between the Division Naval Gunfire Officer (NGFO) and all four of the destroyers, and forward spotters also could use this net if the need arose.

In this phase of the corps advance, Marines in the CAM Division ran into the strongest opposition, and they were stopped the first day by about 200 Japanese in a ravine west of Hill 94. With the help of the close-in naval gunfire adding its weight to artillery, air, and infantry weapons, this opposition was overcome by noon of 24 January when the CAM Division made contact with the 25th Division on the high ground above Kokumbona. Although some of the fighting had been most difficult, the Japanese were pulling back slowly. It appeared that they would probably establish strong defenses farther west.

Actually there would be more stiff fighting on the island, but no all-out stand of Japanese on a strong line of defense, and no more Japanese reinforcements to face. Tokyo and Rabaul had called new signals, and General Hyakutake was withdrawing his troops. The situation now was reversing itself. The U. S. operation, starting as a shoestring, had slowly added other cords in a warp and woof of fabric with a definite pattern. But the Japanese conquest string had ended in the Solomons and New Guinea, and never had a firm knot tied in the end of it.

Affairs in New Guinea suffered when Hyakutake's reserves were diverted from a planned reinforcement there to the November attempt to retake Guadalcanal. Now a small force of Japanese had met with disaster trying to recapture Port Moresby from across the Owen Stanley Mountains, and the 50,000 troops General Imamura brought down from Java to reinforce Hyakutake would have to be used in New Guinea. Around 15 December the Japanese decided to evacuate Guadalcanal and build up new defenses farther north in the Solomon chain. The starving troops on the island would fight delaying actions toward Cape Esperance, and they would be evacuated in detachments from that point by fast destroyers. Commanding these destroyers would be Rear Admiral Tomiji Koyanagi, former chief of staff of the *Second Fleet*. He had replaced the wounded and exhausted Admiral Tanaka, who now was on his way to the home islands where he would serve on the *Naval General Staff*.

XIV Corps maintained the momentum of its western advance by resupplying its attacking divisions over the beach at Kokumbona, where the Tokyo Express had often unloaded, and ordering the attack to push on toward the Poha River, a stream some 2,500 yards beyond Hyakutake's former headquarters village. The 2d Battalion, 27th Infantry met opposition in the high ground south and west of Kokumbona, but this was overcome in attacks of 24 and 25 January, and units of the regiment reached the Poha before dark on the 25th. (See Map 28, Map Section)

FINAL PURSUIT

After the corps advance reached the Poha River, intelligence sources began reporting a new buildup of Japanese ships at Rabaul and in the Shortlands, and the Allied command concluded that the enemy was ready for still another attempt to retake Guadalcanal. Admiral Halsey deployed six task forces south of Guadalcanal, and General Patch recalled the 25th Division from the western advance to bolster the perimeter. It was the same problem General Vandegrift had faced so many times in the past, but now there were more troops and the western attack did not have to be completely stopped. Pursuit of the Japanese was assigned to the CAM Division.

This estimate of Japanese intentions slowed pursuit of the enemy and probably aided their escape, but the mistake was an honest one. Actually the Japanese strength at Rabaul had been mounting, and the basic intelligence was good. But this time the activity in the Bismarcks and the Shortlands was the result of Japanese plans to complete the evacuation of Guadalcanal and to start new defensive installations closer to Rabaul.

By this time the Japanese had nearly completed their withdrawal to evacuation areas around Cape Esperance, and when regiments of the CAM Division launched their new attacks early on 26 January they advanced rapidly along the narrow coastal corridor against slight opposition. Naval gunfire again was employed, but once more it fired in deep support at targets of opportunity and to interdict the coastal trail forward of the advancing troops. (See Map 29)

The Marines and soldiers gained 1,000 yards the first day and 2,000 yards the second. Opposition now was such that General Patch on 29 January brought the 182d Infantry back to the perimeter and ordered the 147th Infantry to continue the pursuit while the 6th Marines covered the rear of the Army regiment. The advance

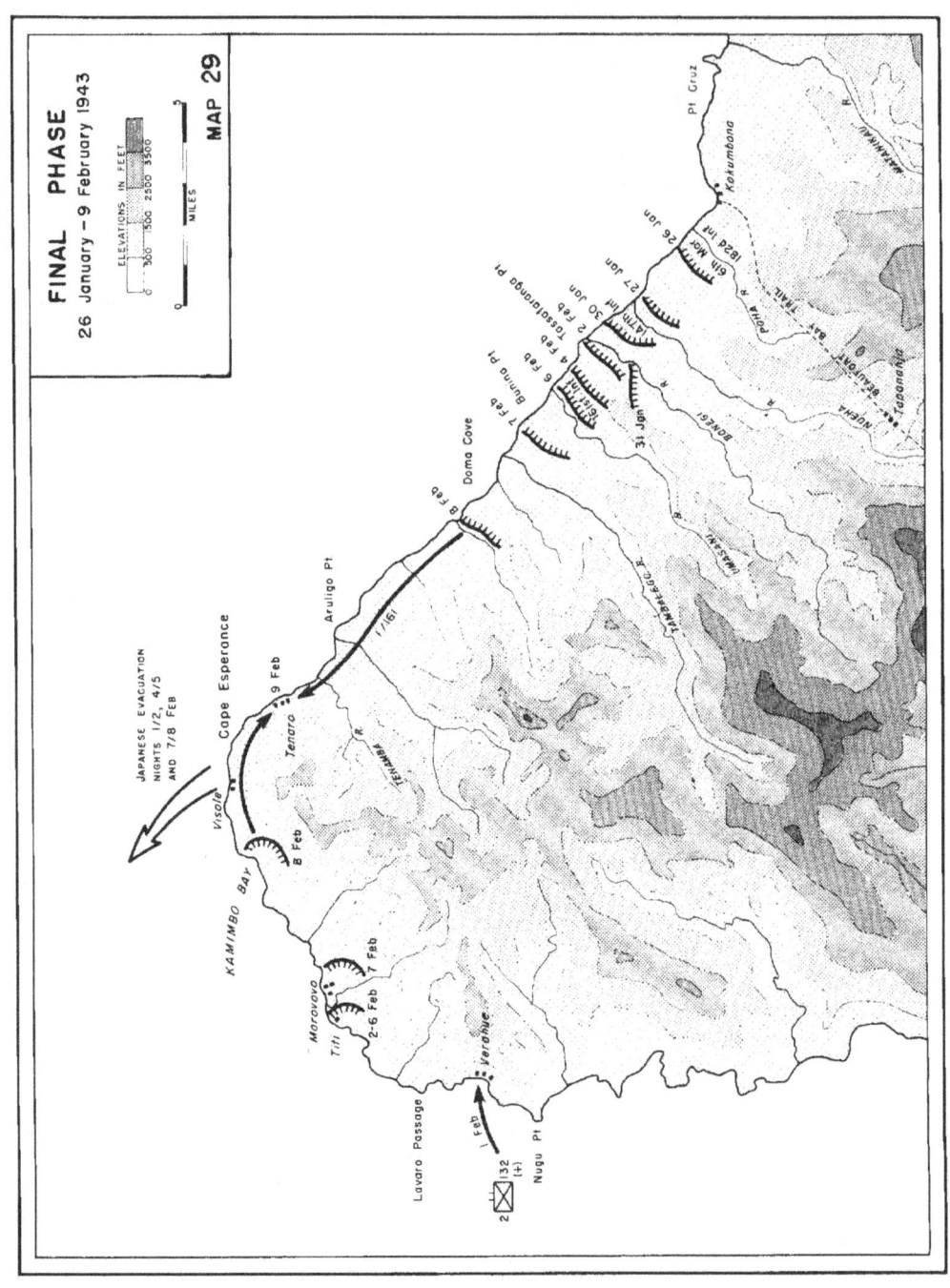

resumed on 30 January, and the soldiers ran into resistance near the mouth of the Bonegi River about 2,000 yards northwest of the Poha. There the units fought until 2 February when the Japanese withdrew. The U. S. force advanced again next day, and on 5 February the 147th held up 1,000 yards short of the Umasami River, a stream some 2,500 yards northwest of Tassafaronga Point.

Meanwhile, to form a new trap for the retreating Japanese, General Patch on 31 January dispatched the reinforced 2d Battalion, 132d Infantry around Cape Esperance to land near the western tip of the island. From that point the battalion was to advance to Cape Esperance and cut off the Japanese line of retreat. After landing early on 1 February at Verahue, the force advanced to the village of Titi, nearly a third of the way to the cape. By 7 February this force was ready to push on from that village, and the north coast attack was prepared to advance beyond the Umasami River.

By this time the 147th Infantry had been relieved at the Umasami by the 161st Infantry of the 25th Division, and on 8 February this regiment reached Doma Cove some eight miles from Esperance. On the same date 2/132 arrived at Kamimbo Bay a short distance from the tip of the island, and on 9 February the two units met at the village of Tenaru on the coast below the high ground of the cape. Only token resistance had been met in these final days. Evacuation of the Japanese from the island had been completed on the night of 7-8 February.

The Guadalcanal campaign was over. When the two units met at Tenaru village, General Patch sent to Admiral Halsey a message announcing "Total and complete defeat of Japanese forces on Guadalcanal. . . . "[11] From a hazardous early step up the long island path toward Tokyo, the Allies had gained a solid footing which would become an all-important base until after the mounting of the final offensive against Okinawa two years later.

Happy to hear the news that Guadalcanal was at last secured—but hardly disappointed that they had not been there for the final chase—were the veterans of the 1st Marine Division in Australia, the 2d and 8th Marines in New Zealand, and the 1st Raider and 1st Parachute Battalions in New Caledonia. These old island hands were resting, fighting off recurring attacks of malaria, getting the jungle out of their blood, and already training for their next campaign.

EPILOGUE

Guadalcanal was the primer of ocean and jungle war. It was everything the United States could do at that moment against everything the Japanese could manage at that place. From this the Americans learned that they could beat the enemy, and they never stopped doing it. The headlines from Guadalcanal did more for home front morale than did the fast carrier raids of 1942's winter and early spring, for at last Americans had come to grips with the enemy; and the outcome of this fighting added in the bargain a boost to the spirit of the Pacific fighting man. The benefits from official

---

[11] To which Halsey replied in part: "When I sent a Patch to act as tailor for Guadalcanal, I did not expect him to remove the enemy's pants and sew it on so quickly . . . Thanks and congratulations." FAdm Halsey and LCdr J. Bryan, III, *Admiral Halsey's Story* (New York: McGraw-Hill Book Co., 1947), 148.

and unofficial circulation of lessons learned there by the Army, Navy, and Marines were many and far-reaching.

Veterans of all ranks from all branches of the service came home to teach and spread the word while many more stayed on to temper the replacements coming out to the war. Barracks bull sessions and bivouac yarns added color and not a little weight to the formal periods of instruction. Thus was the myth that the Japanese were supermen shattered, and the bits of combat lore or the legendary tall tales and true which begin, "Now, on the 'Canal . . ." still have not entirely disappeared from the Marine repertoire.

General Vandegrift summed it up in a special introduction to *The Guadalcanal Campaign*, the historical monograph which contains the Marine Corps' first study of the operation:

> We struck at Guadalcanal to halt the advance of the Japanese. We did not know how strong he was, nor did we know his plans. We knew only that he was moving down the island chain and that he had to be stopped.
>
> We were as well trained and as well armed as time and our peacetime experience allowed us to be. We needed combat to tell us how effective our training, our doctrines, and our weapons had been.
>
> We tested them against the enemy, and we found that they worked. From that moment in 1942, the tide turned, and the Japanese never again advanced.

Likewise, Guadalcanal was more than just another battle for the Japanese, but the lesson they learned there was a bitter one. The occupation which they started almost on a whim had ended in disaster, and from this they never quite recovered. Captain Ohmae summed it up:

> . . . when the war started, it was not planned to take the Solomons. However, the early actions were so easy that it was decided to increase the perimeter defense line and to gain a position which would control American traffic to Australia. Expansion into the Solomons from Rabaul was then carried out. Unfortunately, we also carried out the expansion at the same time instead of consolidating our holdings in that area. After you captured Guadalcanal, we still thought that we would be able to retake it and use it as an outpost for the defense of the empire. This effort was very costly, both at the time and in later operations, because we were never able to recover from the ship and pilot losses received in that area.[12]

Unfortunately for the Japanese there were very few lessons from Guadalcanal that they could put to effective use. In a sense this was phase one of their final examination, the beginning of a series of tests for the military force which had conquered the Oriental side of the Pacific, and they failed it. After this there was neither time nor means for another semester of study and preparation. Admiral Tanaka had this to say about the operation and its significance:

> Operations to reinforce Guadalcanal extended over a period of more than five months. They amounted to a losing war of attrition in which Japan suffered heavily in and around that island . . . There is no question that Japan's doom was sealed with the closing of the struggle for Guadalcanal. Just as it betokened the military character and strength of her opponent, so it presaged Japan's weakness and lack of planning that would spell her defeat.[13]

The Allies entered this first lesson with sound textbooks. In the field of amphibious warfare, Marine doctrine hammered out in the peacetime laboratory now could be polished and improved in practice and supported by a rapidly mobilizing industrial front at home. Modern equipment which everybody knew was needed began to flow out to the test of combat. There

---

[12] *Ohmae Interrogation*, 474.
[13] *Tanaka Article*, II, 831.

it took on refinements and practical modifications, as doctrines and techniques improved. New models continued to arrive and were quickly put to use in the hands of now-skilled fighting men.

For example, landing craft which went into mass production aided the tactical aspects of amphibious assaults and also lessened the logistical problems at the beachhead. Improved communications equipment made it possible for the Marine Corps to improve and make more effective many of the special organizations and operational techniques which previously had been little more than carefully-sketched theory. Air and naval gunfire liaison parties experimented with on Guadalcanal later became the efficient tools of integrated warfare that Marines had been confident they could become. Improved equipment brought improved technique, and thus began a continuous cycle of increasing efficiency which made the final amphibious assaults by cooperating U. S. forces at Iwo Jima and Okinawa remarkable models of military precision.

This strength of new equipment and ability enabled the Allies to take command of the strategy in a contest in which the enemy had been able to set his men for a checkmate before the contest began. The psychology of total war found expression for the front-line Marine in his observation that "the only good Jap is a dead one." But an even better one was the one bypassed and left to ineffective existence on an island in the rear areas: he cost the Allies less. Strength gave the Allies this capability to bypass many garrisons.

Likewise Guadalcanal proved that it often was cheaper and easier to build a new airfield than to capture and then improve one the Japanese had built or were building. This coincided well with the basic amphibious doctrine long agreed upon: never hit a defended beach if the objective can be reached over an undefended one. Together these principles sometimes made it possible for the Allies to land on an enemy island and build an airfield some distance from the hostile garrison. This the Marines did in November 1943, at Bougainville. A perimeter was established around the airfield, and there defenders sat waiting for the Japanese to do the hard work of marching over difficult terrain to present themselves for a battle if they so desired. It was a premeditated repeat of the Guadalcanal tactic, and when the Japanese obliged by so accepting it, they were defeated.

All services, units and men in the Pacific, or slated to go there, were eager to learn the valuable lessons of early combat and to put them into practice. For the Marine Corps, an important factor in the continuing success of the advance across the Pacific was the delineation of command responsibilities between the naval task force commander and the amphibious troop commander.

Late in this first offensive General Vandegrift was able to initiate an important change in naval thinking concerning the command of amphibious operations. The general and Admiral Turner had often disagreed on the conduct of activities ashore on Guadalcanal, and Vandegrift had maintained that the commander trained for ground operations should not be a subordinate of the local naval amphibious force commander. His theory prevailed, and in the future the amphibious troops commander, once established ashore, would be on the same command level as the naval task force commander. Both of them would be responsible to a common superior.

With this point cleared, and with the valuable lessons of Guadalcanal combat a part of his personal experience and knowledge, Vandegrift as a lieutenant general became commander of the I Marine Amphibious Corps in the fall of 1943 and was able to guide an ever-expanding fighting force already involved in new actions in the Solomons. Later, on 10 November 1943, he left the Pacific to become the eighteenth Commandant of the Marine Corps.

The cost of Guadalcanal was not as great as some later operations. Total Army and Marine casualties within the ground forces amounted to 1,598 men and officers killed and 4,709 wounded. Marines of the ground forces killed or dead from wounds numbered 1,152; and 2,799 were wounded and 55 listed as missing. In addition 55 individuals from Marine aviation units were killed or died of wounds while 127 were wounded and 85 missing.[13] Defeat for the Japanese was more costly. Although some 13,000 enemy soldiers were evacuated from Guadalcanal for new defensive positions farther north, more personnel than this had lost their lives on the island. Japanese sources list approximately 14,800 killed or missing in action while 9,000 died of wounds and disease. Some 1,000 enemy troops were taken prisoner. More than 600 enemy planes and pilots also were lost.

Combat shipping losses were about even for the two opponents. The Allies and the Japanese each lost 24 fighting ships, with the loss amounting to 126,240 tons for the Allies and 134,839 tons for the Japanese.

There would be bigger battles later. There would be tiny atolls for which the Japanese would demand higher prices on shorter terms. And far away to the north a dead volcano waited to be the backdrop of a photograph which would become the symbol of the entire island war ahead. But nothing could take from Guadalcanal its unique spot in history. The first step, however short and faltering, is always the most important.

---

[13] A tabulation of Marine casualties appears in Appendix D.

APPENDIX A

Bibliographical Notes

This history is based principally on official Marine Corps records: the reports, diaries, orders, etc., of the units or activities involved in the specific operations described. Records of the other armed services have been consulted where pertinent. On matters pertaining to operations at high strategic level, the authors have drawn on the records of the U. S. Joint Chiefs of Staff (JCS).

Because this volume spans a considerable period of time and deals with a wide variety of activities, the same records seldom overlap from one part of the book to another. These are fully cited in the text and will be discussed separately as applicable to specific parts. Except as otherwise noted such records are on file at, or obtainable through, the Records and Research Section, Historical Branch, G-3, Headquarters, U. S. Marine Corps.

There are, however, a number of published works of general interest more widely cited throughout this volume. The more important of these are listed below.

Books

Jeter A. Isely and Philip A. Crowl, *The U. S. Marines and Amphibious War*. Princeton: Princeton University Press, 1951. This deals with the evolution of amphibious doctrines, tactics, and materiel and their application in the Pacific. This excellent study was undertaken by the history faculty of Princeton University at the behest of the Marine Corps. In no sense an official history, the conclusions it contains were arrived at independently by the authors and researchers who compiled it.

Samuel Eliot Morison, *History of United States Naval Operations in World War II*, Volumes III, IV, V. Boston: Little, Brown and Company, 1948, 1949, 1950. The volumes cited bear the individual titles: *The Rising Sun in the Pacific; Coral Sea, Midway and Submarine Actions;* and *The Struggle for Guadalcanal.* Although he disclaims his work as official, Rear Admiral Morison (USNR, Retired) undertook the monumental project on naval order and has carried it through with all possible support of the Navy. The author ranks as one of our leading writers and historians, and the whole series is highly readable and reliable. A few minor errors of fact that crept into the first editions are being corrected in subsequent printings.

Robert Sherrod, *History of Marine Corps Aviation in World War II*. Washington: Combat Forces Press, 1952. This is another unofficial history undertaken at the request, and with the support, of the Marine Corps. The title is self-explanatory, but the author gives some account of the earlier days of Marine Corps Aviation. It is by far the most comprehensive treatment of this subject now in existence.

E. B. Potter (Editor), *The United States and World Sea Power*. New York: Prentice-Hall, Inc., 1955. This large (963 pages) single-volume history is the work of twelve faculty members of the Department of English, History and Government, U. S. Naval Academy. It is extremely comprehensive in scope, covering naval history from ancient operations to today. As a result comparatively few of its chapters are applicable to Marine Corps operations in World War II. It furnished the authors of this book, however, much valuable background.

Ernest J. King and Walter Muir Whitehill, *Fleet Admiral King: A Naval Record*. New York: W. W. Norton & Co., Inc., 1952. This somewhat heavy-handed tome sheds many interesting sidelights on high-level decisions and how they were arrived at.

William F. Halsey and J. Bryan, III, *Admiral Halsey's Story*. New York: McGraw-Hill Book Company, Inc., 1947. This popular treatment of one of the most spectacular figures in the Pacific war presents eyewitness descriptions of many striking and important events.

Masuo Kato, *The Lost War*. New York: A. A. Knopf, 1946. Kato, a Japanese news correspondent in Washington at the time of Pearl Harbor, was interned and then repatriated in the civilian exchange ship. He understands thoroughly both Japanese and U. S. points of view. His "inside story" presents vividly political, military, and civilian conditions in Japan as the war developed and sheds much light on why they developed as they did on the enemy's side.

United States Strategic Bombing Survey, *The Campaigns of the Pacific War.* Washington: U. S. Government Printing Office, 1946. This is a report of USSBS (Pacific) Naval Analysis Division. It attempts to present the broad picture of the war through brief descriptions of the various campaigns, but unfortunately was prepared too soon after the event to gain deep perspective. The text contains many factual inaccuracies. This book is of great value, however, in presenting translations of many enemy documents that reveal Japanese wartime thinking.

United States Strategic Bombing Survey, *Interrogations of Japanese Officials,* 2 vols. Washington: U. S. Government Printing Office, 1946. This is a companion report to *Campaigns* (above) and similarly is of value in telling the Japanese side of the story.

Part I

INTRODUCTION TO THE MARINE CORPS

Official Documents

Annual Reports of the Commandant of the Marine Corps constitute the basic primary source relied upon in tracing the growth and development of the Marine Corps throughout the period under consideration. These are supplemented by pertinent reports at lower levels, as indicated in the text. More detailed breakdown of personnel statistics derives from study of contemporary muster rolls.

In dealing with the evolution of amphibious doctrine Marine Corps and Navy manuals pertaining to landing operations, issued during the period under discussion, are the principal sources. Files of Headquarters Marine Corps have been consulted in tracing the origin and development of the Fleet Marine Force. These files, together with those of the Navy Department Bureau of Ships and Senate Report No. 10, Part 16, 78th Congress, 2d Session, *Additional Report of the Special Committee Investigating the National Defense Program,* form the basis for the discussion of the development of landing craft and amphibious vehicles.

The reports of the units assigned to the Iceland occupation force, supplemented by command correspondence files, provided the thread of the narrative. Especially valuable are the official letters written by General Marston to various officers at Headquarters Marine Corps giving his personal and professional commentary on the operation.

Unofficial Sources

Letters of comment on draft manuscripts, interviews, and in the case of the Iceland operation, the extensive notes, correspondence, and draft narratives of Lieutenant Colonel John L. Zimmerman, have supplemented official material. Especially useful in providing background information on the amphibious tractor was an interview with Lieutenant Colonel Ernest E. Linsert, a participant in most of the initial stages of its development.

It was permissible to keep a diary in an overseas theatre for the first few months of the war; there was no prohibition, naturally, against the keeping of diaries in peacetime. General Oliver P. Smith, who served as battalion commander of 1/6 throughout the Iceland occupation, kept such a diary and made a copy of it available to the Historical Branch, G-3, Headquarters Marine Corps. The diary is doubly valuable because General Smith has included extensive comments elaborating on the necessarily brief daily entries. The resulting 132-page typescript goes far toward giving the reader the on-the-spot "feel" of the operation.

Books and Periodicals

William H. Russell, "Genesis of FMF Doctrine: 1879–1898," *Marine Corps Gazette,* April–July 1951. In this four-part article, Professor Russell of the Naval Academy discusses the earliest recorded debates within the naval establishment on the amphibious problems which developed following the Navy's transition from sail to steam.

General Holland M. Smith, "Development of Amphibious Tactics in the U. S. Navy," *Marine*

BIBLIOGRAPHICAL NOTES

Corps Gazette, June–October 1948. General Smith probably contributed more than any single individual to the developments which he discusses in this authoritative five-part article.

John H. Russell, Jr., "Birth of the Fleet Marine Force," *U. S. Naval Institute Proceedings*, January 1946. As Assistant Commandant, General Russell conceived the FMF essentially as it exists today; as Commandant, he guided it through its early formative years.

Holland M. Smith and Percy Finch, *Coral and Brass*. New York: Charles Scribner's Sons, 1949. In this autobiographical volume, General Smith touches again on the early struggles dealt with in his *Gazette* series and carries the story through the Pacific war.

Major General John A. Lejeune, "The United States Marine Corps," *Marine Corps Gazette*, December 1923. In this article, General Lejeune, then Commandant of the Marine Corps, expresses the prevailing Marine Corps thought on advance base operations.

Brigadier General Dion Williams, "Blue Marine Corps Expeditionary Force," *Marine Corps Gazette*, September 1925. In this article, General Williams discusses the Army-Navy amphibious maneuver held in Hawaiian waters in 1925.

Lieutenant Colonel Victor J. Croizat, "The Marines' Amphibian," *Marine Corps Gazette*, June 1953. Lieutenant Colonel Croizat, in this article, relates the story of the amphibian tractor.

Stetson Conn and Byron Fairchild, "The Framework of Hemisphere Defense," MS of a forthcoming volume in the series, *United States Army in World War II*, has been most useful in presenting the Army's viewpoint of the problems presented by the Iceland operation. Dr. Fairchild also made available the final draft manuscripts of several chapters he wrote for a further OCMH volume on Army operations in the Eastern Atlantic (as yet untitled) which detail the progress of the occupation and examine Iceland's peculiar command situation.

Part II

WAR COMES

Official Documents

Reports of the units involved, as cited in the text, form the basis of the narrative of Marine garrison activities in Samoa and the 14th Naval District. All Marine records on Guam were either destroyed or captured and the reconstruction of the action on 8–10 December is largely taken from the post-captivity report of the island's governor.

The primary source of information on the actions of the United States and Japan in the period immediately before, during, and just after the Japanese raid on Pearl is Senate Document No. 244, 79th Congress, *Report of the Joint Committee on the Investigation of the Pearl Harbor Attack*. In addition to the basic report of the findings of the committee, there are 39 volumes of hearings, testimony, and exhibits which touch on every facet of the story. The record of the hearings and the appended documents constitute a unique 10,000,000-word examination of a military disaster.

Unofficial Documents

Unofficial reports, personal letters, notes and interviews of numerous individuals, and on occasion unpublished manuscripts, have been drawn upon to supplement official material where pertinent. An especially valuable source of information has been the comments of key participants in the actions described who reviewed draft manuscripts of this history as well as drafts of previous campaign monographs. Unofficial comment of this type, as cited in the text, has been especially helpful in developing a fuller story of the initial action at Midway.

Books and Periodicals

In dealing with the broader aspects of the war and decisions and events on a high strategic plane, two volumes of the Army's official history *United States Army in World War II* have been most useful. They present a lucid account of thought and planning at Chief of Staff level with very detailed citation of sources consulted:

Mark S. Watson, *Chief of Staff: Prewar Plans and Preparations*. Washington: Historical Division, Department of the Army, 1950.

Maurice Matloff and Edwin M. Snell, *Strategic Planning for Coalition Warfare 1941–1942*. Washington: Office of the Chief of Military History, Department of the Army, 1953.

Major O. R. Lodge, *The Recapture of Guam*. Washington: Historical Branch, G-3 Division,

Headquarters Marine Corps, 1954. While this monograph is primarily concerned with the operations on Guam in the summer of 1944, it does include a narrative of the Japanese capture of the island which is the basis for this volume's story.

Thomas Wilds, "The Japanese Seizure of Guam," *Marine Corps Gazette*, July 1955. This article by an accomplished Japanese translator is the only published narrative taken from enemy sources of the capture of the island and is essential to a clear picture of the operation.

PART III

DEFENSE OF WAKE

Official Documents

Official records pertaining to the defense of Wake ceased to exist with the atoll's capture by the Japanese, save for the dispatches which got through to Pearl Harbor and the reports carried out by Major Bayler several days prior to the final struggle, as related in the narrative.

Upon his return after release from Japanese prison camp, Colonel Devereux requested each of his surviving officers to submit to him an informal report concerning his part in the operation. From study of the material thus obtained and the promptings of his own memory, Devereux then prepared his official report for submission to the Commandant of the Marine Corps. Colonel Paul A. Putnam submitted a similar report as CO of VMF-211. These comprise the basic sources from which the version of the operation contained herein derives.

Unofficial Documents

Eighteen officers submitted informal reports to Colonel Devereux, and six of these later filled out a special questionnaire prepared by the Historical Branch. These papers, together with copies of pertinent correspondence and notes and transcriptions of interviews with individuals, are on file in Marine Corps Archives.

Books and Periodicals

The defense of Wake figures more or less incidentally in all of the works of general interest previously described. But comparatively little has been published about the details of the operation itself. Since it was so narrowly a Marine action, the other services have shown little interest in studying it, and within the Corps few remain who know much about it. The following works, however, are deemed worthy of mention:

Lieutenant Colonel Robert D. Heinl, Jr., *The Defense of Wake*. Washington: Historical Section, Division of Public Information, Headquarters Marine Corps, 1947. This is the official Marine Corps historical monograph from which the version in this book has been adapted.

James P. S. Devereux, *The Story of Wake Island*. Philadelphia: J. B. Lippincott Company, 1947. This work prepared by the commander of the Wake defense with some professional literary assistance does not pretend to be a history, but it does contain a number of human interest sidelights not found elsewhere.

Lieutenant Colonel Walter L. J. Bayler, *Last Man off Wake Island*. Indianapolis: Bobbs-Merrill Company, 1943. This book was rushed to publication to shed timely light on an event currently before the public eye. Memories of the events during his stay on Wake were still fresh in Colonel Bayler's mind at the time of writing; but, of course, he did not see the final battle.

Lieutenant Colonel Robert D. Heinl, Jr., "We're Headed for Wake," *Marine Corps Gazette*, June 1946. Lieutenant Colonel Heinl, then a first lieutenant, was a member of the abortive relief expedition and here gives a full account of that little understood event from the point of view of those engaged in it.

PART IV

MARINES IN THE PHILIPPINES

Official Documents

Just before the fall of Corregidor an American submarine took off a load of escapees and a scant haul of the records of units that had fought the Japanese on Luzon. Fortunately, these records included the daily journals of the 4th Marines operations and intelligence sections plus a very few other papers and reports, mostly interleaved in the journal copy books. For some reason, not now known, this contemporary material has been ignored until the writing of this volume. In the few previous accounts which mention Marine action in the Philippines, there are a number of direct contradictions to the entries in these journals. None of these errors are particularly serious, however, and where it was possible they have been corrected in this version of the action.

A number of the official reports cited, including that of the 4th Marines, were drawn up long after the events they describe by participants who survived captivity. The details of these reports are somewhat suspect since the accounts are distillations of memory, carefully hidden notes, and those few official papers of the period that were available when the reports were prepared. It is not difficult to find minor errors in these reports, but on the whole they are quite valuable.

The cited narratives compiled by Admirals Hart and Rockwell, together with their supplementary postwar comments on naval activities in Asiatic waters, have been very helpful in establishing the background of the Navy and Marine Corps contribution to the defense of the Philippines.

Unofficial Documents

A number of undated informal reports submitted by survivors of the 4th Marines, presumably written right after the war, form the largest body of information about the Marine part in the Philippines operation. These reports are frequently cited in the text. Of almost equal importance are the letters of comment received from over 25 survivors who read the preliminary draft of this part. These men were able to clear up many puzzling matters of command relationship and small unit action that were left unanswered in official documents and the personal accounts mentioned above. The narrative of the fighting in the East Sector on Corregidor is drawn in large part from these letters and unofficial reports.

A Marine reserve officer, Captain Grant J. Berry, has compiled an interesting story of the 4th Marines in the Philippines, much of it based upon correspondence with survivors. He used this material to write his master's thesis at the University of California in 1951. A copy of the thesis and a portion of his correspondence with former members of the 4th Marines is on file in the Marine Corps Archives.

Japanese Sources

Following the close of the war, the U. S. Army's Historical Section, G-2, General Headquarters, Far East Command, sponsored and directed the preparation of a series of monographs entitled *Japanese Studies in World War II*. These were prepared by Japanese commanders and staff officers who had participated in the various Pacific campaigns; and they were compiled from reports, notes, and consultation with key survivors. These translated studies have been checked carefully against all other available sources and found to be remarkably accurate. In the case of the early Philippines campaign several of these monographs have been consulted and the two-volume study of Fourteenth Army operations has been used frequently to give the enemy viewpoint. This particular monograph is very uneven in quality but it includes a wealth of information available nowhere else.

Books and Periodicals

Louis Morton, *The Fall of the Philippines*, Washington: Office of the Chief of Military History, Department of the Army, 1953. Dr. Morton's book, is another of the volumes of the *United States Army in World War II* series. It presents what is easily the most comprehensive and thorough treatment of this subject yet to appear in print.

Wesley F. Craven and James L. Cate (Editors), *Plans and Early Operations, January 1939 to August 1942—The Army Air Forces in World War II*. Chicago: University of Chicago Press, 1948. This is the first of a series of official histories, subsequent volumes of which will be cited throughout this history when Army air operations have a bearing on the narrative of Marine action.

General Jonathan C. Wainwright, *General Wainwright's Story*, Robert Considine (Editor). Garden City, N. Y.: Doubleday and Company, Inc., 1946. Although much of this book is devoted to General Wainwright's experiences as a Japanese prisoner, the early portions shed some interesting first-hand sidelights on the fighting on Bataan and Corregidor.

Kazumaro Uno, *Corregidor: Isle of Delusion*, Shanghai: Press Bureau of the Imperial Japanese Army Headquarters in China, 1942. This propaganda booklet, printed in English, contains a number of second-hand accounts of enemy experiences in the seizure of Corregidor. The book has been used principally to give personality to the enemy side of the action. A photostatic copy of this book is held by the Office of the Chief of Military History.

Hanson W. Baldwin, "The 4th Marines at Corregidor," *Marine Corps Gazette*, November 1946–February 1947. One of today's leading analysts and writers on military subjects carefully combed the 4th Marines' report, the personal narratives of survivors mentioned above, and consulted numerous individual participants in compiling his detailed four-part article on the stand of the regiment on Corregidor. The primary fault of the study is that it failed to utilize the existing 4th Marine journals and therefore has perpetuated a number of minor errors regarding the combat organization and strength of the regiment.

First Lieutenant William F. Hogaboom, "Action Report—Bataan," *Marine Corps Gazette*, April 1946. Lieutenant Hogaboom died while he was a prisoner of war but his narrative, secretly compiled during captivity, survived him and was published under this title. Hogaboom participated in both of the major Marine actions in the Philippines, Longoskawayan Point and Corregidor's defense.

Lieutenant Colonel William F. Prickett, "Naval Battalion at Mariveles," *Marine Corps Gazette*, June 1950. This article by a survivor of 3/4 who talked to many participants in the Longoskawayan action disagrees in some few respects with the official version of this action given in Commander Bridget's report. Prickett's story is in much more detail, however, than any official history, and well worth reading.

Part V

DECISION AT MIDWAY

Official Documents

This account of Marine activities on Midway is based mainly on the reports and diaries of the units participating: the 6th Defense Battalion and MAG–22. Also consulted were reports, plans, and official correspondence at higher levels: CinCPac, Commandant Fourteenth Naval District, etc., some of which are cited in the text.

Unofficial Documents

In course of preparation of the historical monograph on which this account is mainly based, Lieutenant Colonel Robert D. Heinl, Jr., carried on extensive correspondence with individuals who held key positions on Midway before and during the attack. Many of these he interviewed personally. Some of this documentation is cited in the text; much more, of incidental interest, is on file in Marine Corps Archives.

Books and Periodicals

As with preceding descriptions of naval operations, the previously cited sources have been relied on. In addition, the following works have been extensively consulted and used for this part:

Lieutenant Colonel Robert D. Heinl, Jr., *Marines at Midway*. Washington: Historical Section, Division of Public Information, Headquarters Marine Corps, 1948. This is the historical monograph which, much-edited and re-worked, forms the foundation for the present account.

M. Fuchida and M. Okumiya, *Midway: The Battle that Doomed Japan*. Annapolis: U. S. Naval Institute, 1955. This is an excellent account of the battle from the Japanese side of the action.

Vice Admiral Chuichi Nagumo, IJN, "Action Report by C-in-C of the First Air Fleet," *ONI Review*, May 1947. This article is simply a translation of what must stand as one of the most revealing documents obtained from the Japanese following the war. It is Admiral Nagumo's official report of the debacle in which he played the leading part. It is frank and factual to a surprising degree, and detailed to the extent of including charts showing the exact location of each bomb hit on each of the four carriers destroyed. It also includes a chronological log of all messages sent and received during the entire period of the approach, action, and withdrawal.

Part VI

GUADALCANAL

Official Documents

In coverage of the strategic planning for Guadalcanal this text cites much official correspondence and planning at top level. The correspondence between Admiral King and General Marshall was obtained from the Naval History Division; material pertaining to the Joint Chiefs of Staff was furnished by the Office of the Chief of Military History, Department of the Army.

As in all operations discussed in this history, those in Part VI are based on the reports of the units concerned. These include action reports, war diaries, etc., of tactical units, and the journals of the various staff sections. At this stage of the war, however, Marines were less experienced in preparing reports than they became later. Command and staff personnel believed fighting to be more important than writing. Thus the documentation on many phases of early operations is fragmentary and incomplete. The 1st Marine Division's "Final Report on the Guadalcanal Operation" was not compiled until several months after the campaign, although much of the material it contains was prepared on the scene.

The Army and Navy were little better than the Marine Corps in this respect; their official documentation also leaves much to be desired. Generally speaking, the records of reporting units are in the custody of the service to which they belong.

Unofficial Documents

In the course of preparing the Marine Corps preliminary monograph on Guadalcanal, Major John L. Zimmerman circulated copies of his preliminary draft among many individuals who participated in that operation. These elicited many factual corrections and cogent comments which are included in the text. He also interviewed some of these officers. Notes or transcriptions of these interviews, together with all pertinent correspondence, are available through Marine Corps Archives.

Books and Periodicals

As the first protracted ground operation of the war, Guadalcanal elicited a spate of published material. Much of this was journalistic in nature; but in addition to these works of general interest, the following apply more narrowly to the historical examination of the campaign:

Major John L. Zimmerman, *The Guadalcanal Campaign*. Washington: Historical Division, Headquarters Marine Corps, 1949. This is the Marine Corps' preliminary study which serves as the groundwork for the present, completely revised and much more complete, account of the battle.

John Miller, Jr., *Guadalcanal: The First Offensive*. Washington: Historical Division, Department of the Army, 1949. This excellent volume is one in the series *United States Army in World War II*, and it has been relied on for much of the interpretation of material pertaining to Army command and operations of Army units.

Wesley F. Craven and James L. Cate (Editors), *The Pacific: Guadalcanal to Saipan*. Chicago: University of Chicago Press, 1950. Volume IV of the series *The Army Air Forces in World War II*, this deals in greater detail with aviation operations than is practical in a general history of the campaign.

Herbert L. Merillat, *The Island*. Boston: Houghton Mifflin Company, 1944. The author participated in operations on Guadalcanal and writes at first hand, and with much human interest, of what he and his fellow Marines experienced there.

Eric A. Feldt, *The Coastwatchers*. New York: Oxford University Press, 1946. Commander Feldt, RAN, organized and commanded that hardy band of rugged individualists who lurked in the jungle behind the Japanese lines and radioed out invaluable information to the Allied forces. Here he tells for the first time the story which was top secret during the war.

Many articles in periodicals were likewise journalistic in nature. They provide valuable sources for information which helps fill the gaps of the official accounts, however, and they have been cited where used in the text. One article bears special mention:

Vice Admiral R. Tanaka with R. Pineau, "Japan's Losing Struggle for Guadalcanal," two parts, *USNI Proceedings*, July and August 1956. This excellent article sheds much light on the Japanese side of the Guadalcanal operation, particularly on the dramatic comings and goings of the Tokyo Express, those determined destroyers and cruisers which guarded the convoys shuttling supplies and reinforcements from Rabaul and the Shortlands to Guadalcanal. With the kind permission of the *Proceedings*, this volume quotes many passages from this article.

APPENDIX B

Chronology

The following listing of events is limited to those coming within the scope of this book, and those forecasting events to be treated in the volumes to follow.

10 November 1775	Continental Congress authorizes raising of two battalions of Marines.
11 July 1798	Congress reactivates Marine Corps.
10 June 1898	Battalion of Marines seizes Guantanamo Bay; preliminary thinking on Advanced Base concept begins.
10 December 1898	Spain cedes Philippines, Guam, and Puerto Rico to U. S.
13 July 1910	Marine School for Advanced Base Training established.
25 April 1915	First modern amphibious assault: British land on Gallipoli.
27 April 1917	First Marine aviation unit formed: "Marine Aeronautic Company, Advanced Base Force."
28 June 1919	Treaty of Versailles gives Japan mandates for German islands in Central Pacific.
23 July 1921	"Operations Plan 712" accepted by Major General Commandant, establishing Marine Corps concept of strategy in the Pacific.
7 December 1933	Fleet Marine Force established.
15 January 1934	*Tentative Manual for Landing Operations* published.
1 September 1939	Germans invade Poland; World War II begins.

1940

7 May	Pacific Fleet ordered by President to remain indefinitely in Hawaiian waters.
5 July	Export Control Act invoked against Japan to prohibit exportation of strategic materials and equipment.
19 July	President signs Naval Expansion Act containing provisions for "Two Ocean Navy."
29 September	Midway Detachment, FMF arrives at Midway.
8 October	U. S. advises its citizens to leave Far East.

1941

12 May	Ambassador Nomura of Japan presents Secretary of State Cordell Hull with Japanese proposal for a "just peace in the Pacific."
27 May	President declares a state of unlimited emergency; he announces that the Atlantic Neutrality Patrol is extended and that Pacific Fleet units have been transferred to the Atlantic.
12 June	All Naval Reserve personnel not in deferred status are called to active duty.
22 June	Germany, Italy, and Romania declare war on Russia and invade along a front from the Arctic to the Black Sea.

CHRONOLOGY

7 July	1st Marine Brigade lands in Iceland. 1st Marine Aircraft Wing forms at Quantico, Va.
10 July	2d Marine Aircraft Wing forms at San Diego, Calif.
15 August	Naval Air Station, Palmyra Island, and Naval Air Facility, Johnston Island, established.
11 September	President orders Navy to attack any vessel threatening U. S. shipping.
14 November	Marines are ordered to leave Shanghai, Peiping, and Tientsin, China.
20 November	Ambassador Nomura presents Japan's "final proposal" to keep peace in the Pacific.
26 November	Secretary of State submits final proposals for adjustment of U. S.-Japanese relations.
27 November	Adm Stark, CNO, sends war warning to commanders of the Pacific and Asiatic Fleets.
30 November	Japanese Foreign Minister Tojo rejects U. S. proposals for settling Far East crisis.
7 December	Japanese attack Pearl Harbor.
8 December	U. S. declares war on Japan. Japan attacks Allied bases in the Pacific and Far East, and lands on Batan Island north of Luzon, P. I., and on east coast of Malay Peninsula. U. S. Marines and other Allied nationals interned at Shanghai, Peiping, and Tientsin, China.
9 December	Japanese occupy Tarawa and Makin Islands in Gilberts.
10 December	Guam surrenders to Japanese landing force.
11 December	U. S. declares war on Germany and Italy. Wake Island defenders repulse Japanese landing attempt. Japanese make additional landings in Philippines.
20 December	Adm E. J. King becomes Commander in Chief, U. S. Fleet.
21 December	Naval defense forces in Philippine Islands move headquarters to Corregidor.
22 December	Japanese land at Lingayen Gulf, P. I.
23 December	Wake Island surrenders to Japanese.
25 December	British surrender Hong Kong.
26 December	Manila, P. I., declared an open city.
31 December	Adm C. W. Nimitz assumes command of Pacific Fleet at Pearl Harbor.

1942

2 January	Manila and Cavite, P. I., fall to Japanese.
11 January	Japanese begin invasion of Netherlands East Indies.
22 January	Allied forces evacuate Lae and Salamaua, New Guinea.
23 January	Japanese occupy Rabaul, New Britain, and land at Kieta on Bougainville in the Solomon Islands.
24 January	Japanese land at Kavieng, New Ireland.
1 February	U. S. carrier task forces raid Japanese positions in the Gilbert and Marshall Islands.

6 February	U. S. and Britain establish Combined Chiefs of Staff (CCS).
8 February	Japanese land at Gasmata, New Britain.
9 February	Japanese land at Singapore.
15 February	Singapore surrenders.
27 February	Battle of Java Sea.
1 March	Battle of Sunda Strait.
8 March	Japanese land at Lae and Salamaua, New Guinea.
9 March	Java surrenders to Japanese, ending conquest of Netherlands East Indies.
10 March	Japanese invade Finschhafen, New Guinea.
11 March	Gen MacArthur leaves Philippines for Australia.
12 March	U. S. forces arrive in New Caledonia.
26 March	Adm King relieves Adm Stark as Chief of Naval Operations.
29 March	Marines arrive at Efate, New Hebrides.
30 March	Pacific Ocean divided into Pacific Ocean Areas under Adm Nimitz, and Southwest Pacific Area under Gen MacArthur.
1 April	Japanese occupy Buka Island, Solomons.
5 April	Manus Island, Admiralties, occupied by Japanese.
9 April	Bataan falls to Japanese.
18 April	Doolittle raid strikes Tokyo, Yokosuka, Yokohama, Kobe, and Nagoya.
2 May	Japanese land on Florida Island, Solomons.
3 May	Japanese occupy Tulagi, Solomons.
4–8 May	Battle of the Coral Sea.
6 May	Corregidor and Manila Bay forts surrender.
12 May	Last U. S. troops in Philippines surrender on Mindanao.
28 May	U. S. forces arrive at Espiritu Santo, New Hebrides.
3 June	Japanese bomb Dutch Harbor; land on Kiska and Attu, Western Aleutians.
4–6 June	Battle of Midway.
14 June	First echelon of 1st MarDiv arrives at Wellington, New Zealand.
19 June	VAdm Ghormley assumes command of South Pacific Area and South Pacific Forces.
25 June	President Roosevelt and Prime Minister Churchill conclude conference in Washington; decision reached for combined efforts to develop atomic bomb.
18 July	Amphibious Force, South Pacific Area, is established under command of RAdm Turner.
21 July	Japanese land at Buna, New Guinea.
7 August	1st MarDiv lands on Florida, Tulagi, Gavutu, Tanambogo, and Guadalcanal in Southern Solomons to launch the first U. S. offensive of the war.
8 August	1st MarDiv wins control of Tulagi, Gavutu, Tanambogo and captures airfield on Guadalcanal.
9 August	Battle of Savo Island forces U. S. ships to retire from Guadalcanal area, leaving control of waters temporarily to Japanese.
17 August	2d Raider Battalion (Carlson's Raiders) land from submarines at Makin Island in the Gilberts. Raid is completed following day.

20 August	First fighter aircraft arrive on Henderson Field, Guadalcanal.
21 August	Marines turn back first major Japanese attack on Guadalcanal in Battle of the Tenaru.
24–25 August	Naval Battle of Eastern Solomons.
13 September	Marines repulse second major Japanese ground attack at Guadalcanal in the Battle of the Ridge.
18 September	7th Marines arrive on Guadalcanal.
11–12 October	Naval Battle of Cape Esperance. U. S. forces under Adm Spruance engage Japanese ships of the "Tokyo Express."
13 October	164th Infantry Regiment of Americal Division arrives to reinforce 1st MarDiv.
14 October	Japanese battleships and cruisers bombard Henderson Field.
18 October	VAdm Halsey relieves VAdm Ghormley as Commander South Pacific Area and South Pacific Force.
20–25 October	Marines and Army troops fight off heavy ground attacks of major Japanese counteroffensive.
26 October	Naval Battle of Santa Cruz Island. U. S. force sustains heavy loss, but checks Japanese movement toward Guadalcanal.
8 November	Allied Expeditionary Force invades North Africa.
12 November	Naval Battle of Guadalcanal (12–15 Nov) begins as Japanese aircraft attack U. S. transports off Guadalcanal.
13 November	RAdm Callaghan's task group of cruisers and destroyers engages Japanese raiding group including two battleships, in second night of Battle of Guadalcanal. U. S. force heavily damaged, but Japanese retire.
14 November	Japanese cruisers and destroyers bombard Henderson Field.
15 November	RAdm Lee with two battleships and four destroyers turns back large Japanese naval group to end naval Battle of Guadalcanal.
16 November	U. S. Army forces land south of Buna, New Guinea.
9 December	MajGen A. A. Vandegrift, CG 1st MarDiv, is relieved by MajGen A. M. Patch, CG Americal Division, as commanding general of Guadalcanal. 1st MarDiv makes preparations to retire from combat zone to rehabilitate and retrain.
17 December	U. S. Army forces begin attacks against Japanese in the Mount Austen area.
1943	
10 January	Gen Patch's XIV Corps on Guadalcanal begins offensive to the west.
23 January	XIV Corps' westward advance captures Kokumbona on Guadalcanal coast.
23 January	U. S.-Australian counteroffensive secures Buna-Sanananda area, New Guinea.
29–30 January	Naval Battle of Rennell Island.

1 February .... Japanese begin to evacuate troops from Guadalcanal.
8 February .... Evacuation of some 11,000 Japanese troops from Guadalcanal is completed.
9 February .... Gen Patch's Cape Esperance envelopment force joins with western advance and Guadalcanal is declared secure.

APPENDIX C

Marine Task Organization and Command List [1]

A. WAKE ATOLL (7–23 December 1941) [2]

MARINE DETACHMENT, WAKE

CO .... Maj James P. S. Devereux

1st Defense Battalion Detachment

CO .... Maj James P. S. Devereux

5-Inch Artillery Group

CO	Maj George H. Potter
Btry A	1stLt Clarence A. Barninger
Btry B	1stLt Woodrow W. Kessler
Btry L	2dLt John A. McAlister

3-Inch Antiaircraft Group

CO	Capt Bryghte D. Godbold
Btry D	Capt Bryghte D. Godbold
Btry E	1stLt William W. Lewis
Btry F (Prov)	MG Clarence B. McKinstry

Separate Batteries

Btry G	Capt Wesley McC. Platt
Btry H	2dLt Robert M. Hanna
Btry I	2dLt Arthur A. Poindexter

Marine Fighter Squadron 211

CO .... Maj Paul A. Putnam

---

[1] Unless otherwise noted names, positions held, organization titles, and periods of service were taken from the muster rolls of the units concerned held in the Diary Unit, FilesSec, RecsBr, PersDept, HQMC. Officers are shown in the highest rank held during the period that they were assigned to the positions indicated.

[2] Because of the incomplete nature of the muster rolls of the Wake Detachment, reference has been made to research conducted by LtCol R. D. Heinl for *The Defense of Wake* (Washington: Government Printing Office, 1947) in order to complete this listing.

B. PHILIPPINE ISLANDS (7 December 1941–6 May 1942) [3]

4TH MARINES (REINFORCED)

CO	Col Samuel L. Howard
ExO	Col Donald Curtis
R-1	Capt Robert B. Moore
R-2	1stLt Robert F. Ruge (To 24Dec)
	LtCol George D. Hamilton (From 25Dec)
R-3	Maj Frank P. Pyzick
R-4	Maj Reginald H. Ridgely, Jr. (To 3Jan)
	Maj Carl W. Meigs (From 4Jan)
HqCo	Capt Robert Chambers, Jr. (WIA 6May)
SerCo	Maj Max W. Schaeffer (WIA 6May)

1st Battalion, 4th Marines

CO	LtCol Curtis T. Beecher
ExO	LtCol Samuel W. Freeny (WIA 29Apr)
Bn-1	Capt Golland L. Clark, Jr.
Bn-2	Capt Golland L. Clark, Jr.
Bn-3	LtCol Samuel W. Freeny (WIA 29Apr)
Bn-4	1stLt Ralph R. Penick
HqCo	1stLt Golland L. Clark, Jr. (To 25Dec)
	Capt Lewis H. Pickup (From 26Dec)
A Co	Maj Harry C. Lang (KIA 5May)
	Capt Lewis H. Pickup (From 5May)

---

[3] After 28Feb42, no muster rolls reached HQMC from the 4th Mar and information presented after that period was taken from the comments of survivors on draft listings and the few existing records of the regiment's actions on Corregidor.

B Co — Capt Paul A. Brown (WIA 4May)
    1stLt Allan S. Manning (Actg From 5May)
D Co — Capt Noel O. Castle (KIA 6May)
BnResCo — 1stLt Robert F. Jenkins, Jr.

2nd Battalion, 4th Marines

CO — LtCol Herman R. Anderson
ExO — Maj John J. Heil
Bn-1 — 1stLt Hugh R. Nutter (To 28Dec)
    Capt Lloyd E. Wagner (From 29Dec)
Bn-2 — 1stLt Hugh R. Nutter (To 28Dec)
    Capt Lloyd E. Wagner (29Dec–6Jan)
    1stLt Sidney F. Jenkins (From 7Jan)
Bn-3 — Maj John J. Heil
Bn-4 — Capt Austin C. Shofner
HqCo — 1stLt Austin C. Shofner (to 4Jan)
    Capt Lloyd E. Wagner (From 5Jan)
E Co — Maj James V. Bradley, Jr.
F Co — Capt Lloyd E. Wagner (To 28Dec)
    Capt Clyde R. Huddleson (From 29Dec)
H Co — Capt Benjamin L. McMakin (WIA 26Mar)
BnRes Co — Capt Austin C. Shofner

3d Battalion, 4th Marines

CO — LtCol John P. Adams
ExO — Maj Andrew J. Mathiesen
Bn-1 — Capt George R. Weeks (To 31Dec)
    Capt John W. Clark (From 1Jan)
Bn-2 — Capt William F. Prickett
Bn-3 — Maj Andrew J. Mathiesen
Bn-4 — Maj Carl W. Meigs (To 4Jan)
    Capt Roy L. Robinton (From 5Jan)
HqCo — Capt George R. Weeks (To 31Dec)
    Capt John W. Clark (From 1Jan)

I Co — Maj Max Clark (WIA 24Apr, 29Apr)
K Co — Capt John W. Clark (To 31Dec)
    Maj George R. Weeks (From 1Jan)
L Co — 2dLt Willard D. Holdredge (To 23Dec)
    1stLt Howard L. Davis (24–31Dec)
    Capt Willis T. Geisman (From 1Jan, WIA 20Apr)
M Co — Capt Ted E. Pulos
BnResCo — 1stLt Clarence E. Van Ray

4th Battalion (Provisional), 4th Marines

CO — Maj Francis H. Williams (WIA 29Apr, 6May)
Bn-1 — Capt Calvin E. Chunn, USA (WIA 6May)
Bn-2 — Capt Calvin E. Chunn, USA (WIA 6May)
Bn-3 — 1stLt Otis E. Saalman, USA
Bn-4 — Ens John McClure, USNR (WIA 6May)
Q Co — Capt Paul E. Moore, USA
R Co — Capt Harold E. Dalness, USA
S Co — Lt Edward N. Little, USN (WIA 6May)
    1stLt Otis E. Saalman, USA (From 6May)
T Co — Lt Bethel B. Otter, USN (KIA 6May)
    Capt Calvin E. Chunn, USA (From 6May, WIA 6May)

Regimental Reserve

CO — Maj Stuart W. King (To 17Feb)
    Maj Max W. Schaeffer (From 18Feb, WIA 6May)
O Co — Capt Robert Chambers, Jr. (WIA 6May)
P Co — 1stLt William F. Hogaboom

C. MIDWAY ISLANDS (4–5 June 1942)

6TH DEFENSE BATTALION (REINFORCED)

CO — Col Harold D. Shannon
H&S Btry — Capt William P. Spenser

MARINE TASK ORGANIZATION AND COMMAND LIST

22d ProvMarCo... 1stLt George E. Metzenthin
23d ProvMarCo... Capt Boyd O. Whitney

5-Inch Artillery Group

CO	LtCol Lewis A. Hohn
H&S Btry	LtCol Lewis A. Hohn
Btry A	Maj Loren S. Fraser
Btry B	Capt Rodney M. Handley
Btry C	Capt Donald N. Otis
7" Btry	Capt Ralph A. Collins, Jr.
7" Btry	Capt Harold R. Warner, Jr.
3"/50 Btry	Capt Jay H. Augustin
3"/50 Btry	Capt William R. Dorr, Jr.

3-Inch Antiaircraft Group

CO	Maj Charles T. Tingle
H&S Btry	MG Maurice C. Pulliam
Btry D	Capt Jean H. Buckner
Btry E	Maj Hoyt McMillan
Btry F	Capt David W. Silvey
Btry G (S/L)	Capt Alfred L. Booth

Machine-Gun Group

CO	Maj Robert E. Hommel
H&S Btry	2dLt George K. Acker
.50 Cal Btry	Maj William E. Boles
.30 Cal Btry	Capt Edwin A. Law

3-Inch Antiaircraft Group, 3d Defense Battalion

CO	Maj Chandler W. Johnson
H&S Btry	Maj Chandler W. Johnson
Btry D	Maj William S. McCormick
Btry E	Maj James S. O'Halloran
Btry F	Capt Arnold D. Swartz
Btry K (37mm)	Capt Ronald K. Miller
Btry L (20mm)	Capt Charles J. Seibert, II

2d Raider Battalion Detachment

CO	Capt Donald H. Hastie
Co C	Capt Donald H. Hastie
Co D	1stLt John Apergis

MARINE AIRCRAFT GROUP 22

CO	LtCol Ira L. Kimes
H&S Sqn	1stLt Charles F. Hurlbut
VMF-221	Maj Floyd B. Parks (MIA 4Jun)
	Capt Kirk Armistead (From 4Jun)
VMSB-241	Maj Lofton R. Henderson (MIA 4Jun)
	Maj Benjamin W. Norris (MIA 4Jun)
	Capt Marshall A. Tyler (From 4Jun)

D. GUADALCANAL (7 August 1942–8 February 1943) [4]

FIRST MARINE DIVISION (REINFORCED)

Division Headquarters
(7Aug42–8Dec42)

CG	MajGen Alexander A. Vandegrift
ADC	BriGen William H. Rupertus
CofS	Col William C. James (To 21Sep)
	Col Gerald C. Thomas (From 21Sep)
D-1	Col Robert C. Kilmartin, Jr. (To 21Sep)
	Maj James C. Murray, Jr. (From 22 Sep)
D-2	LtCol Frank B. Goettge (MIA 12Aug)
	LtCol Edmund J. Buckley (From 14Aug)
D-3	LtCol Gerald C. Thomas (To 20Sep)
	LtCol Merrill B. Twining (From 21Sep)
D-4	LtCol Randolph McC. Pate (To 21Oct)
	LtCol Raymond P. Coffman (21Oct–25Nov)
	LtCol William S. Fellers (From 26Nov)
HqBn(Orgd 2D)	LtCol Edwin J. Farrell

1st Amphibian Tractor Battalion
(7Aug42–22Dec42)

CO	LtCol Walter W. Barr

1st Aviation Engineer Battalion
(18Sep42–8Feb43)

CO	Maj Thomas F. Riley

---

[4] Unit commanders are listed only for those periods when their units are entitled to battle participation credit as indicated by the dates below unit designations. In the case of Marine air units, many of which participated in the battle as flight or advance echelons only, the unit commander who was actually in the Guadalcanal area is shown where muster rolls reveal this information.

1st Engineer Battalion
(7Aug42–22Dec42)

CO — Maj James G. Frazer (To 24Oct)
Maj Henry H. Crockett (From 25Oct)

1st Medical Battalion
(7Aug42–22Dec42)

CO — Cdr Don S. Knowlton, MC (To 14Dec)
LCdr Everett B. Keck, MC (From 15Dec)

1st Parachute Battalion
(7Aug42–18Sep42)

CO — Maj Robert H. Williams (WIA 7Aug)
Maj Charles A. Miller (8Aug–5Sep)
Capt Harry L. Torgerson (6–8Sep)
Maj Charles A. Miller (9–17Sep)
Capt Harry L. Torgerson (From 18Sep)

1st Pioneer Battalion
(7Aug42–22Dec42)

CO — Col George R. Rowan (To 19Sep)
Maj Robert G. Ballance (From 20Sep)

1st Raider Battalion
(7Aug42–16Oct42)

CO — Col Merritt A. Edson (To 20Sep)
LtCol Samuel B. Griffith, II (From 22Sep, WIA 27Sep)
Capt Ira J. Irwin (From 27Sep)

1st Service Battalion
(7Aug42–22Dec42)

CO — LtCol Hawley C. Waterman

1st Special Weapons Battalion
(7Aug42–22Dec42)

CO — LtCol Robert B. Luckey (To 15Oct)
Maj Richard W. Wallace (From 16Oct)

Forward Echelon, 1st Tank Battalion
(7Aug42–22Dec42)

CO — Maj Harvey S. Walseth

1st Marines
(7Aug42–22Dec42)

CO — Col Clifton B. Cates
1st Bn — LtCol Lenard B. Cresswell
2d Bn — LtCol Edwin A. Pollock (To 22Sep)
LtCol William W. Stickney (From 24Sep)
3d Bn — LtCol William N. McKelvey, Jr.

5th Marines
(7Aug42–9Dec42)

CO — Col Leroy P. Hunt (To 19Sep)
Col Merritt A. Edson (From 21Sep)
1st Bn — LtCol William E. Maxwell (To 28Aug)
Maj Donald W. Fuller (30 Aug–11Oct)
Maj William P. Thyson, Jr. (12Oct)
Maj William K. Enright (13–23Oct)
Maj William P. Thyson, Jr. (24–30Oct)
Maj William K. Enright (From 31Oct)
2d Bn — LtCol Harold E. Rosecrans (WIA 11Sep)
Capt Joseph J. Dudkowski (11–17Sep)
LtCol Walker A. Reves (18–24Sep)
Capt Joseph J. Dudkowski (25–30Sep)
Maj David S. McDougal (From 1Oct, WIA 8Oct)
Maj William J. Piper, Jr. (8–11Oct)
Maj Lewis W. Walt (From 12Oct)
3d Bn — LtCol Frederick C. Biebush (To 21Sep)
Maj Robert O. Bowen (From 22Sep)

MARINE TASK ORGANIZATION AND COMMAND LIST

7th Marines
(18Sep42–5Jan43)

CO	Col James C. Webb (To 19Sep)
	Col Amor LeR. Sims (From 20Sep)
1st Bn	LtCol Lewis B. Puller (WIA 8Nov)
	Maj John E. Weber (9–17Nov)
	LtCol Lewis B. Puller (From 18Nov)
2d Bn	LtCol Herman H. Hanneken (To 17Nov)
	Maj Odell M. Conoley (18–28Nov)
	LtCol Herman H. Hanneken (From 29Nov)
3d Bn	LtCol Edwin J. Farrell (To 21Sep)
	LtCol William R. Williams (From 24Sep)

11th Marines
(7Aug42–22Dec42)

CO	BriGen Pedro A. del Valle
1st Bn	LtCol Joseph R. Knowlan (To 18Oct)
	LtCol Manly L. Curry (18 Oct–27Nov)
	LtCol Donovan D. Sult (28Nov–20Dec)
	Maj Lewis J. Fields (From 21Dec)
2d Bn	LtCol Edward J. Hagen (To 19Oct)
	Maj Forest C. Thompson (20–30Oct)
	Maj Lewis A. Ennis (1–5Nov)
	Maj Forest C. Thompson (6–11Nov)
	Maj Lewis A. Ennis (12–30Nov)
	Maj Forest C. Thompson (From 1Dec)
3d Bn	LtCol James J. Keating
4th Bn	LtCol Melvin E. Fuller (To 26Oct)
	Maj Carl G. F. Korn (27–31Oct)
	Capt Albert H. Potter (From 1Nov)
5th Bn	LtCol Eugene H. Price (To 30Oct)
	Maj Noah P. Wood, Jr. (From 1Nov)

2d Raider Battalion
(4Nov42–17Dec42)

CO	LtCol Evans F. Carlson

3d Barrage Balloon Squadron
(8Sep42–8Feb43)

CO	Capt Robert C. McDermond

3d Defense Battalion
(7Aug42–8Feb43)

CO	Col Robert H. Pepper (To 28Nov)
	LtCol Harold C. Roberts (29Nov–11Jan)
	LtCol Samuel G. Taxis (From 12Jan)

Detachment A, 5th Defense Battalion
Redesignated 14th Defense Battalion, 15Jan43
(8Sep42–8Feb43)

CO	LtCol William F. Parks (To 5Dec)
	Col Galen M. Sturgis (From 5Dec)

9th Defense Battalion
(30Nov42–8Feb43)

CO	Col David R. Nimmer (To 2Feb)
	LtCol William J. Scheyer (From 3Feb)

SECOND MARINE DIVISION

Advance Echelon, Division Headquarters
(4Jan43–8Feb43)

CG	BriGen Alphonse De Carre
CofS	Col George F. Stockes
D–1	Maj Lawrence C. Hays, Jr. (To 5Feb)
	Capt Percy H. Uhlinger (From 6Feb)
D–2	Maj Thomas J. Colley
D–3	LtCol John H. Coffman (To 21Jan)
	LtCol Jesse S. Cook, Jr. (From 21Jan)
D–4	Maj George N. Carroll

2d Special Weapons Battalion

(7Aug42–8Feb43)

CO	LtCol Paul D. Sherman (To 8Jan)
	Maj Guy E. Tannyhill (9–12Jan)
	LtCol Paul D. Sherman (From 13Jan)

2d Marines

(7Aug42–31Jan43)

CO	Col John M. Arthur
1st Bn	LtCol Robert E. Hill (WIA 11Nov)
	Maj Wood B. Kyle (From 11Nov)
2d Bn	LtCol Orin K. Pressley (To 14Dec)
	Maj Ewart S. Laue (From 14Dec)
3d Bn	LtCol Robert G. Hunt

6th Marines

(4Jan43–8Feb43)

CO	Col Gilder D. Jackson, Jr.
1st Bn	LtCol Russell Lloyd
2d Bn	Maj Raymond L. Murray
3d Bn	Maj William A. Kengla

8th Marines

(2Nov42–8Feb43)

CO	Col Richard H. Jeschke
1st Bn	LtCol Miles S. Newton (To 22Nov)
	LtCol Joseph P. McCaffery (From 23Nov)
2d Bn	LtCol John H. Cook, Jr.
3d Bn	LtCol Augustus H. Fricke

1st Battalion, 10th Marines

(4Nov42–8Feb43)

CO	LtCol Presley M. Rixey

2d Battalion, 10th Marines

(4Jan43–8Feb43)

CO	Maj George R. E. Shell

3d Battalion, 10th Marines

(7Aug42–8Feb43)

CO	LtCol Manly L. Curry (To 17Oct)
	LtCol Donovan D. Sult (18Oct–27Nov)
	LtCol Manly L. Curry (From 28Nov)

2d Aviation Engineer Battalion

(30Jan43–8Feb43)

CO	Maj Charles O. Clark

11th Defense Battalion

(17Jan43–8Feb43)

CO	Col Charles N. Muldrow

MARINE AIR UNITS

Headquarters Detachment, 1st Marine Aircraft Wing

(3Sep42–8Feb43)

CG	MajGen Roy S. Geiger
CofS	BriGen Louis B. Woods
W-1	LtCol Perry O. Parmelee (To 20Nov)
	Capt James G. Hopper (21Nov–20Dec)
	LtCol Thomas G. Ennis (From 21Dec)
W-2	LtCol John C. Munn
W-3	Col Lawson H. M. Sanderson (To 31Dec)
	Col Christian F. Schilt (From 1Jan)
W-4	Col Christian F. Schilt (To 31Dec)
	LtCol Albert D. Cooley (From 1Jan)
HqSq-1	Capt Herman J. Jesse

Forward Echelon, 2d Marine Aircraft Wing

(26Dec42–8Feb43)

CG	BriGen Francis P. Mulcahy
CofS	Col Walter G. Farrell
W-1	2dLt Robert E. Coddington
W-2	LtCol Elmer H. Salzman

MARINE TASK ORGANIZATION AND COMMAND LIST 393

W-3	LtCol Joe A. Smoak (To 29 Jan)
	LtCol William C. Lemly (From 30 Jan)
W-4	LtCol Franklin G. Cowie
HqSq-2	Maj William K. Snyder

Marine Aircraft Group 14

(16 Oct 42–8 Feb 43)

CO	LtCol Albert D. Cooley (To 17 Dec)
	Col William O. Brice (From 19 Dec)
HqSq-14	Capt Claude J. Carlson, Jr. (To 17 Nov)
	Capt Stanley M. Adams (From 18 Nov)
SMS-14	Maj Arthur R. Stacey

Marine Aircraft Group 23

(20 Aug 42–4 Nov 42)

CO	Col William J. Wallace
HqSq-23	MG Harland W. Bond (To 24 Oct)
	LtCol Charles L. Fike (From 25 Oct)
SMS-23	2dLt Joseph A. Pawloski

Advance Detachments, Marine Aircraft Group 25

(3 Sep 42–8 Feb 43)

CO	LtCol Perry K. Smith
HqSq-25	Maj Leonard W. Ashwell (To 17 Nov)
	Capt Dave J. Woodward, Jr. (From 18 Nov)
SMS-25	Maj Leonard W. Ashwell (To 23 Dec)
	Capt Ralph R. Yeaman (From 24 Dec)

Marine Fighter Squadron 112

(2 Nov 42–8 Feb 43)

CO	Maj Paul J. Fontana (To 31 Dec)
	2dLt Alexander A. Case (1–6 Jan)
	Maj Paul J. Fontana (From 7 Jan)

Marine Fighter Squadron 121

(2 Oct 42–28 Jan 43)

CO	Maj Leonard K. Davis (WIA 11 Nov, To 16 Dec)
	MG William F. Wilson (17–31 Dec)
	Maj Donald K. Yost (From 1 Jan)

Marine Fighter Squadron 122

(12 Nov 42–8 Feb 43)

CO	Capt Nathan T. Post, Jr. (To 21 Nov)
	Capt James R. Anderson (22 Nov–10 Dec)
	2dLt John F. Tenvole (11–23 Dec)
	Maj Elmer E. Brackett, Jr. (24–29 Dec)
	Capt Nathan T. Post, Jr. (30 Dec–11 Jan)
	Maj Elmer E. Brackett, Jr. (From 12 Jan)

Flight Echelon, Marine Fighter Squadron 123

(3 Feb 43–8 Feb 43)

CO	Maj Edward W. Johnston

Flight Echelon, Marine Fighter Squadron 124

(3 Feb 43–8 Feb 43)

CO	Maj William E. Gise

Marine Scout-Bomber Squadron 131

(11 Nov 42–8 Feb 43)

CO	LtCol Paul Moret (To 20 Nov)
	Capt Jens C. Aggerbeck, Jr. (From 21 Nov)

Marine Scout-Bomber Squadron 132

(1 Nov 42–19 Jan 43)

CO	Maj Joseph Sailer, Jr. (KIA 7 Dec)
	Maj Louis B. Robertshaw (From 7 Dec)

448777 O—58——27

Marine Scout-Bomber Squadron 141
(23Sep42–17Jan43)

CO_____ Maj Gordon A. Bell (KIA 14Oct)
1stLt Wortham S. Ashcroft (From 14Oct, KIA 8Nov)
1stLt Robert M. Patterson (8–11Nov)
2dLt Walter R. Bartosh (12–17Nov)
Maj George A. Sarles (18Nov–16Dec)
Capt Claude A. Carlson, Jr. (From 17Dec)

Marine Scout-Bomber Squadron 142
(12Nov42–8Feb43)

CO_____ Maj Robert H. Richard

Flight Echelon, Marine Scout-Bomber Squadron 144
(5Feb43–8Feb43)

CO_____ Capt Roscoe N. Nelson

Flight Echelon, Marine Utility Squadron 152
(21Oct42–8Feb43)

CO_____ Maj Elmore W. Seeds

Flight Echelon, Marine Photographic Squadron 154
(10Nov42–8Feb43)

CO_____ LtCol Elliot E. Bard

Flight Echelon, Marine Fighter Squadron 212
(17Aug42–21Nov42)

CO_____ LtCol Harold W. Bauer (KIA 14Nov)
Maj Frederick R. Payne, Jr. (From 14Nov)

Marine Fighter Squadron 223
(20Aug42–16Oct42)

CO_____ Maj John L. Smith

Marine Fighter Squadron 224
(30Aug42–2Nov42)

CO_____ Maj Robert E. Galer

Flight Echelon, Marine Scout-Bomber Squadron 231
(30Aug42–14Nov42)

CO_____ Maj Leo R. Smith (To 18Sep)
Capt Ruben Iden (From 19Sep, KIA 20Sep)
Capt Elmer G. Glidden, Jr. (From 20Sep)

Marine Scout-Bomber Squadron 232
(20Aug42–2Nov42)

CO_____ LtCol Richard C. Mangrum

Marine Scout-Bomber Squadron 233
(25Dec42–8Feb43)

CO_____ Maj Clyde T. Mattison (To 19Jan)
Capt Elmer L. Gilbert (From 20Jan)

Flight Echelon, Marine Scout-Bomber Squadron 234
(28Jan43–8Feb43)

CO_____ Maj William D. Roberson

Marine Observation Squadron 251
(19Aug42–8Feb43)

CO_____ LtCol John N. Hart (To 29Oct)
LtCol Charles H. Hayes (30Oct–30Nov)
Capt Ralph R. Yeaman (1–7Dec)
Maj William R. Campbell (8–10Dec)
Maj Joseph N. Renner (From 11Dec)

Marine Utility Squadron 253
(3Sep42–8Feb43)

CO_____ Maj Harold A. Johnson (To 11Oct)
Maj Henry C. Lane (From 12Oct)

APPENDIX D

Marine Casualties[1]

Location and date	KIA		DOW		WIA		MIAPD		KDPOW		TOTAL	
	Officer	Enlisted	Officer	Enlisted	Officer	Enlisted	Officer	Enlisted	Officer	Enlisted	Officer	Enlisted
Marines												
Guam (7–10 Dec 41)	---	4	---	1	---	13	---	---	---	5	---	23
Wake Atoll (7–23 Dec 41)	4	46	---	---	6	38	---	6	---	13	10	103
Philippines (7 Dec 41–6 May 42)	43	267	---	5	33	324	---	16	14	225	90	837
Midway Islands (7 Dec 41–6 Jun 42)	2	8	1	---	14	25	23	14	---	---	40	47
Makin (17–18 Aug 42)	1	17	---	---	2	14	---	12	---	---	3	43
Guadalcanal (7 Aug 42–8 Feb 43)	71	1,026	11	98	223	2,693	52	246	---	---	357	4,063
Naval Medical Personnel Organic to Marine Units												
Philippines (7 Dec 41–6 May 42)	---	---	---	---	2	---	---	---	3	25	5	25
Guadalcanal (7 Aug 42–8 Feb 43)	8	23	1	4	15	86	---	---	---	---	24	113

[1] These final Marine casualty figures were compiled from records furnished by Statistics Unit, PersAcctSec, (RecsBr, PersDept, HQMS. They are audited to include 26 Aug 52. Naval casualties were taken from NavMed P-5021, *The History of the Medical Department of the Navy in World War II*, 2 vols (Washington: Government Printing Office, 1943), II. 1–84. The key to the abbreviations used at the head of columns in the table follows: KIA, Killed in Action; DOW, Died of Wounds; WIA, Wounded in Action; MIAPD, Missing in Action, Presumed Dead; KDPOW, Killed or Died while a Prisoner of War. Because of the method used in reporting casualties during World War II a substantial number of DOW figures are also included in the WIA column.

APPENDIX E

First Marine Division
Operation Order—Guadalcanal

FIRST MARINE DIVISION
FLEET MARINE FORCE
Wellington, N. Z.
[20 July 1942][1]

OPERATION ORDER
No. 7-42

Maps: H. O. CHART #2896 (Solomon Islands) reproduced by D-2 Section.
   D-2 Section Map North Coast Guadalcanal Island—Lunga Point to Aola, 9 Sections, 15 July, 1942, RF 1/24,000.
   D-2 Section Map Tulagi and adjacent islands, 7/14/42, (4 sheets) c RF 1/12,000.
   D-2 Section—Special map Tulagi—1/12,000, 15 July, 1942.

TASK ORGANIZATION

(a) *COMBAT GROUP A* [5th Mar, Reinf] (less Combat Team #2 (less Btry E 11th Marines))	Col. LeRoy P. Hunt, USMC.
(b) *COMBAT GROUP B* [1st Mar, Reinf]	Col. Clifton B. Cates, USMC.
(c) *TULAGI GROUP* 1st Raider Bn Combat Team #2 (less Btry E 11th Marines)	LtCol. Merritt A. Edson, USMC.
(d) *GAVUTU GROUP* First Parachute Battalion	Maj. Robert H. Williams, USMC.
(e) *SUPPORT GROUP* 1st Eng Bn (less Cos A, B, & C) 11th Marines (less 1st, 2d, 3d and 4th Bns) 1st Spl Wpns Bn (less 1st & 3d Pl Btry A) 1st Pion Bn (less Cos A & B)	Col. Pedro A. del Valle, USMC.
(f) *DIVISION RESERVE* 2d Marines (Reinforced) (less Combat Team A)	Col. John M. Arthur, USMC.
(g) *FLORIDA GROUP* Combat Team A.	Maj. Robert E. Hill, USMC.
(h) *THIRD DEFENSE BATTALION*	Col. Robert H. Pepper, USMC.

1. See Annex A Intelligence

Naval Attack Force will furnish naval gunfire and air support (see Annexes B and C gunfire and air support plans respectively). Minesweepers will cover landing of FLORIDA GROUP by concentrations on BUNGANA ISLAND [south of Halavo Peninsula] and GAVUTU.

---

[1] With the exception of the information in brackets which was added to assist the reader, this operation order is an *exact* transcription of a copy of the original order contained in *Final/Rept*, Phase I, Annex F. Map Nos. 13, 14, and 15 of this volume should be used as references with the order.

FIRST MARINE DIVISION ORDER—GUADALCANAL

2. This Division will attack and destroy the hostile garrisons of TULAGI, GUADALCANAL, GAVUTU, and MAKAMBO by simultaneous landings on D day. It will then organize and defend those islands.
For Transport Area, Line of Departure, beaches, objectives, Boundaries see Operation Overlay Annex D.

3. (a) Land on Beach RED at Zero Hour with 2 CTs in assault on a front of 1600 yards seize beachhead (see operation overlay). When passed through by Combat Group B, Combat Group A (less CTs #2 & 3) attack toward LUNGA with its right resting on the shore line. Seize the line of the TENARU RIVER. Combat Team #3 attack and seize line of woods running southeast from TENAVATU [eastern flank of Red Beach] (see operation overlay). Hold that line until relieved by Support Group. Then operate as directed by Task Organization Commander.

(b) Land on Beach RED at Zero Hour plus 50 minutes (see operation overlay) pass through right of Combat Group A and attack on magnetic azimuth 260°. Seize grassy knoll 4 miles south of LUNGA POINT. Be prepared for further advance.
Formation—Column of battalions echeloned to the left rear. Maintain contact with Combat Group A on right.

(c) Land on front of 500 yards on Beach BLUE at H hour, and seize that portion of TULAGI ISLAND lying northwest of line A (see D-2 Section Special Map TULAGI 1/12,000, 15 July 1942). Fire GREEN STAR CLUSTER to call for five minutes air and naval bombardment of TULAGI southeast of line A, after H plus 1 hour. Upon completion of bombing and lifting of naval gunfire, attack and seize the remainder of TULAGI ISLAND. Upon completion seizure of TULAGI ISLAND 1st Raider Bn reembark at Beach Blue and report completion of reembarkation to Division Headquarters, prepared for further landings. Upon seizure of TULAGI, control passes to Commander Combat Team #2. Combat Team #2 then reembark sufficient troops and seize MAKAMBO ISLAND, then organize and defend those islands. Following seizure of TULAGI and MAKAMBO, and of GAVUTU and TANAMBOGO by 1st Parachute Battalion, relieve 1st Parachute Battalion with one rifle company plus one machine gun platoon.

(d) Land on east coast of GAVUTU ISLAND at H plus 4 hours, and seize that island, then seize TANAMBOGO. Fire GREEN STAR CLUSTER to call for five minutes naval gunfire on TANAMBOGO ISLAND. Reembark upon relief prepared for employment elsewhere.

(e) Land on Beach RED on order, assume control of 2d and 3d Battalions 11th Marines, provide artillery support for the attack, and coordinate AA and close in ground defense of Beachhead area.

(f) Be prepared to land Combat Team B less all reinforcing units on GAVUTU ISLAND at H plus 4 hours. Be prepared to attach Combat Team C less all reinforcing units to the TULAGI GROUP.

(g) Land 1st Battalion 2d Marines (less one rifle company and one machine gun platoon) on promontory at x3022 [Halavo Peninsula] at H hour plus 30 minutes and seize village of Halavo. Then support by fire the attack of the 1st Parachute Bn on GAVUTU. Land one (1) rifle company reinforced by one machine gun platoon at H minus 20 minutes in cove at W7837 [Haleta] and seize and hold point to southeast thereof.

(h) Execute following on order:

(1) Land Battalion less 1/3 AA elements on Beach RED. These pass to CO Support Group on landing. Assist in AA defense of beach area.

(2) Land 1/3 AA elements on TULAGI and GAVUTU, and provide AA defense that area.

(x) (1) Land tanks with combat groups and move to cover near east boundary of beachhead. Tanks not to be committed except on division order.

(2) Land 1st and 3d platoons Battery A Special Weapons Battalion on flanks of beach and furnish AA defense beach area, 1st Platoon to right 3d platoon to left. These revert to battalion control upon landing of Headquarters 1st Special Weapons Battalion.

(3) Scout cars will not land.

(4) All artillery of combat troops will be landed with those groups and pass to control 11th Marines upon landing 11th Marines Headquarters.

(5) Assistant Division Commander will command operations in TULAGI-GAVUTU-FLORIDA Area.

4. See Administrative Order.

5. (a) See Annex E, Signal Communication.

(b) Command Posts afloat:
    1st Mar Div   MC CAWLEY (AP10)
    Combat Group A   AMERICAN LEGION (AP35)
    Combat Group B   BARNETT (AP11)
    TULAGI Group   APD
    GAVUTU Group   HEYWOOD (AP12)
    Support Group   HUNTER LIGGETT (AP27)
    Division Reserve   CRESCENT CITY (AP40)
    FLORIDA Group   PRESIDENT JACKSON (AP37)
    3d Defense Bn   ZEILIN (AP9)

(c) Axis of Signal Communication all units:
CP afloat—locations ashore to be reported.

(d) Use local time, zone minus eleven (zone suffix letter Love), in all communications with Division.

BY COMMAND OF MAJOR GENERAL VANDEGRIFT

W. C. JAMES,
Colonel, U. S. Marine Corps,
Chief of Staff.

APPENDIX F

Military Map Symbols

SIZE SYMBOLS

•	Squad
• •	Section
• • •	Platoon
I	Company or Battery
I I	Battalion or Squadron
I I I	Regiment or Air Group
x	Brigade
x x	Division or Wing

UNIT SYMBOLS

☐	Basic Unit
∞	Air
LVT	Amphibian Tractor
△	Antiaircraft
• DB	Defense Battalion
E	Engineer
•	Field Artillery
⊠	Infantry
⊠ Para	Parachute
⊠ Prcht	

UNIT SYMBOLS

P	Pioneer
⊠ Rdr	Raider
⊠	Tank

MISCELLANEOUS SYMBOLS

⌐ flag	Command Post
△	Observation Post
/	Boundary (battalion)
✚	Aid Station (battalion)

EXAMPLES

1L • 1DB	1st Sec, L Btry, 1st Def Bn
B ⊠ 5	Co B, 5th Mar Regt
⊠ 1Rdr	1st Rdr Bn
• II	11th Mar Regt
2 △ 7	OP, 2d Bn, 7th Mar Regt
⊠ 1	CP, 1st Mar Div

APPENDIX G

Guide to Abbreviations

AA	Antiaircraft
AAA	Antiaircraft Artillery
AAF	Army Air Force
ABC	American-British-Canadian
ABDA	American-British-Dutch-Australian
Acct	Accounting
Act	Action
ADC	Assistant Division Commander
Adm	Admiral
Adv	Advance
AF	Asiatic Fleet
Air	Aircraft
AKA	Attack Cargo Ship
Amer	American
Amtrack	Amphibian Tractor
An	Annual
Anzac	Australia-New Zealand Area
AP	Navy Transport
APA	Attack Transport
APC	Small Coastal Transport
APD	Destroyer Transport
AR	Action Report
Arcadia	U. S.-British Conference (December 1941–January 1942)
AsFlt	Asiatic Fleet
ATIS	Allied Translator and Interrogator Section
"Avenger"	TBF-#, torpedo-bomber made by Grumman
B	Base
B-17	Army heavy bomber, the "Flying Fortress"
BAR	Browning Automatic Rifle
Bd	Board
BLT	Battalion Landing Team
BM	Boatswain's Mate
Bn	Battalion
Br	Branch
Brig	Brigade
BriGen	Brigadier General
Btry	Battery
Bu	Bureau
BuEng	Bureau of Engineering
BuShips	Bureau of Ships
C	Combat
CA	Coast Artillery
Cactus	Code Name for Guadalcanal
Cal	Caliber
CAM	Combined Army & Marine
Capt	Captain
"Catalina"	PBY patrol bomber made by Consolidated-Vultee
CCS	Combined Chiefs of Staff
Cdr	Commander
CG	Commanding General
Ch	Chief
Chap	Chapter
Chmn	Chairman
CinC	Commander in Chief
CMC	Commandant of the Marine Corps
CNO	Chief of Naval Operations
CO	Commanding Officer
Co	Company
CofS	Chief of Staff
CofSA	Chief of Staff, U. S. Army
Col	Colonel
Cont	Continuing
Com	Commander; Commandant
Comb	Combined
Comm	Communication
CP	Command Post
C&R	Construction & Repair
Cru	Cruiser
CSP	Communication Security Publication
CT	Combat Team
CTF	Commander Task Force
CTG	Commander Task Group
CWO	Chief (Commissioned) Warrant Officer
D-1	Division Personnel Office(r)
D-2	Division Intelligence Office(r)
D-3	Division Operations Office(r)
D-4	Division Logistics Office(r)
DA	Department of the Army
"Dauntless"	SBD-#, scout-bomber made by Douglas
DC	Dental Corps (Navy)

400

GUIDE TO ABBREVIATIONS

Def	Defense
Dept	Department
Des	Destroyer
Dev	Development
"Devastator"	TBD-#, torpedo-bomber made by Douglas
Dir	Director
Disp	Dispatch
Div	Division
Doc	Document
DOW	Died of Wounds
DUKW	Amphibious Truck
Encl	Enclosure
Eng	Engineer
Enl	Enlisted
Ens	Ensign
ExO	Executive Officer
Ext	Extension
F4F-#	"Wildcat" fighter made by Grumman
FAdm	Fleet Admiral
FEAF	Far East Air Force
FEC	Far East Command
Flex	Fleet Landing Exercise
Flot	Flotilla
Flt	Fleet
FMF	Fleet Marine Force
FO	Forward Observer
For	Force
Fourteen	14th Naval District
G-2	Intelligence Office(r), Division or above
Gar	Garrison
Gen	General
GHQ	General Headquarters
Gnd	Ground
GPO	Government Printing Office
Gru	Group
Gun	Gunnery
Hist	History; Historical
H. O.	Hydrographic Office
Hq	Headquarters
HMSO	His (Her) Majesty's Stationery Office
HQMC	Headquarters Marine Corps
H&S	Headquarters & Service
Hydro	Hydrographic Office
IBC	Iceland Base Command
IJA	Imperial Japanese Army
IJN	Imperial Japanese Navy
Inf	Infantry
Inst	Instruction
Is	Island
J	Joint
JAG	Judge Advocate General
JASCO	Joint Assault Signal Company
JCS	Joint Chiefs of Staff
JIC	Joint Intelligence Center
JG	Junior Grade
Jnl	Journal
"Kate"	Japanese torpedo-bomber
KDPOW	Killed or Died While a Prisoner of War
Lan	Landing
Lant	Atlantic (Fleet)
LCdr	Lieutenant Commander
LCM	Mechanized Landing Craft
LCVP	Vehicle and Personnel Landing Craft
LST	Tank Landing Ship
Lt	Lieutenant
Ltr	Letter
LVT	Landing Vehicle Tracked
LVT(A)	Landing Vehicle Tracked (Armored)
MAG	Marine Aircraft Group
Maj	Major
Mar	Marine(s)
MarCor	Marine Corps
MAW	Marine Aircraft Wing
Mbr	Member
MC	Marine Corps; Medical Corps (Navy)
MCEC	Marine Corps Educational Center
MCO	Marine Corps Order
MCS	Marine Corps Schools
MD	Marine Detachment
Med	Medical
Memo	Memorandum
MG	Marine Gunner; Machine Gun
MGC	The Major General Commandant of the Marine Corps
MI	Military Intelligence
MIA	Missing in Action
MIAPD	Missing in Action, Presumed Dead
Mil	Military
MIS	Military Intelligence Service
MLR	Main Line of Resistance
Mm	Millimeter
Mph	Miles per hour
MS	Manuscript
MSgt	Master Sergeant
MTB	Motor Torpedo Boat
NAD	Naval Ammunition Depot

NAS	Naval Air Station	RM	Royal Marine(s)
Nav	Navy; Naval	RMA	Royal Marine Artillery
ND	Navy Department	RN	Royal Navy
NHD	Naval History Division	SBD-#	"Dauntless" scout-bomber made by Douglas
NGF	Naval Gunfire		
NOB	Naval Operating Base	SB2U-#	"Vindicator" scout-bomber made by Vought-Sikorsky
NRMC	Naval Records Management Center (Alexandria, Va.)		
		SCAP	Supreme Commander Allied Powers
NSD	Naval Supply Depot		
OCMH	Office of the Chief of Military History, U. S. Army	Sch	School
		Sec	Section
		Sen	Senior
Off	Officer(s)	Sep	Separate
Ofl	Official	Ser	Service
ONI	Office of Naval Intelligence	SFCP	Shore Fire Control Party
OP	Observation Post	Sgt	Sergeant
OPlan	Operation Plan	Sixteen	16th Naval District
OpOrd	Operation Order	S/L	Searchlight
Ops	Operations	SM	Special Manual
P&P	Plans and Policies Division, Headquarters Marine Corps	SMS	Marine Service Squadron
		SNLF	Japanese Special Naval Landing Force
PAA	Pan American Airways		
Pac	Pacific (Fleet)	So	South
Para	Parachute	Spl	Special
Pat	Patrol	Sqn	Squadron
PB	Patrol Boat	SS	Special Staff
PBY	"Catalina" patrol bomber made by Consolidated-Vultee	SSgt	Staff Sergeant
		SWPA	Southwest Pacific Area
PC	Patrol Craft	TAGO	The Adjutant General's Office
Pers	Personnel	TBD-#	"Devastator" torpedo-bomber made by Douglas
Phib	Amphibious		
Phil	Philippine	TBF-#	"Avenger" torpedo-bomber made by Grumman
Pion	Pioneer		
Pl	Platoon	TF	Task Force
Proj	Project	TG	Task Group
Prov	Provisional	Tng	Training
POA	Pacific Ocean Area	T/O	Table of Organization
POW	Prisoner of War	TQM	Transport Quartermaster
PT	Motor Torpedo Boat	Trans	Transport
QM	Quartermaster	TSgt	Technical Sergeant
R-2	Regimental Intelligence Office(r)	U/F	Unit of fire, a unit of measurement for ammunition supply. It represents a specific number of rounds of ammunition per weapon.
R-4	Regimental Logistics Office(r)		
RAAF	Royal Australian Air Force		
RAdm	Rear Admiral		
RAN	Royal Australian Navy	US	United States (Fleet)
RCT	Regimental Combat Team	USA	United States Army
Rdr	Raider	USAFFE	United States Army Forces in the Far East
Rec	Record(s)		
Reinf	Reinforced	USFIP	United States Forces in the Philippines
Rept	Report		
RF	Representative Fraction (Map Scale)	USMC	United States Marine Corps
RLT	Regimental Landing Team	USN	United States Navy

GUIDE TO ABBREVIATIONS

USNI	United States Naval Institute
USNR	United States Naval Reserve
USS	United States Ship
USSBS	United States Strategic Bombing Survey
VAdm	Vice Admiral
VF	Navy Fighter Squadron
"Vindicator"	SB2U-#, scout-bomber made by Vought-Sikorsky
VMF	Marine Fighter Squadron
VMJ	Marine Utility Squadron
VMSB	Marine Scout-Bomber Squadron
VP	Navy Patrol Squadron
VS	Navy Scouting Squadron
W-1	Wing Personnel Office(r)
W-2	Wing Intelligence Office(r)
W-3	Wing Operations Office(r)
W-4	Wing Logistics Office(r)
Watchtower	Code name for the Guadalcanal-Tulagi Operation
WD	War Department
WDC	War Documents Center
Wes	West
"Wildcat"	F4F-#, fighter made by Grumman
WO	Warrant Officer
WPL	War Plan
Wpns	Weapons
WW	World War
YP	Small Patrol Craft
"Zero"	Japanese fighter

APPENDIX H

Unit Commendations

THE WHITE HOUSE
WASHINGTON

Citation by
THE PRESIDENT OF THE UNITED STATES
of
The Wake detachment of the 1st Defense Battalion, U. S. Marine Corps, under command of
Major James P. S. Devereux, U. S. Marines
and
Marine Fighting Squadron 211 of Marine Aircraft Group 21, under command of
Major Paul A. Putnam, U. S. Marines
and
Army and Navy personnel present

"The courageous conduct of the officers and men who defended Wake Island against an overwhelming superiority of enemy air, sea, and land attacks from December 8 to 22, 1941, has been noted with admiration by their fellow countrymen and the civilized world, and will not be forgotten so long as gallantry and heroism are respected and honored. They are commended for their devotion to duty and splendid conduct at their battle stations under most adverse conditions. With limited defensive means against attacks in great force, they manned their shore installations and flew their aircraft so well that five enemy warships were either sunk or severely damaged, many hostile planes shot down, and an unknown number of land troops destroyed."

FRANKLIN D. ROOSEVELT.

UNIT COMMENDATIONS

GENERAL ORDERS
No. 21

WAR DEPARTMENT,
WASHINGTON, *April 30, 1942*

Citation of units in the United State Forces in the Philippines.—As authorized by Executive Order 9075 (sec. II, Bull. 11, W. D., 1942), a citation in the name of the President of the United States, as public evidence of deserved honor and distinction, is awarded to the following-named units. The citation reads as follows:

The Harbor Defenses of Manila and Subic Bays and Naval and Marine Corps units serving therein, United States Forces in the Philippines, are cited for outstanding performance of duty in action, during the period from March 14 to April 9, 1942, inclusive.

Although subjected repeatedly to intense and prolonged artillery bombardment by concealed hostile batteries in Cavite Province and to heavy enemy aerial attacks, during the period above-mentioned, and despite numerous casualties and extensive damage inflicted on defensive installations and utilities, the morale, ingenuity, and combat efficiency of the entire command have remained at the high standard which has impressed fighting men the world over.

On March 15, approximately 1,000 240-mm projectiles were fired at Forts Frank and Drum, and large numbers of lesser caliber projectiles struck Forts Hughes and Mills. Again on March 20, over 400 240-mm shells were fired at Fort Frank and a lesser number at Fort Drum, while enemy air echelons made a total of 50 attacks on Fort Mills with heavy aerial bombs.

During the entire period all units maintained their armament at a high degree of efficiency, while seaward defense elements executed effective counter battery action. Antiaircraft batteries firing at extreme ranges exacted a heavy toll of hostile attacking planes, and Naval and Marine units from exposed stations assured the defense of the beaches and approaches to the fortified islands. By unceasing labor and regardless of enemy activity, essential utilities were restored and the striking power of the command maintained unimpaired.

As a result of their splendid combined efforts, ruggedness, and devotion to duty the various units and services comprising the Harbor Defenses of Manila and Subic Bays frustrated a major hostile attempt to reduce the efficiency of the fortified islands.

Units included in above citation: 59th Coast Artillery, 60th Coast Artillery (AA), 91st Coast Artillery (PS), 92d Coast Artillery (PS), Headquarters and Headquarters Battery, Harbor Defenses of Manila and Subic Bays, Medical Detachment, Ordnance Detachment, Quartermaster Detachments (American and Philippine Scouts), Finance Detachment, 1st Coast Artillery (PA) (less 2d Battalion), Company A, 803d Engineer Battalion (Aviation) (Separate), detachments DS Army Mine Planter Harrison (American and Philippine Scouts), 4th U. S. Marines, U. S. Navy Inshore Patrol, Manila Bay area, Naval Force District Headquarters Fort Mills, Naval Forces Mariveles Area Philippine Islands, Battery D, 2d Coast Artillery (PA), 1st Platoon Battery F, 2d Coast Artillery (AA), (PA), 2d Platoon Battery F, 2d Coast Artillery (AA), (PA).

(A. G. 201.54 (4-12-42))

BY ORDER OF THE SECRETARY OF WAR:

OFFICIAL:
J. A. ULIO
Major General
The Adjutant General

G. C. MARSHALL
Chief of Staff

General Orders } WAR DEPARTMENT
No. 22 Washington, *April 30, 1942*

Citation of units of both military and naval forces of the United States and Philippine Governments.—As authorized by Executive Order 9075 (sec. II, Bull. 11, W. D., 1942), a citation in the name of the President of the United States as public evidence of deserved honor and distinction, is awarded to all units of both military and naval forces of the United States and Philippine Governments engaged in the defense of the Philippines since December 7, 1941 to 10 May 1942.

A. G. 210.54 (4–12–42). (Closing date auth. by W. D. G. O. #46 of 1948)

By Order of the Secretary of War:

G. C. MARSHALL
Chief of Staff

Official:
J. A. ULIO
*Major General
The Adjutant General*

THE SECRETARY OF THE NAVY,
Washington.

The President of the United States takes pleasure in presenting the PRESIDENTIAL UNIT CITATION to

MARINE AIRCRAFT GROUP TWENTY-TWO

for service as set forth in the following

CITATION:

"For conspicuous courage and heroism in combat at Midway Island during June, 1942. Outnumbered five to one, MARINE AIRCRAFT GROUP TWENTY-TWO boldly intercepted a heavily escorted enemy bombing force, disrupting their attack and preventing serious damage to island installations. Operating with half of their dive-bombers obsolete and in poor mechanical condition which necessitated vulnerable glide bombing tactics, they succeeded in inflicting heavy damage on Japanese surface units of a large enemy task force. The skill and gallant perseverance of flight and ground personnel of MARINE AIRCRAFT GROUP TWENTY-TWO, fighting under tremendously adverse and dangerous conditions, were essential factors in the unyielding defense of Midway."

For the President.

FRANK KNOX,
Secretary of the Navy.

THE SECRETARY OF THE NAVY,
Washington.
The Secretary of the Navy takes pleasure in commending the

SIXTH DEFENSE BATTALION, FLEET MARINE FORCE, REINFORCED,
for service as follows:

"For outstanding heroism in support of military operations prior to and during the Battle of Midway, June 1942. Assuming a tremendous operational and service load in preparing defenses of Midway against anticipated Japanese attack, the officers and men of the SIXTH Defense Battalion carried on intensive night battle training, completed and installed underwater obstacles, unloaded and distributed supplies, emplaced guns and constructed facilities for stowing ammunition and for protecting personnel. Alert and ready for combat when enemy planes came in to launch high and dive-bombing attacks and low-level strafing attacks on June 4, they promptly opened and maintained fire against the hostile targets, downing 10 planes during the furious 17-minute action which resulted in the destruction of the Marine galley and mess-hall, equipment, supplies and communication facilities. Working as an effective team for long periods without relief, this Battalion cleared the debris from the bomb-wrecked galley, reestablished disrupted communications, and serviced planes, thereby contributing greatly to the success of operations conducted from this base. The high standards of courage and service maintained by the SIXTH Defense Battalion reflect the highest credit upon the United States Naval Service."

All personnel attached to and serving with the SIXTH Defense Battalion, Fleet Marine Force, Reinforced, consisting of the SIXTH Defense Battalion, attached personnel of the Third Defense Battalion, 22nd and 23rd Provisional Marine Companies and "C" and "D" Companies of the Second Raider Battalion are authorized to wear the NAVY UNIT COMMENDATION Ribbon.

JOHN L. SULLIVAN,
Secretary of the Navy.

The Secretary of the Navy,
Washington.

4 February 1943.

Cited in the Name of
The President of the United States
THE FIRST MARINE DIVISION, REINFORCED
Under command of
Major General Alexander A. Vandegrift, U. S. M. C.

CITATION:

"The officers and enlisted men of the First Marine Division, Reinforced, on August 7 to 9, 1942, demonstrated outstanding gallantry and determination in successfully executing forced landing assaults against a number of strongly defended Japanese positions on Tulagi, Gavutu, Tanambogo, Florida and Guadalcanal, British Solomon Islands, completely routing all the enemy forces and seizing a most valuable base and airfield within the enemy zone of operations in the South Pacific Ocean. From the above period until 9 December, 1942, this Reinforced Division not only held their important strategic positions despite determined and repeated Japanese naval, air and land attacks, but by a series of offensive operations against strong enemy resistance drove the Japanese from the proximity of the airfield and inflicted great losses on them by land and air attacks. The courage and determination displayed in these operations were of an inspiring order."

Frank Knox,
Secretary of the Navy.

The Secretary of the Navy,
Washington.

The Secretary of the Navy takes pleasure in commending the

NINTH MARINE DEFENSE BATTALION

for service as follows:

"For outstanding heroism in action against enemy Japanese forces at Guadalcanal, November 30, 1942, to May 20, 1943; Rendova-New Georgia Area, June 30 to November 7, 1943; and at Guam, Marianas, July 21 to August 20, 1944. One of the first units of its kind to operate in the South Pacific Area, the NINTH Defense Battalion established strong seacoast and beach positions which destroyed 12 hostile planes attempting to bomb Guadalcanal, and further engaged in extensive patrolling activities. In a 21-day-and-night training period prior to the Rendova-New Georgia assault, this group calibrated and learned to handle new weapons and readily effected the conversion from a seacoast unit to a unit capable of executing field artillery missions. Joining Army Artillery units, special groups of this battalion aided in launching an attack which drove the enemy from the beaches, downed 13 of a 16-bomber plane formation during the first night ashore and denied the use of the Munda airfield to the Japanese. The NINTH Defense Battalion aided in spearheading the attack of the Army Corps operating on New Georgia and, despite heavy losses, remained in action until the enemy was routed from the island. Elements of the Battalion landed at Guam under intense fire, established beach defenses, installed antiaircraft guns and later contributed to the rescue of civilians and to the capture or destruction of thousands of Japanese. By their skill, courage and aggressive fighting spirit, the officers and men of the NINTH Defense Battalion upheld the highest traditions of the United States Naval Service."

All personnel attached to and serving with the NINTH Defense Battalion during the above mentioned periods are authorized to wear the NAVY UNIT COMMENDATION Ribbon.

JOHN L. SULLIVAN,
Secretary of the Navy.

THE SECRETARY OF THE NAVY,
Washington.

The Secretary of the Navy takes pleasure in commending the

FIRST SEPARATE ENGINEER BATTALION

for service as follows:

"For exceptionally meritorious service in support of military operations on Guadalcanal, December 10, 1942, to February 27, 1943; Tinian from August 20, 1944, to March 24, 1945; and Okinawa from April 14 to September 2, 1945. Faced with numerous and difficult problems in engineering throughout two major campaigns, the First Separate Engineer Battalion initiated new techniques and procedures in construction, repair and maintenance, executing its missions under adverse conditions of weather and terrain and in spite of Japanese shellings, artillery fire, bombing raids, sickness and tropical storms. Technically skilled, aggressive and unmindful of great personal danger, the officers and men of this gallant Battalion constructed, developed and maintained vital routes of communication, airfields and camp facilities; they served as combat engineer units in performing demolitions, mine detection and disposal and bomb disposal tasks in support of various units of the Fleet Marine Force; and they built bridges and repaired air-bombed air strips toward the uninterrupted operations of Allied ground and aerial forces. Undeterred by both mechanical and natural limitations, the First Separate Engineer Battalion completed with dispatch and effectiveness assigned and unanticipated duties which contributed immeasurably to the ultimate defeat of Japan and upheld the highest traditions of the United States Naval Service."

All personnel attached to the First Separate Engineer Battalion during any of the above mentioned periods are hereby authorized to wear the NAVY UNIT COMMENDATION Ribbon.

JAMES FORRESTAL,
Secretary of the Navy.

Index

Aaron Ward, 353
Abbott, Capt R. A., 327
Abe, RAdm H., 227
Abe, RAdm K., 129–130
ABC–1, 85
ABDA (American-British-Dutch-Australian) Command, 86
Adak, 215
Adams, LtCol J. P., 162, 164, 168, 171
Advanced base activities, 8–10, 64
Africa, 59, 85
Agana, 76, 78
Air attacks. *See* Aircraft.
Aircraft
  Allied
    aerodynamics safety, 18
    air-ground coordination, 18. *See also* Communications.
    air-ground "armored packets," 18
    aerial photographs, 126, 147, 243, 245
    aerial searches, 79
    close support, 297, 299, 319
    fire power, 17
    liaison, 18
    navigation, 18
    observation, 19, 254, 298, 320
    oxygen system, 280
    procurement, 53
    revetments, 102, 106, 110, 123
    self-sealing fuel tanks, 104, 279
    tactics, 18
    wing tanks, 241
    types
      B–17s, 99, 162, 221, 225, 229, 241, 245, 280, 293, 327–328, 344, 354–355, 362
      B–25s, 209
      B–26s, 224, 363
      bombers, 157, 164, 280, 350, 365
      C–47s, 280, 328*n*
      carrier planes, 210, 230, 241, 258–259, 355
      dive bombers, 207, 212, 223, 226–227, 263, 267, 279–280, 299, 339, 354
      Dutch, 78–79, 123

Aircraft—Continued
  Allied—Continued
    types—Continued
      fighters, 81, 87, 163, 217, 219, 226, 259, 263, 294, 354, 365
      F2A–3s, 216, 225
      F4Fs, 66, 101–102, 107–108, 110, 120, 128, 207, 219, 223, 225–226, 241, 279, 291–292, 294–295, 302–303, 326, 336, 343*n*, 362
      liaison, 254, 373
      Lockheed Hudsons, 363
      observation, 254, 325, 339
      OS2Us, 363
      P–38s, 362
      P–39s, 328, 336, 343*n*, 344, 362
      P–40s, 180
      P–400s, 280, 297, 299, 308, 323, 328, 343*n*, 362
      patrol, 36, 66, 70–71, 81–83, 98, 211, 292, 294, 352
      PBYs, 78, 80–81, 89, 102, 104, 123, 126–127, 161, 163, 165, 216, 221, 277, 328, 363
      photographic planes, 241
      R4Ds, 280, 328*n*
      SBDs, 207, 219, 224–229, 267, 269, 279, 292, 294–295, 305, 311, 316–317, 323, 327–328, 336, 339, 343*n*, 344, 362
      SB2Us, 216, 219, 224–225, 229
      scout bombers, 73, 75, 305
      seaplanes, 360
      TBDs, 226–227
      TBFs, 224, 305, 311, 323, 362
      torpedo bombers, 207, 212, 226, 305, 339, 354
  German, 55
  Japanese, 16, 62, 71, 73–74, 79, 108–111, 125, 128–129, 131, 159, 164–165, 170, 185, 187, 201, 211, 224, 241, 275–276, 279–280, 292, 335, 336, 339
    types
      bombers, 70–71, 76, 107, 112, 115, 121, 123–127, 163–165, 170, 181–182, 185, 189, 220, 223, 258, 275, 292, 294–295, 302, 326–327, 352

413

Aircraft—Continued
  Japanese—Continued
    types—Continued
      carrier planes, 119, 128, 230
      dive bombers, 70–71, 73, 128, 143, 147, 152, 163, 170, 221, 223, 227, 258
      fighter planes, 70–71, 73, 127–128, 151, 163, 165, 170, 218, 227–228, 292, 294, 326
      floatplanes, 227, 260, 291
      flying boats, 121, 123–124, 221
      Kates, 221, 228, 339
      Kawanishi 97s, 115, 121, 123, 218, 224, 228
      observation planes, 275, 327
      seaplanes, 263
      torpedo bombers, 71, 221, 228, 259, 352
      Vals, 221, 223
      Zeros, 128, 221, 223–225, 227–228, 292, 294, 297, 302, 328, 335–336
Air support. *See* Aircraft.
Airfields
  Allied, 36, 64, 68, 99, 102, 106, 108–109, 115–116, 123, 130, 133–134, 136–137, 139, 141, 148–149, 162, 210, 212, 238–239, 241, 255–256, 274–277, 280, 283, 294, 299, 327–328, 336, 346, 352–354, 360
  Japanese, 163–165, 238, 258, 347
Air units, Allied. *See also* Marine units, Air.
  Chinese Air Force, 60
  Philippine Army Air Corps, 180, 188, 191
  Royal New Zealand Air Force, 241
  Royal Australian Air Force, 237
  U. S. Army Air Corps, 100, 156, 163*n*, 191, 241, 280
  Air, Asiatic Fleet, 175, 177
  Aircraft, Battle Force, 68, 100
  Aircraft, South Pacific, 241
  Cactus Air Force, 292–295, 302, 311, 317–320, 323, 326–327, 335–336, 343, 345, 362
  Far East Air Force, 162–164, 170
  21st Air Group, 363
  24th Air Group, 363
  25th Air Group, 363
  26th Air Group, 363
  5th Bombardment Group, 363
  11th Bombardment Group, 293, 363
  69th Bombardment Squadron, 363
  12th Fighter Squadron, 363
  67th Fighter Squadron, 280, 323, 327
  68th Fighter Squadron, 363
  70th Fighter Squadron, 363

Air units, Allied—Continued
  Flight 300, 292, 323
  3d Pursuit Squadron, 177
  3d Reconnaissance Squadron (RNZAF), 363
  VP–12, 363
  VP–21, 78–79, 81, 216
  VS–1–D14, 89–90
  VS–3, 305
  VT–8, 305
Akagi, 215, 223, 227
Akebono, 79–80
Akizuki, 325
Alameda, 50*n*
Alamo, 155
Alaska, 214
Alchiba, 253
Aleutians, 214–215, 218
Alhena, 250, 253
American-British staff conversations, 36, 63
American Legion, 253
American Samoa. *See* Samoa.
Ammunition. *See also* Weapons.
  Allied, 21, 68, 71, 79, 104, 107, 112, 144, 157, 163–164, 167–168, 172, 188, 217, 257, 260, 270, 276–277, 295, 310–311, 316, 321, **348**
    dumps, 164, 297
    magazines, 66, 99, 112, 217
    types
      armor-piercing, 16
      bombardment, 16
      bombs, 108, 120, 122, 126, 181, 183, 209, 212, 269, 276, 293, 297, 328, 355
      .50 caliber, 120, 133
      5-inch, 112, 114, 119, 268
      machine-gun, 114, 195
      mechanically-fused, 163
      90mm, 297
      105mm, 306
      rifle, 73
      6-inch, 26
      small arms, 104, 114, 250
      3-inch, 103, 111–112, 114, 136, 144
      tracer, 193
      torpedoes, 212–213, 227, 328, 351, 365
      20mm, 108
  Japanese, 327, 357, 364, 367
    types
      armor-piercing, 353
      bombardment, 326
      bombs, 71, 73, 108, 121, 125, 126, 163, 165, 170, 185, 190, 200, 207, 212, 218, 223–225, 258, 279, 295, 305, 323, 326–327, 339

INDEX 415

Ammunition—Continued
  Japanese—Continued
    types—Continued
      8-inch, 327
      mortar, 141, 330
      6-inch, 117
      torpedoes, 71, 212, 221, 224, 227, 311, 339, 353
      240mm, 190
Amphibian vehicles
  amphibian tractor, 32–33, 256, 270, 276, 320, 329
  Christie amphibian, 23, 32
  DUKW, 34
  LVT, 32–34
  LVT (A), 33–34
Amphibious doctrine and techniques, 7–8, 11, 14–15, 23, 51, 254, 372–373. *See also* Logistics; Planning.
Amphibious equipment, 23–24, 30. *See also* Amphibian vehicles; Ships.
Amphibious exercises, 22, 52
Anchor and chrysanthemum device, 285
Anderson, LtCol H. R., 171
Anopheles mosquito, 239
Antiaircraft fire, 42, 68, 71, 73, 95, 140, 162, 241, 258–259, 352, 357
Anti-Axis powers, 155
Antiboat obstacles, 113, 190
Antigua, 54
Antilles, 54
Antisubmarine missions, 89, 363
Anzac area, 84, 84n, 205, 209, 235, 238
Aoba, 129, 325
Aola Bay, 285, 343, 348, 363
Aotea Quay, 249
Aparri, 164, 166
Apergis, 1stLt J., 219
Apia, 89–90
Apra Harbor, 76
Arashi, 365
ARCADIA Conference, 85
Argonaut, 285
Arizona, 107, 113
Argentia, 39, 54
Armistead, Capt K., 223
Armistice, 9
Army ground units (Allied). *See also* Marine units, Ground.
  Australian Imperial Force, 237
  Canadian Army, 36
  New Zealand Army, 250

Army ground units (Allied)—Continued
  Philippine Army, 155–157, 164–167, 172, 190n, 191, 200
  Philippine Constabulary, 156, 172, 190n, 191
  Philippine Scouts, 156, 156n, 179–180, 190n, 191, 194
  United States Army, 5, 7, 11, 14, 21, 30, 31, 33, 34, 37, 39, 43–46, 42, 54–55, 63, 71, 74, 86–88, 156, 166, 187–188, 190n, 236, 242n, 295, 297, 321, 323, 326, 329, 336–337, 349, 358, 360, 369, 372
  United States Army Forces in the Far East (USAFFE), 156–157, 161–164, 165n, 166–167, 173, 175–176, 178–179, 182
  United States Forces in the Philippines (USFIP), 182, 184, 189–190, 199–200
  Headquarters Samoan Area Defense Force, 90
  Iceland Base Command, 44
  Luzon Force, 182
  Service Command (Bataan), 175, 177
  I Philippine Corps, 172, 176, 179–180
  II Philippine Corps, 172, 176, 180
  XIV Corps, 362, 362n, 366–369
  North Luzon Force, 167
  South Luzon Force, 166–167
  1st Infantry Division, 52, 54
  2d Constabulary Division, 175
  25th Infantry Division, 342, 351, 360, 362, 366–369, 371
  31st Philippine Division, 167
  71st Philippine Division, 175, 177
  Americal Division, 238, 324, 328, 342, 348, 362, 362n, 365–368
  CAM (Composite Army-Marine) Division, 368–369
  Philippine Division, 156, 156n
  59th Coast Artillery Regiment, 198
  60th Coast Artillery Regiment, 171
  27th Infantry Regiment, 360, 366, 368
  35th Infantry Regiment, 360, 366–367
  132d Infantry Regiment, 348, 360, 365–366
  147th Infantry Regiment, 342–343, 363, 367–369, 371
  161st Infantry Regiment, 360, 366, 371
  164th Infantry Regiment, 324, 326, 328–329, 333, 334n, 337, 337n, 348–351, 357, 360, 360n
  182d Infantry Regiment, 348, 352, 357–358, 360, 360n, 366, 368–369
  101st Medical Regiment, 360n
  26th Philippine Scout Cavalry Regiment, 166
  45th Philippine Scout Regiment, 183
  57th Philippine Scout Regiment, 179

Army ground units (Allied)—Continued
  101st Quartermaster Regiment, 360n
  Americal Division Reconnaissance Squadron, 360n, 365–366
  244th Coast Artillery Battalion, 342n, 357
  57th Engineer Combat Battalion, 360n
  Field Artillery Battalions
    221st, 360n
    245th, 360n
    246th, 347, 363
    247th, 360, 360n
  Infantry Battalions
    1/132, 360
    1/147, 342
    1/164, 334–345, 348, 358
    1/182, 358
    2/132, 366, 371
    2/164, 334–336, 348–350
    2/182, 358
    3/164, 336, 348, 358
    3/182, 366
  British Solomon Islands Defense Force, 285
  Guamanian Insular Force Guard, 76, 76n
  Guamanian Insular Patrol, 76
  301st Chemical Company, 177
  35th Reconnaissance Troop, 366
  26th Signal Company, 360n
  Army Air Corps Detachment, Wake, 103n, 104, 106
Arndt, Sgt C. C., 281
Arnold, LtGen H. H., 85, 342
Arthur, Col J. M. 250, 261, 269n, 345, 350
Arthur, SSgt R. O., 101n, 108
Artillery
  Allied, 8, 16–18, 29, 38, 48, 50, 156, 180–182, 189, 256, 290, 306, 319–320, 334–336, 342–343, 345, 358. *See also* Marine units.
  Japanese, 172, 178, 181, 184–185, 187, 192–193, 195, 198, 202, 286, 299, 301–302, 316, 322–323, 330, 332–333, 337, 354, 358
Aruba, 54n
Asagumo, 325, 356
Asanagi, 129
Ashe, Capt G. B., 253–254
Ashurst, Col W. W., 160
Asia, 59
Asiatic Fleet. *See* Naval units (Allied).
Assistant Commandant of the Marine Corps, 13, 44
Astoria, 114, 131, 229, 254, 260
Atabrine tablets, 239
Atago, 356

Atlanta, 353
Atlantic, 5, 24, 37, 40, 53–54, 63, 342
Atlantic Conference, 42
Atlantic Fleet. *See* Naval units (Allied).
Atoga, 355–356
Attu, 215
Auckland, 242
Australia, 61, 84, 86–88, 155, 205, 209, 230, 235–239, 243, 247, 351, 360, 372
Australian and New Zealand Army Corps, 84n
Australian Mandated Territory of New Guinea, 243
Axis Powers, 47, 53, 59, 61, 63, 85
Ayarami, 356
Azores, 30–31, 38, 55–56

Bagac, 173, 176–177, 180
Baggage, 250
Bagley, 260
Bahamas, 3, 54
Bahm, LCdr G. H., 27n
Bailey, Maj K. W., 263, 315
Baker Island, 115
Baldinus, Lt L., 293
Baldwin, H. W., 191n
Bales, LtCol W. L., 89, 89n
Balesuna River, 245
Ballard, 316
Banana wars, 199
Banzai charges, 329, 334, 339
Barbed wire. *See* Defenses.
Barber's Point, 73
Barnes, BM1stCl J. E., 132n, 137
Barnett, 253
Barninger, Lt C. A., 117–118, 128, 148; Capt, 140; LtCol, 110n, 140n
Barracks, 111, 160–161, 168, 171
Barrett, BriGen C. D., 70n, 90
Barton, 353
Base development, 152
Basilone, Sgt J., 335, 335n
Bataan, 17, 84, 155, 166–168, 171–173, 175–177, 179–185, 187–189, 192–193, 195, 199–200, 202
Batan Island, 163
Battery Crockett, 171, 188, 190
Battery Point, 185
Battery Geary, 171, 188, 190
Battleship row, 71
Battleships. *See* Ships.
Bauer, Maj H. W., 279; LtCol, 362
Bauer, K. J., 216n
Bayler, Maj W. L. J., 100, 102, 104n, 108, 121n, 124, 125n, 127, 216n, 217; LtCol, 98, 98n

INDEX

Beaches. *See also* Defenses; Shore Party.
  Beach Blue 266, 269–270
  Beachmaster, 20
  Beach party, 20–21
  Beach Red, 254, 258, 269
  dumps, 260, 276
  marking, 20
Bearn, 54
Beaufort Bay, 367
Beecher, LtCol C. T., 171, 189, 194; BriGen, 189n
Bell, Maj G. A., 327
Bellatrix, 253
Benham, 356
Benson, Maj W. W., 223
Beri-beri, 187
Bermuda, 54
Berry, Capt G. J., 189n
Betelgeuse, 252–253, 352
Biebush, LtCol F. C., 256
Binu, 350
Bismarck Archipelago, 62, 78n, 205, 237–238, 275, 302, 310, 369
Bivouac areas, 20
Blacksmith shop, 111, 125
Blitzkrieg, 47
Bloch, RAdm C. C., 75, 79; Adm, 65n
Blockade run, 276
Block Four River, 290–291
Bloody Ridge, 305–306, 308–310, 313, 315–316, 329–330, 333, 336–337, 347, 360
Blue, 260
Blue Goose, 328
Boat Rig A, 29
Boatswains' pipes, 71
Boise, 324–325
Bomb racks, 104
Bombs. *See* Ammunition.
Bone, LtCol B. A., 83
Bonesteel, MajGen C. H., 43–44, 46
Bonegi River, 371
Booth, 1stLt A. L., 79; LtCol, 79n
Borneo, 84, 172, 301
Borg-Warner Corporation, 34
Borth, MG H. C., 110, 121
Bottomside, 169, 171, 181, 183, 195, 201
Bougainville, 237, 243, 259, 322, 373
Bowen, Maj R. O., 345
Branic, Sgt J. H., 283
Brazil, 56
Bremerton, 50
Brice, LtCol W. O., 343; Col, 362
Bridges, 256, 258, 278, 288, 344, 347, 351. *See also* Engineer operations.

Bridget, Cdr F. J., 175, 175n, 177–180
Briggs, PlSgt R., Jr., 334
Brisbane, 258
British Chiefs of Staff, 86
British Commonwealth, 61, 84n
British Empire, 5
British Guiana, 54
British Solomon Islands Protectorate, 237, 243
Brook, Capt C. B., USN, 185n
Brown, Maj L. A., 160
Brown, Capt P. A., 190, 192
Brush, Capt C. H., Jr., 285, 288; Maj, 285n
Bryan, B., 134n
Bryan, LCdr J., III, 371n
Bubbling Well-Nanking Roads, 159
Buchanan, 263, 268–269, 324, 352
Buckley, LtCol E. J., 281n
Buckner, Capt J. H., 80, 217
Bugles, 71, 73
Buka, 243
Buna, 238
Bunkers. *See* Defenses.
Buoys, 19
Bureau of Construction and Repair, 24, 26–27, 29, 32
Bureau of Engineering, 24
Bureau of Ordnance, 68
Bureau of Ships, 28, 31, 33–34
Burma, 62, 86
Burrows, 82
Burton, Capt C., Jr., 216; LtCol, 216n
Bushido spirit, 322, 335
Butler, J. R. M., 35n
Buzzard Patrol, 357

CAA homing tower, 83
Caballo Island, 169, 181
Cadres, 48
Caldwell, Lt T., 292; LCdr, 323, 323n
Calhoun, 253
California, 14
Call to Arms, 71, 105–106, 161
Callaghan, RAdm D. J., 252, 325–355
Camouflage, 103, 107, 110, 117
Camp Elliott, 38, 46, 51–52, 88
Camp Holcomb, 160
Camp Lejeune, 52
Canada, 16, 35
Canberra, 260
Cannon, 1stLt G. H., 79
Canopus, 164, 175, 180, 187
Canton Island, 87

Cape Cod, 10
Cape Esperance, 253–254, 260, 325, 343, 351, 353, 356, 365, 367, 369, 371
Cape May, 24
Cape of Good Hope, 342
Cape York, 327
Carabao Island, 169, 181
Carderock, 50
Carey, 1stLt J. F., 217; Capt, 223
Cargo nets, 19
Caribbean, 5, 8–9, 14, 38, 52–54
Carl, Capt M., 292
Carlson, LtCol E. F., 262, 285, 342, 348, 350
Caroline Islands, 10, 63, 96
Carpenter's Wharf, 264–265
Carr, MessSgt G., 137
Carriers. *See* Ships.
Castor, 100
Castle, Capt N. O., 192, 197
Casualties
    Allied, 73–74, 78, 80, 88, 109, 111, 122, 125, 152, 164–165, 171, 180, 189–190, 194, 197, 200, 207, 230, 267, 269–270, 279, 283, 285, 291–292, 299, 308, 310–311, 315–316, 320–322, 327, 337, 339, 349–350, 353, 359, 374
    Japanese, 74, 120, 137, 146, 149, 152, 180, 196, 200, 247, 266, 269–270, 283, 285, 290–291, 299, 308, 317, 320–321, 332, 337, 345–346, 350, 374
Cate, J. L., 163n, 235n
Cates, Col C. B., 248, 256–257, 290
Causeways, 267
Cavalry Point, 185, 192–193, 198
Cavite, 157, 162–164, 168–170, 181, 184, 189
Cebu, 301
Central Pacific, 64, 75, 83–84, 96, 214, 253. *See also* Pacific.
Cereal, 249–250
Chambers, Maj J., 264
Chambers, Capt R., Jr., 188, 195–196, 198
Chaney, Lt H. F., Jr., 327
Chappell, Maj C. J., Jr., 216
Charleston, 38–40
Charleston, 7, 7n
Cheney Ravine, 168
Cherry Point, 52
Chester, 207
Chicago, 260
Chief of Naval Operations (CNO), 13–14, 33–34, 37, 39, 44, 65, 67, 85, 96
Chikuma, 129, 143n, 227
China, 11, 59–60, 84, 157–158, 160–161, 301, 322
China Sea, 159

Chinwangtao, 158, 160
Chitose, 291–292, 325
Choiseul, 243, 259
Chokai, 327, 354
Christmas Island, 87
Chunn, Capt C. E., 188n, 198
Churchill, Prime Minister W. S., 35, 35n, 36–37, 40, 42–43, 86
Civilian construction contractors, 52, 65–66, 81–82, 95, 98–99, 104, 122
Civil War, 16
Clark, Maj C., 362
Clark, Capt G. L., Jr., 195, 199
Clark Field, 100
Classified documents, 124
Clearwater, 32–33
Clemens, Capt W. F. M., 285, 285n
Clement, LtCol W. T., 160n, 161; Col, 179
Clothing, 38–39, 170, 277
Coast defense. *See* Defenses; Weapons.
Coast Guard. *See* Naval units (Allied).
Coastwatchers, 320, 326, 353
Coconut plantations, 243, 297
Collins, MajGen J. L., 360, 366
Colors, national, 149, 199
Combat loading, 19–20, 38, 248–249. *See also* Logistics.
Combined Chiefs of Staff (CCS), 85–87
Commandant of the Marine Corps, 10–11, 13, 29–30, 32–33, 44, 262
Commander in Chief, Asiatic Fleet (CinCAF), 158–161, 165n
Commander in Chief, Pacific Fleet (CinCPac), 84, 114, 131, 143, 218, 236
Commander in Chief, Pacific Ocean Area (CinCPOA), 87
Commander in Chief, United States Fleet (CominCh), 84–85
Command relationships, 15, 43, 46, 240–241, 373
Commander, U. S. Naval Forces, Europe, 85
Communications
    Allied, 8, 18, 27, 102, 209, 348
      air-ground, 18, 108, 110
      trans-Pacific cable, 65, 108
      failure, 137, 144, 151, 162, 192, 197
      panels, 297
      radio, 79, 105, 111, 131, 138, 152, 160, 265, 297–298, 316, 347, 367
      radio intercept, 157
      runner, 192
      semaphore, 316
      testing, 79

INDEX 419

Communications—Continued
    Allied—Continued
        wire, 68, 103, 105, 108, 110, 132, 137, 152, 189–190, 192, 256, 290, 306, 334
    Japanese
        flares, 76, 82, 136, 138, 195, 198, 305–306, 323
        radio, 258, 264, 286, 332
        ship-to-shore, 285
        telephone, 333
Command posts, 18, 66, 79
Communist Cominform, 59
Concrete battleship, 169. *See also* Fort Drum.
Conderman, 2dLt R. J., 100, 100n, 102, 108
Condit, K. W., 92n
Condition Red, 335
Congress, 52–52, 75
Conn, S., 35n
Conoley, Maj O. M., 337
Constitution, 3–4
Construction. *See* Engineer operations.
Continental Congress, 3
Continental Marines, 3
Convoys, 39–40, 43, 46. *See also* Ships.
Cooley, Col A. D., 362
Copra, 243
Coral formations. *See* Terrain.
Coral Sea, 205, 209–210, 212, 214–215, 218, 227, 230, 235, 237–238, 286
Corpus Christi, 50n
Corregidor, 84, 87, 155, 157, 167–171, 173, 175, 179, 181, 183–185, 188–190, 192–193, 196, 198, 200–202
Corregidor Marines, 202. *See also* Marine units.
Cory, Lt R., 281
Cosmoline packing, 160
Coulson, PlSgt R. L., 146–147
Counteroffensives
    Allied, 303, 337
    Japanese, 283, 319–320, 330, 334–337, 343, 345, 351, 353, 359
Cox, Capt J. D., 316
Crace, RAdm J. C., 210
Cram, Maj J., 328
Crane, Capt E. J., 263, 268
Craven, W. S., 163n, 235n
Creek-Seminole Indian Wars, 4
Crescent City, 250–253
Cresswell, LtCol L. B., 258, 290–291
Crowl, P. A., 8n
Croizat, LtCol V. J., 32n
Cruisers. *See* Ships.
Crutchley, RAdm V. A. C., 241

Cuba, 38
Culebra, 8–10, 14, 18n, 23, 26, 29–30
Cunningham, Cdr W. S., 99, 102–103, 106, 106n, 107, 117n, 124–126, 134, 140–141, 143–148; Capt, 99n, 126n
Cunningham Field, 52
Curacao, 54n
Curry, LtCol M. L., 271n
Curtis, MajGen H. O., 42
Cushing, 353
Custer, 1stSgt S. A., 281

Daggett, LCdr R. B., 27, 27n
Dalness, Capt H. E., 197–198; Maj, 185n
Damage control teams, 71
Danish King, 35
Davidson, 2dLt C. R., 100n, 107n, 121, 128
David Taylor Model Basin, 50
Davis, LtCol H. L., 162n
Davis, Maj L. K., 326
Davits, 24, 28
De Carre, BriGen A., 360
Defenses
    Allied
        antitank obstacles, 290
        armor plate, 279
        barbed wire, 114, 181, 190, 193, 220, 313, 334
        beach defenses, 17, 68, 121, 126–127, 167, 171, 179–181, 185, 188, 190, 201, 313
        bunker, 110
        coast and harbor, 67, 157, 168
        dummy guns, 112–113, 127
        emplacements, 99, 103, 110, 112, 126–127, 181, 185, 190, 192, 310, 337
        field fortifications, 288, 290, 330
        foxholes, 79, 99, 107, 109–110, 161, 170, 188, 192, 305–306, 313, 323, 332, 337
        gun turrets, 169
        personnel shelters, 103, 109–110, 124, 168
        positions, 109, 126, 128, 134, 152, 173
        sandbags, 103, 107, 112, 121
        tank trap, 195
        trenches, 181, 198
    Japanese
        caves, 269
        dugouts, 269–270
        foxholes, 270, 320
        emplacements, 268, 308, 313, 367
Del Monte, 162
del Valle, Col P. A., 313
Denmark, 35, 35n, 36n, 53
Demountable tracks, 23

Dengue fever, 245
Denver Battery, 193–199
Dessez, Capt J. H. S., USN, 175
Dessez, LtCol L. A., 88
Destroyers. *See* Ships.
Detonator magazines, 99
Devereux, Maj J. P. S., 99–100, 102, 104–106, 108, 112–113, 117, 117n, 118, 121, 126, 132, 134, 136, 136n, 137–138, 138n, 139, 139n, 140–144, 147–149, 151; Col, 96n, 107n, 130n
Dewey, Adm G. F., 7
Diamond, G., 92n
Dierdorff, Capt R. D., USN, 95n
Diesel fuel. *See* Fuel.
Dill, Gen Sir J., 42
Dixon, LCdr R. E., 211n
Docks, 243
Dockside equipment, 249
Doma Cove, 371
Doolittle, LtCol J. H., 207, 209, 218
Downing, SSgt C. E., 197n
Drydocks, 74
Drysdale, Maj D. B., 36n
Dugout Sunday, 335, 343
Duhamel, Father A. C., 283, 285n
Duke of York & Albany's Maritime Regiment of Foot, 3. *See also* Royal Marines.
Dumps. *See* Supply.
Duncan, 324–325
Dunedin, 33, 50
Dungeas Beach, 76, 78
Dutch Guiana, 54n
Dutch Harbor, 214
Dynamite, 109–110, 112, 125, 220
Dysentery, 182

Early warning equipment, 65, 103, 109, 122, 150, 162, 192. *See also* Radar.
East Asia, 237
Eastern Hemisphere, 36n
Eastern Island, 80, 216–217, 219, 223
East Indies, 62, 84, 86, 322
East Sector, 171, 189–195, 197, 199, 201
Edson, LtCol M. A., 248; Col, 264–265, 298–299, 303, 305–306, 308, 315, 315n, 316, 320, 343–345, 347
Edson's Ridge. *See* Bloody Ridge.
Efate, 88, 238–239, 279–280
Egypt, 342
El Fraile Island, 169
Ellice Islands, 239
Elliott, 253, 259

Ellis, Maj E. H., 8–9, 9n, 10
Elrod, Capt H. T., 100n, 107n, 109–110, 112, 119–120, 141
Emperor's birthday, 189
Engineer operations
 building equipment, 277
 construction, 45, 64, 66, 112
 dirt-moving equipment, 250
 hand tools, 66, 89, 114, 276–277, 279
 heavy equipment, 74, 88, 99, 104, 109, 125, 311
 Japanese equipment, 258, 274, 330
 Japanese units, 386, 301–302, 323, 329, 354
 pneumatic tampers, 294
 power shovels, 274
 safety, 18,
 units, 8, 20, 38, 48, 74, 274, 276–277, 279, 290, 294–295, 303, 311, 313, 343–344. *See also* Naval units; Marine units.
Emplacements. *See* Defenses.
England, 35, 42
Enright, Maj W. K., 344
Enterprise, 65–66, 74, 101–102, 114, 205, 207, 209, 214, 218, 221, 226–228, 242, 247n, 252, 263n, 280, 292–293, 311, 339, 342, 352, 354
Equipment. *See* Supply.
Ericsson, 249n
Erskine, Maj J. C., 264n
Espiritu Santo, 239, 241–242, 261, 280, 293–294, 302, 305, 310–311, 322, 327–328, 343–344, 354, 357, 362, 376
Esprit de corps, 46
Eureka. *See* Landing craft.
Europe, 18, 38, 47, 53, 55–56, 59, 61, 63, 85, 342
Everglades, 32
Ewa Mooring Mast Field, 48, 68, 71, 73, 101, 279
 See also Airfields.
Expeditionary service, 8–9, 13
Explosives, 250, 274, 291

Fairchild, B., 35n
Far East, 5, 7, 63, 95, 155
Farenholt, 324–325
Faroe Island, 40n
Fassett, Col H. S., 115, 115n
Featherstone, 270
Feldt, Cdr E. A., 237n
Ferguson, QMClk F. W., 195–196, 198; Capt, 161n
Ferrell, GunSgt H. M., 176n; MG, 191n, 193–194
Few, PlSgt F. L., 281
Field glasses, 333

Fields of fire, 305
Fighter 1, 295, 326–328, 335–336, 362. *See also* Airfields.
Fighter 2, 362. *See also* Airfields.
Fiji Islands, 84, 87–88, 230, 237–238, 242, 247, 250, 252–253, 259, 279
Fike, LtCol C. L., 279
Fink, Ens C., 293
Finschhafen, 237
Fire-control equipment, 82, 103, 107, 110, 112–114, 118, 127, 138, 148, 152, 190, 325, 355. *See also* Radar; Weapons.
Fitch, RAdm A. W., 362
Flag. *See* Colors, national.
Fleet landing exercises (Flex), 14–15, 20–21, 26
    Flex 4, 26
    Flex 5, 27, 29–30
    Flex 6, 27, 30
Fleet Training Publication 167, 14, 17
Fleming, Capt R. E., 229, 229*n*
Fletcher, 353
Fletcher, RAdm F. J., 115, 130–131, 143, 205, 207, 210–211, 218, 218*n*, 221, 224, 226, 229, 229*n*, 230, 237–238, 240; VAdm, 242, 250*n*, 252, 258–259, 291–292
Florida, 32
Florida Island, 237–238, 243, 247–248, 253–254, 260, 263, 268, 270
Fomalhaut, 253
Fontana, Maj P. J., 343
Food. *See* Supply.
Food Machinery Corporation, 33–34
Ford Island, 71, 73, 101
Formosa, 160, 162–163, 165, 172
Fort Drum, 169, 171, 181, 184, 193
Fort Fisher, 16
Fort Frank, 169, 181, 184
Fort Hughes, 169, 171, 180, 193
Fort Mills, 168–171
Fort Storey, 32
Fort Wint, 167
Forward observers, 18
Foss, Capt J. J. 326, 336
Fowel, MSgt R. 316
Fox, Col W. J., 362
France, 9, 53–54, 59, 137
Fraser, Capt L. S., 217; LtCol, 79*n*
Frazier, Lt K. D., 292
Free French, 90
Freeman, Air Chief Marshal Sir W., 42
French Guiana, 54*n*
French High Commissioner for the Antilles, 54

Frueler, Capt H. C., 100*n*, 104*n*, 109, 119–120, 122–123, 128
Fubuki, 325
Fuchida, M., 205*n*, 215*n*, 230, 238*n*
Fuel, 157, 250, 259, 277, 327
    aviation, 108, 225, 277, 311, 326
    bulk, 107
    diesel, 117, 125, 277
    drums, 108
    dumps, 268
    gasoline, 21, 99, 164, 277, 280
    Japanese, 277, 286
    tanks, 82, 117, 223
Fuel-drum floats, 344
Fuller, 253
Fuller, MajGen J. F. C., 7
Funafuti, 239
Fungus infections, 245
Fundamentals of teamwork, 92
Furumiya, Col, 337
Furutaka, 129, 325

Galer, Capt R. E., 279; Maj, 295
Galley, 223
Gallipoli, 16
Galloping Horse, 366–367
Gaomi, 269
Garage, 111, 125
Gas masks, 107
Gasoline. *See* Fuel.
Gavaga Creek, 349
Gavutu, 238, 243, 247–248, 263, 267–271
Gay, Ens G. H., 227*n*
Gay, P., 134*n*
Geary Point, 188
Geiger, Col R. S., 17; BriGen 297–298, 311, 324, 327–328, 336, 343, 362
General Quarters, 71
Generators, 136
Geneva, 59
Geraci, LtCol F., 274
German Consulate, 36
German submarines, 35–36, 53–55, 63, 342
Germany, 37, 40, 53–56, 59–60, 63, 342
Ghormley, VAdm R. L., 236, 236*n*, 237, 239–240, 240*n*, 241–242, 250, 250*n*, 252, 259, 262, 276, 302, 305, 311, 324, 341
Gibraltar, 38, 170
Gifu Pocket, 365–367
Gilbert Islands, 62, 115, 205, 207, 239, 253, 285, 363
Gizo Harbor, 301

Gleason, S. E., 35n
Glidden, Capt E. G., 224n
Godbold, Capt B. D., 138, 141-142, 142n, 151; LtCol, 121n, 127n
Goettge, LtCol F. B., 243, 247, 281, 281n
Goto, RAdm A., 210
Government Ravine, 171, 188, 195
Government Track, 276
Gragg, Sgt R., 140
Grassy Knoll, 256-257
Graves, 1stLt G. A., 100n, 108-109
Graves, Cpl L., 138-139, 141
Great Britain, 35-37, 47, 53, 61-63, 85
Great East Asia War, 155
Greeley, 2dLt R. W., 142
Greenland, 36n
Greenport Basin and Construction Company, 24
Greenslade, RAdm J. W., 55
Greey, LCdr E. B., 99, 99n, 127
Gregory, 253
Gridley, 270
Griffin, Col R., 90
Griffith, LtCol S. B., II, 315, 315n
Guadalcanal, 15-16, 19, 22, 237-239, 241-243, 245, 247-248, 253-254, 257-259, 261-271, 275-277, 279-280, 283, 285-286, 288, 291-292, 294, 297-298, 301-302, 310-311, 317, 322-324, 327, 330, 333, 336, 339, 341-343, 346, 350-357, 359-360, 360n, 362-367, 369, 371-374
Guadeloupe, 54n
Guam, 7, 7n, 9, 64, 75-76, 78, 78n, 84, 95, 106, 115, 286
Guamanians 76, 78
Guantanamo Bay, 5, 8, 10, 16, 38
Gulf coast, 24
Gwin, 356

Haiti, 9, 11, 17
Halavo Peninsula, 263
Haleta, 263
Haley, Lt G. L., 327
Hall, LtCol R. K., 334-336
Halsey, VAdm W. F., 114, 205, 207, 209, 218; Adm, 218n, 341-342, 352-354, 355n, 359, 369, 371, 371n
Halstead, PFC W. C., 146
Hamilton, MG H. B., 292
Hamilton, Capt J. H., 107
Hamilton, TSgt W. J., 101n, 107n, 109, 111, 120, 122-124
Hampton Roads, 27
Handley, 1stLt R. M., 80

Hand pumps, 102
Hanna, 2dLt R. M., 134, 136-137, 139-141, 148, 152; 1stLt, 134n
Hanneken, LtCol H. H., 320-321, 333, 336-337, 347, 347n, 348-349
Hara-kiri, 293, 308
Harmon, MajGen M. F., 240, 275-276, 280, 324, 362
Harris, 1stLt W. F., 192, 194-195
Hart, LtCol J. N., 241
Hart, Adm T. C., 155n, 157, 157n, 158, 158n, 159, 161, 161n, 164-165, 165n, 166-167
Haruna, 225, 326
Haskin, QMSgt J. E., 196
Hastie, Capt D. H., 219
Hatsuyuki, 325
Hauck, Capt H. H., 198
Havannah Harbor, 239
Hawaiian Islands, 5, 7, 7n, 9, 11, 62, 64-66, 68, 78, 83-84, 87-88, 95-96, 101, 123, 143, 215, 218-219, 238, 249, 253, 351, 360
Hayashio, 351, 356
Hayate, 118, 120
Hayes, Maj C. H., 276
Hayes, Cdr T. H., 170n
Haynes, Capt R. M., 218
Hazelwood, Cpl H. R., 79
Heel Point, 98, 141, 147
Heinl, 1stLt R. D., Jr., 115; LtCol, 4n, 5n, 64n, 113n, 130n, 216n, 265n, 342n
Helena, 324-325, 344, 348, 353
Helm, 260
Helmets, 107
Henderson, 158
Henderson Field, 279-280, 292-295, 298, 302-303, 308, 310-311, 314, 317, 323-324, 326-327, 333, 335, 337, 339, 343-346, 350-355, 357, 360, 362, 364. *See also* Airfields.
Henderson, Col F. P., 367n
Henderson, Maj L. R., 217, 224-225, 279
Hepburn Board, 64, 75
Hepburn Report, 95
Hermle, Col L. D., 38
Herring, Capt G. W., 264
Hesson, AD1stCl J. F., 123-124
Hetherneck, Lt(jg) R. G., 170n
Hevenor, H. P., 107n, 127
Heywood, 241, 253
Hickam Field, 71, 74, 106
Higgins, A., 24, 26-28, 30
Higgins boats. *See* Landing craft.
Hiei, 353-354
Hill, LtCol R. E., 263; Col, 269n

Hill 53, 367
Hill 54, 365
Hill 55, 365
Hill 56, 365
Hill 66, 363–364, 366
Hill 67, 329, 333
Hill 90, 368
Hill 94, 368
Hill 98, 368
Hill 148, 367, 269
Hill 208, 265–266
Hill 230, 265
Hill 281, 264–265
Hirokawa Maru, 355
Hiroyasu, Col, 337
Hiryu, 25, 127–130, 143, 227–228
Hitler, 36n, 38, 40, 47, 53–54, 56
Hitokappu Bay, 62
Hogaboom, 1stLt W. F., 162n. 175–177, 188, 192, 194–196
Hohn, Maj L. A., 98–99, 99n; Col, 80n
Hoists, 279
Holcomb, LtGen T., 44, 85n, 262, 333n, 341, 342n, 360n
Holden, 2dLt F. J., 100n, 108
Holdredge, 1stLt W. C., 175–178
Holewinski, Cpl R. J., 134
Hollingshead, 2dLt B., 68n
Homma, LtGen M., 155, 172–173, 176, 180–182, 184, 199–200
Hong Kong, 84
Hoover, VAdm John S., 55
Horii, MajGen T., 78n
Hornet, 207, 209, 214, 218, 226, 303, 311, 339
Hospitals, 104, 109, 111–112, 183. *See also* Medical activities.
Howard, Col S. L., 157–158, 161, 165, 167, 170, 180, 187, 189, 194; BriGen, 156n; LtGen, 181n
Howland Island, 115
Huizenga, 2dLt R. M., 160; Capt, 161n
Hull, Secretary C., 36n
Hunt, Col L. P., 41n, 248, 298, 315n
Hunt, LtCol R. G., 269
Hunter Liggett, 253, 259
Huston, CWO T. W., 269n
Hvalfjordur, 36, 45
Hyakutake, LtGen H., 286, 301, 322–323, 326, 328–329, 343, 346–347, 349–351, 353, 357, 364, 368–369
Hydrographic charts, 245. *See also* Maps.

Iberian peninsula, 55
Ibushi, K., 132n
Iceland, 35, 35n, 36, 36n, 37–46, 56
Icelandic Government, 35–37
Ichiki, Col K., 286, 288, 290–292, 297, 299, 301–302, 306, 308, 313, 322–324
Ilu River, 245, 256–258, 275, 288, 290, 299, 302, 306, 308, 313, 329
Imamura, Gen H., 364, 369
Imperial Palace, 209
India, 86
Indiana, 342
Indianapolis, 81
Indian Island, 50
Indian Ocean, 237
Indispensable Strait, 243
Indonesia, 286
Indo-China, 59–60, 155, 182
Infantry Point, 185, 192–193
Infiltration, 266
Inouye, VAdm N., 96, 115, 129–130
Intelligence
　Allied, 237, 242, 247
　Japanese, 62, 143
International Settlement, 158
Iron Bottom Sound, 325
Isely, J. A., 8n
Isolationist tendencies, 47
Isuzu, 354
Italy, 59, 63
Ito, MajGen T., 347n, 350
Iwo Jima, 373

Jabor Town, 207
Jachym, 2dLt J. J., 283, 285
Jack, LtCol S. S., 362
Jackson, CWO C. R., 159n
Jackson, Col G. T., 360
Jaluit, 114, 207
Jamaica, 54
James Ravine, 168, 185, 201
Japan, 8, 10, 53, 59–61, 63, 65, 78, 85, 95, 155, 209, 231, 357, 364, 372
Japanese Army star, 285
Japanese combat correspondent, 132
Japanese evacuation of Guadalcanal, 371, 374
Japanese delegates, 59
Japanese installations, 207, 247, 258
Japanese Units
　Army
　　Eighth Area Army, 364
　　Fourteenth Army, 165–166, 172–173, 180, 182, 184

Japanese Units—Continued
  Army—Continued
    Seventeenth Army, 286, 301, 322, 329, 332, 337, 349, 364
    2d Division, 314, 323, 327, 333, 358, 364
    4th Division, 182, 184–185
    7th Division, 286
    16th Division, 165–166, 172, 176, 182, 184
    18th Division, 301
    21st Division, 182
    38th Division, 323, 329, 346, 347n, 350–351, 358, 364
    48th Division, 164, 166, 172
    55th Division, 78n
    5th Air Group, 163, 170, 172
    35th Brigade, 286, 288, 301
    65th Brigade, 172–173, 176, 182
    Kawaguchi Force, 299, 301, 308, 310–311, 314, 317, 322
    South Seas Detached Force, 78
    2d Formosa Regiment, 164
    4th Infantry Regiment, 301, 308, 314, 319, 321–322, 329, 332, 364
    16th Infantry Regiment, 328–329, 334, 336–337, 364
    20th Infantry Regiment, 176–177
    28th Infantry Regiment, 286, 301
    29th Infantry Regiment, 329, 334–337, 364
    61st Infantry Regiment, 185, 193–194, 196
    124th Infantry Regiment, 301, 323, 329, 364
    144th Infantry Regiment, 78n
    228th Infantry Regiment, 350, 364
    229th Infantry Regiment, 354, 364
    230th Infantry Regiment, 328–329, 347, 354, 364
    Ichiki Force, 286, 288n, 290, 291, 294, 299, 301, 310, 317, 322, 364
    20th Independent Mountain Artillery Battalion, 322
    6th Independent Rapid Gun Battalion, 329
    7th Independent Rapid Gun Battalion, 329
    3d Light Trench Mortar Battalion, 329
    antiaircraft units, 322
    antitank units, 301, 323, 329
    engineer units, 185, 286, 301–302, 322–323, 329, 354
    medical units, 323
    mortar units, 185, 322–323
    mountain artillery units, 185, 322, 329
    signal units, 301
    service troops, 172
    tank units, 185, 322–323

Japanese Units—Continued
  Navy
    Naval General Staff, 62, 369
    Combined Fleet, 62, 96, 129, 228n, 230, 235, 346
    Second Fleet, 228, 339, 355–356, 369
    Third Fleet, 339
    Fourth Fleet, 75, 96, 115–116, 129
    Eighth Fleet, 238, 260, 286, 291, 301, 325, 350, 356
    Eleventh Air Fleet, 162, 165, 170, 325
    Southeastern Fleet, 346
    Advance Expeditionary Force, 215
    Aleutian Screening Force, 215
    Carrier Striking Force, 210, 215, 221, 226–227
    Midway Covering Force, 210–211
    Midway Invasion Force, 228
    Midway Main Body, 215, 229
    Midway Neutralization Unit, 78
    Midway Occupation Force, 215, 221
    Outer Seas Forces, 325
    Second Mobile Force, 214–215
    Submarine Force, 228
    Aleutian Screening Group, 228
    Port Moresby Invasion Group, 210–212
    Carrier Division 2, 127, 129
    Cruiser Division 6, 114–115, 129–130, 142
    Cruiser Division 7, 228
    Cruiser Division 8, 129–130
    Cruiser Division 18, 129
    Combat Division 3, 326
    Destroyer Division 15, 326, 350, 355
    Destroyer Division 24, 301
    Destroyer Division 29, 118
    Destroyer Division 30, 119
    Destroyer Division 31, 326
    Twenty-Fourth Air Flotilla, 107, 110, 115–116, 123, 253, 264
    Air Attack Force One, 107, 115
    Air Attack Force Three, 115
    Destroyer Squadron 2, 291
    Destroyer Squadron 4, 114
    Destroyer Squadron 6, 116
    2d Maizuru Special Naval Landing Force, 129–130, 133, 136, 140–144, 146–147, 149, 152
    3d Kure Special Naval Landing Force, 327
    5th Yokosuka Special Naval Landing Force, 286, 288, 293
    5th Defense Force, 76
    Tulagi Communication Base, 264

INDEX

Japanese Units—Continued
  Navy—Continued
    Special naval landing force troops, 96, 116, 133, 136, 143, 149, 293
Jarvis, 259
Java, 62, 86, 167, 172, 369
Jellicoe, Earl, 238*n*
Jenkins, 1stLt R. F., Jr., 187, 192; LtCol, 170*n*, 192*n*
Jeschke, Col R. H., 342
Jetties, 243
Jintsu, 291, 293, 299
Johnson, Maj C. W., 219
Johnston Island, 64–66, 68, 75, 81–84, 114
Joint Action of the Army and Navy, 11
Joint Board of the Army and Navy, 11, 14, 55
Joint Chiefs of Staff, 85, 85*n*, 86, 86*n*, 87–88, 235–236, 342
Joint Planning Committee, 54
Jonasson, Prime Minister H., 39*n*
Jones, 1stLt L. A., 216
Jolo Islands, 172
Josselyn, Lt H. E., 264*n*
Juneau, 353
Junyo, 339
June, MSgt R. M., 138*n*

Kaga, 215, 223, 227
Kagero, 293
Kahn, Lt(jg) G. M., 109*n*, 112
Kajioka, RAdm, 116–117, 118*n*, 119, 129–132
Kako, 129
Kalbfus, RAdm E. C., 32
Kaluf, Maj J., 32
Kaminbo Bay, 371
Kashima, 96
Kato, M., 60*n*
Kawaguchi, MajGen K., 288, 301–302, 305–306, 308, 313, 322–324, 329, 334*n*, 335
Kawaguchi, Capt S., IJN, 225*n*
Keene, Cdr C., 103
Keene, LtCol J. W., 164*n*
Kelly, Capt C. W., Jr., 316
Kentucky, 41
Kessler, 1stLt W. W., 119, 132, 142, 142*n*, 143
Key West, 5
Kimes, Maj I. L., 217
Kimmel, Adm H. E., 95–96, 114
Kindley Field, 169, 193, 200
King, RAdm E. J., 21–22, 55; Adm, 84–85, 87–88, 235–236, 242, 242*n*, 247–248, 276*n*, 341–342, 351; FAdm, 84*n*

King, MajGen E. P., Jr., 182, 182*n*, 183
King, Maj S. W., 171, 171*n*, 180
Kinkaid, RAdm T. C., 339, 354
Kinney, 2dLt J. F., 101*n*, 109–110, 121–122, 122*n*, 123–124, 128; 1stLt, 102*n*, 107*n*, 121*n*
Kinryu Maru, 291, 293
Kinugawa Maru, 355
Kinugasa, 129, 299, 325, 327, 354
Kirishima, 225, 353, 355–356
Kirn, LCdr L. J., 305
Kisaragi, 120
Kiska, 215
Kittyhawk, 219
Kiyokawa, 129, 133
Kliewer, 2dLt. D. D., 101*n*, 109, 111, 122, 124, 136, 141, 142*n*, 148; 1stLt, 149*n*
Kobe, 209
Kodiak, 50*n*
Kokomtumbu Island, 270
Kokumbona, 280, 283, 288, 298, 301, 308, 314–315, 317–318, 326, 329–330, 333, 337, 344–345, 349–350, 357, 363–364, 367–369
Kokumbona River, 343
Koli Point, 285, 308, 345–350, 363
Kondo, RAdm N., 215, 228–229, 339; VAdm, 355–356
Kongo, 326
Kongo Maru, 119–120
Konoye Cabinet, 60
Konoye, Prince, 60
Konryu Maru, 119
Korean War, 4
Koro Island, 247, 252
Koyanagi, RAdm T., 369
Kuku Point, 104, 117–119, 146
Kukum, 275–276, 311, 316–317, 326, 328, 362
Kukum River, 258
Kuniholm, Bertel E., 36
Kuriles, 62
Kurita, VAdm T., 326
Kurusu, Ambassador S., 60–61
Kusaka, VAdm J., 325
Kwajalein, 115, 119, 129, 207
Kyle, LtCol W. B., 268*n*

Lae, 207, 237
Laffey, 324, 353
Lake Pontchartrain, 28
Lamon Bay, 166
Landing Boat Development Board, 27

Landing craft
  Allied
    control procedures, 19–20
    development, 23–34
    types
      barges, 24, 322
      Bay Head boats, 24
      Bureau, 26–28, 31–32
      Eureka, 24, 26–28, 30–31
      fishing boats, 27
      Freeport boats, 24
      general, 252, 254, 257, 263, 268, 277, 283, 316–317, 322, 347, 373
      Higgins, 27–28, 31–32, 81, 277, 317
      launches, 29, 180
      LCMs, 32
      LCTs, 367
      LCVPs, 28
      lifeboats, 24
      lighters, 23–24, 29–32, 110, 276–277
      ramp, 23, 28–29, 256
      Red Bank boats, 24
      rubber boats, 344
      sea skiffs, 24
      sea sleds, 24
      surf boats, 24
      Troop Barge A, 23–24
      wave guide boats, 19
  Japanese, 28, 117, 128, 130, 133–134, 137–139, 144, 158, 177, 184–185, 189, 192–196, 301, 317, 364
Landing exercises, 10–11, 14, 17, 20, 23. *See also* Fleet exercises; Rehearsals.
Landing operations
  Allied, 19, 23–24, 26, 30
  Japanese, 19, 172, 177, 180, 184, 189, 192, 201
Lang, Maj H. C., 190, 192
Langer, W. L., 35n
Lansdowne, 348
Lapiay Point, 177–179
Larkin, LtCol C. A., 73; Col, 101
Larsen, Lt H. H., 305
Larsen, Col H. L., 88; BriGen, 89–90
Lash, J. P., 37n
Layton, Capt E. T., USN, 253n
League of Nations, 47, 59
League-mandated islands, 59
Leahy, Adm W. D., 85
Lee, RAdm W. A., 324, 354–355, 355n, 356–357, 364
Lee, CMG W. A., 160
Leech, Col L. L., 38

Legaspi, 165
LeHardy, LCdr L. M., 252
Lehtola, E., 134n
Lejeune, MajGen J. A., 10, 10n, 11
Lend-Lease, 37
Leslie, 2dLt D. M., 316–317
Lever Brothers, 243
Lewis, 1stLt W. W., 108, 138, 148; LtCol, 112n
Lexington, 73–74, 79, 114, 131, 210, 212
Libra, 253, 352
Life magazine, 32
Life rafts, 365
Limay, 192
Limited national emergency, 47
Lingayen Gulf, 165–166, 172, 184
Linsert, Maj E. E., 28, 33; LtCol, 28n
Lisbon, 55
Listening posts, 288
Little, 253
Little, Lt E. N., 197–198
Little Creek, 32
Little, MajGen L. McC., 32
Lodge, Maj O. R., 75n
Logistics, 19, 21–22, 257
London, 35, 236
Long Island, 279
Longoskawayan Point, 177–180
Loomis, Maj F. B., Jr., 82
Louie the Louse, 305, 323, 326–327. *See also* Aircraft, Japanese.
Louisiades, 211
Louisville, 207
Low Countries, 53
Lubricants, 276
Lunga area, 247, 257–258, 276, 280, 292, 294, 302, 310–311, 313–314, 319, 322–323, 326–327, 336, 345–347
Lunga beaches, 247, 254
Lunga perimeter, 298, 302, 319, 332–333, 336, 342, 349, 351–352, 358–360, 363
Lunga Point, 247–248, 275–276, 288, 298, 301, 323
Lunga River, 238, 245, 258, 276, 283, 297, 303, 305, 313, 329–330, 333, 336, 343
Lunga Roads, 324
Luzon, 157, 162–166, 169, 172, 181, 184, 225
Lyon, LtCol J. V., 164n

MacArthur, Gen D., 87, 156–157, 165–167, 169, 172–173, 175, 179, 181–182, 200, 235–236, 241, 342
MacFarland, 328n

Machine shop, 111, 125
Maginot Line, 18
Mahan, RAdm A. T., 151
Majuro, 115
Makambo Island, 270
Makin Atoll, 115, 205, 207, 285
Malaita, 243, 352
Malanowski, PlSgt A. P., Jr., 317
Malaria, 182, 184, 239, 245, 310, 323, 328, 332, 359, 371
Malaya, 62, 84, 86, 155, 157, 162
Maleolap, 207
Malinta Hill, 169, 171, 185, 187, 192–193, 199, 201
Malinta Tunnel, 194–195, 197–198
Malleck, Sgt D., 148
Malnutrition, 173, 182, 328, 359
Manchuria, 59, 201
Maneuvers, 8–10, 52
Mangrum, LtCol R. C., 279, 294, 323, 323n
Manila, 7, 84, 159, 161–167, 172
Manila Bay, 7, 157, 159, 163–164, 166, 168, 172, 184, 201
Manley, 299
Manning, 1stLt A. S., 192, 199
Manual for Naval Overseas Operations, 14
Maps
  Allied, 18, 243, 247
  Japanese, 147, 185, 265
Marcus Island, 207
Marianas, 64, 95
Marine Corps Equipment Board, 24, 28, 32–33
Marine emblem, 4
Marine units
  Air
    1st Marine Aircraft Wing, 19, 48, 52, 56, 297, 319, 324
    2d Marine Aircraft Wing, 48, 56, 362
    1st Marine Aircraft Group, 47
    2d Marine Aircraft Group, 47
    MAG–11, 48, 343
    MAG–13, 90
    MAG–21, 48, 68, 69n, 73, 100–101
    MAG–22, 217, 219, 220n, 221, 230
    MAG–23, 238, 279, 295, 297, 299
    MAG–25, 280
    Marine Aviation Detachment, Midway, 217
    VMF–111, 90
    VMF–121, 326
    VMF–211, 66, 68, 74, 100, 100n, 101–102, 104, 106, 108–109, 112, 113n, 120–121, 123–124, 126, 128, 134, 136–137, 139, 148, 150, 152, 343
    VMF–212, 238, 241, 279

Marine units—Continued
  Air—Continued
    VMF–221, 81, 114n, 121, 126, 130, 216–217, 223, 225
    VMF–223, 279, 291–292, 323
    VMF–224, 279, 295
    VMF–252, 68
    VMO–151, 90
    VMO–251, 241, 276
    VMS–3, 47
    VMSB–132, 343
    VMSB–141, 327
    VMSB–231, 73–75, 79, 81, 100, 216, 279, 295
    VMSB–232, 68, 100n, 279, 292, 323
    VMSB–241, 217, 223, 223n, 224–225
  Ground
    Marine Corps Headquarters, 22, 28
    Marine Corps Schools, 14
    Fleet Marine Force, 11, 13, 14, 32, 47–48, 51–52, 54
    Fleet Base Defense Force, 13
    I Corps (Provisional), 38
    I Marine Amphibious Corps, 341, 374
    1st Marine Division, 38, 48, 52, 52n, 56, 90, 236, 239–240, 243, 247–249, 252n, 261, 293, 341, 351, 359–360, 362, 367n, 371
    2d Marine Division, 38, 46, 48, 52, 56, 69, 88, 248, 360, 362, 366, 368, 368n
    1st Marine Brigade, 18, 47
    1st Marine Brigade (Provisional), 39–40, 44, 54, 54n, 55
    2d Marine Brigade, 47, 88–90, 92, 205
    3d Marine Brigade, 90, 90n
    Marine Defense Force, 14th Naval District, 113
    1st Marines, 245n, 248, 256–258, 261, 275, 283, 295, 299, 302–303, 313, 329, 360
    2d Marines, 38, 248, 248n, 250, 252, 261–262, 269–271, 310, 343–345, 350, 360, 366, 371
    4th Marines, 157–159, 159n, 161, 161n, 165–167, 170, 175, 178–181, 183, 187, 189–191, 194–195, 198–202
    5th Marines, 26, 47n, 54n, 248–249, 256, 261, 275, 281, 283, 302, 313, 315n, 318–321, 336, 343–344, 360
    6th Marines, 38–39, 42, 46, 47n, 360, 366–369
    7th Marines, 90, 240, 241n, 241, 248, 310–311, 313, 313n, 318–321, 323, 329, 333, 337, 337n, 348–349, 360
    8th Marines, 38, 88–89, 205, 241, 342, 345, 349, 350–351, 358, 360, 366–367, 371

Marine units—Continued
  Ground—Continued
    11th Marines, 248, 261, 275, 281n, 283, 303, 306, 313, 329, 332, 343
    Whaling's Group, 319–321, 343
    Amphibian Tractor Battalions
      1st, 261, 275, 303, 313
      2d, 261, 270
    Artillery Battalions
      1/10, 54n, 342, 348
      1/11, 90, 261, 310, 313, 319
      2/10, 39, 88–89
      2/11, 275, 283, 298, 319
      3/10, 261
      3/11, 275, 283, 290, 319
      4/11, 261
      5/11, 275, 283, 298, 305–306, 308, 319
    Aviation Engineer Battalions
      1st, 362
      2d, 362
    Defense Battalions
      1st, 65–67, 73, 75, 79–80, 82, 83, 96, 98–100, 103–104, 109n, 110, 113, 125–126, 128, 134, 137, 147, 150
      2d, 56, 88–89, 205
      3d, 65–67, 73, 75, 113, 219, 230, 249, 252, 261, 294, 298, 313, 329, 335, 357, 359n
      4th, 66–67, 75, 81, 113–114, 126, 130, 216–217, 238–239
      5th, 38–39, 41–42, 46, 298, 310–311, 342, 342n
      6th, 65–67, 79–80, 216–217, 221, 223, 230
      7th, 67–68, 88–90
      8th, 90
      9th, 342, 363
    Engineer Battalions
      1st, 39, 54n, 250, 261, 275, 290, 303, 308, 344
      2d, 69, 74, 261
    Infantry Battalions
      1/1, 256, 258, 285, 290
      1/2, 263, 268–271, 343, 365–366
      1/4, 159, 162, 167, 170–171, 187, 189–196, 198–199
      1/5, 27, 256, 258, 281, 298, 337, 344–345
      1/6, 45
      1/7, 314–317, 320, 333–334, 336–337, 348–349
      2/1, 256, 288, 288n, 290, 302
      2/2, 270–271, 343
      2/4, 159, 171, 187n, 199, 201

Marine units—Continued
  Ground—Continued
    Infantry Battalions—Continued
      2/5, 248, 256, 261, 266, 271, 298, 302, 305–306, 315–317, 320, 344–345
      2/6, 45
      2/7, 320, 333, 336–337, 339, 347–349
      3/1, 256, 306, 308, 319, 329–330, 333
      3/2, 268–269, 271, 311, 313, 318–319, 329, 333, 343, 344n, 345, 350
      3/4, 170–171, 175, 199, 201
      3/5, 256, 281, 283, 320, 344–345
      3/6, 45
      3/7, 90, 329, 333, 336, 343, 348
      4/4, 187, 187n, 188, 191, 197
      Reserve Bn, 4th Marines, 171, 180, 191, 195–196
    Medical Battalions
      1st, 54n, 261
      2d, 39, 361
    1st Parachute Battalion, 248, 261, 267, 269, 270–271, 298–299, 311, 359n, 371
    Pioneer Battalions
      1st, 257, 261, 275, 303, 313, 329
      2d, 261
    Raider Battalions
      1st, 247–249, 252, 261, 264, 298, 315, 317, 320–321, 359n, 371
      2d, 219, 262, 266, 285, 342, 348, 350
      2d Provisional, 262
    Raider-parachute battalion, 303, 305–306
    1st Samoan Battalion, 67–68, 88
    1st Separate Marine Battalion, 161n, 162–164, 164n, 168–169, 175
    Service Battalions
      1st, 261
      2d, 39, 261
    1st Special Weapons Battalion, 275, 290, 305, 313, 329
    Scout-sniper detachment, 1st Marine Division, 318–319, 333, 343
    Tank Battalions
      1st, 258, 261, 329
      2d, 39, 261, 269
    1st Base Depot, 242
    Chemical troops, 9, 38–39, 54n
    Embassy guard detachments, 157–158, 160–161
    Marine Barracks Detachment, Olongapo, 161
    Marine Barracks, Pearl Harbor Navy Yard, 64
    1st Military Police Company, 261

Marine units—Continued
  Ground—Continued
    1st Scout Company, 39, 261
    Signal Companies
      1st, 39, 261
      2d, 261
      JASCO, 367
    Security guard detachments, 54
    Ships' detachments, 13, 50
Mariveles, 157, 162, 167–168, 170, 173, 175–180, 182
Marshall, Gen G. C., 43, 85, 87, 235–236, 275
Marshall Islands, 10, 62, 81, 95–96, 110, 129, 131, 207
Marston, BriGen J., 39, 41n, 42, 42n, 43–44, 44n, 45–46; MajGen, 360, 360n
Marston matting, 276, 295, 362
Martinique, 38, 54, 54n, 55
Marushige, RAdm K., 129
Maruyama, LtGen M., 327, 329–330, 332–333, 334n, 335–337, 337n, 364
Maruyama Trail, 330, 333, 337
Mason, Pilot Officer C. J., 258–259
Matanikau, 281, 298, 314, 316, 318, 320, 336, 363–364
Matanikau River, 245, 280–281, 308, 314–317, 319–320, 323, 329–330, 333, 343, 347, 351–352, 358, 365
Matloff, M. E., 37n
Maya, 354
Maxwell, LtCol W. E., 256, 298
Mbangai Island, 270
McAlister, 1stLt J. A., 117, 132n, 144, 146–147
McAnally, Cpl W. J., 140–141
McBrayer, Capt J. D., Jr., 161n
McBride, BriGen A. C., 175
McCain, RAdm J. S., 241–242, 276–277, 362
McCalla, 324
McCaul, Maj V. J., 130, 143
McCawley, 46, 250, 253–254, 259, 268, 324, 326
McClure, Col R. B., 366
McCormick, Maj W. S., 223n
McCulloch, Col W. A., 366
McDowell, Cdr R. S., 26; Capt, 27n
McKean, 253, 299
McKean, Maj W. B., 247
McKelvy, LtCol W. N., Jr., 308, 313, 319n
McKinistry, MG C. B., 112n, 128, 134, 142, 144, 146–147
McMillin, RAdm G. J., 75n, 76, 76n, 78
McMorris, RAdm C. H., 114n
McNarney, LtGen J. C., 242n
McNulty, LtCol W. K., 76

Mead, Lt G. H., Jr., 283
Meade, 357
Medal of Honor, 80, 335
Medical activities. *See also* Hospitals; Casualties.
  aid stations, 66, 74, 112, 148
  dispensaries, 223
  evacuation, 20, 270
  medicines and equipment, 104, 111, 170, 172
  medical units, 20, 48, 239
  naval, 66, 75, 104, 161
Mediterranean, 55
Melanesia, 237
Mercurio, MGunSgt J., 192
Merizo, 78
Merrillat, Capt H. L., 235n
Messhalls, 125–126, 223
Metapona River, 347, 349
Metcalf, LtCol C. H., 9n
Metze, Capt A. F., 160n
Mexican War, 4, 16
Mexico, 9
Miami, 50n
Michisdio, 354
Middle East, 85, 87
Midway, 48, 62, 64–66, 68, 73–75, 78–81, 84, 92, 95, 130, 143, 151, 214–219, 221, 223–231, 235–238, 279, 286, 291–292
Middle Sector, 171, 194
Middleside, 168, 171, 181, 190, 199
Middleside Barracks, 170
Mikawa, VAdm G., 238, 260, 291, 299, 301, 325, 350, 356
Mikuma, 229
Mili, 207
Military police, 21
Miller, Maj C. A., 266, 268
Miller, Col E. B., 14
Miller, Capt E. F., 327
Miller, Dr. J., Jr., 235n, 332
Mindanao, 162, 172, 301
Mine fields, 137, 141, 148, 157, 181, 189–190, 200. *See also* Defenses; Weapons.
Miners, 243
Minneapolis, 114, 352
Miquelon, 54n
Missionaries, 237
Mission, Marine, 3, 11
Mississippi River, 24, 51n
Mize, MSgt K. W., 187n
Mobile reserve, 132, 134, 136–137, 141, 149, 151
Mochizuki, 118, 143

Mogami, 229–230
Monroe Doctrine, 5, 36
Monssen, 263, 268, 353
Moon, Lt A. L., 265n
Mo Operation, 210
Moore, MajGen G. F., 156n, 169–170, 198
Moore, Col E., 326
Moore, Capt P. C., 197
Morison, Capt S. E., 114n, 126n; RAdm, 40n, 62n, 205n, 214n, 215n, 225n, 227n, 235n, 337n, 342
Morrison Hill, 171
Morrison Point, 185
Morton, L., 156n, 200n
Moser, Col R. D., 18n
Moses, BriGen E. P., 28, 28n, 33
Mt. Austen, 245, 248, 256–258, 308, 314–315, 330, 333, 337, 358, 363, 366
Mt. Bataan, 173
Mt. Natib, 173, 176
Mt. Pucot, 177–179
Mt. Silanganan, 173
Mugford, 258
Mulcahy, BriGen F. P., 362
Munn, LtCol J. C., 297
Munro, SM1stCl D. A., 317
Murakami, Capt Y., 301
Murakumo, 325, 325n
Murray, RAdm G. D., 324
Mutsuki, 293
Mutsuki, 118, 143

Naganami, 365
Nagano, Adm O., 62
Nagara, 227, 353, 355
Nagoya, 209
Nagumo, VAdm C., 62, 215, 224, 226–227, 227n, 228, 228n, 339
Nakaguma, Col T., 319, 321–322, 324
Nakamura, Ens T., 109n
Nalimbiu River, 347–349
Nashville, 209
Nasu, MajGen Y., 329, 334–337
National Guardsmen, 37, 43
Native bearers, 350
Native scouts, 285, 288, 298, 302
Natsugumo, 325, 325n
Nauru Island, 115
Nautilus, 227, 285
Naval air base program, 66
Naval Gunfire
    Allied, 11, 15–18, 207, 241–242, 252–254, 256, 263, 265, 267–270, 352, 366–369, 373

Naval Gunfire—Continued
    Japanese, 129, 297, 318, 351, 353
Naval Units, Allied. *See also* Ships; Task Organizations.
    British Home Fleet, 40n
    U. S. Coast Guard, 21, 24
    U. S. Navy, 3–5, 7, 10, 11, 14, 17, 18, 21, 23, 24, 26–30, 32, 33, 40, 44–46, 50, 53, 55, 64, 69n, 71, 74, 76, 76n, 86–87, 90, 99, 157, 175, 190n, 205, 236, 241–242, 260, 295, 297, 303, 311, 372
    Asiatic Fleet, 69, 76, 157, 164
    Atlantic Fleet, 10, 21–22, 28, 85
    Pacific Fleet, 62–64, 69–71, 74, 81, 84, 87, 95–96, 98, 113, 157, 205, 209, 214–215, 228
    U. S. Fleet, 5, 10, 13, 32, 84, 214
    Amphibious Force, South Pacific, 252n, 262
    South Pacific Forces, 236
    U. S. Naval Forces in Europe, 236
    14th Naval District, 64, 66, 70n, 75, 124
    16th Naval District, 157
    Atlantic Squadron, 27 30
    Cub-1, 276
    Guamanian naval militia 76, 76n
    Naval battalion, Mariveles, 175–176, 178–180
    Philippine Inshore Patrol, 180
    6th Naval Construction Battalion, 295, 326, 362
    18th Naval Construction Battalion, 363
    NAD, Burns City, 50n
    NAD, Cavite, 175, 178, 180
    NAD, Lualualei, 69, 74
    NAS, Cape May, 50n
    NAS, Ford Island, 69, 71
    NAS, Jacksonville, 50n
    NAS, Kaneohe, 71
    NAS, Key West, 50n
    NAS, San Diego, 51
    NAS, Wake, 104, 111–112, 115, 136
    NSD, Oakland, 50n
    Naval Magazine, Indian Island, 50
    Naval War College, 10
    Norfolk Navy Yard, 29
    Pearl Harbor Navy Yard, 62, 64, 69
    Transport Division A, 253
    Transport Division B, 253
    Transport Division C, 253
    Transport Division D, 253
    Transport Division E, 253
    Transport Division 12, 252–253, 276
    Transport Squadron 26, 247
Navigation, 20, 102, 123

Navy Department, 13, 27, 31, 54, 89, 157–158, 166
Navy Department Continuing Board for the Development of Landing Boats, 28, 30
Nazis, 35, 47
Ndeni, 252, 261, 310–311, 323, 324, 342
Near East, 61
Neches, 114, 131
Neosho, 210–211
Netherlands, 54, 61–62, 84
Netherlands East Indies, 78, 155, 157
Neuse River, 52
Neutrality Patrol, 37
Neutrality Zone, 63
Neville, 253
New Britain, 236
New Caledonia, 86, 88, 209, 230, 237–238, 324, 343, 360, 360n, 371
Newfoundland, 54n
New Georgia Group, 243, 301
New Guinea, 86, 207, 209, 236–238, 301, 322, 342, 346, 368–369
New Hebrides, 86, 88, 238–239, 241, 259, 262, 279–280, 293, 295, 311, 339, 353
New Ireland, 236
New London, 8
New Orleans, 24, 28, 31
New Orleans, 352
Newport, 8
New River, 14, 21, 31, 38, 52, 90
New World, 54
New York, 45–46, 54
New Zealand, 36, 61, 84, 86–87, 89–90, 155, 205, 230, 236, 239, 243, 248–250, 257, 360, 366, 371
Nggela Group, 243, 270
Niagara Peninsula, 16
Nicaragua, 11, 17–18
Nickerson, Maj L., 264
Nichols Field, 100, 163
Night glasses, 79
Nimitz, Adm C. W., 84–85, 87, 143, 215, 218–219, 224, 235–236, 236n, 237, 240, 242, 247, 250, 262, 276n, 302, 305, 341–342
Nissen hut, 42
Nisshin, 325
Nomura, Ambassador, 60
Norfolk, 27, 31, 51
Norris, Maj B. W., 224–225
North African operation, 31, 342
North Carolina, 52
North Carolina, 242, 311
North Dock, 168
Northampton, 207, 352

North Pacific, 214. *See also* Pacific.
North Point, 192–193
Norway, 53
Noumea, 240–242, 252, 260, 324, 341, 359
Noyes, RAdm L., 242, 259

Oahu, 48, 66, 68–69, 69n, 70–71, 74–75, 81, 106, 113, 130–131, 279, 285
O'Bannon, 353
Oboro, 129
O'Brien, 311
Observation post, 105
Ocean Island, 115
O'Connell, Maj M. V., 298
Odilia, Sister, 285n
Ohmae, Capt T., IJN, 120n, 346, 346n, 357n, 363, 372
Oil. *See* Fuel.
Oite, 118, 120
Oka, Col A., 301, 333n, 337, 339, 367
Okinawa, 371, 373
Okinoshima, 237
Okumiya, M., 205n, 215n, 230
Olongapo, 157, 159, 161, 165, 167
Open Door policy, 59
Operation Bolero, 342
Operation Shoestring, 237, 257, 260
Organizational loading, 249. *See also* Logistics.
Orient, 59, 65, 75
Orion, 173, 176, 180
Orkney Islands, 40n
Orndorff, Col C. A., 366
Orote Peninsula, 76
Osaka, 209
Otter, Lt B. B., 197–198
Oude-Engberink, Father H., 285n
Outposts, 288, 303
Owen Stanley Mountains, 207, 238, 369

Pacific, 9, 10, 38, 45, 52, 53, 59–61, 63–64, 69, 76, 84, 84n, 85–88, 152, 207, 214, 235–237, 241, 249, 262, 286, 310, 339, 341, 355, 357, 359, 367, 371–374
Pacific Ocean Area, 86–87
Pacific War, 160, 230
Packs, 257, 348
Pagoda, 327
Pago Pago, 67–68, 89–90, 205
Paige, Maj Gen H. R., 39n
Palaus Islands, 10, 160, 165, 288, 301–302
Palmyra, 64–66, 68, 75, 83
Panama, 10

Panama Canal, 38, 53
Pan American World Airways, 65, 75, 80, 106, 109
Parker, MajGen G. M., Jr., 167, 172–173, 176
Parker, LCdr T. C., 183n
Parks, Maj F. B., 223
Parris Island, 38, 46, 51, 51n, 52
Patch MajGen A. M., 238–239, 360, 360n, 362, 366–367, 369, 371, 371n
Pate, LtCol R. McC. 249
Patrol Craft 32, 129, 130, 133–134, 136, 142
Patrol Craft 33, 129, 130, 133–134, 136
Patrols, 180, 275, 280–281, 283, 285, 288, 308, 315, 318, 328, 330, 333, 345, 347, 349–350
Patterson, 260
Patterson, Lt R. M., 328
Peacock Point, 98, 102–103, 108, 110–113, 117–118, 124, 130, 134, 136–137, 139–140, 143
Peale Island, 98–99, 103, 105, 111–112, 115, 119, 121, 123–124, 127–128, 132, 134, 138, 141–144, 147, 151
Pearl Harbor, 5, 33, 43, 45, 48, 50, 56, 62, 64–70, 73–76, 78–79, 81–84, 86–89, 101, 107, 113–114, 125, 127, 130–131, 143, 155, 157, 160–161, 205, 207, 209, 212, 214–216, 219, 236, 241, 252, 253, 262, 286
Pefley, Maj A. R., 67 ; BriGen, 65n
Peiping, 157, 159–160
Penguin, 76
Pensacola, 352
Pepper, Col R. H., 252, 313
Peshek, 2dLt M. E., 176n
Pew, Lt (jg) L. A., 177
Phase Line A, 264
Philadelphia, 8, 51
Philippine Clipper, 106–107, 109, 127
Philippine Insurrection, 7
Philippine Islands, 7, 9, 75, 84, 86–87, 95, 99–100, 155–163, 166, 172, 176, 181–182, 189n, 200–201, 286, 301, 322
Photo reconnaissance. *See* Aircraft.
Pickett, Col H. K., 64, 67, 69, 70n, 73–75, 83
Pickup, Capt L. H., 192–194, 197
Pineau, R., 235n
Pistol Pete, 326–327, 330, 335, 343, 345, 352. *See also* Artillery, Japanese.
Planning
　Allied, 36, 62–63, 201, 254
　　Japanese, 96, 130, 150, 184, 200–201, 209, 215, 286, 288
Planters, 243, 247, 257
Platt, Capt W. McC., 103–104, 128, 134, 137, 144, 146–147, 151 ; LtCol, 104n, 132n

Poha River, 343, 345, 357, 369, 371
Poindexter, 2dLt A. A., 132, 134, 136–137, 141, 147, 149, 151–152 ; LtCol, 126n, 132n
Point Cruz, 281, 316–320, 344–345, 347, 350, 354, 357–358, 363, 366–367
Poland, 47
Pollock, LtCol E. A., 288n, 290
Pond, Lt Z. A., 292
Ponies, 41
Porter, 339
Portland, 353
Port Moresby, 209, 237–238, 322, 346, 369
Port Royal, 51
Port of embarkation, 20
Portugal, 55–56
Post exchange, 51, 223
Potter, E. B., 5n
Potter, Maj G. H., 134, 139, 141–142, 142n, 143 ; Col, 132n
Potter's Line, 142, 148
Pound, Adm of the Flt Sir D., 42
Powerhouse, 79, 82, 223
Pratt, LCdr M. L., 281
Preliminary bombardment
　Allied, 150, 192
　Japanese, 150, 185, 200, 202
Presidential Unit Citation, 360
President Adams, 250, 253, 268, 270
President Harrison, 158–160
President Hayes, 250, 253, 268
President Jackson, 250, 253
President Line's dock, 159
President Madison, 158–159
Pressley, Maj O. K., 270
Preston, 356
Price, MajGen C. F. B., 90
Prickett, LtCol W. F., 178n ; Col, 176n
Prisoners, 20, 78, 200–201, 247, 258, 270, 311, 367
Puller, LtCol L. B., 314–316, 320–322, 333–336, 348–349
Pulos, Maj T. E., 181n
Pumps, 279
Putnam, Maj P. A., 100n, 101–102, 106–107, 107n, 108, 110–111, 117, 119, 123, 126, 136, 139, 139n, 140–141, 152 ; Col, 96n
Pye, VAdm W. S., 143
Pyzick, Col F. P., 201n

Quail, 179
Quantico, 9, 11, 13, 14, 24, 28, 29, 32, 33, 39, 47, 48, 50–52

INDEX

Quartermaster stocks. *See* Supplies.
Quinauan Point, 177, 180
Quincy, 254, 260
Quinine, 184, 239
Quonset Point, 50n

Rabaul, 78n, 205, 210, 212, 235–238, 241, 253, 257, 259, 264, 274, 280, 286, 293–294, 301–302, 305, 308, 310, 316, 320, 322, 328–329, 334–336, 346, 350–351, 355, 357, 363–364, 368–369, 372
Radar, 70, 79, 98, 103, 105, 109, 114, 150, 152, 162–163, 170, 217, 221, 275, 325–326, 353, 355–356
Radio. *See* Communications.
Raiders. *See* Marine units.
Railhead, 160
Rainbow-5, 63–64, 75. *See also* Planning.
Ralph Talbot, 260
Ramsey Battery, 185
Ramsey Ravine, 169, 171
Rape of Nanking, 59
Rations. *See* Supply.
Raysbrook, Sgt R. D., 316
Reconnaissance, 17, 48, 65, 89, 241. *See also* Aircraft.
Recruit depots, 51, 92
Reefs, 133, 137
Regulus, 98
Rehearsals, 129, 184, 242, 252
Reifsnider, Capt L. F., USN, 253
Reinforcements, 310, 339
Rekata Bay, 260
Rendezvous area, 19
Rennell Island, 322, 324
Replacements, 52, 92, 92n
Reserves, Marine, 48, 53
Revolutionary War, 3
Reykjavik, 36, 40–42, 45–46
Ridgely, Maj R. H., Jr., 159, 170
Rifle range, 51
Riley, Maj T. F., 362
Ritidian Point, 76
Roads, 41, 89, 98, 173, 175–177, 268, 308, 336, 369
Robert, RAdm G., 54–55
Rochester, 168
The Rock, 168, 170–171, 175, 178, 183–185
Rockey, LtGen K. E., 23n
Rockwell, RAdm F. W., 162, 163n, 164, 166–167, 169, 175
Roebling, D., 32–34
Rogers, Maj O., 316
Roi, 107, 110, 116, 123–127, 130, 207
Rongelap, 131

Roosevelt, E., 37n
Roosevelt, President F. D., 23, 31, 37–39, 39n, 42, 47, 53, 55, 60, 85–86, 86n, 113, 155, 342
Roper Poll, 47n
Roscoe, T., 190n
Rose, LtCol M., 4n
Rosecrans, LtCol H. E., 248, 266, 315
Rosenman, S. I., 40n
Rowan, Col G. R., 257
Royal Marines, 3, 4, 36
Royal Navy, 210
Rupertus, BriGen W. H., 247, 265, 268, 269n, 298, 333n, 348, 348n, 349
Russell Islands, 243, 354, 356
Russell, BriGen J. H., 13
Russell, W. H., 5n
Russia, 38, 40, 53, 56, 60
Rust, MG E. S., 283
Rutledge, R. R., 137
Ryujo, 292
Ryukyu Islands, 160, 166

Saalman, 1stLt O. E., 185n, 198, 200n ; Maj, 187n
Sackett, Capt E. L., USN, 175n
Sacramento, 83
Sado Maru, 299, 301
Sailer, Maj J., Jr., 343
St. George's Channel, 259
St. Louis, 207, 219
Saint Lucia, 54
Saint Pierre, 54n
Saipan, 76, 129, 133
Salamaua, 207, 237
Salt Lake City, 324–325
Salt tablets, 257
Samoan Islands, 5, 64, 67, 84, 88–90, 92, 92n, 205, 209, 230, 237–240, 248–249, 310, 342
Samoan Marines. *See* Marine units.
San Clemente, 14, 26
San Cristobal, 243, 322
San Diego, 9, 11, 38, 46–48, 50, 51, 51n, 65, 67–68, 81, 88, 114, 205, 207, 248–249
Sand Island, 65, 78–80, 216–217, 219–220, 223, 225
Sand Islet, 81–83
San Francisco, 209
San Francisco, 114, 324–325, 344, 348, 352–353
Sangley Point, 162–163, 168
San Jose, 169
San Juan, 50n
San Juan, 263–264, 267, 339
Sano, LtGen T., 350, 364

Santa Cruz Islands, 236, 252, 310, 335, 339, 342–243
Santa Isabel, 243, 260
Santo Domingo, 9, 17
Saratoga, 81, 114–115, 130, 143, 216, 242, 252, 263n, 292, 302–303, 311, 323n
Sasapi, 264
Sato, Col G., 185, 192–193, 196
Sato, Capt T., IJN, 350, 356, 365
Savaii, 89–90
Savo Island, 238, 243, 253, 260, 298, 325, 327, 353–357
Schaeffer, Capt M. W., 171n; Maj, 188, 194–198
Schooner pilots, 257
Scotland, 40n
Scott, RAdm N., 324–326, 353
Scott, Gen W., 16
Seabees, 276–277, 279, 295, 342, 362–363. *See also* Naval units, Allied.
Seadromes, 64–65
Sea Horse complex, 367
Sealark Channel, 243, 247, 253, 259–260, 276–277, 294–295, 303, 305, 311, 322–323, 325–326, 328, 330, 335, 339, 345, 347–348, 353–356
Seaplane hangars, 80, 223
Seaplane ramps, 73, 78, 99, 267
Searchlights, 8, 65, 80, 103–104, 113, 144, 146, 169, 190, 193, 356
Sebree, BriGen E. B., 348, 348n, 349–350, 357, 362
Secretary of State, 36
Secretary of the Navy, 30–31
Secretary of War, 44
Segilau, 365
Selective Service, 37, 53
Sendai, 355
Shanghai, 157–159, 161
Shank, Dr. L. M., 109n, 112
Shannon, LtCol H. D., 79–80, 216, 219
Shaw, Cdr J., 253n
Sheep, 41
Sherrod, R., 120n
Sherwood, R. E., 47n
Shetland Islands, 40n
Shima, RAdm K., 237
Shipmasters, 243
Shipping losses, 374
Ships. *See also* Landing craft.
  Allied
    auxiliaries, 74, 157, 164, 241
    battleships, 24, 39, 71, 74, 218, 241–242, 291, 311, 324, 342, 352, 354–356
    cargo, 39, 41, 65, 88, 205, 241–242, 252

Ships—Continued
  Allied—Continued
    carriers, 54, 74, 87, 114, 130–131, 209–212, 214–215, 218, 224, 228, 235, 240, 242, 250, 259, 291–292, 311, 339, 352, 354
    Coast Guard cutters, 54n
    commercial, 24, 26, 88, 164
    control vessels, 19
    cruisers, 24, 39, 74, 157, 207, 209, 218, 228, 241–242, 260, 263, 267, 291, 311, 322, 324, 339, 344, 348, 351–353, 357
    destroyers, 36, 39, 53, 70, 74, 131, 157, 207, 209–210, 218, 228, 241–242, 250, 258–260, 263, 291, 311, 316, 322, 324, 339, 344, 348, 351–354, 356–357, 367, 368
    destroyer transports, 38, 242, 252–253, 276, 299, 335
    dredges, 83, 99
    escort carriers, 279
    gunboats, 157–158
    LSTs, 34
    mine layers, 74, 324
    mine sweepers, 76, 81, 164, 179, 242, 311
    motor torpedo boats, 116, 164, 167, 177, 181, 350, 354, 365
    oilers, 114, 131, 209–210
    paddle-wheel steamships, 32
    picket boats, 19, 31
    seaplane tender, 81, 100, 114, 219
    submarines, 65, 131, 157, 164, 166, 168, 181, 189, 189n, 207, 217–218, 227, 229, 285–286, 352
    submarine tenders, 164, 175
    supply, 66, 82, 277
    target, 74
    trading schooners, 245
    transports, 17, 19, 24, 28, 38–39, 98, 158, 205, 241–242, 249, 252, 254, 259–260, 295, 311, 324, 326, 352
    tugs, 335
    yard craft, 164, 322, 335
  Japanese
    auxiliaries, 117
    battleships, 214–215, 225–226, 228, 291, 326, 339, 352–356
    carriers, 62, 78, 82, 129–131, 143, 210–211, 214, 224–228, 230, 286, 291, 325, 339, 353
    cruisers, 82, 96, 116–120, 129–130, 136, 139, 143, 143n, 211, 214–215, 226–229, 259, 283, 288, 291–292, 295, 299, 303, 324–27, 336, 339, 352–357

INDEX 435

Ships—Continued
  Japanese—Continued
    destroyers, 78–80, 82, 96, 116–120, 129–130, 143, 143n, 147, 149, 179, 214, 226, 228–229, 275, 283, 288, 291–293, 301, 303, 305, 324–325, 335–336, 339, 351–357, 364–364, 369
    destroyer-transports, 116–117, 120, 129, 133–134, 136, 291, 293, 301, 323
    floatplane tender, 129, 133
    gunboats, 196, 211
    mine layers, 129, 207, 237
    patrol craft, 134
    submarines, 16, 70, 74, 81–83, 96, 116, 122, 130, 205, 214, 252, 275, 294
    tankers, 78–79
    transports, 116, 118–120, 221, 291–293, 299, 327–328, 352, 354–358
Shirayuki, 325
Shiriya, 79
Shock, Capt T. M., USN, 207
Shoho, 210–211
Shoji, Col T., 334–335, 347, 347n, 349
Shokaku, 210, 212, 339
Shore fire control. *See* Naval gunfire.
Shore party activities, 20–22, 240, 257–258. *See also* Supply.
Shortland Islands, 259, 301, 322, 346, 350–351, 354–355, 369
Signals. *See* Communications.
Simard, Cdr C. T., 79–80, 219; Capt, 221, 224, 229
Simpler, LCdr L. C., 302
Sims, 210–211
Sims, Col, 348
Singapore, 84, 86
Sitka, 50n
The Slot, 259, 288, 301, 305, 325, 328, 346, 352, 354–355, 364–365
Smith, 339
Smith, MajGen H. M., 21–22, 28, 28n, 30–31, 55
Smith, LtGen J. C., 18n
Smith, Lt J. J., 268
Smith, Maj J. L., 279, 292, 294, 323
Smith, Maj L. R., 279, 295
Smith, Gen O. P., 35n, 45n
Smoke screens, 17, 119, 254, 306
Snell, E. M., 37n
Snellings, QMClk H. L., 196
Sniping, 194, 198, 308, 337
Society Islands, 87
Soji, RAdm A., 229n

Solomon Islands, 92, 209–210, 236–239, 243, 252–253, 257–259, 275, 280, 286, 290–291, 294, 310–311, 322–324, 326, 335, 341–342, 346, 348, 351, 353, 363, 368–369, 372
Solomon Sea, 235
Songonangona Island, 270
Soryu, 127–131, 143, 215, 227
Sound-flash equipment, 275, 317. *See also* Fire control equipment.
South America, 54n, 55–56
South Dakota, 339, 354–356
Southeast Asia, 61, 86
South Pacific, 83–84, 90, 155, 205, 218, 236–237, 240, 249, 275, 277, 279, 302, 311, 324, 340–342, 351, 353–354, 362, 364. *See also* Pacific.
Southern Resources Area, 61–62
South Seas Islands, 96
Southwest Pacific, 67, 83, 86–87, 236, 241–243. *See also* Pacific.
Soviet intervention, 60
Spain, 56
Spanish American War, 5, 7, 7n
Spaulding, Cpl J., 281
Spearfish, 189–190
Special naval landing force. *See* Japanese units, Naval.
Spencer, FltLt, 268
Sperling, Capt W. E., 264; Maj, 264n
Spruance, RAdm R. A., 207, 218, 218n, 221, 224, 226–230
Staging area, 92
Standing Operating Procedure, 22
Stark, Adm H. R., 37, 39, 44, 85, 85n
State Department, 54
Steel matting. *See* Marston matting.
Stefansson, V., 36
Steiger, G. N., 59n
Sterrett, 344, 348, 353
Stern anchor, 23
Stevens, PFC R. L., 147
Stiff, Maj H., 264n
Strategic defensive, 63
Strategic panorama, 342
Strategic reappraisal, 75, 84
Subic Bay, 157, 167, 184
Submarines. *See* Ships.
Suez Canal, 342
Sugar, 249
Sumatra, 62, 86
Sumay, 76
Sumiyoshi, MajGen, 329–330, 332–333, 335

Supply. *See also* Shore party activities.
  artillery, 217
  aviation, 104, 217
  construction, 125
  dumps and storage, 20, 45, 111, 257, 276–277
  equipment, 23, 81, 276–277
  food, 277, 357
  Japanese emergency measures, 364
  Japanese stocks, 276, 310, 327, 354
  movement of supplies, 257
  munitions. *See* Ammunition.
  quartermaster stocks, 88
  rations, 21, 104, 167, 170, 172–173, 182, 249, 261, 311, 313, 330, 364
  spare parts, 276
  stowage, 11
Supreme Commander of the SWPA (CinCSWPA), 87
Surf, 24, 26, 276
Surrender of Corregidor, 199
Surrender of Wake, 147
Suva, 279
Sweeney, Lt E. J., 269
Sweeney, Maj J. B., 264n
Sweeney, SgtMaj J. H., 196
Sweeney, LtCol W. C., 225
Sylvia, Sister, 285n

Taivu Point, 288
Takagi, VAdm T., 210–212
Takao, 355–356
Talafofo Bay, 78
Tambor, 229
Tanambogo, 243, 247–248, 263, 267–271
Tangier, 81, 114–115, 126, 130–131, 143, 216
Tanikaze, 143n
Tanaka, RAdm R., 286, 288, 291–293, 299, 301, 327, 346, 350–351, 354–357, 364–365, 369, 372; VAdm, 235n
Tanks. *See* Weapons.
Tarawa, 62, 115
Tarpaulins, 110
Tasimboko, 298, 301–302
Task Organizations
  TF 7, 131
  TF 8, 207
  TF 11, 114, 131, 242, 250n
  TF 14, 114, 130–131, 143
  TF 16, 209, 218, 242
  TF 17, 210, 218
  TF 18, 242
  TF 61, 242

Task Organizations—Continued
  TF 61.1, 242
  TF 61.2, 242
  TF 62, 250, 253, 261
  TF 63, 242, 276
  TF 65, 311
  TG 62.2, 253
  TG Yoke, 247, 253–254, 263
  TG X-Ray, 247, 253–254
Tassafaronga, 327–328, 350–351, 356, 364–365
Tassafaronga Point, 371
Tatsuta, 117–120, 129
Tenaru, 371
Tenaru River, 245, 256, 288, 292, 308, 313, 347
Tenavatu River, 256
Tenryu, 117–120, 129
Tentative Landing Operations Manual, 14–15, 17, 19–20, 23
Tenyo Maru, 129
Terrain. *See also* Reefs; Roads; Vegetation.
  caves, 179
  cliffs, 177
  coral formations, 98–99, 264, 266
  hills, 176, 193, 305
  interior lagoon, 98
  jungle, 170, 177, 181, 243, 245, 256–257, 275, 298, 302, 308, 330, 336
  mountains, 41, 173, 243
  mud, 276
  ridges, 173, 177, 192, 243, 302, 305, 313, 330
  rivers and streams, 243
  sand dunes, 66, 290
  swamps, 239, 245
  tableland, 283
  valleys and ravines, 173, 243, 298, 320, 330, 344
Teruzuki, 356, 365
Tetere, 283, 285
Teters, D., 95, 99
Tharin, Capt. F. C., 100n, 108–109, 119, 121, 124, 148
Thomason, Capt J. W., Jr., 4, 4n
Thorpe, LtCol H. R., 263n
Tientsin, 157, 159–160
Timor, 62
Tinsley, Capt W. B., 269
Tisdelle, Maj A. C., 182n
Titi, 371
Todd, 1stLt C. S., 78
Tojo, Gen H., 60, 326
Toki Point, 103, 121, 132, 138
Tokyo, 96, 184, 209, 286, 308, 341, 368, 371
Tokyo Bay, 78

Tokyo Express, 288, 322–325, 327–328, 343, 345–346, 352, 355, 363–364, 369
Tokyo raid, 207
Tomonaga, Lt J., 224
Tone, 129, 143*n*, 224, 227
Tonga Islands, 88
Tongatabu, 88, 238, 241
Tongue Point, 50*n*
Topside, 168, 171, 181, 190, 194
Torpedoes. *See* Ammunition.
Traders, 243
Trails. *See* Roads.
Training
  Allied, 17, 45, 51–52, 156, 188, 218
  Japanese, 184
Transport quartermaster, 20, 250
Trenton-Princeton campaign, 3
Triangulation, 245
Trinidad, 54
Tripartite Treaty, 59
Triton, 104
Truk, 115–116, 286, 288, 293, 299, 301–303, 322
Trundle, 2dLt W. B., 23*n*
Tsugaru, 129
Tsuji, N., 108*n*
Tulagi, 210, 235–238, 242–243, 245, 247–248, 253–254, 261, 263, 266, 268–271, 277, 292, 295, 298, 302, 310–311, 322, 323, 344, 348, 354, 357, 360, 362
Tulagi Bay, 248
Tumon Bay, 78
Tunnel stern, 24
Turnbladh, E. T., 92*n*
Turner, RAdm R. K., 240, 242, 248*n*, 250, 250*n*, 253–254, 257, 259–262, 268, 274, 285, 310, 310*n*, 311, 324, 341, 343*n*, 352–353, 373
Tuttle, Col W. B., 343, 348, 363
Tutuila, 67–68, 88–90
Twining, LtCol M. B., 245
Two-ocean navy building program, 53
Tyler, Capt M. A., 223*n*, 229

Uchida, Lt K., 133, 141*n*
Ugaki, RAdm M., 228*n*
Umasami River, 371
Umstead, 1stLt F. G., 217
United States, 5, 7, 7*n*, 8–9, 11, 33, 36–37, 47, 50, 53–56, 59–63, 68, 69*n*, 78, 84–85, 95, 156–157, 236
United Kingdom, 342. *See also* Great Britain.
Units of fire, 170, 250, 260. *See also* Ammunition.

Unloading, 20, 22, 100, 257. *See also* Shore party activities.
Uno, K., 191*n*
Upolu, 89–90
Urakaze, 143*n*
Ushio, 79–80, 80*n*
Uzuki, 293

Vandergrift, BriGen A. A., 44*n*; MajGen, 239–240, 240*n*, 241–243, 245*n*, 247–248, 250, 252, 252*n*, 254, 257–260, 262, 267–268, 274–275, 280, 288, 290–291, 294, 297–299, 303, 310, 310*n*, 311, 313, 315, 319–321, 323–324, 330, 333*n*, 341–343, 343*n*, 345–351, 359–360, 360*n*, 363*n*, 369, 372–373
Van Ness, Col C. P., 271*n*
Vegetation, 29, 41, 66, 140, 149, 173, 178, 187, 243, 245, 256–257, 266, 277, 290, 295, 297, 305, 313, 327, 330
Vehicles
  Allied. *See also* Amphibian vehicles; Weapons.
    bomb-handling trucks, 279
    bulldozers, 66, 99, 274, 295
    carts, 279
    dump trucks, 274, 294
    flatbed lorries, 250
    gasoline trucks, 279–295
    graders, 66
    motorcycles, 167
    prime movers, 256
    radio vans, 106
    scout cars, 38
    searchlight trucks, 146
    tractors, 23
    trucks, 66, 71, 107, 112, 125, 151, 167, 250, 256, 276–277
  Japanese
    carts, 274
    gas locomotives, 274
    hopper cars, 274
    road rollers, 274
    trucks, 276, 295
Vera Cruz, 9, 16
Verahue, 371
Versailles, 9
V-J Day, 80*n*
Vichy Government, 54, 59
Vieques, 14
Vigan, 164, 166
Vila, 238
Vincennes, 209, 254, 260
Virgin Islands, 47, 48

Virginia, 51
Vogel, MajGen C. B., 341
Vouza, SgtMaj, 285n, 288n

Wade, LCdr E. M., 194n
Wade, GunSgt T. Q., 137
Wainwright, MajGen J. M., 167, 172–173, 176, 179–180, 182, 189, 199–200; Gen, 155n, 157n
Wait, Capt L. W., 264, 266; Maj, 345
Wake Atoll, 62, 64–66, 68, 75, 78–82, 84, 95–96, 98–99, 101–104, 106–107, 109–117, 120–121, 123–127, 129, 131, 134, 139, 143, 147, 150, 207, 253
Wake Island, 48, 98–99, 103, 105, 111, 116, 127, 130–131, 133–134, 136, 138, 140–144, 147–148, 151–152, 216
Walke, 356
Walker, LtCol T. J., Jr., 90
Wallace, LtCol W. J., 217, 217n; Col, 295
Wallis (Uea) Island, 90
Ward, 70
War Department, 156, 182
War of 1812, 16
Warehouses, 249
Washing-machine Charley, 305, 317, 323, 326. *See also* Aircraft, Japanese.
Washington, 324, 354–356
Washington, D. C., 35–36, 38, 60, 76, 85, 87, 89, 237, 240, 341–342
Washington, Gen G., 3
Washington Naval Disarmament Treaty, 59, 75
Wasp, 242, 250, 263, 263n, 267–268, 292, 303, 311
WATCHTOWER, 237, 239–240
Water supply, 104
Water tank, 105, 297
Water towers, 82, 195, 198
Watson, M. S., 62n
Wavell, Gen Sir A. P., 86
Weapons, *See also* Ammunition.
  Allied
    antiaircraft guns, 38, 50, 71, 103, 134, 230, 275
    antiboat guns, 194
    BARs, 160, 178, 317
    cannon, 173
    coast defense guns, 50, 65, 131, 140, 193
    depth charges, 70
    8-inch guns, 169
    81mm mortars, 178–179, 266, 347
    .50 caliber machine guns, 33, 65, 67, 74, 76, 79–80, 103–104, 108, 114, 122, 127, 131, 134, 136–137, 140–141, 147, 162, 169–171, 176, 190

Weapons—Continued
  Allied—Continued
    5-inch guns, 66–67, 79–80, 82–83, 98, 103–104, 114, 117–118, 121, 131, 134, 138, 140, 147–148, 152, 217, 275, 294, 355, 357
    flame throwers, 367
    14-inch guns, 168–169
    grenades, 114, 137, 141, 144, 148, 178, 195, 297, 332
    machine guns, 33, 42, 71, 73–74, 78, 83, 136–137, 144, 146, 151, 160–161, 165, 171, 178–179, 191–193, 195–196, 217, 291, 306, 320, 334, 337
    mines, 8, 114, 136, 157, 168, 220
    molotov cocktails, 220
    mortars, 171, 179, 192–193, 198, 266, 306, 316, 320–322, 334, 336, 345
    mountain howitzers, 179
    naval guns, 16, 180
    155mm guns, 23, 169, 342, 349, 352
    155mm howitzers, 275
    105mm howitzers, 256, 275, 305
    pistols, 71
    rifles, 73, 78, 148, 178, 188, 196, 306, 320
    7-inch guns, 67, 81, 216–217
    75mm guns, 169, 179, 191, 193
    75mm half-tracks, 275, 332, 345
    75mm pack howitzers, 256, 275, 290, 342, 349
    6-inch guns, 68, 169, 267
    60mm mortars, 264–265
    submachine guns, 141, 160
    tanks, 29–31, 34, 38, 83, 151, 183, 219–220, 258, 269, 291, 308, 367
    10-inch guns, 169
    3-inch guns, 42, 65, 67–68, 73–74, 76, 80–81, 83, 98, 103–104, 107–108, 111–112, 114, 124–125, 127–128, 131, 134, 136, 138–140, 144, 147–148, 162–163, 169–170, 175–176, 190, 216–217, 219
    3-inch Stokes mortars, 198
    .30 caliber machine guns, 34, 65, 67, 74, 76, 104, 114, 118, 132, 136, 140–141, 146, 171
    37mm guns, 33–34, 171, 190–193, 219, 290, 330, 335–336
    12-inch guns, 168–169, 190
    12-inch mortars, 169, 179, 190
    25-pounders, 342
    20mm guns, 219
    2.95-inch mountain pack howitzer, 177
  Japanese
    antitank mines, 291

INDEX 439

Weapons—Continued
  Japanese—Continued
    antitank guns, 308
    bayonets, 141, 291
    field pieces, 329, 345
    5-inch guns, 129
    flame throwers, 291
    14-inch guns, 353
    infantry cannon, 116
    grenades, 141, 144, 291, 320, 334
    grenade launchers, 116, 291
    howitzers, 178
    machine guns, 116, 139–141, 146, 177–179, 193–195, 198, 268, 283, 291, 330, 334–336
    mortars, 140, 178–179, 198, 290, 306, 315–316, 330, 332–333, 337–338
    mountain howitzers, 198
    observation balloons, 187
    150mm howitzers, 317, 326, 329, 342
    105mm guns, 181
    100mm guns, 329
    pistols, 291
    rifles, 177–178, 198, 268, 291, 334
    75mm mountain guns, 184
    70mm guns, 290–291
    6-inch guns, 118
    small arms, 139, 141, 303, 316, 322, 334, 348
    swords, 147, 291
    tanks, 172, 199, 329–330, 332
    37mm guns, 330, 332, 345
    240mm howitzers, 184, 189
Weather, 41, 89, 245, 249, 252, 320, 276, 295, 330, 334–335, 347
Webb, 2dLt H. G., 101n, 108
Weber, Maj J. E., 349
Weir, Maj K. H., 274; LtCol, 297
Welin Company, 27
Wellington, 239, 242, 248–249, 260
Wells, Capt E., 345
Wells, 1stSgt N. W., 192
Western Hemisphere, 35–36, 36n, 37, 40, 47, 53–55
Western Samoa. *See* Samoan Islands.
West Indies, 54n
West Sector, 194
Whaling, Col W. J., 319, 319n, 320, 344–345, 347
Whangpoo River, 159
Wheeler Field, 71
White House, 31, 86n

White, 2dLt P. R., 217
Whitehill, Cdr W. M., 84n
Wilds, T., 75n
Wilkes Island, 98, 103, 105, 110, 113, 115–116, 118, 121, 124–125, 127, 130, 133–134, 137, 139, 142–144, 147–149, 151
Williams, BriGen D., 11n
Williams, Capt F. H., 168; Maj, 187–188, 194, 197–199,. 200n
Williams, Maj R. H., 248, 267
William Ward Burrows, 295
Wilson, 260
Wilson, Capt H. S., 103n, 106
Wilson, President W., 44
Wire. *See* Communications.
Woods, Col L. E., 297; BriGen, 343, 362
Working details, 20, 42, 45
World War I, 4, 8–9, 44, 50, 51, 54n, 59, 107, 137, 168, 199
World War II, 4, 9–10, 17, 19, 32, 46, 63, 80
Worton, MajGen W. A., 44n
Wotje, 123, 207
Wright, 99–100, 102, 216
Wright, RAdm C. H., 351
Wright, PlSgt J. E., 127

Yamaguchi, RAdm T., 227
Yamagumo, 325
Yamamoto, Adm I., 62, 214, 214n, 215–216, 228, 230, 235, 237, 346, 349, 351, 353
Yamamoto, Cdr T., 346n
Yamatsuki Maru, 355
Yamaura Maru, 355
Yangtze Patrol, 158
Yangtze River, 157
Yankee Imperialism, 54
Yayoi, 119–120, 143
Yokosuka, 286
York, 16
Yorktown, 205, 207, 210–212, 214, 218, 221, 226–230
Young, Capt C., USN, 353
Yubari, 116–118, 120, 129, 136, 139
Yunagi, 129

Zeilin, 252–253, 324, 326
Zimmerman, Maj J. L., 35n, 235n, 240n, 253n
Zuiho, 339
Zuikaku, 210–211, 339

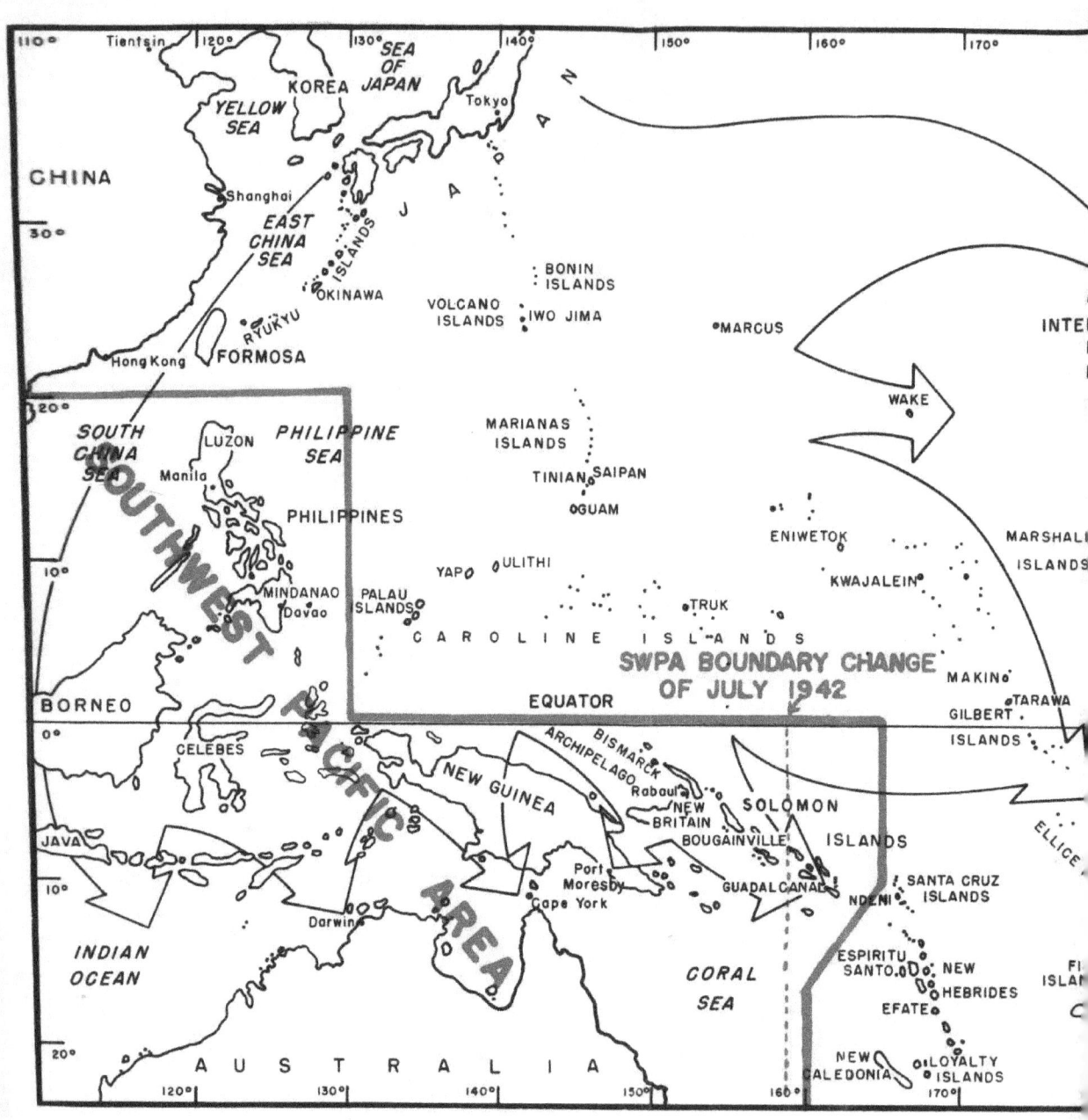

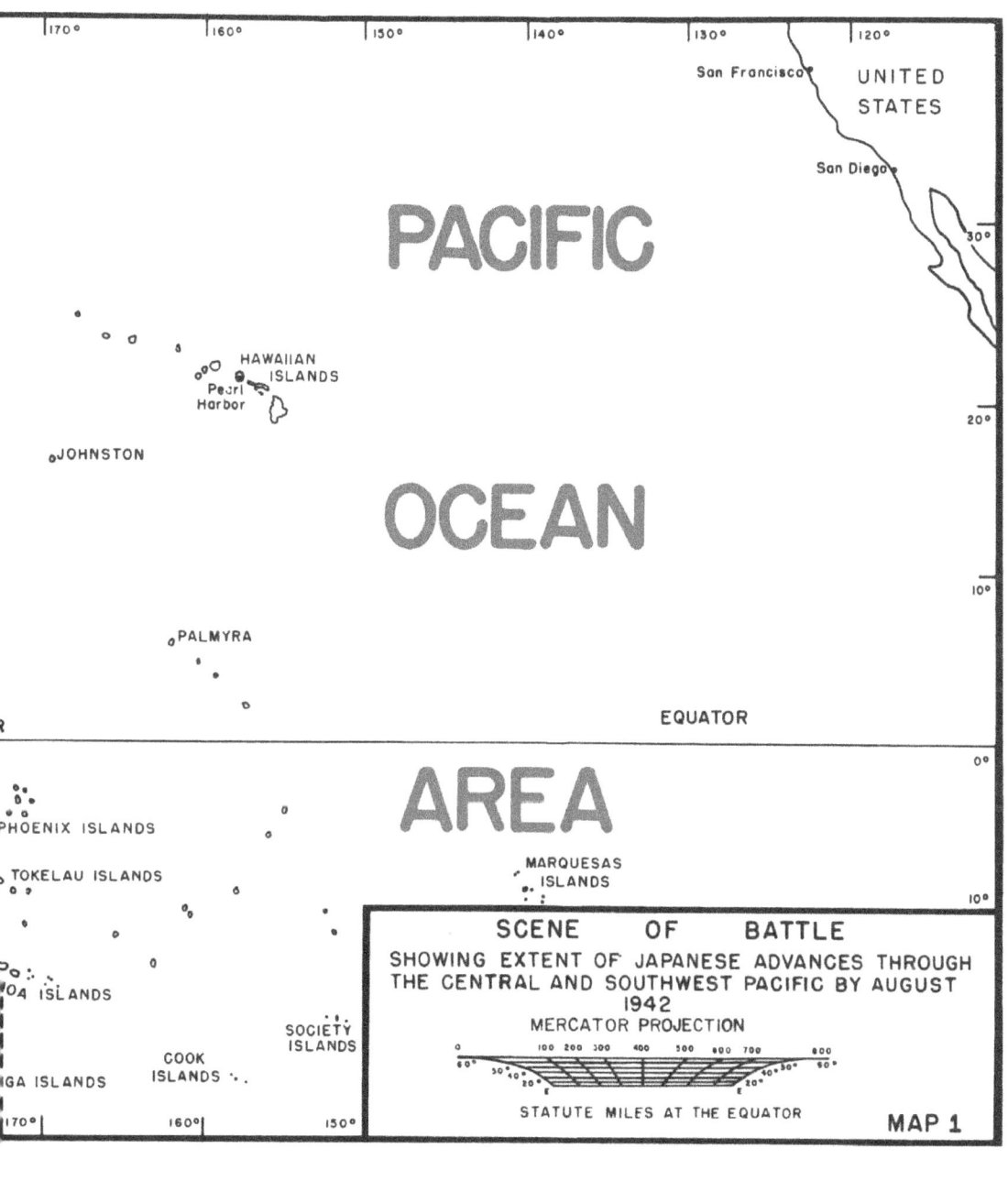

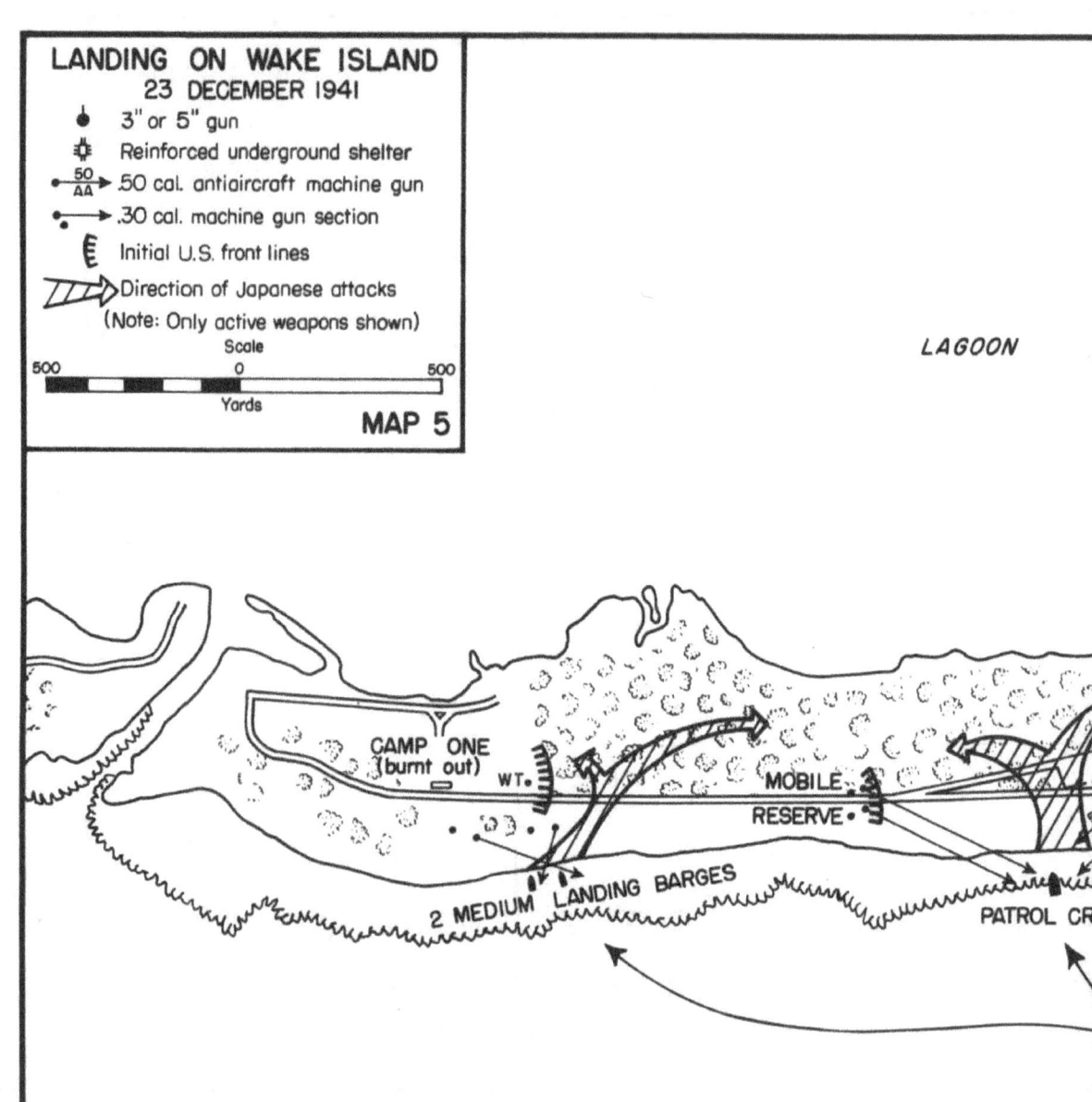

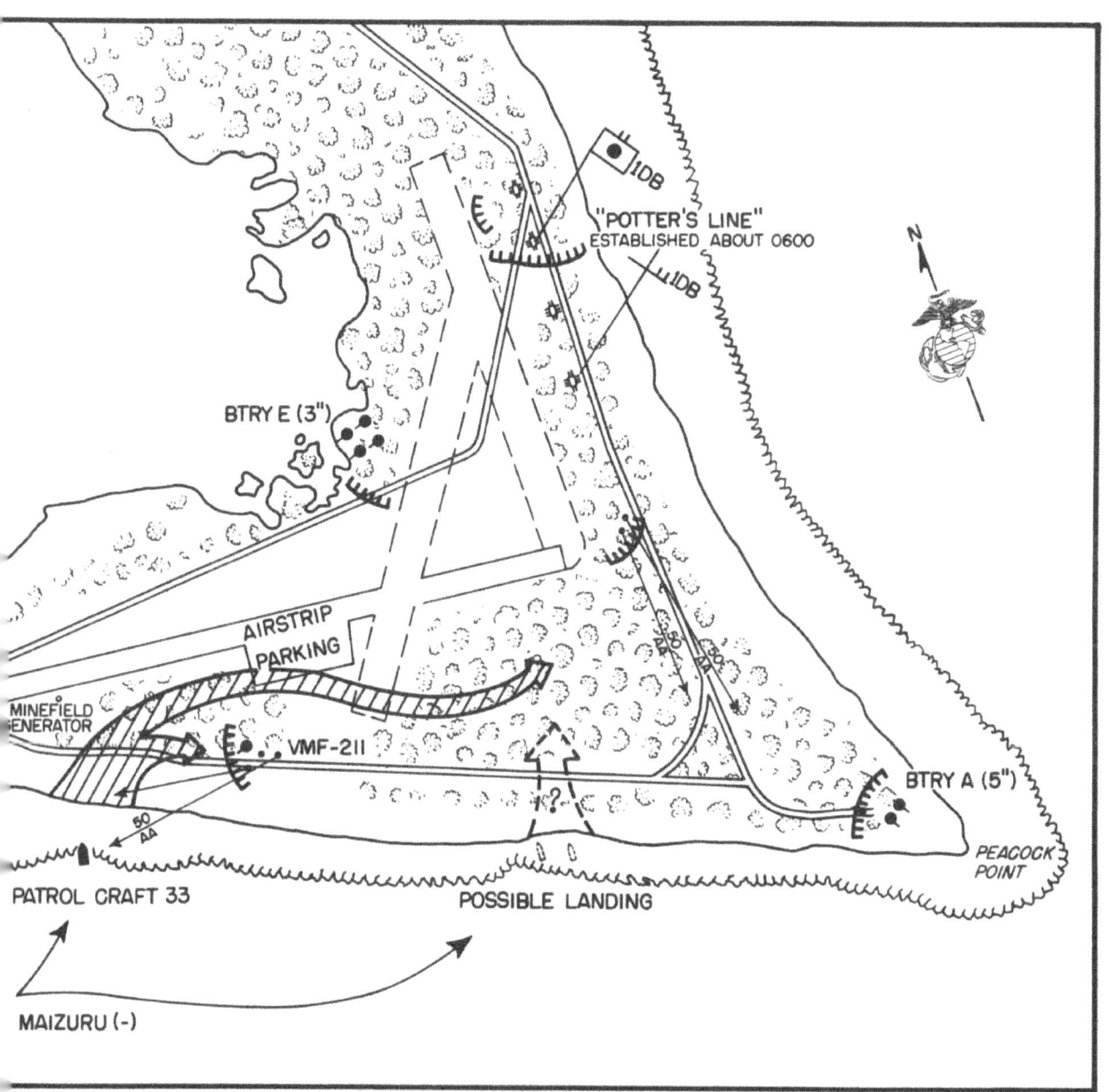

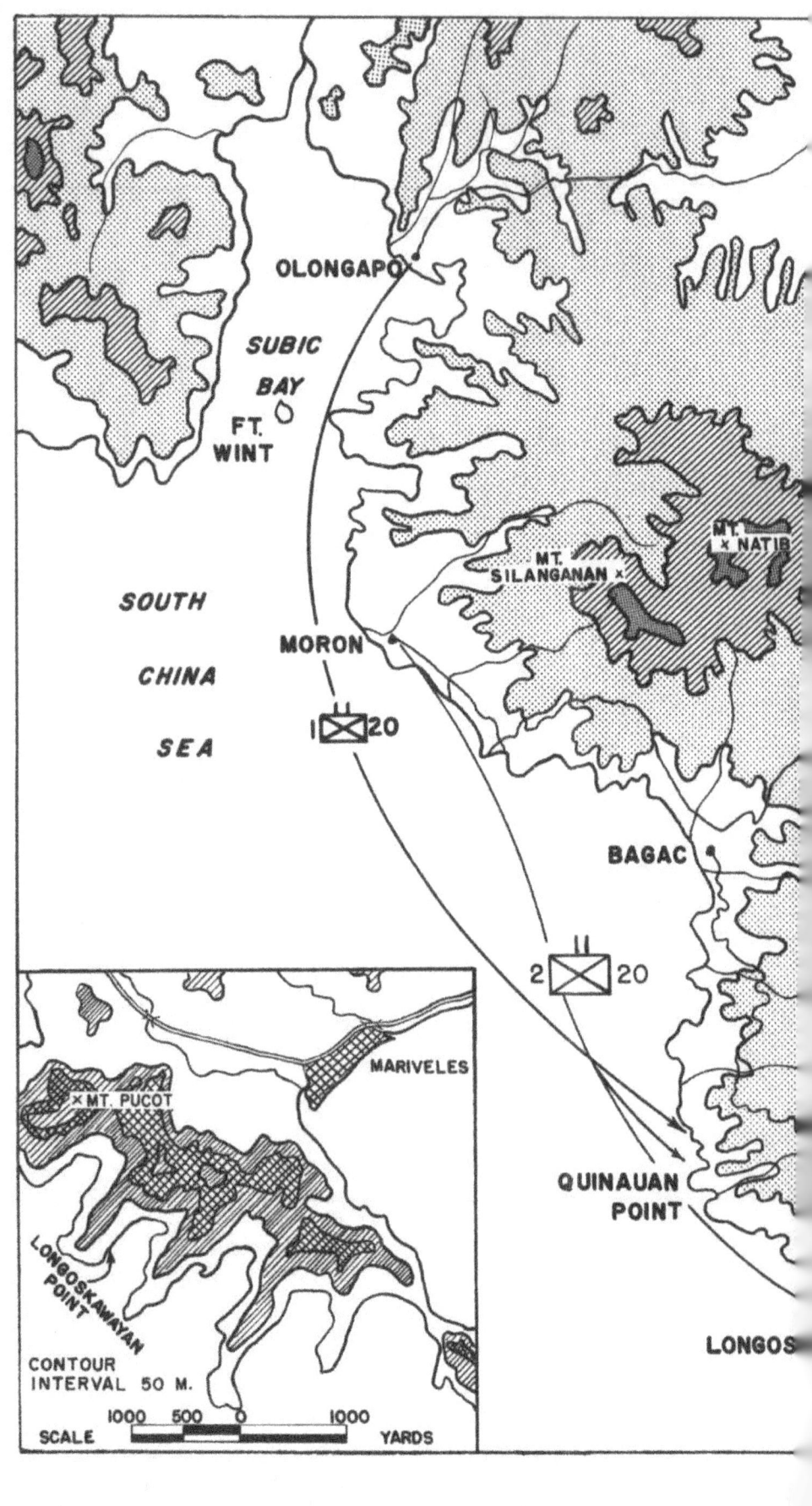

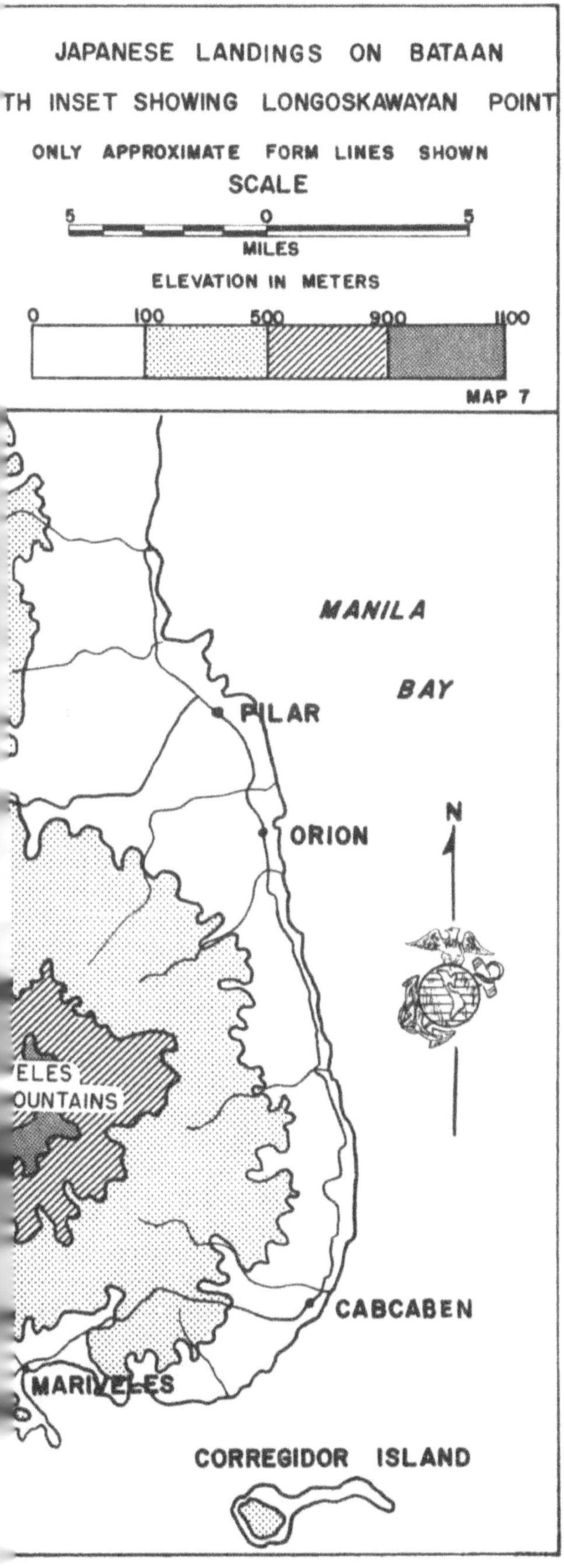

JAPANESE LANDINGS ON BATAAN
WITH INSET SHOWING LONGOSKAWAYAN POINT

ONLY APPROXIMATE FORM LINES SHOWN

SCALE

5　　　　　0　　　　　5
MILES

ELEVATION IN METERS

0　　100　　500　　900　　1100

MAP 7

MANILA BAY

PILAR

ORION

N

ELES
OUNTAINS

CABCABEN

MARIVELES

CORREGIDOR ISLAND

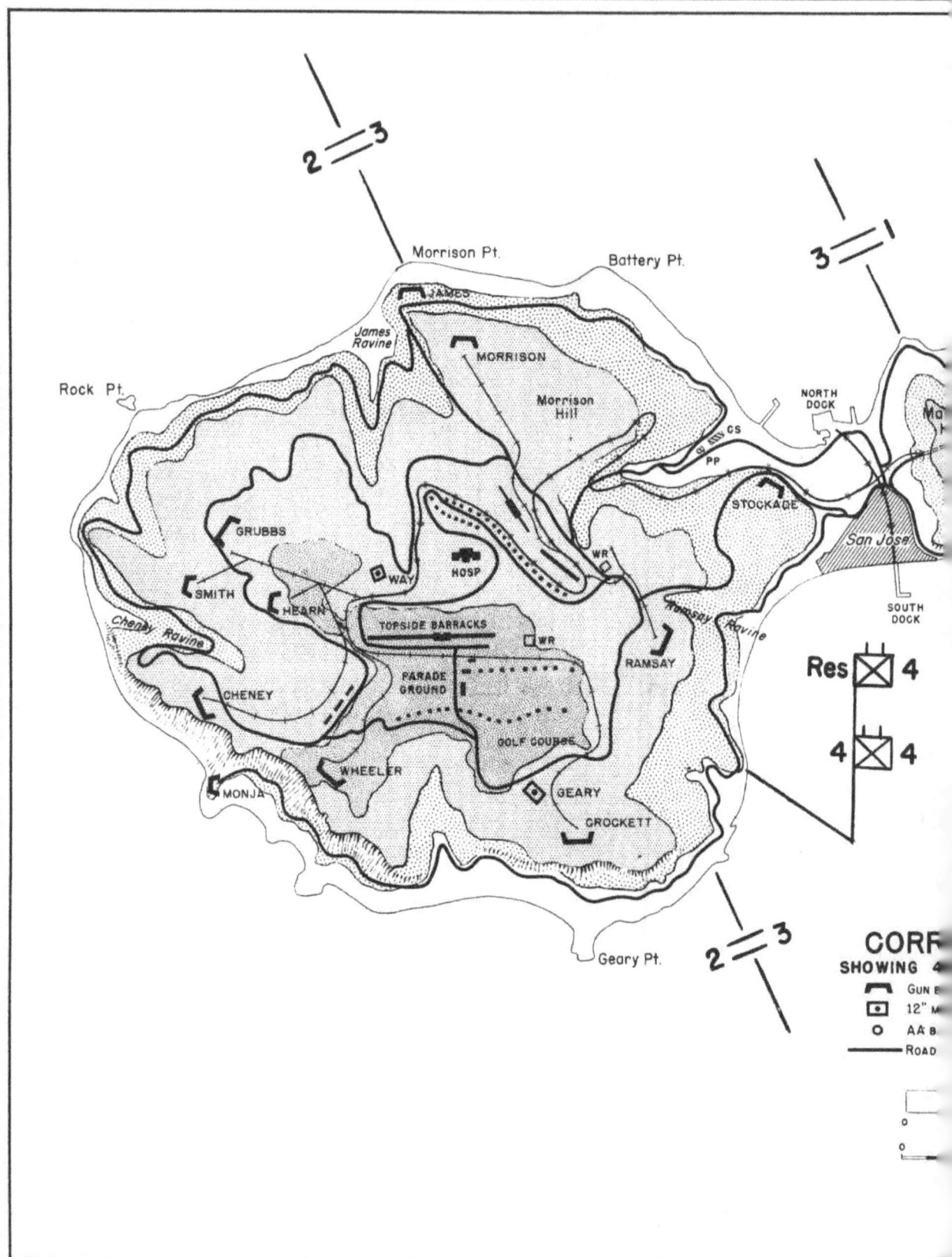

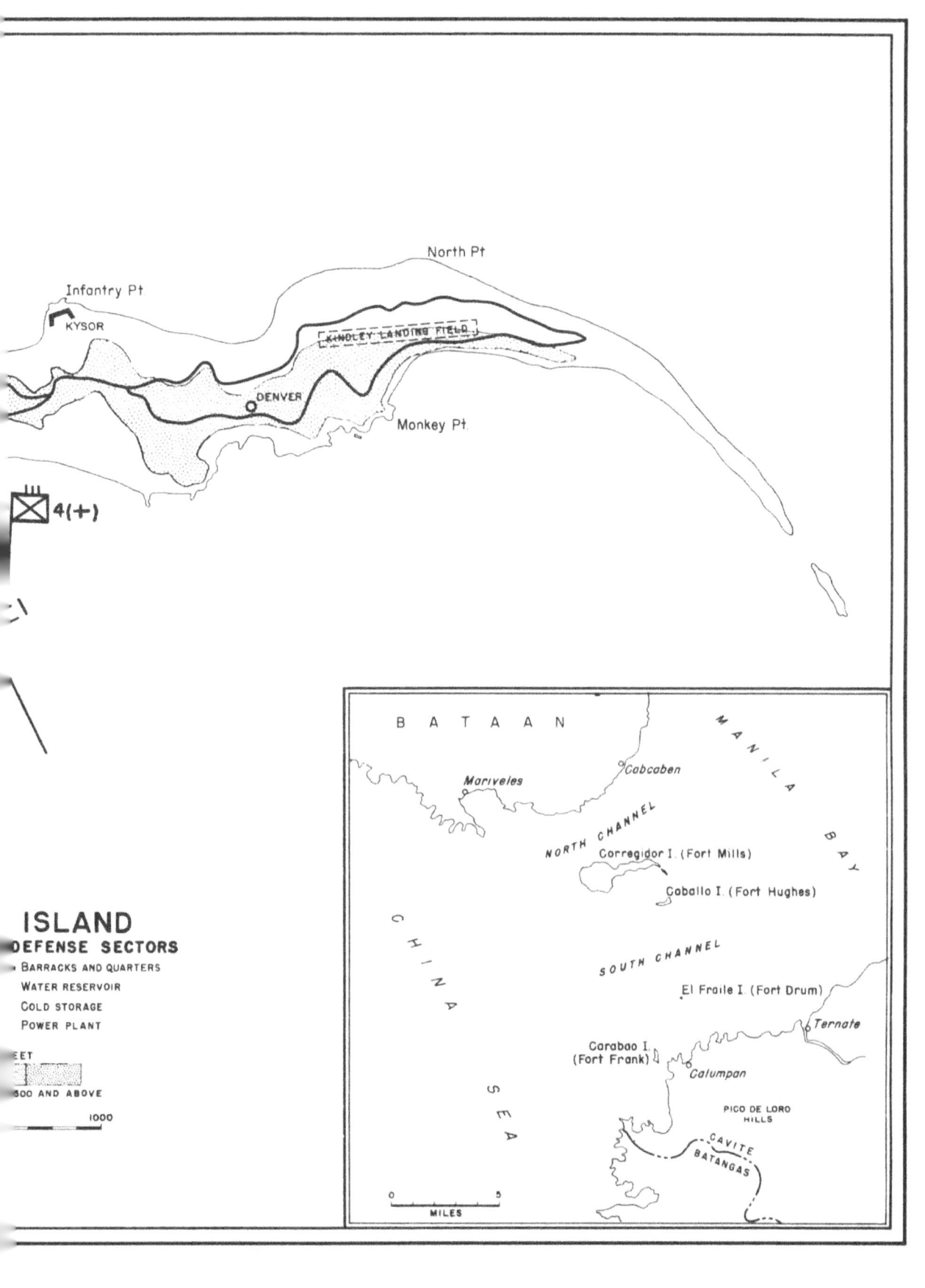

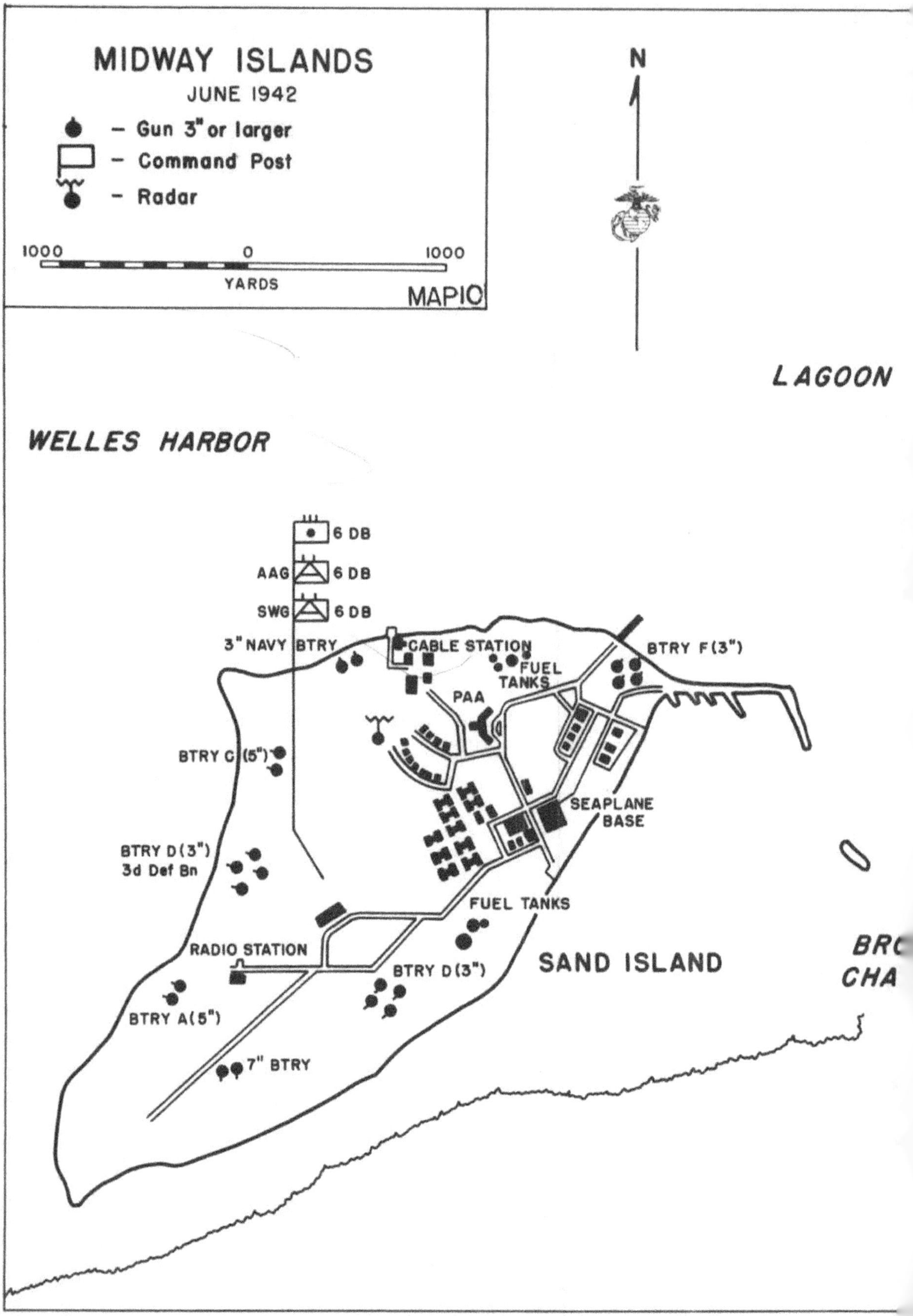

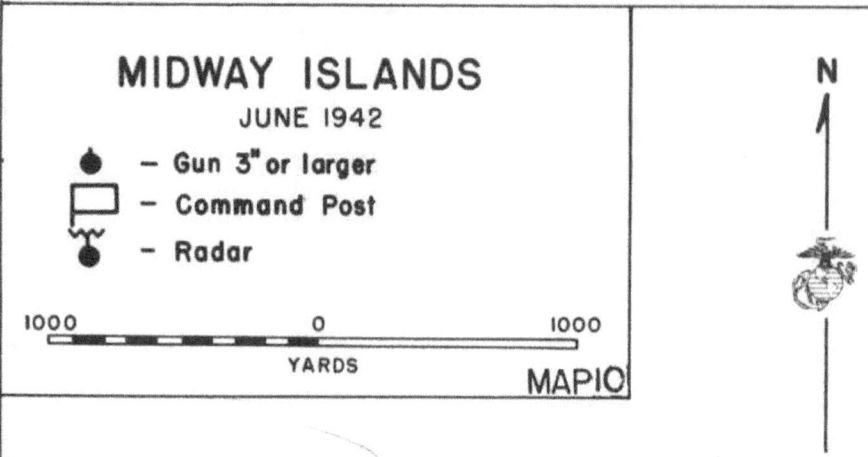

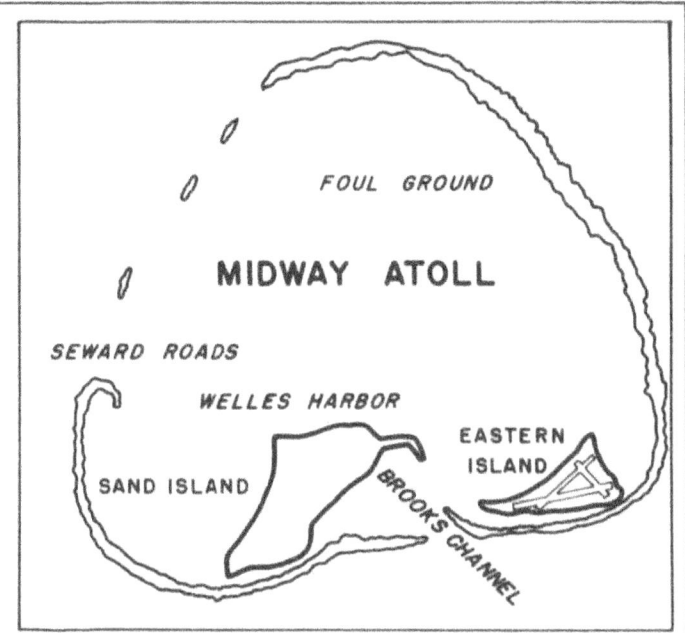
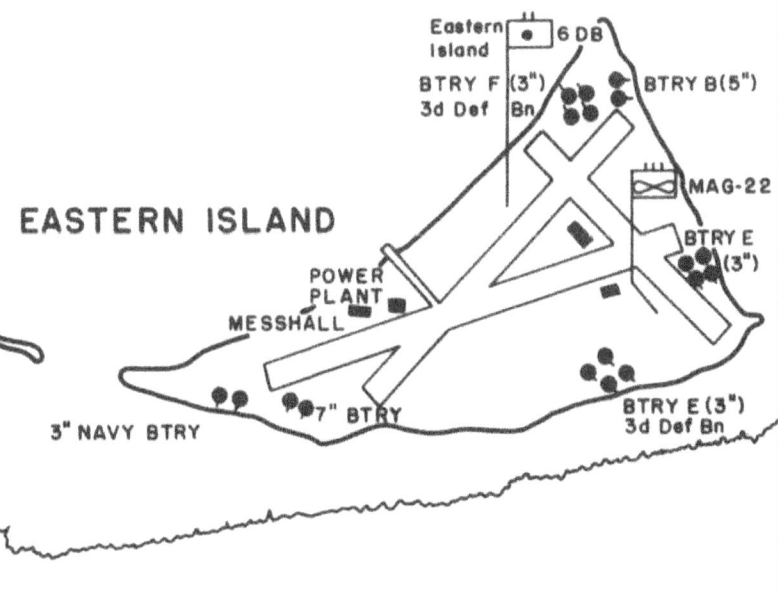

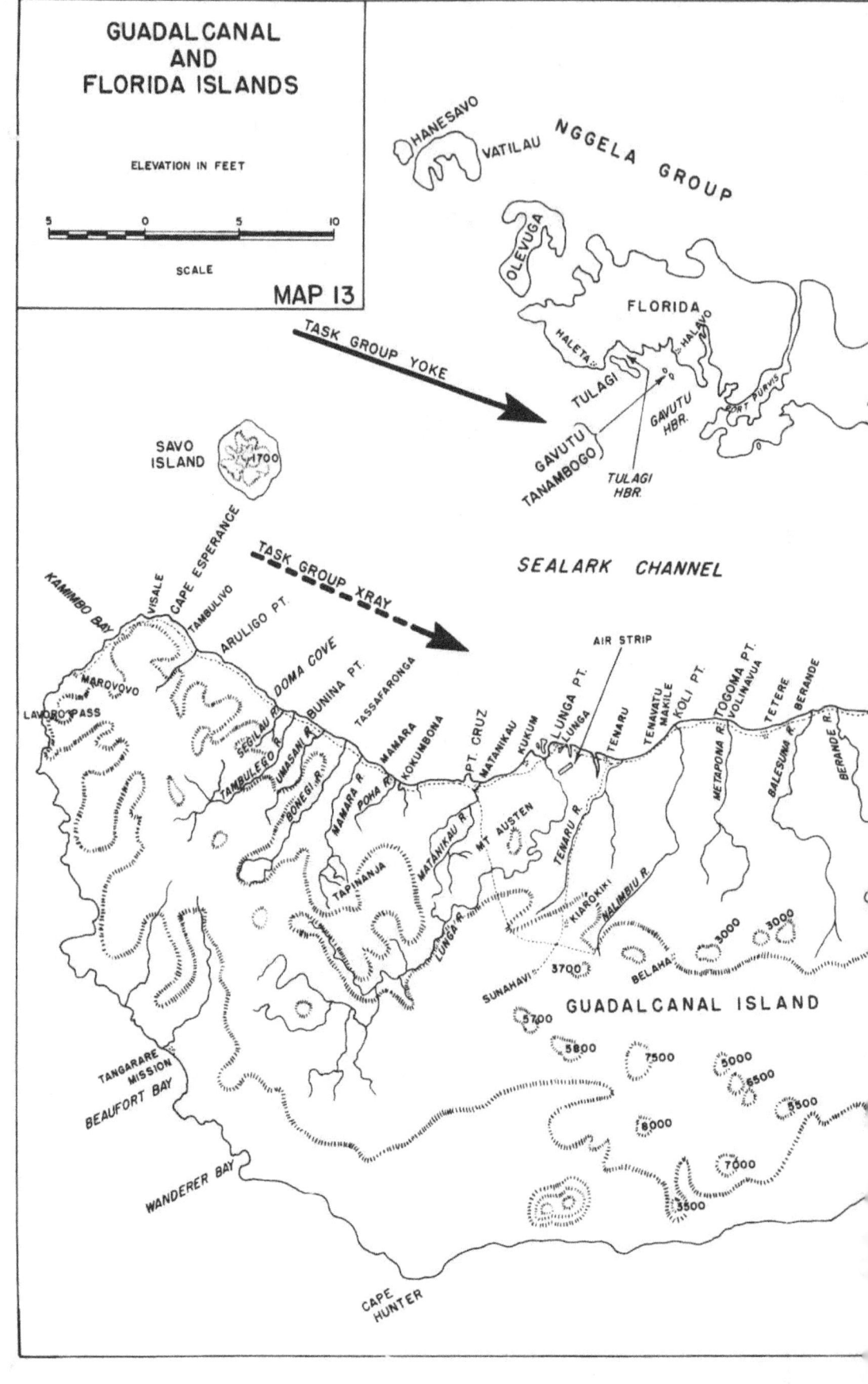

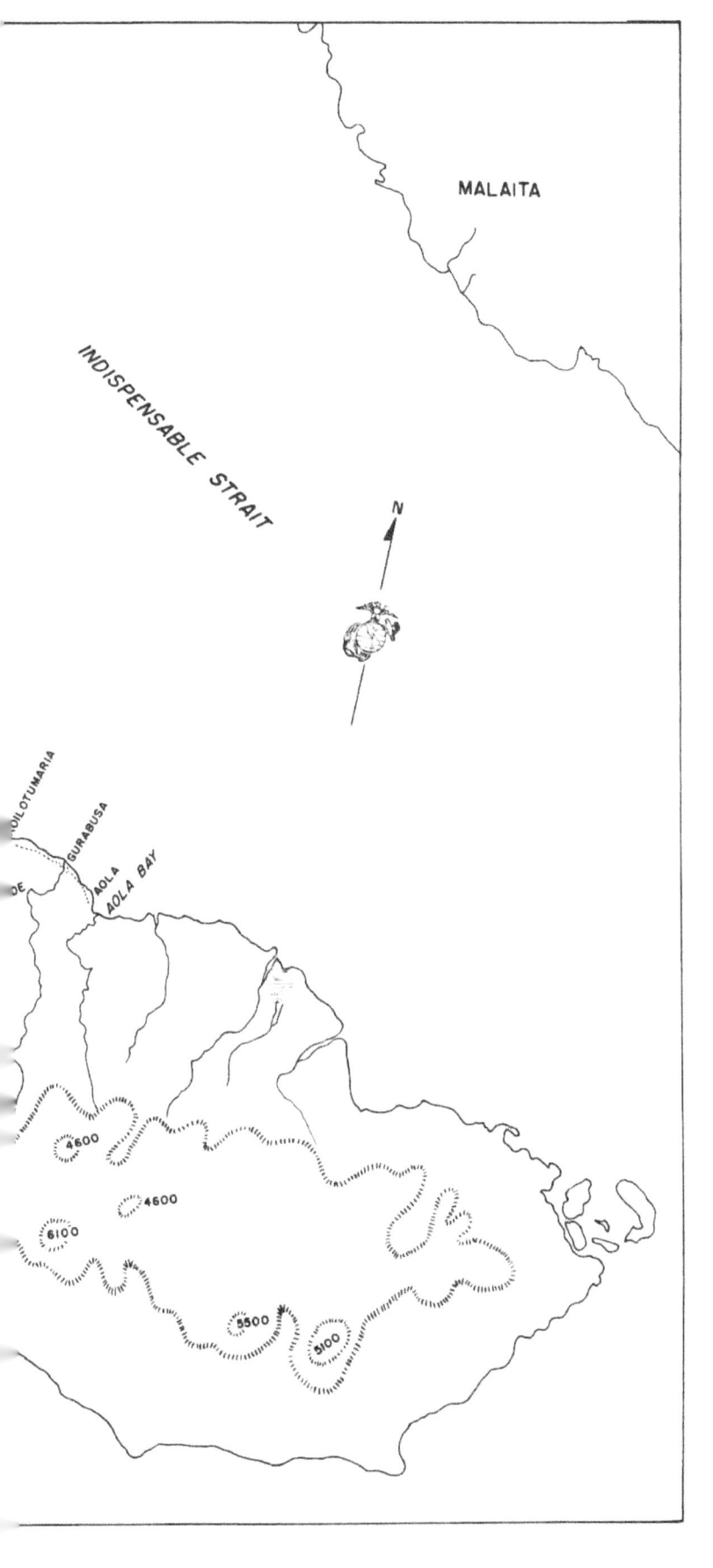

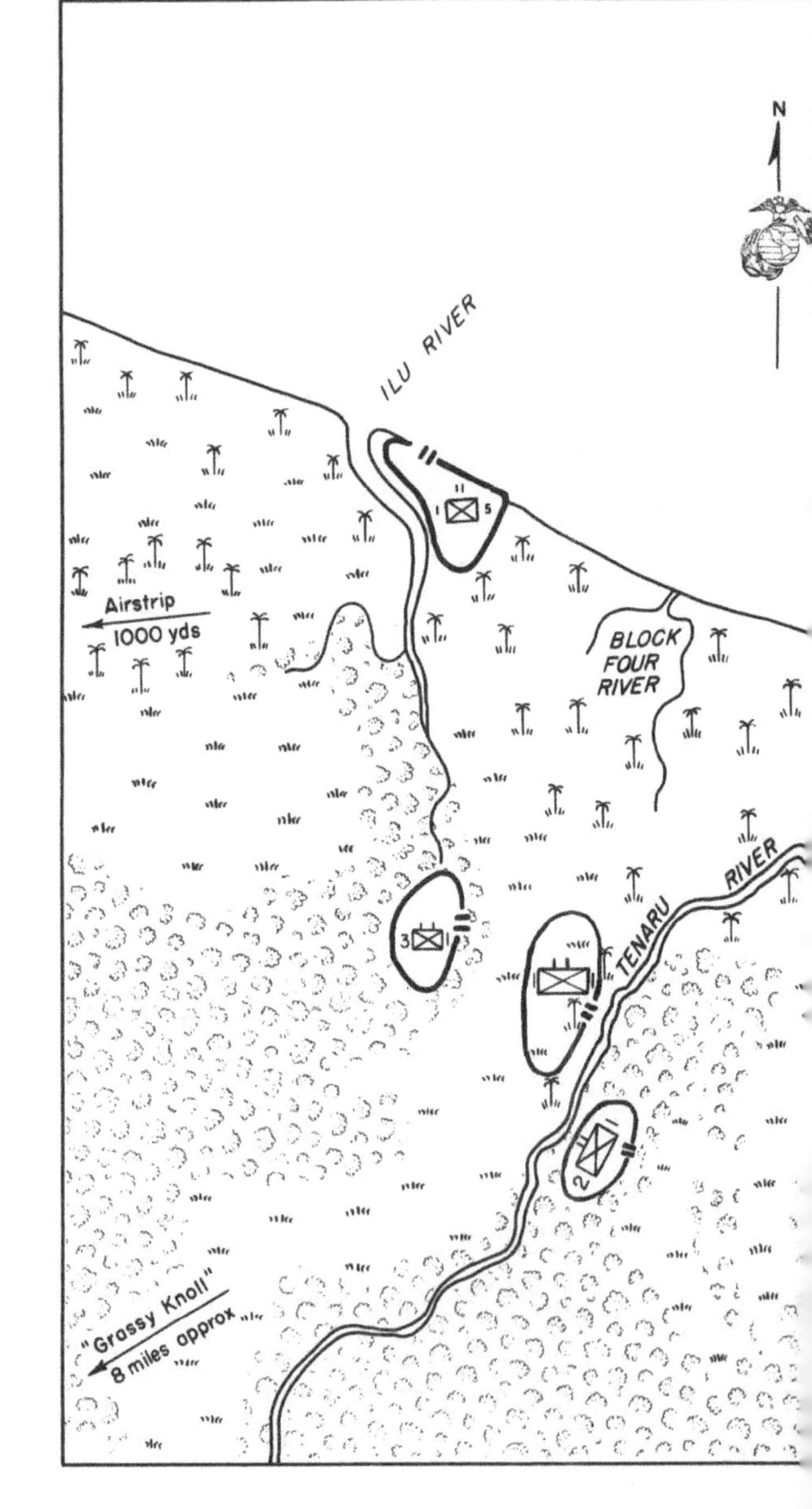

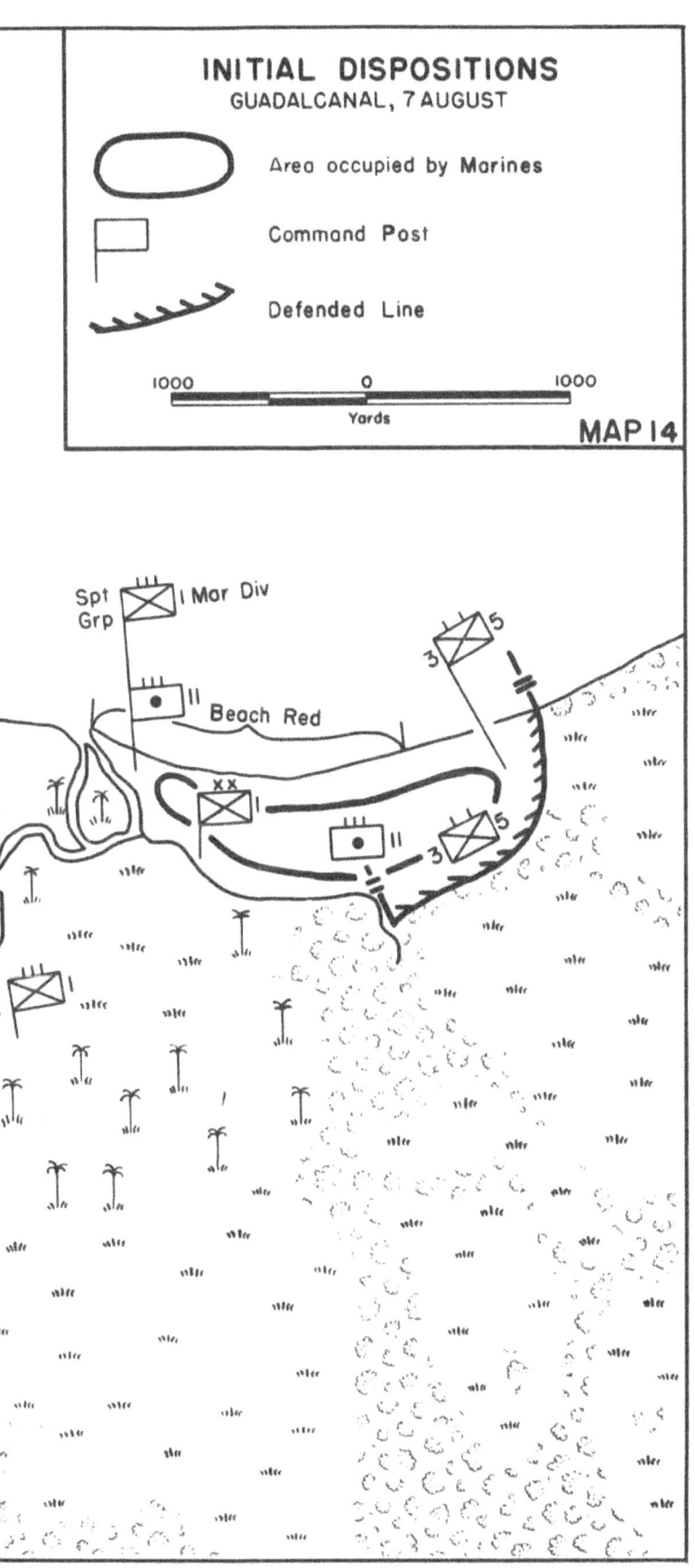

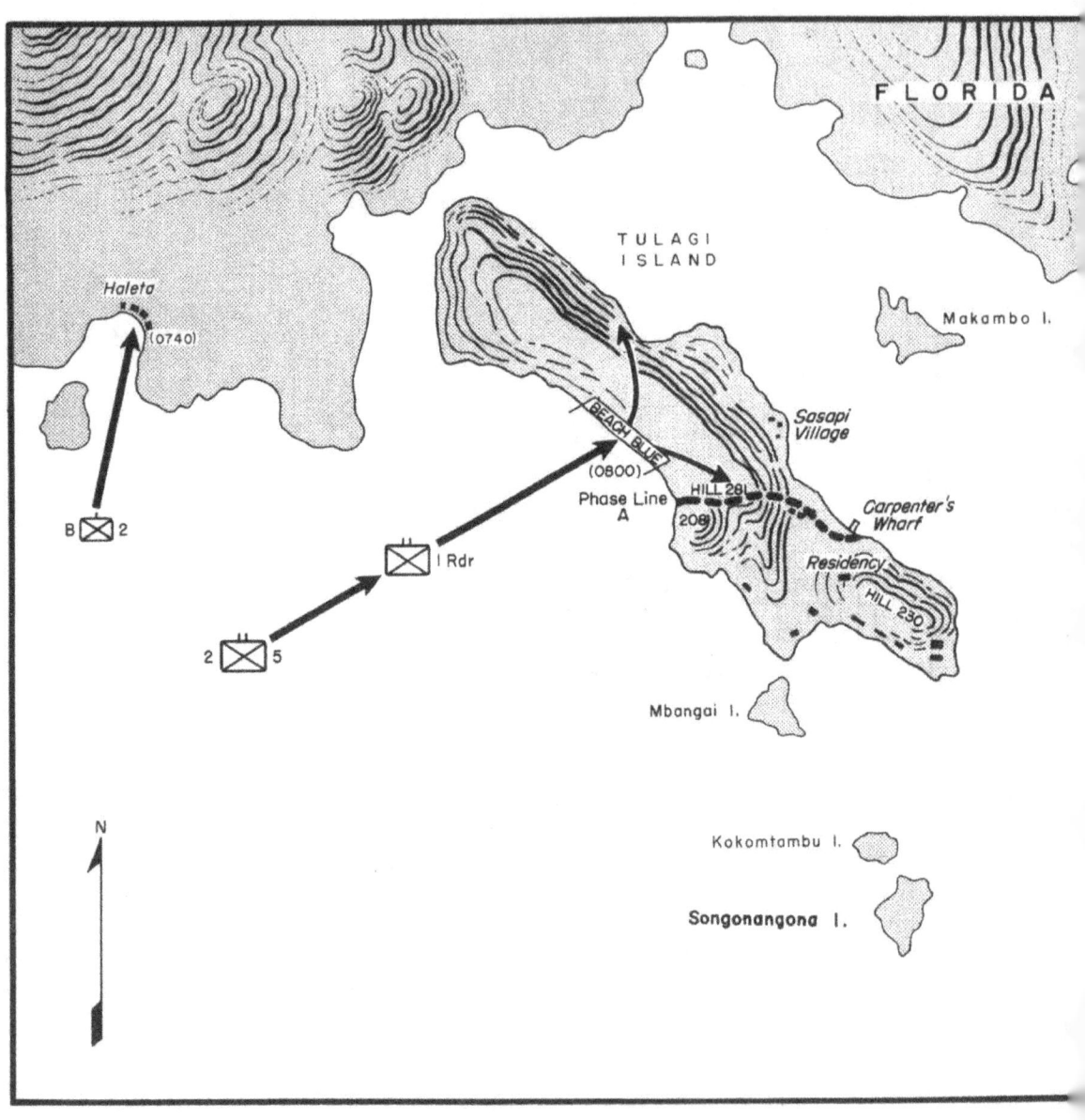

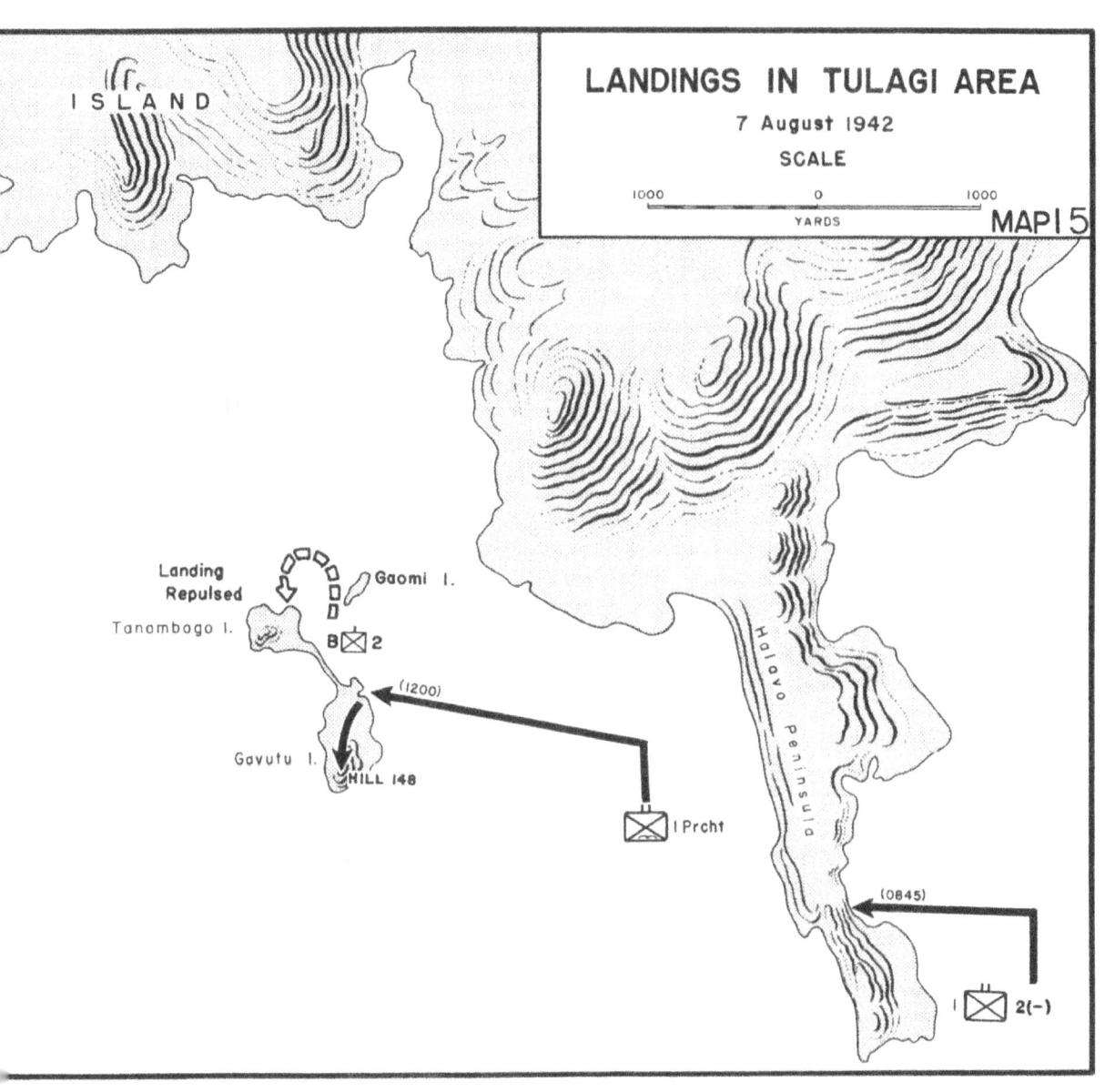

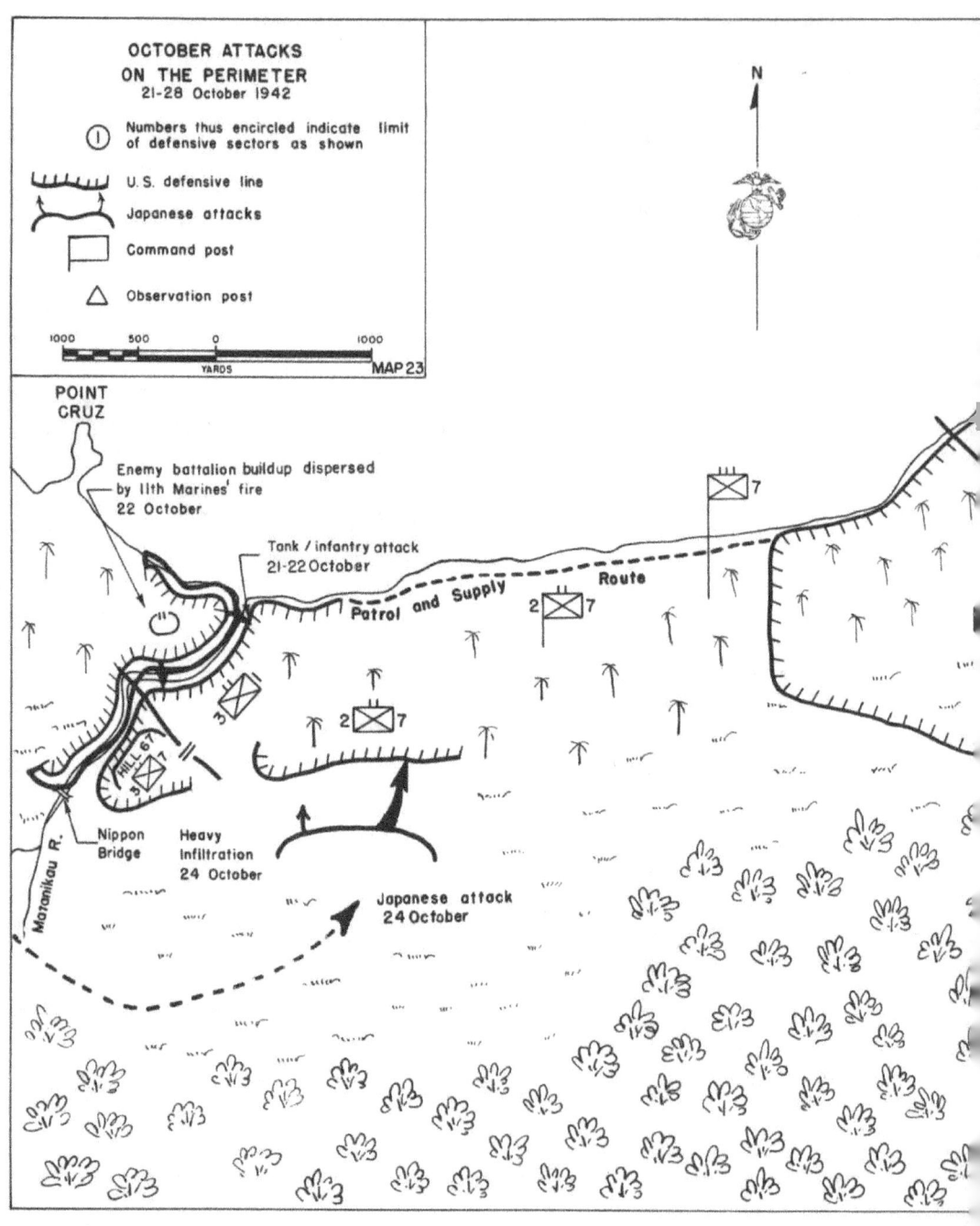

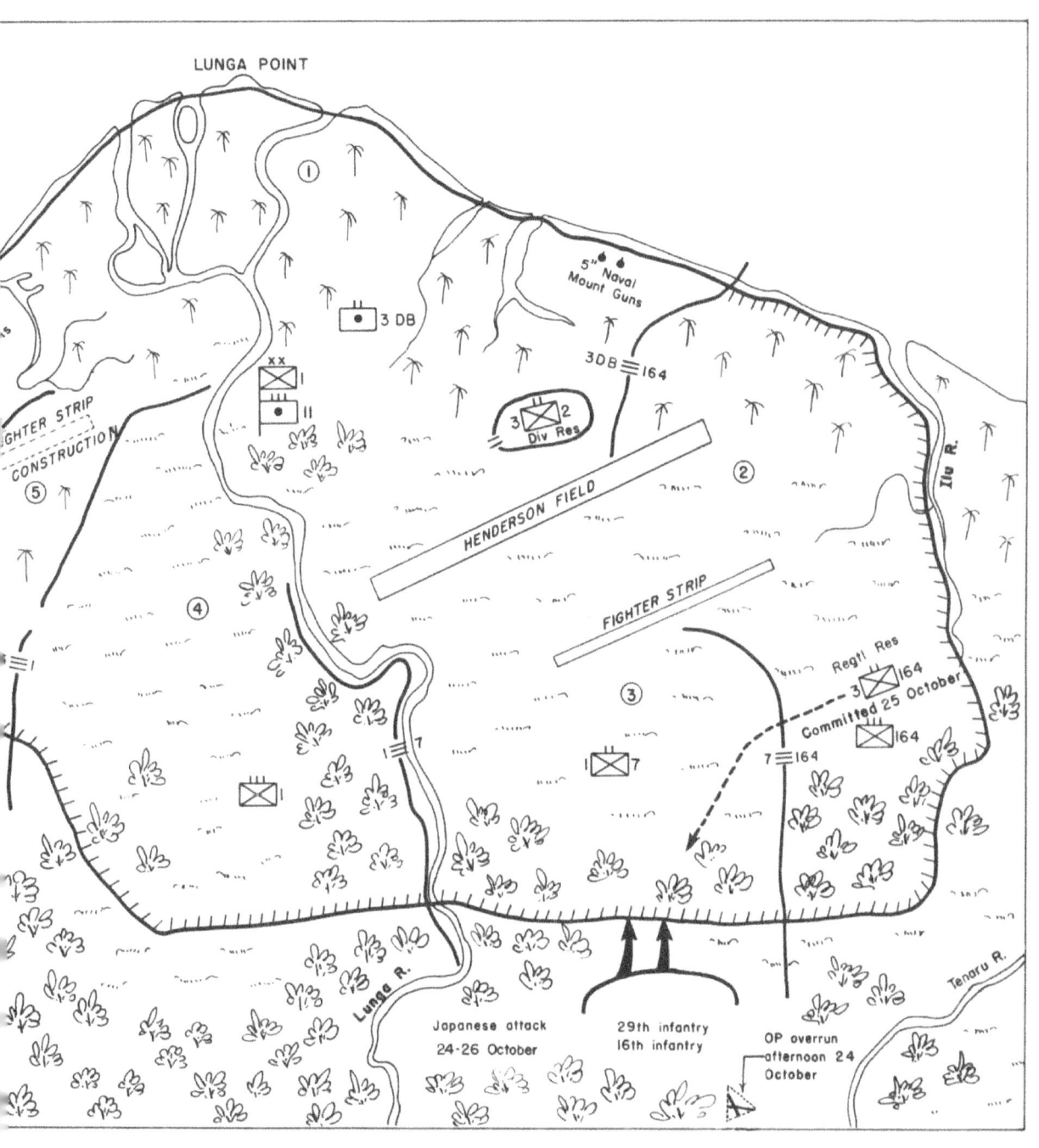

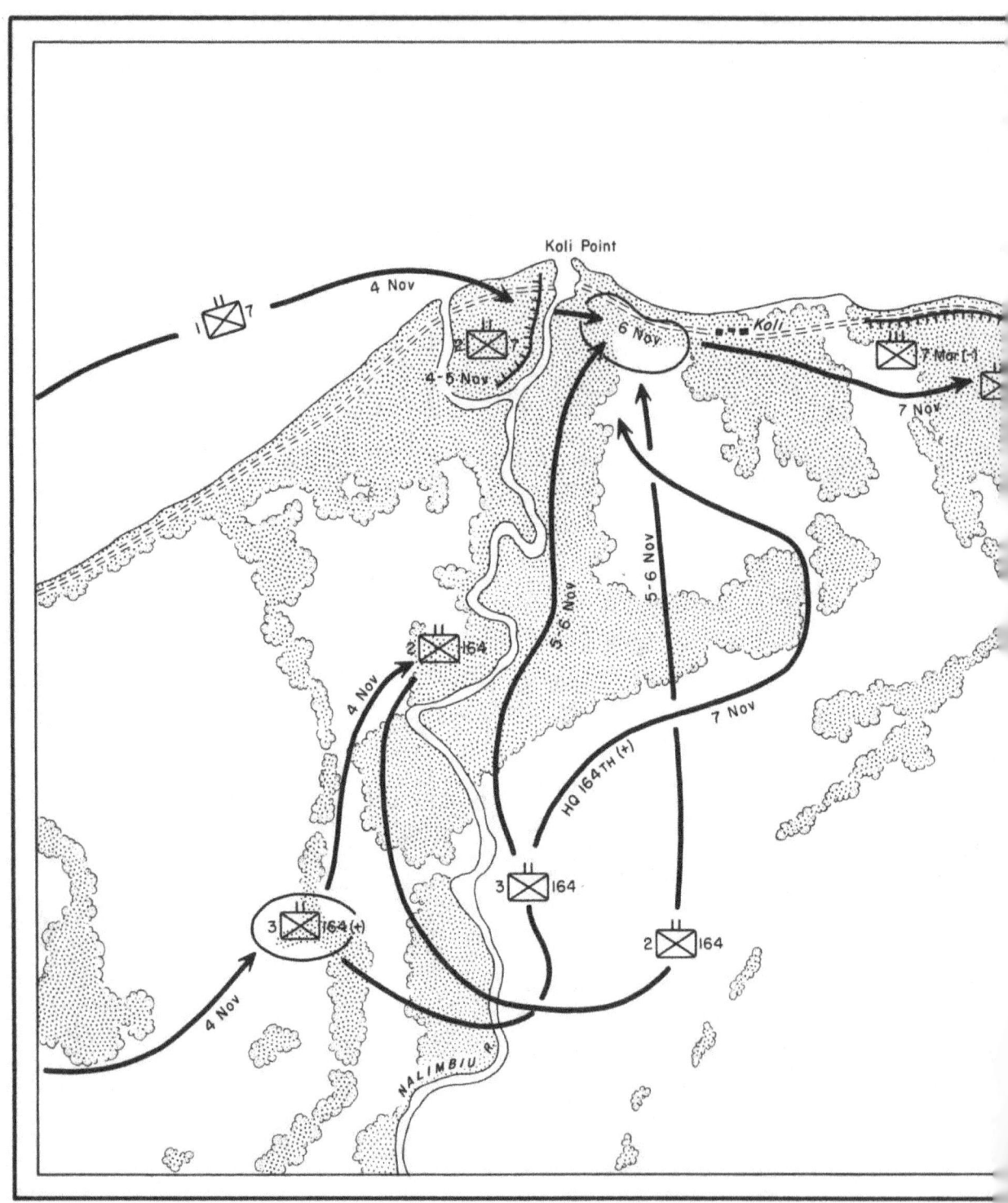

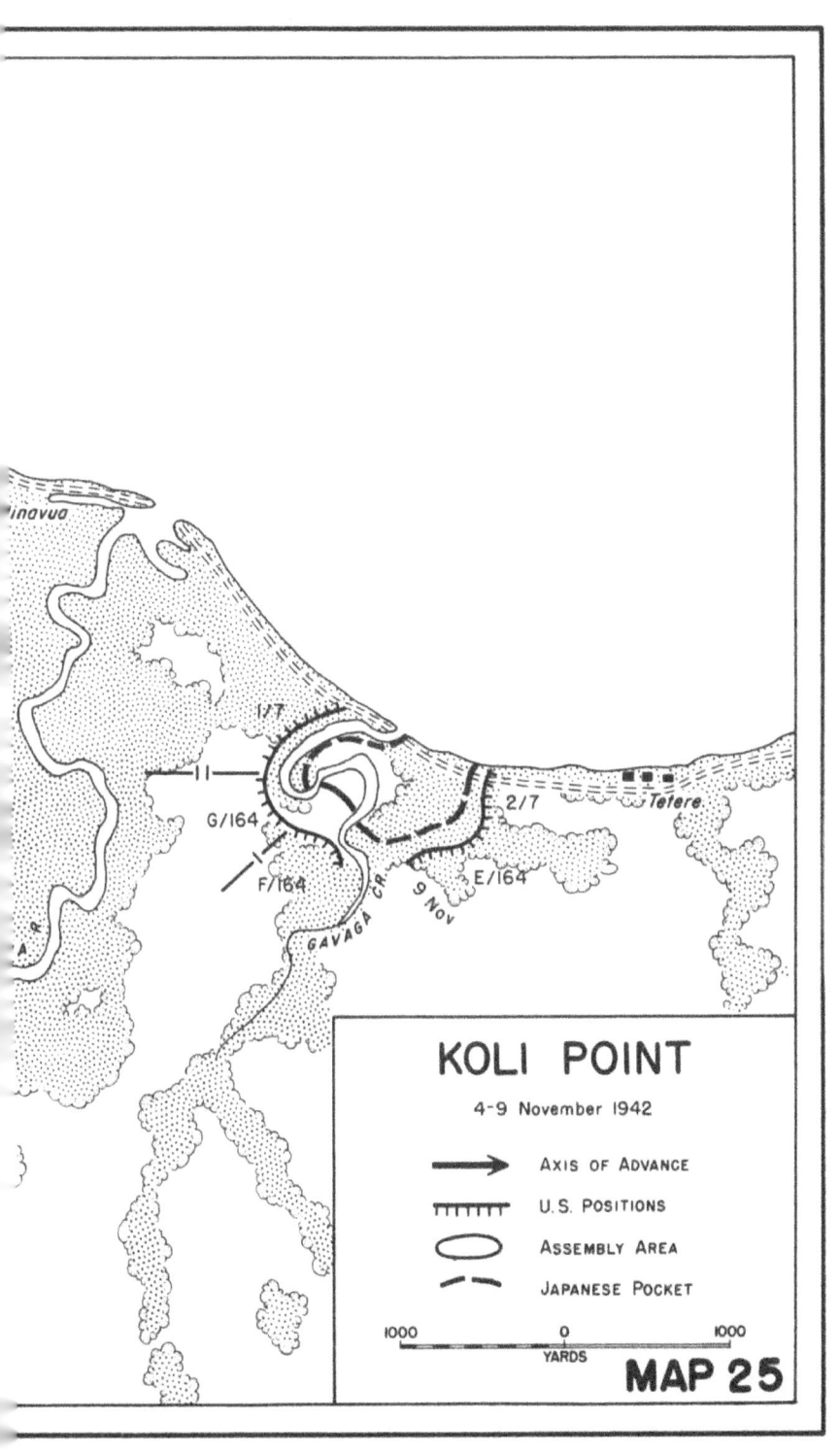

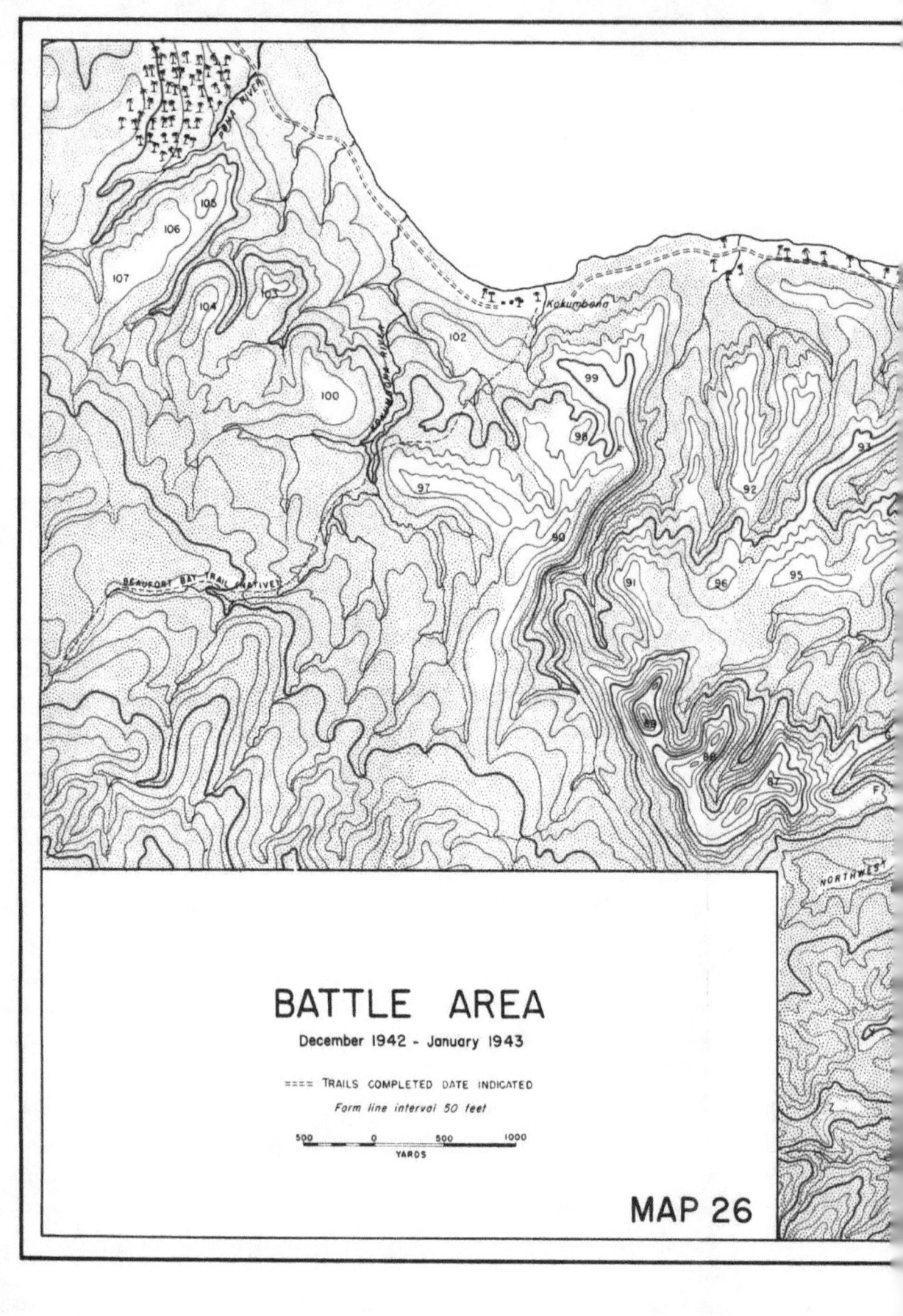

BATTLE AREA
December 1942 - January 1943

==== TRAILS COMPLETED DATE INDICATED

Form line interval 50 feet

MAP 26

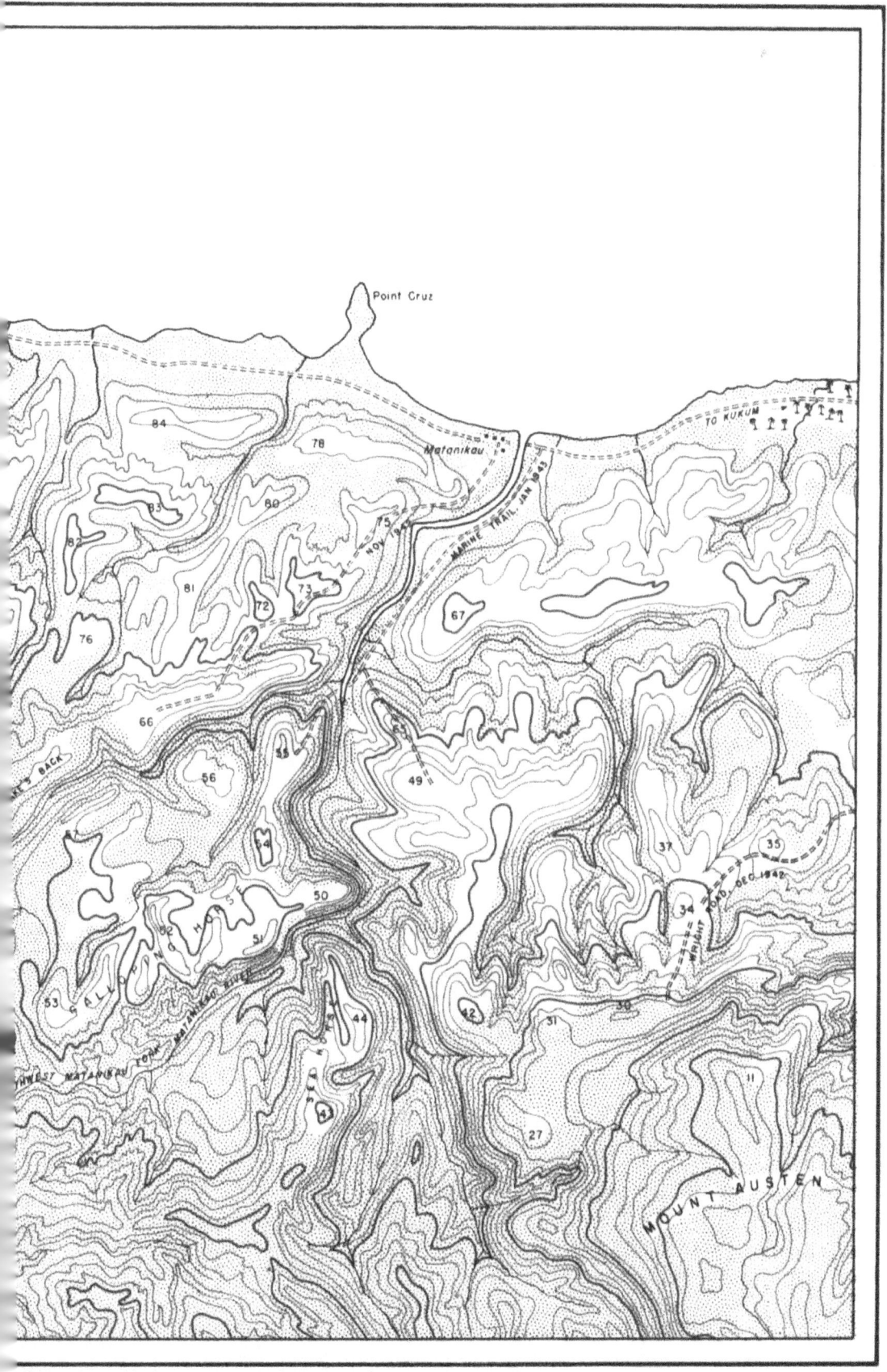

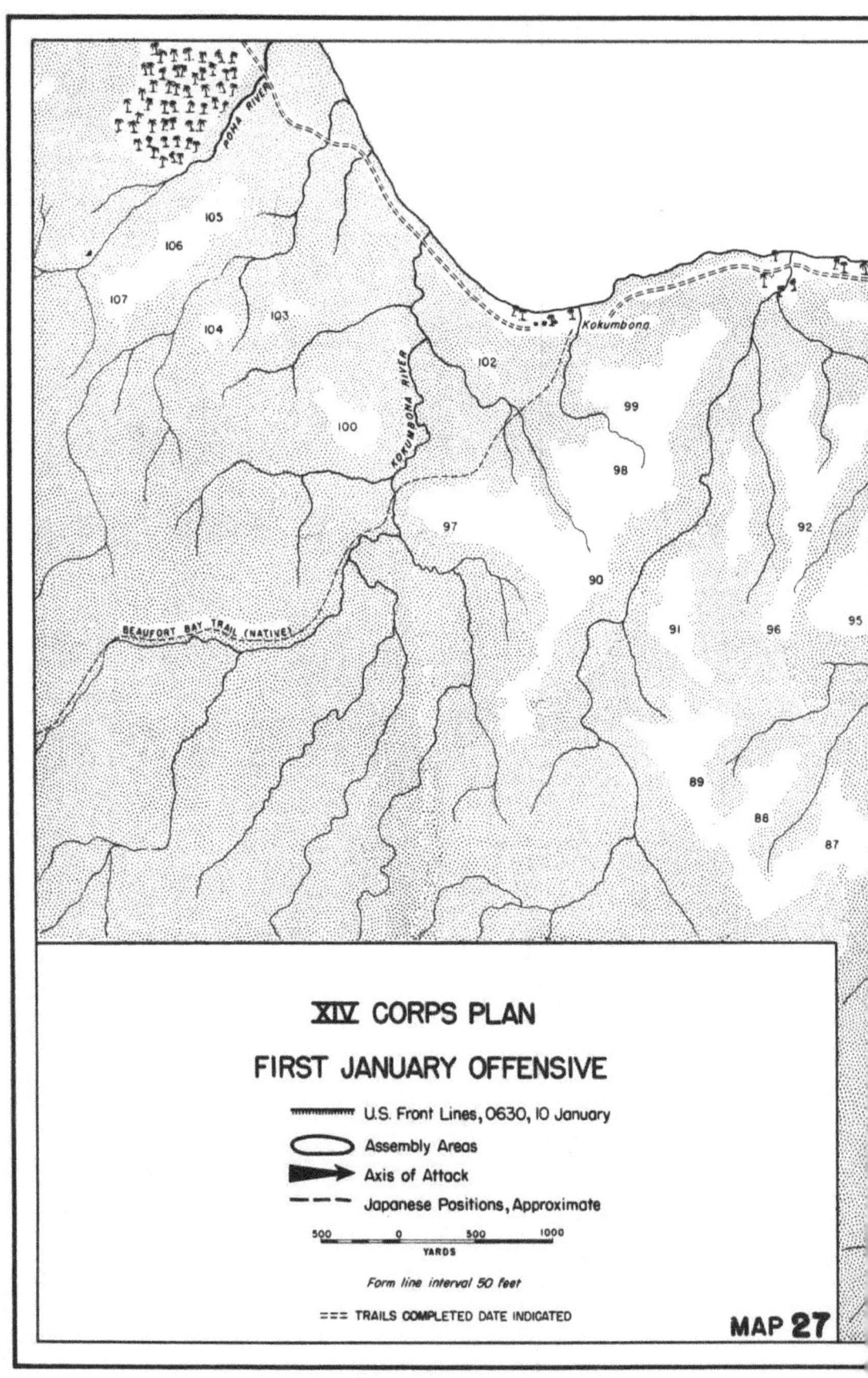

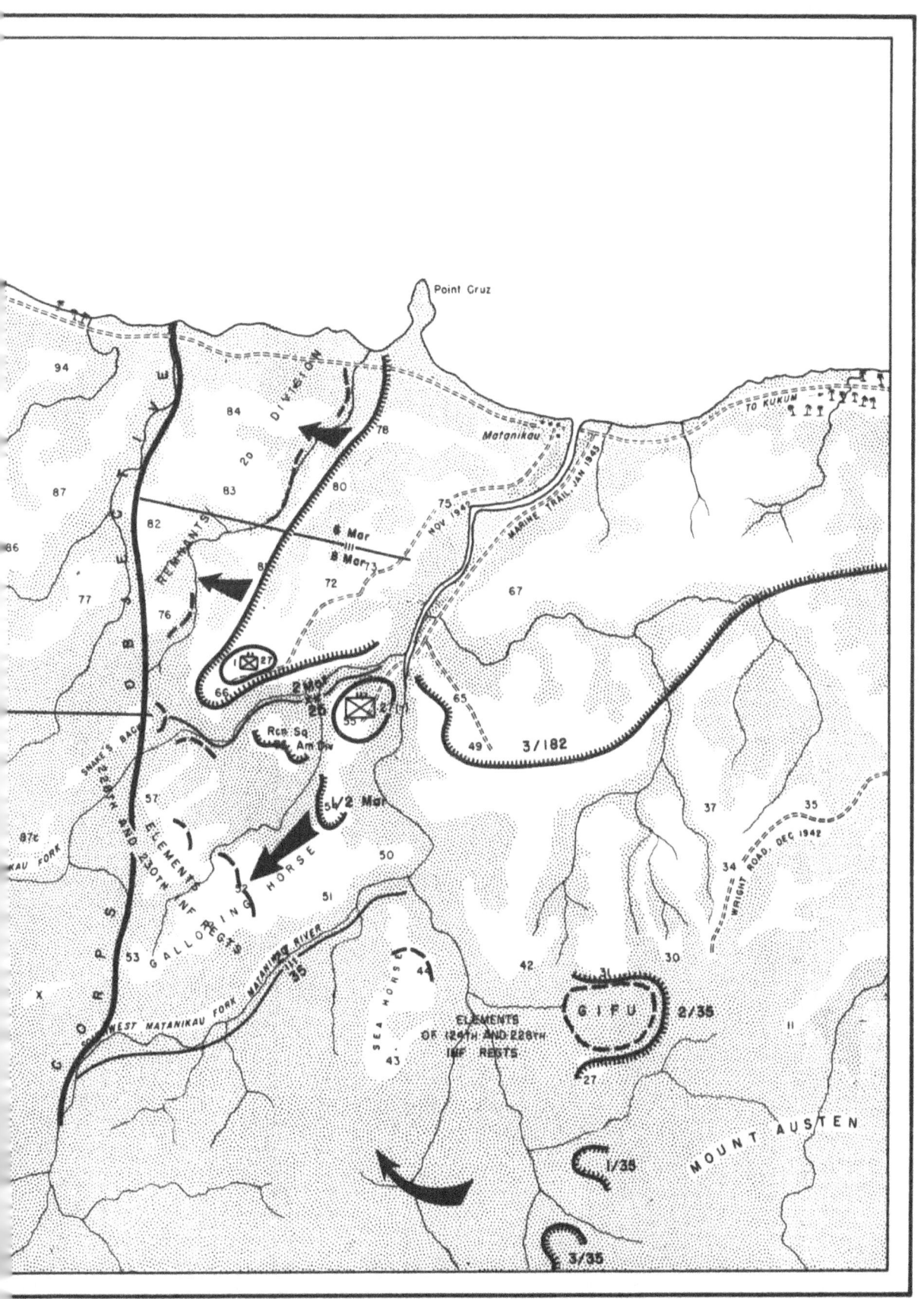

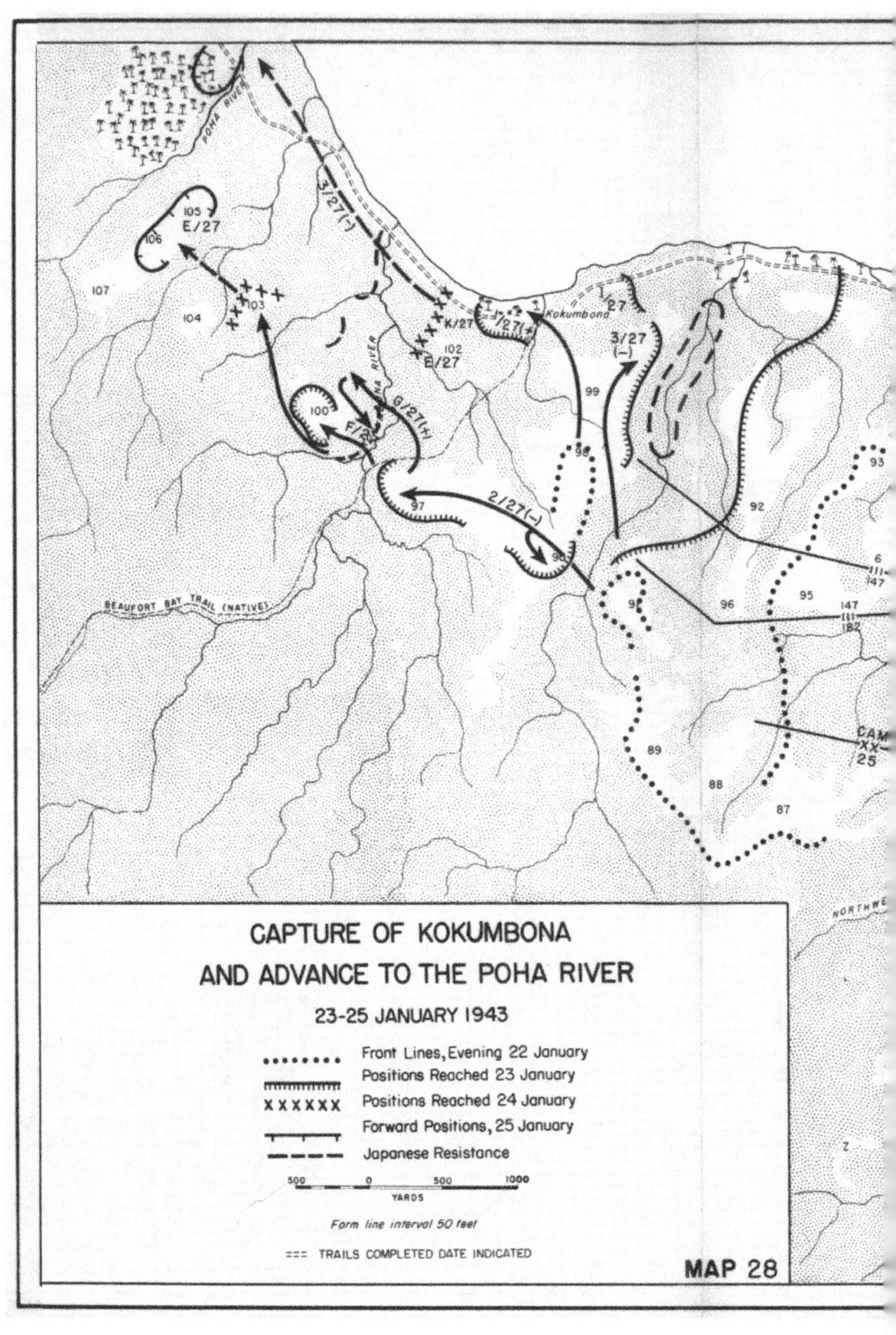

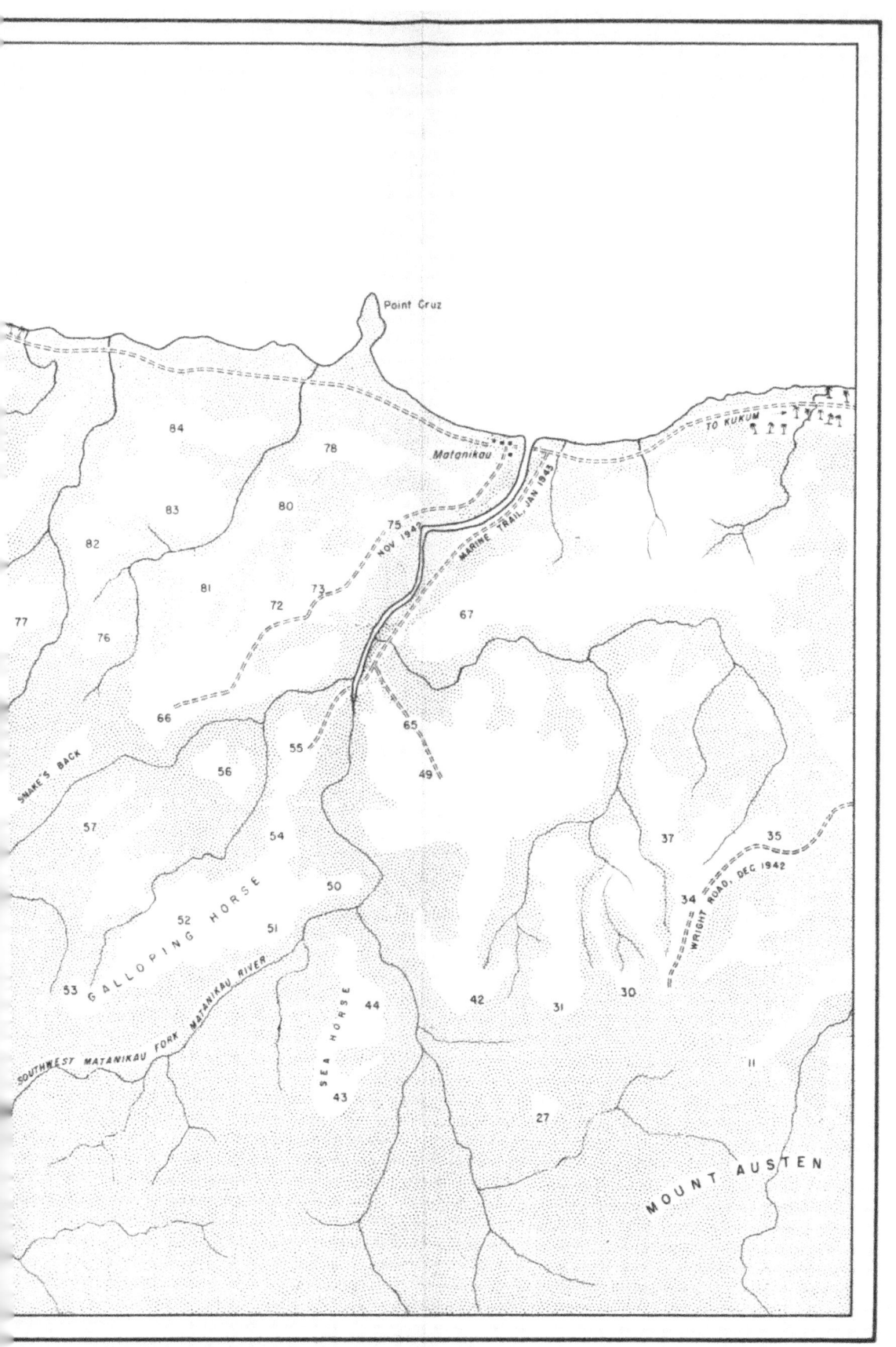